THE CRISIS OF DEMOCR

Centrist Politics under the Secon

CU00862874

For my parents,
Duncan and Lesley

The Crisis of Democracy in Spain

Centrist Politics under the Second Republic,
1931–1936

NIGEL TOWNSON

sussex
ACADEMIC
PRESS

BRIGHTON • PORTLAND

Copyright © Nigel Townson 2000

The right of Nigel Townson to be identified as author of this work has been asserted in
accordance with the Copyright, Designs and Patents Act 1988.

2 4 6 8 10 9 7 5 3 1

First published 2000 in Great Britain by
SUSSEX ACADEMIC PRESS
PO Box 2950
Brighton BN2 5SP

and in the United States of America by
SUSSEX ACADEMIC PRESS
5804 N.E. Hassalo St.
Portland, Oregon 97213-3644

All rights reserved. Except for the quotation of short passages for the purposes of criticism
and review, no part of this publication may be reproduced, stored in a retrieval system, or
transmitted, in any form or by any means, electronic, mechanical, photocopying,
recording or otherwise, without the prior permission of the publisher.

British Library Cataloguing in Publication Data
A CIP catalogue record for this book is available from the British Library.

Library of Congress Cataloging-in-Publication Data
Townson, Nigel.
The crisis of democracy in Spain : centrist politics under the Second Republic, 1931–1936
/ Nigel Townson.
p.   cm.
Includes bibliographical references and index.
ISBN 1–898723–19–2 (hc : alk. paper) — ISBN 1–898723–95–8 (pb : alk. paper)
1. Partido Republicano Radical—History.   2. Spain—Politics and government—
1931–1939.   I. Title.
JN8395.R4 T68   2000
324.246'02—dc21   99–059288

Typeset and designed by G&G Editorial, Brighton
Printed by Bookcraft Ltd, Midsomer Norton, Bath
This book is printed on acid-free paper

Contents

―――――

Acknowledgements

My first debt is to Peter Burke for initially stimulating my interest in the history of Spain – sorry that the Millenarian movements were jettisoned for the lure of the 20th century. My second debt is to Paul Preston, who has patiently directed the research upon which much of this text is based. He has not only provided steadfast support and encouragement in relation to the doctoral thesis but also in relation to the publication of the book. The British Academy, the Vicente Cañada Blanch Foundation, and the University of London are all to be thanked for their indispensable financial support. Thanks, too, to Martin Blinkhorn and Helen Graham, my doctoral examiners, for their constructive criticisms and suggestions. The staff at the Archivo de Salamanca, the Archivo Diego Hidalgo, the Ateneo de Madrid, the Fundación Pablo Iglesias, the Fundación Juan March and the Archivo del Tribunal Supremo were – if not necessarily elsewhere – distinguished by their efficiency and cooperativeness.

I am extremely grateful to the many people who have discussed the Republic with me over the years, especially Andrés de Blas Guerrero, Mercedes Cabrera, Fernando del Rey, Edward Malefakis, Manuel Requena Gallego, Timothy Rees, and above all Santos Juliá and Enrique Montero Hernández. A special debt of gratitude is due to José Alvarez Junco not just for his openhanded hospitality but also for his indefatigable enthusiasm and unusual capacity for dialogue – qualities that make him an outstanding teacher as well as scholar. Heartfelt thanks to all those who tackled early drafts of the book: Enrique González Calleja and Shayne Mitchell, who each commented on a chapter, my father, Duncan Townson, who reviewed the bulk of the book with his usual meticulousness as well as helped with the index, and José Alvarez Junco and Helen Hills, who both found the time and energy to grapple with the manuscript in difficult personal circumstances. None, of course, are responsible for the errors and omissions. I should also like to thank Anthony Grahame at Sussex Academic Press for his forebearance and guidance.

Throughout the work's lengthy gestation my parents, Duncan and Lesley, have provided unflagging succour and encouragement. My parents-in-law, Angel and Susa, gave generously of their time in relation to the family during the final stages. No one has been more important during the writing of this book than my wife, Susana, not just for her editorial comment and bibliographical back up, but also for the cheery and stoical manner in which she has tolerated the seemingly endless time dedicated to the book. In particular she has borne most of the responsibility for our newly-born daughter, Sonia, without whom this book would not be the same either.

Abbreviations

———

I Political parties, trade unions amd other organizations

AR   Acción Republicana – Republican Action, the party of Manuel Azaña

BOC   Bloc Obrer i Camperol – Trotskyist Worker and Peasant Bloc

CEDA Confederación Española de Derechas Autónomas – the Spanish Confederation of Autonomous Right-wing Groups, the principal force on the right from its foundation in early 1933

CNT   Confederación Nacional del Trabajo – the anarcho–syndicalist National Confederation of Labour

DLR   Derecha Liberal Republicana – the Republican Liberal Right, the conservative republican party under Niceto Alcalá-Zamora and Miguel Maura

DRV   Derecha Regional Valenciana – the Valencia affiliate of the CEDA

FAI   Federación Anarquista Ibérica – the dominant extremist group within the CNT

FIRPE Federación de Izquierdas Republicanas Parlamentarias Españolas – the parliamentary alliance of left–republican parties

FNTT Federación Nacional de Trabajadores de la Tierra – the landless labourers' union, the largest within the UGT

IR   Izquierda Republicana – the Republican Left, Azaña's new party from April 1934

JAP   Juventud de Acción Popular – the militant youth section of the CEDA

JONS Juntas de Ofensiva Nacional-Sindicalista – an early fascist formation

ORGA Organización Republicana Gallega Autónoma – the leading left–republican party in Galicia

PCE   Partido Comunista de España – the Spanish Communist Party

PNV   Partido Nacionalista Vasco – the Basque Nationalist Party

PRD   Partido Radical Demócrata – the Radical–Democratic Party under Diego Martínez Barrio

PRRS   Partido Republicano Radical Socialista – the Jacobin Radical–Socialist Party

PRRSI   Partido Republicano Radical Socialista Independiente – the Independent Radical–Socialist Party

PSOE   Partido Socialista Obrero Español – the Spanish Socialist Workers' Party

PURA   Partido de Unión Republicana Autonomista – the Valencia affiliate of the Radical Party

UFNR   Unión Federal Nacionalista Republicana – the Nationalist Republican Federal Union, a left–republican party from Catalonia

UGT   Unión General de Trabajadores – the General Union of Workers, the socialist trade union movement

UR   Unión Republicana – the left–centre party established in September 1934

2 Archives and sources

ADH   Archivo Diego Hidalgo

AMB   Archivo Martínez Barrio

AS, P-S Archivo de Salamanca, Sección Político-Social

ATS   Archivo del Tribunal Supremo

DSCC   Diario de las sesiones de las Cortes Constituyentes

DSC   Diario de las sesiones de Cortes

Prologue

The story of the Spanish Second Republic of 1931 to 1939 has long been overshadowed by that of its tragic climax – the Civil War of 1936 to 1939. Historians have tended to project back on to the first six years of the regime the ideological extremes of the last three. As a result, the left and right of the political spectrum have received a disproportionate amount of attention. This has obscured above all the role of the more centrist republicans, who were peripheral during the war, but dominated politics before the military insurgency of July 1936. In fact, all the presidents, all the prime ministers, and the overwhelming majority of the ministers during the *ante bellum* period were republicans. Yet for many years the left, swayed by the certainties of Marxism, dismissed the republicans as belonging to the inherently treacherous "bourgeoisie", while for the authoritarian right, the republicans were a radical mutation of liberalism, the dreaded virus that had eaten away at the soul of Spanish society since the early nineteenth century. By infecting Catholic Spain with parties, parliaments, and the popular will, liberalism had been responsible for the nation's imperial reverses, for the decadence of the nineteenth and twentieth centuries, and for the general loss of "spiritual unity" and "greatness". The conflagration of 1936 to 1939 was ultimately blamed, too, on the anti-Catholic and anti-Spanish influence of liberalism. In short, both left and right had a vested interest in debunking the republicans. During the Transition of the late 1970s from dictatorship to democracy, the republican form of government, associated with the tumult of the 1930s as well as the proverbial instability of the First Republic of 1873–4, was again rejected. Instead, the monarchy, at once a symbol of continuity and change, became the framework of consensus. Neither ideologically nor politically could the republicans win.

Since the early 1990s the republicans have been somewhat rehabilitated.[1] Much attention has been devoted to the figure of Manuel Azaña, the left–republican Prime Minister between 1931 and 1933 and in 1936, and President from 1936 to 1939. This is partly because he provides the most compelling vision of a democratic and reformist Republic, partly because of the remarkable personal testimony which he bequeathed in the form of his diaries, and partly because his exertions to reconcile the "Two Spains" during the Civil War echoed the consensual sentiments of post-Francoist Spain. No doubt his stature as a cultivated intellectual and writer has made him more attractive still to "bourgeois" historians. For the Francoist regime, Azaña was a *bête noire*. Today, the Spanish left and right alike lay claim to his political legacy.[2] Yet the allure of Azaña – with whom the republican cause has often been confused – has done little for the studies of the left republicans as a whole. Only two monographs on the national left–republican parties, Acción Republicana and the Radical–Socialist Republican Party, have been published. Even here, the shadow of Azaña looms large; one of the two books is titled *Azaña en el poder* ("Azaña in Power") – only the subtitle revealing that it deals with "The party of Acción Republicana".[3] By contrast, studies of the Basque and Catalan republicans have been boosted considerably by the resurgence of regional nationalism since the 1970s.[4]

It is no coincidence that the most neglected of all the republican parties is also the most reviled: the Radical Republican Party, which has generally been regarded as a corrupt and cynical enterprise that was the epitome of pork-barrel politics. The unfavourable press arises in large part from the fact that the Radicals fell from power following a brace of scandals, one of which, the "Straperlo", became a byword for the black market in 1940s and '50s Spain. This image has been reinforced by earlier venal associations, such as the *cal, yeso y cemento* ("limestone, plaster and cement") scandal of 1910 and the relationship with Juan March, the Mallorcan mogul whose fortune was initially based on smuggling. Moreover, sympathizers of the Second Republic have interpreted the fact that the Radical Party governed in alliance with the non-republican right from the end of 1933 to late 1935 as a betrayal of the republican cause. Allegedly acting as a stepping stone for "fascism", the Radical Party is also regarded as having played a crucial role in a process of political polarization which resulted in civil war. For most historians, the self-serving cupidity and opportunism of the Radicals ran diametrically counter to the self-sacrifice and idealism that supposedly characterized the 1930s in Spain. This vision of the Radical Party as a force that lacked ideological commitment is accentuated by its pragmatic, centrist politics, which were bereft of the crusading, doctrinaire zeal that characterized the parties to the left and right. Accordingly, the Radicals were far removed from the romantic image of a Spain torn between competing ideologies which has so appealed to foreign historians. Finally, the Radical Party has been ignored because its origins, which lie in the Lerrouxist movement of 1901–8 in Barcelona, are viewed as much more path-breaking and quixotic. Indeed, this has inspired some of the most outstanding studies of twentieth century Spanish political history, in particular Joaquín Romero Maura's *"La rosa de fuego"* and *El Emperador del Paralelo* by

José Alvarez Junco.[5] The world-weary, graft-ridden party of the 1930s suffers by comparison. In sum, the Radical Party has excited little respect and even less research.[6]

The "Black Legend" of the Radicals is certainly not unfounded but it has invariably eclipsed their real significance under the Second Republic. In 1931 the Radical Party, by far the largest of the republican parties, formed an essential part of the republican–socialist governments; in 1932–3, it was the principal source of opposition to the left/republican–socialist administrations; and from 1933 to 1935, it was the main force in government. In a regime often considered to have been in thrall to the extremes of left and right, the Radicals constituted a centrist option of redoubtable proportions: up to the general election of February 1936, no party won more parliamentary seats or occupied more ministerial departments. Yet only one study has been dedicated to the Radical Party during the Republic, *El Partido Republicano Radical* by Octavio Ruiz Manjón, which was published over 20 years ago. There is nothing in English.[7]

This book modifies the historiographical imbalance by reappraising the nature, role, and achievement of the Radical Republican Party under the Spanish Second Republic of 1931 to 1936. **Chapter I** traces the party's history from its origins as a revolutionary, working-class movement in Barcelona at the turn of the century to its transformation into a moderate, mainly middle-class force of national dimensions by the time of the Republic in 1931. Particular attention is paid to the ideological, organizational, and social metamorphoses which were wrought by the foundation of the Radical Party in 1908, and the extent to which these left indelible imprints on the new political formation. Also examined is the evolution of the party's relationships with those forces, especially the left republicans and socialists, that were to shape its trajectory in the 1930s. Above all, an endeavour is made to delineate the elements of continuity and change in the party up to the Republic.

Chapter II covers the period from the fall of monarchy in April 1931 to the general election for the Constituent Cortes two months later. A crucial issue addressed here is how and why the Radicals differed from the left republicans in confronting the challenge of the nascent regime's consolidation. More broadly, the Radicals' aims and aspirations are compared and contrasted to those of its allies in the provisional government of April to June 1931. I shall examine how the party was changed by the exigencies of mass politics, especially the influx of urban and rural middling classes. Finally, the expectations surrounding the Radical Party at the time of the June 1931 general election, and the reasons for its success, are considered.

The central struggle within the ruling majority between the Radicals and the socialists, its repercussions for relations within the republican camp, and the fashion in which these cumulative tensions were refracted through the constitutional debate and the two Cabinet crises of late 1931, is the focus of **Chapter III**. Why, in December 1931, the Radicals ruptured the republican–socialist government is considered at length, as are the consequences for the stability of the regime. Also explored for the first time is the question of the party's corruption, focusing on the scandal involving the Radicals and Juan March in November 1931.

The rationale and resonance of the Radicals' opposition to the left/republican–socialist administration under Manuel Azaña during the first half of 1932 is the guiding theme of **Chapter IV**. Inextricably linked is the vertiginous growth of the party in the provinces and the way in which this determined its assault on the ruling bloc. **Chapter V** offers the only detailed account to date of the part played by the Radicals in the attempted *coup d'état* of August 1932 by unravelling the tangled skein of military and civilian strands that made up the conspiracy.

Chapter VI tackles the strivings of the Radicals to rebuild their bridges with the left republicans, culminating in the party's first and last national congress under the Republic in October 1932. The Congress is scrutinized for the light it sheds on the party's organization, its social base, the personality cult surrounding its *jefe* (or "boss"), Alejandro Lerroux, and for its political reverberations. The relaunch of the Radicals' opposition in late 1932 is reconsidered in view of the recently published diaries of the Prime Minister.[8] Why, despite the mounting disillusionment of the socialists, the revival of the right, and the escalating socio-economic agitation, the republicans failed during the turbulent summer of 1933 to form an all-republican administration is the chapter's other main theme. Of critical importance in this context is the breakdown in relations between the Radicals and the left republicans during the drawn-out governmental crisis of September to October 1933.

The extent to which the general election of November 1933, overseen by a Radical-led Cabinet, was a vindication of the Radicals' two-year campaign of opposition is examined in **Chapter VII**. A crucial question is why the Radical Party, having previously collaborated with the left republicans and socialists, now formed a parliamentary majority in alliance with the non-republican right. The nature of this arrangement, notably the extent to which the Radicals and the right shared a common agenda, is an overarching theme in this and the following chapters. Of particular concern is the extent to which events in Madrid were shaped by relations between the Radical Party and its new-found allies in the provinces – a subject which has received little attention up to now. Another thread that runs through the rest of the book is whether the Radicals' strategy of integration advanced the consolidation of the Republic or whether, on the contrary, it merely converted them into an instrument of the authoritarian right. The corruption of the Radicals is subjected to further examination: in what it consisted, how it shaped party policy and politics, and whether it set them apart from the clientelist practices that characterized Spanish political life. **Chapter VIII** re-examines the causes and consequences of the Radical schism of May 1934, including a reassessment of the role of the Masonic lodges.

Chapter IX seeks to provide a fresh perspective on the Radical government of April to October 1934, invariably portrayed as a weak caretaker administration, by reviewing the way in which it dealt with an ever-widening opposition front, ranging from the socialists and left republicans to the regional nationalists and the Radicals' own right-wing allies. A recurring issue of the Radical Party's period in power, discussed here at length, is the degree to which the legislative labours of the Constituent Cortes of 1931–3 were defended or demolished. The chapter closes with the CEDA's entry into the government in October 1934, the left-wing uprisings that followed, and an evaluation of the extent to which these were due to the policies of the ruling centre–right alliance. The dramatic shift in the balance of power that took place after the October events and the resulting intensification of the rivalry between the Radicals and the right provides the centrepiece of both **Chapters X** and **XI**, which focus on the struggle not just at the national level but also attempt to relate it to the escalating confrontation at the provincial level.

Chapter XII tackles the Cabinet crisis of September 1935 and the eruption of the "Straperlo Scandal". In evaluating the causes of this labyrinthine affair, I draw on the judicial investigation of the special magistrate, Ildefonso Bellón, the first time these papers have been analysed. The impact not only of this scandal, but also of the "Tayá Affair", which burst upon the political scene a few weeks later, is related to the crumbling of the ruling coalition and the precipitate collapse of the party. A final, critical issue addressed is the extent to which the Radical Party contributed to the collective tensions of the spring and summer of 1936.

In assessing the trajectory of the Radical Party under the Republic, this book endeavours to establish whether the centre could have played a greater stabilizing role or whether Spain was in fact divided into two irreconcilable camps that were fated to clash. A quintessential corollary is whether the Second Republic of 1931 to 1936 should be studied in its own right or whether it was, indeed, a mere prelude to civil war.

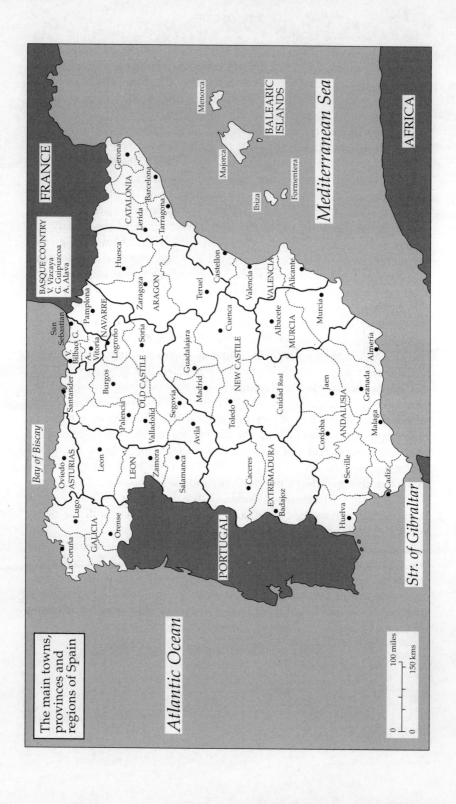

The main towns, provinces and regions of Spain

FRANCE

BASQUE COUNTRY
V. Vizcaya
V. Guipuzcoa
A. Alava

Bay of Biscay

Atlantic Ocean

San Sebastian
Santander
Oviedo
Lugo
La Coruña
Orense
GALICIA
ASTURIAS
Leon
LEON
Zamora
Salamanca
Burgos
Palencia
Valladolid
OLD CASTILE
Avila
Segovia
Madrid
Toledo
NEW CASTILE
Caceres
Badajoz
EXTREMADURA

V. Bilbao
A. Vitoria
G.
Pamplona
NAVARRE
Logroño
Soria
Zaragoza
ARAGON
Huesca
Teruel
Cuenca
Guadalajara
Ciudad Real

PORTUGAL

Huelva
Seville
Cadiz
Cordoba
Malaga
Jaen
ANDALUSIA
Granada
Almeria
Albacete
MURCIA
Murcia
Alicante
VALENCIA
Valencia
Castellon

CATALONIA
Gerona
Barcelona
Lerida
Tarragona

Ibiza
Majorca
Formentera
Menorca
BALEARIC ISLANDS

Mediterranean Sea

AFRICA

Str. of Gibraltar

0   100 miles
0   150 kms

I

From Revolution to Reform
The origins and evolution of the Radical Party, 1901–1931

The origins of the Radical Republican Party could be said to lie in the "Disaster of '98". In 1898 Spain lost the remnants of its empire – Cuba, Puerto Rico, and the Philippines – to the United States of America. If the material blow to Spain was considerable, the psychological one was colossal. A widespread, if nebulous, clamour for the "regeneration" of a "decadent" nation rose up. The region that was most affected by the "Disaster" was Catalonia. The social and political upheaval caused by the events of 1898 not only revived the moribund republican movement there, but the loss of the Cuban market together with the insensitivity of central government to the plight of local business also led to the formation of a Catalanist party, the Lliga Regionalista. Thus in the general election of May 1901 the republicans and the Lliga between them destroyed the "*turno pacífico*" – the rotation in power of the two oligarchical dynastic parties by means of rigged elections – in Barcelona. A new era in Spanish politics had begun. One of the new republican deputies was a newspaper editor by the name of Alejandro Lerroux.[1]

Born in 1864, Lerroux was the son of a lowly-paid army veterinary surgeon. After deserting from the army as a teenager, he worked in a variety of jobs before making his mark in the 1890s as the editor of the daily newspaper *El País*. Physically powerful, with broad shoulders, he was audacious, brash, and energetic, as well as bristling with bonhomie and charm, possessing what is known in Spanish as *don de gentes* – a way with people. He was astute, too, relying heavily as a politician on his instinct rather than his negligible educational and intellectual formation. As a radical, republican journalist he fought numerous duels and under-took polemical public campaigns. Indeed, it was *El País*'s dogged defence of those held and tortured at the "Montjuich" prison in Barcelona for their alleged involvement in a terrorist act of 1896 that established Lerroux's name in Catalonia.[2]

Beginning in the late 1890s, Lerroux built up a revolutionary, largely working-class movement in Barcelona that was to dominate politics there for much of the first decade of the twentieth century.[3] By forging a new basis for collaboration between the republicans and the working class, he was to create the first mass party in Spanish history. Rather than the traditional and elitist casinos, *círculos*, and committees – which constituted the so-called "parties of notables" – he made consumer co-operatives, lay schools, and trade unions the cornerstone of a more participatory republican politics. In 1903 the first "Popular Picnic", attended by thousands of families, took place. In 1906, the Lerrouxists – not, as is often assumed, the socialists – opened the first *Casa del Pueblo* ("House of the People") in Spain, this embracing a clinic, a library, a theatre, a billiards room, and a cafe. A bakery and a co-operative that provided insurance, pension schemes, and legal aid were later added. In effect, the Lerrouxists had created a welfare state within the state. Lacking the independent means and the same access to government of the dynastic parties, the Lerrouxist movement exploited the Barcelona town hall in order to fund both itself and its clientage networks. These were also supplied by bringing public services under municipal control and by improving conditions for the council workers. The eight-hour day and a minimum wage, for example, were introduced.[4] Another novel feature of the movement was its "populism". This can be defined as a politics geared to the mobilization of support through the demagoguery of a charismatic leader who deploys a rhetoric based on the idea of a vaguely-defined "people" and which is regarded as being in opposition to evil oligarchic, or anti-popular, elements (hence "populism"). Naturally, the nature of this inter-classist appeal – moralistic, emotional and anti-intellectual – reduced ideology to a mainly decorative or formal role.[5] Moreover, in drawing on the strike and protest movement which had been unleashed in the Catalan capital after the "Disaster", Lerroux had identified himself with the anarchists' revolutionary goals rather than with the more evolutionary approach of the socialists. As a republican, however, he never sought to create an authentically revolutionary, wholly working-class party, and key ideological differences remained. His "revolutionary" discourse, in consequence, was always sufficiently vague and ambiguous to disguise his essentially reformist aims. None the less, Lerroux had mobilized working-class opinion, breathed new life into the republican movement, and presented the Restoration system with a redoubtable challenge.[6]

In December 1901 Lerroux, together with the dashing young writer Vicente Blasco Ibáñez and the journalist Rodrigo Soriano, founded the Federación Revolucionaria. This merged into the Unión Republicana in March 1903 under the temperate leadership of Nicolás Salmerón, a President of the First Republic of 1873–4. The Unión proved a success insofar as it won 36 seats in the 1903 general election,[7] but it was soon transformed by the "¡Cu-cut!" affair. In November 1905, a military mob ransacked the satirical Catalanist weekly *¡Cu-cut!* and the conservative daily *La Veu de Catalunya* as a manifestation of the army's resentment at Catalan regionalism. The government, rather than punish the insubordination, passed the Law of Jurisdictions in 1906, which placed all alleged offences against the armed forces as well as *la Patria* (or motherland) under the jurisdiction of the army, thereby granting it a monopoly on patriotism. In defending the Catalans, the Unión helped create a new opposition alliance, "Solidaridad Catalana" (Catalan Solidarity). This placed Lerroux in an extremely difficult predicament. Not only did Solidaridad include the Lliga, his principal foe in Catalonia, but it was also hostile to the army. Lerroux, in keeping with a long-standing republican tradition and in particular the strategy pursued by the Progressive leader Manuel Ruiz Zorrilla (in whose party he had been active in the 1890s), believed that the collaboration of sympathetic elements in the army was essential for the Republic to triumph. The ensuing clash between *Solidarios* and *Antisolidarios* led to an assembly in June 1907 in which Lerroux was subjected to a barrage of accusations ranging from corruption to murder. The only alternative was to found his own party. A new force duly emerged in January 1908 – the Radical Republican Party.[8]

The establishment of the Radical Party signalled an almost complete rupture with the Barcelona movement. Organizationally, it was to be a nationwide, as opposed to regional or municipal, entity. Ideologically, the rhetoric of revolution gave way to reformism as the party underscored its "realism" and "responsibility" in readiness for the exercise of power. Thus the often inflammatory anticlerical propaganda of the past was replaced by a stress on change by legal, as opposed to violent, means. Sociologically, it was not so much the working class as the middle classes at which the movement's populist appeal was directed. Consequently the "revolution" was to be confined to a purely political transformation that would be channeled and capitalized upon by the middle classes, not the insurgent working class. None the less, the Lerrouxists still aspired to be the revolutionary working class's de facto political representative. By taking advantage of the anarcho–syndicalists' rejection of "bourgeois" politics – a stance that hardened with the formation of the Confederación Nacional del Trabajo (CNT) in 1911 – the Radicals managed to forge an "alliance of convenience". As a result, anarcho–syndicalist votes were exchanged for logistical and political protection; party centres were used for workers' meetings, the Radical press acted as a union bulletin board, and leading politicians such as Rafael Guerra del Río and Emiliano Iglesias acted as lawyers for the unions as late as 1919. In essence, the Radicals and anarcho–syndicalists had achieved a mutually beneficial division of labour rooted in their respective political and trade union spheres. The informal alliance with the anarcho–syndicalists notwithstanding, the Radical Party represented an alternative to the workers' organizations to the left and to the monarchists to the right. From its very inception, therefore, the Radical Party was neither a left- nor a right-wing force, but a centrist one.[9]

The transformation of the Lerrouxist movement was reflected in the "law and order" ticket that was presented in the Barcelona municipal elections of 1909. Made up of businessmen, professionals, and property owners, it did not include a single worker. Many of the Catalan old guard, originally workers, soon became *nouveau riche* businessmen or lawyers – "bourgeois bohemians". Lerroux himself was greatly changed by his exile of 1908–9 in Argentina – undertaken in order to avoid jail after he had lost a court case concerning a defamatory newspaper article – where he became involved in an array of business ventures. Indeed, his return to Spain in November 1909 had been delayed by two months as a result of further commercial dealings in London and Paris. "I'm not yet rich," as he declared in 1912, "but I propose to be so." That same year, he founded the Banco Español de Obras Públicas. His entrepreneurial activities further extended to mining companies, the thermal waters at Coslada (near Madrid), and the spa at Baños de Montemayor in Caceres province. His lifestyle, in contrast to his politics, was revolutionized as cars, jewels, servants, and a hotel in O'Donnell Street, just a stone's throw from the central Retiro Park in Madrid, became his. The trappings of the revolutionary working-class leader had been cast aside for those of a self-made man of the bourgeoisie. His fraudulent law degree, obtained in 1922 at the age of 58, was a further expression of his desire to supersede his origins as a Grub Street journalist for the status of a respected member of the professional middle classes. Yet his metamorphosis was merely that of the movement writ large.[10]

The new-found priorities of the Lerrouxists were revealed by their reaction to the "Tragic Week" of July 1909 in Barcelona. This was a spontaneous uprising sparked by the embarkment of conscripts for the unpopular war in Morocco in which rioters, seizing upon the Catholic Church as the most visible symbol of the *ancien régime*, sacked a hundred religious buildings. The heavy-handed response of the authorities was directed above all at the Barcelona Radical Party, which had done much to fan the flames of revolt. Although the repression enhanced the Lerrouxists' reputation as an anti-system force, they did little to save Francisco Ferrer Guardia, the anarchist educator who had been a source of support for Lerroux during his early years and who had been targeted by the authorities as a scapegoat, from the firing squad. At the national level, the Radicals, while underlining their populist identification with "*el pueblo*" by celebrating the events of July 1909 as the "Glorious Week", distanced themselves from the rising's revolutionary overtones. Indeed, the "Tragic Week" was something of an embarrassment to the reformist Radical Party, less radical, ironically, than its predecessor.[11]

For the Radical Party to establish itself as a truly national entity it was crucial that Madrid replaced Barcelona as its epicentre. To this end, an impressive social centre was inaugurated, numerous neighbourhood centres were put in place, and a national newspaper – *El Radical* – was set in motion in March 1910. The dazzling launch attracted many of the country's most prestigious young thinkers, including the philosopher and journalist José Ortega y Gasset, the academics and future socialists Julián Besteiro and Fernando de los Ríos, and writers such as Pío Baroja and Jacinto Benavente. A nationwide recruitment drive was also undertaken. The goal was to construct not just a national party but the dominant force within the opposition.[12] In 1909 the Radical Party united with other republican parties and the socialists to form the most ambitious anti-dynastic front yet under the Restoration, the Conjunción Republicano-Socialista. In the general election of 1910, the Conjunción did promisingly, securing 36 seats including seven Radicals and the first ever socialist deputy, its leader Pablo Iglesias.[13] Later that year, however, the Radicals were discredited by the so-called *cal, yeso y cemento* ("limestone, plaster and cement") corruption scandal, which involved the misappropriation of local taxes in the Barcelona *ayuntamiento* (town hall). The pellulation of the Radicals had initially been exposed by their Catalan rivals, but the socialists seized on the affair, too, in order to expel the Radical Party from the Conjunción. It can be argued that the socialists were eager to disqualify the party because it threatened their own position, especially in Madrid. The clash was to mark the beginning of a long and conflictive relationship.[14]

The scandal of 1910 had a devastating impact on the Radical Party. Not only was it abandoned by the intellectuals and writers, but it subsequently proved unable to conquer Madrid, a severe setback for its national project. Worst of all, the Radicals were to be associated for ever after with the stench of corruption. A play of 1912, "The Redeemer of the People" by Adolf Marsillach, crystallized the popular image of the Radical Party as corrupt and cynical. However, as Joan Culla stresses, the Radicals' administrative venality in the Barcelona town hall was "proverbial from the times of the dynastic parties and in the twentieth century it was employed by elements of all tendencies". Moreover, the Radicals plundered the public purse not so much for their personal enrichment as to finance the Barcelona party and to feed its clientage networks. Local candidates would promise, if elected, to be "the friend of everyone". This was understandable insofar as Radical politicians, unlike many dynastic ones, did not have independent incomes to draw on. Exploitation of local government was also a means of opening up the channels of influence within a highly restrictive economic and political system. Undoubtedly there was a sector within the party for which the relationship between politics and pellulation became inverted over time; that is to say, the exercise of public office became a mere extension of their business activities. The most glaring example was that of Juan Pich y Pon, the former tinsmith who built up a company that employed twenty-five workers before moving on to the higher echelons of industry and finance as well as the presidency of the Chamber of Urban Property. For Lerroux, who, in addition to a 75-year lease on the Baños de Montemayor spa and the purchase of the hotel in Madrid had acquired a four-house estate at San Rafael in the Guadarrama mountains north of the capital, the two worlds were to be indissolubly linked.[15]

Needless to say, the "*cal, yeso y cemento*" affair badly damaged the Radical Party's Barcelona flagship. The following year, 1911, the Radicals lost the overall majority on the town council. The subsequent decline in the local party was manifested in the atrophying of its organization, the haemorrhaging of activists, the fetid infighting, and its ebbing powers of popular mobilization. All of which was reflected in the ever more wretched electoral results. In the 1914 general election, the Radical Party had to reach an agreement, the so-called "Pact of San Gervasio", with the Catalanist UFNR in order to challenge – unsuccessfully, as it happened – the Lliga, now the hegemonic force in Barcelona. These setbacks were partly the result of Lerroux's absence from Catalonia, but they were also a function of the contradictions between the party's national priorities and those of the more leftist Barcelona organization. Yet the Radical Party's advancement at the national level was far from spectacular. Having lost the backing of the intellectuals in 1911 and of its strongest local affiliate, the Valencia-based PURA, in 1912, the Radical Party made little progress, winning a mere four seats in the general election of 1914. It has even been questioned whether the decline of the party in Barcelona was compensated for by its rise in the rest of the nation.[16]

The Radical Party was able to relaunch itself as a leading opposition force as a result of the First World War. Neutral throughout the hostilities, Spain was none the less deeply divided between "germanófilos" and "aliadófilos". The most prominent "aliádofilo" – through a mixture of principle and pragmatism – was Alejandro Lerroux. On the one hand, the Radical Party, inspired by the French Republic and its Radical–Socialist Party, was naturally francophile, while many Radicals regarded the conflagration as a final reckoning between progress and reaction. On the other hand, the Radicals sought to sharpen the tensions within the Restoration system in order to hasten the republic's coming. In the meantime, the Radical leader made capital out of the conflict by selling cereals, mules, wine, and other products to the allies, while the party press appears to have received financial backing from the French Radical–Socialists in exchange for promoting the Allied cause.[17]

The tensions generated by the divisions over the European war and by its socio-economic repercussions climaxed with the greatest political crisis in Spain in forty years. In the summer of 1917, the government was challenged by the Juntas Militares de Defensa, a sort of unofficial trade union made up of junior officers, the Assembly of Parliamentarians, which was composed of the republicans, socialists, and other forces including the Lliga, and, lastly, the organized working class. The dissident officers were aggrieved at plummeting salaries and the promotions system, but had no political programme. The Assembly, convoked as a result of parliament's suspension and which can be seen, as Sebastian Balfour observes, as "the culmination of efforts since the Disaster to create a modernizing and democratic alternative to the ruling political order", demanded elections for a constituent Cortes. Furthermore, the Unión General de Trabajadores (UGT) and CNT threatened to launch a general strike in support of the Assembly's goals. The crisis of legitimacy that had afflicted Spain since 1898 had become a full-blown crisis of state. Partly out of adherence to nineteenth-century republican tradition and partly to avoid a revolutionary upheaval, the Radical leader, for whom the army was "the most vibrant organ of those that make up the nation", was most inclined to the seizure of power by means of a *pronunciamiento* (coup d'état). Yet he was also prepared to overthrow the monarchy in a legal fashion by backing the Assembly. Indeed, the Radicals strengthened the Parliamentarians' case by insisting that the Lliga had to be included in the Assembly if it was to have sufficient support and credibility to outface the monarchy. Moreover, the Radicals did not flinch at the possibility of bringing the Restoration to its knees by means of worker mobilization. In fact, they regarded the general strike of August 1917 as simply one more piece in the wide-ranging offensive against the monarchy – though aspiring to channel the workers' protest via the parties. By pursuing a reformist strategy alongside a revolutionary one, the Radicals underlined their fundamentally pragmatic outlook. In the end, the contradictions within the opposition, together with the state's monopoly on force and the temporal unity of the monarchist parties, proved too much. The Juntas, ambiguous towards the Parliamentarians, hostile towards the workers, and having rejected Lerroux's overtures, reached a settlement with the government. The Assembly was later torpedoed by the decision of the Lliga, alarmed at the increasing radicalism of its allies, to join the government. Finally, the general strike was crushed by the strategic and physical superiority of the state, a hundred workers being killed in the process. Symptomatic of the Radical Party's failure to topple the regime was the fact that Lerroux, as a result of his subversive activities, had to flee to France in order to elude arrest.[18]

By 1918, a decade after its foundation, the Radical Party had signally failed to establish itself as a national political force. In the general election of that year, its candidates were limited overwhelmingly to Andalusia, Catalonia, and the Levante. What is more, the party won just a single seat.

The year before, the party newspaper, *El Radical*, had closed, heavily in debt. As Lerroux admitted before parliament in 1913, "there is, in fact, no republican party: there are republican masses, there are eminent republican men, thinkers, intellectuals; but an organic, positive force, no".[19] The aborted hopes of the party magnified the already considerable profile of its charismatic leader. During the early Barcelona years, Lerroux had accumulated a great deal of power in his hands, this being enhanced by his elevation into a national leader with the establishment of the Radical Party. Needless to say, this identification of the party with the person stunted the Radical Party's institutional and democratic evolution. The rules and regulations that supposedly governed its existence were irrelevant in the face of the Godfather-like authority of the *jefe*. Prior to the Second Republic, for example, not a single congress was held in order to discuss and develop the party's national organization. Those bodies that did function, such as the National Junta, merely rubber-stamped the decisions of Lerroux. Accordingly, references to the activities of the Junta scarcely exist. Instructions handed down by the national leadership were signed by the *jefe* and began "my desire is . . . ". The interpreter of doctrine, the orchestrator of propaganda, and the arbiter of disputes, was Lerroux, and Lerroux alone.[20]

From 1918 to 1923 the Radical Party accentuated its conservative profile as the boom of the First World War gave way to a sharp economic downturn and widespread social strife. During the "Bolshevik Triennium" of 1918–20, crop-burnings, riots, and strikes engulfed Andalusia, while from 1919 to 1921 Barcelona was hit by a wave of violence as employers, disillusioned by the limits to legality, turned to *pistoleros*, the unions responding in the same mode. In the midst of the agitation, the Radical Party offered itself, in Lerroux's words, as "the mediator between the social classes in struggle"; that is to say, as a "Third Way" between the unfettered capitalism of the right and the anti-capitalist collectivism of the left – a guarantee of "harmony between capital and labour". On the one hand, the Radicals, determined to head off a revolutionary convulsion, promised the working-class reform and rights within the framework of a republic. On the other, the Radicals assured the middle class that they would eschew the "social catastrophe" that the monarchists appeared unable to avert by enforcing law and order and by thwarting "the red dictatorship". In the same vein, the Radicals vouched to treat the Catholic Church with care and consideration. Essentially, the Radical Party was endeavouring to broaden the area of its support through the incorporation of more conservative classes. To the same end, Lerroux ardently defended Spain's Moroccan colony – "the *pueblo* that doesn't have colonies is a dead *pueblo*" – as well as the armed forces. His attendance at a banquet in 1923 in honour of the young Francisco Franco, a military hero of the colonial wars, symbolically united the two causes.

Finally, the Radical Party stressed that the transition to the Republic would be characterized by the maintenance of law and order and by minimizing the role of popular mobilization. In short, the Radical Party was projecting itself as an orderly alternative to the monarchy – the "guardian of change".[21]

The shift of the Radical Party to the right was not entirely surprising given its proximity to the Restoration system. On numerous occasions the Radical Party had backed the Liberals against the Conservatives, reviving for example the "Maura No!" campaign of 1907 to 1909 from 1910 to 1915. It had also acted on the Liberals' behalf in relation to the left, such as by extenuating strike movements. As a result, Lerroux was consulted by Liberal administrations on the leading matters of the day and granted personal favours (such as in relation to the purchase of the Madrid hotel), while Radical politicians gained access to the corridors of power. In the process, the Radical leader had managed to carve out a niche for himself, albeit a peripheral one, within the political establishment. It was widely suspected that he secured his parliamentary seat for Cordoba in 1914 through the intervention of the authorities.[22] In the same spirit, the Radicals reached a modus vivendi with the dynastic Catalan party, the Lliga, in the 1910s. Rhetorically hostile to the Lliga, in reality the Radicals cooperated with it in relation to the Mancomunidad, the Barcelona World Fair, and in the day-to-day running of the city of Barcelona and the Catalan region. They even became "crony capitalists" by collaborating, for example, in the establishment of the Fabricación Nacional de Lámparas Eléctricas in 1917. In effect, the partnership between the Radicals and the *Lligistas* was a mutually beneficial arrangement that kept the Conservatives and Liberals out of Catalonia.[23] At the national level, the Radical Party was often closer to the arepublican Reformists and the left-wing of the Liberal Party, especially the faction headed by Santiago Alba, than to the republican parties. In fact, by the early 1920s it was understood that if Alba and the Reformist leader, Melquiades Alvarez, achieved power, the Radical Party would second their efforts to reform the regime from within. If they were unsuccessful, however, they would consider backing the transition to a Radical-controlled Republic. Yet Lerroux was even prepared to go beyond his dealings with liberal monarchists. In 1918 and again in 1920, he surreptitiously met Alfonso XIII himself. The king, in turn, publicly praised the "statesman-like qualities" and "talent" of the Radical leader. Thus Lerroux was even prepared – should the circumstances dictate – to provide the monarchy with a left-wing option. Indeed, this marked the culmination of the Radical Party's goal – evident since its foundation – to integrate itself into the Restoration system.[24]

Ultimately, however, the Radical Party was a centrist force that looked both ways. In Catalonia, for instance, it not only made common cause with the Lliga and the Liberals, but also with the left-wing Catalanist UNFR, the socialists, and the CNT. Similar shifts can be observed on an ideological plane. Often regarded as an inherently anti-Catalan force, the Radicals none the less backed the demands for greater Catalan autonomy throughout much of the period from 1914 to 1922. The pragmatism of the Radical Party is exemplified by the fact that in 1920 – the year when Lerroux conferred for a second time with Alfonso XIII – it hosted the high-profile National Congress of Republican Democracy in Madrid, the most impressive republican gathering since the Unión Republicana Congress of 1903. The National Congress was attended by 1,461 delegates, most of whom were Radicals from Catalonia, Andalusia, Extremadura, the Canary Islands, and Madrid. Ostensibly designed to provide the varie-gated republican forces with a greater sense of unity and purpose, in reality the Congress was held in order to relaunch the Radical Party both in propagandistic terms – by demonstrating that it had a viable programme for the nation's problems – and in practical terms by attracting and assimilating numerous provincial parties.[25] Still, in the 1920 general election the Radical Party won only five seats, while the republicans overall, bereft of the alliance with the socialists, sank to under twenty. The following year, Lerroux's prestige within republican and Radical circles alike plunged as a result of his personal backing for the government's Moroccan policy, which resulted in the disastrous defeat of Annual in July 1921 in which 10,000 Spanish soldiers died. His standing did not improve when, following an interview in September 1921 with his arch-enemy, Antonio Maura, he expressed an interest in collaborating with the Conservative-led government. In late 1922 and early 1923, however, the Radical leader attempted to re-establish his opposition credentials by pursuing a "campaign of responsibilities" over the Annual catastrophe, which included the demand that the king abdicate.[26]

The ease with which the *coup d'état* of General Primo de Rivera triumphed in September 1923 was in part a measure of the weakness of the anti-dynastic opposition and in particular of the republicans. Indeed, the republicans were, as Ben-Ami observes, "at the height of a process of disintegration and in a mood of frustration because of their failure to change the political system either through conspiracies or by legal means". Despite the fact that the *Blasquistas* (the followers of Blasco Ibáñez) in Valencia had shown as early as 1894 that the dynastic parties could be overthrown in the urban arena, that the "Disaster" of 1898 had been a monumental blow for the Restoration regime, and that the collapse of the *turno pacífico* in 1913 had made stable politics impossible, the republi-cans had been unable to break the monarchists' hold on the nation's political life. Not even during the crises of 1917 and 1918–23 did the republicans represent an authentic alternative to the crumbling of the dynastic parties. Even in the cities, the republicans' support was often uncertain. In Madrid, for example, the Conjunción won 41,650 votes in 1910 but less than half this six years later. Once the Conjunción folded in 1919, the republicans garnered no more than 9,000 votes out of an electoral roll of over 140,000. Yet they had won 27,400 votes in 1903. The republicans' ideological fuzziness and their failure to hammer out a common programme was accentuated by the lack of support from the intellectuals. Neither the "Generation of 1898" nor that of 1927 was republican, while that of 1914 was initially sympathetic, but abandoned the republican cause for the "accidentalism" (that is to say, neutrality in relation to the form of government) of the Reformist Party under Melquiades Alvarez. "Our propaganda," as Lerroux declared before the Cortes, "is more rhetorical than substantial, it is verbalistic, it is inorganic: we have not succeeded in reaching the heart of the *pueblo* except through the declaration of programmes whose content the majority of us ignore." Neither had the republicans been characterized by their organizational unity. The Unión Republicana of 1903 had been split by the formation of the Radical Party in 1908 and then sunk by that of the Reformist Party in 1912. The next unificatory enterprise, the Conjunción Republicano-Socialista, lost its leading left-wing republican force with the exit of the Radicals in 1911 and its main right-wing one with that of the Reformists two years later. Besides, the relationship between the republican cause and the socialists was always ambiguous. As orthodox Marxists, the socialists were not so much republicans as accidentalists or arepublicans for whom the republic – a merely "bourgeois" form of government – was simply a staging post on the road to socialism. As a result, the republicans and socialists were at once allies and antagonists. In Madrid, to take an example, the socialists grew at the republicans' expense following the Conjunción's collapse in 1919. Further, there can be little doubt that the republicans had undermined their appeal as an alternative through their integration into the Restoration system. The Radicals were not an exception insofar as all the republicans benefited to a greater or lesser extent from official influence. The most extreme example was that of the Reformist Party which, by declaring its accidentalism in 1913, gave up the best prepared of the republican forces to the Restoration.[27]

By the advent of the Dictatorship, the Radical Party, despite being the largest of the republican forces, still did not represent a truly national entity. It was limited to Andalusia, Aragon, the Canary Islands, Catalonia, and the Levante, and had failed to supersede its urban middle-class origins, its social base lying largely amongst lawyers, teachers, civil servants, shopkeepers and small-scale industrialists. Nor had the party been able to arrest its decline in Barcelona, which, despite the organization's vicissitudes there, remained a fundamental point of reference. The situation in the Catalan capital had been made even worse by the "quasi civil war" of 1921–3 over the leadership of Emiliano Iglesias, the wily

Galician with the handlebar moustache who was Lerroux's right-hand man there. Nationwide, the Radical Party scarcely existed in at least a third of the provinces, while the general election results continued to make depressing reading: in 1919, the party obtained three deputies, and in 1920 five. In 1923, it achieved the highest total yet of twelve. Still, this was no more than 3 per cent of the seats in the Cortes.[28] The *coup d'état* of General Primo de Rivera was greeted by Lerroux with the declaration that "if I am needed, I am waiting the order, the call, the request". On the assumption that the military's rule would be fleeting, the Radical leader was offering himself as the "guardian" of the return to constitutional normality. The assumption proved misplaced. The dictatorship not only lasted for six years, but it was also to have no need of the republicans.[29]

The opposition of the Radical Party to the military regime of 1923 to 1930, like that of the other republican forces, veered between benevolence and impotence. Party life was limited mainly to sports events and small gatherings, including the inevitable acts of homage to the *jefe*. Absent were the political meetings and other means of mobilization on which the party thrived. "Like the veteran soldiers of Napoleon," as the Radical organ, *El Progreso*, put it, "we, who follow Lerroux, can say: 'The guard dies, but never surrenders'." This was partly due to the prohibitions on political activity, but also, during the early years, to a patent lack of will. There were those, most notably Pich y Pon, who cooperated fulsomely with the regime, though the scale of such collaboration cannot remotely be compared to that of the socialist trade unions, the UGT, which joined forces with the dictator in an endeavour to implement their corporatist goals and to destroy their arch rival, the now illegal CNT.[30]

The restrictions on normal political life led the republicans into conspiracy. Shortly after the *pronunciamiento* of September 1923, Lerroux wrote to Blasco Ibáñez that a coup would soon finish off the regime, but such optimism was designed more to keep the "sacred flame" of republicanism alive than anything else. The following year, the Radical leader was approached by the dissident General Cavalcanti, but this came to nothing as he was sent by the dictator to the Balkans.[31] More important was the formation of the Alianza Republicana in February 1926, the first step towards the coordination of the republican opposition. A loose-knit federation made up of the Radical Party, the Federals, and the Catalan Republican Party under Marcelino Domingo, the Alianza also included Acción Republicana, a group of Madrid-based intellectuals founded the year before. The Alianza soon claimed to have the support of 450 local groups and an overall membership of just under 100,000. The Junta, which included Lerroux, Domingo, and Manuel Azaña of Acción Republicana, managed to coordinate the numerous groups and, despite the manifold constraints, to achieve a minimal level of activity. Like all the attempts at republican unity before it, the Alianza was soon beset by discrepancies and divisions. The main cleavage was between the "old" and the "new" republicans. The "new" republicans, who included Azaña and Domingo, placed a greater emphasize on social reform, the politicization of the working class, and more democratic forms of participation. The "old" republicans – above all Lerroux – were criticized for their perceived conservatism and "caudillismo".[32]

The divergences within the Alianza were crystallized by the reaction to the Radical leader's article "Collaboration and Revolution" of April 1929 in which he called for a "national government of all the political groups" that would determine the nation's fate by means of a constituent Cortes. By placing "national sovereignty" above the Republic, Lerroux incurred the wrath of his allies, for whom he was far too conciliatory towards the *ancien régime*. Two months later, the Federals abandoned the Alianza together with intellectuals such as Gregorio Marañón, Ramón Pérez de Ayala, and Luis Jiménez de Asúa, who, along with José Ortega y Gasset, would later form the quasi-party Agrupación al Servicio de la República (Group at the Service of the Republic). That same month, another section of the Alianza, headed by Marcelino Domingo and the writer and former Radical deputy Alvaro de Albornoz, left to form the Radical–Socialist Republican Party (PRRS). Desperate to escape the populist dogma and personalism of "historical republicanism", the new force aspired to a synthesis of republicanism and socialism that would amount to a republican entity "to which workers could adhere".[33] Strategically, Domingo and Albornoz aimed to take advantage of the fast-growing enthusiasm for the republican cause so that they could return to the Alianza from a position of strength. Indeed, it was the partial lifting of restrictions in July 1929 and the mushrooming of support for the republicans that allowed the Alianza to weather the myriad splits. As its activities increased, so did its membership – by mid-August to 150,000. Many of the local, provincial and regional groups that, having emerged from their enforced hibernation, joined the Alianza were effectively co-opted by the Lerrouxists, making it more than ever their creature. In late 1929 and early 1930 the Radical Party held regional assemblies in Barcelona, Huelva, La Coruña, Valencia, and Madrid. "Which opposition party in Spain," as *El Progreso* asked, "could offer such a number of branches upholding the ideal?" Moreover, the Radical *jefe*, as Federal leader Hilario Ayuso admitted, was still the "axis of Spanish republicanism".[34]

The Radical strategy was shaped by two central ideas. First, the fear of revolution. The republic should not be born, Lerroux affirmed, amidst "street tumults against the social order", as this would condemn it to "death by another sword". Thus in "Collaboration and Revolution" he had called for a national government because "the Soviet . . . was on the point of emerging". In other words, the "tragedy" of a "social revolution" had to be avoided by means of the triumph of a "political revolution" –

that is to say, one controlled by the parties and the politicians, not one swept away on a tide of popular insurgency. Intimately linked to the defence of the "political revolution" was the contention that the republicans had to broaden their base of support. The Radical leader made it plain in early 1930 that the republicans not only had to unite, but that they also had to reach out to other sectors of society, ranging from the extreme left to non-republican opposition forces. This was not, Lerroux explained in a letter of June 1929, an "absurd evolution" but "a strategy designed to attract to our side new people". Accordingly, his propaganda was aimed not at "the traditional republicans, but at the new ones and at the enemies of the present regime". He was convinced that, as he underlined in a speech in Valencia in late 1930, there existed an alarming lack of people sufficently "prepared to organize a new state". Only by creating as broad an anti-dynastic front as possible did the Radical leader believe that a controlled transition to the republic be guaranteed. Above all else, however, Lerroux stressed the need for the republicans to come together. The door of the Alianza, therefore, was left open for the return of the breakaways. First, the Federals rejoined the fold. Next, the Alianza agreed to coordinate its activities with both the PRRS and the new Galician formation, the ORGA. By the end of May 1930, as a result, all the republican forces except the Catalans had been brought within a tactical alliance.[35]

The surge in opposition to the Dictatorship was due not so much to the strength of the republican movement as to mistakes of the regime's own making. Primo de Rivera's confrontations between 1928 and 1930 with the army, the intellectuals, the Catalan nationalists, and with the students and university lecturers rapidly politicized the middle classes. The climax to this process of deterioration was the bursting of the economic bubble and the regime's subsequent inability to halt the plummeting of the peseta. The republicans were able to take advantage of the burgeoning discontent precisely because the military dictator – who had been manifestly unable to create his own political system – had demolished the foundations of the monarchist parties. Primo de Rivera probably created more republicans than the republicans themselves. Yet it was only once the Dictatorship fell in January 1930 that the republican movement swoll at a dizzying rate, filling the void left by the dynastic parties. The incorporation of the shock-headed Niceto Alcalá-Zamora, a former monarchist minister, in April 1930 was a major boost to the republican cause. Moreover, he was joined by the saturnine Miguel Maura, son of Antonio Maura, a symbol of conservative, monarchist Spain. Three months later, they established the Derecha Liberal Republicana (DLR) with a view to securing a "Republic of order" that would protect the interests of the conservative classes. The republican mobilization reached its crescendo with the meeting of 28 September 1930 in the Madrid bullring. By this stage, the Radical leader had shifted strategy. Earlier in the year, he had still maintained that a constituent Cortes should decide the future of the monarchy. Now, however, he insisted that abdication was the only solution to the ongoing crisis. Not only were four of the eight speakers at the Madrid rally Radicals, but their *jefe*, according to a newspaper report, "magnetized the crowd".[36]

The high profile of the Radicals at the September meeting contrasted vividly with their treatment at the gathering of republican leaders a month earlier in the Basque resort of San Sebastian. This was designed to take the opposition a step further by incorporating the Catalans and by launching a committee to organize the "revolution". Having achieved the first objective, the party leaders set about nominating the "Revolutionary Committee". The Radical Party's historical and political importance notwithstanding, the ambiguous relationship of Lerroux with the monarchy and his reputation for graft made him deeply distrusted by his colleagues. The personal hostility of Miguel Maura towards the Radical leader – the bête noire of his father – also played its part. As a result, the director of the Committee was not to be Lerroux, but Alcalá-Zamora – a convert of four months' standing. In fact, the Radical *jefe* was not included in the Committee at all. Worse still, he was not put on the substitute list either. He was, however, included in the *troika* that was entrusted with the task of approaching the working-class organizations. Yet even here, Lerroux was marginalized. He was to deal with neither of the two main movements – the anarcho–syndicalists or the socialists – but with the peripheral Spanish Communist Party (PCE), a move that was made even more tactless given his notorious anti-Soviet sentiments.[37] There could be little doubt that the Radical leader had been treated extremely shoddily. He himself regarded the proceedings as "an insult and an offence" that sought "my elimination". In reality, his colleagues had tried to balance the Radical leader's status as "the black sheep" with his undoubted popularity. Thus Marcelino Domingo later recalled that Lerroux "gave us goose pimples" and that he was considered as "dangerous as the police itself", but that he was accepted as a "necessary evil" as there were "few republicans and the few existing remnants obeyed the discipline of Don Alejandro". Yet the ostracism of the Radical *jefe* at San Sebastian was not only, as Maura admits, "an offence", but also counterproductive, as it was considered impossible to construct the republic "against him". The error was compounded by the fact that the Revolutionary Committee acted "without counting on him".[38]

The Radicals were further marginalized two months later when it came to the selection of the "provisional government". The two key posts of Prime Minister and the Minister of the Interior went to the erstwhile monarchists, Niceto Alcalá-Zamora and Miguel Maura. It was suggested – before he had arrived at the meeting – that Lerroux should be given the

Ministry of Justice, but Maura objected that the Radical *jefe*'s acolytes would then be found auctioning court sentences in the centre of Madrid. Upon arrival, Lerroux declared his interest in the Ministry of the Interior, but, despite contending that he had been the "embodiment" of the republican cause since the outset of Alfonso XIII's reign, he was shunted into Foreign Affairs – one of the most marginal ministries given the overwhelming importance of domestic politics and Spain's low international profile.[39] Quite rightly, Lerroux also protested at the fact that the Radicals had been given just one Cabinet seat. As a result, the taciturn Sevillian Diego Martínez Barrio was chosen by the provisional government for the yet-to-be created Ministry of Communications. However, this was yet another minor department which, to make matters worse, would bring the Radical minister into conflict with the socialist-dominated postal unions. Altogether, the Radical Party had come out of the negotiations extremely badly. They occupied two low-ranking departments, while the PRRS occupied the ministeries of Education and Public Works. Even worse, the socialists, who, as recently as the National Congress of 1928 had poured scorn on the republicans, collared three mainstream departments: Economy, Labour, and Justice. At least the incorporation of the socialists signified that a common republican–socialist front had at last been established.[40]

Despite the groundswell in support for the republican cause, the Revolutionary Committee still aimed to come to power by means of a *pronunciamiento*. Many of the early insurrectionary schemes had been the product of isolated individuals and groups rather than all-embracing enterprises. However, the Alianza participated, if only peripherally, in the "Sanjuanada" rising of 1926, while taking a more active role in the coup attempt of former Prime Minister Sánchez Guerra in January 1929.[41] Of Lerroux's commitment there can be no doubt. His conspiratorial activities had so far put him behind bars in 1926 and 1928. He later confided to a friend that "the police did not leave me in peace" and that his subversive exertions had made him lose 12 kilos in weight. In early 1930 Martínez Barrio was involved in the preparations for a *pronunciamiento* in Andalusia. The limitations to the Committee's coercive resources were revealed by the thwarted uprising of December 1930, which was held in conjunction with a socialist general strike. Such was the suspicion of the Radical leader – it was thought that he might be playing a double game – that he had been given little responsibility in organizing the insurrection. No one in the provisional government, Maura relates, had "the slightest confidence" in Lerroux, regarding him as "extremely dangerous". Yet the Radical leader, as he had demonstrated in 1917, was perfectly prepared to bring the monarchy down by violent means if the opportunity arose. Spurned by his allies, Lerroux had in fact set up his own, parallel, revolutionary committee.[42]

Following the débâcle of December 1930, most of the provisional government ended up either in jail or exile. Lerroux, with the likely connivance of the regime, remained in Madrid. Despite being given control of the Revolutionary Committee, he remained isolated. The jailed members of the provisional government refused to accept Lerroux's nominations as intermediaries, causing yet another "great disappointment" for the Radical *jefe*. Still, he not only tried to rally the socialists and the republicans, but also urged the provincial committees not to let up in their offensive against the monarchy. Moreover, he endeavoured to win over the army and Civil Guard to the republican cause, going so far as to meet General Sanjurjo, the head of the Civil Guard. But Lerroux's contacts were restricted largely to the Radical Party, while his support within the army was circumscribed. As a result, the Lerroux-led Committee's greatest contribution to the anti-dynastic campaign was the widespread dissemination of clandestine propaganda.[43]

The so-called *Dictablanda* (Soft Dictatorship) of General Berenguer, who had come to power on Primo de Rivera's fall, finally succumbed on 14 February 1931. The General's attempt to return to constitutional normality had been stymied above all by the abstention campaign of the republican–socialist alliance. In a further attempt to return to constitutional rule, the new premier, Admiral Aznar, announced municipal elections for 12 April. The Radicals were convinced that this was a trap, but they participated in the elections out of discipline to the Republican–Socialist Coalition. The elections were converted by the anti-dynastic opposition into a plebiscite on the monarchy's future. In the rural areas, the regime's grip on the electorate proved undiminished, but in the towns and cities the opposite was true: the Republican–Socialist Coalition defeated the monarchists in nearly all the nation's fifty provincial capitals. On 14 April, the king went into exile. The Republic had triumphed. The Radicals, like their allies, were astonished that the regime had come about as a result of the municipal elections. Lerroux in particular had, finally, achieved "the dream and goal of all the aspirations of his life".[44]

The ambiguity that had epitomized the Radical Party prior to the Republic was at once its strength and weakness. On the one hand, the Radical Party had been distrusted, if not disdained, by the other republican and socialist forces for its symbiotic relationship with the monarchy. On the other hand, the Radical Party had demonstrated the value of compromise by working alongside forces both to its left and its right. Indeed, the future of the Republic was likely to be shaped to an important extent by the interplay between the crusading principles of the left and the centrist pragmatism of the Radicals.

II

"A Republic for all Spaniards"
The Radical defence of change and continuity,
April to June 1931

The Second Republic was swept into being on 14 April 1931 on a wave
of euphoria as people flooded onto the streets in towns and *pueblos*
throughout Spain to celebrate the proclamation of the newly-born regime.
Many middle-class, and some upper-class, citizens, greeted the new order
with even greater alacrity than they had the military dictatorship eight
years earlier. Hitherto staunchly monarchist institutions, including
landowners' associations and religious bodies, were sufficiently impressed
by the precipitous collapse of the Restoration to declare their allegiance
to the nascent regime. Such was the expectation following the disasters of
Alfonso XIII's reign that many people embraced the Republic as the long-
awaited panacea for the nation's ills. The spontaneous transformation of
the streets and squares into a "fiesta" of the anti-monarchist *pueblo* was
therefore a fitting finale to a process which had seen the *ancien régime*
toppled by plebiscite rather than *pronunciamiento*. As one observer noted,
"the Republic is the work of the people".[1]

Spain's first democratic regime in the twentieth century none the less
faced a formidable series of obstacles if it was to be consolidated, let alone
fulfil the widespread expectations of reform placed in it. The first problem
was that the Republic emerged on the cusp of the Great Depression of the
1930s. Admittedly, the Spanish economy, protected by high tariff walls
and dependent only to a limited extent on import–export markets, escaped
relatively lightly in comparison with the major western economies.
However, several leading industries, most notably construction, the
metallurgical industries, and mining in Asturias, as well as the agrarian
export sector, were badly damaged by the 1929 Crash. In addition, the
boom of the 1920s, the greatest in Spanish history, had come to a shud-
dering halt, leaving in its wake the greatest debt in Spanish history. For
the politicians of the Republic, the most explosive issue thrown up by the
recession was unemployment. The scourge of escalating unemployment
was compounded by chronic structural underemployment in industries

such as construction, but above all in agriculture, the largest single sector of the economy. In those areas dominated by the huge landed estates, or *latifundios*, especially in the south, the landless labourers, or *jornaleros*, usually found themselves without work for five or six months of the year. The recent winter drought and a succession of poor harvests made the situation in the spring of 1931 even worse. The economic setbacks of 1929–31 were to shape events under the Republic substantially, especially as regards relations between the workers and employers, in both the cities and the countryside.[2]

The very nature of the transition from the monarchy to the Republic, whereby king Alfonso XIII had peacefully abandoned the country following the unexpected result of the municipal elections of 12 April, can plausibly be seen as a further obstacle to the regime's consolidation as well as a constraint on the reformist aspirations of the anti-monarchist *pueblo*. By deserting the king out of sheer expediency rather than through an identification with the republican cause, the principal pillars of the *ancien régime*, especially the army, the church, and the landowning oligarchy, had not only managed to preserve their extant social and institutional might, but also indicated that they, even allowing for the progressive or moderate elements within each institution, would almost certainly act as a constraint on change. Had the monarchy been overthrown by revolutionary or violent means, as opposed to the brief and bloodless transition of 12–14 April, the balance of power might have been radically different.

By contrast with the institutional intactness of the *ancien régime*, the political forces of the monarchy had disintegrated. While the two dynastic parties, the Liberals and Conservatives, had been dismantled under the Dictatorship, Primo de Rivera's own party, the Unión Patriótica, had failed to survive the regime which had created it. However, those forces which would inevitably be mobilized in defence of the interests of the old regime had redoubtable resources to draw on. First, *caciquismo*, the backbone of the Restoration system, was alive and well. This had been amply demonstrated by the April elections when the monarchists, despite having been trounced by the republicans in the towns and cities, had none the less triumphed in the countryside through the machinations of the local party bosses, or *caciques*. Only by means of far-reaching administrative, agrarian and other reforms would the *caciques'* clout be diminished, let alone eliminated. Second, the right would still be able to count on extensive backing, whether of a financial, organizational, or social nature, from the institutional pillars of the former regime. Politically speaking, the monarchists may have been displaced, but the eventually reorganized forces of the right, given the socio-economic and institutional reserves at their disposal, would almost certainly wield considerable influence under the new regime.

By comparison to those of the *ancien régime*, the republican–socialist coalition's resources were decidedly meagre. The republican movement was divided into the numerous local and provincial groupings that made up the weakly integrated national bodies as well as a number of independent regional parties. Of the national entities, Acción Republicana, still a mere group as opposed to a party, was limited to a skeletal structure in a few provinces, while the PRRS possessed a more extensive organization, but fell far short of a genuinely nationwide party of mass proportions: three months into the Republic, the Radical–Socialist Party had no more than 45,000 affiliates.[3] A third party, the DLR, was a fledgling body circumscribed by the personal influence of its two founders, the Catholic ministers Alcalá-Zamora and Miguel Maura.

The Radical Party was undoubtedly the largest and best organized of all the republican parties, yet it remained more of a congeries of highly autonomous regional and provincial bodies held together by the charismatic figure of Lerroux rather than a truly national party. In much of Spain, especially in the countryside, the Radicals' presence was negligible or non-existent. The national republican parties were, therefore, characterized by their organizational fragmentation, paltry financial resources, and an overwhelmingly urban social base in a country where nearly half the working population was still employed in the agrarian economy. Of all the forces that made up the republican–socialist coalition, the most organized and well supported was the socialist movement, the vast bulk of which was made up of its trade unions, the UGT. But the socialists, like the republicans, were far from truly national in scope. Only in 1930 did the UGT begin to attract substantial support in the rural areas, while neither the UGT nor the Partido Socialista Obrero Español (PSOE) had ever managed to establish themselves in Spain's greatest industrial area, Catalonia. On the contrary, the leading workers' organization in Catalonia, as in many other parts of Spain such as Gijon, Huesca, Seville, and Zaragoza, was the CNT. Yet the anarcho–syndicalists did not form part of the republican–socialist coalition. In fact, the CNT had a highly ambiguous attitude towards the new regime, having backed the anti-monarchist movement largely to secure an amnesty for its prisoners and to be able to organize itself more freely under a more liberal regime. For its part, the Communist Party, of little importance nationwide but significant in certain localities such as Seville, declared war on the Republic as a bourgeois tyranny from the outset. The backing of the workers' movements for the Republic was therefore equivocal at best, hostile at worst.[4]

The inability of the republican–socialist alliance to overthrow the monarchy by coercive means had been cruelly exposed by the abortive *coup d'état* of December 1930. In particular, the Radical leader, Alejandro Lerroux, had signally failed to realize the dream cherished throughout his long years in opposition of coming to power by means of a nineteenth-century-style *pronunciamiento*. Now that the republicans and socialists had finally taken command of the State, they were in a stronger position than before – especially as the monarchists were demoralized and in disarray – to carry out a thoroughgoing revolution by means of force. However, the republican rulers lacked the will, strategy, and, in all probability, the military support for such an enterprise. In any case, the pacific nature of the transition, subsequently acclaimed by Lerroux as "a history lesson for the entire world", and the vertiginous surge in support for the anti-monarchist cause following the fall of the military dictatorship in January 1930, had convinced the republicans that a democratic parliamentary regime would enjoy sufficient support and legitimacy to satisfy the variegated expectations placed in it. The scrupulously legalistic approach undertaken by the provisional government was embodied in the Judicial Statute issued on the day of the Republic's proclamation, which stated that elections would be held to a constituent Cortes in order to draw up a democratic constitution. The Cabinet's fastidious approach, personified in the legalistic figure of Prime Minister Niceto Alcalá-Zamora, reflected a collective desire to implant a regime that, in contrast to the arbitrary practices of the monarchy, would be beyond reproach and therefore acceptable to all Spaniards.[5]

The overriding challenge to the provisional government was to consolidate the Republic by effectively channelling the diverse expectations of the anti-monarchist *pueblo* as well as integrating, or neutralizing, those sectors of society which were actively hostile. The contradiction at the heart of the opposition to the monarchy, which ranged from industrialists to landless labourers, shopkeepers, artisans, landowners, unskilled workers, and the professional classes, and which embraced many former monarchists along with the uncommitted middle classes, the "*clase neutra*" (the neutral class), is that it was a populist movement brought together by a common opposition, but bereft of a common vision or programme. In reality, the crowds that thronged the squares and streets of Spain on 14 April in joyous celebration of the Republic's proclamation harboured a multitude of disparate, often opposing, hopes. The numerous working-class organizations, ranging from the dominant division between the UGT and the CNT to the Communist Party, the Catholic unions, and the republican workers, were characterized by powerfully antagonistic ideologies and interests.

The panorama presented by the middle classes, in comparison with the sectarian schisms of the organized working classes, was even more perplexing. Despite the myriad republican parties, these accounted for only a part of the middle classes. Traditionally, an even greater segment lay completely beyond the orbit of republican politics: the Catholic middle classes. The fault line between the republican and religious middle classes represented a fundamental challenge to the Republic's consolidation, especially in view of the paramountcy of anticlericalism in republican political culture. The religious cleavage also affected the working and upper classes, though to a lesser extent. In overall terms, the middle classes were divided between Catholics and anticlericals, regional nationalists and centralists, radical, progressive and conservative republicans, as well as between republicans, who included some Catholics, and non-republicans. Nor should the *clase neutra*, that vaguely defined segment of the middle classes which had not committed itself fully to the monarchy and which remained to be convinced, along with many monarchists, by the Republic, be forgotten. In short, the varied expectations of the heterogeneous middle classes posed a fundamental problem for the stability of the Republic.

Conflicting class interests had to be accommodated by a provisional government that was itself divided amongst socialists, conservative and left-wing republicans, Catalan and Galician nationalists, and recent Catholic converts to the republican cause. While the socialists and left-wing republicans, including the progressive Catalan and Galician nationalists, were all committed to the idea of reform, they did not share a common programme or even a set of proposals. Indeed, the left republicans were more concerned with institutional and cultural reform than the socialists, for whom socio-economic issues were foremost. And while the left republicans and socialists maintained that the Republic was meaningless if divorced from substantive reform, the Radical Party, together with the DLR, believed that the establishment of parliamentary democracy was the overriding goal. Starkly contrasting visions of the Republic, however, were to be found not just between the parties but within them too. The UGT leader Francisco Largo Caballero had collaborated with the Dictatorship of Primo de Rivera in order to further the unions' corporatist concerns, not least at the cost of its arch-rival, the anarcho–syndicalist CNT. He had fought for the Republic not for the sake of democracy but to advance the interests of the socialist trade unions. For Largo Caballero, the Republic was a mere staging post on the road to socialism. By contrast, Indalecio Prieto, the dominant figure within the Socialist Party, who had refused to collaborate with the Dictatorship as a matter of principle, viewed a reformist Republic as an end worth defending in itself.[6]

The Radical Party, too, harboured divergent visions of the new regime. It is not surprising to discover, given the Radicals' populist background, that the party contained widely differing views on issues such as Catalan autonomy, the Catholic Church, and agrarian reform, but there were also profound divisions over wider questions of political principle. For example, the Barcelona party's pork-barrel view of politics did not coincide with that of many others, including the Seville party under Martínez Barrio, nor did Lerroux's *Zorrillista* fixation with nineteenth-century-style *pronunciamientos*. Broadly speaking, the party was divided into "old" Radicalism, centred on the Barcelona party and with much in common with the political practices of the dynastic regime, and "new" Radicalism, which placed a greater stress on democratic procedure and drew its strength from regional sections such as the Tenerife and Seville parties. Such differences, however, were less apparent in the Radical Party than in the socialist movement on account of Lerroux, whose charismatic leadership invariably managed to subordinate genuine political differences. Within Acción Republicana and the Radical–Socialist Party, fewer fundamental differences in outlook were to be found at the outset of the Republic, though the Radical–Socialists were soon to distinguish themselves by their huge variety of opinions on issues of reform.[7] Overall, the provisional government was characterized by its diversity of views and the corresponding lack of a shared vision or programme.

A further handicap for the provisional government was the lack of experience and expertise of its own ministers. Most of the Cabinet had served in a legislative capacity as parliamentary deputies, but only Alcalá-Zamora had national-level executive experience, although Largo Caballero had participated in Primo de Rivera's Council of State. The ministers were hampered too by their very conception of change. Reliance on a stunted and loosely integrated state as the main instrument of reform to the neglect of other means of change was a highly questionable approach, given the intractability of structural problems such as caciquismo and the strength of vested interests such as the Catholic Church and the army. Another critical constraint on the republicans' room for manoeuvre was the poverty of economic thought, as reflected in a slavish adherence to the orthodoxies of a balanced budget and low taxes – which may also have been a reaction against the state interventionism of the Primo de Rivera years. Yet the challenges of a global recession, the monumental debts inherited from the Dictatorship, and the tenuous fiscal resources of the Spanish state demanded a more creative response. Symptomatic of the republicans' indifference to economic matters was the appointment of a socialist, Indalecio Prieto, as Minister of the Economy, despite his glaring lack of macroeconomic experience and the destabilizing impact that his appointment would have on the business world.

The Spanish Second Republic was the last in a long line of European republics formed in the aftermath of the First World War, including Germany, Austria, Czechoslovakia, and Poland, and in the 1920s such as Ireland and Greece. Neighbouring Portugal had gone over to a republican state as early as 1910. Yet most of these republics had subsequently given way to authoritarian regimes or would soon do so. In other words, Spain embraced republican democracy at precisely the moment when many other such regimes in Europe were moving in the opposite direction. In this sense, Spain certainly *was* different. The provisional government had to confront the diverse expectations of its popular base as well as its own divisions and deficiencies in the context of a worldwide economic depression just as the tide of democracy in Europe was ebbing.

It was therefore with a view to consolidating the Republic, and the position of the republican–socialist coalition within it, that the provisional government resolved to maintain its unity at least until the general election in June 1931 for the Constituent Cortes. Discrepancies within the ruling alliance were kept to a minimum despite the sweeping, if not controversial, nature of the reforms which it was to carry out by decree over the next three months. However, the most controversial aspect of the agrarian reform – the redistribution of land – was left to the Constituent Cortes precisely in order to avoid conflict within the Cabinet. The most urgent task facing the government was the unemployment crisis in the countryside, especially in the south. Thousands of labourers and their families were living in abject misery, often struggling for their very survival. The Minister of Labour, Francisco Largo Caballero, took advantage of the situation to pass a far-ranging package of labour reforms. Most notable amongst these was the creation of the *jurados mixtos*, or mixed juries, which would arbitrate in disputes between workers and employers. Unlike the *comités paritarios* (joint committees) set up under the Dictatorship, the new committees were extended beyond the cities to the countryside, as well as being granted greater powers. Another key measure was the *términos municipales* edict forbidding landowners from contracting labour outside their municipality until all local hands had been employed. This would not only raise local employment and wages by restricting the supply of labour, but also protect the trade unions by preventing them from being broken by the introduction of migrant labour. The extraordinary surge in support for the socialists in the rural areas during the regime's first year was due in large measure to the *términos municipales* initiative. In addition, one of the trade unions' long-standing demands, the eight-hour day, was finally realized in the decree of 1 July. These edicts further strengthened wages as overtime payments would now have to be made to labourers that worked *de sol a sol*, from dawn to dusk, during the harvest. Otherwise, more workers would have to be taken on. Finally, the *laboreo forzoso*, or obligatory cultivation, decree sought to enforce the above measures by ensuring that landowners continued to cultivate their land.[8]

The socialist-inspired labour legislation of April–July 1931 had far-reaching implications. First, despite the absence of an agrarian reform law, it represented a radical realignment of the rural socio-economic order. Traditionally, the landowners, exploiting their monopolization of local institutions such as the *ayuntamiento* (town or village council), the courts, and the Civil Guard as well as the zealous backing of the church, the consent of provincial and national authorities, and above all the constant surplus of hired hands, had held almost absolute sway over the landless labourers. The greatest abuse had taken place in the south on account of its *latifundios*, or huge estates, and the swarms of workers who were dependent on them for employment. The socialist-inspired reforms transformed the rural status quo by finally allowing the workers to organize and defend themselves against the landowners; in other words, by contesting the hegemony of the proprietors. By contrast, the urban employers, or *patronal*, were more accustomed to negotiating with the trade unions, having participated most recently in the *comités paritarios* under Primo de Rivera. Although the *jurados mixtos* represented less of a novelty to the urban employers than to the landowners, the early months of 1931 had none the less seen the *patronal* in open rebellion against the alleged impartiality of the *comités*. Assemblies held in January 1931 at the local level by the Defensa Mercantil Patronal, which represented 14,000 Madrid shopkeepers and tradesmen, and at the national level a month later, had called for withdrawal from the *comités*. It was clear, from the outset, that the *jurados mixtos* and other labour measures would cause fierce resistance from both the rural and the urban employers. Second, Largo Caballero's reforms were designed to improve not so much the lot of workers *per se* as that of *socialist* workers. The legislation, like that under the Dictatorship, was intended not only to entrench the socialists, its authors, within the state, but also, given that the CNT would not take part in statist schemes as a matter of principle, to win the anarcho–syndicalist rank-and-file over to the UGT by demonstrating the advantages of state socialism. In other words, the provisional government failed to exploit the unresolved struggle within the CNT between the revolutionary FAI and the more moderate, syndicalist leadership to try and bring the anarcho–syndicalist movement into the new regime. On the contrary, the attempt of the UGT to further its own interests at the expense of the CNT was merely a rerun of events under the Dictatorship. Yet the distancing of the anarcho–syndicalists from the new regime would only serve to destabilize it by heightening social and economic tension. Overall, the far-reaching labour reforms passed within weeks of the Republic's establishment cut both ways. On the one hand, they marked a substantial advance for those workers affected. On the other hand, the decrees, by alienating both the employers and the CNT, caused the first fissures within the anti-monarchist *pueblo*.[9]

Other reforms tackled by the provisional government during its early days included the efforts of the Radical–Socialist Minister of Education, the bespectacled former teacher and journalist Marcelino Domingo, to transform the state system, especially through the provision of primary schools. Traditionally, no area of reform had been attached greater importance by the republicans than education. In republican culture, enlightenment was the key to progress. In 1930, illiteracy still stood at between a quarter and a third of the population, while 60 per cent of children received no education at all.[10] Domingo's principal aim was "to sow Spain with schools". A decree of 12 June provided for the building of 27,151 new primary schools, 7,000 of which were to be completed by the beginning of the next academic course. Additional measures included the decree of 6 May, which made religious instruction in state schools optional, and the innovative edict of 29 May, which set up the Pedagogic Missions in order to take culture, such as in the form of theatre troupes, to the *pueblos*.[11]

The provisional government's other major target for reform was the armed forces. The Acción Republicana Minister of War, the tough-minded if owlish intellectual Manuel Azaña, aimed to "republicanize" and modernize the military. The first goal was undertaken principally by the decree of 25 April which endeavoured to diminish the bloated officer corps – estimated at three times its required size – by allowing officers to retire on full pay. As a result, 8,000 out of 21,000 officers, including a majority of generals, took early retirement. The second goal, however, was doomed from the start by a lack of public money. In effect, modernization was reduced to restructuring the armed forces in an effort to save money; a decree of 25 May halved the number of divisions from 16 to 8, another of 3 June slimmed down the "Army of Africa" in the Moroccan Protectorate, while yet another eliminated four of the seven military academies. Azaña also cut back the army in other ways; the infamous Law of Jurisdictions of 1906, by which military courts could put civilians and publications on trial for having insulted the armed forces, was abolished on 17 April.[12]

Altogether the reforms-by-decree, despite their wide-ranging and sometimes radical nature, did not create any major confrontations within the provisional government. Certainly the Radicals' closeness to the *patronal* and their remaining links with the CNT gave them ample reason to take issue with the reforms of Largo Caballero. However, the Radicals, like the other members of the government, eschewed confrontation in the belief that the Republic's consolidation and their own immediate electoral fortunes demanded that the republican–socialist coalition remain united at least until the elections for the Constituent Cortes had taken place. Despite the Radicals' conservative image within republican–socialist circles, they were far from hostile to the reformist spirit which pervaded the provisional government. In Lerroux's first major public speech, on 7 June in Valencia, he fulsomely praised the reforms of Azaña and Domingo as "magnificent". He could have given voice to criticism of the socialist-inspired labour reforms and Prieto's stewardship of the economy by the CNT and the *patronal*, but instead he kept his counsel in the name of governmental unity.[13]

Indeed, in his own capacity as a minister, Lerroux demonstrated that he was an enthusiastic advocate of the spirit of "regeneration". He seized upon the imminent meeting of the Council of the League of Nations, to be held in May, to establish his own reformist credentials. The policy of the Spanish monarchy towards the League of Nations had been listless and uncommitted, culminating in 1926 in its petulant withdrawal as a result of the League's refusal to grant Spain a permanent seat on the Council. Lerroux signalled his determination to break with this undignified record by announcing that the Republic, unlike the monarchy, which had been content to send a career diplomat to the League's proceedings in Geneva, would be represented at the Council by the Minister of Foreign Affairs in person. He eagerly identified the Republic with the League, contending that the latter's ideals of collective peace and security were a natural extension of the former's democratic and pacifist values. While the monarchy, he insisted in Geneva shortly before the Council met, had kept Spain isolated, the Republic would demonstrate its commitment to a more elevated "international ideal" by vigorously backing the League's pursuit of "world peace". On 20 May, in his inaugural speech before the Council, Lerroux insisted that the activities of the League had always been avidly followed by the Spanish republicans. At last, he declared dramatically, "Spain stands by you", to which the President of the Council, Mr Curtius, replied, "We stand by Spain". Lerroux again stressed that the government of the Spanish Republic was determined to strengthen its "cordial" relations with all other countries and to support zealously the work of "this fraternal organization".[14] On his return to Spain, Lerroux recommended to the Cabinet that foreign policy should be drawn up in accord with the principles of the League, thereby acquiring an "moral elevation" that would enhance the Republic's international standing. To that end, he suggested, the government should prepare thoroughly for the Council's next meeting in September – when Spain would occupy the presidency – and for the Conference on Disarmament early in 1932. There is little question that Lerroux's enthusiastic advocacy of the League of Nations was entirely in tune with the government's own determination to break with the monarchist past. Lerroux's high-profile baptism as Minister of Foreign Affairs received enthusiastic press coverage back in Spain. The leading republican daily El Sol, for example, lauded the minister's "great speech" before the Council, going so far as to describe the "great eloquence" of his – in reality, extremely shaky – French.[15]

Another area of Lerroux's ministerial performance to receive a good deal of public scrutiny was the new departmental appointments. In a society permeated by a clientelist mentality whereby the personal was to a great extent political, the temptation for republican ministers was to reward the loyalty of expectant supporters with jobs in the public sector. Lerroux, in fact, was the epitome of a clientelist "Godfather", spending a considerable part of each day either drafting "recommendations" on behalf of "clients" or else receiving them personally in great numbers.

Paris-Soir calcuated that he received hundreds of visits on a quotidian basis, once counting 425 in a single day.[16] The Radical leader had an additional motive for favouring his own supporters in that the diplomatic corps, membership of which was a particular source of prestige for aristocrats and upper-class individuals of independent means, was a notorious monarchist stronghold. However, in May, Miguel Maura, in keeping with the spirit of the Judicial Statute, issued a circular which expressly prohibited the dismissal of a public employee on political grounds alone. Socialist minister Indalecio Prieto was therefore prevented by fellow ministers from replacing staff at the state-run tobacco company, the Compañía Arrendataria de Tabacos, with party appointees. Lerroux, in his introductory speech to the staff at the Ministry of Foreign Affairs, explicitly stated that no one would be dismissed on account of their monarchism. Despite the opposition of the sub-secretary, he then proceeded to confirm – as he explained in a letter to the monarchist daily *ABC* – that those that had passed the civil service exams prior to the Republic would still be permitted to take up their positions. This is not to say, however, that the minister did not take into account the political leanings of those working under him. On the contrary, within a fortnight of taking up office Lerroux had a report drawn up detailing the political leanings of all the civil servants at the Ministry of Foreign Affairs. Estimating that the number of monarchist functionaries, which stood at 44, was nearly double the number of republicans, of whom there were 23, the study none the less classified 78 as "civil servants at the service of the nation"; that is to say, under a third were monarchists. In effect, Lerroux had provided himself with the wherewithal to avoid politically-motivated confrontations with his civil servants, while keeping within the guidelines laid down by Miguel Maura. Where necessary, however, Lerroux took a more confrontational line. In reshuffling the diplomatic corps Lerroux suspended the existing regulations, causing an outcry as the ever-vigilant *ABC* claimed that his initiative contradicted the stance of the Minister's inaugural speech to his staff. Lerroux defended his action on the grounds that it was in accordance with the "interests of the Republic, which are those of Spain".[17]

By contrast with the state functionaries, the posts of ambassador and certain other high-ranking officials were regarded as political appointments in the gift of the minister concerned. In his memoirs Miguel Maura relates the frenzy that accompanied the allocation of the civil governors as each republican party vociferously promoted its own candidates, often despite their individual qualifications for such an exigent post. Indeed, the "recommendations" made by the republican parties were so baldly sectarian – Marcelino Domingo, amazingly, recommended the owner of a shoeshine "saloon" in Madrid's central square, the Puerta del Sol – that many of the civil governors were dismissed by Maura only a month later on the grounds of sheer incompetence.[18] The same "jobs-for-the-boys" mentality prompted the establishment by a number of ministers of "*juntas de defensa de la República*", or "committees for the defence of the Republic", to limit the number of recent republican converts who were able to gain entry to their departments. Despite his reputation, Lerroux displayed a marked reluctance to nominate party loyalists for ambassadorial and other prominent posts. For example, he did not chose a party member as his under-secretary but a career diplomat, Francisco Agramonte y Cortijo. No doubt in the case of the ambassadors this was largely, if not wholly, due to the fact that these nominations were subject to scrutiny by the Cabinet. Thus Lerroux's first ambassadorial appointment, that of the writer Ramón Pérez de Ayala to the prestigious London posting, was a politically popular decision that reflected a desire to designate members of the liberal "great and the good", mostly taken from artistic and academic circles, as well as reflecting, it must be admitted, the lack of expertise within republican circles in the field of international diplomacy. A notable exception was the Oxford University-based polymath Salvador de Madariaga, an experienced international bureaucrat as well as an academic and writer, who was appointed to the Washington embassy.[19] Meanwhile, the eminent historian Américo Castro was assigned to the Embassy in Berlin, Luis de Zulueta, a writer, to the Vatican, and the left-wing socialist Julio Alvarez del Vayo to Mexico. Lerroux offered Paris to the liberal doctor and writer Gregorio Marañón, but he turned the offer down. Designations made from within the diplomatic corps also seem to have had a liberal bent. For example, the eventual appointment as Ambassador to France of Alfonso Dánvila, a diplomat, historian and novelist (a volume of whose writings had recently been published under the inauspicious title of *Las luchas fratricidas en España*, or "Fratricidal Struggles in Spain"), was greeted enthusiastically by *El Sol* on the grounds that he was "a man beloved and admired in this house". Only to a limited extent did the Radical leader attempt to reward his own supporters with top-level postings abroad: his old crony Juan José Rocha was made Ambassador to nearby Lisbon, while Fernando Gasset and José Estadella – neither of whom was a member of Lerroux's inner circle – were offered the posts for Cuba and Argentina, but both declined.[20]

Undoubtedly Lerroux's ambassadorial appointments, together with his performance in Geneva, lent him a certain prestige within republican circles, but his impact on Spanish public opinion was limited. This was partly due to a general lack of interest in foreign affairs, but mainly to the fact that the country was overwhelmingly occupied by its immense domestic challenges. Lerroux had departed for Geneva with the consent of the Cabinet but, in his words, "without discussion or observations": no guidelines had been approved, let alone an agreed-upon policy or even a provisional stance as regards the leading international questions of the day, such as on disarmament, reparations, and the Great Depression.

Given that Spain was a second-rank power with few overseas possessions, there were inherent limits to what he could hope to achieve on the international stage. As Lerroux recognized, the Republic could not intervene "actively", its presence being limited to "the mere fact" of taking part in international deliberations and the possibility of exercising "a greater moral influence".[21] The peripheral status of international affairs in comparison with domestic politics compounded Lerroux's sense of grievance at being given such a minor ministry in the first place. He later lamented that "not one colleague" expressed any interest either in the affairs of the League of Nations in general or in the role of Spain in Geneva in particular, the other ministers being too absorbed by internal affairs to pay any attention to his external exploits, "as if Spain was on the moon". As a result, Radical colleagues urged Lerroux to seek a higher profile ministry. Manuel Marraco, the party spokesman on economic affairs, called on him in a private letter as early as April to take up the much more prestigious post of Minister of the Economy if, as seemed likely at the time, the socialist Indalecio Prieto, overwhelmed by the economic crisis, vacated the post. Juan Giró Prat also wrote to Lerroux from Barcelona pressing him to occupy the Ministry of the Interior. Yet it was too late for such changes, resignations or reshuffles aside.[22]

Like Lerroux, Martínez Barrio, the other Radical Cabinet member, headed a department of secondary status, the Ministry of Communications. He, too, however, was distinguished by his efforts to break with the monarchist past. On taking possession of the ministry, Martínez Barrio declared stirringly that "on the ruins of an outdated Spain" there would be built "a new Spain". As minister, he therefore proposed to return to the postal and telecommunications workers "that status, that prosperity" which had been denied them by the monarchy. Over the following months he was to fulfil this goal to a great extent through a series of measures which considerably strengthened the corporate employees' associations. Given the Radical Party's close links to the *patronal*, Martínez Barrio's reconciliatory approach to the postal unions was, if anything, an even greater demonstration than Lerroux's of the party's commitment to reform. However, his achievement was obscured by the ministry's relative unimportance as well as by the greater coverage dedicated to the Radical leader.[23]

The accomplishments of the Radical ministers may have been in tune with the spirit of renewal that pervaded the provisional government, but for a more precise idea of the party's vision of the Republic one has to turn to its propaganda. The first speech delivered by the Radical leader was at a banquet held to commemorate the first anniversary of the death of the republican reformer Basilio Paraíso. Following the 1898 "Disaster", Paraíso, in collaboration with that indefatigable advocate of reform, Joaquín Costa, and with the initial political backing of Lerroux, had tried to mobilize the urban and rural middle classes through the Unión Nacional in an endeavour to open up the political and social channels of influence of the Restoration system. Few figures in the pantheon of republican heroes could have been more representative of the Radical Party at the outset of the Republic than Basilio Paraíso. As a self-made businessman and reformer within the republican tradition, he personified the party's predominant values of change within an absolute respect for private property and the maintenance of law and order. He, like Costa, came from Aragon, one of the Radical Party's bulwarks. Lerroux paid fulsome homage to Paraíso, as well as invoking the memory of other republican luminaries such as Ruiz Zorrilla, Pi y Margall, Salmerón, and Costa. Other highly symbolic acts followed. In May, on his way through Paris in his capacity as Minister of Foreign Affairs, Lerroux ordered a wreath to be placed on the grave in the south of France of the republican leader and world-famous novelist Vicente Blasco Ibáñez. He was even willing to pay homage to the party's traditional rivals, if current allies, the socialists. On 20 April, Lerroux visited the main civil cemetery in Madrid to place flowers on the graves of venerable republicans as well as at the mausoleum of the socialist founder Pablo Iglesias. On his way back into Madrid, he joined the head of a 150,000–strong crowd that was making its way from the central Plaza de la Independencia to Iglesias' final resting place.[24]

The Radical leader's second speech was delivered at the elitist Casino de Madrid on 4 May before a distinguished audience of the "Great and Good", such as the philosopher José Ortega y Gasset, as well as numerous politicians, including recent converts from the Constitutionalist cause (those monarchists, or sympathisers, who had sought a solution to the Restoration's crisis throught a constituent Cortes), such as Melquiades Alvarez. Having implored the "aristocracy" of talent before him to serve the Republic as it lacked "men", Lerroux specifically identified the former Constitutionalist leaders, Santiago Alba and Melquiades Alvarez, now republicans, as the potential "escort" of the regime. He went on to invite those parties which stood outside the republican camp to enter it on the grounds that only by becoming as representative as possible would the Republic eschew the dangers of the extreme left and right. Obviously, the Radical leader's appeal on this occasion was directed not so much at the regime's long-standing supporters as those who had flocked recently to its banner in addition to those that remained to be convinced by it. Clearly Lerroux did not believe that the Republic would survive with the backing of traditonal republicans and socialists alone. On the contrary, the inherent limitations of the republican–socialist coalition persuaded him that the regime not only had to consolidate the support of the anti-monarchist *pueblo* of 1930-1, but also had to reach out to other sectors of society. The Radicals' stress on reconciliation rather than reform as the key to the

Republic's consolidation set them apart from their left republican and socialist allies from the very beginning of the regime.[25]

Indeed, the Radical Party's defence of a Republic rooted in consensus rather than conflict had more in common with the Catholic ministers, Niceto Alcalá-Zamora and Miguel Maura, and the former Constitutionalists than with the forces of the left. The extent to which the aspirations of the Radicals and ex-Constitutionalists coincided was underlined over the following weeks. A major speech by Melquiades Alvarez in Madrid on 25 May echoed the concerns hitherto voiced by Lerroux, while the manifiesto published that month by Santiago Alba reflected in its very title – "For Spain, With the Republic" – the Radical preoccupation that the regime should be as nationally representative as possible. Moreover, Alba's slogan that "the Republic is for all Spaniards" was adapted by Lerroux as the guiding theme of his own propaganda, especially during the general election campaign in June. At the same time, the personal and organizational ties between the Radicals and the ex-Constitutionalists were strengthened. In May, Alba greeted Lerroux as a "friend and colleague". Shortly after, Alba, having denied that he was going to set up his own party, ordered his own supporters to enter the Radical Party. Seemingly this was the first step towards the integration of the former monarchist minister himself, the Catalan leader Francisco Cambó insisting that Alba was already "a soldier within the ranks of Lerroux". Later the same month, Lerroux and Melquiades Alvarez also met, and, by all accounts, found themselves in general agreement on the main issues of the day. Certainly the incorporation of the former Constitutionalists into the Radicals' orbit can be seen as part of their broader aim, already made explicit by Lerroux, of consolidating support for the regime and party alike amongst the more moderate sectors of the anti-monarchist *pueblo*. Many of the ex-Constitutionalist leaders were notable *caciques*, Melquiades Alvarez in the region of Asturias and Santiago Alba in Leon province. Likewise, Manuel Burgos y Mazo, another former Constitutionalist and monarchist minister, who, like Alba, instructed his supporters to enter the Radical Party, was the dominant figure in the southern province of Huelva. Valuable support was even provided by the ex-Constitutionalists outside their heartlands, as shown by the influx into the Radical Party of *Albista* rank-and-file in the city of Zaragoza and the adhesion of *Albista caciques* such as Edmundo Alfaro in Albacete province. Consequently the backing of former Constitutional *caciques* helped the Radicals reach out into many areas, above all rural ones, where they were hitherto weakly implanted. Establishing themselves in the countryside constituencies was obviously crucial to the Radicals if they were to occupy the centre–right of the political spectrum in the face of competition from, amongst others, the DLR. It was no coincidence that while Lerroux had publicly embraced the ex-Constitutionalists, he had made no move to forge links with the DLR. Whereas the former Constitutionalists, tainted by their monarchist past and circumscribed by their localized political bases, were strategic, if not ultimately subordinate, allies for the Radicals, the DLR leaders Alcalá-Zamora and Miguel Maura were their potential political rivals, both within and without the Cabinet.[26]

In the short term the developing relationship with the former Constitutionalists was complementary to the Radicals' alliance with the forces that made up the provisional government. At the first meeting of the Alianza Republicana under the Republic, on 27 April, all three parties, comprising the Radical Party, Acción Republicana, and the Federals, reaffirmed their commitment to the republican–socialist coalition by agreeing to maintain it for the forthcoming general election. In the meantime, the Alianza itself was to be strengthened by renewing publication of the *Boletín de Alianza Republicana*. The Alianza also underlined its republican pedigree by agreeing on the need to combat the entry, "already noticeable in a number of regions", of monarchist *caciques* who disfigured "the revolutionary labour".[27] Clearly the Radical Party was pursuing a dual-track strategy whereby it contributed towards the consolidation of the left-dominated ruling republican–socialist coalition while cultivating relations with the more right-wing ex-Constitutionalists. This was hardly surprising. The Radicals' ambiguity partly reflected their strong populist roots, but was principally a function of their centrist position within the regime, making it inevitable that the party would look both to left and right in the search for support.

In the meantime, the Radical leader in particular tended to adopt a low profile as regards all domestic or potentially controversial issues, as revealed by his reaction to the dramatic events of 10–12 May. On 10 May the members of a Monarchist Circle, located on the central avenue of Alcalá Street, angered passers-by by playing an amplified version of the *Marcha Real*, the monarchist anthem, out onto the street. Following a thwarted attempt to enter the Circle, the growing crowds tried to storm the nearby monarchist daily, *ABC*, resulting in a clash with the Civil Guard which left two people, a local doorman and a 13-year-old boy, dead. Indignant crowds now swelled the central streets and squares of Madrid but the Cabinet, at meetings held on the evening of the 10th – on this occasion, at the Ministry of the Interior building at the very heart of the disturbances in the Puerta del Sol – and on the morning of the 11th, refused to turn to the Civil Guard to contain the mounting disorder, not to mention the threat of church burnings. This was because the Civil Guard, with its distinctive leather tricorn hats and olive-green uniforms, was widely reviled as the most visible face of monarchist oppression. Its sanguinary suppression of the *ABC* demonstration, which, after all, had been directed against monarchist provocation, served only to confirm such prejudices. Within the Cabinet, the most adamant opponent of the

Civil Guard was Manuel Azaña, who, in contrast to his normally reserved demeanour, declared defiantly that "all the convents of Madrid are not worth the life of a single republican". The government's refusal to countenance the deployment of the Civil Guard, despite the fact that on the morning of the 11th religious buildings began to go up in flames, finally prompted the increasingly exasperated Minister of the Interior, Miguel Maura, to resign. The authorities later declared a state of alarm, calling out the army to restore order in order to avoid using the Civil Guard. However, the deteriorating situation, along with the implications of a split within the provisional government so soon after the Republic's advent, prompted the Cabinet to accept the return of Maura on his terms. Even so, he proved unable to prevent the spread of the incendiarism the following day to the southern cities of Malaga, Seville and Valencia.[28]

As a belligerent backlash against the defenders of the monarchy, the *quema de conventos*, or religious burnings, of 11–12 May no doubt gave expression to the deep-seated antagonism felt by many sections of Spanish society towards the *ancien régime*. In terms of the Republic's consolidation, however, the incendiarism proved counterproductive by alarming Catholics in particular and property owners in general. Especially disturbing for conservative opinion was the fact that the provisional government, headed by a Catholic premier and with another Catholic as Minister of the Interior, had appeared indecisive and inept. Not surprisingly, relations between the government and the Catholic Church, the placatory efforts of the Papal Nuncio and a number of moderates within the church hierarchy notwithstanding, deteriorated rapidly thereafter. On 17 May, Maura expelled the confrontational Bishop of Vitoria from Spain, provoking yet another Cabinet crisis as Alcalá-Zamora, aggrieved at not being consulted by Maura, threatened to resign. The passing of an edict on religious freedom five days later scarcely improved matters. Worse still, on 25 May, the Primate, Archbishop of Toledo, the intransigent and saturnine Pedro Segura, was deposited over the border on the government's orders. The bishops responded on 3 June with an outspoken attack on the government.[29]

The May church burnings, the first major public disorders under the Republic, had presented the Radical Party with an outstanding opportunity to advertise its law and order credentials. However, the Radical leader was notable by his absence. It has often been pointed out that Lerroux's role was limited by the fact that he had had to travel to Geneva for a League of Nations' Council session. Maura, in his detailed account of the crisis, states that Lerroux was unable to attend the Cabinet meeting on the evening of the 10th as he was already on his way to Geneva. In reality, the Radical leader was still in Madrid on the night of the 10th, his departure for Geneva, as the contemporary press accounts show, taking place at 10.30 a.m. the next morning – half an hour after the first burnings started and another half an hour before the Cabinet was due to meet again. Given the gravity of the situation and the fact that the League of Nations' Council did not meet until nearly a week later, it is difficult to explain why Lerroux should leave as scheduled on the morning of the 11th. Martínez Barrio, who met Lerroux at the railway station before he departed, having himself hurried up overnight from Seville, recalls that Lerroux gave the overwhelming impression that he was eager to leave, claiming that his departure, as agreed upon with the President, would project an image of serenity – a claim which Martínez Barrio, for one, did not find convincing.[30] In other words, Lerroux abandoned Spain just as the Republic's first major governmental crisis blew up. He claims in his auto-biographical account of the period, *La pequeña historia*, to have publicly condemned the incendiarism at the time, but this was not in fact the case. It appears that the Radical leader did not want to compromise his imme-diate future by taking a clear-cut stand. Undoubtedly Miguel Maura is right in claiming that had Lerroux been present in the Cabinet he would not "have dared put his authority at risk by demanding the suppression of the disorders". On the contrary, Lerroux preferred to keep his political powder dry until the republican–socialist government had given way to a new one, whether as a result of the general election or after the passing of the Constitution. In other words, he was not concerned with the provi-sional government, but with the administration that replaced it. The Radical leader, as Martínez Barrio later recalled, simply "crossed his arms anew and continued with his strategy of awaiting patiently for the collapse of the heterogenous provisional government".[31]

The inhibition of Lerroux can partly be explained by the Radicals' ambiguous centrist position, but his reluctance to engage with realities sat uneasily with the urgent task of overhauling the party in order to meet the unprecedented demands of mass politics. A snapshot of the party's strengths and weaknesses at the outset of the Republic had been provided by the April municipal elections. The Radicals' greatest support, like that of the other republican parties, lay in the urban areas. In Seville, 19 of the Republican–Socialist Coalition's 32 victorious candidates were Radicals. Much the same occurred in Valencia where the Radicals secured 21 of the Coalition's 32 seats. In the Aragon region, where over 60 per cent of the elected councillors were republicans, the Radical Party was the strongest republican force. In the city of Zaragoza the Radicals supplied 11 of the Coalition's 16 councillors. Besides, all three Aragonese capitals – Huesca, Teruel, and Zaragoza – would have Radical mayors. The party did well, too, in a number of Galician towns. The only shock was in Barcelona. Of the 21 Radical candidates, who formed the bulk of the Coalition's list of 32, only 13 were elected. In contrast, the recently-formed Catalan left-wing party, the Esquerra Republicana de Catalunya, won 25 seats. There were still a good many towns, such as Albacete, Burgos, Cadiz,

Guadalajara, Salamanca, San Sebastian, Valladolid and Zamora where the Radicals won few if any seats. Indeed, there were numerous areas throughout Spain where the Radicals had made a strictly limited impression: Asturias, the Basque country, and Navarre in the north, Old and New Castile in the centre, and provinces such as Badajoz, Cadiz, Huelva, Jaen and Murcia in the south. In nationwide terms, the Radical Party, despite being by far the largest of the republican parties, enjoyed little or no support in at least a third of the country. Neither in scope nor in structure could the party be regarded as a fully articulated national political organization. Reflecting the strength of localism in Spain, many of the Radicals' apparent bastions were not so much branches of the Party as highly autonomous local entities which were mere affiliates. This was illustrated by their nomenclature. Neither the Seville party nor the Valencian one were known as the "Radical Party" but as "Izquierda Republicana" and the "PURA" respectively. Significantly, the head of Izquierda Republicana, Diego Martínez Barrio, deputy leader of the national party, admits in his memoirs to having dealt little with Lerroux prior to the Republic. Izquierda Republicana did not join the Radical Party until November 1931 – seven months after the Republic was proclaimed. Similarly, the PURA, founded not by Lerroux but by Vicente Blasco Ibáñez, affiliated to the Radical Party only a year earlier, in 1930. In reality, the Radical Republican Party was not so much a national party as a network of highly autonomous regional and provincial bodies centred on the charismatic figure of Lerroux. The April elections also reveal that the party's populism and its strong local roots had produced a heterogeneous and inter-classist, if overwhelmingly urban, social base. Certain territorial sections, such as Valencia, still retained a substantial working-class following as well as informal links with the CNT. However, the bulk of the party's base lay amongst the middle classes, especially civil servants, teachers, artisans, and professionals, as well as amongst shopkeepers, traders, and entrepreneurs. Overall, the commercial and industrial sectors, otherwise known as the *patronal*, constituted the greatest single contingent. Local leadership was drawn largely from the same urban strata: members of the *patronal* formed the biggest group, while lawyers represented the second largest.[32]

In spite of the fact that the cornerstone of the Radical Party was the commercial and industrial classes, scrutiny of the relationship between the party and the *patronal* has been almost completely neglected. More specifically, the *patronal*, unlike the trade unions and the agrarian associations, has received limited attention from scholars. The national *patronal* organizations, such as the Confederación Gremial Española and the Confederación Patronal Española, founded in 1914, and the Federación de Industrias Nacionales, established in 1924, were neither truly national in scope, nor strongly integrated. The Federación was a vehicle for the interests of the Basque metallurgical industries and the railway construction companies. The Confederación Gremial, which defended the interests of shopkeepers, small traders, and businessmen, was also limited in scale: in 1932 it had only 17,637 members, who employed a mere 78,409 workers. Its effectiveness was further circumscribed by a highly autonomous structure, making it difficult to orchestrate demands at the national level. The Confederación Patronal, finally, was also made up of small businessmen, but unlike the Gremial it embraced the construction industry as well as being more widely supported. In late 1933 the Confederación claimed roughly 70,000 members, and employed at least 160,000 workers. A further contrast between the two Confederaciones was that whereas the Patronal sought to replicate the workers' organizations by setting up an "employers front", the Gremial took a more moderate, if not democratic, line, rejecting participation in the Dictatorship's National Assembly of 1926, defending the *comités paritarios*, and, later, the *jurados mixtos* of the Republic as well. The emphasis of the Confederación Gremial was therefore on accommodation, that of the Patronal on confrontation.[33]

The links between the Radical Party and the urban employers at the national level are difficult to discern. A formal, institutional relationship between them was out of the question as the *patronal* declared itself apolitical, preferring a more flexible role as a lobby group. Informal ties in terms of overlapping personnel, such as that between the UGT and the Socialist Party or between the landowners' associations and the right, are scarce, too. The highest-ranking link is that of Mariano Marraco, the twin brother of the leading Radical politician Manuel Marraco, who was president of the Confederación Gremial between 1917 and 1920. In 1931, however, there were few Radicals prominent within the *patronal* at the national level, by contrast with the monarchist and non-republican parties. Finally, there were the ideological affinities. Like the Radical Party, the Confederación Gremial, for example, claimed to represent "the interests, sentiments and ideology of the middle class majority". The voicing of common concerns, especially the maintenance of law and order and low taxation, served to reinforce the identification between them although issues of such a general nature were inevitably echoed by other conservative parties.[34]

Plotting the relationship of the Radical Party with the employers' groups is hindered too by the fragmentation of the *patronal*, itself a product to a great extent of the Spanish economy's marked localism and structural heterogeneity. Organizationally, the *patronal* was divided by sector as well as by territory. Alongside the few national-level bodies, numerous regional, provincial, and municipal ones existed. Doctrinally and strategically, there were differences within each locality and even sector, further complicating the picture. The result was a myriad of bodies of varying size and scope amongst whom co-ordination at the national level was invariably precarious and fraught. The relative unity of purpose and structure of the UGT and even of the landowners' associations was superior to that of the *patronal*. The very fragmentation of the employers' groups in both organizational and ideological terms, along with their pronounced a-politicism, made it inherently difficult for the Radical Party to establish a relationship at the national level. Yet, even within these parameters, the Radicals did not forge especially close ties with the *patronal*. Both the monarchists and the accidentalist right, embodied in the embryonic Acción Nacional, appear to have had stronger links to the employers. Compared to the personal, institutional, and doctrinal ties that bound the socialists to the UGT or the right-wing parties to the agrarian associations, the Radicals' relationship with the *patronal* at the national level was relatively weak.[35]

In fact, the real strength of the Radical Party's relationship with the *patronal* is to be found at the local level. It is in the chambers of commerce, the mercantile centres, the associations of shopkeepers, and other local and provincial bodies that the Radicals are to be found, whether in their capacity as members, organizers, or as permanent officials. Moreover, a very substantial sector of the party's activist base was drawn from the *patronal*. Broadly speaking, around a quarter of all Radical representatives at the local level were from the industrial and commercial property-owning classes. Nearly as great a proportion of the deputies elected by the party to the Constituent Cortes in the June 1931 general election were from the same strata. Many Radicals who were lawyers also acted on behalf of the *patronal*, both big and small. Among the Radical politicians who would later be elected to the Constituent Cortes, there were a number of spokesmen or agents for major economic concerns, including Ricardo Samper for the Valencian orange growers, Andrés Orozco for the export companies of the Canary Islands, and Manuel Marraco for the Aragonese sugarbeet industry, as well as Emiliano Iglesias and Alejandro Lerroux himself, amongst others, as political fixers for the vast, often secreted interests of the Mallorcan magnate Juan March. Only by taking into account the local ties and connections between the Radical Party and the *patronal* does the massive overlap in interests between the two become apparent. The *patronal* was, as a result, the single most important sector within the party.[36]

The Radical dream, in fact, was manifested in the life story of the entrepreneurial Marraco twins. Of lower middle-class commercial origins, their father owning a chemist's shop on Manifestación Street in central Zaragoza, both brothers outgrew their origins to become directors of large economic entities. While Mariano became president of the Mutualidad Mercantil, of the Quintana Company, and director of a *patronal* organization, the Centro Mercantil Industrial de Zaragoza, his brother Manuel worked his way up to become director of the Alcoholera Agrícola del Pilar – from the sugarbeet industry, a leading sector of the Aragonese economy – as well as director of two *patronal* bodies in Zaragoza; the Asociación de Labradores and the Cámara Oficial de Comercio e Industria. Both brothers were also prominent at the national level. Mariano headed the Confederación Gremial between 1917 and 1920, and again in 1934, while Manuel, in October 1931, was made director of the nationwide Banco de Crédito Local. He later moved on to become director of the Bank of Spain. Had it not been for the opposition of the socialist Indalecio Prieto, Manuel Marraco might have been a minister in the provisional government instead of Martínez Barrio. The Marraco twins thus crystallized the hopes and aspirations of inumerable Radicals, opening up the channels of economic and political influence to lower middle class entrepreneurs such as themselves. An even greater paradigm of the Radical spirit was the party leader himself. As a self-made man whose varied economic interests included a hotel, a country estate, a spa resort, and numerous other enterprises, Lerroux was the living embodiment of the ideals of the party he had founded.[37]

The Radical Party may have been the most important vehicle of all the national republican parties for the *patronal*, but it was not the only political party to represent the interests of the employers. Amongst those to whom the *patronal* would also look under the Republic were the accidentalist Acción Nacional (later merged into the CEDA), the monarchist organizations, as well as regional parties such as the Lliga, the PNV, and the DRV. Still, it should be borne in mind that, generally speaking, the *patronal*, unlike the agrarian associations, was prepared to work within the Republic. As a result, the *patronal* harboured greater expectations of the republican Radical Party than of any other party under the new regime. These expectations were heightened by the appointment of the socialist Indalecio Prieto as Minister of the Economy and by the climate of economic uncertainty, as reflected in the massive flight of capital abroad and the sudden fall of the peseta, which clouded the Republic's early months.[38] There was widespread hope that, if – as seemed possible at the time – Prieto stepped down, the Radical leader himself might replace him. Manuel Marraco wrote to Lerroux, as early as 21 April, that "those that defended law and order" were convinced of "the beneficial effect" if this occurred. The *patronal* was concerned not only by the economic situation but also by the new-found strength of the trade unions. From Barcelona, one of the strongholds of the CNT, the Radical industrialist Juan Giró Prat wrote to Lerroux two days after Marraco that "the big industrialists" believed that if he was made Minister of the Interior he would be able to end "this chaotic state" and force the anarcho–syndicalists and communists to obey the law.[39] Naturally, such expectations were to become even more acute with the application of the socialist-inspired labour decrees of April to July

1931 as well as with the growing number of strikes and increasing social conflict as the unions began to flex their muscles.

The Radicals strove not just to consolidate their support among traditional urban sectors such as the *patronal* but also to extend it to new ones. As a result, monarchists in many parts of Spain joined the Radical ranks. For example, the maverick monarchist, ex-premier and chief *cacique* of Guadalajara province, the Conde de Romanones, instructed his followers in Barcelona to join the Radical Party. To the northwest, in Zaragoza, the Radical Party was joined by numerous followers of Santiago Alba and Melquiades Alvarez as well as former *Sánchezguerristas* and Liberals, though many others were rejected. Farther northwest, in Logroño, numerous members of the Monarchist Circle also signed up with the Radicals. However, an even greater imperative for the Radicals was to extend their social base into the rural areas. As the April elections had manifestly demonstrated, the weakest area of support for both the republicans and the socialists was the countryside. This perception had informed the socialists' massive recruitment drive amongst the *jornaleros*, or landless labourers, soon to establish their union, the Federación Nacional de Trabajadores de la Tierra (FNTT), as the largest single one within the entire UGT.[40] In some rural areas, such as parts of Aragon, Galicia and Valencia, the Radical Party already had a certain backing but overall, in spite of the growth of 1930–1 in regions such as Castile La Mancha, the Radical presence was still unimpressive. Yet expansion into the countryside was vital, especially while the right was still struggling to rejuvenate its material and moral forces, if the Radical Party was to convert itself into a national political contender. The paramountcy of extending the party's support among the rural electorate was illustrated by a letter to the national leadership from the writer and Radical supporter Eloy Soriano Díaz in Badajoz. He stressed that the "the positive force" in Badajoz province was the "farmers and stockbreeders" and that if the Radical Party defended their interests it would win the support of "an enormous and unconditional mass". Nor did the Radicals flinch at the prospect of winning over former monarchist *caciques*. A fortnight into the Republic, for example, Lerroux was informed that if the party secured the backing of a well-disposed "rich landowner and ex-Liberal *cacique*" in the *pueblo* of Torredonjimeno in Jaen province the monarchists would lose the majority in the town hall to the "Governmental Party".[41]

The fact is that in many areas the Radical Party became a leading refuge for ex-monarchist *caciques*. A prime example is the region of Castile La Mancha. In the province of Albacete, for instance, the Radical Party was joined by the powerful Ochando family. Made rich by the process of *desamortización* (the sale of church lands) in the first half of the nineteenth century, the Ochandos had been major *caciques* throughout the Restoration period, initially for the Conservative Party but then, from

1880, for the Liberal Party. They dominated one of five electoral districts in the province, that of Casas Ibáñez, to the extent that application of the *"turno pacífico"* there was never a foregone conclusion. Under the Primo de Rivera Dictatorship, the Ochandos kept their options open by backing the *Somatén* (Primo de Rivera's civilian militia) while maintaining links with the Liberal Party. Once the Republic came, however, the Ochandos promptly entered the Radical Party. The same was true of many other *caciques* in the region. The dominant *caciques* in the Albacete district of Yeste, the Alfaro family, previously *Albistas*, also joined the Radicals. Indeed, the Alfaros provided the Albacete party with its provincial leader, Edmundo Alfaro. In Cuenca, the neighbouring province to the north, the party was joined by none other than José María Alvarez Mendizábal, not only a prominent landowner and *cacique* but also a former Liberal deputy, as well as a direct descendant of Juan Alvarez Mendizábal, the architect of *desamortización* in the 1830s and 1840s. In another Castilian province, Ciudad Real, the party incorporated a number of prominent ex-monarchists, including the former deputy and *cacique*, Germán Inza.[42]

The entry of *caciques* and monarchists into the Radical Party was not confined to Castile La Mancha. A similar story is to be found in Aragon. In Zaragoza province many outlets of Primo de Rivera's official party, the Unión Patriótica, became branches of the Radical Party overnight. In the neighbouring province of Teruel, the *cacique* and industrialist José Rivera, a former member of the Dictatorship's *Somatén*, joined the Radical Party and was soon rewarded with a leading role in the provincial organization.[43] In the south, there was a veritable influx of *caciques* and monarchists into the Radical Party. In Huelva, for instance, the province's leading bigwig and ex-monarchist minister, Manuel Burgos y Mazo, signed up with the Radicals. *Caciques* in Badajoz and Granada, along with numerous former monarchist supporters, also enlisted in the Radical ranks. In Murcia, supporters of Juan de la Cierva, the last dynastic Minister of the Interior and the province's chief *cacique*, joined the Radical Party. In Seville the Radicals accommodated the erstwhile monarchist deputies Manuel Blasco Garzón and Antonio Rodríguez de la Borbolla. Another former monarchist deputy to back the Radical cause was José Rosado Gil.[44]

Then and since the Radicals have been robustly criticized for converting the party into what one contemporary publication described as "a nest of *caciques*". Prior to the general election, *El Socialista* stopped short of criticizing the Radical Party explicitly – presumably in the interest of governmental harmony – but it did lambast the Radical's informal allies, the former Constitutionalists, as "our worst enemies" precisely because they were monarchist converts to the republican cause. The ex-Constitutionalists, in the socialist organ's view, were therefore "a thousand times more pernicious" than declared monarchists. Indeed, *El*

Socialista repeatedly criticized "converts" as a greater danger to the regime than its overt enemies because their new-found republican identity would allow them to "continue enjoying the fruits of power to the advantage of their interests". Thus the entry of *caciques* into the republican parties was an "extremely grave danger" for the Republic. Much the same view is found in many histories of the Second Republic. Moreover, the socialists clashed in the provinces over the Radical accommodation of *caciques*. In Zaragoza, for example, the socialists abandoned the *ayuntamiento* (local council) in June in protest at the conduct of the Radical mayor and civil governor, but at heart was a dispute over the incorporation of *caciques*. The socialists returned to the town council a few days later, but the electoral alliance had been ruptured.[45]

In terms of the Republic's consolidation the integration of monarchists into the republican parties was not a counterproductive move *per se*. First, the rural electorate had been monarchist not by choice but through conformism, even coercion. The Restoration system had not allowed the countryside to exercise an independent vote, but had "fixed" the ballot through the Ministry of the Interior in collaboration with the *caciques*. The relatively free urban vote in April had demonstrated that disillusionment with the monarchy was almost universal. Many rural "monarchists", struck by the support for the nascent regime and the total eclipse of the monarchy, had embraced the Republic in good faith. Second, the power of the *caciques*, rooted as it was in the debility of the Spanish state and relations of socio-economic dependency, required a wide-ranging series of reforms in order to be reduced, let alone eliminated. A start had already been made with the socialist-inspired labour and property decrees as well as the appointment of republican civil governors, but further measures, including a meaningful agrarian reform, were still necessary. In the meantime, it was obviously in the interests of the Republic that the *caciques'* resources be marshalled in the name of republicanism rather than in that of forces which were essentially hostile to the regime.

In any case, it would be a mistake to assume that the Radical Party was the exclusive refuge of *caciques* and erstwhile monarchists. On the contrary, all the republican parties were joined by monarchists. This phenomenon has been well documented in the case of Castile La Mancha by Manuel Requena Gallego. Prior to the Republic the republican presence in this vast region was extremely weak. Only two of the five provinces that make up the region, Ciudad Real and Toledo, had more than a minimal presence. After the Republic's advent, monarchists throughout Castile La Mancha flooded into the republican organizations. There is no doubt that the Radical Party, as shown above, profited substantially from this process. However, the Radicals were not the only ones. In the case of Albacete province, the republican party to benefit most from monarchist-fuelled growth was not one of the conservative republican parties such as the Radical Party – despite the entry of *caciques* – or the DLR, but a left-wing republican party, Acción Republicana. This requires some explanation. During the course of 1930 and the early part of 1931, two friends of Manuel Azaña based in Albacete, Enrique Martí and Arturo Cortés, began to organize Acción Republicana in the province, but with limited results. However, once the Republic arrived, monarchists flocked to the Acción Republicana banner, the Conservative *cacique* for Alcaraz, for example, offering "the district to the Minister of War, Señor Azaña". The reason for this sudden change in fortune was simple enough: the civil governor was Arturo Cortés.[46] Although many of the monarchist newcomers, and in particular the *caciques*, had little ideological affinity with Acción Republicana, they joined the group because their chief priority was to keep in with the powers-that-be. What mattered above all to these sectors was to maintain the web of clientelist interests upon which their political and socio-economic influence rested. Often crucial to this web was a reciprocal relationship with the provincial, and, through them, the central authorities. Many monarchists therefore entered the republican fold to defend their clientelist networks *vis-à-vis* the state authorities, whether monarchist or republican.

However, the political affiliation of the civil governor, powerful as it was, was not the only criteria by which ex-monarchists judged the republican parties. Any governmental party that had an organizational presence in a particular area, or was in the process of acquiring it, had the opportunity to attract supporters of the former regime. In Ciudad Real, for example, the DLR-affiliated governor was able to build up the DLR in the province from nothing, but the Radicals were also able to capitalize on their pre-republican presence there. In Toledo, the distribution of republican newcomers was evenly spread between the DLR, the Radical Party, and the left-wing Radical Socialist Party. Nor were the socialists entirely immune to the incorporation of ex-monarchists: in Albacete province, the party was joined not just by workers and progressive members of the middle classes, but also by a former leader of the *Somatén*. During the first few months of the Republic, the influx into the republican parties in Castile La Mancha was so great that Acción Nacional, the non-republican right-wing group set up under the auspices of *El Debate*, and other non-republican entities encountered severe difficulties recruiting members. It was also the case that many monarchists temporarily withdrew from the political scene altogether. In Albacete, for example, the monarchist *caciques* Martínez Acacio and the Marqués de Montortal retired momentarily from provincial politics rather than join a republican party or continue fighting as monarchists. The mass entry of monarchists into the republican parties that characterized Castile La Mancha took place to varying degrees in all the rural regions. Much the same process occurred, for example, in Galicia. In many areas where the republicans were weak or non-existent, branches of the former dynastic parties, often under the patronage of local *caciques*, simply switched their affiliation from monarchist to republican. In Vigo, for instance, supporters of the former monarchist minister Bugallal renamed their centre the "Democratic Republican Casino" and reversed their portrait of him. Likewise, the Liberal Party in Orense declared that it was now republican.[47]

The reason for the accommodation of monarchists by the republicans in rural areas was to strengthen their parties. Monarchist supporters were often taken on board because the local republican parties had few members. Indeed, many local parties lacked organizers, speakers, and other officials. Ironically, ex-monarchists of political experience were often necessary for the very functioning of the republican parties. As the intellectual and writer Miguel de Unamuno noted in a speech in Albacete, "it is not the republicans who have created the Republic, but the Republic that has created the republicans".[48] In rural Spain the consolidation of the republican parties and of the Republic itself demanded the assimilation of former monarchists. Conversely, many monarchists, impressed by the wave of euphoria in favour of the new regime and by the fact that the monarchy was a lost cause, threw in their lot with the republicans. The rural political scene cannot be interpreted solely in terms of the relations between republicans and monarchists. Under the monarchy, roughly one sixth of the adult male population had been entitled to vote. The Electoral Law of 8 May 1931 extended the suffrage to all males over the age of 23, thereby increasing the number of potential voters by a factor of four. Consequently the republican parties were not just integrating former monarchists but also many new, first-time voters.

The large-scale influx of former monarchists into the republican parties not only triggered a torrent of criticism from *El Socialista*, but also substantial protest from within the republican parties themselves. At the national level, fears had already been expressed at the Alianza meeting on 27 April that the entry of former monarchist *caciques* into the republican parties would end up "distorting the revolutionary labour". There was also extensive criticism from the Radical Party in the provinces at the sudden conversion of monarchists to republicanism. The local branch in the *pueblo* of Sarinena in Huesca province wrote to the national party that those that "yesterday were staunch monarchists, today call themselves republicans" and that it was convinced that on first possible occasion "they will betray us". In the south, the Radical outlet in Munera in Albacete province protested to Madrid that in the *pueblo*, as well as the neighbouring one, there were republicans that "stink as they are the dregs of the illiterate and rural *caciquismo*". In Alicante province the Radicals clashed with the republican organization of the former monarchist minister Joaquín Chapaprieta as it allegedly contained ex-*Upetistas* (members of the Unión Patriótica, the official party under the

Dictatorship), ex-monarchists, and "pseudo socialists". Elsewhere in the province the Radical Socialist Party was denounced to Lerroux by local Radical militants as comprising "a deputy, three mayors and two judges" from the Dictatorship, not to forget the "eternal *cacique* disguised according to the latest fashion" who will "crush us with his preponderance". "Don Alejandro, where can we find the truth?", they pleaded.[49]

Despite the party's reputation as a haven for ex-monarchists, many Radicals objected to their incorporation into the party as a matter of principle. There was also a sense of personal resentment at having to share power with their former rivals, if not enemies. The assimilation of erstwhile monarchists created acute internal tensions in numerous sectors of the party, especially where former monarchists became local Radical leaders overnight. The recently formed committee in Ibiza was denounced to the national party by a veteran councillor as "a failure and an absurdity" for including Eugenio Bonet Riera, mayor under the Dictatorship, "the most hated man in Ibiza and an utterly slippery and unpredictable individual", as well as Isidoro Macabich, author of anti-republican articles and "the great enemy" of the Republic. The committee, according to the local activist, was made up of "the greatest enemies of your ideas". The only solution, he concluded, was to "de-authorize them because they bring together the scum of Ibiza". Similar ructions were caused within veteran ranks by the monarchist influx in the Orense party in Galicia, as revealed to the Radical leader by S. Quintas, a local activist. He claimed not only that "extremist *caciques*" had managed to become Radical officials, but that the new local party boss was Osbaldo Basalo, mayor under the Dictatorship and a life-long monarchist. In Quintas' opinion, Basalo had joined the Radical Party merely to maintain his position as "factotum of the situation". Once selected as a Radical candidate for the Constituent Cortes, he had become "more of a *cacique* than ever", threatening people with, amongst other things, deportation. He scarcely knew the republicans while his house was a "clerical centre where they conspire openly against the Republic". Naturally, the traditional Radicals were mortified that under the new regime "we will continue being mocked and persecuted by the same ones that did it as monarchists". The Republic, Quintas concluded damningly, "is digging its own grave, delivering itself into the arms of its eternal enemy".[50]

Parallel protestations took place in Castile La Mancha. The Radicals of Valdepeñas in Ciudad Real province rejected "the impatient and false republicans" in a letter to the national headquarters. Of particular concern was the "*cacique*" Germán Inza, who was allegedly doing everything possible to promote those who a few days ago were "our most bitter enemies". Elsewhere, such tensions nearly caused the Toledo party to split. Similarly, in Andalusia serious internal difficulties were generated in the Huelva provincial party following the entry of the former monarchist *cacique* Burgos y Mazo and his supporters. The emergence of an ex-monarchist as head of the Logroño party *did* result in a split, the dissidents forming the Autonomous Radical Party. These divisions within the Radical Party were no doubt motivated in part by personality clashes and the disgust of veteran Radicals at having to share power with their former foes, but there was also a conviction in many parts that the accommodation of former monarchists was a Trojan horse that threatened to destroy the Republic from within.[51]

The influx of monarchists into the Radical Party, despite the internal opposition, was actually accelerated by the decision to hold rerun municipal elections at the end of May. These elections have been unjustly neglected by historians as they played a crucial role in the early history of the Republic.[52] Although the republicans had triumphed in the towns in April, they had been resoundingly defeated by the monarchists in the countryside. The provisional government therefore set about "republicanizing" the Republic by undermining the monarchists", and in particular the *caciques*", hold on the rural electorate. The Minister of the Interior, Miguel Maura, issued a decree, which he himself later admitted was "somewhat arbitrary", inviting complaints from local communities regarding the 12 April elections. While the complaints, virtually all of which concerned alleged monarchist abuses, were being examined, steering committees comprising republicans and socialists were set up by the civil governors in the local authorities affected, thereby ensuring that many of the monarchists who had been elected on 12 April never took up their seats.[53] Overall, there were just over 2,500 complaints from local councils. The government was perfectly frank about its purpose. Given the difficulty of examining "with care" every single complaint, it declared in a decree of 13 May, new elections would be held wherever there existed a "well-founded suspicion" that the popular will had been "falsified and oppressed". This would meet the government's aim of ensuring that all the local councils had, prior to the general election in June, emerged from the "popular, authentic suffrage". Clearly the *raison d'être* for the precipitous May elections was to improve the chances of the republican–socialist coalition in the general election. According to Maura, three functionaries processed all the protests in a mere two days, as a result of which 5 per cent were anulled. In fact, over 2,000 *pueblos* held rerun elections.[54] In many provinces the number of councils affected was extremely high: in Albacete 52.3 per cent, Ciudad Real 47.4 per cent, Granada 69.5 per cent, Seville 71.3 per cent, Toledo 49 per cent, while in Cadiz 59.6 per cent of the localities were affected. The *pueblos* selected for a new round were not so much those where there was proof of irregularity as those where the republicans and socialists had a chance of winning. Few elections were therefore repeated in provinces such as Cuenca and Guadalajara where monarchist *caciques* were deeply entrenched and the republicans virtually non-existent. Likewise, elections held in localities where the republicans and socialists had already triumphed in April were intended to strengthen their position still further.[55]

A protest campaign mounted by the right at the sectarian nature of the elections was rapidly defused by the republican backlash over the events of 10–12 May.[56] There were objections from republicans too at the new round of elections. Some wanted to be declared victors without the elections taking place at all, others feared that another vote would put the April victory in peril, and still others were afraid that hostile *caciques* would defeat them yet again. The civil governor of Zaragoza, for example, received a petition from over 30 *pueblos* demanding that the ballot should be postponed as the monarchists' control over the electorate remained undiminished. In some cases the protests were motivated by the support of the civil governors for the *caciques* against local republicans. In the *pueblo* of Montemolin in Badajoz province the sudden replacement of a republican–socialist steering committee at the behest of the civil governor by one comprising the *caciques*' appointees resulted in a bloody confrontation in which a Civil Guard and one civilian died.[57]

The rationale for the May elections was further illustrated by the overt interventionism of the civil governors. Politically neutral in theory, the republican civil governors, like the monarchist ones before them, invariably went to great lengths to promote the cause of the particular party which had sponsored them. Albacete's Acción Republicana civil governor and the DLR appointees for Ciudad Real, Cuenca, and Toledo, for example, not only applied intense pressure on reticent *caciques* so that they backed the governors' parties but also travelled the length and breadth of their provinces in support of party candidates. Similarly, many members of the steering committees – which were technically limited to carrying out emergency functions – abused their position by campaigning actively on behalf of republican candidates and even, despite the law, standing themselves. Some monarchists reacted to the new balance of forces by temporarily retiring from local politics, while others stood in the election as "Agrarians" or "Independents", but many, given the coercion of the republican authorities together with the tidal wave of pro-republican euphoria and the belief that the monarchy had gone for good, were persuaded that it was in their best interests to join the republicans. In Albacete, for example, a third of the republican candidates on 30 May had stood as monarchists just over a month earlier.[58]

The success of the provisional government's May election offensive in disarming the monarchists can be guaged by the fact that in most parts of Spain the Republican–Socialist Coalition either collapsed altogether or else had to compete against one or more of its own parties. The coalition's prompt disintegration was symptomatic of the lack of opposition. In Galicia the coalition appeared to be in tatters, with separate candidatures being presented for the PSOE, ORGA, and Republican Agrarian Party in Vigo alone, with violent clashes taking place between the Radical Party and ORGA in La Coruña, and with individual lists in Pontevedra being submitted for the DLR, the Republican Agrarian Party, and the Republican–Socialist Coalition. In the south, the coalition often competed against parties that only a month earlier had formed part of it. In Badajoz, for instance, separate Radical and Socialist lists took on the Coalition ticket. By contrast, in Alicante the coalition split in two as the Radical–Socialist Party and socialists joined forces against an alliance of the DLR and Radical Party. A kaladeiscopic variety of lists also emerged in Andalusia. While in Jaen the coalition fought separate socialist and republican candidatures, in Huelva the coalition collapsed completely as the Radicals and socialists took one another on. In the city of Seville, the coalition theoretically held, but in many districts the parties were found to be competing openly against one another. In Valencia, the Republican–Socialist Coalition splintered into an "Alianza de las Izquierdas" ("Alliance of the Left"), consisting of the Radical Party, Acción Republicana, the PURA, the PRLD, and PSOE, a DLR candidature, one for the Conjuntionist Party, and another for the Federal Democratic Republican Party. In Castile La Mancha there was also a considerable diversity of coalitions and lists although in the majority of constituencies either a republican–socialist coalition or a purely republican one was presented.[59]

Given its greater conservatism and more extensive organization, the Radical Party would have expected to do better than the left republicans in those rural constituencies where the May elections were celebrated. However, there were other, distinctly traditional, factors to be taken into account, above all that of the civil governors. Certainly the results indicate that the governors played an extremely influential part in the outcome. In Albacete, Acción Republicana, which had only begun to organize itself in the province in 1930, won nearly 40 per cent of the province's seats. The DLR, which had no party network to speak of in either Ciudad Real or Toledo province prior to the Republic, secured 33 per cent and 45 per cent of the councillors respectively. Even though the nationwide results issued by the Ministry of the Interior for the May elections are far from complete, they none the less reveal that the strategy of "republicanization" in the countryside had been a resounding triumph. Of the 5,300 seats covered by the Ministry, 4,640 – that is to say, 80 per cent – had been won by republicans and socialists, just over a third of them on the coalition ticket. According to these figures, the republicans and socialists secured 2,995 councillors outside the coalition ticket, of which 141 were for the Alianza Republicana and 1,438 for the Radical Party and its regional affiliates such as the PURA. This would give the Radicals 48 per cent of all the republican and socialist seats won outside the ticket, a figure that rises to more than half if one makes the conservative assumption that the Radicals would have cornered at least 70 of the Alianza's 141 seats.[60]

For a more accurate breakdown of the election results, one must turn to the available local studies. These demonstrate, if anything, that the republican victory was even greater than the official picture indicates. *Pueblos* that a few weeks before had been impregnable fortresses of monarchism were now not just republican territory, but overwhelmingly so. In Seville province, for example, the monarchists did not win a single one of the 889 seats on offer. In the three provinces of Castile La Mancha for which figures are available – Albacete, Ciudad Real and Toledo – the monarchists obtained just ten out of 1,223 councillors ie less than one per cent of the seats, while the republicans won 77 per cent and the socialists 21 per cent. A similar story emerges in many other parts of the country. In Cadiz province, the monarchists won a paltry 11 out of 425 seats, the republicans and socialists securing 349 between them. In Granada, where 140 of the province's 201 municipalities held elections, the monarchists and non-republicans were swamped by the socialists and republicans. Of the 985 seats contested in Valencia, the PURA won 547, or 56 per cent of the total, while the monarchists secured 12, the accidentalist DRV 22, and the "Independents", many of whom were probably monarchists, 74.[61]

Yet the victory of the republican and socialist forces in the May elections was only one of sorts. The real victor in much of the country was, as always, the *cacique*. In provinces such as Cuenca and Guadalajara the republican authorities barely attempted to tackle the entrenched monarchist caciquismo. It could be argued that in many other localities the electorate, much as it had done under the monarchy, continued to vote for the government list. In effect, the *caciquismo* of the Restoration had been supplanted by that of the Republic. It was no coincidence that in Albacete, for example, electoral participation was highest in those areas where the *caciques* were most powerful, while it was lowest in *pueblos* where the republicans and socialists dominated.[62] However, it can also be argued that the co-optation of monarchist voters and *caciques* into the republican camp was a step in the right direction. Their integration strengthened the republican parties and by extension the regime itself by ensuring that many monarchists were at least within the system, not outside it. For the sake of the Republic, assimilation was better than alienation. The obvious drawback was that many local authorities were in the hands of former monarchists who were likely to oppose the government's reforms by delaying, distorting, and even destroying them. This would shift the regime at the local level to the right.

Realistically, the *caciques'* influence was never going to be easily reduced, let alone extirpated, given the deep-seated nature of the socioeconomic and institutional roots that sustained them. Certainly a start had been made with the drawing up of larger constituencies under the

Electoral Law of 8 May 1931 and the battery of labour and agrarian edicts enacted during the regime's first months, but obviously further measures, including reform of the landholding structure, were essential. The general election looming, the provisional government therefore took a pragmatic line by advancing the immediate political interests of the republican parties and the Republic alike through the integration of former monarchists. The danger that many local republican parties would become mere vehicles for the interests of former monarchists would have to be offset by vigilant provincial and national authorities. In the meantime, the May ballot had served its purpose in preparing the ground for the republican–socialist triumph in the general election a month later. The campaign in May had greatly accelerated the organization of the republicans and socialist parties in the rural domain as well as giving them an instructive propaganda dry run. It had also enabled the incoming civil governors to flex their electoral muscles. Most importantly, the May elections shifted the balance of rural power towards the republicans and socialists, who would now be in a position to influence the outcome of the general election in June. In many ways, the May elections were a vindication of the Radical contention that the integration, not rejection, of monarchists was the key to the regime's consolidation.[63]

The Radicals' vision of the Republic was spelt out more fully during the general election campaign that followed on the heels of the May municipal poll.[64] The keynote of the Radicals' propaganda was, in the words of Lerroux, the "National Ideal" of a Republic not only "for the republicans, but also for all Spaniards". "The affirmation of the Republic, the consolidation of the Republic", was, he declared on 26 June before an audience in Valencia of over 40,000 people, "my greatest concern". The party aimed to accommodate not just traditional republicans, but also recent converts to the republican cause together with those, including moderate Catholics and monarchists, which were still sceptical of the new regime. Only through the "reconciliation" of those that until "yesterday viewed one another as enemies" would the new regime be consolidated. "The Republic has been won", as Lerroux put it succinctly in Barcelona, "it is necessary now to preserve it".

Throughout the campaign the Radicals made it plain that they were a party of law-and-order. For the Radicals, the upholding of order provided the regime with the essential framework for reconciliation and consensus-building. Once the Republic's "enemies", the party leader claimed before a conservative audience in Burgos, realized that the new regime was "the guarantee of your conscience, of your home, of your property and of your rights", they would give it their support. In other words, the defence of law and order implied the defence of many other rights, including those of property and religion, held dear by the conservative classes. It also reassured property owners that the Radicals would take a firm line against the agitation of the property-less classes. This conservative facet of the Radicals' appeal was given full rein by Lerroux in an interview shortly after the general election in which he compared his own preoccupation with law and order with that of the French politician Louis Thiers, responsible for crushing the Paris Commune of 1871. However, this did not mean that the Radicals welcomed their former foes unreservedly. Lerroux insisted that the Republic had to be ruled by republicans. He also called on republicans to "supervise" the political evolution of their erstwhile enemies. Newcomers ambitious for public office would therefore have to serve a period of "penitence".

Nor should the Radical leader's chest-thumping over law-and-order be interpreted as a denial of reform. On the contrary, the Republic, he declared grandly in Valencia, was not "a station of arrival but a point of departure". Lerroux lavished praise on his Alianza ally, Manuel Azaña, for his "magnificent" military decrees. He also dedicated an effusive encomium to the Radical–Socialist minister, Marcelino Domingo, for his educational reforms. This was underscored by an emotional account of a recent visit to the gravely ill Manuel Cossío, a co-founder of the pioneering secular educational body, the *Institución Libre de Enseñanza*. Lerroux enthusiastically endorsed the building of schools and the raising of teachers' salaries, going so far as to claim later in the campaign that the universal provision of state education would eradicate "the social problem". He also called for the provision of free university education. Somewhat optimistically, the Radical leader estimated that the Republic's educational reforms would convert Spaniards into the "sovereigns of the world economy". In the same reformist spirit, Lerroux drew attention during the campaign to his own achievements as Minister of State by identifying the diplomatic aims of the Republic with the pacific and democratic ideals of the League of Nations.

A more ambivalent attitude was adopted by the Radical Party in relation to the Catholic Church. On the one hand, the party, in keeping with republican tradition, upheld the separation of church and state, the freedom of worship, and restrictions on the activities of the religious communities. On the other hand, the Radical leader was repeatedly to stress that reform of the church should not amount to "revenge". Indeed, on 14 June, in the pious city of Burgos, he sought to reassure Catholic onlookers not only by accepting that the vast majority of Spaniards possessed a "Catholic conscience", but also by claiming that religious pluralism would not undermine Catholicism in Spain as it had remained the dominant faith in countries as diverse as Belgium, France, the USA, and England – an observation that did not do a great deal of credit to his status as Minister of Foreign Affairs, but much for his conservative credentials. Finally, he emphasized that, having exchanged views with the Nuncio and a number of bishops in person, there were no fundamental points at dispute between himself and the Catholic Church. The Church, in short, was safe in his hands.[65] The Radicals' ambivalence towards established religion was an attempt to tread a fine line between Catholics and republicans. This was illustrated by Lerroux's claim in Barcelona that the May church burnings marked an improvement in historical terms insofar as the anticlerical agitators had targeted the convents but not the religious personnel nor the churches. "Is there not an evident advance?", he pleaded rhetorically. However, as a seasoned politician, Lerroux took care to modify his interpretation of the May events according to his audience. In Burgos he limited himself to observing that there had been "not one personal assault" and that the people had readily assisted the stricken clergy, while in Caceres he declared that the crowds had attacked "that which in whose religiosity they do not believe: the religious communities". He also remonstrated with the Catholics in Caceres on the grounds that on the day of the Republic's proclamation a religious procession had gone ahead in the city without the slightest hitch and that they, therefore, were obliged to respond in kind. The Radicals' ambiguous stance on religion was partly a response to the very heterogeneity of the middle classes, but it was also due to the imperatives of the party's centrism as it aimed to appease republican and Catholic opinion alike.

A similar ambivalence characterized the Radical Party's approach to the key question of agrarian reform. On the one hand, the Radical leader assured the audience in Burgos that the Republic was not going to "sweep away private property", nor was it going to transform "the rich into poor". On the other hand, in Barcelona, he denounced the "evident social injustice" of a system which meant that for many tenant farmers the land was nothing more than a "grave" in which they mixed their "bones in order to enrich the landowners still further". He therefore urged the creation of an "army of rural citizens in . . . support of a progressive republic". These contrasting claims notwithstanding, Lerroux consistently maintained that land could only be seized through indemnification and that a hasty reform would result in "the economic ruin of Spain". Nevertheless, Lerroux accepted that the Constituent Cortes would eventually have to subject "the bourgeoisie" to "fair and just norms". Another burning issue was the question of Catalan autonomy, though Lerroux only dealt with this at some length in the Barcelona speech, where he took a moderate line, limiting himself to recognising Catalonia's right to autonomy as outlined in the San Sebastian Pact.

The characteristic ambivalence of the Radicals' electoral campaign was summed up in their leader's claim that "I am conservative when confronted by anarchy but revolutionary when faced by stagnation". This appeal was largely a product of the party's centrism along with its residual populism. Neither of the left nor of the right, the Radicals sought a midway space between the two of, in Lerroux's phrase, "moderation and serenity". In pursuit of the politics of consensus, the Radical leader called upon the left to show restraint in the exercise of power, while urging the right to integrate itself into the new regime. The Radicals themselves hoped to become the catch-all party of the heterogenous middle classes. In Valencia Lerroux had lambasted the monarchy for alienating the professional classes from public life, while appealing for their support in the building of the new regime. Aware of the brittle nature of the Republic's support, the Radicals were concerned not only to strengthen support amongst the urban middle classes but also to reach out to the rural middle strata where the republican presence was still weak and circumspect. In terms of the regime's consolidation, the Radical Party therefore fulfilled an essential integrative function by attracting many doubters and former monarchists to the republican fold.

The overriding moderation of the Radicals' propaganda should not obscure the party's perennial populist streak. Demagogic demands rooted in the paramountcy of "social justice" were liberally splattered throughout Lerroux's speeches. In Badajoz he called for a "new era" in which "men who live at the expense of others" would no longer exist. Likewise, he envisioned in Barcelona the end of "the anomalous situation" in which "some work and do not eat and others who eat but do not work". In true populist style, he expressed a profound faith in the *"pueblo"* and in particular the working class. In Valencia, for example, he claimed that "peace" depended on the "will of the people, of the organized proletariat". Such populist harangues may seem somewhat anachronistic, but they appealed to the old guard while mobilizing a wide-ranging social base that embraced not just the fragmented middle classes but also a substantial working-class segment in provinces such as Valencia.

Clearly the Radical vision of progress without, as Lerroux put it, "precipitations", but within an absolute respect for law and order, placed a greater stress than either the left republicans or the socialists on reconciliation rather than reform as the path to the regime's consolidation. Whereas the left was determined to republicanize the nation, the Radicals were more concerned to nationalize the Republic. Nevertheless, the Radical agenda, however vague and insubstantial, was firmly rooted within the spirit of renewal that characterized the provisional government. The Radical proposals for reform of the church and the land may have been heavily qualified, but Lerroux had none the less conceded during the campaign that these were issues upon which the Constituent Cortes would have to reach a final resolution. Moreover, the Radicals explicitly aligned themselves with the parties of the ruling coalition. Not only did the Radical leader fulsomely praise the reforms of the left republicans, but he also, despite the unpopularity of the socialists among patronal and CNT circles, eschewed any overt criticism of the PSOE ministers. In particular, Lerroux refused to take advantage of the misfortunes of the socialist

Minister of the Economy, Indalecio Prieto, as the peseta plunged by 22 per cent and capital fled abroad, by presenting himself before the business community as a greater guarantor of the economic order. In Valencia, where the Radical Party shared the platform with the PSOE, he attributed the fall of the peseta and the general economic uncertainty to a lack of confidence that would soon be superseded by the stabilizing influence of the Constituent Cortes's labours. Further, the Radical leader celebrated the fact that the republicans, after so many years of confrontation, had reached an understanding with the socialists. The Radical campaign cannot therefore be equated with that of the right-wing forces that rued the passing of, in Lerroux's words, "the dictatorial monarchy".

The relative unity of the provisional government was not reflected in a nationwide electoral alliance. In theory, the Radical Party, along with Acción Republicana and the Federal Party, had agreed at a meeting of the Alianza Republicana on 27 April that the Republican–Socialist Coalition should be maintained for the general election. In practice, the Coalition suffered multiple fractures, resulting in an astonishing variety of electoral arrangements within not just individual regions but even single provinces. As in the case of the May elections, these splits, given the disarray of the opposition, were more a symptom of the Coalition's strength than its weakness. Certainly wherever the Radical Party was confident of winning the outright majority, as in a number of constituencies in Andalusia, Aragon, Galicia, and the Levante, it unceremoniously ditched its allies in order to gain more deputies. Such strategic considerations were often sharpened by marked ideological and socio-economic differences. This was especially true in Andalusia and Extremadura, but also in other regions such as Aragon. In much of the south, as well as in Ceuta, Melilla, and Tenerife, the Radicals were the main alternative to the socialists. In Cadiz, Ciudad Real, Caceres, Cordoba, and the central province of Toledo the Radicals allied with the DLR against the Socialists. In Alicante, the two parties faced one another alone. Likewise, in not one of the three Aragonese provinces did the Radicals ally with the socialists: whereas in Huesca the Radicals confronted the Radical–Socialist Party on their own, in Teruel and both the Zaragoza constituencies, a Republican Coalition, which included the Radical Party, took on the socialists. Yet there were also many provinces where the balance of electoral forces led the Radicals to ally with the socialists against one or other of the left-republican parties. In Murcia, for example, the Radical Party joined forces with the PSOE and Acción Republicana in fighting the PRRS, while in the northern province of Burgos the Radicals again aligned themselves with the PSOE against the PRRS. In the southeastern city of Valencia, the Radical Party joined forces with Acción Republicana and the PSOE in opposition to the DLR and PRRS.[66] Further up the coast in Tarragona the Radical Party found itself once more up against the PRRS, this time in alliance with the

Esquerra. In Galicia, a veritable mosaic of local alliances, pacts, and feuds produced the most bewildering variety of electoral arrangements in the entire country. Thus in La Coruña the Radical Party joined forces with the PSOE against the ORGA, the left-wing republican autonomy party, and lost, while in Pontevedra the Radicals stood alongside the ORGA, and won. In Orense, the Radicals, despite publishing the best-selling Radical paper in the country (*La Zarpa*), found themselves obliged to make a pact with the socialists, though this allowed them to hold off the combined forces of the ORGA, PRRS, and the Nazonaluista Repubrican. In Lugo, meanwhile, the Radicals presented one of three separate lists, only to be soundly thrashed by the ORGA. Fraud, however, led to a second round in which the Coalition was resurrected and the Radicals secured four more deputies.[67]

The internal tensions generated within the Radical Party by the influx of newcomers and the selection of electoral candidates and allies resulted in a number of localized splits. Probably the gravest schism occurred in the province of Ciudad Real. Dissent within the provincial party had initially been sparked by the decision of the local leadership, taken without prior consultation of the rank-and-file, to forge an electoral alliance with the DLR. The final catalyst for the split was the selection of Germán Inza, a former monarchist deputy and leading *cacique*, as a Radical candidate at an Alianza assembly on 17 June. As the dissidents, who claimed to represent "the majority" of the province's *pueblos*, explained in a letter to the national party, the conservatism of the local leadership had given them no option but to unite with "the true Republic of the left"; namely, the Radical–Socialists and socialists. Another ideologically-motivated confrontation took place in the northern coastal town of Santander where the youth section broke away from the party because an electoral arrangement with the socialists had not been reached.[68] Further fissures of varying degrees of seriousness also occurred in Caceres, Las Palmas, Logroño, and Oviedo, though they do not seem to have seriously damaged the party at the national level. Nationwide, the Republican–Socialist Coalition held in its entirety in only 11, or 17 per cent, of the 63 constituencies. In another 27 the Coalition competed against at least one other party from the ruling coalition. This was sometimes done with a view to winning not only the majority positions on the ticket, but the minority ones, too. However, there were also numerous cases where the coalition had simply fallen out over the distribution of seats or for ideological reasons. Further, in twenty-five constituencies, or 40 per cent of the total, the coalition had collapsed completely. Consequently in the vast majority of constituencies the Coalition did not hold, this being due in at least half of them to irreconcilable differences.[69]

The Radical election campaign was rapturously received by the moderate republican press. *El Sol* heralded Lerroux, "a republican apostle", as "the leading figure of the Republic". Applauding the Radical leader's "conciliatory intelligence", the republican daily believed that he held the key to the regime's immediate future and would ensure that it was ruled in a "measured and decisive" fashion. Lerroux was, in short, "the Figure of the Future".[70] A vigilant interest in the Radical leader's electoral performance was also taken by the non-republican right. The only politician to appear on the cover of the monarchist *ABC* throughout the entire campaign was Lerroux, and not just once but on three separate occasions. The coverage of the Catholic, accidentalist *El Debate* was distinguished by the fact that it was even more thorough than that of the foremost Radical daily, *El Progreso*. Headlines such as "I do not accept anything other than obedience before the law" endeavoured to underscore the affinity between the Radical leader and the the non-republican right. Equally, the right-wing press eagerly seized upon what divided, rather than united, the Radicals and their allies. *El Debate*, for instance, favourably contrasted the moderation of Lerroux's speech in Valencia on 7 June with the "subversive" nature of Azaña's contribution at the same meeting. Both *ABC* and *El Debate* readily interpreted the electoral differences within the republican–socialist camp as a sign of its imminent disintegration, the latter claiming in early June that the coalition's "great heterogeneity" had already led to its "fatal division". While *El Debate* acclaimed Lerroux as the "Principal Figure [upon whom] converge all eyes", *ABC* proclaimed him "a great man".[71]

Clearly the non-republican right, still disorganized and demoralized, was courting the Radicals as a potential ally because of its own debility. Obviously, this was a purely strategic consideration as the ideological differences between the Radicals and the traditional right, particularly over the church and education, meant that the Radical Party could never represent the interests of the Catholic right. By contrast, and more surprisingly, both the monarchists and the accidentalists turned their backs completely on the DLR, headed by the Catholic ministers, Alcalá-Zamora and Miguel Maura. First, as former monarchists, Alcalá-Zamora and Miguel Maura were perceived to have betrayed the monarchy, an original sin of which Lerroux could never be accused. Second, Alcalá-Zamora, and in particular Miguel Maura, were held to have failed unforgivably in their duty as Catholics during the May church burnings. As Angel Ossorio y Gallardo, a former monarchist himself and friend of Miguel Maura, later wrote, "from that moment on the hatred of the right for him grew and they treated him for ever as if he – Catholic by conviction and by blood – had personally set fire to the temples". *ABC* judged that a Lerroux government would have been more likely than the Alcalá-Zamora administration to have upheld "public order", judging that the Radical leader "merits more confidence as far as the monarchists and all the elements of order are concerned". The DLR's search for a union of the republican and

Catholic traditions probably made it unpalatable to the accidentalists in the final analysis, as well as to the monarchists, for obvious reasons. This made it highly improbable that the DLR could have received the backing of the forces of the traditional right. In any case, the DLR, even if it did manage to establish itself, would represent a threat to Acción Nacional. *El Debate*, already busily involved in the promotion and organization of Acción Nacional, therefore rejected the DLR's pretentions and anticipated instead the creation of a "genuine and loyal" party. For the accidentalist right, the Radical Party was acceptable precisely because it was not so much a rival as a potential, if provisional, ally. What the traditional right expected from Lerroux was spelt out by a prominent, though unidentified, politician in *El Debate* two days before polling day. The anonymous figure – probably Gil Robles given that *El Debate* was Acción Nacional's mouthpiece – predicted that the San Sebastian coalition would be ruptured by the growing conflict between the Radicals and the Socialists. The non-republican right would then back the Radicals until such time as its own forces were sufficiently organized to stand on their own two feet.[72]

Spain's electoral landscape was transformed by the June 1931 general election. Under the Restoration, the republican and socialist parties had never obtained 50 parliamentary seats in an election. They now captured over 400 of the 470 available seats, the opposition being reduced, as in the May municipal elections, to a rump. The Radical Party, having presented around 150 candidates nationwide, notched up a final tally of 94 seats, 82 more than ever before. The one party to surpass the Radical total was the PSOE with 117 deputies. Of the national republican parties, the PRRS was the only one to approach the Radicals with 58 deputies, while Acción Republicana won 26 seats and the DLR 27. Of the leading regional republican parties, the Esquerra secured 26 and the ORGA 21. The Radical Party was therefore the largest republican party by far, the combined totals of any three of the four most numerous left republican parties – the PRRS, Acción Republicana, the Esquerra, and the ORGA – being required to supersede the Radical aggregate.[73]

Nearly half (forty-three), of the Radical deputies came from the party's traditional heartlands of Andalusia, Aragon, Galicia, Santa Cruz de Tenerife and Valencia. In Santa Cruz de Tenerife the Radical Party won two-thirds of the deputies, in Aragon and Valencia over half, in Seville just under half, and in three of the four Galician provinces roughly a third of the seats on offer. The Barcelona party's humiliating defeat in April was converted into outright crisis as the Esquerra monopolized 26 of a possible 29 deputies. The Radicals could not muster a single seat. In overall terms, however, the Radicals had not only greatly enhanced their electoral profile in established areas of support, but also made significant inroads into many constituencies, above all in the countryside, where its presence hitherto had been limited at best. In Seville province, for example, the party won a third of the seats, yet only a month before the election it had local branches in only 15 per cent of the *pueblos*. Constituencies that were predominantly rural or conservative, or both, such as Avila, Badajoz, Burgos, Cuenca, Leon, Murcia, and Toledo, were now represented by Radical deputies. The Radical Party, in common with the other republican parties, had not only widened but also considerably altered the nature of its social base by embracing the rural electorate. In absolute terms, though, the Radical Party was still more of an urban creature than a rural one.[74]

The kaleidoscopic change which had taken place since 14 April in the Radical Party's grassroots make-up was only partially matched at the national level. A number of deputies, such as José María Alvarez Mendizábal, José Borrajo, and Vicente Cantos, were former monarchists, but they still did not amount to more than a fraction of the party. Socially, the party remained overwhelmingly urban in outlook: over 40 per cent of the deputies were lawyers. Much the same was true of the Radical Socialist Party and to a lesser extent of Acción Republicana, but whereas practically a quarter of the Radical parliamentary party came from the business world, virtually none of the left republican deputies – less than one per cent, in fact – were from the same sector. By contrast, Acción Republicana contained a high proportion of academics, while the Radical Socialist Party had more journalists and other writers in relative terms than either Acción Republicana or the Radical Party. These striking variations in social composition help elucidate the parties' differing outlooks: whereas the left republicans were more ideologically-led and focused on institutional and cultural reform, the Radicals' more pragmatic concern with law-and-order as well as their greater hostility towards the trade unions derived to a notable degree from their business base, virtually non-existent in the left republican parties at the national level.[75]

Both moderate republican opinion and the non-republican right hailed the Radical triumph. For *El Sol* Lerroux was "the victorious man", while *ABC* stated plainly that the Radical leader had the support of sectors "that, without accepting either the Republic or all the doctrine of Señor Lerroux, desire an order and legality that guarantees all interests and all rights". For his part, Lerroux judged that the electoral outcome "places upon my shoulders a great responsiblity": in other words, the possibility of becoming prime minister.[76]

III

The Struggle with the Socialists
The fight for supremacy within the Republican–Socialist Coalition, July to December 1931

No sooner had the results of the general election been announced than the first fissure appeared in the Republican–Socialist Coalition. Such was the success of the Radicals, embellished by Lerroux's personal triumph in six individual constituencies, that there was widespread speculation that they were about to form a government. Indalecio Prieto, the portly and pugnacious PSOE minister, reacted vigorously to the rumours by asserting on 30 June that an administration presided over by the Radical leader would not count on "the collaboration nor the support nor the confidence" of the Socialist Party. To add insult to injury, he went on to praise the avowedly conservative and former monarchist Alcalá-Zamora for his "loyalty and correctness" enthusing that it would be difficult to find a man who "satisfies us more completely" as premier. Unauthorized by the party leadership, Prieto's outburst none the less reflected the dominant mood within the socialist movement. The President of the party's National Committee, Remigio Cabello, judged his observations as "correct and opportune", while fellow minister Largo Caballero reminded the press of the unofficial nature of Prieto's remarks, but added that few in the socialist movement would disagree with him. Clearly the socialists believed that a Radical-led administration would place in jeopardy the reforms so far achieved as well as those to come under the Constituent Cortes, a conviction no doubt influenced by the developing conflict in the provinces between the two parties' social bases. Underlying this was the sectarian consideration that the Radicals might displace the socialists as the leading force within the Cabinet, a fear that drew on the traditional rivalry between them. In response, the Radical leader displayed greater political adroitness than the socialist minister by pointing out, quite correctly, that it was still "premature" to talk of the next government. In the meantime, he regarded the socialists' ministerial collaboration as "indispensable".

Certainly the consolidation of the Republic would not have been furthered if the Republican–Socialist Coalition had broken up in the immediate aftermath of the general election. It did not take long before all the ruling parties recognized as much. From this point of view, Prieto had jumped the gun in attacking the Radicals and created an unnecessary obstacle to collaboration within the government.[1]

Prieto's proverbial impetuosity had none the less given expression to the socialists' heartfelt abhorrence of the Radical Party. For the socialists, the Radicals embodied everything that was worst about the republican movement: an archaic residue of historic republicanism whose alleged conservatism, opportunism, and corruption made them both ideologically hostile and politically untrustworthy. In short, the Radicals were necessary if deeply undesirable allies. By drawing attention to the Radicals as a potential threat to the reformism of the Republic, Prieto had implicitly associated them with "the forces of the right", an identification that would become increasingly explicit. This was to prove a constant failing of the left and in particular of the socialists. By rejecting the Radical Party for its conservatism, the socialists were alienating a substantial segment of the middle classes whose support was of considerable importance for the consolidation of the regime. And by associating the fundamentally centrist Radicals with the right, the socialists were grossly underestimating the real, currently submerged, threat to the Republic from the non-republican right. Instead, the left should have encouraged the emergence of a moderate conservative option around the Radical Party that was thoroughly integrated into the regime. By casting the party onto the shores of the right, the socialists were guilty of placing reform above the Republic rather than seeking to merge the two. Change, ultimately, could not be divorced from consolidation. Rejection of the Radicals may have been a virile sign of ideological purity in the short term but it was politically counterproductive in the long run.

Indalecio Prieto's robust disqualification of Lerroux's party can also be seen as the opening salvo in a socialist effort to discredit the Radicals and strengthen the links with the left republicans. Relations with the left republicans were of crucial importance to both the PSOE and the Radical Party as they held the balance of power within the Cortes: either party could form a majority government in alliance with them. In an exclusive interview with *El Sol* a few days after the clash with Prieto, Lerroux alluded to the pivotal role of the left republicans by stressing that although relations between the parties were still in a state of flux, the socialists would do well to remember not only that the Alianza Republicana commanded a greater number of parliamentary seats than the PSOE but also that the Radical Party could call on the support of other republican forces.[2] In effect, he was contesting the socialists' status as the most influential parliamentary minority while laying claim to the left republicans.

The Prieto–Lerroux exchange thereby anticipated the struggle between the socialists and the Radicals for the control of the ruling majority.

At least Prieto's declarations had the virtue of making it clear that the Radicals would be unlikely to have the support of the socialists in forming a government. Indeed, the Radicals could probably count not only on the opposition of the socialists but perhaps also, at least in the immediate future, on that of the Radical–Socialists, who had made a point of publicly backing the socialist minister. The other Alianza parties, the Radicals' only clear-cut allies, did not command enough votes to permit the Radical Party to constitute a majority administration. As Lerroux explained to the parliamentary group, a Radical-led administration, confronted by "passionate and extraneous parliamentary groups, of an unjustified ill-will", would achieve nothing more than "a sterile and absurd labour". Consequently the Radical leader reacted to the rumour in late July that he was about to head an Alianza-based government by saying that it would be "a folly" if the present government did not continue in power. To be Prime Minister now, he insisted, would be "the greatest upset of my life". "Above all else", Emiliano Iglesias emphasized, "we are parliamentarians and we have no appetite for power".[3] Or, as Lerroux put it, "the later power comes to me, the better for me and for my party".

Unable to form their own government in the short term, the Radicals' overriding priority was for the Constituent Cortes to fulfil their principal mission of drawing up a new founding charter as soon as possible. Once the Constitution was out of the way, explained the party's spokesman Rafael Guerra del Río in an interview on 2 August, the Radicals would aspire to the formation of an all-republican government. According to the decree of convocation, the Constituent Cortes, following the passing of the Constitution, would have to undertake "the complementary laws". However, the Radicals were decidedly vague as to how long, in their view, parliament should remain in session. Guerra del Río limited himself to asserting rhetorically that once an all-republican administration was formed "the real revolution" would unfold, while Lerroux told *El Sol* in a more circumspect vein that he doubted that "everything can be discussed in these Cortes". In fact, as Guerra del Río and Martínez Barrio revealed in a private conversation with Azaña in early August, the Radicals' real aspiration was for the Cortes to be dissolved as soon as the Constitution had been passed. This was partly because the Radicals believed that they had little or no possibility of forming a stable majority government under the Constituent Cortes. But there was also another reason. The Radicals were convinced that, once liberated from the shackles of the Republican–Socialist Alliance, the party would be in a position to enhance considerably its parliamentary presence. Indeed, the sooner new elections were held, the more likely the party would be able to take advantage of the uncertainty of the conservative classes, as reflected in the high level of abstention in June, along with the political disarray that still reigned on the right. As Lerroux put it in a speech in Santander, he was supported by a huge section of public opinion for whom he was their saviour. Hence the Radicals' anxiety for the Constitution to be passed as soon as possible. Within a month of the Cortes opening, Lerroux went so far as to warn in a speech in Soria against the danger of "converting the parliament into a convention" on the grounds that this could result either in "a dictatorship or, what is worse, an anarchic situation". Hence, too, the Radicals' confidence that the next parliament would be theirs. As the Radical leader predicted in July to a French publication, "the axis of Spanish politics will be the Radical Party. The revolution has been made in order to apply a doctrine that is identical to our programme". Thus no sooner had the Constituent Cortes met than the Radical Party began to look forward to its end. "The dissolution", as Azaña observed, "is the coveted ideal of Lerrouxism".[4]

Confronted after the election by the combined hostility of the socialists and the Radical–Socialists, the Radicals set about shoring up their support within the Alianza Republicana by requesting that it convene before the Cortes opened. Two meetings were held, one for the Alliance's National Council alone and another three days later with the parliamentary parties also in attendance. The press release following the National Council's meeting on 10 July stated that the Alianza constituted "a single parliamentary bloc". The relief of the Radicals was palpable. "The Alianza has taken shape", trumpeted the PURA organ El Pueblo. "The Republic", it concluded triumphantly, "possesses an instrument of power, a left-wing that is defined, prepared". El Socialista, outraged at Azaña's apparent backing for Lerroux, dismissed their partnership as an unholy alliance. In reality, the Alianza was not as united as Radical propaganda would have it. At both meetings the Acción Republicana leader, Manuel Azaña, made it plain that his party was determined to maintain its independence and not to become yet another autonomous republican party swallowed up by the Radical Party. When Lerroux, at the second meeting, spoke of the two parties' "parliamentary unity", Azaña immediately corrected him, adding that they were "allies, but without any confusion". Privately, the Acción Republicana leader regarded the Alianza as a means of maintaining the government coalition until the Constitution had been passed and of preventing the Radical Party from drifting to the right. In consequence, the Alianza was not a "single bloc" but a provisional conjunction of forces whose future together was far from assured. Its fragility was a further indication of the vulnerability of the Radicals' position at the outset of the Cortes.[5]

The opening of the Constituent Cortes on 14 July, Bastille Day, was intended to be not just a heavily symbolic nod of gratitude towards the French Republic as the perpetual paradigm of the Spanish republican movement, but also as a portent of the revolutionary changes to come. Despite this expectation, the Radical *jefe*, leader of the largest republican party and renowned for his parliamentary oratory, was notable by his absence. Indeed, during the period up to the beginning of the debate on the Constitution on 27 August, he delivered not a single discourse in the Cortes. By contrast, he gave three speeches outside the Cortes. Lerroux was clearly more eager to catch the ear of the provinces rather than that of parliament. This was partly a ploy to avoid prolonging the Constituent Cortes and even prejudicing the formation of an all-republican government once the Constitution had been passed by exacerbating differences with the Radicals' government allies, but it also reflected his lack of interest in the proceedings, his dwindling energies (the fixed nature of his routine whereby he retired early in the evening soon became common lore), and a certain conceit. There is no question that the Radical leader could have raised his party's national profile considerably without antagonizing his allies by participating more in the life of the Constituent Cortes, but his own personal requirements appeared to override those of the party.

The extra-parliamentary speeches given by Lerroux in August shared much in common with the electoral campaign, though they placed a greater stress upon the "capture of hearts and minds" in an effort to build upon the expectation aroused by the party's success in June. As he exclaimed on 13 August in Colmenar Viejo, a small agrarian town north of Madrid, the Republic should not be the "patrimony of the republicans, but of all Spaniards, so that they can march together along the path of history and so that tyranny, neither in the form of a monarchy nor of a dictatorship, rises up again". The message of the Radical leader was directed in particular at those sectors of the middle classes that had yet to commit themselves to a republican party. Against a background of increasing labour unrest, the most vivid illustration of which was the CNT's violent general strike in Seville the previous month, he was eager to reassure the property-owning classes of his commitment to law and order. "Without order, without authority and without law neither progress nor liberty are possible", he declared. However, as in the general election, Lerroux's message looked both ways at once. His appeal was directed not only at the newcomers but also at the party's traditional supporters. For "a long time", he declared, the traditional republicans would have to watch over the newcomers as they were "our enemies", while also surveilling the actions of the army, the teaching profession, and especially the clergy. In uncompromising terms, he went on to say that the ministers of the church, many of whom were still "fanatical and backward and regressive", should not be allowed to act as "ministers of reaction and enemies of liberty". In the same vein, the non-republicans within the professions would have to be regarded as "smiling enemies who maybe carry in their sleeves . . . the dagger that they wish to plunge in our breasts". This fighting talk on behalf of the republicans was combined with a vibrant defence of reform. The coming of the Republic did not amount to a change in political regime alone but, he stressed in Soria on 10 August, a "transformation so radical, that a new history of Spain begins". But, as in the election campaign, his own proposals for reform were moderate and vague. He demanded that there should be indemnification for those whose land was redistributed while insisting that the "social problem" would take "several generations" to solve, though adding that he was more than ready for the Cortes to have the final word on these issues.[6] Once again, the Radical leader's propaganda retained a strong inter-classist flavour which demonstrated that his appeal was not aimed exclusively at the middling classes. More at home in the realm of populist generalities than in that of policy detail, he reassured the audience in Colmenar Viejo that "I am from the *pueblo*", claiming to be much more at ease in the company of "humble crowds", landless labourers, and small landowners than in that of diplomats, national politicians, and urban society. He also promised, if made premier, to carry out a "labour of justice" so that those without land would have "a patrimony that would represent bread for their children and hope in their lives". Finally, in true demagogic style, Lerroux turned on its head the argument of those to his left who insisted that the Republic should be for the republicans, by arguing that the reason why the Republic should be "for all Spaniards" was so that "the *pueblo* will always govern".

The Radical leader's last speech in August, delivered in the major Castilian town of Valladolid on the 23rd, was also the most important. Here Lerroux placed a far greater emphasis than in the previous addresses on the need to consolidate the Republic by widening its social base. According to the Radical *jefe*, there was no act more radical or left-wing than "the defence and conservation of the Republic", but the republicans could not hope to win over the majority of Spaniards to the new regime if the parties limited themselves to the role of "a tabernacle where they go to preserve the faith". On the contrary, they would not grow, if, "on the pretext of defending the purity of their doctrines", they were to place "a barrier at the door, a screen through which a certain type of people could not pass". To be definitively consolidated, the Republic required the assistance of "all the social classes", including as well that of former monarchist politicians – following a period of "penitence" – such as Melquiades Alvarez and Santiago Alba. The Valladolid speech differed from those in Colmenar Viejo and Soria not only because of a greater stress on integration, but also as a result of a much more placatory approach towards non-republicans. On the one hand, Lerroux contended that the state bureaucracy, army, clergy, teaching profession, and the judiciary all had to be reformed. If, on the other hand, those affected did not collaborate loyally with the Republic "nor will they be traitors". Indeed, he went so far as to claim that many convinced royalists offered "better guarantees than the recent arrivals, those that come to see if they can milk the system". Clearly this was a speech tailored to the needs of its predominantly conservative audience. A more accommodating tone was also detectable in the Radical leader's treatment of the Catholic church. While declaring his own laicism ("Not only am I laic, but my household is as well") and defending the separation of church and state, he also took pains to stress that this did not amount to "civil war" nor was it a "punishment". Even more significantly, he defended the rights of Catholics, like those of any other social group, to form religious communities in accordance with the Law of Associations, on the grounds that "the majority" of Spaniards were Catholic. Such appeasement, however, was complemented by a determination to stand up to the church in other areas. Lerroux rejected the church's monopoly of education, arguing instead that the state should do everything possible to promote public sector education "however possible" so that within a generation or two Spain found itself "at the head of civilization". He also found fault with the religious seminaries, calling in colourful language on the state to ensure that they were not converted into "a factory for the castration of mentalities".[7]

On account of Valladolid's status as a heartland of pious conservatism, the Radical leader's address there was distinguished by his effort to win over non-republicans, though its chief purpose did not differ from that of the previous speeches in attempting to please traditional supporters while extending the party's base. Undoubtedly Lerroux was right to insist that the imperatives of a more democratic politics made it essential that the republican parties should seek to consolidate and expand their support. High abstention levels among the conservative classes in the general election along with growing opposition both on the left and the right to the regime's reformist measures already indicated not only that much of the anti-monarchist *pueblo* had not yet been converted into a pro-republican one, but also that many monarchists remained to be convinced by the Republic. The task confronting the republicans was, for the sake of the regime, to win over as many sectors of society as possible. The Valladolid speech epitomized the Radical effort to integrate, rather than alienate, the conservative middle classes before the non-republican right offered them a new, anti-republican, home.

Though the Radical leader had neglected parliament for the provinces, his extra-parliamentary speeches in August scarcely amounted to a concerted campaign of propaganda. A similar lack of energy and purpose characterized the overhauling of the party's national organization to meet the challenge of mass politics. Yet this was an urgent undertaking, partly because the Radicals had just emerged from seven years of relative political inactivity under the Dictatorship, but mostly because they now faced a monumental task of assimilation as numerous regional and provincial parties along with many thousands of individual citizens flooded into the party. As well as revamping the national organization, the Radicals also had to tackle those provinces, nearly a third in all, where the party's presence was still skeletal or virtually non-existent. In August, a new organizational blueprint for the party was finally unveiled. A mere two pages long, the new Regulations proposed the creation of a National Council to improve national-level coordination, a path-breaking provincial structure, and an annual general congress.[8] Nevertheless, the leadership's lack of drive, the party's lack of resources, and the provincial bodies' lack of unity meant that the plan's application would be hesitant, uneven, and often polemical. In fact, it was not until well into 1932 that the August Regulations were enforced in the provinces. What can be termed the party's "democratic deficit", a function of Lerroux's overarching personalistic power, was reflected in the fact that the National Council was never properly formed. In the meantime, Martínez Barrio relates that because of Lerroux "all my efforts to ensure that the General *Junta* met with regularity were dashed by his passive and disdainful resistance". Moreover, by the end of 1931 the party had still not held a national congress. This was not only in stark contrast to the left–republican parties, both Acción Republicana and the PRRS having held two congresses by October 1931, but also a lost opportunity in terms of the party's reorganization and its projection at the national level. The absence of a congress again revealed the party's organizational shortcomings as well as Lerroux's unwillingness to expose himself to the criticism, let alone control, of the lower echelons. Another symptom of the Radical Party's inability to relaunch itself in 1931 was the failure to establish a national party paper. Unlike the socialists, the Radicals had no truly nationwide organ of their own, so that, like the left republicans, they had to make do with sympathetic republican dailies such as *El Sol* and *El Liberal*.[9]

The conservative tone of the Radical leader's Valladolid address did not go down well with his Alianza partners. At a meeting of the Acción Republicana parliamentary group two days later, several deputies went so far as to call for the Alianza's dissolution, but Azaña, though privately regarding the speech as "deplorable", counselled calm on the grounds that there was no purpose to be served in confronting the Radicals before the Constitution had been passed. Nevertheless, the Valladolid speech stiffened the already considerable resistance within the ruling majority to the Radical Party's goal of securing for itself the decree of dissolution once the Constitution had been passed. Two weeks earlier, Azaña, in discussion with Martínez Barrio and Guerra del Río, had stressed that, unlike the Radical Party, Acción Republicana was in favour of passing the complementary laws and budget during the current parliament. Yet, in Valladolid, Lerroux still entertained the idea of a prompt dissolution.

Opposition within Acción Republicana to such a move, as illustrated by the meeting of the parliamentary group on 25 August, was soon evident. Early in September, Alcalá-Zamora added his support by assuring Azaña in person that, if elected president, he would refuse to give Lerroux the decree of dissolution. Further support for the Acción Republicana position came from the Radical–Socialists and socialists, thereby reducing the Radicals to a minority of one. Certainly the left republicans and socialists had their own particular reasons for opposing an early dissolution in that, in contrast to the Radicals, they were unlikely to enhance their parliamentary strength in a new round of elections. Reinforcing this opposition was the conviction that the Radicals' aspiration of heading a government with a decree of dissolution was not so much a legitimate ambition as a purely opportunistic move that smacked of dynastic modes. In other words, the Radicals' allies were convinced, not without reason, that Lerroux, just like the monarchist politicians before him, aimed to manufacture a majority for his party in the next parliament by the "old ways". Naturally, the Radicals' government allies, determined to break with the undemocratic practices of the Restoration, were firmly set against such a move, Azaña denouncing it in his diary immediately after the Valladolid speech as a "*coup d'état*". In a similar vein, Alcalá-Zamora, despite his own credentials as a prominent *cacique* in Cordoba and Jaen, told Azaña in private on 8 September that a parliamentary majority "manufactured by force" would destroy the Republic. The Radical Party's much-cherished objective of a prompt dissolution was looking increasingly untenable.[10]

Whether or not the Radicals would head the next government was a question over which the ruling majority was divided. Socialist minister Indalecio Prieto, as was made clear during an informal discussion between several ministers on 4 August, declared himself implacably opposed to Lerroux becoming prime minister on the grounds that the venal excesses of the monarchists would be a "thing of cherubims" in comparison with the Radicals. By contrast, fellow socialist De los Ríos was convinced that the Radical Party had to rule in order to weaken its appeal. Miguel Maura told Azaña in private that "the experience" of Lerroux had to be gone through. Like De los Ríos, he believed that, for the sake of the regime, the Radical Party should not be permitted to go into opposition as a focus of conservative discontent. On the contrary, Lerroux should be disarmed by having him "fenced in" within the government. In fact, Maura aimed to leave the government himself in order to win over "the uncouth, conservative middle class". If the Radicals also left they would obviously represent a major threat to his own political project. Yet it was unclear how an all-republican government under the Radicals could be formed in the face of the opposition of the Radical–Socialists. Maura had already suggested to Azaña back in July that by becoming "the axis of the combination" he would attract the Radical–Socialists and other forces who were loathe to deal with Lerroux directly. This scenario, too, was fraught with difficulties. Azaña refused, above all because of the Radicals' reputation for corruption, to form part of a predominantly Lerrouxist government – even if "the Republic was going to fall". Participation would be dependent on the Radicals forming a minority within the Cabinet so that Lerroux in particular was swaddled by people that made him "inoffensive".[11]

In fact, an alternative Prime Minister to the Radical leader was already being worked upon by the time of the Valladolid speech. As already established, Prieto, at the intra-ministerial discussion on 4 August, had advocated an all-republican government headed by Azaña with the parliamentary backing of the socialists. Three days after Lerroux's speech, the socialist deputies Luis Araquistain, the ideologue of Largo Caballero, and Juan Negrín, the dynamic rector of the Madrid Complutense University, visited Azaña in person to press him, like Prieto, to consider becoming prime minister with the extra-governmental support of the socialists. Obviously, the socialists wanted Azaña as prime minister because Acción Republicana was ideologically much more in tune with their reformist aims than the Radical Party. Strategically, an alliance of Acción Republicana with the PSOE, together with the PRRS, could establish a dominant left republican–socialist axis within the ruling majority, effectively marginalizing the Alianza Republicana. Acción Republicana, a relatively small party, had the added advantage of not representing a threat to the socialists' position within the governing coalition.

Azaña, however, was not in accord with this proposal as he wanted the socialists to stay in the government. At the meeting of 28 August with Araquistain and Negrín, Azaña had reiterated his opposition to the socialists' departure. He also seems to have agreed with Lerroux's verdict that he was still too inexperienced to be prime minister. As a result, Azaña was inclined, as his diary reveals on 1 September, to a government headed by the Radical leader but offset by an ample non-Radical presence. He expanded on this view in a discussion with a number of other ministers on 9 September. Despite Prieto's continued plea for Azaña to head the next government, the Acción Republicana leader contended that "the Lerroux card" had to be played on the grounds that a left republican–socialist government presided over by himself, and with the Radicals in opposition, would be prematurely exhausted, leaving the Radical Party as "master" of the situation. The ruling majority also had to "retain" the Radical Party so that it would not shift further to the right. Not only did this satisfy the Radicals insofar as Martínez Barrio had maintained during the discussion that the Radicals would not participate in a predominantly republican government that was not presided over by Lerroux, but also, promisingly, it met with the approval of the Radical–Socialist leader Marcelino Domingo. Without the backing of the PRRS, the Azaña proposal would not be able to prosper.[12]

Undoubtedly the Valladolid speech had played its part in convincing Azaña that, as Maura had argued, the Radicals had to be prevented from drifting to the right by being penned in within the government. Further, Azaña was now of the view, as De los Ríos had contended, that Lerroux had to be made prime minister in order to exhaust his political capital. What is striking about these twists and turns within the ruling majority is the fear and loathing that the Radicals evince. They are seen in almost wholly negative terms, as a dangerous substance that has to be handled with care. Equally, the debate about whether or not the Radical leader should become prime minister of the following government is regarded purely as an exercise in damage limitation. This approach naturally reflects an appreciation of the parliamentary and extra-parliamentary support commanded by the Radicals. There is little regard, however, for the positive contribution made by the Radicals to the consolidation of the Republic. Not only did they represent many traditional republicans but they also attracted much moderate opinion to the republican cause. The integrative function of the Radicals was largely ignored by the left on the grounds that this involved forces to its right. Underlying this disregard was an overestimation of the stability and strength of reformist opinion as embodied in the left republican–socialist majority in the Cortes and a corresponding underestimation of the potential of the traditional right. For much of the left, especially the socialists, the Radical Party *was* the right. The left republicans and socialists were motivated not so much by the integration of the Radical Party as by its neutralization. Such a negative assessment would inevitably shape the manner in which relations between the Radicals and their government partners were eventually worked out.

The growing differences between the Radical Party and Acción Republicana were exacerbated by a hard-hitting speech from Azaña before the Acción Republicana Congress on 13 September, which can be seen as a riposte to the Radical leader's Valladolid address. Rather than seek to appease monarchist and conservative opinion as Lerroux had done, Azaña went on the offensive, calling for the crushing of *caciquismo* and the extirpation of all opposition from within the state bureaucracy "surgically". He also differed profoundly from the Radicals over their immediate strategic goals. To begin with, he insisted that the complementary laws had to be passed by the Constituent Cortes, not the next parliament. This cannot have come as too much of a surprise to the Radicals, as it was merely a public restatement of the position Azaña had defended in private since early August. But the speech did contain a genuine shock. Since the constitutional debates had got underway in late August there had been a burgeoning consensus in favour of an all-republican administration once the Constitution was out of the way. Minister of the Interior Miguel Maura, for example, had affirmed that the next Cabinet would be a "a broad all-republican" one. The hitherto hostile Radical–Socialist leaders also appeared to be prepared to collaborate with a Lerroux-led government. A number of leading socialists, such as Minister of Justice Fernando de los Ríos, were inclined, too, towards a strictly republican government. Andrés Saborit, right-hand man to Julián Besteiro, affirmed that the PSOE would form "a benevolent opposition", as well as accepting that the "axis" of the next government should be the Radical leader. Azaña, however, now declared that the make-up of the next government was irrelevant as long as it passed the complementary laws "within the spirit of the current majority within the Cortes". This was a tremendous setback for the Radicals. Their strategy was being undermined not on one but two fronts: not only was Azaña publicly proposing to extend the life of the Constituent Cortes – exactly what the Radicals had been resisting – but he was also indifferent as to whether a purely republican administration was formed or not. Moreover, the Acción Republicana leader backed up his proposals with a thinly-veiled warning for Lerroux: a decree of dissolution granted to a prime minister that did not possess a parliamentary majority would be equivalent to "a *coup d'état*". Furthermore, if the majority at the next election was manufactured *cacique*-style by the Ministry of the Interior "to serve the interests of one party" – namely, the Radical Party – the Republic "would be finished immediately, because this would be equivalent to a dictatorship". The admonition could scarcely have been more explicit: if the Radicals dissolved the Constituent Cortes prematurely and deployed the undemocratic methods of the *ancien régime* for their own sectarian ends they would meet with the outright opposition of the left.[13]

The significance of Azaña's rejection of the Radical strategy lay not just in his status as the Radicals' chief ally. He was also the leading figure within the government around whom the left republicans and the socialists were now coalescing. His failure to endorse the establishment of a purely republican administration after the Constitution not only carried considerable weight with the other left-wing forces, but also provided succour to those in favour of a republican–socialist government. On 12 September the socialist leader Largo Caballero, in widely-reported declarations to the press, maintained that the complementary laws had to be passed by the current parliament, and, echoing Azaña, that a premature dissolution of the Constituent Cortes would amount to the "act of an intolerable dictatorship". To make matters worse for the Radicals, he, unlike fellow minister De Los Ríos, defended the continuation of the socialists in the next government. Already out of tune with the left republicans and the socialists over the complementary laws, the Radicals also found themselves losing ground over the question of the composition of the next government.[14]

Faced by the consensus on the left over the complementary laws, the Radicals were forced to retreat. The day following Azaña's speech, Martínez Barrio, in Lerroux's absence, accepted that the complementary laws and the budget would have to be approved by the Constituent Cortes after the Constitution, though he did not specify either the number of laws to be undertaken or the time given over to them. Naturally, the developing left republican–socialist axis sharpened the conflict between the socialists and the Radicals. *El Progreso*, in an editorial on 26 September, declared bluntly that the greatest single obstacle to the formation of an all-republican government, which, it contended, would be more in tune with the country's needs than a republican–socialist one, was the Socialist Party. The socialists, according to the Radical daily, were determined to destroy the Radicals because they realized that the Radical Party would supersede the PSOE at the next general election. Martínez Barrio also told the press that a choice had to be made: either a socialist-led government was formed, in which the Radicals would play no part, or else a Radical-led, all-republican one. Similarly, Lerroux, on his return from Geneva, declared that the next administration should be "homogeneous, whether of a socialist tendency or of a republican tendency". He also made it clear where his own preference lay: "the hour has not yet arrived for the Socialist Party to govern". However, the Radicals were clearly on the defensive, their initial strategy crumbling through a lack of support as they called for an all-republican administration which not even their closest ally, Acción Republicana, advocated.[15]

A parliamentary vote taken a week after Lerroux's Valladolid speech, which concerned the suspension of a number of newspapers, saw the Radical Party side with the right against the socialists and left republicans. On the left, this was widely perceived as the first vote to mark the true division of forces within the Cortes. The judgement, however, was to prove premature. Certainly in the discussion on the entirety of the constitutional project between 27 August and 15 September, the Radical Party were to the right of the socialists and left republicans in defending such issues as the creation of a Senate and strong executive powers for the President. But the Radicals were also decidedly to the left of the conservative republicans and non-republican right on questions such as education and religion. The Radicals, in short, occupied the middle ground. More importantly, during the subsequent two-and-a-half month debate on the Constitution's individual articles the Radicals neither found themselves isolated by their centrism nor in consonance with the non-republican right. Indeed, the main fault line within the ruling majority was to be revealed by the debate on the Constitution's very first article on 16 September. The socialist-inspired draft of this article had described the new regime in somewhat triumphalist tones as "a Republic of workers". Too Marxist in tone for a centrist, largely middle-class party such as the

Radical Party, its deputies withdrew from the chamber in disgust and urged their ministers to abandon the government too. As Radical spokesman Guerra del Río explained, the party objected to the idea that the Republic was "of a particular class", as well as being concerned that the regime might be viewed from abroad as aligned with the Soviet Union. The Radical protest eventually resulted in a compromise whereby the Republic was described as one of "all classes". The dispute over the first article, however, had not been a straightforward clash between the Radicals and the socialists. On the contrary, the Radical Party had been backed by its Alianza ally, Acción Republicana, while the socialists had been supported by the PRRS. This, in fact, was to be the principal cleavage within the ruling majority during the course of the constitutional debate: on the one hand, the PRRS and PSOE, and, on the other, the Radical Party and Acción Republicana.[16]

The confrontation over the first article may have established the predominant pattern of voting within the ruling majority, but the inevitably wide-ranging nature of the constitutional debates resulted in a considerable variety of alignments. For example, in the debate of 22–27 September on Catalan autonomy, the socialist and national republican parties, despite the terms of the San Sebastian Pact and the crucial importance for the Republic of retaining the support of the Catalans, were drawn together by a common antipathy towards the Catalan nationalists. Although the principle of Catalan autonomy was not ultimately at stake, the lack of enthusiasm of the government parties was reflected in their limited interventions and the fact that these tended to favour the central state at the expense of the region, an eventuality that was made possible by the very vagueness of the San Sebastian Pact. Of particular importance was the amendment presented by Largo Caballero granting the central authorities exclusive competence in the area of social legislation. Although the Prime Minister called on the ruling parties to vote against the amendment in order to avoid the Esquerra's threatened withdrawal from the Cortes, numerous Radical and Acción Republicana deputies chose to abstain while half of the Radical–Socialist deputies actually voted for the socialist proposal.[17] Loyalties shifted once again in the vote on women's suffrage. During the debate on 1 October, the Radicals had joined both the Radical–Socialists and Acción Republicana in opposing the extension of the suffrage to women, whereas the socialists – on this occasion in alliance with the right – defended the measure. However, the property debate on 6 October resurrected the original divide between the Alianza and the PSOE and PRRS. On this occasion, the Radical–Socialists and socialists managed to overturn narrowly a Radical amendment, backed by most of Acción Republicana, to the socialist-promoted Commission text. Even more aggrieved than the Alianza parties by the outcome was the republican right. Prime Minister Alcalá-Zamora promptly resigned from the Constitutional Commission, though he later returned as a moderate amendment, presented by the group "Al Servicio de la República", became the basis of a compromise.[18]

Attitudes on constitutional matters did not just vary between the parties, but also within them. The Radical whips sometimes had to exert extreme pressure, such as on the vote on Catalan autonomy, to achieve some semblance of unity. There were also numerous unauthorized interventions, in particular by the moustacheoid maverick Emiliano Iglesias. His outbursts of 21 October over Catalan autonomy and that of 4 November against the socialists had to be disowned in parliament by party spokesmen. Political immaturity also played its part. Such was the Radicals' resentment at the socialist-inspired draft of the first article on 16 September that, later that day, they supported the proposition that the Republic should become a federal state, even though this conflicted with party doctrine. Moreover, the proposition went against the criteria of both the Commission and the government. If the speaker, socialist Julián Besteiro, had not avoided a vote being taken at the last minute, the Radical Party might have seriously damaged the governmental coalition.[19]

The indiscipline of the left–republican parties was equally bad, if not worse. The PRRS and Acción Republicana, in contrast to the Radical Party, were embryonic parties with no parliamentary experience behind them. Azaña declared in private that he could not preside over a government that included the Radical–Socialist Party as it was "full of ungovernable and impetuous people". The blatant lack of control of the two Radical–Socialist ministers over their own deputies was notorious. No other party could match the PRRS for the frequency and outright idiosyncracy of its deputies' unauthorized interventions, drawing as it did on a veritable gallery of demagogues, including Eduardo Ortega y Gasset, Juan Botella Asensi, José Antonio Balbontín, Ramón Franco, and Joaquín Pérez Madrigal. The lack of comprehension between Acción Republicana and the PRRS, Azaña believed, stemmed not from their ideological differences but the temperamental abyss that separated them. Less prone than the PRRS to fragmentation, Acción Republicana none the less suffered a series of split votes during the early stages of the constitutional debates. Such was the exasperation of Acción Republicana's parliamentary leader, José Giral, at the indiscipline that he attempted to resign on more than one occasion. Perhaps the most notable incident occurred when the votes of a number of Acción Republicana deputies managed to overturn the Radical amendment to a socialist-inspired property clause. An incandescent Azaña threatened to resign as party leader should such an act of rebellion happen again. Indiscipline of this order was of considerable importance given the tightness of many of the final votes.[20]

The ill-discipline that characterized the republicans was in part an obvious symptom of the internal tensions generated by the ideological disparities within each party. Certainly in the case of the Radical Party, the constitutional debates were an inadvertant showcase for its ideological diversity. The cultural and economic heterogeneity of the Radicals' social base together with the party's perennial populism gave rise to curious contrasts, if not contradictions, in outlook. Although the party as a whole opposed the introduction of the female suffrage, the most determined and articulate proponent of the vote for women was the Radical deputy and lawyer Clara Campoamor.[21] Equally, the Radicals may have prided themselves on their anticlerical heritage, but one of their most outspoken figures was a Catholic cleric, the bombastic abbot Basilio Alvarez. He made his mark in the Constituent Cortes with a demagogic tour-de-force in which he denounced the Commission's draft constitution as anticlerical, hostile to the family, and "confused", as well as suffering from "a coldness incompatible with the heat of our country in ebullience". Yet such ideological diversity was not the exclusive preserve of the Radicals. While the differences within Acción Republicana were fuelled by the confrontations between a clearly identifiable left and right wing, the clashes within the PRRS drew on a striking variety of doctrinal currents, ranging from anarcho–syndicalist sympathizers to conservative republicans.[22]

What did set the Radicals apart from the left republicans was the negligible contribution of their leader to the constitutional proceedings. Controversial topics such as the religious question caused him positively to flee from the chamber. Yet even decidedly less polemical subjects such as his own area of ministerial expertise, foreign affairs, were also eschewed. In fact, this was one of the least controversial areas of the constitutional debate, in which the Radical leader, generally eager to highlight his achievements as minister, could easily have shone. However, he did not make one speech on the many articles which touched on international affairs and which amounted to the most progressive constitutional statement in Europe. Astonishing as it may seem, Lerroux, despite his outstanding reputation as a parliamentary orator and despite heading the largest of the republican parties, made not a single contribution to the constitutional proceedings during the entire three months. This cannot be attributed solely to his admittedly lengthy stays in Geneva as Minister of Foreign Affairs, partly because he avoided speaking in the Cortes when he was in Spain and partly because he deliberately extended his sojourns at the League of Nations in order to avoid domestic affairs. As a populist *caudillo*, Lerroux had always been more interested in language as a means of popular mobilization than as an instrument of ideological and intellectual scrutiny. In the circumstances, Lerroux's horror of doctrinal debate and his immediate strategic goal came conveniently together in his desire to dissolve the Constituent Cortes as soon as possible. For Lerroux, the sole purpose of the current parliament was to pass the Constitution –

which he regarded largely as a legalistic formality – into law before dissolving itself. The Radical leader's indifference and failing energies also explain why he made no effort to speed up the constitutional debates by, say, seeking time-saving compromises between conflicting parties.[23]

The invariable absence of the Radical leader from the constitutional debates no doubt detracted from the performance of the party as a whole. Overall, the Radical contribution to the constitutional debates was distinguished neither by its intellectual input nor by its strategic skill. The parliamentary party, Martínez Barrio recalls, "acted arbitrarily in the chamber. The deputies fought amongst themselves without Lerroux admonishing or correcting them".[24] Probably Clara Campoamor, in the debate on women's suffrage, made the most notable contribution by a Radical deputy on a particular issue, though, ironically, she was speaking against the party's official line. The Radical Party's poor performance during the constitutional proceedings could perhaps be put down to the fact that, in comparison with the left republican parties, it contained fewer lawyers and intellectuals and many more businessmen and traders, accustomed more to the quotidian give-and-take of politics than to the ideological nuances of parliamentary debate. Yet lawyers formed the largest occupational sector within the Radical parliamentary group. In any case, the PRRS, despite being ideologically and intellectually more driven than the Radical Party, displayed an incoherence and lack of prowess during the debates that did not exactly distinguish it either. Superior to both parties was Acción Republicana, whose principal speakers, such as Gabriel Franco, Mariano Ruiz Funes, Eduardo de Ramos, and above all Manuel Azaña, were academics and writers. As a result, the Radical contribution to the constitutional proceedings lay not so much in the quality of its oratory as in the sheer quantity of its votes.

In the second week of October the Cortes undertook discussion of the most polemical constitutional issue of all, the religious question. As on so many matters, the Radical position was far from clear-cut. Lerroux's days as an anticlerical firebrand may have been more than two decades old, but the activities of his "Young Barbarians" during the early 1900s and the Radicals' tangled involvement in the "Tragic Week" of 1909 were indelibly etched into the collective memory of Spanish political culture. Anticlericalism, in principle, still occupied a leading place amongst the party's doctrinal tenets. As if to prove as much, Guerra del Río, an erstwhile "Young Barbarian" himself, declared before parliament on 10 October that "we do not believe that anyone is to our left". He proposed not only that church and state be separated but also that the ecclesiastical associations be dissolved and the orders banned from education. However, the Radical leader was not so keen to take up the anticlerical torch. In declarations to the press shortly before the debate, Lerroux accepted the separation of church and state, but, in contrast to Guerra del

Río, said that the religious associations should be made subject to a Law of Associations and not be dissolved. More generally, in his speeches during the summer the Radical leader had treated the Catholic Church with caution, claiming that it deserved respect because the majority of Spaniards were Catholics and warning repeatedly against its "persecution".[25] Eager to expand the party's base amongst the conservative classes, Lerroux was endeavouring to tread a fine line between republican and Catholic opinion. On the one hand, he did not want to alienate the Catholics by adopting an overtly anticlerical posture, while, on the other hand, he could not repudiate either the party's own doctrine or the great many Radicals who remained convinced anticlericals. There were, to be sure, more Masons amongst the Radical ranks than in any other republican party, including figures such as Diego Martínez Barrio, shortly to be made Grand Master of the Gran Oriente Español, the principal Masonic organization in Spain. The dilemma over the religious question was borne of the party's centrism. Lerroux resolved it by abandoning the religious debate to the party spokesman, Guerra del Río, while explicitly refusing to take part in the debate himself.[26]

In any case, Guerra del Río's proposals were no match for the more stridently anticlerical measures put forward by the socialists and Radical–Socialists. The approach of the Radical–Socialists in particular was vividly illustrated by minister Alvaro de Albornoz's apocalyptic call for no more transactions with "the irreconcilable enemy". Moreover, the socialists presented a proposal, with the support of the Radical–Socialists, that was so far to the left of the posture defended by the Radical Party and Acción Republicana that Azaña feared that, if passed, it would provoke the resignation of the Catholic ministers, Alcalá-Zamora and Maura. Although Azaña's speech of 13 October has often been portrayed as a radical attack on the church, as symbolized in his utterance that "Spain is no longer Catholic", it was in fact an effort to seek a compromise with the socialists which would detach them from the more extreme Radical–Socialists. In an effort to achieve it, Azaña had given ground by incorporating the dissolution of the Jesuits into the Constitution, rather than leaving it for a special law, and above all by depriving the religious orders of their educational functions, which would now be assumed by the state. The strategy worked, the socialists not only withdrawing their alternative but, along with the Radicals, successfully backing the more moderate dictum defended by Azaña. This was a rare outcome insofar as the Radicals and socialists had voted together, but not insofar as the greater moderation of the Alianza parties had once again prevailed over the more extreme position of the Radical–Socialists and socialists.[27]

It is striking that the difficult compromise finally reached over the religious question had been achieved by Azaña, not Lerroux. Yet the Radical leader had been personally involved, along with Alcalá-Zamora and De los Ríos, during the preceding months in the negotiations with the Vatican in an attempt to hammer out a solution to the religious problem before the constitutional debate took place. Indeed, it was precisely for this reason that Alcalá-Zamora had recalled Lerroux from Geneva in early October. Although the negotiations did not prosper, the Radical leader, who had distinguished himself during the talks by his accommodating attitude towards the church, had undertaken to continue the search for a solution. His refusal to participate in the constitutional debate was therefore a grave disappointment to both Prime Minister Alcalá-Zamora and the church hierarchy. However, this was entirely in accord not only with Lerroux's generally inhibited attitude towards the constitutional debates but also with his desire not to exacerbate the party's centrist dilemma. This was illustrated by the decision of the parliamentary party, despite its ostensible anticlericalism, to exercise a free vote on the religious articles. Equally symbolic was the fact that Lerroux did not even wait for the final vote, having gone home to bed.[28]

Despite the strenuous effort of the Minister of War, Manuel Azaña, to strike a workable compromise over the religious question, the eventual solution as embodied in article 26 of the Constitution was still too much for the Catholic ministers, Alcalá-Zamora and Maura, who both resigned abruptly on 14 October. Their resignation was motivated not by the religious debate alone but also by the direction which the talks over agrarian reform had taken recently, especially the rejection of Alcalá-Zamora's proposals by a parliamentary committee. Approval of article 26 proved to be the final straw. There is no doubt that, integral as anticlericalism was to republican culture, article 26 was a strategic mistake. First, it ruptured the Republic's founding pact. The spectacle of Alcalá-Zamora and Miguel Maura, the leading Catholic converts to the republican cause, breaking with the republican–socialist coalition only six months into the new regime did not favour its consolidation. The likely damage was accentuated by the fact that Alcalá-Zamora, hitherto the president-in-waiting, now committed himself publicly to the revision of the offending clauses. Second, the offending article provided the non-republican right with the ideal banner around which to mobilize support against the regime. "Today, against the Constitution", as Acción Nacional leader José María Gil Robles declared in parliament, "stands Catholic Spain".[29] Consequently article 26 boosted the right-wing campaign against the Republic while losing it much goodwill amongst moderate opinion. The destabilization of the regime from the right, in addition to that promoted from the left by the CNT and Communists, was thereby enhanced. By playing into the hands of the right, the Constitution's anticlerical clauses, a result above all of the ideological zeal of the Radical–Socialists, had in fact been too hasty and too radical for the regime's own good.

Selection of the new prime minister took place at a meeting of the Cabinet on 14 October. Given that the socialists refused to occupy the premiership, Miguel Maura, the first to speak, stated baldly that the choice was between Lerroux and Azaña. Without a moment's delay, the Radical leader proposed that the Acción Republicana leader, rather than himself, should be the prime minister. The endorsement of Lerroux was enthusiastically embraced by the rest of the Cabinet.[30] Through his industry and expertise at the Ministry of War and the revelatory impact of his parliamentary oratory – his speech of 13 October was to prove the most memorable discourse of the entire constitutional proceedings – together with his obvious leadership qualities, Azaña had certainly established himself as the outstanding figure of the government. This was all the more impressive given his lack of political experience at the national level as well as contrasting vividly with the muted performance so far of Alejandro Lerroux, the seasoned republican veteran. But there were also powerful strategic reasons for backing Azaña as premier. For the socialists and Radical–Socialists, Azaña was the ideal choice: he shared many of their ideas, kept Lerroux out of the premiership, and would be able to maintain the unity of the republican–socialist coalition at least until the Constitution had been passed. This was because Acción Republicana, as the only party that enjoyed good relations with the Radical–Socialists and socialists on the one hand and the Radicals on the other, was in a pivotal position within the Cabinet. Azaña had the additional advantage for the socialists of heading a small party that did not threaten their position within the ruling majority.

Lerroux's eager backing of Azaña for the premiership was ostensibly motivated by the belief that the Radical Party would be unable to form a stable majority government under the Constituent Cortes. If he came to power, the Radical leader was convinced that, as he stated in a public letter shortly before the reshuffle, "parliament, in its majority, would dedicate itself to procuring our failure, and, principally, mine". This interpretation, though, is highly debateable. Azaña, as his diary shows, did not want to assume the premiership yet, believing that it was too soon.[31] Had Lerroux expressed a determination to occupy the post, Azaña would not only have supported him but also would have been in a position to play a key role in persuading the Radical–Socialists and other left republican groups to do the same. Nor was the opposition of the socialists a foregone conclusion. Fernando de los Ríos, for one, was convinced that the Radicals had to head a government, if only to discredit them and clear the way for the left. Indeed, from the point of view of the left, this would have been an optimum moment for Lerroux to have taken up the premiership. The Radicals' room for manoeuvre would have been tightly circumscribed by the republican–socialist majority. In particular, the Radicals' commitment to the complementary laws would have been strengthened while their options for slipping into opposition as the natural alternative to the ruling republican–socialist coalition would have been significantly reduced. In fact, Lerroux had backed Azaña for the premiership precisely in order to avoid being penned in by a republican–socialist majority bent on exploiting the left-wing majority within the Constituent Cortes in order to pass a substantial number of laws. He also did so in the belief that the Azaña administration would fail before too long. As the Acción Republicana leader wrote in private at the time, "I am like a condemned man, waiting for them to execute me." He later referred to the government as one that was considered "dead and a failure by its opponents from the moment it was born". In other words, the Radical leader aimed to come to power on the back of the Azaña administration's downfall so that he could assume the premiership with the decree of dissolution in his hand. This was, in Martínez Barrio's words, the "secret desire" of his leader. To be more exact, Lerroux had calculated that Azaña would last a mere two months before giving way to him as "the master" of the government. In the envisaged general election, the Radicals, by drawing much like the monarchists on the illicit means of influence at the disposal of the authorities, would greatly increase their parliamentary presence. As a result, the Radical leader would return triumphantly to office for a period of stable rule before, perhaps, retiring gracefully from the political scene as President of the Republic.[32]

The replacement of the Catholic ministers by left republicans and in particular the elevation of Acción Republicana leader Manuel Azaña to the premiership shifted the government perceptibly to the left. The new balance of power within the Cabinet made the struggle between the Radicals and socialists starker than before. Five days later, on 19 October, Lerroux delivered in Santander his first mayor public speech in nearly two months. Whereas twenty-three years before he had given a speech in Santander which, in marking the foundation of the Radical Party, had divided the republican movement, he now called for its unity, a "coalition of all the republicans". He contended that a Radical-led government would respond to the "enormous quantity" of people that did not regard itself as properly represented in the current Cortes. For them, Lerroux was, in his own dramatic words, "the lifebuoy on which the shipwrecked person pins his hope of salvation". This was, in the context, an appeal directed at those sectors that were hostile to the socialists. Largo Caballero was quick to riposte that the socialists could not remember an occasion on which the Radicals had supported them. None the less, Lerroux stuck to his guns, lamenting before the press that the socialists should take offence at his words, but maintaining that the socialists "even in opposition" would constitute "an indisputable asset". The most tangible manifestation of the fast-developing conflict between the two parties at the national level was the Radical obstruction of several socialist-backed bills at the parliamentary committee stage. The socialist ministers were especially infuriated at the Radicals' blocking of Indalecio Prieto's reform of the banking system.[33]

A typical illustration of the grassroots struggle at this time is provided by a Radical activist from Madrid. The local party, he informed Lerroux, was backed by "traders, industrialists and manufacturers" who were "terrified" by the trade unions' demands for enormous wage-rises and by the death threats to property owners. Not surprisingly, the rumour in November that Largo Caballero was about to become prime minister had produced "little less than a heart attack" amongst the Radical supporters. Naturally, these groups looked to Lerroux as "the only one capable of saving the situation". The greatest area of conflict was the south where the nature of the two parties' respective social bases – the socialists drawing the bulk of their support from the landless labourers and the Radicals from the property-owning middle classes – centred the struggle on the labour legislation in addition to that for the control of local government. This is well illustrated by the confrontation in the *pueblo* of Chimeneas in Granada province. The Radical supporters, as a local member explained to the national leadership, were "farmers and landowners, people of order", whose position had been greatly undermined by the introduction of the new labour legislation. Socialist authorities apparently forced them to employ workers whatever the weather, even though the landowners were convinced that this contravened "the existing provisions". From the *pueblo* of La Cumbre in Caceres province a local activist called on the party to send a speaker to the *pueblo* so as to convince the landowners that "abusive contracts have no place in relation to the provisions which the Republic is implementing". In fact, there was a constant stream of complaints from local Radical branches to the national party at the socialists' alleged abuse of power. A typical case is that of the Radical group from Arjona in the province of Jaen, one of the most strife-ridden areas, which complained to Madrid that the PSOE majority on the local council was involved in illegal financial dealings. Convinced of the socialists' misdoings, they pleaded for a representative of the civil governor to be sent in order for the council's accounts to be inspected.[34]

Relations between the Radical Party and PSOE were scarcely improved by the tendency of the socialist press, much-inclined to reduce the complexities of Spanish politics to an overriding Manichean struggle between left and right, to dismiss the Radicals as little more than stooges of the right. *El Socialista*, in its repeated attacks on the Radical leader, readily identified his interests with those of the reactionary forces that were hostile to the regime, accusations which Lerroux denounced before his parliamentary group as "a vileness". On 25 October the socialist organ claimed that the ideological differences between the Radicals and the non-republican right would eventually be swept aside in order to form a "united national bourgeois front" against the socialist movement, the "*caudillo* of the forces of the right" being none other than Lerroux himself. By contrast, the socialists, "the only force that gives impetus to the revolution", represented "the firmest enemy of the reactionary right-wingers". Such Marxist certainties were lent a certain credence by the fact that the more open struggle with the Radicals coincided with a concerted right-wing press campaign, motivated in large measure by Prieto's proposed reform of the banks, against the socialists. Further credibility was given to this interpretation by the willingness of Largo Caballero to associate the Radical opposition with that of the non-republican right. In replying to Lerroux's assurances that the socialists would serve a valuable function outside the government, the socialist minister exclaimed before the press that "the forces of the right" were committing a terrible mistake in "deviating us from collaboration in the government", adding darkly that if the socialists left the Cabinet they would join forces with "other sectors that are today in opposition to the government". The socialists' simplistic identification of the Radicals with the non-republican right served the Republic ill insofar as it undermined the very coalition that had initially established the regime as well as making the prospects of a future reconciliation that much less rosy.[35]

The resumption in hostilities between the Radicals and socialists served the purpose of the Radical Party insofar as they resurrected the question as to whether or not the next government should be an all-republican one. However, the Radical cause in favour of a strictly republican administration was setback by a sudden deterioration in relations with Acción Republicana. In the constitutional debate of 21 October on education in the regions, particularly in Catalonia, the Radicals presented an amendment to the motion put forward by the left republicans, including Acción Republicana. On this occasion, the socialists actually found themselves in agreement with the Radicals. If the Radicals and socialists had joined forces, the left republican bill would have been overthrown. However, such was the enmity between the Radical Party and the PSOE that the socialists, rather than vote with the Radicals, decided to present their own amendment. This gave Azaña the opportunity, the following day, to visit Lerroux in order to persuade him, once the Radical amendment had been defeated, to vote with the other republicans against the socialists. The Prime Minister was concerned that the socialist proposal, if passed, would provoke a serious conflict with the Catalans, possibly leading to the withdrawal of their deputies from parliament as well as placing the position of the Catalan minister, Luis Nicolau d'Olwer, in jeopardy. The Radical leader acceded to Azaña's request, though not before overcoming fierce resistance from within his own party.[36] Still, the reconciliation between the Radicals and Acción Republicana did not last long. In the vote of 28

October on the unicameral parliament, Acción Republicana sided with the socialists and against the Radical Party. The Radicals were most aggrieved. "In the Alianza there is turbulence", Azaña confided to his diary. But worse was to follow. In the vote on the procedure for the election of the President, Acción Republicana once again joined forces with the PSOE and the PRRS rather than the Radical Party. This time, Azaña noted, the Radicals were "furious. They claim that Acción Republicana is a loved one that has been unfaithful". On Friday 30 October Azaña called a Cabinet meeting in order to defuse the growing tensions between the Radicals and the rest of the ruling majority at which it was agreed that the parties would show greater solidarity towards one another. The next morning, however, the socialist ministers visited Azaña in person to complain that the measures taken the day before were insufficient to tackle the Radical opposition. Consequently another Cabinet meeting was held that Saturday evening at which Lerroux, "'the bogeyman'", as Azaña observed wrily, explicitly agreed to cease his party's obstruction. The immediate problem may have been solved, but the two parties remained deeply antagonistic towards one another. Despite the Cabinet resolution, *El Socialista* continued to denounce the Radical Party for "demonstrating daily its intransigent hostility to socialism and its conservative and reactionary sentiments".[37]

In view of the manifest unease within the governmental coalition, the Prime Minister brought the Cabinet together yet again on 3 November, though this time for lunch in the convivial surrounds of the Lhardy, a high-class francophile restaurant near the Cortes. The principal reason for the gathering was to ascertain the ministers' opinion as to the future of the government once the Constitution had been dispatched with. The last to speak was Lerroux, who, in keeping with the opinions already expressed – Largo Caballero having repeated that a premature dissolution of the Constituent Cortes would amount to a *coup d'état* – affirmed that the present government should carry on after the Constitution in order to carry out the complementary laws and any other laws made necessary by circumstance. Only then, he averred, would the moment have arrived "to examine the convenience of a political change". A provisional list of the complementary laws was then drawn up, although no time limit was set for their completion. Faced by an overwhelming majority in favour of the current administration's continuity, the Radical leader did not force the issue of an all-republican government. Outright confrontation at this juncture, especially in view of the recent ructions with the socialists and Acción Republicana, would obviously have been counterproductive. "Once more", as Martínez Barrio comments, Lerroux made "the temporary sacrifice of his desires". The likelihood is that the Radical leader still believed that the government would collapse before long through the sheer weight of its own contradictions. A revealing commentary on the point of view of Lerroux's inner circle is provided by the observations made at the time by Emiliano Iglesias. The parties that made up the ruling majority, in Iglesias' opinion, were "openly hostile, without cohesion and without discipline and without any interior satisfaction". The Radicals in particular were "uncomfortable and unwelcome", and, if they did not leave the government soon, there would be an "explosion". Clearly the Radical leadership anticipated a fundamental shake-up of the government as a result of the tensions within the ruling majority, although whether that would lead to an all-republican administration or the Radicals' departure it was still too soon to say.[38]

Having finally reconciled themselves with their colleagues over the thorny issue of the complementary laws, the Radicals became embroiled in yet another dispute only a few days later, this time as a result of a corruption scandal. This originated in the Commission of Responsibilities, which had been set up under the Republic in order to investigate and prosecute abuses of public power under the dictatorship of General Primo de Rivera. One of the figures under investigation was the Mallorcan magnate Juan March. The bald, beak-nosed multi-millionaire had already made his fortune, largely through the smuggling of tobacco, by the time he was 34. Under the Dictatorship, he had founded the Banco March in 1926, and, a year later, added the North African tobacco monopoly to what was now a vast and varied business empire. Shortly after the Republic was established, March was arrested and charged with offences arising out of the concession of the tobacco monopoly. Republican culture had, in its stress on private austerity and public probity, endeavoured to set itself apart from the sleaze and official favouritism that characterized the monarchy. The investigation of March, a symbol for the left of all that was most corrupt and perfidious about the *ancien régime*, was a signal of the new regime's determination to break with the past.[39]

While under examination by the Commission, March, who in the meantime had obtained parliamentary immunity by winning a seat in the general election, defended himself before the Cortes on 5 November. The Commission, he claimed, was persecuting him, as shown by the fact that not one of its sessions passed by without some aspect of his activities being subject to scrutiny. As this was true and as the proceedings of the Commission were held in secret, an investigation was immediately launched in order to discover March's "Deep Throat". The Radical deputy Jaime Simó Bofarull, a member of the Commission, stepped forward, apparently eager to clear his name. He explained before both the Commission and a secret session of the Cortes that a fellow Radical, Emiliano Iglesias, had offered him money in exchange for voting on behalf of March and for influencing the opinion of the other members. Iglesias, who denounced the claims as "a monstrosity", was found guilty and, along with March, declared "morally incompatible" with the Cortes, a finding, however, which did not deprive either one of them of their seats or parliamentary privileges. Worse still, Rafael Guerra del Río, the Radical parliamentary spokesman and also a Commission member, was implicated in the scandal too for allegedly having informed March, via an intermediary, of the Commission's deliberations. He, however, was cleared, there being no clear-cut evidence, but the ambiguous judgement reproached him for his (unproven) indiscretion and suggested that he leave the Commission.[40]

The fact that Emiliano Iglesias should have been exposed as aiding and abetting the cause of Juan March could not have come as a terrible shock to his parliamentary colleagues. Whereas Guerra del Río enjoyed a relatively upstanding reputation, the flashily-dressed, fast-living Iglesias, one of Lerroux's closest associates, had always been regarded as something of a spiv. It is worth recalling that Iglesisas had been rejected by the Revolutionary Committee as an intermediary between its jailed members and the Radical leader. Although claiming to have met March on only two occasions, Emiliano Iglesias had in fact been linked to March for almost two decades, acting in Barcelona as a lawyer for March's commercial interests, as a personal intermediary between March and Lerroux, and eventually as a friend and advisor. In other words, the March connection with the Radicals not only went back a long way, but it also went right to the top. The Commission scandal confirmed the view of many on the left that the Radical Party was little more than a corrupt by-product of the *ancien régime*, a throwback to what *El Socialista* described as the politics of "nepotism and conspiracy": a shabby clique of discredited politicians who were not merely unsuitable standard bearers for the Republic but unworthy and even immoral.[41]

The Commission scandal, however, must be placed in perspective. The Radicals were far from the only politicians to be linked to, or to benefit from the largesse of, Juan March. While his closest political ally was probably that section of the Liberal Party under the leadership of Santiago Alba, March being an intimate friend of his and having been elected as an *Albista* deputy in 1923, his network of political friendships also embraced republican politicians such as Marcelino Domingo, Miguel Maura, and the eminent doctor and writer, Gregorio Marañón, now a deputy in the Cortes for the "Al Servicio de la República" group. The socialists, too, had their ties to March, the Mallorcan section of the Socialist Party having accepted the construction of, according to the socialist deputy José Prat, a "magnificent" *Casa del Pueblo* in 1924.[42] Of the many newspapers which had come under March's control at one time or another there was the right-wing *Informaciones*, the left-wing *La Libertad*, as well as, it has often been alleged, the anarcho–syndicalist *La Tierra*. In truth, there was a certain incoherence, and even hypocrisy, in the Republic's investigation of March. By its very activities, the Commission, which was made up exclusively of members of parliament, was flaunting the traditional separation of powers between the legislature and the judiciary. Back in 1930, the Revolutionary Committee had no compunction in approaching him on several occasions to bankroll the "revolution", nor in promising him immunity from prosecution if he did so. The fact that March, a convinced monarchist, had eventually refused to cooperate, even refusing a plea from his old-time business and political associate Alejandro Lerroux, gave the impression that the republicans were motivated, at least in part, by revenge. This impression is heightened by the knowledge that the Radical–Socialist Angel Galarza, who, in his capacity as chief prosecutor and as a member of the Commission, had spearheaded the investigation of March, was an intimate ally of one of March's greatest enemies, Francisco Bastos.[43] Once the initial investigation into March had collapsed because of a lack of evidence, Galarza, as Carolyn Boyd points out, "pursued from the Cortes his vendetta against the financier". Azaña himself was concerned at the extent to which Galarza regarded the pursuit of March as a personal question. By contrast, the republicans continued to deal with, and favour, other powerful financiers such as Horatio Echevarrieta, a long-time ally of Indalecio Prieto. Furthermore, Azaña, the efforts of the Commission of Responsibilities notwithstanding, approached March the following year to see if he would back the Portuguese revolutionaries. There was, in fact, a growing gulf between the Commission and the government. Indeed, the prime minister eventually came to regard the Commission's efforts as time-wasting and counter-productive, not least because it made the Republic appear sectarian and petty.[44]

The extreme if not excessive zeal with which both Iglesias and Guerra del Río were pursued by the Radical–Socialist and socialist members of the Commission was indicative of the fact that underlying the attempt to expose March was a determined effort to smear the Radicals by association. As Azaña recognized at the time, the prosecution of the Radicals was to a great extent politically motivated. Once Iglesias had been found guilty, the Radical Party swiftly endeavoured to distance itself from him by censuring his conduct and by calling upon the aberrant deputy to renounce his seat. This did not prevent *El Socialista* from pouncing on the affair by publishing a special flysheet, "A Likely Danger", in which it concluded damningly that the Radical Party was bereft of "the necessary moral authority" to form a government.[45] In fact, the socialists had made something of a career out of exposing Radical corruption for their own ends. The infamous *"cal, yeso y cemento"* scandal of 1910 had been heavily exploited by the socialist leader Pablo Iglesias in order to tarnish the Radicals, then a major rival, and eject them from the Republican–Socialist Coalition. As in 1910, the socialists were attempting to take advantage of a scandal in order to discredit the Radicals. Of course, there could be no denying that Iglesias, Lerroux, and other Radicals were associates of March, but they represented only a fraction of the national party. Even in the Barcelona party, where the bulk of March's Radical contacts lay, his collaborators amounted to no more than a small minority. Simó Bofarull, who had denounced Iglesias, was himself from the Catalan party and a long-time political colleague of Iglesias. In reality, the March connection was very much the work of the Barcelona cabal centred on Lerroux. Certainly the conduct of Martínez Barrio, who was effective leader of the party during the course of the Commission scandal given Lerroux's absence, could not be faulted. The socialist deputy Juan-Simeón Vidarte claims in his memoirs that the socialists were not out to discredit the Radicals as a whole but "the immoral group, especially Lerroux's favourite", but such a distinction was not made by El Socialista, nor was it often made by the socialists in general. In this particular case, the Socialist Party was eager to discredit and even disqualify the Radicals so as to make their own goal of dominating the ruling majority that much easier.[46] The Radicals reacted to the El Socialista smear by threatening to rupture the ruling majority if the socialist parliamentary party upheld the daily's defamatory claims. In yet another secret session the socialists, now under pressure from the Prime Minister to seek a solution, managed to mollify the Radicals by praising their support for the government and by assuring them in private that the views of El Socialista did not necessarily reflect those of the parliamentary party. Still, the damage had been done. The socialist organ had achieved its aim of discrediting the Radicals further in the eyes of the left by drawing attention to the alleged moral gulf that existed between the Radical Party's ancien-régime venality and the left's democratic civic probity. Indicative of the Radicals' weak standing was the acceptance of the socialists' apology as sufficient. As Azaña observed, the Radicales "contented themselves with little".[47]

The Commission scandal further tarnished the image of a party that was under increasing assault from the left-wing press for its conservative leanings. The former Radical deputy and journalist, Roberto Castrovido, now a Acción Republicana deputy, denounced in the pages of El Progreso on 1 November an alleged campaign of vilification directed at the Radical Party, protesting in particular at the portrayal of its leader as a "demagogic dictator", while the Madrid party issued a public statement in protest at the attacks. Illustrative of the febrile climate was a rumour that Lerroux was about to resign the party leadership for the presidency, a possibility that was immediately dismissed by a Radical spokesman. Though unfounded, the rumour was none the less symptomatic of an undeniable problem for a party that was so closely identified with its founder-leader: the lack of leadership. Lerroux, as Martínez Barrio writes, "had assumed the role of the Great Absent One". Since the 24 August

Valladolid speech, Lerroux had delivered no more than one single speech, having been out of Spain for much of the period. He returned just before the October crisis – and only then at the insistence of the Prime Minister.[48]

There was, in fact, a very good reason for the Radical leader's absence from Spain. He had left for Geneva in order to assume the presidency at the League of Nations' XII General Assembly as well as for the 65th ordinary session. Initially, he had built on his promising impression in May, giving a stirring speech in which he had highlighted the "perfect harmony" between the principles of the League and "the new Spain", defended the League against recent attacks, as well as resurrected the spirit of world peace that had informed the League's founding principles. His role in Geneva, however, was transformed by the "Mukden incident" of 18/19 September, which heralded the outbreak of hostilities between Japan and China. This was an international crisis of colossal proportions that was to bring into question the *raison d'être* of the League and, in the process, the whole basis of Spanish foreign policy. There is no doubt that the scope and severity of the conflict, poorly covered in Spain, was not fully appreciated by Lerroux's Cabinet colleagues, absorbed as they were in domestic affairs. The gravity of the situation along with Spain's occupancy of the presidency obliged the Radical minister to remain at the League, but it soon became apparent that his woeful French, his poor grasp of international affairs and of the workings of the League, made him more of a bane than a bonus in the circumstances, causing acute embarrassment among diplomatic circles. As he himself commented to Salvador de Madariaga, "sometimes one has to make a fool of oneself for one's country". Still, rather than hand over to Madariaga, or pass the presidency on to another country, Lerroux preferred to carry on in Geneva. Consequently there is some justice to the complaints emanating from Madrid that the Radical leader was avoiding his domestic commitments by staying on at the League. Indeed, this was a time when many of the most important articles of the Constitution, especially those dealing with religion, were being discussed. In fact, Alcalá-Zamora wanted Lerroux back in Spain to help reach a settlement with the Vatican on the religious question before the constitutional debate. When, finally, the Radical *jefe* did return, he protested before his own party – who needed him, too – that he had required more time at the League. Shortly after, he attempted to return to Geneva, only to be publicly reprimanded by the Prime Minister. Further credence is given to the view that Lerroux avoided his domestic responsibilities by his blatant uninterest in the constitutional proceedings. He did not even find time to speak on one of the numerous articles devoted to foreign affairs. Nearly three months after the Constituent Cortes had got underway, he finally intervened, if only briefly, on 14 October, though merely to draw attention to his own role in the recent Cabinet reshuffle.[49] Nor was the Radical leader doing that much more outside parliament.

There was, he pointed out himself in Santander, "an enormous quantity of public opinion" which looked to the Radical Party. Yet not enough was being done to meet that expectation. Indeed, the Santander speech was his only one in nearly two months. Moreover, the Radical Party, in contrast to the other republican parties, had still not held a national congress.

Vividly contrasting with the lackadaisical approach of the Radical leader was the bustling activity of the party's leading social sector, the *patronal*. The sweeping series of socialist-conceived labour reforms passed during the regime's first few months prompted the *patronal* to organize an ongoing campaign of protest against the measures. In September 1931 the Federación Nacional de Círculos Mercantiles y Asociaciones Libres held a mass meeting at which the arbitration boards were lambasted for their "lack of justice" while the *patronal*'s other principal concern, the necessity of upholding "public order and respect for all authority", was also highlighted. In the same vein, the Defensa Mercantil Patronal of Madrid reacted to the crisis in the capital's trading sector by denouncing the new labour regulations "not out of rebelliousness but on the grounds of impossibility", before holding a grand assembly in November as the climax to a series of local meetings and assemblies. At the November assembly, the shopkeepers and traders, while affirming their loyalty to the Republic, criticized both the socialist Minister of Labour, Largo Caballero, and the arbitration boards for their sectarianism. Yet the Radical leader did little to address or assuage these concerns. Nor could his absence from Spain be justified by the favourable publicity generated by his performance in Geneva. The overwhelming impression is that Lerroux was waiting on events, rather than influencing them. His approach was shaped partly by his ebbing energies but also by a mixture of conceit and misguided aloofness.[50]

Voice was given to the growing frustration amongst those sectors that had pinned their hopes on the Radical Party by *El Sol* in an outspoken editorial on 11 November. The republican daily highlighted the contrast between the enormity of the problems confronting the country, particularly the "difficult and delicate" political situation, with the inhibited response of the Radical leader. Rather than engage with the challenges that confronted the country, Lerroux, who in the Cabinet had spoken "extremely little" and in the Cortes "nothing", had eschewed them through his "systematic absence" and by adopting the posture of "an enigma, a sphinx". What the Radical leader had to do was demonstrate "what he is, as soon as possible". Such criticisms made little, if any, impact on the Radical leader. Three days later he abandoned Spain once again, not to return until 7 December. As in October, the Radical leader reappeared on the national political scene just in time for a government crisis.

The Constitution was finally passed on 9 December 1931 by a crushing majority of 360 votes to 21. The Republic's founding charter, shaped above all by the Weimar Constitution, was essentially a centre–left document. Naturally, the Radical Party, along with all the other parties of the ruling coalition, voted in favour. The Radical contribution had lain not so much in the Constitution's ideological content – despite the non-existent contribution of the Minister of Foreign Affairs it contained the most far-reaching pacifistic statement of any Constitution in Europe – as in the moderating influence of its sheer weight of numbers together with Acción Republicana. The immediate task now facing the Constituent Cortes was the election of the president. Two months earlier, Niceto Alcalá-Zamora, the president-in-waiting, had stormed out of the government in protest at the Constitution's religious clauses, vowing to campaign against the offending articles until they had been satisfactorily revised. At a stroke, he appeared to have dashed his chances of becoming president. An obvious alternative was Lerroux. No doubt the prestige and grandeur of the presidency would have appealed greatly to the vain and ageing Radical leader, crowning a long and turbulent career in the service of the republican cause with, as Azaña wittily put it, a "magnificent retirement". As early as July, however, Lerroux had firmly rejected the idea of being a candidate on the grounds that "he should be independent and I am not. I am bound to a political discipline". In fact, the identity of the Radical Party was so intimately bound up with that of its charismatic founder-leader and mentor that an immediate divorce between the two was difficult to conceive.[51]

In August, the Radical Party had, along with the other parties of the ruling majority, declared its support for the candidature of Alcalá-Zamora. However, once he left the cabinet in October the ruling majority found itself bereft of a presidential candidate. The new Prime Minister, Azaña, along with several other ministers, was immediately attracted to the idea of elevating Lerroux to the presidency. Azaña saw this as an opportunity to solve "the problem" of the republican parties; that is to say, he calculated that in Lerroux's absence the Radical Party would break up, allowing him to form a "big left-wing party". Credence was given to this conjecture by the information that up to twenty of the party's deputies were thinking of joining Acción Republicana. As a result, Azaña interpreted Lerroux's constant declarations of his desire to govern as no more than a ruse to placate his own party. Similarly, the Radical leader's aloofness from the political affray was seen as a means of indicating his suitability for the presidency. Yet when a socialist minister, the mellifluous Fernando de los Ríos, approached the Radical *jefe* in the aftermath of the October reshuffle to explain that the socialists were prepared to back him as a replacement for the unstable Alcalá-Zamora, Lerroux rejected the offer point blank. The Radical leader, who regarded the socialist move as a clumsy attempt to remove him from party politics, refused to take the bait because he, like Azaña, believed that the party, "without the binding that holds it together like a sheaf of wheat", would fall apart if he took up the presidency, thereby leaving the socialists as the undisputed masters of the political scene. The Prime Minister's belief that Lerroux did not seek the presidency because of the protests of his fellow Radicals is rejected by the *jefe* himself, who insists in *La pequeña historia* that the party would have accepted his decision "with resigned disgust". Indeed, his ascendancy over the party was such that it is quite inconceivable that it could have prevented him from taking up the presidency. In any case, Lerroux's political ambitions were so inextricably bound up with those of the Radical Party that it is difficult to imagine him renouncing the opportunity to seize the maximum prize in party politics – the premiership, as opposed to the secondary, often ceremonial role, of the presidency. His ambition, as Lerroux told Azaña in private, was to be Prime Minister. If he proved successful as premier, he would then aspire to the presidency. In sum, there is no evidence that Lerroux sought the presidency in 1931. Rumours at the end of October that Lerroux was about to be designated as a candidate for the presidency were therefore dismissed by Guerra del Río as "a joke".[52]

As the socialist ploy to persuade the Radical leader to become a presidential candidate did not prosper, the Cabinet had agreed at the Lhardy restaurant on 2 November that an approach would be made to Alcalá-Zamora to see if he would accept the presidency in exchange for renouncing his opposition to the Constitution. There was a certain urgency to the undertaking as the constitutional debate was nearing its end and the ruling majority did not yet have a candidate. Two days later, Alcalá-Zamora accepted the government's terms, only to create yet another headache for the government by renouncing his candidacy in early December – a matter of days before the election. His decision was motivated by the overturning of a proposed article to the Constitution which would have guaranteed a *congrunea vitalicia* for the rural clergy. The envisaged measure had been defeated above all by the Radicals, who, along with other republicans, were aggrieved at the prominent – and, in their view, inappropriate – role played by Alcalá-Zamora in defeating a Radical resolution to phase in the women's suffrage. Thus another chance presented itself to elect as president someone other than Alcalá-Zamora, who, it was generally agreed, was "mad". Still, after considering a number of candidates, the Cabinet fell back on the "madman". On 10 December, the day following the passing of the Constitution, Alcalá-Zamora was duly elected as the first President of the Republic.[53]

From the point of view of the Radicals, Alcalá-Zamora was in many ways the ideal president. As a former dynastic minister who had embraced the republican cause prior to the fall of the monarchy, he embodied the Radical vision of the Republic: namely, that union of monarchism and republicanism wherein lay the stability of the new regime. Not only did his conservative views share much in common with the Radicals' own, but also his own diminuitive party, the Progressive Party, a product of the DLR's break up in August, did not represent a threat to the Radical Party. Everything indicated that the president would prove to be an asset to the Radical cause rather than an obstacle.

By contrast, the left republicans and socialists, despite the latter's good personal relations with Alcalá-Zamora, had more reason to pause. The president's conservatism might work against their reformist ambitions. Furthermore, Alcalá-Zamora may have renounced his intention to alter the Constitution, but the depth of his convictions – he had, after all, resigned as Prime Minister and momentarily, though none the less genuinely, placed his presidential nomination in jeopardy – indicated that he might favour those parties which shared his revisionist views. Admittedly, this was a remote prospect at the time, but a possibility nevertheless. Another consideration for all the parties was that as Prime Minister Alcalá-Zamora had already proven to be a thoroughly meddlesome figure, threatening to reproduce many of the interventionist traits of king Alfonso XIII, as well as being disturbingly, if not destabilizingly, touchy and impulsive. Most of those that voted for him did so, according to Azaña, "without enthusiasm and many disgustedly".[54] At least it could be said that Alcalá-Zamora's election made sense insofar as he provided the Republic with a legally scrupulous figurehead of authority whose presence might well serve to disarm the doubts of many monarchists and Catholics regarding the regime.

As the constitutional debate had neared its end, speculation over the next government had naturally become rife. The first point at debate was the likely composition of the government. On 18 November the National Executive Council of the Radical Party had voted in favour of the republican–socialist administration under Azaña persisting in its present, or a similar, form so as to carry out the complementary laws. A more detailed exposition of the party's position was given by Martínez Barrio five days later in a speech in Castellon. The deputy leader stated that the party backed the continuation of the same government as long as an agreement was established beforehand on the number of complementary laws to be passed by the Constituent Cortes and the time given over to them. If no agreement could be reached, the largest parliamentary party – that is to say, the socialists – should be given the opportunity to form a government. The Radicals would take no part in a socialist-led administration, although they would support it "nobly" from outside. If, on the other hand, the socialists did not form a government, the Radical Party had the right to try and constitute an all-republican government. In this case, however, the Radicals were prepared to make a major concession by not insisting that Lerroux should be prime minister. This can be seen as an effort by the Radicals to appease the left, in particular the socialists, as well as reflecting Lerroux's belief that he would be unable to govern with the Constituent Cortes. Yet it was also consistent with the Radicals' hidden agenda; namely, to come to power on the back of Azaña's failure. The Radicals did not want to damage their political standing by governing an unstable left-wing administration with the socialists in opposition, but to keep themselves in reserve, ideally coming to power just in time to organize the next general election.[55] In replying to a questionnaire of *El Heraldo*, the parliamentary spokesman, Guerra del Río, also called for the continuation of the republican–socialist government as long as the Prime Minister was a republican. On leaving the country for Geneva and later from abroad, Lerroux, like Martínez Barrio, defended the continuity of the government, the carrying out of the complementary laws, and the refusal of the Radicals to enter a socialist-led administration. In the lead up to the change of government, he made it abundantly clear that he did not want to be Prime Minister instead of Azaña. On the day of his return from Paris, 7 December, the Radical leader, in a private meeting with Azaña, again expressed his support for the current administration and his lack of interest in heading a Cabinet under the Constituent Cortes. For the Radicals to head a government, as he put it bluntly to the press, "we would need the decree of dissolution". One thing was the Radicals' official line in keeping with the Lhardy agreement, and another the party's desired outcome. A substantial body of opinion within the party, if not the majority, wanted to break with the socialists. At the Assembly of the Madrid provincial organization on 30 November, there were repeated assaults on the PSOE. Deputy López de Uribe denounced the PSOE as the "socialist *fascio*", while another, Velarde, manifested the collective hope that "we have been called to witness the failure of the Socialist Party". *El Progreso* continued to insist, as exemplified in an editorial on 24 November, that there was no solution other than an all-republican, Radical-led government given that the socialists were still not prepared "to assume power". The Radical leaders themselves indicated that their ideal choice was an all-republican administration. In Castellon, Martínez Barrio may have defended the present government's continuity, but he also declared "honourably" that it was time to form an all-republican one. While not so explicit, the Radical leader liked to dwell on the possibility that the socialists, "for one reason and another", quit the Cabinet, thereby paving the way for an all-republican one. The Radicals' desire for an all-republican administration was confirmed by a behind-the-scenes approach made to Azaña by Martínez Barrio. Shortly before his Castellon speech, Martínez Barrio told the Prime Minister's under-secretary confidentially – though almost certainly with a view to this reaching the premier – that he was in reality in favour of an all-republican government. In fact, the Radical view was strongly shared by its Alianza partner, Acción Republicana. The Acción Republicana National Council and parliamentary party, at a joint meeting on 30 November, voted against the continuation of the socialists in the government. Acción Republicana vice-president, José Giral, publicly affirmed that the next administration should be an all-republican one. Azaña, too, was momentarily inclined to a purely republican government, commenting to the President on 1 December that the republicans and socialists could not continue in power together. "This is not a government, it's a committee", he affirmed.[56]

By contrast, the PRRS leaders were firmly opposed to a republican government. Albornoz, as he made clear in a speech in Badajoz on 22 November, wanted a strong left-wing government with a socialist as Prime Minister. Domingo, on the other hand, took a more moderate line. Writing in *El Liberal* on "The Next Government" he defended the continuity of the present government. The opposition of the Radical–Socialists to a strictly republican administration was one reason why the Radicals did not press their case, clearly judging it to be a counterproductive move. Another reason in favour of a softly-softly approach was that the socialists had not yet taken a final decision. Certainly Largo Caballero was as convinced as ever, as declarations to the press show, that the socialists should remain in the government, but neither De los Ríos nor Besteiro were of the same mind. Indalecio Prieto, in a long and reflective speech delivered on 7 December, admitted that he was bedevilled by doubts, but inclined overall to leave the government. "The disorientation", Largo Caballero admitted a week before the reshuffle, "continues". On 15 November *El Sol* may have speculated that a socialist-led administration under Largo Caballero might be formed, but, two weeks later, it was decidedly of the opinion that "the idea that a republican bloc will govern is becoming stronger by the day", the only unknown factor being whether the Prime Minister would be Azaña or Lerroux.[57] Still, the Radicals did not press their case for a strictly republican government. In particular, the Radical leaders and press alike avoided criticizing the socialists. The restraint of *El Progreso* was manifested in its regular expressions of "hurt" at the socialists' more hostile comments.[58] As the outcome of the imminent reshuffle appeared increasingly to turn on the resolution adopted by the socialists, the Radicals appeared to have decided that confrontation with their principal rivals would prove counterproductive. Once again, the Radicals were waiting for events to turn their way, rather than acting on them.

The second question at debate in relation to the forthcoming reshuffle was the number of complementary laws to be undertaken by the next administration, and the time required for their parliamentary passage. At the Lhardy meeting of 2 November the Cabinet had drawn up a provisional list of laws. There were, in fact, wildly divergent views as to how many laws should be passed, and how much time should be dedicated to them. As a result, the debate over the complementary laws in November as the constitutional debates reached their end became extremely heated.

While the socialists and Radical–Socialists lobbied for as long a list as possible, the Radicals fought to reduce it as much as possible: whereas Lerroux spoke of the current parliament not going much beyond the spring of 1932, Alvaro de Albornoz insisted that the Constituent Cortes would require two years to fulfil its objectives. Near the end of the month the socialist and Radical–Socialist parliamentary groups, which defended the complementary laws as "consubstantial" with the Republic, drew up a list of 24 complementary laws in the form of a provisional bill to be considered by the Cortes, estimating that one to two years should be permitted to pass all of them. The Radicals were outraged. All the list lacked, Martínez Barrio commented ironically, was a bill which stated that "the constituent deputies could transfer the post to their sons and daughters and grandchildren". A counter-offer of five laws was made by the Radical Party, although a number of its deputies recognized that, as the party was in a minority within the government, the demands of the socialists and Radical–Socialists would probably have to be accepted. However, the Radicals' resistance was reinforced by that of Alcalá-Zamora, who threatened not to stand as the ruling majority's presidential candidate if confronted by such a list.[59] The mounting dispute over the complementary laws was temporarily defused by the decisive intervention of the Prime Minister in the Cabinet meeting of 1 December. Azaña, who rapidly dismissed the idea of the list in the form of a bill as an undue limitation upon the future president and a declaration of the Constituent Cortes on the matter as pointless, persuaded the Cabinet instead to leave the matter to the next government. The list of complementary laws would be presented to parliament as part of the new Cabinet's programme, and, if the Cortes was not in agreement, then another government would have to be formed. Although a "minimum list" of seven or eight laws appears to have been accepted by all sides, the complementary laws remained a point at contention. The Radical leader, on his return to Spain on 7 December, insisted that an agreement had to be reached before a government could be formed. In his view, the laws should be as few as possible and should not occupy the Constituent Cortes beyond the autumn of 1932. The lack of concordance over the complementary laws therefore heightened the climate of uncertainty surrounding the looming Cabinet reshuffle.[60]

On 9 December, three days before the Azaña administration resigned, the Alianza held a meeting specially requested by the Radicals to discuss the forthcoming reshuffle. Deputies from both the Radical Party and Acción Republicana unleashed a torrent of complaints from the provinces concerning the socialists. The only solution, the two deputy leaders, Martínez Barrio and José Giral, concluded, was to form a strictly republican administration. Azaña, however, had changed his mind. He now defended the socialists' continued governmental presence on the grounds that if they were in opposition the life of the government would be made impossible. The Radical leader, rather than dispute Azaña's viewpoint, delivered a speech of endorsement, the proposition of the Prime Minister thereby being carried. For the Radicals, the meeting seemed to serve no other purpose than to strengthen their presence in preparation for the reshuffle, Lerroux commenting to the press afterwards that the gathering's *raison d'être* had been to "form a strong minority". Surprisingly, the Radical leader did not try to win the deputies over to the idea of an all-republican government, even though this would not have been difficult; not only was there widespread dissatisfaction among both parties at the alliance with the socialists, but the Radical deputies far outnumbered the Acción Republicana ones. Once more, Lerroux seems to have avoided direct confrontation at all costs, neither tackling Azaña over his change in stance, nor adding his voice to the myriad criticisms of the socialists, even commenting to the press in a placatory tone that the Radicals "were not against the socialists". Instead, the Radical leader preferred to let events take their course rather than shape them himself.[61]

Azaña presented the government's resignation on the afternoon of Saturday 12 December. The following morning, the President consulted the political leaders. The Radical *jefe* recommended the formation of a republican–socialist administration headed by Azaña, "the concourse of the socialists", he specified, "being necessary". At 9 p.m. that Sunday evening the President invited Manuel Azaña to form the new Cabinet. Conscious of the Radical leader's self-importance, Azaña first went to Lerroux's house. There he gained the Radical *jefe*'s unconditional support for a republican–socialist administration similar to the previous one. Later that night, Azaña approached the PRRS and PSOE for their collaboration. Upon receiving the request, the socialist parliamentary party, expectantly waiting in the Cortes in "permanent session", launched into a heated discussion as to whether the party should in fact continue in power or not. After a lengthy debate, it was decided, late into the night, to carry on, this being communicated to Azaña shortly before he reached home at 2 am. Later that Monday morning, at around 10.30 a.m., Azaña also received the acceptance of the Radical–Socialists. At this point, Azaña was expecting to form a Cabinet of three socialists, two Radical–Socialists, and a brace of Radicals, in addition to a single ORGA member and one from Acción Republicana; much like the previous administration. Determined to replace Prieto at the Ministry of the Economy, the premier had offered the post on Monday morning to the Catalan Jaume Carner, who accepted later that afternoon. The Cabinet, at last, was complete. Azaña's final task was to visit Lerroux in order to brief him on the outcome of the reshuffle. The Prime Minister, however, was in for a shock. The composition of the new government, Lerroux revealed, placed him in "a very difficult position", adding that the parliamentary party would have to vote on the matter the following morning. Given the Radical *jefe*'s sway over the party, this was obviously a foregone conclusion – as it proved. The Radicals, in short, were out of the government.[62]

Why did the Radicals abandon the republican–socialist government? In his memoirs, the Radical leader claims that, in his first meeting with Azaña, on the evening of the 13th, he specified that the socialist presence would have to be substantially reduced if the Radicals were to remain in office. The fact that this was not done, he explains, prompted the Radicals' withdrawal. At the consultative meeting with President Alcalá-Zamora earlier that day, Lerroux, as he told the press afterwards, had made it plain that the Prime Minister should not be a socialist. However, he made no mention of the number or distribution of socialist ministers. No reference is made to this either in Azaña's account of the exchange with the Radical leader later that evening. On the contrary, Azaña wrote in his diary that Lerroux "does not make any observations, nor does he set any conditions: repeats that I can count on him for everything". Nor did the Radical leader challenge this version of events as recalled by Azaña before the Cortes during the presentation of the government on 17 December. As a result, there is no basis, either in the private or public sources, to Lerroux's claim. Only at the second meeting, on the 14th, does he, according to Azaña's account, refer to the increase in the "socialist preponderance", along with the stagnation in the number of Radical ministries, as a motive for leaving the government. Yet there is no foundation to this claim, either. The socialists had the same number of ministeries as before. Nor were their newly-appointed departments of Labour, Education, and Public Works of greater importance than those which they had hitherto occupied. When Azaña asked Lerroux why he had not raised the matter before, he replied unconvincingly that "it would not have been correct". The fact that the Radical leader did not attempt to negotiate any of these matters with the Prime Minister at either meeting makes his explanation of the Radicals' departure even less convincing. What is clear, however, is that the number and distribution of ministries in the new government was not the *cause* of the Radical Party's exit, but a pretext.

Neither was the cause of the crisis the Radical leader's desire to be Prime Minister. He had made it crystal clear, both before and during the reshuffle, in public and in private, that, as the Constituent Cortes were "hostile" to him, he was not interested in heading a government unless, as he reminded Azaña on the 13th, he had the decree of dissolution in his hand. Nor, in the end, did the complementary laws present a stumbling bloc. Lerroux told Azaña that the number of laws was not an issue. His only caveat was, as he had informed the president, that the Radical Party could not accept the agrarian reform project as it stood. So why did the Radical leader repeatedly defend the continuity of the republican–socialist government, but then reject it? In keeping with the hands-off approach which had so far characterized the Radical leader's political strategy under the Republic, Lerroux was waiting to see which way the tide turned. In this case, the Radical decision depended on the resolution adopted by the Socialist Party. Over the previous weeks the Socialists had been genuinely divided as to whether or not they would remain in power. Had the social- ists finally opted, late into the night of the 13th, to leave the government, the Radicals would almost certainly have stayed in order to reap the bene- fits of an all-republican administration: namely, a greater influence than before over the government and in particular a greater say in the timing of the dissolution and the organization of the elections. The decision would have gone down well, too, with the party's supporters on account of the widespread grassroots conflict with the socialists. Conversely, for the Radicals to have refused participation in an all-republican adminis- tration would have been profoundly counterproductive as it would have placed the onus on the socialists to return to the government as well as damaging the party's relations with the left republicans.

Once, however, the socialists voted to remain in the government, the Radical leader almost certainly decided not to. It was only after the socialist decision had been taken that the Radicals, in contrast with Lerroux's failure to present any conditions to Azaña on the 13th, began to bemoan the make-up of the Cabinet. Thus Martínez Barrio, on the morning of the 14th, having heard that the railways were to be brought under the control of the Ministry of Communications, expressed alarm at the prospect of dealing with the rail unions as well as his general dissatis- faction at the unfolding reshuffle. Other Radical deputies criticized the distribution of ministries, contending that the Radical Party should receive the same number of posts as the PSOE. Several prominent Radicals spec- ified that the party should occupy the Ministries of Justice and Industry in addition to that of Foreign Affairs. It is unlikely that such objections would have been raised without the encouragement, express or otherwise, of the *jefe*. On the contrary, these censures served an evident purpose in preparing the ground for the Radicals' later withdrawal. Lerroux himself spoke out on the afternoon of the 14th, declaring ominously that the "time for transactions" had arrived. However, at the final meeting with Azaña later that day, he made no effort whatsoever to renegotiate the Radicals' position within the Cabinet. In reality, his decision had already been taken. The ostensible postponement of that decision until the Radical Party had deliberated the following day was mere window dressing, a means of justifying the leader's individual decision on collective grounds. If, at the first meeting, the Premier had offered more seats to the Radicals, while the socialists had remained in office, the Radical leader would have been placed in a dilemma. Azaña, however, took Lerroux at his word. Lerroux, by contrast, failed to keep his.[63]

The Radicals' hidden agenda for the reshuffle was revealed by their observations in its aftermath. The official statement of the party claimed cryptically that the Prime Minister's proposals had failed to respond to the "political direction which in our judgement the country currently requires". What this meant was spelt out by the Radical leader, who complained that "they believe that the hour has not yet arrived for liberal republican democracy to govern". Martínez Barrio was even more explicit in his declarations to the press in Seville a few days later. The Radicals, he explained, had aspired to a government that would last three months, after which Lerroux would head an all-republican administration with the decree of dissolution. In other words, the Radicals went into opposition because an all-republican administration had not been formed, or, put another way, because the socialists had not left the government. Over the following weeks and months Lerroux was to refer repeatedly in his public speeches to the Cabinet reshuffle of December 1931. In *La pequeña historia* he returns to the subject time and time again. The justification is always the same: the socialists' continuation in power. Yet Lerroux invariably portrays this as the outcome of a robust exchange of opinions in which he made his objections to the socialists abundantly clear, whereas in reality the Radical leader ambushed Azaña once the Cabinet had been put together.[64] What cannot be denied is that the Radical leader's decision to separate from the republican–socialist administration was in keeping with the mood of the party as a whole. As the Madrid provincial party assembly of 30 November and the Alianza meeting of 9 December had vividly demonstrated, the rank-and-file were bitterly opposed to the socialists. In many areas, especially the south, supporters of the two parties clashed constantly. Admittedly, there was conflict too between the left republicans and the socialists, but this was largely restricted to the rural areas. Furthermore, the left republicans, unlike the Radicals, coincided on many issues with the socialists both ideologically and strategically.

By abandoning the government, the Radicals were effectively sticking to the strategy envisioned after the general election; that is to say, of assuming the premiership just in time to oversee the dissolution of the Constituent Cortes, and, by influencing the electoral process, ensuring a Radical-led majority in the next parliament. Since the Constituent Cortes had not been dissolved following the passing of the Constitution, as the Radicals had originally desired, this would now be achieved by coming to power as the natural alternative to the republican–socialist administration. "The Radicals", as Azaña lucidly observed in his diary, "in competition with the socialists, want to be in opposition in order to be the reserve and dissolve the Cortes. They want the rest of us to wear ourselves out so that they can come to power one day as a guarantee of order."[65]

The decision of Prime Minister Azaña to stick with the PSOE rather than opt for an all-republican government was perfectly understandable insofar as the reformist agenda which he envisioned for the Constituent Cortes would make greater progress with the socialists in, rather than out of, power. In particular, the socialist presence would greatly restrain the UGT, a matter of considerable importance given that the other main trade union organization, the CNT, was already hostile to the regime. Nevertheless, the Radicals' withdrawal from the ruling coalition was a major blow. The governing alliance had been effectively reduced to the progressive middle strata, the socialist working class, and those rural property owners that had backed the left republicans. With the exit of the Radical Party, by far the largest of the republican parties, the government's social base was deprived of a substantial swathe of the urban as well as rural middle classes along with regionally important sections of the working classes. So far confronted by the anarcho–syndicalists and Catholic opinion, the Azaña administration would have to contend in future with that of the middle class majority. Within the chamber of the Cortes the balance of power still lay firmly with the centre–left, but within the country at large this had shifted towards the centre–right with the Radicals' withdrawal from office. The key question was whether the government had a broad enough base for its far-reaching programme of reform, especially as the opposition generated by the measures passed hitherto would become even more vociferous as a result of the Radicals' exit from the government. Conflict over the labour reforms in particular would augment considerably given that the Radical Party was the closest ally of the *patronal* amongst the republican parties. The sweeping series of reforms still to come, including Catalan autonomy, agrarian reform, and further anticlerical initiatives, would inevitably create an even greater backlash. The challenge for the Azaña administration was to maintain, if not increase, its popularity rather than to sacrifice the consolidation of the regime to reform.

As the republican–socialist government's programme of reform advanced and the distance which separated it from the opposition became ever greater, there was a danger that the Radical Party might drift to the right in search of allies. There was a possibility that this would become a self-fulfilling prophesy given the contempt in which the party was held by both the left republicans and socialists. Having come into being largely as a reaction against the politics of the Radicals, the left republicans heartily despised Lerroux and his party. For the left republicans, the Radicals represented the putrid, and unprincipled, remnants of historical republicanism. Azaña's writings show that he was repelled by the Radicals' dynastic-style venality and politicking, while the Radical–Socialists regularly censured the Radicals for their alleged conservatism. The socialists' rejection of the Radicals was, if anything, greater still. Permeated by past rivalries and hatreds, the socialists already regarded the Radical Party as a right-wing, "bourgeois" force. In fact, a leading justification of the socialists for remaining in power had been to protect the reformist programme of the republican–socialist coalition against the threat of reaction – which included the Radicals. These fears had been expressed most recently by Indalecio Prieto in his speech of 7 December. He declared that a "great battle" was developing between the socialists, who would absorb "all that is vigorous" in the republican parties, and "the reactionary and clerical elements", who would mop up the rest of the republicans. The fundamental flaw in this argument was that the Radical Party was not an anti-reformist, right-wing entity, but a pragmatic, centrist one. However, the traditional hostility of the socialists for the Radicals, together with their Manichean Marxism and the conviction that the traditional right had been made irrelevant, led them to believe otherwise. The Radicals were, as their performance in the provisional government and the constitutional debate showed, a force for moderation, but they were not *anti*-reformist. By constantly marginalizing the Radicals in ideological terms by painting them as reactionary, the socialists were effectively helping to alienate them from the republican–socialist camp. Yet the consolidation of the new regime, and of its reforms, required that the republican parties extend their social bases. By incorporating the urban as well as the rural property-owning classes, the Radicals were performing a valuable integrative function. Clearly the consolidation of the Republic was better served by assimilating these elements into a republican party, however corrupt and attached to the political practices of the *ancien régime*, than to lose them to the right. Just as the socialists grossly underestimated the resurgent strength of the right, so they ignored the perils of rejecting the Radicals. By sidelining the Radicals and those social sectors which they represented, many of which, such as the *patronal*, were prepared to work within the new regime, the socialists in particular and the left in general were guilty of placing the regime at risk for the sake of ideological purity. And by not welcoming the establishment of a moderate republican party, the left was playing unnecessarily into the hands of the right. Ultimately, the scorn and derision heaped on the Radicals was short-sighted and self-destructive. Integration rather than alienation of the Radicals would have done much to strengthen a regime, which, at the end of 1931, was far from consolidated. As a result, a more suitable solution to the December reshuffle, in terms of the reformist task which the left republicans and socialists had set themselves, might well have been a reversal of the socialists' and Radicals' roles. By remaining in power, the Radicals would have been constrained by the left republicans within the Cabinet and by the socialists without. The Radical Party would almost certainly have been amenable to just such a scenario. Lerroux had suggested in the interview with *Ahora* in November that the socialists should leave the government and become "a brake so that the republican governments do not let themselves be pushed too far to the right" as well as act as a stimulus for the "reformist works that our country urgently needs". In terms of the regime's future, such an outcome may well have been more apposite.[66]

IV

In Search of a Strategy
The vicissitudes of the Radical opposition, January to August 1932

The Radicals' abandonment of the republican–socialist government naturally created enormous expectation amongst the opposition. This embraced not just conservative republican opinion but also the non-republican right, currently bereft of a major opposition party of its own. The Catholic publication *El Financiero* declared that while it did not share many of the Radical Party's ideas, a Lerrouxist government would at least embody "an initial solution of order and of peace and of possible co-habitation. Later, only God can say". Likewise, *La Nación* stressed that, though the Radical leader did not represent "the maximum guarantee", the propertied classes should back him as the "least worst option" who offered "order and peace". *El Noticiero Universal*, too, regarded him as a defender of "spiritual peace and collective confidence". Clearly the qualified rapture of right-wing and Catholic opinion for the Radicals was circumstantial, but it none the less converted the Radical Party into the cynosure of anti-government sentiment. Moderate and conservative opinion now looked to the Radical Party as the alternative to the Azaña administration.[1]

At the national level, the Radicals' immediate support was limited to the ex-Constitutionalists, though Miguel Maura, despite his ill-disguised hostility if not contempt for Lerroux, soon began to make overtures.[2] At the provincial level, the party was flooded by a wave of newcomers which was second only to that of the Republic's early weeks. Also detectable in certain local councils was a shift in political alignment as the Radicals teamed up with non-republicans in opposition to the left republicans and socialists. Old Castile, a conservative and agrarian region where the Radicals were traditionally weak, illustrates these changes well. In Zamora province, according to *El Socialista*, the remants of the Unión Patriótica and "*caciques* of all sorts" entered the Radical Party, while in the capital the Radicals allied with the monarchists against the socialists and Radical–Socialists. In neighbouring Palencia, the Radical committee in the capital was co-opted by former monarchists, who included the new president. To the south, in Avila province, there was an influx of *caciques* into the party. Much the same occurred in many other parts of the country. In the north-eastern province of Teruel numerous *caciques* enlisted in the Radical Party, while in Galicia, in the north-west, countless Radical groups fell under the sway of ex-monarchists. In the south, in Murcia, former supporters of Alfonso XIII's last Minister of the Interior, Juan de la Cierva, now a political exile in Biarritz, poured into the party.[3] In Cadiz, the dynastic Liberals voted en masse at a congress in February 1932 to solicit their enrolment in the Radical Party. In Albacete, the Radicals, who only began to organize themselves there in earnest in 1932, received a cascade of erstwhile monarchists, such as supporters of Santiago Alba, leading landowners such as Francisco and Miguel Jiménez de Córdoba, eight Liberal–Democrat councillors in Hellín, a substantial cross-section of Liberals and Conservatives in the capital (including town councillors), ex-Upetistas and members of the *Somatén* in Corral-Rubio, the followers of the Yeste county *cacique*, Antonio Alfaro Gironda, and, finally, the Ochando family of the Casas Ibáñez district, amongst the most influential landowners in the entire province. No doubt the claim of *La Tierra* that "the active elements of all the populations look to Lerroux" was an exaggeration, but it was far from groundless.[4]

To judge by the left-wing press, the Radical Party grew almost entirely due to the entry of *caciques* and monarchists. In reality, many sectors of "the middle and neutral classes" looked to the Radical Party, the National Secretary, Manuel Torres Campañá, explained, as they did not want "to take up extreme positions". "The Spanish middle class," as Martínez Barrio stresses in his *Memorias*, "wanted to follow a moderate line that was equidistant from conservative intolerance and demagogic fury." The Radical appeal was directed above all at the conservative, with a small "c", middle classes. For example, in Alicante, a republican stronghold, the party, in stiff competition with the PRRS, implored the national headquarters to send either Martínez Barrio or Lerroux himself to the city so that it could take advantage of the widespread sympathy for the Radicals. Indeed, by the end of the year, the Alicante party had grown by 5,000 members, a much bigger rise than in 1931.[5] The Radical Party attracted left republicans, too. In Albacete, despite the influx of monarchists, the party was joined by *Azañistas* from La Roda, Radical–Socialists from the capital and Hellín, and even a prominent socialist figure from Yeste. Nor did the party necessarily align itself with monarchists in an indiscriminate fashion. In Santander, the veteran Radical Isidro Mateo was elected as mayor in the summer with the backing of monarchists, but he later resigned on the orders of Lerroux. Still, three months later, the Radicals joined forces with the monarchists to force the resignation of the socialist mayor. This, however, caused a seismic split in the party, "destroying",

El Socialista relates, "the Radical ranks".[6] Nor was the Radical recruitment drive aimed exclusively at the agrarian heartlands. On the contrary,
the Radical leader addressed a banquet at the Hotel Ritz in Barcelona on
27 February for no less than 1,500 representatives of industry, commerce,
and the banking world, all of whom had joined the party. "Commerce,
the banks, industry, property", declared Lerroux, "that which I lacked".
The groundswell of expectation surrounding the Radical Party emanated
from many quarters. As the Prime Minister noted nervously, "there's a
Lerrouxist fever".[7]

   The upsurge in support for the Radicals in the wake of their departure
from the government created further tensions in the party, as well as
sharpening existing ones. The principal fissure was between old and new
activists, who clashed over questions of both power and principle. Many
party veterans deeply resented sharing power with recent recruits, especially if they were erstwhile enemies. Indeed, one former monarchist, now
a Radical, claimed in a letter to the Radical *jefe* that "jealousy, egoism,
ambitions" and the conviction that the newcomers might "anul certain
influences" had prevented the entry "in many cases" of "valuable
elements, both in terms of numbers and quality". Such struggles were
invariably embittered, as well as justified, by ideological discrepancies.
The Barcelona party, for example, was divided between traditional
members and those who, the national leader was informed, were "without
doctrine, without republican tradition and supporters, above all in the
pueblos". However, the newcomers, as another correspondent remarked,
backed "the new trajectory of your governmental programme". The
Logroño party split later in the year as a result of a struggle between the
moderates and those that aspired to a party that was "frankly left-wing".
Political differences also provoked a horrendous split in the Salamanca
party, in September 1932, as a result of which 65 branches representing
7,000 affiliates – half the provincial party's entire rank and file – joined
the Autonomous Republican Party.[8] Part of the problem was the rapid
promotion of newcomers. A vivid illustration is provided by the fratricidal
feud that engulfed the Murcia party in 1932. In the 1931 general election
the Radicals won four of the eleven seats, converting it into one of the
province's leading political players. Following the Radical exit from the
government, a fierce debate ensued as to how the followers of the
province's most powerful *cacique*, Juan de la Cierva, should be accommodated. By the spring, the "Ciervistas", headed by the Radical deputy
José Cardona and the president of the *Diputación* (provincial government), Pascual Murica, both recent converts, had, in defiance of the
Provisional Junta's authority, created a parallel organization. Provincial
leader Manuel Rivera, himself a veteran, explained to the Radical leader
in a letter of 22 April that "the question at heart is if the Radical Party of
Murcia is to be a republican party which can be joined by those that were

not before, and who sincerely wish to collaborate in a *republican* manner, or if it is to be the same old *Ciervista* party that until now has been dominant with the same *caciques* in each *pueblo* and using identical methods". To resolve the feud, Lerroux brought in an outsider, but he, too, proved unable to unite the two sides. A meeting of the Provincial Junta in July also failed to overcome what a local deputy, Salvador Martínez-Moya, described as "the lamentable problem". The inability of the Junta to forge a consensus between the warring factions condemned the party, Martínez-Moya concluded despondently, to a "sterile, Byzantine struggle, without carrying out a single propaganda act and without organizing the disorganized".[9]

The Radical Party's internecine conflicts did not always revolve around the struggle between old and new republicans. The two camps were sometimes brought together by a common enemy. Early in 1932, veterans and newcomers alike of the Quintanar de la Orden party in Toledo joined forces against "three or four traditional republicans and the monarchist *cacique* elements". In the case of Huesca province, the party did divide into two competing bands but, as José María Azpíroz has stressed, "one cannot simplify saying that the traditional members defended the pure republican ideals against the recent arrivals". A traditional Radical bulwark, the Huesca party was split by the affair of the "Provincial Steering Committee", which pitted recent recruits, including the young lawyer Manuel Sender (brother of the writer Ramón Sender, himself an anarchist), in alliance with established members such as Sixto Coll against a coalition, led by the mayor of Huesca, Manuel Gómez, that also drew on new and old militants alike. While the "regenerationists" wanted to purge the *Diputación* (provincial government) – hitherto a source of public sector patronage – of dynastic functionaries found guilty of irregularities, the "integrationists" took a softly-softly approach. This was, at heart, a dispute over how the institutions of the monarchy should be adapted to the Republic. Under Sixto Coll's presidency of the Steering Committee between April and August 1931, the "regenerationists" had sacked monarchist employees despite being constrained by the Minister of the Interior, Miguel Maura, who, in accordance with the provisional government's guidelines, adopted a moderate stance. Once the "integrationists" gained control of the Committee, they proceeded to appoint many of the functionaries previously dismissed. Moreover, in September 1932, Coll having regained control of the Committee a month earlier, the national party came down firmly on the side of the "integrationists". The Huesca party was rent asunder. Many joined the recently created Republican Autonomous Party, while others, including Manuel Sender, enlisted in Acción Republicana. In certain areas, such as Albacete, the Radical Party suffered little discord, but many provincial bodies were afflicted by rifts and ructions which, in a notable number of cases, resulted in damaging schisms. Internal tensions were to an extent an inevitable result of the demands of democratic politics as all the parties struggled to come to terms with the mass entry of newcomers, but in the Radical case these were accentuated by the party's marked social heterogeneity, itself a product of its inter-classist message, as well as by its rapid promotion of recent recruits. Even Martínez Barrio, whose integrity as a republican was beyond dispute, objected at the Seville Congress in March to a motion in favour of a two-year executive ban on new members. The failure to address the challenge of integration properly caused a constant haemor-rhaging of the Radical Party during the first biennium, thereby prejudicing its appeal and the corresponding growth of its social base. It was a ques-tion that the Radicals were never to resolve.[10]

Once the Radicals left the government in December 1931 their rela-tions with the socialists had inevitably become even more acrimonious. In a speech on 24 January 1932, the moderate Martínez Barrio had drawn a dramatic parallel between contemporary Spain and the revolutionary Russia of 1917, asserting that the socialists were aiming to replicate the triumph of the Bolsheviks and that, by extension, Azaña was their Kerenski.[11] Yet the conflict between the Radicals and the socialists was not merely a product of their rivalry at the national level, but was also powerfully shaped by the mounting struggle in the provinces between the workers and employers. This was a result of rising unemployment, the severe winter of 1931–32, which affected agricultural and construction labourers in particular, and the negotiations over the contracts to be drawn up in accordance with the new labour legislation. Numerous inci-dents testify to the heightened tension between the parties' social bases. At a public meeting in Cazorla (Cordoba), the Radical speakers had stones thrown at them because, *El Socialista* explains, they were "on the side on the *patronal* class". In the *pueblo* of Beas (Huelva), a Radical member, assaulted on leaving the Casino by a stick-wielding socialist, turned on his aggressor and shot him dead. In Cañete la Real (Malaga), the socialists attacked a Radical meeting, while shouting "death to Lerroux" at their own gathering. At another meeting, attended by the parliamentary deputy Antonio García Prieto, PSOE councillors incited the crowd to assault the Radical centre. In the province of Granada, urban professionals and rural landowners swelled the ranks of the Radical Party in refuge from what a local leader described as "the horrible damage that the socialists are doing to us with the indignant and *cacique* politics" of minister and provincial leader Fernando de los Ríos. The struggle in Granada, as the rest of Spain, was centred above all on three areas: the application of the labour legis-lation, the upholding of law and order, and the control of the *ayuntamientos*. In March, for example, the Radical branch in Chauchina, a *pueblo* of 4,000 people, denounced the socialist mayor, "an uncouth, rude and vulgar individual" who had allegedly served 17 years for murder, for persecuting Radical employers and workers alike. Not only did the socialists prevent labourers from the party from working in the fields but they also had them repeatedly arrested on false grounds. Unless a solution was forthcoming, the party warned Lerroux, "a catastrophe will take place any day".[12]

Such was the antipathy between the Radicals and the socialists that "Confidential Reports on the Socialist Performance" were compiled by the former. The Toledo party's dossier, for instance, alleges that the socialist authorities discriminated against non-socialist workers, embezzled public funds, and aided their members in subverting the law. It was even said that one of the PSOE deputies for Toledo, Domingo Alonso Jimeno, otherwise known as "The Toad", had once been fined 500 pesetas for the "exploitation of minors" and that, despite his political credentials, was an intimate friend of the Conde de Casafuerte. It was also claimed that the President of the Workers' Society in the *pueblo* of Las Navas was a "killer" who had not only murdered a shepherd but also the director of the prison where he was subsequently held, that the socialist mayor of Cebolla, who had previously belonged to the *Somatén*, incited workers to rob the houses of landowners, and that a socialist doctor from Escalona was the "promoter of all the disorders in the province". The report, despite the party's anticlericalism, even detailed acts against the church. In one *pueblo*, it affirms, a PSOE mayor ordered the removal of crucifixes from all the school classrooms before handing them over to "the boys so that they could smash them into splinters and throw them down the toilet".[13]

In spite of the heightened conflict with the socialists and the expectation surrounding the party, the Radicals did not go into outright opposition to the republican–socialist administration in an attempt to maximize their appeal as a conservative counterpoint. Instead, the Radicals presented "a ministerial opposition". In reality, they aimed to drive a wedge between the left republicans and the socialists in order to bring about the establishment of an all-republican government. The spearhead of the Radical strategy was its anti-socialism. The Radical Party, as the focus of middle class resentment, would thereby become the natural alternative to the Azaña administration. In this way, a "transitory situation", as the Radical leader described it, would soon be brought to a close.[14] The Radicals' priorities were promptly illustrated by their reaction to a series of sanguinary clashes involving the Civil Guard. The first occurred in Badajoz province in the southwestern region of Extremadura, one of the poorest areas of the country, where vast estates worked by surplus armies of landless labourers predominated. The shift in the balance of power against the property owners since the advent of the Republic – due to the election of left-wing councils and the labour reforms – made relations between the landowners and the workers increasingly

fraught, as reflected in the fact that there were over eighty stoppages in
the province in 1931. In December 1931, the FNTT called a strike in
protest at the civil governor, Manuel Alvarez Ugena, and the Civil Guard
as a result of the uneven enforcement of the labour legislation. In the
impoverished *pueblo* of Castilblanco, lost in the remote "Extremaduran
Siberia", the strikers were dispersing after the stoppage when the Civil
Guard attempted to hurry them along in a typically heavy-handed fashion.
A tussle ensued between the four Guards and the workers as a result of
which a labourer was shot, and died. In a Dantesque explosion of popular
hatred the villagers set upon the Guards and savaged them by gouging out
eyes, dismembering limbs, and crushing skulls. All four were killed.[15]

The blood-letting at Castilblanco crystallized two crucial dilemmas for
the Republic; first, the fundamentally undemocratic impunity with which
the forces of public order continued to act, and, second, the monumental
difficulty of satisfying the expectations of reform unleashed by the new
regime in a society characterized by gaping inequalities – especially in the
midst of a recession and by means of a weak state. The incident was an
early indication of the grassroots conflict between the socialists and the
republicans as the polemical civil governor was a member of Acción
Republicana. Further, the socialists' principal foes in the province were
the Radicals. A Radical deputy for Badajoz, the Madrid-based notary
Diego Hidalgo, who was originally from the province and known for his
book *Un notario español en Rusia* ("A Spanish Notary in Russia"),
compiled a report on the Castilblanco confrontation. Firmly identified
with the Radicals' conservative wing, having joined the party in the 1920s,
Hidalgo took an unflinching law-and-order line, attributing the massacre
to the propaganda of socialist extremists, especially a local PSOE deputy,
the flamboyant art critic and journalist of German origin Margarita
Nelken, as well as the Badajoz FNTT leaders, while robustly defending
the Civil Guard. He referred revealingly to the latter, without which
Extremadura "could not live", as "la Benemérita", a term of affection
(meaning "the worthy"), while condemning the socialists for fomenting
unrealistic expectations in what he described disparagingly as "the uncul-
tured mass". In the Cortes, the Prime Minister affirmed that no single
party could be held responsible for the events in the Extremaduran *pueblo*.
Although the socialist and Radical deputies clashed over the incident, the
Radicals took care not to attack either the government as a whole or the
left republicans over the affair.[16]

Less surprisingly, the Radical Party did not take issue with the Azaña
administration over a series of violent assaults in the wake of Castilblanco
by the Civil Guard. These abuses of the law by one of the very institutions
designed to uphold it, including the killing at Epila in Zaragoza province
of two CNT members and that at Jeresa in Valencia which left four dead
and thirteen wounded, amounted to a protracted vendetta by the

"Benemérita" for its own losses in Castilblanco. The backlash climaxed with the massacre on 5 January at Arnedo in the province of Logroño. A dispute between the local UGT and the unyielding owner of a shoe factory, Señor Muro, who had repeatedly reneged on his promise to take back a number of workers, eventually resulted in a strike. On the day of the stoppage, a meeting took place at the town hall between the civil governor, the lieutenant colonel of the Civil Guard, and a number of businessmen and town councillors, all of whom conceded that the workers would have to be readmitted. At the very moment this agreement was being negotiated, the strike march, at the head of which were women and children, was wending its way through Arnedo. Suddenly, the Civil Guard opened fire on the protestors. In all, eleven people, including five women, were killed, while nineteen more were wounded, five of whom would not be able to work again. One Civil Guard was slightly hurt by a stray bullet. The shooting, ordered by lieutenant Juan Corcuera y Piedralita, had only ceased when the lieutenant colonel had rushed out of the town hall. Although Martínez Barrio denounces the incident in his memoirs as a "barbaric act", the Radicals did not hold the Civil Guard to account in the Cortes. This was not just to avoid criticizing the government and in particular the republican Minister of the Interior, the lugubrious Santiago Casares Quiroga, but also to reinforce their "law and order" image.[17]

Nor did the Radical Party confront the republican–socialist administration over the repression of the CNT's first major insurrection against the Republic later that month. The rising began as a strike by the miners of Fígols in Catalonia on 19 January but quickly assumed revolutionary proportions while spreading to other parts of the Alto Llobregat and Cardoner. The army and Civil Guard required five days to quell the rebellion. However, the CNT's National Committee which, like the Catalan Regional Committee, had been caught completely unawares by the revolt, gave orders on the 23rd for a "stoppage in all Spain", but only a sprinkling of *pueblos* in the Levante and Aragon responded. By 28 January, the entire movement had been quashed. Despite the Prime Minister's severe orders – he had told the Cabinet that it would be crushed "with the greatest violence", anyone holding a gun being shot on sight – no one died. On 10 February 104 *Cenetistas*, including Buenaventura Durruti and Joan García Oliver, were deported to a penal colony in Equatorial Guinea. In the Cortes, despite the persistence of informal ties between the CNT and the Radical Party, the latter did not assail the government over the summary justice meted out to the anarcho–syndicalists. The only protestations were those of a handful of Federal and Radical–Socialist deputies.[18] Over the following weeks, the Radical Party further expressed its support for the Azaña administration by backing its programme of laicization, with which the left republicans were particularly identified, including the secularization of the cementaries.[19]

Throughout these parliamentary debates the Radical leader had been conspicuous by his absence. In fact, for the first two months after the party left the government he gave not a single speech of note. Bored with the leading questions of the day and the minutae of reform, he generally eschewed the Cortes. Nor, too, did he respond to the pleadings of Martínez Barrio to convene the recently-created National Council. Instead, he often retreated to his country estate at San Rafael in the Guadarrama mountains north of Madrid or to the spa town of Baños de Montemayor in the province of Caceres to take the waters for his rheumatism.[20] He satisfied his vanity in the meantime, as well as enhancing his establishment profile, by accepting the presidency of the Círculo de Bellas Artes and that of the Press Association.[21] As in the winter of 1931, the Radical *jefe* exuded a mixture of reserve and complacency that was designed, his deputy recalls, to create "an equivocal, reticent silence, charged with menace". This may have generated ever greater expectation, but it also projected an ambiguous image that made the left republicans more, rather than less, wary of him. "The silence of Lerroux" was finally broken by the announcement that he would deliver a speech in Barcelona on 11 February. The act, however, was delayed by the deportation of the Llobregat insurgents from Barcelona. On 11 February, as a result, the Radical leader gave an in-depth interview to the leading republican daily *El Sol*. On the one hand, he explained, the government should "develop its programme" by passing as many complementary laws as "it judges necessary". On the other hand, the socialists should leave office for the good of "the Republic, the government and the Socialist Party itself" and facilitate the formation of an all-republican Cabinet. The Radicals would then aim to dissolve the Cortes as soon as possible on the grounds that, he insisted, "they are hostile to me". In other words, he was at once for and against the government. In reality, his acceptance of its programme was merely designed to placate the left republicans so as not to prejudice the formation of an administration together. Clearly the Radicals' goal was to dominate an all-republican government, dissolve the Constituent Cortes, and then hold a general election that would considerably strengthen the party's parliamentary position.[22]

The expectation surrounding the Radical leader's speech was heightened by its delay as well as by the decision to switch the venue from Barcelona to Madrid, and in particular to the most spectacular arena the capital had to offer: the recently-completed Plaza de Toros, the largest bullring in the world. The build-up to the speech in the party press provides a graphic illustration of the personality cult that surrounded the Radical leader. As founder and figurehead of the Radical Party, Lerroux is acclaimed not merely as synonymous with the Radical Party and as "the embodiment of historic republicanism", but also, in a revealing comment on the party's populist origins, as "the *caudillo* of the *pueblo*". Lionized as "the axis, the centre of the national expectation . . . the man of the present and of the future", he was also hailed as the only man capable of carrying out the "necessary, constructive labour that would show the people the route to salvation, the only possible route to salvation". In short, the party and the personae were inseparable.[23]

Eventually, on 21 February, the Radical leader spoke before a crowd of 40,000 people, many having journeyed to Madrid from Andalusia, Aragon, Asturias, the two Castiles, Catalonia, Extremadura, Galicia and Valencia, while a far greater number listened in by radio.[24] The keynote of the speech was that the socialists, who had produced a "state of alarm" throughout the country and were regarded by many as a "threat", should abandon the government. The *pueblo* had voted in the Republic for it to be ruled not in the interests of a particular class or party – that is to say, the socialists – but "in a republican manner". By contrast with the current administration, an all-republican one would consolidate the regime by ruling "for all Spaniards". This required, Lerroux noted, that the Radicals should "live in peace with all the republican fractions". The reason was obvious: the Radical Party could not govern, he admitted candidly, without "the collaboration, with the solidarity" of the republicans. Indeed, for the next few years the Cabinet would have to be "all-republican", otherwise the republicans would be at the mercy of any "vigorous minority of the right". The second aim of the speech was to take advantage of the expectation surrounding the party to net as many new recruits as possible. The Radical *jefe* averred that the electoral triumph of 12 April 1931 had been due not to the vote of the established republicans but to that of the anti-monarchist *pueblo*. The republicans, therefore, had no option but to embrace the anti-monarchist sentiment if the nascent regime was to be consolidated. Resisting newcomers with "daggers drawn" and by demanding "clean blood, history and tradition" would merely be counterproductive. Only by representing all classes would the Republic avoid becoming "divorced from the country" or, worse still, the "dictatorship of a party or the dictatorship of a social class" – in other words, a socialist tyranny. Accordingly, the Radical Party opened "its arms to all those who want to join it and obey its discipline". By implicit contrast with the socialists, it was not incompatible with any belief or class but would collaborate with all those that sought "a labour of pacification". Thus the two halves of the speech were united by a common theme: the Radicals' opposition to the socialists.

The inherent ambiguity of the Plaza de Toros meeting lay in the endeavour to separate the socialists from power without alienating the left republicans and thereby jeopardizing the formation of a strictly republican administration. The Radical leader sought to appease his former allies by claiming that the speech was not one of outright opposition, by insisting that future relations with the socialists should be "cordial", and by contending that, once out of office, they would serve a fundamental role by monitoring the progress of the government while acting as a counterweight to the right.[25] This was counteracted, however, by his stance on reform. Support for the Catalan Statute, a compromise acquired at San Sebastian in August 1930, was vague and uncertain. On the church, he was resigned rather than committed, accepting the measures hitherto passed into law as a fait accompli but hinting heavily – "religious persecution, no; no more" – that he would not back any substantial future initiatives. He conceded that the latest agrarian reform bill might produce a "real" change, yet upheld a gradualist approach by defending indemnification, a stage-by-stage schedule, and by concluding that the entire project should be the "work of Romans". The Radicals' lack of sympathy for the left republican programme of reform was evident. Another major obstacle was that the formation of a purely republican administration was regarded by the Radical Party as inseparable from a prompt dissolution of the Cortes. An indefinite prolongation of the Cortes would be viewed by public opinion, Lerroux affirmed, as the "kidnapping of the national sovereignty", or even as "a parliamentary dictatorship". Yet the left republicans refused to consider the matter before the lengthy list of laws complementary to the Constitution had been completed. Ultimately, the failure of the speech to reach out convincingly to the left republicans was a function of the Radicals' balancing act. By looking at once to the right, in an effort to attract conservative opinion and enhance the party's support, and to the left, in a bid to win over the left republicans, the Radicals ran the risk of convincing neither. The quintessential ambiguity of the Radical Party's stance was crystallized by Lerroux's cry, "Confronted by reaction, revolutionary. Confronted by anarchy, conservative".[26]

Judging by the reaction to the Plaza de Toros speech, the balancing act of the Radical leader was not a success. The non-republican right did not consider itself alluded to as Lerroux had defended both the anticlerical reforms and the Catalan Statute. While the Radicals' informal allies, the former Constitutionalists, were more or less content, Miguel Maura was not, as he had anticipated a more right-wing speech. On the left, *El Socialista* made predictable fun of the address' ambivalence by characterizing it as "indecisive, stuttering, contradictory", and ridiculing the Radical Party as "not on the right, nor on the left nor in the centre; not in front of, nor behind, the Republic". More seriously, Largo Caballero condemned those, such as the Radical leader, that sought to bring the Cortes to a close before the complementary laws had been passed. Otherwise, he warned, in an intemperate outburst which revealed the extent to which the socialists identified the new regime with their own reforms, they would declare "civil war". Progressive republican opinion, too, was highly critical. *El Sol* thought the speech incoherent. The Prime

Minister viewed it as a disloyal act which made future collaboration with the Radicals even more problematic. "It makes the all-republican government of which I was thinking once we separate from the socialists much more difficult", he noted. The Radical leader's simultaneous appeals to left and right had, in effect, cancelled one another out.[27]

The Plaza speech had struck at the heart of Azaña's vision of the Republic. He aimed to create a bloc of progressive republicans, consisting of Acción Republicana, the PRRS, the ORGA, the Federals, and the Esquerra, as the pivotal force of the regime, with the socialists to the left and the Radical Party and other conservative republicans to the right. This required that the reformist agenda undertaken in alliance with the socialists should be completed during the course of the Cortes and that the Radicals should form a "loyal" opposition, thereby permitting the formation of an all-republican administration once the socialists had left.[28] Lerroux's discourse had upset these calculations. First, the Radicals were utterly at variance with the left republicans over the nature and duration of the Cortes. Second, the two camps diverged profoundly over the role of the socialists. The left republicans considered that the integration of the socialist movement into the Republic by means of reform was indispensable for the regime's consolidation. By contrast, the Radicals held that the accommodation of the heterogenous middle classes was the key to its stabilization. As a result, the Radicals envisioned a broader political spectrum in which they, rather than the left republicans, would be the pivot. In effect, the Radicals and the left republicans were competing to become the arbiter of republican politics. Mixed in with these strategic and ideological considerations there were of course personal ones. The longer the republican–socialist administration lasted, the stronger Azaña's position as Prime Minister became. This might be threatened by the claims of the Radical leader should an all-republican administration be established. From the point of view of Lerroux, a purely republican government would provide him with his only chance of becoming Prime Minister under the current Cortes, but, given the improbability of manufacturing a stable majority, the premiership was solely of interest to him once he had the decree of dissolution in his hand.

Having failed to persuade the left republicans that the formation of an all-republican administration was imperative, the Radical *jefe* was comforted by the conviction that the Plaza de Toros speech had served as an "act of presence"; that is to say, he had demonstrated that public opinion was with the Radical Party, not the government. As he told the press, the Cortes was against him, "the opposite of what occurs to me with the country".[29] Such was the party's euphoria in the aftermath of the speech that, as a "highly representative" Radical disclosed to *El Sol*, it believed that, by exploiting the divisions within the ruling coalition, the Azaña administration would soon be toppled. The Radical ploy, however, failed. In opposing a number of Carner's economic measures on 24 February, the Radicals ended up voting with the right rather than splitting the republican–socialist majority. Still, Lerroux assured the press that the government's survival was not guaranteed for long.[30] Underlying this goal of bringing the Azaña administration down lurked his personal enmity for the Prime Minister. In the Plaza de Toros speech, the Radical leader, despite the intention to appease the left republicans, could not avoid a sarcastic swipe at Azaña for his "loyalty" towards Alcalá-Zamora during the October reshuffle.[31] In private, the Radical *jefe* accused the premier of having "expelled" him from power. Later, in *La pequeña historia*, he mocks Azaña as "a 'great man'" and reviles him for "his ambition" – in other words, for having eclipsed the Radical leader as the foremost republican figure. Certainly this rivalry sharpened the desire of the Radicals to overthrow the government. Lerroux, as the Prime Minister noted in his diary, hoped that "I will blow up in a few weeks". Nor is this surprising. The Radicals had, after all, abandoned the government precisely in order to precipitate the downfall of the republican–socialist administration.[32]

Relations with the government were unlikely to have been improved by the Radical leader's speech at the Ritz Hotel in Barcelona on 27 February before an audience of 1,500 members of the business community. Such was the show of support that, *El Sol* exclaimed, "never has the Ritz given a banquet like that celebrated last night". Even greater resonance was given to the event by the fact that it took place against a backdrop of mounting socio-economic conflict, 139 strikes having taken place in the first three months of 1932. The protests of the *patronal* at the strikes for their supposed "political and almost always revolutionary character" and for often allegedly involving "coercion, assaults on property, and violations of the law" had inundated the Ministry of the Interior. Consequently the violent incidents at Castilblanco and Arnedo were widely perceived by employers as merely the tip of the iceberg. Locally, the Catalan *patronal* regarded itself as trapped between the central government and the CNT, which refused, for ideological reasons, to abide by the state-engineered labour legislation and which, to make matters worse, was no where stronger than in Barcelona. Future prospects of industrial harmony had been dealt a severe blow earlier in the year by the triumph of the FAI and its radical allies within the CNT. Accordingly, the anarcho–syndicalists' first full-blown uprising against the Republic, which took place in Catalonia itself the previous month, appeared to presage an escalating spiral of strikes and insurrections. The *patronal*'s two overriding obsessions – public order and the socialists' continuation in office – were dealt with head on at the Ritz. First, Lerroux denounced the "wild strikes" and the "constant agitation" as well as criticizing the authorities' lack of "protection against the violence". Second, he blamed the state of the economy, "which is suffering a convulsive fever", and the lack of "moral confidence" – as reflected above all in the flight of capital abroad and the withdrawal of money from circulation – on the Azaña administration but in particular on the socialists. Underlying the call for an all-republican executive as the panacea for the nation's ills was a dramatic warning: unless public confidence was restored, a "collapse of such a nature" might take place that the government might be forced to turn to "a miraculous saviour, perhaps a soldier". Such dire predictions, apart from reiterating the extent to which the Radical leader's outlook was still shaped by the praetorian politics of the nineteenth century, were unlikely to enhance the stability of the regime. It was just as well that the comment, overshadowed by the Madrid speech, received little attention.[33]

Relations between the Radicals and the left republicans deteriorated rapidly thereafter as the rhetoric of a "ministerial opposition" increasingly failed to match reality. On 9 March, the Radical Party allied in parliament with the right in combatting the suspension of a number of papers, including *El Debate*, the mouthpiece of Acción Popular. There were terrible scenes in parliament as the Radicals, following a provocative remark by Prieto, waved their fists and bayed at a taken-aback Prime Minister. The gravity of the occasion notwithstanding, Lerroux, who had seconded the motion at dispute, was to be found not in the Cortes but at the tea rooms of the Ritz, a few yards down the road. It was a gesture typical of his complacent leadership which did nothing for his standing with the left republicans. The suspension of the newspapers together with the decision to deprive all military conspirators of their assets fuelled a public debate as to whether or not Azaña, like Mussolini, was a dictator. An intensely annoyed Prime Minister attributed this to the frustration of certain Radicals, notably the thrusting young deputy for Badajoz Rafael Salazar Alonso, that the government had not yet fallen. The claim in *La Voz* that, in Lerroux's words, the Radicals' intentions were "cordial, conciliatory, collaborative" and that they were not bent on the overthrow of the republican–socialist administration bore little relation to their actions.[34]

By mid March, the Prime Minister was convinced that the refusal of the Radicals to pursue a "loyal" opposition was rapidly undermining the prospect of an all-republican administration. On 13 March he observed in private that "they insist on quarreling at all costs". Four days later, he commented bitterly in his diary that "they are making things impossible". That same day, the National Council of Acción Republicana and its parliamentary group reached the conclusion that the Radicals' obstruction had left the Alianza Republicana "dead as a dodo", though this was not made public in case the arrangement with the Radicals could be resuscitated at some point in the future. Similarly, the Acción Republicana Congress of 26–28 March stopped short of declaring the Alianza finished, but it left the National Council free to do so when it saw fit. Not having met since the Radicals had left the government, the Alianza had been put on ice.[35] The cooling of relations between the Radicals and left republicans was illustrated by a speech on 20 March by José Giral, the Acción Republicana deputy leader who had until recently defended an all-republican administration, in which he declared that his party had more in common with the socialists and the PRRS than the Radicals. A further symptom was the talk in March of creating a "cartel" of left republican parties. The idea was to provide the variegated forces of the republican left with a framework for greater parliamentary and electoral collaboration as well as the wherewithwal to form a Cabinet on their own should the socialists depart. The "cartel", in effect, would replace the Alianza Republicana. In the event, the left-republican vehicle did not take shape until later in the year, but the fact that the possibility had first been raised in March was another sign of the burgeoning divide within the republican camp. A further symptom was the decision of the Prime Minister to join a Masonic lodge that same month. This was a purely political move that was designed to challenge the Radicals in one of their bastions and even to win over some of their more liberal elements. Not surprisingly, Azaña's incorporation into the Masons catalyzed a bitter struggle within the movement throughout 1932. El Progreso lamented that whereas the Radicals had always aimed to further the unity and understanding of the republicans, the left republicans had gone out of their way to isolate the Radical Party. In reality, the parliamentary opposition of the Radicals together with the Plaza de Toros speech had brought relations since 1931 to their lowest point yet.[36]

The unleashing of a concerted propaganda campaign by the Radicals in March and April, designed to complement their parliamentary opposition, made the breach between the republicans wider still. The spring offensive was of nationwide proportions, meetings being held in all but two of the provinces over the weekend of 19–20 March, for example, while more than 60 individual rallies took place at its close on 14 April, the first anniversary of the Republic. Effectively launched by the Radical *jefe*'s speeches in Madrid and Barcelona, the campaign was in part a recruitment drive. Lerroux, eager to build on the expectation surrounding the party now that it was out of government, exhorted former monarchists and others to rally to the Radical banner. "There is no right to close the doors to anyone", he proclaimed. This open-door policy did not just reflect the will of a republican leader that had co-habited cosily with monarchists for many years, but was also embraced enthusiastically by the irreproachable figure of Martínez Barrio. At the Seville party's congress in March, he exclaimed that "it does not bother me that the Radical Party is now joined by all those that served . . . until yesterday the cause of Don Alfonso Bourbon". The justification of the Radicals was nothing if not pragmatic. As the traditional republicans alone would not have secured the electoral triumph of 12 April 1931, all those that had voted for the Republic had as much right, the Radical leader explained, as "the veterans to be considered as republicans". The republicans, by not welcoming the *pueblo* into their midst and by not overcoming their organizational deficiencies, ran the risk of turning sympathizers of the regime into "our enemies". Whilst admitting that "what interests us is our very own organization", Lerroux stressed that all the parties had to broaden their base in order to guarantee the "definitive stability of the Republic". "We need", he declared in Valencia, "the concourse of all the social classes", though adding that the country had to be "governed by republicans". Dismissal of the Radical argument as a self-serving justification for the influx of monarchists into the party ignores the fact that if the Republic was to be consolidated as a parliamentary democracy the republicans had to extend their support far beyond their traditional circles. The Radicals contended that even the conservative classes had to be incorporated, otherwise they would swell the ranks of those hostile to the regime. It was, therefore, especially important that the republicans grasped their opportunity while the right was still struggling to reorganize itself. From this perspective, the determined recruitment drive of Acción Popular (which changed its name from Acción Nacional in April 1932) in 1932 was a timely warning for the republicans.[37]

The Radicals' spring campaign, as the slogan of "Law, responsibility, and authority" indicated, was directed above all at the middle classes. "Law-and-order" was defended not just as a traditional demand of the propertied classes but also, the Radical leader insisted in Valencia on 20 March, as "the guarantee that we are going to live in the order that is essential for the spiritual peace and mutual and reciprocal tolerance that permits the discussion, even with the greatest passion, of the most contrasting doctrines". The party's propaganda also retained a strong reconciliatory, inter-classist component that underpinned its centrism. For instance, the speech delivered by Lerroux before the Madrid party on the anniversary of the Republic was devoted to the historic campaigns of Montjuich and Almadén fought on behalf of the workers. Even when addressing businessmen at the Ritz Hotel in Barcelona, he emphasized that the greatest injustices had been suffered by the working class and that the differences between the classes had to be eliminated so that all men, "without a mentor", could regard one another as "brothers".[38]

Spearheading the party's appeal, however, was its antisocialism. On 10 April, before 12,500 people in the Ciudad Real bullring, the Radical *jefe* made his most outspoken attack yet on the socialist movement. Heavily exploiting the middle classes' fixation with law-and-order, he upbraided the socialists for "the anarchy" of their local councils, "which constantly violate the law", and for embracing "all those that go about robbing olives, assaulting property, setting churches alight, making social co-existence impossible, compromising the existence of the Republic". He held the "party politics" of the socialists responsible not only for the economic crisis but also for the general lack of confidence in the government. Finally, he rebuked them for not having left the Cabinet in December 1931. Indeed, the call of the Radicals for the socialists to leave office became a clamour during the spring campaign. Martínez Barrio, in a high-profile interview with *Blanco y Negro*, urged them to withdraw from the Azaña administration for the sake of the regime.[39] In the same vein, the Radical press railed ceaselessly against the socialist movement for causing the nation's "dismay", for perpetuating the division of the republicans, and for being, in short, "against the Republic". The anti-socialist thrust of the Radicals' propaganda fulfilled the same role as the "anti-*pueblo*" in populist discourse: it mobilized the broadest possible support as the central plank in the party's recruitment strategy and addressed their overriding political objective – the removal of the PSOE from power. After all, it was the sectarianism of the socialists which had thwarted the formation of a government "for all Spaniards"; that is to say, of an all-republican administration by means of which the Radicals could have engineered a prompt dissolution of the Constituent Cortes. By mid April, *El Progreso* concluded that there existed "not one tie of affection or cordiality" between the Radicals and the socialists.[40]

By contrast, the Radicals generally avoided explicit censure of the left republicans during the campaign in the conviction that this would prejudice the formation of a strictly republican government. The Radical *jefe* characterized his propaganda not as a "discourse of opposition" but as a series of "fraternal warnings", while hinting at the complicity between the republicans by affirming that he had not spoken in the Cortes in order to avoid creating further problems for the Azaña administration. By defending the anticlerical legislation, including the recent expulsion of the Jesuits, he also endeavoured to underline the Radicals' reformist links with their former republican allies. Nevertheless, this strategy was deeply flawed. First, the identification with the agenda for change of the left republicans was decidedly lukewarm. The Radical Party defended a much more moderate agrarian reform, had severe reservations over the Catalan Statute, and put forward no proposals of their own for change.[41] Second, the Radical critique of the socialists' "party politics" was in effect one of the entire government. The failure to separate out criticism of the PSOE from that of the administration as a whole was exemplified by the campaign keynote: namely, that the Azaña government was divorced from the country. "It is necessary to recognize", the Radical leader claimed in Valencia, "that each day public confidence is more and more removed" from the government. Like the *patronal*, he stressed that the lamentable state of the economy was the most evident manifestation of the loss of public confidence. Unlike the government, the Radical Party did not embody a "party interest" but "a state of opinion" which sought a "change in politics" that would benefit all Spaniards. Public opinion, in other words, was with the opposition, not the government. Finally, the Radicals were unlikely to win the left republicans over by resuscitating a ploy strongly reminiscent of the *ancien régime* – by appealing not to parliament but to the head of state in order to force a change in government. Certainly Lerroux's gushing peroration for the President in Valencia can be interpreted as a thinly-disguised plea for Alcalá-Zamora to act upon the supposed divorce between Cortes and country. There can be little doubt that the propaganda campaign in March and April worsened rather than improved relations between the republicans. It was symptomatic that Lerroux's last speech, delivered before the Madrid party on 14 April, should annoy the left republicans considerably by boasting that the latter would have to approach the Radicals in order to form an all-republican andministration rather than the other way around.[42]

Although the spring campaign did little to advance the Radicals' immediate goal of toppling the government, it did give another boost to the party's growth. In Seville province, to take one example, the party had branches in only 15 per cent of the *pueblos* in May 1931, yet by March 1932 this had risen to 85 per cent and, by October 1932, to 100 of the province's 102 *pueblos*. By the summer of 1932, an organizer in Asturias was able to report to the national leader that few *pueblos* in the region were without a party outlet. One of the most spectacular surges took place in Albacete. Only at the beginning of 1932 did the Radicals begin to organize themselves there in earnest, yet, ten months later, they had branches in 62 per cent of the province's *pueblos*.[43] Altogether, 1932 was the year when the Radical Party consolidated itself as a mass-based entity insofar as the reorganizational blueprint announced in August 1931 was largely enforced. By October 1932, the party had 3,806 branches nationwide. The available information, which has to be treated with care given the scarcity of reliable data, indicates that the Radicals may well have had at least 250,000 members – considerably more than Acción Republicana's 40,000 in March 1932 or the 73,000 affiliates of the PRRS in June 1932.[44] Still, notable shortcomings to the party's articulation as a national body persisted, such as its institutional weakness, its sparse presence in many regions, and the fact that localism, as revealed by the correspondence between the provinces and Madrid, remained deeply entrenched. Furthermore, the restructuring of the party created its own set of problems. An outstanding example is provided by the Cadiz party. In January 1932 its overhaul was entrusted to a specially appointed provincial committee. An acrimonious battle was thereby unleashed between four of the province's deputies, who defended the party's republican pedigree, and the fifth, and last, Santiago Rodríguez Piñero, who vigorously defended the integration of former monarchists and other non-republicans. Rodríguez Piñero was denounced by his fellow deputies on the grounds that the party "cannot and should not be a fetid manure heap on which one tries to tip all the filth of the past monarchist regime". As the two sides were unable to reach a consensus, the national leadership had to intervene. This, in keeping with its approach elsewhere, backed those – in this case, Rodríguez Piñero – in favour of a more accommodating recruitment policy. The triumph of the "Piñeristas" was crowned at the Gaditan provincial congress in October 1932. The four dissident deputies not only forfeited control of the provincial committee and of the *Libertad* newspaper, but, at the next general election, of their nominations as Radical candidates.[45]

In Catalonia, too, there was vigorous resistance to the reorganization. The four provincial parties, a special circular of 22 June made clear, were to be brought under the auspices of the Barcelona group in order to prepare them for the challenge of the Catalan Statute. However, the national leadership also took advantage of the circular to promote newcomers to leading positions. Antonio Montaner, a Barcelona figure, wrote to Lerroux in July that the circular had been received with "a spirit of disgust" as the new provisional committees were unrepresentative. He even feared that if the old and new Radicals "fell out", the pull of the Esquerra to the left and that of the Lliga to the right would threaten the Barcelona party with "dissolution". None the less, the circular was approved by both the Barcelona and Gerona provincial parties at their August assemblies. The Tarragona party presented a different story altogether. Though the party had grown greatly since the regime's advent through the incorporation of the "neutral classes" and "members of other parties", local leader Pedro Loperena explained to the Radical *jefe* in July, the designations for the new provincial bodies had been met with "general astonishment and stupor". Those nominated to head the Tarragona party, the "scarcely recommendable" Ricardo Guasch and Pedro Pilón, would, Loperena believed, cause "enormous damage". Indeed, at the congress later that month nineteen of the thirty-six delegations – the other seventeen abstaining – backed the motion of the provincial committee and local Radical deputy Jaime Simó y Bofarull to abandon the Radical Party rather than subordinate themselves to the "old Liberal *caciquismo*" and the Barcelona machine. In short, the Tarragonese party had suffered a shattering split.[46]

The turmoil caused by the reorganization undoubtedly contributed to the disastrous performance of the Radicals in the Catalan regional elections in November 1932. In Barcelona, having been rejected as an ally by the Esquerra, the party went to the polls alone. Such was the situation that Lerroux returned to Catalonia in October in order to take personal control of the campaign. At least in Gerona, Lerida, and Tarragona the

Radical Party managed to join forces with other centre–right parties. Still, the Radical Party did not win a single seat. By contrast, the Radical dissidents in Tarragona – a measure of the damage wrought by the schism earlier in the year – obtained four deputies. The letters of Pich y Pon, the Radical leader's righthand man in Catalonia, chart the Radicals' subsequent decline in the region in 1933. Not only did the party persist with its "old-fashioned style" in the Barcelona town hall, but it also continued to meet with considerable resistance to the reorganization. Plagued by internal feuds and bereft of an overall sense of direction, the Catalan Radical Party was in a desperate state. A further symptom was the decline of *El Progreso*. By early 1932, the party organ was in considerable difficulty. Publication was suspended for a week in March. Although the paper's "transformation" by means of the introduction of "modern material means" was announced, sales continued to decline. By April 1933, Lerroux was informed, sales had slipped to a "truly exiguous" level. By July, the paper was only selling 3,000 copies daily – a loss of 80 per cent since 1927. A public appeal was then launched, but this fell 13,000 pesetas short. In September 1933, the paper folded.[47]

Ferocious in-fighting erupted not just in those provincial parties where there already existed a sizable sector of veteran opinion. On the Republic's establishment, the Radical Party in Granada, restricted to a sliver of the middle classes in the capital, was "without organization, without members and without life". In the June 1931 general election the party was excluded from the Republican–Socialist Coalition by the socialists for having become a "nest of *caciques*". Following the election, in which the Radicals won not one of the thirteen seats, the party was led by Fernando Gómez de la Cruz, proprietor of *La Publicidad* newspaper. Support grew amongst small and medium landowners, especially those on the province's periphery, who, bereft of a political vehicle, looked to the Radicals as a defence against the socialists. At the same time, the party embraced the *clientela* of *caciques* from the dynastic Liberal Party, including that of Natalio Rivas (a close personal friend of Lerroux and former Minister of the Interior) in the Alpujarra, of Manuel Lachica y Mingo in La Vega and of Montes Jovellar in the Alhama area, as well as agents of big landowners such as Jiménez Molinero. The Radicals' populist message also attracted skilled workers and employees in the towns along with middle-class professionals and employers. The appeal of the Radicals for the property-owning classes was further enhanced by the precipitate collapse of both the DLR and the Democratic Republican Party in the province. Nevertheless, the Radical *jefe* estimated that the party could do better still. In 1932 he persuaded José Pareja Yébenes, the white-haired rector of the University of Granada and founder of the Republican Autonomous Party (PRAG) who had been elected as a parliamentary deputy in June 1931, to overhaul the party as the new provincial leader. This made good sense

insofar as the PRAG boasted four deputies, several Granada city councillors, and a network of local branches. Pareja Yébenes was also effective
leader of the Agrupación al Servicio de la República in Granada. He was
urged by Lerroux to attract "traditional elements of republican democracy and many others of a liberal or apolitical origin" and to include in
the reorganizing committee "the greatest number of tendencies, political
interests and elements attached to the Radical programme". The relaunch
was therefore designed to bring together a number of differing tendencies
by drawing on the infrastructure of the PRAG. However, the Provincial
Committee rejected the authority of the PRAG leader, Gómez de la Cruz
denouncing him to the Radical leader as politically "detestable", as "a
slave" of the socialist minister from Granada Fernando de los Ríos, and
as "useless". He disputed that the party, now "very well organized",
needed to be restructured at all, or that it could attract any further
support. The threat represented by Pareja Yébenes was not only perceived
in personal terms – the reorganization would almost certainly dislodge
many of Gómez's "people" – but also in ideological ones as the PRAG,
unlike the Radical Party, had allied with the socialists in the 1931 election. As in the case of Cadiz, the backing of the national party proved to
be decisive. The triumph of Pareja Yébenes was none the less achieved at
a cost. The party split, the dissidents forming the Republican Independent
Party.[48]

The Radical propaganda of March and April 1932 powerfully complemented the opposition of the *patronal*. Late in 1931, it had initiated a
far-ranging protest against the workers' control bill before it reached the
Cortes. By denouncing Largo Caballero's essentially moderate proposal
for "destroying the bourgeoisie" and for subjugating the economy to
"foreign economic pressures", the employers' associations successfully
portrayed the envisaged measure as a revolutionary tool at the service of
shadowy overseas' interests that would devastate Spanish business. The
campaign, together with the hostility of the CNT and the indifference of
the UGT, ensured that the bill never left the committee stage. The *patronal*
had claimed a notable scalp. The Unión Económica's Congress in late
April signalled a further advance by bringing the urban and rural
employers together for the first time. At the Congress, the landowning
oligarchy won the backing, or at least the quiescence, of industry and
commerce in combatting the agrarian reform as "a frank and evident
attempt at nationalization". Echoing Lerroux's Plaza de Toros speech in
February, the Assembly demanded the socialists' removal from the
Cabinet while warning the government that "without us the country's
stability will not be forthcoming".[49]

In May the Cortes undertook discussion of two of the Azaña administration's most crucial legislative projects, the Catalan Statute and the
agrarian reform bill. Inevitably, both provoked the visceral opposition of

the right: the latter because it struck at the heart of the landowning oligarchy's socio-economic interests and the former because the question of decentralization had acquired traumatic proportions for conservative opinion since the loss of empire in 1898. Of even greater concern were the latent divisions within the ruling majority, leading the Prime Minister to subject the two bills to simultaneous discussion in an effort to ensure the backing of the centrally-minded socialists for the Statute, and that of the Catalans, unaffected by the agrarian reform, for the other bill. Despite the left's vision of the Radical Party as a right-wing force awash with *caciques*, it did not have a clearcut stance on the agrarian question. While some deputies, such the prominent landowner from Cuenca, José María Alvarez Mendizábal, regarded the bill as too radical, others, including the auto-didactic schoolteacher from Cordoba, Eloy Vaquero, who had distinguished himself in the fight against southern landowners (as recalled in his book of 1923 "From the Drama of Andalusia. Recollections of Rural Struggles and Citizens"), thought the proposals "extremely moderate". A compromise was struck by alighting on the cigar-puffing notary from Badajoz, Diego Hidalgo, who had spoken previously on agrarian affairs. Still the Radical stance was unclear: Hidalgo, though claiming to represent the party's general point of view, spoke in a personal capacity. As a result, a veritable array of Radicals held forth on the issue. Ricardo Samper, the bespectacled PURA deputy, admitted that the party harboured a "variety of nuances", ranging from "frankly progressive ideas" to those "of a prudent and moderate tone", but maintained that in their synthesis lay "the balance". In reality, the Radicals were partly chan-neling the protest of the property-owners affected by the reform and partly endeavouring to drive a wedge between the left republicans and the social-ists by highlighting the differences between them while offering a "republican" alternative. Yet the Radicals failed to exploit the very real divisions within the governing coalition effectively, in large measure because there was little sympathy on the left for Diego Hidalgo's semi-official position. Moreover, the two tendencies within the party ended up neutralizing one another. The appeal to the left republicans was further undermined by the Radicals' spasmodic tendency to exploit discussion of the bill to score political points. The final result was that the Radical Party, despite the commendable efforts of Diego Hidalgo, failed to offer a coherent alternative to the government's proposal. In any case, the Radicals, like the ruling majority – through a combination of disinterest and the fatigue engendered by the simultaneous discussion of the Catalan Statute – paid insufficient attention to the agrarian bill. In July, Hidalgo reproached parliament for the fact that, although agriculture was "the foundation of the economy in Spain", the agrarian measure was being debated "in the midst of the indifference of everyone". The deputies' predominantly urban background, the greater interest of the republicans in institutional rather than socio-economic change, and the importance to the ruling majority of the Esquerra ensured that the bill continued to be neglected. Little was done to offset the situation by the weak, and frequently absent, Minister of Agriculture, Marcelino Domingo, or by a Prime Minister who, apart from failing to remove his feckless minister, made few contributions of his own to the proceedings.[50]

Over the Catalan Statute, the Radicals were also strongly divided. Some, such as the PURA deputies and Eloy Vaquero, were in favour, while a sizable minority, including the Aragonese deputies, Alvarez Mendizábal, and Salazar Alonso were utterly opposed. Struggling to reconcile the two camps was a third sector, the largest in the party, but still no clear-cut position emerged. Although the Radical leader maintained that the party would back the government as long as it did not "affect national unity", in practice the Radicals assailed numerous clauses, especially those concerning education, finance, justice, and language. By dragging out the initial debate on the bill from 6 May to 3 June, the opposition took a heavy toll of the ruling bloc. In the final debate on the initial reading, the Prime Minister pleaded with the Radicals to ally with the majority and guarantee the Statute's future. Rather than heed the call, the Radical *jefe* tried to exploit the ruling coalition's divisions over the Statute.[51] During the subsequent discussion of the individual articles, the Radicals joined forces with the right in an attempt to force the government's withdrawal from the debate, partly by wearing it down through sheer exhaustion and partly by endeavouring to play up the differences within it. For the Radical Party, in other words, the Statute was merely another means of overthrowing the Azaña administration. As an exasperated premier declared before the Cabinet on 8 July, "the Radicals are not at all interested in the Statute. What they want is to overthrow the government". Obstruction of the Statute had graver consequences for the Radicals' relations with the left republicans than that of the agrarian reform. Azaña staked the future of his administration on the Catalan bill. "To withdraw the Statute", he wrote grimly, "would be the defeat of our programme and the downright failure of the government". By opposing the Statute, the Radicals were effectively challenging the continuity of the republican–socialist government. In so doing, they had taken a highly calculated risk; namely, that they could bring the Azaña administration down without prejudicing the formation of an all-republican one afterwards.[52]

The tension between the Radicals and the government was further accentuated by the resurfacing of the Juan March affair. In February, the Cortes, to the annoyance of the socialists and the delight of March's defenders, had failed to agree on whether or not he should be prosecuted. The decision had been put off because the Prime Minister himself was in negotiation with the tobacco tycoon. Azaña sought his support for the Portuguese revolutionaries as the original backer, Indalecio Prieto's ally, the Basque shipbuilder Horacio Echevarrieta, had run into financial difficulties. The Mallorcan magnate, the Prime Minister noted in his diary, "could be useful to the Republic". The negotiations, however, fell through as March's conditions – a public pardon and recognition of his role – proved unacceptable. Consequently the March case was re-examined in a secret session on 8 June. This debate, together with the public one on 14 June, were amongst the most dramatic of the entire Constituent Cortes. The Radicals leapt to March's defence. "I will not give up this man defenceless", exclaimed Radical deputy Fernando Rey Mora, adding that there was insufficient proof to proceed. The accused himself pointed out that the Supreme Court had already thrown out the evidence for which he had been arrested in 1931 while maintaining that the tobacco concession which had been withdrawn under the Republic was not illegal. Given that the March case was viewed by the ruling majority as a demonstration of republican virtue, inquired Gil Robles, why did the former Minister of the Economy, Indalecio Prieto, adjudicate March's tobacco monopoly to a company in which a close associate of his, Horacio Echevarrieta, had a leading stake? The whiff of hypocrisy was strengthened by the knowledge that Prieto's replacement, Jaume Carner, had suggested in Cabinet that the concession should be reawarded to March as he offered the best deal. Even though the Cabinet was opposed to such a move, the Prime Minister continued to parley with the mogul. It should also be remembered that the Revolutionary Committee had approached March on several occasions for financial backing. Had March backed the Revolutionary Committee, or even the Portuguese revolutionaries, he probably would not have been investigated by the Republic. Despite the high-minded moralizing, he was ultimately viewed in highly pragmatic terms. Yet the Republic was playing with fire. As Carner, who, from his time as a lawyer and businessman in Barcelona, knew March well, warned: "either the Republic makes him submit, or he will make the Republic submit". The following day, 15 June, Juan March was sent to prison. The Radicals were outraged.[53]

In an effort to improve relations between their respective camps, the Radical leader and Prime Minister met twice in June. On the first occasion, Lerroux, as an act of goodwill, alerted Azaña to the preparations for a military rising. Yet the premier regarded the warning as "unnecessary and sterile", believing that the Radical *jefe*'s real purpose in meeting was to sound him out over the state of the ruling majority. Two weeks later, the Prime Minister tried to break the deadlock over the Statute by securing the collaboration of the Radicals, Lerroux having recently defended the measure in parliament against the accidentalist leader, José María Gil Robles. This encounter, however, backfired too: Azaña was again convinced that the Radical leader was interested not in the Statute but in the plans of the ruling majority, particularly the time required to complete its legislative labours. The Prime Minister informed the Cabinet on 8 July that an agreement with the Radicals was out of the question as they were determined to use the Statute in order to overthrow the administration. Lerroux and Azaña had lost a valuable opportunity to reverse the steady slide in relations between the Radicals and the government. These meetings laid bare, once again, the personal incompatability of the two republican leaders. "We were unable to understand one another", laments Lerroux in *La pequeña historia*. Underlying the strategic manoeuvres lay a dispute over the purpose and duration of the Constituent Cortes. For the Radicals, stabilization of the regime lay in a new round of elections and the incorporation of the conservative classes, while for the left republicans this lay in the modernization of Spanish society. Accentuating this divergence lay the left republicans' reservations in relation to the Radicals' political modes and mores. First, they were inclined to the behind-the-scenes politicking reminiscent of the monarchy rather than the more open parliamentary culture of the Republic. Indeed, the premier was convinced that the Radicals had dubbed him a "dictator" earlier in the year precisely because he had defended the paramountcy of parliament. Unlike them, he categorically refused to transform republican politics into "a plaything of friends and colleagues".[54] Second, the Prime Minister, in common with the left as a whole, judged that "Lerrouxism is corruption and politics as business". Certainly the Radicals' unabashed defence of Juan March in parliament and their subsequent exertions in favour of his release – the party leader protesting that "what has been done and what continues to be done is lamentable" – did little to persuade him otherwise. He was even persuaded, as he told José Ortega y Gasset and Fernando de los Ríos, that the Radicals would not serve under him as he would oppose their venality.[55] Finally, Azaña was horrified by what he regarded as the Radicals' opportunism. He was appalled to discover during the discussion of the Catalan Statute that the Radicals, who had voted against many of the bill's articles, had offered the Esquerra to pass the bill by decree in exchange for its support: "can one be more immoral?", he asked himself incredulously. The Radicals, he was sure, wanted power "however" and that they would even join forces with the monarchists to get it. He also feared that, just when the right was whipping up opinion in the press, parliament, and the barracks in favour of a military uprising, the Radical leader, out of sheer ambition, would end up "inciting some soldier to intervene". A Lerrouxist government, characterized by its "spirit of 'old politics' that stinks", the Prime Minister concluded gloomily, would represent a devastating setback for the regime by resurrecting the rancid politics of the *ancien régime*.[56]

The Prime Minister's withering indictment of the Radicals was strongly overdrawn. Many Radicals, such as Basilio Alvarez, Clara Campoamor, Antonio Lara, and Martínez Barrio, bore little relation to Azaña's characterization of the party. The striking of secretive, monarchist-style deals was far from the exclusive preserve of the Radicals. Neither, as Indalecio Prieto's activities revealed, was the potential abuse of power for commercial reasons. Azaña's unflinching vision was very much that of an austere intellectual whose meteoric rise in politics had left him untouched by years of quotidian politicking and compromises. This is not to deny that a section of the Radical Party, including its leader, was deeply imbued by a traditional, wheeler-dealing view of politics. Yet it was precisely for this reason that the left had to be wary of letting the Radicals slip from the ruling majority's orbit. Their pronounced pragmatism, as the premier himself perceived, might well lead them to collaborate with the right. However, the left republicans and socialists alike were blinded by their Jacobin morality and doctrinaire outlook. Certainly the Radicals were more than eager to mend their bridges with the left republicans, but the Prime Minister refused, as he put it to the Cabinet on 8 July, "to promise Lerroux that he will govern straightaway and that I myself will open for him the door . . . because such a way of conducting politics cannot prevail under the Republic, and, of course, is incompatible with me". Nor would he attempt to disarm the Radicals' opposition by, for example, negotiating over secondary matters or by expressing a willingness to collaborate in the future. In short, Azaña lacked the political adroitness necessary to take advantage of the Radical leader's flexibility. Yet the more the left isolated the Radicals, the more likely they were to fulfil its very worst fears. The left's self-righteous rejection of the Radical Party was therefore a sacrifice of stability to principle which the regime could ill afford.[57]

The dangers of alienating the Radicals from the ruling majority were vividly illustrated by the speech of Lerroux in Zaragoza on 10 July. This was given just as the government was struggling to overcome the determined opposition of both the right and the Radical Party to the Catalan and agrarian reform bills against the background of rumours of a military plot to overthrow the Azaña administration. The political climate was probably more tense that at any time since the Radicals had left the government seven months earlier. In Zaragoza, Lerroux voiced serious reservations in relation to the educational, public order, and fiscal aspects of the Catalan bill, but, despite the vociferous protests of the crowd, he did not denounce the Statute as such. Nor did he reject the agrarian proposals out of hand. On the contrary, he argued, amidst a rambling appraisal, that landless labourers and tenants should themselves become landowners, while affirming vaguely that his own approach would be "eclectic" as the problem was "as varied as the *pueblos*". Yet again the Radical *jefe* insisted that public opinion was not on the side of the republican–socialist administration, but on that of the Radical Party. Inside the Cortes, he admitted, "I am a minority", but outside it, "I am a majority, because I have public opinion on my side". Only the formation of an all-republican Cabinet would resolve this predicament. This was prevented not so much by the left republicans as the socialists, "assassins of liberty" who were exercising "a type of dictatorship" over their allies. A thinly-veiled appeal was made to the President – "he who has the obligation to set the pulse of politics" – to break the deadlock by withdrawing his support from the government. Thus far, the Radical *jefe* had nothing new to say, the more violent tone towards the socialists notwithstanding. However, he had a shock in store. He denounced the Azaña administration for provoking "acts of rebellion which cannot be repressed by force alone" and which, moreover, "are not without reason". That is to say, unless the republican–socialist government gave way to an all-republican one the army might well rise up. The Radical leader, in short, was blackmailing the government.[58]

The ruling parties were naturally outraged by the Radical leader's speech. A socialist "Manifesto" denounced the appeal to the President as "anti-democratic, anti-republican and anti-constitutional" and the succour offered to the right as "suspicious and inopportune". The socialists responded, too, with an anti-constitutional gesture of their own by declaring that the dissolution of the Constituent Cortes would be "a *coup d'état*" to which they would react with a general strike. Lerroux retorted provocatively that only one of two dictatorships was possible; a socialist one, "which is already being exercised", or a military one, which would be established "as a logical response to the attitude of those gentlemen who are dividing those of us that should be governing". Such dire threats, the culmination of the Radicals' precipitate campaign to force the creation of an all-republican administration and the dissolution of the Constituent Cortes, were irresponsible and shocking. Republicans and socialists alike had turned to the army in order to overthrow the monarchy, but the Radical leader was looking to exploit anti-democratic yearnings within the army to the benefit of his own political ends under the Republic. This ran the risk of undermining, if not destabilizing, the regime. Not surprisingly, the Zaragoza speech brought relations with the left republicans to their nadir. The Prime Minister in particular was driven to distraction by the Radical *jefe*'s most brazen attempt yet to subvert the parliamentary order. In his diary, Azaña commented despairingly that "this adventurism of Lerroux . . . could leave me with my work half completed and destroy it easily. It would be a question of abandoning politics".[59]

Amidst much expectation, the Radical leader addressed the Cortes on 19 July. As in February, he failed to back up his extra-parliamentary threats in parliament. He first assured the Cortes that he did want to offend "any" party. Nor had he said "anything new" in Zaragoza. On the contrary, his demand for power, justified by the "grave damage" caused to the country by the current administration, had been made on many previous occasions. Finally, he informed the chamber of his endeavour to inform the Prime Minister of the alleged *coup* preparations; in other words, the warning of 10 July had been made not on behalf of the Radical Party, but of the Republic. In effect, the Radical leader was trying to keep his options open by avoiding a rupture with the left republicans. His inconsistency, however, did little for his standing in the eyes of his former allies. In particular, the Prime Minister was perplexed as to why Lerroux was informed of "the intrigues of the military . . . what do they expect of him?"[60]

V
Plotting for Power
The attempted *coup d'état* of 10 August 1932

Exactly a month after the Radical leader's Zaragoza speech, his threat became reality – a section of the army backed by civilians rose up against the Republic.[1] The authorities, as the diary of the President and that of the Prime Minister confirm, were well informed about the ill-coordinated putsch. It was organized, recalls Martínez Barrio, "in view of everyone".[2] In Madrid, beginning at 4.00 a.m., the insurgents tried to storm the Ministry of War, from where the Prime Minister was overseeing the government's operations, and the Palace of Communications, both of which looked onto the central Plaza de Cibeles. They failed to seize either objective; the Assault Guards under the Director General of Security, Arturo Menéndez, saw them off at the Ministry, while a Civil Guard detachment foiled the attack on the Palace. Nine of the assailants died and nine more were wounded, while the security forces suffered five injuries.[3] In the provinces, the rebels fared little better. In Cadiz, Cordoba, and Granada, the insurrection got nowhere. General González Carrasco, chief coordinator in Granada, had to go into hiding before being whisked by car to the French border by the Marqués de las Marismas del Guadalquivir. Nor did any of the northern garrisons declare themselves. Once the Madrid uprising had folded, General Barrera, its director, flew straight to Pamplona but was unable to rouse either the army or the Carlists there. He then sought refuge in Biarritz, only to fly back into Spain, this time to Seville, the one city where the *pronunciamiento* had triumphed.[4]

Unlike the others, the operation in Seville, directed by General Sanjurjo, had faced no resistance, both the army and Civil Guard units in the Andalusian capital joining the rebels. The General installed himself in the Palacio de Casa Blanca, declared a state of war, replaced the local authorities, and, in the classical tradition of the *pronunciamiento*, issued a manifesto. This proclaimed the establishment of a dictatorship but did not mention the restoration of the monarchy. Instead, it lambasted the Azaña administration and the Constituent Cortes for having brought the nation to the brink of "ruin, of iniquity and of dismemberment".[5] Sanjurjo's insurgency, seemingly, was directed against the government but not the Republic. In the meantime, the General paid court to the Andalusian aristocracy and other monarchists, including Acción Popular and FEDA activists. His main source of civilian support, however, was the Carlists. Once it became clear that the Madrid and other revolts had been thwarted, the Sevillian rebellion was doomed, especially as the troops under Sanjurjo refused to fight those on their way down from the capital. The flight of General Barrera had been in vain. The next day, the 11th, Sanjurjo fled for the Portuguese border but was apprehended at Huelva. A resounding failure, the *pronunciamiento* became known as the "Sanjurjada".[6]

The first conspiratorial activities against the Republic had begun back in 1931. There was not one plot but several, which drew on an array of civilian and military groups ranging from declared enemies of the regime such as Alfonsists, Carlists, and fascists, to former Constitutionalists and military officers alienated by the army reforms. By the end of 1931, there were essentially two main strands. The first was centred on the Alfonsine monarchists. This was probably hatched following the May events of 1931 but it did not acquire any substance until the end of the year, being led by Generals Barrera, Ponte, and Cavalcanti with the financial and organizational backing of numerous aristocrats and other monarchists. Of particular importance was the exile community in Biarritz, which revolved around the former minister Juan de la Cierva but also embraced José Calvo Sotelo and Eduardo Aunós, both ministers under Primo de Rivera. These conspiratorial activities elicited the Alfonsists' first approach, in April 1932, to the fascist regime in Italy for material backing, the Minister of Air, Italo Balbo, promising 200 machine guns and ammunition as well as planes.[7] The second plot turned on the efforts of the former Constitutionalists, who had become rapidly alienated by the regime. Manuel Burgos y Mazo, for example, had already reached the conclusion that the Republic was heading for a "soviet and irremediably to anarchy". His private papers reveal that the organization of the Constitutionalist conspiracy fell "almost exclusively on Melquiades Alvarez and on me, and above all on me", although Santiago Alba was also involved. Having approached Sanjurjo, without success, as early as November 1931, Burgos y Mazo none the less won over General Goded to the conspiracy. As he regarded the support of the Civil Guard as "absolutely indispensable", Burgos also obtained the somewhat unenthusiastic backing of General Cabanellas, the replacement for Sanjurjo as head of the Civil Guard.[8]

During 1932, the conspiracies gained momentum as more and more military officers signed up. Especially important was the adherence of General Sanjurjo. This tubby, moustachioed figure with bulging eyes was probably the most popular figure in the Spanish armed forces, largely

because he was the hero of the so-called "pacification" of Morocco in the
1920s (for which he earned the title of the Marqués del Rif), but also
because of his affable, down-to-earth character.[9] Having played an important role in the transition from the monarchy to the Republic by keeping
the Civil Guard strictly neutral, he quickly became disillusioned at the
direction the new regime was taking. The massacre of four Civil Guards
at Castilblanco in December 1931 prompted him to criticize the government publicly. The revenge killings by the Civil Guard, climaxing at
Arnedo on 5 January 1932, caused Azaña effectively to demote Sanjurjo
to the Carabineros. Through an intermediary, the General warned
President Alcalá-Zamora that, although he was not in favour of a *pronunciamiento*, "if the circumstances oblige me ...".[10] In fact, by the spring
of 1932 Sanjurjo had committed himself to the conspiracy.

In spite of General Sanjurjo's incorporation, the conspiracies remained
a motley venture bereft of a common strategy or programme. An immediate restoration of the monarchy, should the *pronunciamiento* triumph,
was out of the question, not only because it would be extremely unpopular, but also because the Constitutionalists as well as many of the recently
recruited military, including Sanjurjo and the leaders of the key Seville
garrison, initially sought a conservative republic. Theoretically, the insurgents, if successful, would oversee the election of a Constituent Cortes,
which would then decide between the monarchy and the republic. The
monarchists, however, still hoped that a period of military dictatorship
would be followed by a restoration of the former regime. Maladroit organization together with the lack of discretion and misplaced self-confidence
of the plotters – "the fatuity that was characteristic of upper-class monarchists and an excessive confidence in the military's means", believes
Martínez Barrio – made it relatively straightforward for the security
services to infiltrate the conspiracy. Possibly the ease with which the
pronunciamiento of General Primo de Rivera had triumphed in September
1923 – in which, Sanjurjo, as military governor of Zaragoza, had played
a prominent role – helped lull the conspirators into a false sense of security.[11]

In May 1932, the conspirators suffered the first of a series of setbacks.
The leader of the proto-fascist Partido Nacionalista Español, Dr Albiñana,
was exiled to the remote area of Las Hurdes in Caceres, in theory for
having promoted illegal monarchist propaganda but in practice for having
converted his party into one of the conspiracy's civilian channels.[12] On 15
June a number of the praetorian plotters were arrested, amongst them
Generals Barrera and Orgaz. Although Barrera was released not long
afterwards, the retention of Orgaz, a key organizer, was a blow for the
scheme. An even more serious setback was the decision taken in June by
the Carlists, the only conspiratorial element which could boast a mass
civilian base, not to participate in the rising (though members could do so

on a purely individual level). No doubt these events contributed to the heightened tension between civilian and military authorities during the summer of 1932. A speech by Justice Minister Alvaro de Albornoz in Avila on 19 June in which he mocked those officers recently arrested provoked an outraged reaction from Generals Milans del Bosch and Cavalcanti, resulting in the arrest of the latter. Eight days later, a highly-publicized confrontation took place at the Carabanchel parade ground in Madrid between Generals Goded, Villegas, and Caballero and Colonel Mangada as a result of the derogatory attitude of the first three towards the Republic. The decision of the Minister of War to uphold the imprisonment of the republican officer nearly caused the Radical–Socialists to withdraw from the Cabinet.[13]

Despite the evidently monarchist hue of the uprising of 10 August, there was widespread speculation in the aftermath as to whether or not the Radical leader – who, only a month before, had attempted to overthrow the government by the threat of a *pronunciamiento* – might actually have been involved himself. Foremost amongst the conspiracy theorists were the Radicals' arch-rivals, the socialists. *El Socialista* was quick to affirm that the revolt's failure had diverted attention from the "*éminences grises*" that were "morally" implicated. For the socialist daily, the most intriguing feature of the rebellion was the role of those who now protested their loyalty to the Republic but were, in fact, "traitors to the latter and traitors to the uprising". In the Cortes, a Catalan deputy accused a "certain party" – while directing his gaze at the Radical benches – of "suspicious" behaviour. Tellingly, it was not Lerroux, but Martínez Barrio, who leapt to the defence of the party. More damagingly, the Prime Minister condemned those who had been moved by "personal spite, frustrated ambition", yet were "far from thinking as the enemies of the Republic thought". Like the *El Socialista* editorial, this could be interpreted as a swipe at the Radical leader. In fact, the socialist parliamentary party, as deputy Juan-Simeón Vidarte recalls, suspected "a double game of Lerroux". Further credence was lent to these conjectures by General Sanjurjo himself, who made it plain that while he had done his duty "other gentlemen cannot say the same".[14]

Could there have been any truth to the speculation swirling around the Radical leader? Alejandro Lerroux had been associated with the army in one way or another all his life. His father had been a veterinary surgeon for the army, and, along with Lerroux's elder brother – the role model for the young Alejandro – fought in the Carlist Wars of the 1870s. As a boy, Alejandro once ran away from home in an ill-fated attempt to join the army. Later, he was accepted as a recruit by the General Military Academy in Toledo, but was unable to take up his post because his brother had squandered the pledged financial support on gambling. Worse still, by failing to report at the Military Academy on time, Lerroux was declared a deserter, so that when he came to live in Madrid, in 1886, he had to adopt a pseudonym (the uninspiring "Manuel García"). In spite of this setback, Lerroux always professed a "great love for the army". Certainly his childhood affection for the army not only carried over into adulthood but also played a critical role in his political career. During the first three-quarters of the nineteenth century, the weakness of civil society invariably converted the army into the arbiter of political life. All parties regarded the *pronunciamiento* as a perfectly legitimate means of coming to power. The architect of the Restoration of 1875, Antonio Cánovas, sought to banish praetorian politics from Spanish life. Just one of the four main republican parties under the Restoration, the Progressive Party of Manuel Ruiz Zorrilla, still clung to the *pronunciamiento* as the only route to power. This was the party in which Lerroux was initially active. Indeed, his first political act of importance was to scuttle as a go-between between Madrid and, 30 kilometres to the east, Alcalá de Henares, on behalf of General Villacampa's thwarted *pronunciamiento* of 1886. As a republican revolutionary in the 1890s, Lerroux co-operated mostly with working-class radicals but also with sympathetic elements in the army in an effort to overthrow the monarchy. After the turn of the century, when the focus of his political activity switched to Barcelona, he still embraced violence as a means of change. Most notably, he was involved in the attempts on the king's life in 1905 and 1906. Following the foundation of the Radical Party in 1908, Lerroux began to shed his revolutionary politics for a more reformist outlook. Regicide was renounced, but not the recourse to force. During the crisis of state in 1917, for example, Lerroux sought power via the Juntas de Defensa as well as through the Assembly of Parliamentarians and the workers' movement. During the Dictatorship of Primo de Rivera, the Radical leader continued to seek a military backer in order to come to power. Like Ruiz Zorrilla, he always believed that the Republic would come about by *pronunciamiento* rather than by popular plebiscite.[15]

The establishment of the Second Republic by peaceful means as a result of the municipal elections of 12 April 1931 therefore confounded a life-long belief of Lerroux. Not even this, however, persuaded him to renounce the insurrectionary option. New light is shed on this aspect of the Radical leader's politics by the hitherto uncited writings of Pedro Rico. A former Radical, the roly-poly Rico was to be known under the Republic as an Acción Republicana deputy and mayor of Madrid. During the early months of 1931, he was in close contact with Lerroux. He reveals that while most of the Revolutionary Committee, following the foiled Jaca rising of December 1930, was either in jail or exile, the Radical *jefe* was not merely at liberty in Madrid – as other sources testify – but in negoti-ation with the head of the Civil Guard, General Sanjurjo. In fact, the initial encounter between the two men had been arranged by Rico himself at Lerroux's instigation. At the meeting, the General assured the latter that

the "army will not get involved in any more adventures and there will be
no more dictatorships in its name". This and the following talks, Rico
believes, were instrumental in ensuring that the Civil Guard did not come
to the defence of the monarchy in the aftermath of the municipal elections
of 12 April 1931.[16] Astonishingly enough, Lerroux, vain and self-publi-
cizing as he was, failed to draw this considerable achievement to the
attention of the Revolutionary Committee, the Radical Party, or public
opinion. Martínez Barrio, the Radical deputy leader and a Revolutionary
Committee member, observes, in commenting upon Rico's draft, that the
jefe never spoke of his pre-republican contacts with the General. The only
explanation for this secretive behaviour was that, as Rico concludes,
Lerroux "wanted to keep the General in reserve in order to use him politically". This impression is enhanced by the fact that the relationship with
the General, for whom, Martínez Barrio recalls, Lerroux "never hid his
respect and esteem", was strengthened under the Republic. In June 1931,
Sanjurjo was elected for the Galician constituency of Lugo as an "independent", but with the backing of the Radical Party. When the result was
overturned because of fraud, the General's place in the rerun poll was
taken by his assistant, Ubaldo Azpiazu. The subsequent election of
Azpiazu as a Radical deputy thereby provided a direct line of communication between Lerroux and Sanjurjo.[17]

As early as the summer of 1931, there were rumours that the Radical
leader was involved in a conspiracy. In July, the Minister of War was
informed that a monarchist group was planning a *coup d'état* which
aimed to install a Radical government that would include Sanjurjo. A
month later, Lerroux had to respond in Cabinet to the accusation that he
was implicated in a plot. His defence was far from convincing. In his diary,
Azaña commented that "he creates a bad impression like a man who is
not sure of his authority".[18] Further rumours of the Radical *jefe*'s conspiratorial activities abounded in October and November. No firm evidence
regarding this speculation has emerged, but the Radical Party's own
archive indicates that it may not have been altogether baseless. Following
a meal in October 1931 at the house of the Barón de Vallvert, a former
aide to the king, a Radical politician informed his leader that the Baron's
son, who had been Captain of the Royal Escort, asssured him that within
three months "one of the heirs of Alfonso XIII will be here, ruling in the
company of Lerroux", revealing that his source was the owner of the
monarchist daily *ABC*, Juan Luca de Tena, "and other titled friends".[19]

It is known that Lerroux and Sanjurjo saw one another shortly after
the Castilblanco incident of December 1931. They met in a restaurant in
the company of Martínez Barrio and Miguel Maura.[20] According to the
version in *La pequeña historia*, the three politicians, all ex-ministers,
sympathized with the General's profound misgivings in relation to the
Azaña administration. The Radical leader assured him that the "problem"

would be resolved by a change in government. Still, Lerroux was left with the impression that Sanjurjo's disenchantment marked the "first step towards a conspiracy". Shortly after, following the General's dismissal from the Civil Guard in February 1932, the Radical *jefe* met him again, but this time alone. Lerroux relates that Sanjurjo sought his advice; should he accept a transfer to the Carabineros, an evident demotion? Apparently, Lerroux persuaded him to take up the post as his refusal would be interpreted as an "act of disaffection". Nevertheless, the Radical leader was now convinced that the General was "preparing something subversive". This, he recalls, left him in "spiritual turmoil". He had to make a choice between being "disloyal to a friend" or "disloyal to the Republic". He sought to reconcile his conflicting loyalties by informing the Prime Minister that a coup was being prepared, but without revealing any names. Martínez Barrio, having travelled all the way down to Baños de Montemayor in order to receive the instructions, then had to return to the capital, before retracing his steps as the premier demanded to know the plotters' names. This time, the Radical *jefe* decided to put the case to a prestigious triumvirate of deputies; the philosopher José Ortega y Gasset, the lawyer Felipe Sánchez Román, and the former minister Miguel Maura. All three "men of honour" endorsed the course of action undertaken. Lerroux was convinced that he had done everything possible to thwart a possible *pronunciamiento* "without failing in my duty as a friend and as a gentleman", and, in the process, had exposed "the trap" of Azaña.[21]

There are compelling grounds for believing that the Radical leader's portrayal of his relationship with General Sanjurjo is far from accurate. First, his contact with the General was greater than *La pequeña historia* indicates. They not only met on several occasions before the Republic, but also at least twice in the build-up to the uprising. They were in touch by telephone, too, as the Prime Minister's diaries reveal.[22] Besides, the Radical deputy Ubaldo Azpiazu provided a constant line of communication between them. As Azaña, then Minister of War, noted in July 1931, Sanjurjo "is a real enemy of mine and a very good friend of Lerroux".[23] Second, the latter's memoirs are contradicted by the account which he had published in *La Libertad* after the revolt. In the Madrid daily, the Radical *jefe* admits that General Sanjurjo had in fact offered him power should the *coup d'état* succeed, but claims to have turned the offer down and, in addition, to have told the General that he would denounce the conspiracy to the authorities. The article also reveals that both General Barrera, the chief conspirator, and General González Carrasco, the head of the Granada rising, were anxious to meet him, but he categorically refused. As with Sanjurjo, he made it known to González Carrasco that he would inform the government of his subversive activities. In *La pequeña historia*, there is no mention of Sanjurjo's offer, nor of the approach by the other two generals. It would seem that the *La Libertad* interview was part of

Lerroux's campaign to clear his name. Third, in his memoirs the Radical leader casts himself in the role of an honourable man who did everything possible to reconcile his loyalty to the Republic with his friendship with the General. The well-kept secret of the pre-republican meetings with Sanjurjo suggests otherwise. That such a right-wing figure as the General was Lerroux's friend, to whom he turned for advice in contemplating a putsch against the Republic, is suspicious in itself. Moreover, the Radical *jefe*'s refusal to name the chief conspirator to the government, effectively putting his loyalty to a seditious general above that to the regime, further brings into question his loyalty to the Republic. The complicity between them was underlined by Lerroux's misguided boast after the rising that "I am sure that against me he would not have rebelled". Altogether, there are prima facie grounds for suspecting that his relationship with General Sanjurjo was more than one of mere friendship.[24]

The real purpose behind the first meeting between the General and the Radical leader is partly indicated by the choice of location and companions. This took place over a meal in a well-known restaurant in central Madrid, the companions being Diego Martínez Barrio, universally regarded as an irreprochable republican, and Miguel Maura, a prominent critic of the Radicals of unshakeable convictions. Neither could be construed as a crony of Lerroux. The very nature of the gathering indicates that the latter wanted to demonstrate that he had nothing to hide in his dealings with the General. By contrast, the second meeting took place in very different circumstances. The two men saw one another in the wooded seclusion of the Radical *jefe*'s country estate at San Rafael, with no independently-minded politicians as witnesses. Given the coup's failure, it is hardly surprising that in the interview with *La Libertad*, Lerroux claims to have rejected the General's offer to become the civilian figurehead of the uprising. More implausible still is the account given by Lerroux, both at the time and in his memoirs, of his tip-off to the government. On hearing this version in the Cortes, Martínez Barrio was struck by his leader's "amnesia". In fact, Martínez Barrio had been told of the coup preparations not by the *jefe* but by two Radical deputies, José García Berlanga and José Manteca, both, ironically, former monarchists. Initially, the two deputies had journeyed up to San Rafael to inform Lerroux himself but, as he had left for Baños de Montemayor, they decided to brief the deputy leader back in Madrid. They insisted that a coup, ostensibly directed at the Azaña administration but in reality at the Republic itself, was being organized by Generals Sanjurjo, Goded, and Barrera with civilian backing, which included the ex-Constitutionalists Burgos y Mazo and Melquiades Alvarez, and that it would take place as soon as the parliamentary debate on the Catalan Statute had acquired a "a scandalous character". On his own initiative, Martínez Barrio decided to apprise the Prime Minister of the confidential information as the delay in telling the *jefe* – 300 kilometres away in the province of Caceres, not far from the Portuguese border – might prove fateful. In informing the Prime Minister, however, Martínez Barrio refused, in keeping with his promise to the deputies, to identify the conspirators. Immediately afterwards, he shot down to Baños de Montemayor, where he found Lerroux "content, as always, with himself, and discontented with everyone else". He urged the Radical leader to seize this opportunity not only to thwart the conspiracy but also to resolve his differences with Azaña. By divulging the names of the plotters, he argued, the mistrust that characterized relations between the two leaders would be largely vanquished; "everyone will gain: the parties and the regime". To his amazement, Lerroux dismissed the proposition out of hand. He was not even prepared to seek a "temporary armistice". Nor would he, despite the circumstances, return to Madrid, proposing to stay on at the spa for another two weeks. A compromise solution was reached whereby Martínez Barrio would consult with Ortega, Sánchez Román, and Maura to see if the Radicals should "undertake a new approach in relation to the government". Once in Madrid, the Radical deputy leader was judged by the three luminaries to have fulfilled his duty. He could not be expected to do any more. For his part, Martínez Barrio felt vindicated, having feared that "my concept of the gentleman had blinded me to my duty as a citizen". A meeting with the Prime Minister that same day dispelled his misgivings completely. Azaña commended him for having worked "in conscience", while adding that he already knew who the plotters were.[25]

The Radical leader's account in *La pequeña historia* is, therefore, almost wholly misleading. The Prime Minister was informed of the conspiracy by Martínez Barrio, not Lerroux. On the contrary, the latter was anxious not to inform the authorities, as shown by his strikingly ambivalent response to Martínez Barrio's news. Rather than leap to the government's defence and seek a reconciliation with the premier, the Radical leader opted instead for a face-saving compromise. In reality, he did not want to expose the plotters. Certainly the Radical deputy leader felt that his *jefe* was "sinning by omission". All of which is consistent with Lerroux's attempt to topple the government by blackmail in Zaragoza on 10 July.[26]

The grave doubts raised by the inconsistencies of the Radical leader's account are given further substance by his conduct on the night of 10 August. He left Madrid for San Rafael before the hostilities commenced without advising his deputy, a highly irregular act. He had hastily abandoned the capital, he later claimed, on the initiative of the General Directory of Security. Aware of the uprising's imminence, the authorities wanted him out of Madrid because the insurgents allegedly planned to kill not just the Prime Minister and the Minister of the Interior, but also – on account of his refusal to join them – Lerroux. In fact, he was almost certainly advised to leave Madrid on the purely personal initiative of José Valdivia, a friend and party member who also happened to be the secretary to the Director General of Security. Nor is there any reason to believe that the Radical *jefe* was a target for the rebels. He was probably much more afraid of what the Socialist Youth might do to him in a potentially confused and violent situation. The reception given to the three Radical deputies who presented themselves at San Rafael a few hours after the revolt in order to persuade their leader that his rightful place was in the capital are additional grounds for suspicion. They were shocked that one of his companions, Miguel Galante, a retired soldier and crony of Aurelio Lerroux (the adopted son of the party leader), who had recently been censured by the President for his outspoken views, went out of his way to defend the insurrection. He argued that it was directed not against the Republic but the Azaña administration – precisely the conspirators' own justification. The deputies came away with the strong impression that Lerroux's cabal was actually in favour of the *pronunciamiento*, being "saturated by hate for the government without considering the circumstances".[27]

Following the crushing of the "Sanjurjada", evidence began to emerge that implicated the Radical leader. The defence lawyer for General Sanjurjo, the former Constitutionalist leader Francisco Bergamín, addressed a public letter to Lerroux in which he called on him to confirm that the goal of the rising had been to convoke an election in order to determine the nature of the regime. Bergamín sought to demonstrate by means of a "favourable testimony" that the insurgents' aim had not been to restore the monarchy. Obviously, this indicated that Lerroux possessed privileged knowledge of the *pronunciamiento*. He reacted by persuading Bergamín to issue a statement which averred that he, Lerroux, would never have accepted power at the hands of a coup. However, this failed to address the principal issue as to why he was considered a witness to the rebels' intentions and why the lawyer of Sanjurjo was considered an apposite judge of the Radical leader's democratic convictions. Such queries echoed those of the Prime Minister's prior to the *coup* attempt as to why Lerroux knew of the subversives' "intrigues" and what it was that "they expect of him".[28]

Much more incriminating was the statement given by General Sanjurjo's personal secretary in Morocco, José Matres. Arrested a few days after the rising, Matres made a lengthy statement to the authorities which heavily implicated the Radical leader. According to *El Socialista*'s version of the confession, Lerroux was in intimate contact with the General, not least through the offices of the Radical deputy Ubaldo Azpiazu and Miguel Galante, the ex-soldier who was at San Rafael on the night of the insurrection. Matres further alleged that the Radical *jefe*, hopeful of bringing the government down himself, asked the General to postpone the *pronunciamiento* until after the Zaragoza speech. These revelations, *El Socialista* avowed, were well known in "certain Madrid circles". Manuel Azaña, in his account of the statement in his diary, reiterates Lerroux's plea to Sanjurjo as well as adding that the former was in contact with General Cabanellas, the head of the Civil Guard. The Radical leader rejoined that his loyalty to the Republic had never been in doubt and he challenged the socialists to reproduce their evidence in parliament. For his part, Matres rejected *El Socialista*'s report, though he agreed that parts of it were accurate. However, he failed to specify *which* parts. During the Civil War, in 1937, Azaña had occasion to discuss the statement with the socialist leader Indalecio Prieto and Mariano Gómez, the judge who had presided over the "Sanjurjada" trial. They recalled, Azaña recounts, that Matres's first statement confirmed the "connivance of Lerroux with Sanjurjo". However, the public prosecutor omitted to pass this on to the court. By the time the error was discovered, it was too late. Matres then renounced the statement. He was later absolved, having been defended by the monarchist leader Antonio Goicoechea – himself implicated in the conspiracy. Gómez was convinced that, had Matres' original statement been incorporated into the proceedings, Lerroux would have been put on trial.[29]

Certainly the Prime Minister himself was convinced of the Radical leader's involvement in the *pronunciamiento*. Given the intelligence upon which he could draw, he was in an unusually privileged position to evaluate Lerroux's actions. On 22 July, he received the information that the Radical boss had spoken with Sanjurjo by telephone to inquire as to the state of the army. "They have got something organized", Azaña observed in his diary. The conspirators, he reveals, "count on the support of Melquiades and they expect that of Lerroux".[30] After the insurrection, the Prime Minister made a thinly-veiled reference in parliament to the Radical leader's participation in the *pronunciamiento*. Early in 1933, he wrote that the jailed Sanjurjo "expects everything" from a change in government. In particular, if Lerroux came to power "he would not consent spending one more minute in jail". As Azaña concluded, "Sanjurjo must have a very serious account with Lerroux". Once the Radical leader assumed office, the insurgents of 10 August 1932, including Sanjurjo, did indeed obtain an amnesty. This was undertaken by Lerroux despite the febrile opposition of the President, the threat to the unity of the Radical Party, and the danger that the administration would fall over the issue. Clearly the Radical leader and the General had "a very serious account". The deal, as the judge at Sanjurjo's trial observed, was that "if the movement triumphed, Lerroux would come to power; and if it failed, he acquired the compromise to obtain the amnesty". The President, too, became convinced of the Radical *jefe*'s complicity by the battle over the Amnesty of April 1934. "I understood," he later disclosed, "the compromises contracted by him with Sanjurjo in 1932, which had prevented him from denying the insurgents."[31]

The case against Lerroux is strengthened still further by the prominent role played by certain allies of his in the uprising. It was widely suspected, but unproven at the time, that the former Constitutionalists, who had championed Lerroux's cause from the regime's outset and encouraged their own supporters to enter the Radical Party, were involved. In fact, they organized an entire strand of the conspiracy. Many of the rebellious officers linked to them were also in contact with the Radical leader, most notably Generals Sanjurjo and Goded. Matres, like Azaña, affirmed that Lerroux was also in touch with General Cabanellas, head of the Civil Guard. In the aftermath of the "Sanjurjada", these ties were not so much renounced as reinforced. Both Santiago Alba and General Cabanellas were elected as Radical deputies in the 1933 general election, the former becoming a prominent figure within the party.[32]

An even more formidable ally of the Radical leader involved in the events of 10 August was Juan March. The tobacco tycoon had numerous grounds for being aggrieved with the Azaña administration. Earlier in the year, the government had blocked his bid for the Ceuta and Melilla tobacco concession.[33] He then tried to improve relations with the Azaña administration by aiding the Portuguese revolutionaries, but his conditions were rejected by the Prime Minister. Most crucially, March, having defended himself before the Cortes on 8 June 1932, was jailed a week later on the initiative of the Commission of Responsibilities. Biographies of the magnate offer little direct evidence of his participation in the 10 August plot. The most authoritative one asserts that March's imprisonment resulted "immediately in a generous financial support for those that were discontented with the republican regime and for those that conspired against it", but offers no proof.[34] There are, however, numerous indications of his collaboration. First, he funded the publication *La Correspondencia Militar*, which not only incited the military dissidents to revolt but also served as a vehicle for them. Once the authorities closed the publication down, on 7 July 1932, many of its journalists passed over to the conspiracy.[35] Second, the manifesto for the *pronunciamiento* was drawn up by Juan Pujol, the editor of *Informaciones*, and one of March's men. It is difficult to believe that the Mallorcan mogul, given that he would be one of the leading beneficiaries of a successful *pronunciamiento*, did not help finance the rising. Recent research has shown that he was the greatest contributor by far, at two million pesetas, to a monarchist fund set up in the aftermath of the "Sanjurjada". It is difficult to believe, too, that March's participation did not implicate the Radical leader. Since the Republic's advent, March had rooted for a Lerrouxist government, while the Radical Party had publicly defended his cause in the Cortes. At the time, the Radical deputy Tomás Peire Cabaleiro, like Emiliano Iglesias

before him, was a lawyer for the tycoon.[36] Scarcely surprisingly, it was
widely assumed that the Zaragoza speech had been undertaken on
March's biding.[37] March himself boasted that he had Lerroux in his
pocket. Altogether, the involvement of both the former Constititionalists
and Juan March in the conspiracy makes it even less plausible that the
Radical leader was not himself implicated.[38]

Why, therefore, did the government not press its well-founded suspicions regarding the Radical leader? The Prime Minister, as his
recently-published diaries reveal, was in fact prepared for justice to take
its course. On 23 August, he wrote that the Matres statement could create
"a lot of noise". If, he added six days later, this supported Bergamín's revelations "this could become interesting". The upshot was that Lerroux,
humiliatingly, had to give a statement to the chief of police, but the indictment did not contain enough evidence – the public prosecutor having
failed to pass on Matres's declarations – for him to be put on trial. Like
Burgos y Mazo, who avoided jail "by a miracle" by destroying numerous
documents, the Radical leader managed to cover his tracks. He must
certainly have been well practised in the art of concealment given his
shadowy business dealings and numerous contacts with army dissidents.
He may also have been put on guard by the very unwieldiness of the
conspiratorial enterprise as well as by its lack of a clear strategy and goals.
As a republican, he obviously had a lot more to lose than the declared
enemies of the regime. It is extremely unlikely that he was an organizer or
financial backer of the "Sanjurjada". On the contrary, he kept himself on
the periphery in a somewhat ambiguous position. Indeed, the conspirators, exasperated by his failure to build on the Zaragoza speech by
pressing in the Cortes for a government crisis, suspected him of "a dirty
trick". Yet by keeping himself on the margins, Lerroux could, depending
on the outcome of the rising, either leap forward as a civilian figurehead
or else withdraw stealthily into the shadows. Still, his involvement was
sufficient for a heavy debt to be incurred, as the amnesty of April 1934
demonstrated. Had he been convicted of participation in the "Sanjurjada"
and the Radical Party disintegrated as a result, Azaña might have been
able to realize his project of creating a truly redoubtable republican party
through the incorporation of many Radicals. On the other hand, the political disqualification of Lerroux might have divided the republican
movement irrevocably and severely tarnished the Republic, thereby
playing into the hands of the regime's enemies and forfeiting many of the
gains derived from the rising's repression. By discrediting the right rather
than the Radicals through the "Sanjurjada", the regime, at least in the
short run, probably gained in stability.[39]

This begs the question as to what extent the Radical Party as a whole
was implicated in the "Sanjurjada". The available evidence indicates that
knowledge of Lerroux's undertaking was limited to a handful of intimates.

Few, if any, Radicals were actively involved in the *pronunciamiento* or desired its triumph. The Radical leader's Zaragoza speech of 10 July contrasts starkly with that of his deputy in Seville two weeks later. Martínez Barrio vigorously denounced the alleged conspiratorial activities while insisting that, if the Republic was placed in danger, the party would "defend it and protect it". This is consistent with his own actions on the night of 10 August when he immediately placed himself at the disposition of the government. The contrast is heightened if the dubious reaction of Lerroux's cabal is compared with that of the Seville party, the only Radicals to be put to the test by the insurgency.[40] Indeed, the sole public institution to stand up to the rebels in the Andalusian capital was the town council under the Radical mayor, José González y Fernández de la Bandera. Rather than surrender, he held a special session of the town council, which issued a proclamation against the uprising. The councillors were duly detained by Sanjurjo's troops at the San Hermenegildo barracks.[41] Radicals also comprised half the "Comité de Salud Pública", a committee of civilian resistance, in the capital, while out in the province, another Radical, Dr Puelles, hurtled from *pueblo* to *pueblo* setting up support groups. Not all the Seville Radicals, however, adopted an unambiguous attitude. Antonio Rodríguez de la Borbolla, a former monarchist deputy now on the local Executive Committee, was briefly arrested after the revolt's downfall and made to give a statement, but he was never charged. None the less, Radical criticism of his conduct during the rising, which he put down to "enmity and unjust antipathy", caused him to resign from the party. More generally, the "Sanjurjada" sharpened long-standing tensions between former monarchists and republican veterans within the Seville organization. At a special meeting presided over by Martínez Barrio in early September, the Provincial Junta failed to resolve the ongoing conflict. As a result, the Radical deputy and former monarchist Miguel García y Bravo Ferrer abandoned the party along with his supporters.[42]

Despite the fact that the "Sanjurjada" nearly destroyed his political career, the Radical leader did not renounce the insurrectionary option. Numerous disaffected officers expressed their support for him in the wake of the attempted coup. Colonel José Bermudez de Castro, for example, wrote to him shortly afterwards that the army was not only "disaffected with the present government" but also "feels no enthusiasm for the Republic". There was even a letter from a member of the General Staff, General Pardo, which was strongly sympathetic to the rising. He claimed that the *pronunciamiento* was to be expected, reflecting as it did a broad "protest against the present government and the influence of the socialists", and that Azaña's continuation in office would put at risk "the Republic itself". By contrast, he regarded the events of 10 August as "a continuation of your protests".[43] More seriously, the papers of the Radical

Party reveal that the *jefe* was still in contact with subversive elements within the army. A salient example is that of General Gil-Yuste who, although he did not participate in the 10 August rising, was kept under close surveillance by the authorities thereafter. He rose against the Republic in July 1936, later playing a crucial role in the selection of General Franco as Nationalist leader.[44] Back in March 1933 Gil-Yuste addressed an extraordinarily candid letter to Lerroux. Echoing the Radical and right-wing opposition, he denounced the government as "an odious socialist dictatorship". More radically, he declared that the country would probably have to be saved "in a violent fashion". "To save Spain," he continued, "a lot of blood has to be spilt." To this end, he assured the Radical leader that he could count on the necessary support "at all times". Although the latter's letters to the General have not been discovered, it is apparent from these unguarded remarks that the two men were in sympathy with one another.[45] Further evidence that Lerroux was informed of the conspiratorial activities within the army is shown by a letter amongst his papers from General José Fernández de Villa-Abrille to a certain González Jonte. Dated the 8th of August 1933, the General replies to González Jonte's plea to establish himself as "the saviour of Spain" by protesting his loyalty to the Republic despite the "the black fate that soon awaits me, by contrast, for not accepting". In short, the Radical leader kept the insurrectionary option open.[46]

The Azaña administration seized on the "Sanjurjada" as an opportunity to destroy the myth that, as the Prime Minister wrote in his diary, "if the Republic survives it is because the military allows it". The crushing of the uprising therefore strengthened the regime by discrediting the *pronunciamiento* as a tool of political change and by reaffirming the Republic's democratic principles. In particular, the government took advantage of the attempted coup to deal a heavy blow to the extreme right. Far-right organizations such as the Spanish Nationalist Party and the Valladolid-based JONS were devastated by the repression. One hundred and fourteen papers throughout Spain, including national dailies such as *ABC*, *El Debate*, *Informaciones*, and *La Nación*, were suspended. A total of 5,000 people were detained. Most were soon released, but one hundred and forty-five detainees, including numerous members of the aristocracy, were deported to the harsh environs of Villa Cisneros in the Sahara. Others, including the traditionalist ideologue and writer Ramiro de Maeztu and the young José Antonio Primo de Rivera, son of the dictator and future founder of the Falange, were incarcerated in the more accessible Modelo prison in Madrid. Sanjurjo himself was sentenced to death but the Cabinet, anxious not to create a martyr as the monarchy had done by executing Galán and García Hernández in December 1930, reprieved him. Despite being dispatched to the prison of El Dueso on the north Atlantic coast, he confidently predicted that his release "will not take long".[47]

The events of 10 August marked a watershed in the trajectory of the right under the Republic. As a result of the "Sanjurjada", the long-standing tensions between the "accidentalists" and the "Alfonsists" were brought to a head at the first Congress of Acción Popular on 22–23 October 1932. The latter's insistence on their monarchist identity and the insurrectionary option was rejected by the accidentalists as counterproductive and impractical. Power would not be achieved by legal means if, as one speaker put it, "from six to eight they respect the legal order, according to the rules of Acción Popular, and from eight to ten they take up a rifle and hit the streets". The accidentalists triumphed at the Congress, but at the cost of the Alfonsists' abandonment. The former's original aim of gathering all Catholics under one political umbrella, already undermined by the separation of the Traditionalists and the Carlists from Acción Popular, had been dealt the severest blow yet.[48] None the less, they had gained enormously in terms of strategic and ideological coherence. At the Congress, Acción Popular finally declared itself a political party with a view to creating a mass Catholic movement. Despite the fiasco of the "Sanjurjada", the monarchists still sought to overthrow the Republic by violent means. Recent research had shown that, by drawing on a personal letter from the king, the monarchists rapidly built up a huge war chest of 20 million pesetas. The biggest donor was the jailed Juan March, while the king himself paid 125,000 French francs into yet another fund.[49] Nevertheless, the monarchists at last realized that the downfall of the regime could not be pursued by *pronunciamiento* alone. On 12 January 1933, a monarchist party, Renovación Española, was founded with a view to contesting Catholic and conservative support with the accidentalists. As a result, the "Sanjurjada" at once rejuvenated and fragmented the forces of the right.[50]

VI

The Ambiguous Courtship
The Radicals and the left–republicans, August 1932 to September 1933

The abortive coup of 10 August 1932 transformed the political climate overnight by rallying all the republicans around the government in defence of the regime. In particular, the Radical opposition gave way to a demonstrative display of loyalty towards the Azaña administration. When the Prime Minister called on 18 August for the confiscation, without indemnification, of the land of all those implicated, the uncritical response of the Radicals was, as Martínez Barrio declared before the Cortes, "the Radical Party does not hesitate, the Radical Party does not argue, the Radical Party does not hinder"; when the confiscations were extended in September, however questionably, to the grandees, the Radical Party was again not found wanting; and when, on 9 September, the agrarian reform bill was put to the vote, the Radicals, despite their previous obstruction, stood shoulder-by-shoulder with the government. This *volte-face*, together with the disarming of the right, ensured the bill a prompt passage. That same day, the Catalan Statute, hitherto opposed even more viscerally by the Radicals, was passed into law with their backing. In this case, however, the hostility within the Radical ranks was so great – shortly before the vote, Manual Marraco had denounced the Statute to Lerroux as nothing more than "one more cause of agitation" – that the *jefe* had to postpone a trip to Barcelona in order to ensure that the parliamentary group voted with the ruling majority. Having stressed that the Law embodied "a formula that is not ours", the Radical leader added that his party would treat it "with loyalty".[1]

The resurrection of the spirit of San Sebastian was embraced unreservedly by the overwhelming majority of Radicals, but for the Lerrouxist cabal which had been implicated, however peripherally, in the uprising it signalled a grave setback. The lack of unanimity within the party over the "Sanjurjada" partly explains why the parliamentary group sank, Martínez Barrio recalls, into a "disconcerting decline", but the overriding reason was that the Radical Party had lost all sense of direction, the wind having been taken out of its oppositional sails. By contrast, the governing coalition was rejuvenated by the crushing of the insurrection. Not only did the government finally pass its two most critical bills, but the Radical and right-wing opposition had been defused. Furthermore, recent changes in newspaper ownership hitched three leading national dailies – *El Sol*, *Luz*, and *La Voz* – to the Prime Minister's bandwagon. Unopposed and reunited, the Azaña administration was at its zenith. The new-found sense of purpose was manifested in the vigour with which the Minister of Agriculture and the premier, in contrast to their lacklustre performance during the passage of the agrarian reform bill, tackled the land invasions in Badajoz and elsewhere from the beginning of October 1932.[2]

Radical support for the government in the aftermath of the "Sanjurjada" did not alter the party's immediate goal: the establishment of an all-republican administration. However, the left republicans saw no reason, especially as the logjam of the opposition had been broken, to replace the socialists with the Radicals. Both the Radical–Socialist Party and Acción Republicana, at their respective congresses in September, rejected the need for a strictly republican government. This was not to deny that they foresaw a time when the PSOE would leave office and an all-republican Cabinet be formed. The Prime Minister himself addressed this question, now that his two key bills had been passed and before the socialists debated the matter at their Congress in early October, in a high-profile speech in Santander at the end of September. He believed that the republican–socialist administration should remain in power, but if the socialists departed, an "instrument of left-wing republican government" should be at the ready. This would be based on a parliamentary alliance "without the fusion of the parties, without any sort of confusion between the parties" of around 130 deputies, less than a third of the Cortes, but which would count on the benevolent support of the PSOE. The socialists welcomed the initiative as a guarantee of continuity. A left–republican federation, Prieto commented, would permit the PSOE to leave office in the knowledge that "the significance" of the Republic would be maintained. Once the PSOE had abandoned the government, in other words, the left republicans would still aim to rule with the support of the socialists – not that of the Radicals. On the contrary, the Radical Party did not appear to enter into the Prime Minister's plans. The proposed federation would, in effect, take the place of the Alianza Republicana.[3]

The Radicals immediately made it plain that they, too, wanted to form part of the all-republican body, but the response of the left republicans was unfavourable. Martínez Barrio, in a rare moment of public passion, fulminated that the Radical Party would do everything possible to ruin the scheme. Power, he exclaimed, had been subjected to a "kidnap". Basilio Alvarez later boomed that the divorce between the government and "true opinion" was "absolute" and that, whatever the manoeuvrings of the left republicans, a Radical-led government was still awaited by a "great political mass". Wrath rapidly gave way to *rapprochement*. Martínez Barrio declared in an interview with *Heraldo de Madrid* that "the convergence" of the republican parties was urgent. The Radicals would not only undertake talks with the left republicans in relation to a common programme of government in a spirit of "accommodation", but would also respect all the legislation of the Constituent Cortes while accepting that the remaining laws complementary to the Constitution had to be passed, though quickly. He stressed that the Radicals did not "reject anybody". However, the central plank in the Radicals' campaign of appeasement was yet to come – the National Congress in October.[4]

The *raison d'être* behind the Congress is revealed in a confidential document entitled "Aim of the Congress".[5] The first objective was to raise the profile of the party, eclipsed by the resurgence of the republican–socialist administration in the wake of the "Sanjurjada". A congress was "not only necessary, but indispensable", the document discloses, because "it is urgent to give the country a sense of our strength". Underlying this goal was the desire to dispel the suspicions surrounding the Radicals' role during the uprising of 10 August, or, as the internal report puts it, "present ourselves before the country with a record of republican loyalty". It was especially important to relaunch the party as the left republicans and socialists would all hold congresses in September and early October. A second reason was to establish a framework by which the party's chronic infighting could be resolved. Its vertiginous growth had completely superseded "the old framework", resulting in "grave internal problems" which "should be channeled". In any case, there was considerable pressure in favour of a national congress. This is hardly surprising given that, despite the Regulations of August 1931 and in stark contrast to the other republican parties, the Radical Party had not yet held a national congress.[6]

However, neither the relaunch nor the party's reorganization were to be left to chance. On the contrary, the leadership's greatest fear, the confidential report reveals, was its own rank-and-file. "The greatest inconvenience", the document discloses, would be for the congress to be "drowned by a flood of local complaints" or for it to be dominated by "verbiage, the extremist desire of some, exhibitionism" as this could result in "the coercion by the Congress of the parliamentary group and of the *jefe*". As grassroots' pressure was "inevitable, democratically inevitable", the report recommends that "the inconveniences" should be avoided by calling a "Special Congress". Not only would this ensure that the congress was "limited in extension and in composition" and that all speeches would be approved beforehand by the executive, but also that much of the work would take place in preselected committees. The result would be two hundred and fifty "selected, easily presidable" delegates and only two plenary sesssions. In this way, the congress would achieve its objective of bestowing "authority" on the national leadership. In other words, the congress was conceived as a public-relations exercise stage-managed from above rather than a forum for debate from below. This was underlined by the nature of the proposal made in relation to the conflict in the provinces. "Co-existence", it stated, should be achieved by strengthening "the authority of the *jefe* ... by means of a National Junta". Consequently the first congress to be held under the Republic by the Radical Party was organized not in accordance with the Regulations of August 1931 but, as the extremely short notice and the conference's "special" status indicate, in response to the strategic needs of the leadership in the aftermath of the "Sanjurjada".

The Radical leader's opening address to the Congress on 15 October was in stark contrast to his Zaragoza speech of 10 July. He dwelt at length on what united, rather than divided, the republicans, highlighting the Radicals' commitment to the Constitution and to the spirit of reform that characterized the Azaña administration. In the same placatory vein, he declared that the Radical Party was not an enemy of the Socialist Party. "We cannot," he claimed, "be anything other than followers of this government." Such opportunistic rhetoric did not prevent him from reaffirming the party's opposition, albeit in much more moderate tones than in Zaragoza, by criticizing those reforms "that break the national economy, that make the Republic unsympathetic" and by calling for an all-republican government. He concluded with a homily to a future Radical Cabinet "without extremes" that, unlike the current one, would not be "incompatible with the national economy".[7]

The generally conciliatory tone of the inaugural discourse pervaded the entire congress. The report on the "Position of the Radical Republican Party within the Republic", entrusted to the Galician deputy Gerardo Abad Conde but drawn up in collaboration with the *jefe*, not only rejoiced in the overthrow of "the dynasty, clericalism, and militarism", but also outlined a thoroughly progressive programme. In relation to agrarian reform, to take one example, a veritable shopping list of reforms, including "the handing over of lands to communities of workers and peasants' cooperatives", "agrarian credit", "encouragement of cooperation and mutualism", as well as the subordination of property to "the general interest", the expropriation of land "not only on the grounds of public utility, but also through lack of cultivation and malicious concealment", and the defence of the *jurados mixtos* was presented. There was no hint that much of this far-ranging programme was at variance with the party's position hitherto. The Radical Party was clearly endeavouring to appease the left republicans by demonstrating that it, in accordance with the "left-wing outlook that characterizes the Republic", was just as reformist in outlook. Diego Hidalgo's report on the Radicals' relations with other

parties also exuded conciliatoriness. The Radical Party and left republicans, he declared, were differentiated merely by "a nuance", while in
relation to the Socialist Party, the ideological differences between them
"do not imply enmity nor aggression".[8] Martínez Barrio's keynote report,
entitled "The Future All-Republican Government", advocated the
creation of "a federation of political groups . . . to constitute an instrument of republican government" – exactly as the Prime Minister had
proposed at Santander, except for the inclusion of the Radicals. To that
end, the Radical Party would discuss "in a friendly and cordial manner"
a programme upon which all the republicans could agree, taking as its
starting point the acceptance of everything that the Constituent Cortes
had done to date. Meanwhile, the Socialist Party would fulfil the crucial
"mission of watching over, from the opposition, the fulfilment of the ends
that gave rise to the Republic, and constitute, for the future, a governmental reserve". The entire Special Congress was, therefore, an exercise
in appeasement. The goal was to incorporate the Radical Party into the
federation initially outlined by the Prime Minister as a first step towards
the formation of an all-republican administration.

None the less, the conciliatory plea of the Radical Congress for an all-
republican administration fell on deaf ears. The Radical–Socialist
National Executive Committee, having consulted its regional and provincial bodies, had already told the Prime Minister that his proposed
federation should exclude the Radicals. The deputies of Acción
Republicana agreed on 25 October that the federation should only include
those republicans that supported the government and that, in the circumstances, an administration without the socialists was impossible. The next
day, 26 October, the two left–republican parties announced that the
alliance they were seeking to establish would not include the Radical
Party. The federation's initial organizational efforts in early November
were duly limited to Acción Republicana, the PRRS, the ORGA, and the
Esquerra. This strategy was underscored by Azaña's Valladolid speech on
14 November. The Prime Minister contended that the current government
should continue in power until it had completed its parliamentary
programme and that, once the republican–socialist coalition had come to
an end, the left–republican federation – not an all-republican administration – would allow the Cortes to continue. In other words, the
rejuvenation of the ruling alliance and the discrediting of the right as a
result of the "Sanjurjada" meant that the left republicans had no need, at
this juncture, of the Radicals.[9]

The socialists, for their part, had remained in the government since
1931 to an important extent because they did not want the Radicals to
dominate an all-republican administration. The marked social tensions
between their respective social bases in the provinces was a crucial consideration. Moreover, during the winter of 1932–3, the employers, many of

whom sided with the Radicals, went on the offensive, starting with a rural lock-out in the autumn of 1932. It is no coincidence that the radicalization of Largo Caballero dates from the end of 1932. The growing militancy of the socialist rank and file in response to the employers' obstructionism would erode the socialist leaders' backing for governmental collaboration. But there was more to the hostility between the Radical Party and PSOE than that. Against a long-standing rivalry and their ideological differences, both parties were in competition as the only republican national entities. In particular, both aimed to win over the left republicans, who held the balance of power.

It was, therefore, in the socialists' interest to discredit the Radical Party in the eyes of their left-republican allies as much as possible.[10] Following the Radical Congress, even the moderate socialist deputy Manual Cordero had dismissed the Radicals for their "utter rightism", for attracting "the moneyed and anti-democratic elements", and for their "ever firmer and more manifest support . . . for the capitalist elements, or at least, for those that fight against the proletariat". Yet the socialist stance harboured an implicit idealization of the left republicans. Both Acción Republicana and the PRRS had, like the Radical Party, incorporated landowners and ex-monarchists. Indeed, the left republicans' rural base would come into increasing conflict with the socialists' one, to the extent that this would play a notable role in the eventual dissolution of the republican–socialist coalition. Moreover, the readiness of the socialists to associate the Radicals with the non-republican and monarchist right alike was to ignore the gaping ideological differences that separated them. As the Radical leader lamented at the October Congress, "we are not the enemy because the enemy is the intransigent bourgeoisie, it is the reactionary bourgeoisie, it is the capitalism that does not want to evolve". To reject the Radicals by equating their centrist moderation with "utter rightism" was to narrow the regime unnecessarily and even dangerously. In fact, the socialists' vulgar Marxist vision, which often reduced analysis to a simplistic struggle between "the bourgeoisie" and "the proletariat", was itself an impediment to the consolidation of the Republic. But, as became increasingly obvious during the course of 1933, this was not uppermost in the socialists' minds. They were more interested in change rather than consolidation on the grounds that the Republic had already been consolidated. The left republicans, too, believed that the Republic was theirs for good. Yet they overestimated their own support, while underestimating that of the opposition. Years later, Martínez Barrio, despite having fought side by side with the left republicans and socialists in the Civil War, still judged that "the sectors of opinion that the Señores Azaña and Prieto believed sufficient to govern the Republic were, all together, a minority, and, as a result, vulnerable to a bad wind that would sweep them away". That wind would arrive sooner than they expected.[11]

The Radicals found themselves in a quandry. On the one hand, their appeasement of the left republicans had signally failed to advance the formation of an all-republican administration. It had not even improved relations between them, the Radical Party having been rebuffed over the proposed republican federation. On the other hand, the prospect of the municipal elections in three months time filled the Radicals with dread as they feared a drubbing at the hands of the ruling coalition. This would greatly discredit their opposition by revealing that the country was not divorced from the Cortes. The Radicals therefore decided, as Antonio Lara informed the Prime Minister in person on 16 December, to reactivate their opposition with a view to overthrowing the government before the April elections took place. The change in tack was immediately made evident in the parliamentary debate on the railway strike. Whereas, five months earlier, the Radicals had objected to a subsidy for the railways, they now – in an effort to create a conflict between the UGT and the socialist minister concerned – denounced the projected sum as too little.[12] More importantly, the filibustering of the Radicals led them to target the military budget. The Prime Minister was outraged at their "effrontery", not to mention their "ignorance", in putting forward an unrealistic alternative. The Radicals' defence of a "democratic and pacific" proposal, in contrast to the government's "bellicose and militaristic" plan, was indeed ironic given that at least one of the party's military experts was implicated in the "Sanjurjada". Although Azaña had warned Lara on the 16th that the Radicals would prejudice the formation of an all-republican administration by renewing the obstruction, and in particular if they objected to the military budget, the opposition continued unabated. Indeed, the Radical Party and its allies tried later in the month to deprive the ruling majority of a quorum in the vote on the budget. If, according to the Prime Minister, this "madness" had succeeded, the Cabinet might have fallen. Hardly surprisingly, by the end of 1932 relations between the Radicals and the left republicans had reverted to the pre-Sanjurjada state of, in Azaña's words, "acrimony and violence".[13]

Inadvertently, the Radical obstruction received a major boost as a result of an uprising by the CNT. Originally conceived as a nationwide movement, the insurrection of 8 January 1933 was initiated in Barcelona but spread no farther than the province of Valencia to the south. Only after these actions had been suppressed did news began to filter through of disturbances in the Andalusian province of Cadiz. One of the localities catalyzed by the call to arms was Casas Viejas, a *pueblo* of 2,000 inhabitants 19 kilometres from the town of Medina Sidonia. The local CNT militants rose up on the morning of 11 January and took control of the four-man Civil Guard post. Two of the Guards would later die from the wounds inflicted during the shoot out. At 2 o'clock in the afternoon, a detachment of thirteen Civil Guards entered the village. At this point, many of the peasants involved in the rising fled, while others shut themselves up in their homes. A few hours later, four Civil and twelve Assault Guards under the command of Lieutenant Artal arrived. They attempted to seize those holed up in the mud-and-stone hovel of "Seisdedos", a 72-year-old coalman affiliated to the CNT but who had not been involved in the insurrection. In the assault, an Assault Guard was shot dead. Captain Rojas, who appeared on the scene several hours later with a further forty Assault Guards, ordered the shack to be set on fire. Two people were killed as they fled the hovel while six more were burnt alive, including "Seisdedos" himself. The Guards then searched the *pueblo* for the ring-leaders of the revolt, a 75-year-old, who allegedly cried "Don't shoot! I'm not an anarchist!", being shot dead in the process. Eventually, twelve people were rounded up, of whom only one had taken part in the assault on the Civil Guard post. In a vile climax, Captain Rojas, now soused with brandy, began shooting the prisoners, the other Guards following suit. All twelve prisoners were murdered. Altogether, nineteen men, two women, and a child, all but two of whom were under 20 years of age, had died, along with three Guards.[14]

It was soon established that the repression of the Casas Viejas rising had been sanguinary, but neither the public nor the politicians realized that the prisoners had been shot in cold blood. Before long, however, it was suspected that undue force might have been deployed. During the period leading up to the opening of the Cortes on 1 February, the Radicals fuelled the growing conjecture in order to prepare the ground for an all-out assault on the government. A renewed attack on the socialists was central to the build up. The Madrid daily *El Imparcial*, now aligned with the Radical Party, denounced the "intolerable dictatorship" of the socialists, while *El Pueblo*, the PURA's leading daily, slated "the socialist empire". Martínez Barrio, in a speech on 25 January, indicted the socialists for wrecking the economy, dividing the republicans, and for placing the Republic itself in danger. Equally, Radical deputy Pedro Riera Vidal affirmed in *El Progreso* that the socialists had placed the Republic "in danger".[15] In editorial after editorial, *El Progreso* called for an all-republican administration as the only solution to the nation's ills. In an editorial of 26 January, the Radical daily asserted that the ruling majority was "divorced from the will of the country, is contrary to the harmony of the classes and to the spiritual, social and economic convenience of the majority of the governed". There was, Riera Vidal affirmed, "hunger for a republican government, purely republican, throughout the country". In Orense, Basilio Alvarez thundered against an "anti-republican" government that represented no more than 5 per cent of Spaniards. By contrast, a Radical government would be one of "social peace, of economic restoration". The day before parliament opened, *El Progreso* exclaimed "the government has to be changed in order to restore to the Republic its authority". The following day, in a spirit of expectant crisis, the Radical daily insisted that the Azaña administration had "gravely damaged" the economy, ignited "a civil war" within the working class, and failed in education, public works, and many other areas; "a government, in short, that does not know how to govern". In the same spirit, Guerra del Río declared before the press that the Socialist Party had "failed", the Radical–Socialists were "dispersed", and that the only solution was the Radical Party.[16]

The Radical barrage reached its crescendo with the accusation that the government was implicated in the carnage at Casas Viejas. The day before parliament recommenced, Rafael Guerra del Río, the Radical parliamentary spokesman, disclosed to journalists that there was "evidence of a lack of foresight and of cruelty". Included was the testimony of the mayor of Medina Sidonia, inexplicably removed from his post two days after the events at the nearby *pueblo* of Casas Viejas, that eight men had been shot in cold blood. Indeed, the Radicals had already seized upon Casas Viejas as a symbol of the Azaña administration's failure. "The policies that have been pursued", Martínez Barrio declared to the press the day the Cortes met, "have been buried with the victims" of Casas Viejas. That same day, *El Progreso* claimed that a reshuffle was imminent, while the Radical leader expressed his willingness to bring down a government that was "exhausted in every respect".[17]

Once the Cortes reopened, Guerra del Río lambasted the government for its performance in relation to the massacre in Casas Viejas. The Prime Minister dismissed the attack as pure opportunism, commenting in his diary that the Radical spokesman deserved the prize for "political immorality". Yet the ruling majority's problems had only just begun. The following day, discussion of one of the most polemical pieces of legislation, the bill on Religious Congregations, began. Thus the controversy over Casas Viejas merged with that over the religious bill. On 3 February, the Radical leader seized the moment to assail the entire record of the Azaña administration in a rhetorical tour-de-force. Predictably, he blamed its divorce from "the national conscience", the lack of "spiritual peace" within the country, and the general bankruptcy of the republican–socialist coalition on the Socialist Party. While the government's "social" failure had resulted in the CNT uprising of 8 January 1933, he claimed damningly, its "political" one had climaxed in the attempted coup of 10 August 1932. Indeed, the administration had "failed totally and categorically". Just as predictably, Lerroux exhorted the front bench to give way to an all-republican one. If the government did not resign forthwith, he foresaw a "governmental crisis or a presidential crisis" – a cue for Alcalá-Zamora to intervene. In the meantime, the Radical Party would do everything possible in parliamentary terms "to make the government's labours impossible". The 3 February speech was backed up by the resignation of

Radical appointees from all leading public positions, whether as civil governors, the President of the Court of Accounts, the Director of the Mint, or as representatives at nationalized companies.[18]

Unmoved by the Radical leader's oratorical onslaught, the Prime Minister rejoined uncompromisingly that to bring the government down before its programme had been completed would raise the possibility of a republican coalition that "does not exist, not even in the thoughts of the republicans", destroy the work of the republican–socialist majority, and signal the end of the Constituent Cortes. He went on to give an impassioned defence of the ruling alliance in a speech in Madrid on 14 February. For Azaña, the key was the collaboration with the socialists, which he exalted as "a fundamental experience of universal historical interest". "We might separate one day," he avowed, "but we will come together again in the government or in the opposition in order to complete the task that we have undertaken." This ringing endorsement of the socialists was partly a response to the chronic instability that afflicted the left republican camp. Not only had the FIRPE, beset by ideological and individual clashes, failed to live up to expectations, but also the PRRS had become increasingly divided over government policy since the onset of the Casas Viejas debate. At the same time, the speech was a critique of the Radical Party. The regenerationist vision of the left, rooted in the paramountcy of parliament and a new public morality, was contrasted with that of those "men incapable of possessing this sense of duty or weak men capable of accommodating all the immoralities that continually assault the public power" – an unmistakable reference to the Radicals. He therefore rejected the Radicals' call for the left republicans to unite with the opposition for the sake of the regime on the grounds that the Republic did not need "to save itself from any danger".[19]

The next day, 15 February, the Radical Party initiated an all-out opposition by putting forward hundreds of amendments to a bill concerning public works in the province of Alicante. The government hurdled this particular obstacle by applying the "guillotine" – a procedure which required the votes of the majority plus one – to the first article and by suppressing the rest, but it would be impracticable for the ruling majority to carry on in this way. To make matters worse, the opposition returned to the breach over Casas Viejas. The Radicals aimed to demonstrate not only that the government was behind the excesses but also that the Prime Minister had been misleading parliament from the beginning. In reality, he had received the first evidence of wrongdoing on 9 February. Four days later, he confided in his diary that "I fear the worst". Yet it was another ten days – the day of the debate – before he was informed that thirteen people had witnessed the Assault Guards shoot the prisoners in cold blood. For the Radicals, this was irrelevant. The debate, which the Prime Minister regarded privately as a "repugnant spectacle", was an opportunity to bring the government down.[20] The opposition nearly succeeded. That same day, the Radical–Socialist ministers along with two socialist ones, having reached the conclusion that the government was "broken", told Azaña that, if it was to be subjected to a smear campaign, they would prefer to leave office. The Prime Minister retorted that resignation would be an admission of guilt, the Cabinet later endorsing his position. Just as the republican–socialist administration was regrouping, the PRRS split into two warring camps. The catalyst was the opposition's motion of censure. Those Radical–Socialists headed by Fernando Valera, Ramón Feced, and above all by Felix Gordón Ordás, were in favour of backing the motion as they, like the Radicals, wanted the socialists out of the government. Following a long and vociferous debate within the parliamentary party on the 24th, the pro-government supporters squeezed home by 21 votes to 18 with 3 abstentions.[21] The Azaña administration had been saved, but only just.

However, the Cabinet's calvary over Casas Viejas was not yet over. Five Assault Guards had presented the Radical Party with a statement in which they claimed that the government had instructed them to take no prisoners. "It's a bomb", as one Radical boasted, "that we had in waiting". By the time parliament met again on 2 March, the statement, along with the prospect of the motion of censure, had created enormous expectation. In the Cortes, the opposition speaker, the former Radical–Socialist Juan Botella Asensi, attempted, just like the Radicals on previous occasions, to demonstrate that the shootings in the Cadiz *pueblo* were made inevitable by the government's policies. The Prime Minister thereupon delivered a crushing reply, to which the Radicals failed to respond. Nor did the Radicals disclose the Assault Guards' statement. It appeared that the Radical *jefe*, probably as a result of the premier's redoubtable performance during the debates on Casas Viejas, had developed cold feet. The censure motion was overturned. After all the bravura and bragging in the press and in the corridors of the Cortes, the Radicals had suffered a humiliating defeat. Worse was to follow. The next day, 3 March, Guerra del Río tried once again to link the Cabinet to the killings, but the Prime Minister, in his own words, left him "KO". The Radical leader then rose to disown both Guerra del Río's speech and the Assault Guards' statement, before announcing that he would not speak again on the subject of Casas Viejas. In other words, Lerroux had discredited his own opposition. Five days later, the Prime Minister informed the chamber that Captain Rojas had confessed to carrying out the shootings on the orders not of the Cabinet but of the Director General of Security, Arturo Menéndez. On 15 March, the parliamentary commission of investigation also absolved the government of any direct responsibility. Still, on 15 and 16 March, the Radicals, in the shape of Ricardo Samper, attempted once again to prove otherwise. Kept alive for a month and a half by the opposition, the Casas

Viejas debates finally drew to a close on the 16th. The final vote was a triumph for the Azaña administration with 210 deputies backing it while the opposition, along with five Radical–Socialists, abstained.[22]

The tragedy of Casas Viejas crystallized many of the challenges confronting the Republic. Clearly the initial hopes of agrarian and labour reform under the regime had not been met. Exploited by the landowners and in particular by "The One-Eyed Man", José Vela (held responsible by many locals for both the rising and the repression), it was no coincidence that many people in Casas Viejas had abandoned the reformist UGT for the revolutionary CNT the previous year. Nor had the regime achieved enough in relation to the security forces. It was bitterly ironic that the massacre should have been perpetuated by the Assault Guards, the body created in the aftermath of the May events of 1931 precisely in order to avoid the habitual excesses of the Civil Guard. Casas Viejas also highlighted the Republic's failure to integrate the anarcho–syndicalists. In 1931, the republican–socialist administrations had eschewed the possibility of reaching a modus vivendi with the CNT's moderate leadership. Thereafter, the republican state had regarded the anarcho–syndicalist movement as little more than a problem of public order. Most damagingly of all, Casas Viejas was widely perceived by contemporaries as a failure of the Azaña administration's democratic promise. The tragedy effectively stripped away much of the Republic's moral superiority. Casas Viejas therefore became a symbol of the regime's inability to meet the high, if often unrealistic, expectations placed in it.[23]

The calamity of Casas Viejas marked a watershed in the history of the Azaña administration. Henceforth, it would be widely known as the "Government of Casas Viejas", a smear which would undoubtedly contribute to the electoral defeat of the left republicans and socialists later that year. Responsibility for this collective change in perception lay overwhelmingly with the opposition, but the government's own shortcomings, including the sluggish investigation, should not be ignored. In particular, the Prime Minister's self-righteous insistence that the government's responsibility was limited to the purely judicial, rather than political or moral, sphere was a grievous misjudgement of the national mood. The right had predictably taken advantage of the affair to attack the ruling coalition, but arguably the foremost role lay with the Radicals. Yet their eagerness to torpedo the ruling majority over "Casas Viejas" proved devastatingly counterproductive as it prolonged the life of the Constituent Cortes while poisoning relations with the left republicans. Furthermore, the Radicals' opportunistic campaign did much to tarnish the reputation of the regime which they purported to defend. In this sense, the Radical Party, too, was a victim of Casas Viejas.

Bloodied but unbowed, the Radicals and their allies tried to end the Constituent Cortes by striking a deal with the majority parties. The opposition statement issued on 31 March proposed that the two remaining laws complementary to the Constitution, the bill of Congregations and that relating to the Court of Constitutional Guarantees, should be passed without obstruction as long as parliament, if the President considered it appropriate, was then dissolved. Several ministers suspected that this move would not have been taken without the tacit approval of Alcalá-Zamora. In fact, the President himself had suggested to Martínez Barrio, in a private meeting on 17 March, that if the Radicals left three particular bills unopposed, a Cabinet reshuffle, "going as far as the dissolution of the Cortes", could take place. Alcalá-Zamora's proposal had been considered by the Radical National Executive Committee, but its conditions, including the suspension of the municipal elections and the presentation of no further bills, led the President to desist. Still, the tacit collaboration which had emerged over the bill of Congregations had been subtly strengthened. The statement of 31 March did not involve the President, but the opposition had been able to take advantage of his misgivings. The Radicals and the President had become, in effect, accomplices. However, the statement came to nothing. The Cabinet called Alcalá-Zamora's bluff by asking him to renew his vote of confidence. Too wily for such a manoeuvre, the President did so, thereby taking the wind out of the opposition's sails.[24]

One of the principal spurs for the Radical opposition since December 1932 was the prospect of a resounding defeat in the April municipal elections. On the one hand, the party faced a republican–socialist coalition that enjoyed official backing, and, on the other, a resurgent right that would benefit greatly from the introduction of the female suffrage. By contrast, the Radical Party could only count on the support of the relatively weak conservative republican parties. The Radicals were terrified, at heart, that the elections would expose their claim that the country was divorced from the government. The Catalan elections of November 1932, in which the Radicals had been trounced by the Esquerra, had already dented their credibility on this score. Their anxiety was reflected in doom-laden prophesies of apocalyptic proportions should the elections go ahead. In January, Martínez Barrio solemnly declared that nothing less than civil war might break out if they were held. By mid February, he was averring that, with the republicans in "distinct fronts" and the regime's enemies – that is to say, the right – united, the very existence of the Republic would be placed in jeopardy. By March, the Radical leader was deploying language which was just as dramatic. "The civil war will come," he predicted, "and fascism will burst forth." The elections, he insisted, "make me fear for the Republic": whereas the right would triumph in the cities, the republican–socialist alliance, in order to avoid a repetition in the countryside, would impose its victory through violence. By the end of March, Martínez Barrio was denouncing the municipal poll as a "great mistake" and "serious provocation" which would cause the definitive rupture of relations between the republicans while playing into the hands of the regime's enemies. The Radical leader, for his part, reiterated that "I fear a civil war in the cities and in the countryside a social war".[25]

These alarmist predictions, designed to help force a change in government or at least to abort the elections, revealed the Radicals' fear of the right. This did not concern the monarchists, whose impotence had been highlighted by the failure of the "Sanjurjada", but the non-republicans. Through the incorporation of numerous provincial parties and electoral committees, Acción Popular, established in October 1931, had become the cornerstone of a broad coalition of right-wing forces. The new formation, known by the acronym CEDA (Confederación Española de Derechas Autónomas), held its founding congress between 28 February and 5 March 1933. The leadership was largely from the professional middle classes, but much of the rank-and-file was made up of landowners. The CEDA was a formidable force not only because it had managed to bring together small and middling landowners alongside large ones within the same party, but also because it had forged an alliance of rural and urban property owners. The CEDA was also set apart from the republican parties by its extensive mobilization of women. Almost half the Madrid party, for example, was said to comprise women. Overall, the CEDA boasted 700,000 members, considerably more than any other party. Only the socialist and anarcho–syndicalist trade unions, at their peak, had more members. The Republic, in short, had given birth to the first mass Catholic party in Spanish history. The regression of the right in 1931 had already, in early 1933, given way to resurgence.[26]

Underpinned in part by the ideological, financial, and organizational resources of the agrarian associations, which provided the party with many of its leaders, including José María Gil Robles, the CEDA was above all a creature of the Catholic church. The emergence of first Acción Popular and then the CEDA was in large measure a reaction to the anti-clerical provisions of the 1931 Constitution. Both aimed to rally Catholic opinion around the banner of constitutional revision. Only the ample appeal of Catholicism could bring together such a wide array of social and political forces under the same roof. For the Catholic right, religion and property were, as synthesized in the party slogan of "Religion, Motherland, Order, Family and Property", the twin pillars of State and society. A minority within the Confederación, including Manuel Giménez Fernández, a young law professor from Seville, was in favour of declaring the party's allegiance to the Republic, but the majority, like Acción Popular, adopted the Vatican-inspired doctrine of accidentalism, a formula that permitted Catholic parties to operate within republican regimes without denying either their faith or, even, their monarchism.[27]

Gil Robles later admitted that "the immense majority of the members of Acción Popular were decidedly monarchist", adding that nearly all of them felt an "invincible repugnance" at the idea of declaring themselves republicans. The question as to the CEDA's real nature and aims has been vigorously debated by historians and political scientists alike. Despite the dynastic sentiment that prevailed within the party, the restoration of the monarchy was not necessarily its fundamental objective, in part because of the extreme unpopularity of such a move. The CEDA's overriding goal – in the medium term at least – was the reform of the Constitution. Beyond that, the party aimed to supplant republican democracy by an authoritarian regime based on corporatist, Catholic principles. It has been suggested that the Estado Novo in Portugal provided the most apposite model. In practice, the Cedistas identified themselves most readily with Dollfuss's regime in Austria, while being less enthusiastic towards Nazi Germany and fascist Italy. Certainly the CEDA was not a fascist formation, but its fascination with fascism, as shown by the leadership's visits to Hitler's Germany and Mussolini's Italy, and the apeing of certain traits, including the adulation of Gil Robles as "the Jefe", made its stance equivocal. Unlike the Radical Party, the CEDA renounced both parliamentary democracy and the secular state. Consequently the eruption of the CEDA onto the political scene marked a profound cleavage not just within the middle classes, but within the Republic itself. As a result, the new, accidentalist right represented a colossal challenge to the consolidation of the regime.[28]

The Radical press reacted to the creation of the CEDA with undisguised horror. An El Progreso editorial of 10 March 1933, titled "The Reactionaries on the March", denounced the CEDA as "the fascist formation". "They are the same old lot", it continued, "that come back to life; the defenders of the altar and of the throne; those that yearn for the Inquisition; the rebels of other times who return to defend their hateful privileges which they see are in danger; to renew the civil war. This is the emergence of fascism". Radical deputy Juan Palau denounced "this resurgence of the troglodyte", warning cataclysmically that if they triumphed in the April elections the result would be "the most brutal and antihuman reaction that the peoples of the present modern era have known".[29] It was clear that the CEDA, given its redoubtable resources, represented a serious threat to the Radical Party as a conservative alternative to the Azaña administration. The Radicals' alarmist forecasts in relation to the April municipal elections, motivated in large part by the rise of the right, were largely quelled by the announcement at the end of March that the municipal poll would only cover those local councils affected by article 29, along with those replaced by steering committees in October 1932. Still, the elections involved just under a quarter of Spain's 81,099 councillors, though only 12.89 per cent of the voters. The great majority of constituencies were small, rural localities, above all in Aragon, the two Castilles, and Navarre, which had invariably been under the hegemony of monarchist *caciques* prior to the Republic. For the Radicals, the elections at least had the advantage of taking place in the wake of the Casas Viejas scandal. Even more favourably situated was the right given the recent, high-profile launch of the CEDA, the introduction of the women's suffrage, and the fact that the bill on Congregations was currently being subject to heated parliamentary debate. The Radicals felt acutely threatened by the rejuvenation of the right. *El Progreso* stressed that the right's organization "is perfect" and in particular that its mobilization of the women's vote "is difficult to counteract on the part of our republican women" on the grounds that "the numerical struggle is unequal and the means and resources inferior". Lerroux, too, drew attention to the fact that "the imponderable elements" possessed "great means of defence and intelligence".[30]

Squeezed by the governing coalition to the left and by the CEDA and its allies to the right, the Radicals expressed their willingness at a rally in early April to reach an electoral understanding with the left republicans. Rebuffed at the national level, the Radical Party managed to join forces with them in certain provinces, such as Badajoz, while in others, such as Albacete, Huesca, Zaragoza and to an extent in Toledo it ran alongside the non-republican right. In the majority of cases, the Radicals either stood alone or else with the conservative republicans. Despite the overall weakness of their alliances, the Radicals won more seats than any other republican party: Acción Republicana obtained 1059, the Conservative Republicans of Miguel Maura 1345, and the PRRS 1649, while the Radicals captured 2475. Surprisingly, the Radicals also exceeded the socialists, at 1875. "Crushing victory of the Radical Party," exclaimed *El Progreso* jubilantly. However, the Radical-based coalition, at 4206 seats, did not surpass the republican–socialist one, which totalled 5048. Had the Catalan elections not been delayed the difference in favour of the ruling majority would have been greater still. Moreover, the real victor of the April elections was a reborn right, which overhauled the republican opposition and nearly the government, too, with its 4954 councillors. The Radicals' forebodings in relation to the right had proven well founded. Indeed, the Radical press was to claim that the party had saved the Republic from the "regime's enemies" and was to draw on the resurgence of the right – blamed on the socialists – as an additional motive for the formation of an all-republican government. "No more socialist tutelage! Resignation!", trumpeted *El Progreso*. If not, it warned, the Socialist Party would "ruin the Republic". Overall, the April elections had demonstrated the strength of the Radical Party while highlighting the weakness of its coalition partners. The Radicals must also have been concerned at the fact that they had triumphed in their pre-1931 strongholds, such as Aragon and Valencia, but had made limited headway in new areas.[31]

Following the impressive electoral performance of the right, the republican opposition called on the Azaña administration to reach a truce. On 2 May, the government proposed a cessation in hostilities that would require the passing of two remaining laws complementary to the Constitution along with the bills on Public Order and Rural Leases. The Radicals, Federals, and independent republicans accepted the proposal, but a minority comprising the Conservative Republicans, Progressives, and extremist republicans led by Botella Asensi rejected it. Rather than impose a majority decision, the Radical Party went along with the objectors. In effect, the Radicals upheld the opposition while trying to distance themselves from it.[32] Having failed to secure a truce, the government attempted to accelerate passage of the Congregations bill by guillotining article 31 and by then fusing the remaining ones into a single article. Nevertheless, the ruling majority had to tread warily as it did not want to provide the opposition with a pretext to withdraw from parliament. This would not only hand the right a major propaganda coup but could even result in the dissolution of the Constituent Cortes given the serious misgivings of the President in relation to the bill – who, as the final vote loomed, became "almost insane, tearful, agitated". During the debate on the Congregations bill, the Radicals had defended the government's original measure as this conflicted with the position taken by the parliamentary commission, thereby placing the Cabinet in a difficult position. In the process, they appeared to be taking advantage of confidential information: the fact that the President was secretly opposed to the commission draft. This impression was heightened by the Radical leader's confident assertion in parliament that the Azaña administration would fall as a result of the intervention of the head of state. Finally, on 17 May, the Congregations bill was passed into law by a margin of 228 votes, including those of the Radical Party, which had done so much to impede it. The defence given by Salazar Alonso of its volte-face added further weight to the speculation that the Radicals had been collaborating with the President.[33]

In fact, the opposition of the Radicals *had* benefited from the collusion of the President. As if to confirm the rumours, on 31 May, in the midst of the delay in signing the Congregations bill, Martínez Barrio paid him a visit, a fact that was widely commented upon in political circles. Some Radicals were to boast as a result that the government's days were numbered. It seemed that the Radicals, thwarted in their endeavours to overthrow the republican–socialist majority in parliament, had fallen back on a brace of ploys that were strongly reminiscent of the monarchy: namely, by appealing over the head of the Cortes to the chief of state and by taking advantage of the confidential indications of the President in order to make their opposition more effective. However, the Radicals were not alone. Miguel Maura, too, expected a change in Cabinet to come about through Alcalá-Zamora's intervention. Many republican politicians clearly regarded the President much as their dynastic predecessors had the king. The Prime Minister, distressed at the resurrection of such modes, lamented in his diary that "all the present problems derive from men of the regime".[34]

By now, however, the Radical opposition had become heavily discredited. Not only had the party failed to achieve its objective of bringing the government down, but it had also undermined the stability of both the Constituent Cortes and the regime through its often unprincipled attacks on the ruling majority and its collaboration with the President. Yet the Radicals continued to count on the sympathies of the head of state. In the last week of May, Martínez Barrio proposed a limited truce to the Prime Minister, adding that once it was over "we shall see what winds blow" – an indication that the Radicals hoped, or perhaps even had the assurance, that the President would then intervene. It is ironic that Martínez Barrio himself later recognized that the party was "disposed to sacrifice whatever was necessary in order to overthrow the government".[35]

Predictably, the Law of Congregations outraged the Catholic community. On 2 June the bishops of Spain issued a declaration against the measure. The following day Pope Pious XI added to the clamour by publishing an encyclical, the "Dilectissima nobis", which was even more explicit in its condemnation. The new Law was undoubtedly a tremendous boost to the Catholic right's campaign in favour of constitutional revision. Like article 26 of the Constitution, the Law of Congregations was too extreme and too prompt a measure for the Republic's own good. Rather than advance the consolidation of the regime, this latest anticlerical initiative played into the hands of the Catholic right.[36] As a Catholic, a conservative, and a constitutional revisionist, President Alcalá-Zamora had done his utmost, short of dissolving the Constituent Cortes – including collaborating obliquely with the opposition – to impede the Law. He had registered his disapproval by delaying its signing until 3 June. The outcry from the right and in particular the criticism directed at him by the Catholic community mortified him. The Law brought relations between Alcalá-Zamora and Azaña, always awkward and distrustful, to their nadir. Worse still, the Catholic protest coincided with a resurgence of the Radical–Socialist dissidence at the party Congress, which began on 3 June. The rebels' stance was defended by Gordón Ordás in a Castro-like oration of six hours' length in which he called for the socialists to collaborate from the opposition and for the government to resign, while Marcelino Domingo defended the continuity of the Azaña administration. In the end, a split was avoided, but the conflict still threatened the ruling majority. The Prime Minister chose this moment to change his Cabinet, partly to restructure the unwieldy Ministry of Agriculture, Industry and Commerce, but mainly because the Minister of the Economy, Jaume

Carner, was dying of cancer. The President signalled his lack of support
for the government by opening fullscale consultations. The Cabinet duly
resigned.[37]

"There is no solution but me. Power is almost in our hands", confided
the Radical leader to a colleague once the government stepped down. The
President, who sought a broader Cabinet that would undertake a change
in political direction, first turned to the ruling majority and in particular
its largest parliamentary group, the PSOE. Julián Besteiro, despite being
an outspoken opponent of the party's government collaboration and the
fact that he did not enjoy the support of the socialist deputies, was initially
approached, but predictably declined. Next, another socialist, Indalecio
Prieto, was entrusted with the task of forming an administration that
embraced the Radicals. Both the PRRS and Acción Republicana backed
the endeavour, in the belief that this would discredit the Radical Party's
opposition, but Largo Caballero refused to share power with the Radicals.
More importantly, he persuaded the PSOE's Executive Committee, by a
vote of 28 to 13, of his stance. In all likelihood, the Radicals would have
turned the offer down as participation in a socialist-led administration
would have contradicted their entire opposition campaign. The gauntlet
was then taken up by the Radical–Socialist Marcelino Domingo, but,
having gained the collaboration of Acción Republicana, he fell at the
second hurdle by failing to win over the Federals.[38]

Parliamentary logic dictated that the President should finally have
turned to the largest opposition party, the Radical Party, to form a government. Yet he did not. Lerroux had made it plain that, if asked to establish
a Cabinet, he would aim to form an all-republican one that would dissolve
the Constituent Cortes before too long. Clearly, Alcalá-Zamora did not
yet want to forego one of his two opportunities to dissolve parliament.
That said, it is hard to understand why the President, given that relations
between the government and the opposition made a significant variation
on the Azaña administration extremely unlikely, provoked the crisis at all
if he was not prepared to bring the Cortes to an end. Unless, of course,
the aim of the reshuffle – as the search for an alternative Cabinet from
within the ruling majority reveals – was to eliminate Manuel Azaña from
the premiership. The failure of this ploy forced Alcalá-Zamora back on
Azaña, whom he instructed to assemble a Cabinet irrespective of whether
or not he was able to broaden its base. In the event, Azaña won over both
the Federals and the Esquerra. In accordance with the President's instructions, he also approached the Radical leader but Lerroux, in an act of
conceit, had left Madrid for his estate at San Rafael.[39] In his absence,
Azaña told Martínez Barrio that he wished to incorporate the Radicals
into a republican–socialist Cabinet. As Martínez Barrio retorted that the
Radicals would only form part of an all-republican administration, Azaña
tried a different tack: would the Radicals, he inquired, take part in a

republican–socialist government if he got the PSOE to agree? He added that the government's programme had to be completed before the relationship with the socialists could be reconsidered. Always his goal, this had been "hampered and delayed" by "everyone"; first by the left republicans' fall-out over the FIRPE and then by the Radicals' obstruction. The socialists, as even they recognized, had to leave, but, he clarified, "not expelled nor deceived; it is simply a question of timing". In reply, Martínez Barrio suggested that the Radicals could prop up an all-republican administration from the outside, but this would reduce the government parties to 135 deputies – an unappealing prospect. In any case, Lerroux later informed Azaña that he could not take up the offer as he would be unable to justify it to public opinion. An impasse had been reached. While the Radicals were not prepared to share power with the socialists, the left republicans were not prepared to do without them. The crisis, artificial and unnecessary as it was, had none the less highlighted the shortcomings of the Radicals' opposition. They had failed to secure the establishment of an all-republican administration. Neither had they brought forward the dissolution of the Cortes. On the contrary, this had been delayed by the Radical opposition. It could be argued that the Radicals' obstruction had not only been counterproductive but that, through its opportunism, it had also brought discredit on the Republic itself.[40]

Azaña's aspirations for his third administration were to round off the legislative programme, oversee the partial elections in October and the municipal ones in November, and, having passed the budget, give way to an all-republican government before the year was out. This would allow time to head off the growing radicalism within the socialist ranks and prepare the general election on the basis of a "pact of non-aggression" with the PSOE. The main legislative goal was to pass into law the measures complementary to the Agrarian Reform Law as outlined by the Minister of Agriculture before the Cortes on 20 June. This included a Law of Communal Goods, the creation of a National Agrarian Bank, and, above all, a new Lease Law, a potentially far-reaching measure. Once the Cortes reconvened, the Conservative Republican Party, as a mark of its disgust at the reshuffle's outcome, promptly withdrew. By contrast, the Radical leader recognized that the all-out obstruction had been defeated and announced the adoption of a "normal" oppositional stance. As a result, the Radicals abstained over the motion of confidence, rather than vote against the government. Thereon, they would often aid the ruling coalition. Nor did they second the indefatigable opposition of the Agrarians to the Lease bill.[41]

It was ironic that the new Azaña administration, having disarmed the Radical obstruction, was confronted from the outset by an ever-widening opposition front. Of crucial importance was the fact that the economy reached its nadir under the Republic during the summer of 1933.

Unemployment rose sharply not only as a result of the economic crisis, but also due to the exhaustion of public works funds and the fact that the emigration of the 1920s – 277,000 from 1920 to 1929 – gave way to immigration as more than 100,000 people entered Spain from 1931 to 1933.[42] According to the authorities, unemployment climbed from 446,263 in June 1932 to 618,947 by the end of 1933, though the real figure, given the manifold inadequacies of the official statistics, was much higher, probably as much as double. Its impact was greatly aggravated by the lack of a comprehensive social security system. More than half those without work were from the rural economy, while construction and mining were also gravely affected. Escalating unemployment, together with chronic structural underemployment, radicalized relations between workers and employers in the urban and rural arenas alike. The fight over an ever-shrinking job market further heightened tension between the unions, which embraced the Communist and Catholic sindicates as well as the UGT and the CNT. Hit by the cutbacks of the *patronal*, the impotence of the state, and the rivalry between the unions, the workers fell back increasingly on the strike weapon to protect themselves. Stoppages, having remained at roughly the same level between 1930 and 1932, soared from under 450 in 1932 to over one thousand in 1933. The strikes' extension and duration also augmented as 14 million days were lost in 1933, compared to between three and four million days per annum over the previous three years. Unemployment alone cannot explain the extensive mobilization of workers during the summer of 1933. Many had become sorely disillusioned by the shortcomings in the application of the labour and agrarian legislation. For others, by contrast, the burgeoning agitation reflected their rising expectations as urban wages climbed from a level of 107 in 1930 to 124 in 1933 and rural ones by at least a third in unionized areas.[43] Such tensions naturally sharpened the confrontation between the CNT and UGT. Often regarded as having reached its zenith during the summer of 1933, the CNT, as Julián Casanova has stressed, had in fact been losing members since 1931. Its fall is inseparable from the rise to power of the FAI and other radicals within the CNT. Thus the thousands of affiliates lost to the movement in 1932 and 1933 from traditional industrial sectors were not compensated for by those won amongst construction workers and the unemployed. In Madrid, the CNT may have grown at the expense of the UGT, but in strongholds such as Barcelona, Seville, Valencia, and Zaragoza the anarcho–syndicalists gave ground to the socialist trade unions. The ascendancy of the FAI and other extremists along with the defensiveness born of the movement's decline contributed significantly to worker mobilization in the summer of 1933.[44]

Mushrooming labour agitation and the deteriorating economic situation naturally shaped the most intensive period of *patronal* protest so far. Under the Republic the employers had set about defending their interests not only by rejuvenating existing organizations but also by founding new ones. The Federación Económica de Andalucia (FEDA), established in November 1931 and affiliated to the Confederación Patronal Española, was a prime example. Based in Seville, where the organized working class was divided between the CNT, the UGT, and the Communist Party's most important redoubt in Spain, the Federación was one of the most combative *patronal* associations in the country. During the first months of 1933 Seville was engulfed by a wave of violence, including assassinations by bombs and "*pistoleros*", as the CNT and the Communists battled for control of the city's workers. In March, the FEDA informed the government that, unless it intervened, the local economy would be ruined by a combination of the recession, strikes, and union terrorism. Two months later, still in the grip of a "spiral of terror", the city was hit by the stoppage of the public services, the closure of shops, and a general strike by the CNT and Communists. Over a thousand Sevillian businessmen and shopkeepers stormed Madrid on 7 May in order to register their protest. A delegation met the Prime Minister, the President, as well as Alejandro Lerroux, Miguel Maura, and Gil Robles, although a march through the centre of the capital was banned by the authorities. Back in Seville, the FEDA held a major rally on 19 May, but, the next day, the unions struck back by murdering the association's general secretary, Pedro Caravaca. His funeral, attended by 15,000 people, was converted into an anti-government demonstration. The FEDA's vigorous campaign of protest was a salient illustration of the pressure applied to the government by the *patronal* during the summer of 1933.[45]

Aside from the enforcement of law and order, the overriding grievance of the *patronal* was the socialist-inspired labour legislation, especially the mixed juries. First, the employers complained that the juries, whose casting vote lay with a ministerially-appointed president (invariably a socialist), were politically biased. The fact that in 1933 22,670 of their verdicts were favourable to the workers and about half that number, 12,165, to the employers provided the *patronal* with further ammunition. Second, the mixed juries, designed to institutionalize the power of the socialist trade unions to the detriment of the anarcho–syndicalist movement, were criticized by the employers for making relations with the CNT even more conflictive. Lastly, many businesses, especially small and medium-sized ones, protested that the contractual obligations established by the juries were simply beyond their means. A leading dispute in Madrid, for example, centred on the new regulations approved for the clothes' industry by the Minister of Labour in early 1933. The *patronal* rejected the proposed changes on the grounds that they simply could not be met. The resistance of the employers resulted in the arrest of their representatives, causing an uproar amongst business circles. Yet at a meeting of 18 July, the *patronal* still maintained that the new measures would ruin them.[46]

Like the urban employers, the landowners either revamped old associations or set up new ones in order to meet the challenge of the Republic. The Confederación Española Patronal Agrícola (CEPA), for instance, was created in response to the Law of Associations of April 1932. The CEPA, like the FEDA, lobbied the government vigorously throughout 1933. The main target of the Confederación, whose founding manifesto declared unequivocally "Socialism is the enemy . . . War to those who brought us the war!", was the labour legislation. The negotiations over the new labour contracts, made even more fraught by forecasts of a poor harvest and the recession in certain export sectors, led the CEPA to mount a campaign which climaxed with a rally in Madrid of 14,000 farmers from Guadalajara, Cuenca, Toledo, and Ciudad Real. At the Unión Económica Congress of March 1933 the agrarian associations were able to voice their concerns in common with the *patronal*. Urban and rural property-owners alike, having predictably reserved their most vehement attacks for the socialists on account of their reforms and for having allegedly ruined the economy, called for the overhaul of the entire gamut of agrarian and labour measures and in particular for the revision of the Agrarian Reform Law.[47]

The zenith of the *patronal*'s campaign against the government, coinciding with the peak of the labour agitation, was the Unión Económica's nationwide Congress in July 1933. This was at once a demonstration of the urban employers' strength and weakness. On the one hand, there were, Mercedes Cabrera has calculated, "more than a thousand" associations represented. On the other hand, there was a patent lack of unity within their ranks. Some backed the reform of the *jurados mixtos*, while others demanded their overthrow. Some urged the establishment of a Unión General de Patronos (thereby replicating the centralized structure of the Unión General de Trabajadores), while others defended a Coordinating Committee of extant entities. In the end, the moderates triumphed. The assembly limited itself, therefore, to lobbying for the modification of the *jurados mixtos* (though the employers declared their readiness, should their petition not be met, to undertake other means – "whatever their gravity and transcendence"), and to set up a coordinating body rather than an all-embracing employers' association. In the same spirit, a motion calling for the socialists' ejection from the government was rejected as violating the a-politicism of the *patronal*.[48]

Even since the Radical Party had gone into opposition in December 1931, the *patronal* and the Radicals had powerfully reinforced one another's critique of the Azaña administration. The centrepiece of the *patronal*'s protest – namely, that there was no popular or constitutional mandate for the "socialization" of the economy – was echoed by the Radicals' charge that the *pueblo* had voted for the Republic to be governed by republicans, not socialists. Both the employers and the Radicals held the socialists largely responsible for the deleterious state of the economy, for the alleged lack of political stability, and for much of the public disorder. For the *patronal* and Radical Party alike, the socialists were the quintessential cause of the Republic's woes. The identification between the Radicals and the business world was not merely ideological. Martínez Barrio, for example, addressed the FEDA in May. More importantly, Salazar Alonso gave a speech at the Unión Económica Congress in March in which he criticized the Agrarian Reform Law as destined to "destroy the national wealth".[49]

However, the proximity of the Radicals to the *patronal* should not be overdrawn. It should be stressed that the Radical Party was not a mere conduit for the grievances of the employers' associations. In relation to the Unión Económica Congress in March 1933, for example, the Radical leader observed that he shared "many" of its concerns, but added revealingly that it was neither in his party's interests nor that of the employers themselves for the Radical Party to adopt the Assembly's resolutions. The Radicals kept their distance partly to avoid restrictive electoral commitments, but largely because of the heterogeneous, if not contradictory, nature of their social base. The Radical Party did not want to forfeit its working class following, prominent in Valencia but also evident in other provinces. In March 1933, for example, the *jefe* addressed the Radical Workers' Centre in Madrid. Though the speech was of limited national importance, it was still included in the party's lavishly-produced anniversary album, the *Libro de Oro* of 1935, as proof of the party's commitment to the workers. Moreover, the Radicals' marriage of convenience with the anarcho–syndicalists still retained a certain validity, as shown by Lerroux's appeal to them in his speech before the Cortes of 3 February 1933. It would seem, in conclusion, that the Radicals did not want to limit their inter-classist appeal unnecessarily by identifying themselves too closely with any one socio-economic group. Underlying this, of course, lay the Radicals' view of themselves as mediators in the class war who sought to strike a centrist balance between the extremes of untrammelled capitalism and revolutionary collectivism. This explains why Lerroux went out of his way at the business lunch at the Barcelona Ritz in February 1932 to underline the importance of obtaining "social justice" for the working class.[50]

None the less, the Radical Party, more than any other republican force, gave voice to the concerns of the urban employers. Indeed, the Radical opposition campaign and that of the *patronal* were to reinforce one another constantly throughout the first half of 1933. Their protest was to be amplified by its merger into an ever-wider opposition front that eventually embraced the non-republican right, the conservative republicans, the moderate regional nationalists, the CNT, and the Radical–Socialist dissidents. Neither the Radical Party nor the *patronal*, in contrast to the agrarian associations and the anarcho–syndicalist workers, was anti-republican or even necessarily anti-government, but anti-socialist. Together, they represented a swathe of public opinion which the government ignored at its peril. The danger to the Republic was that the *patronal*, still dominated by moderates, would shift to the right in search of greater protection and, eventually, become disenchanted with the regime itself. The Prime Minister's diaries reveal that, in the worst year so far for the republican economy, he did not attach a great deal of importance to the grievances of the *patronal*. Yet a balance had to be struck over the labour reforms, especially the heavily-politicized mixed juries, for the sake of the regime's stability. The *patronal*'s summer campaign not only magnified the opposition of the Radicals but also fomented the hostility towards the socialists within Radical–Socialist ranks. The PRRS dissidents were led by Felix Gordón Ordás, a veterinary surgeon from Leon who had at one time been active in the Radical Party. He was also President of the Alianza de Labradores, one of the few republican agrarian associations, having clashed earlier in the year with the Minister of Agriculture, fellow Radical–Socialist Marcelino Domingo, over the Lease bill. The programme drawn up by the Radical–Socialist rebels in the aftermath of the June Cabinet reshuffle, which called for the "immediate overthrow" of the Law of *términos municipales*, the liberty of employment (a reference to the UGT's grip on the rural labour market at the expense of the CNT), and the strict neutrality of the *jurados mixtos*, strongly echoed the demands of the *patronal*. The demand that local councils, especially in Andalusia and Extremadura, should be subject to financial inspection was also a response to the complaints of the business sector regarding socialist authorities. Yet the Radicals and Radical–Socialist dissidents were drawn together not just by a common concern for the interests of the employers but for that of the middle classes as a whole. "The Spanish middle class," as the Radical deputy Diego Hidalgo wrote to a colleague, "has for the time being just about requested a 'divorce' from the Republic." Amongst the middle classes there was a deeply-entrenched belief that under the new regime they had lost out to the socialist working class. The mounting dissidence within the PRRS was one more sign that middle-class opinion was shifting against the Azaña administration.[51]

The Radical–Socialist dissidence gathered momentum with the presentation of their own programme-of-government to the PRRS parliamentary party on 14 June. Despite the fact that the rebels did not command a majority amongst the deputies – in contrast to the National Executive Committee – the programme was approved, with slight modifications, on 5 July. Two days later, Gordón Ordás delivered the alternative agenda to the Prime Minister on the understanding that the continuation of the PRRS in the government depended on acceptance of the rebels' demands. The dissidence went a stage further the following day when they took part in a public meeting at Eibar in the Basque country alongside not just the Radicals but also a Federalist and even a member of Acción Republicana. For the Radicals, this represented, in Martínez Barrio's words, "the beginning of an agreement". Moreover, all the speakers called for an all-republican administration. Shortly afterwards, the Radical–Socialist dissidents buttressed their position still further as Gordón Ordás was elected President of the National Executive Committee and, on 13 July, Alvaro de Albornoz bid farewell to both the government and active politics to become President of the Court of Constitutional Guarantees. Ten days later, Gordón Ordás gave a high-profile speech in Madrid that echoed the opposition claims of the Radical Party more strongly than ever. He not only called for the re-establishment of authority and for the modification of the labour and agrarian legislation, but he also vowed to fight the "socialist dictatorship" while urging the republicans to unite around a minimum programme of government. It was a speech which could have been delivered by the Radical leader himself.[52]

The republican–socialist administration was not only being undermined by the schism within the PRRS but also by the President, who, bitterly resentful at Azaña's return to power, had renewed his behind-the-scenes contacts with the Radicals. In June, he let the Radical leader know that "the ball is now in your court". As Lerroux observes in his memoirs, Alcalá-Zamora "held the same opinion as the opposition and he invited the latter to proceed". The President also let Martínez Barrio know that if the socialists left office, he did not want the Radicals to permit Azaña to govern again as "the entire state would enter into crisis". On 24 July, Alcalá-Zamora elaborated on this scheme at his summer residence near Segovia to Martínez Barrio in person. The President proposed to facilitate the creation of an all-republican administration that would not be headed by that "danger" Azaña before granting the Radical leader the decree of dissolution in early 1934. In effect, the President was plotting the government's downfall with the opposition – in clear violation of his mandate.[53]

Events moved fast thereafter. On 26 July, the Radical–Socialist dissidence bore its first fruits as the leaders of the Radical Party, PRRS, Acción Republicana, the Federals, ORGA and of the Catalan republicans agreed to seek "harmony and cordiality within and without the chamber". That same day, Azaña initiated discussion within Acción Republicana over the programme put forward by the Radical–Socialist dissidents. In yet another meeting on the 26th, Sánchez Román, Martínez Barrio, and Gordón Ordás met to elaborate their future strategy. "Union," *El Progreso* predicted, "will be realized probably in the space of a few hours." The next day, 27 July, the Prime Minister and Martínez Barrio exchanged views over the all-republican administration that would replace the republican–socialist one. This flurry of meetings convinced the Radicals that the government was finally about to give way to a strictly republican one. The

Cabinet, *El Progreso* judged, was "floating like a dead body". "Each day," it declared on 28 July, "is the eve of the day of the reshuffle." The government's situation, Salazar Alonso opined, could not be "more critical and more untenable", while Guerra del Río affirmed that the republican "bloc . . . is already formed".[54] Indeed, the Prime Minister himself appeared resigned to a change in Cabinet. Having made the Cortes labour throughout the peak of the summer heat, he was in despair at the sluggish progress made. Neither the ruling majority nor the Minister of Agriculture had so far displayed the vigour and determination necessary to overcome the Agrarians' obstruction to the Lease bill. Criticism of Domingo's performance in Azaña's diary is corruscating. He observes that the Minister's ignorance of agrarian matters "is total", and that he "will do nothing useful".[55] The premier was deeply troubled too at the mounting anti-socialist protest amongst republican circles, not just from within the Radical–Socialist Party but also from within his own party, as well as at the rise of the right and the Machiavellian machinations of the President. As if this was not enough, in July the government lost the support of three leading republican dailies, including *El Sol*. Worse still, they had fallen into the clutches of arch-enemy Juan March. Thus *Luz*'s opinion of the Prime Minister was transformed overnight – he was no longer a "genius", but "stupid". Naturally, the change in ownership benefited the Mallorcan mogul's political allies enormously, foremost amongst whom were the Radicals. By 28 July Azaña had, as recorded in his diary, reached a resolution: "to finish".[56]

Yet the government, despite everything, did not fall. In reality, the republicans still lacked the unity necessary for the establishment of an all-republican administration. First, there was strong resistance from within the republican camp itself to such a government. On 30 July, Marcelino Domingo had replied to Gordón Ordás' speech a week earlier by declaring his unswerving support for the alliance with the socialists. Second, the Prime Minister, his private resolution notwithstanding, was still opposed to a change in the executive. At a second meeting with Gordón Ordás on 27 July, he realized that there had been a fundamental misunderstanding over the Radical–Socialist programme presented to him earlier in the month. Whereas the Prime Minister, advised by the PRRS ministers, believed that the document was merely for discussion, the dissidents viewed it as an ultimatum. The Radical–Socialist ministers were immediately instructed by Azaña to ascertain whether or not the government had their party's unqualified support. On 2 August the Radical–Socialist parliamentary group not only voted for the government, but also, the following day, decided that the programme required further consideration, thereby depriving the document of its status as an ultimatum. The Radical–Socialist dissidence had therefore been dampened, but not defused. In any case, Gordón Ordás's opposition had been undermined by his desire, as publicized at the PRRS's June Congress, to become Prime Minister. He tended, as demonstrated by his attitude to the FIRPE and to other republican leaders during the summer of 1933, to evaluate each situation overwhelmingly in terms of his own personal ambition. This did much to hinder the formation of a common anti-government front. At the meeting of 26 July with Sánchez Román and Martínez Barrio, Gordón Ordás did nothing but "sound us out, advance and retreat". Having failed to formulate a plan, they fell back on the vain hope that the government would fall shortly through a parliamentary defeat. Similarly, Gordón Ordás' speech on 23 July had been flawed by the failure to propose either a framework or a date for the republicans' union.[57]

The republicans' essential problem was that they lacked a common programme or strategy. The collective initiative of 26 July, which merely expressed a generalized desire to cooperate, was stymied by the Prime Minister's rejection of the programme of the Radical–Socialist rebels. Many left republicans did not even agree that an all-republican administration was required. As Azaña asked himself following Domingo's unqualified defence of the socialist alliance on 30 July, "where does this leave the all-republican project?" A final stumbling bloc was the inability of the Prime Minister to reach a compromise with the Radicals. At the meeting of 26 July, Martínez Barrio had urged him to remove the socialists from the government. The Radical deputy leader not only listed the usual arguments in favour of a republican administration, but also warned of a "catastrofe" for the republicans in the November municipal elections if they did not unite. He conceded, nevertheless, that the socialists could not be unceremoniously dumped from the Cabinet and that the government had to fulfil its legislative programme. As a result of this inconclusive exchange, Martínez Barrio had to consult the Radical leader, who, in an effort to reach an agreement, conceded that the prospective republican Cabinet could be headed by Azaña. However, Martínez Barrio was unable to gain access to the Prime Minister until early August, by which stage the latter was no longer interested in a deal, perhaps because the Radical–Socialist dissidence had been quelled in the meantime.[58]

At the epicentre of "that turbulent summer", in Martínez Barrio's words, was the controversy over the socialist movement. The opposition to the socialists, which ranged from the Radicals, CNT, *patronal*, and the forces of the right to the Radical–Socialist dissidents, naturally put the PSOE and UGT on the defensive. Disillusionment had in fact been mounting within socialist ranks since the Congresses of October 1932, partly because of the resistance to their governmental presence but also due to the impact of the economic crisis and the uneven enforcement of the trade union and agrarian legislation. The socialists' anxiety was accentuated by the fact that they had attributed to themselves the pivotal role in the new regime and that they were inclined to identify the latter with their own programme. Correspondingly, they tended to devalue the republicans' contribution and to regard their allies' capacity and loyalty with scepticism. For the socialists, as José Manual Macarro Vera observes, the Republic existed insofar as "it respected the reformist content which they gave it and which they themselves guaranteed with their presence in the government". Largo Caballero, the principal architect of the socialist reforms, did not defend the Republic as a democratic regime on principle but merely as a means by which the socialist movement could win support, entrench themselves within the state, and thereby advance towards socialism. It was this essentially corporatist philosophy which had led the UGT to collaborate with the Primo de Rivera Dictatorship. Whether the UGT worked within a dictatorship or a democracy, these were simply stages, *El Socialista* explained, in "an intelligent tactic". Indeed, Largo Caballero's reforms of 1931–3 were the continuation of those in the 1920s. The goal of the *Caballeristas*, therefore, was not the establishment of democracy, but the defence and advancement of the interests of the organized working class or, to be more precise, of the socialist working class (the socialists were wont to equate the "workers" and "working class" with themselves, largely as a means of denying legitimacy to the claims of their rivals, principally the CNT). In short, the Republic was a means to an end. Though clearly not the same as the accidentalist doctrine of the CEDA, the *Caballerista* vision shared a similarly instrumentalist view of the Republic.[59]

The socialists had been extremely confident, given the republican–socialist alliance's robust parliamentary majority and the paltry presence of the right, that their programme would be realized during the course of the Constituent Cortes. However, the April 1933 municipal elections, when the right re-emerged as a force to be reckoned with, gave the socialists a glimpse of their own political mortality. As support for the Azaña administration waned during the summer of 1933, they became ever more concerned that the legislature might end before their programme had been completed. It was this prospect which was addressed in August by the socialist leaders at the Socialist Youth's summer school. Julián Besteiro, the first to speak, reiterated his view that the socialists should leave office forthwith. He also urged the movement to eschew the "collective madness" of radicalization. Next, the pragmatic Indalecio Prieto stressed that, given the country's development, there were limits to what the socialists could hope to achieve. In a similar vein to Besteiro, he rejected the parallels draw by left-wingers between the situation in Spain and that in Russia in 1917. Predictably, the most belligerent stance, as manifested in speeches at the Pardiñas Cinema in Madrid on 23 July and at the summer school on 15 August, was that of Largo Caballero. It should be remembered that ever since the Radicals had abandoned the Azaña administration in December 1931, the socialists had occasionally reacted to the calls of the Radicals for an all-republican government with extremist threats. In February 1932, following the Radical leader's speech in the Madrid bullring, Largo Caballero declared that if the republicans ejected the socialists from power before time "they would force us to go to civil war". Eight months later, he had reiterated that if the socialists left office this would be "suicide for the socialist movement and for the entire Spanish nation". In March 1933, Manuel Cordero, an otherwise moderate figure, insisted that "if the Republic and democracy fall into the hands of our enemies they would no longer interest us". Two months earlier, a socialist under-secretary had warned that "we would not let a Lerroux government live for a single day". Such threats assumed a different status altogether in Largo Caballero's speeches in the Pardiñas Cinema and at the summer school. For the socialist leader, the disparate forces that confronted the socialists were simply "the common enemy". According to this reductionist view, their triumph, whether this resulted in the return of the traditional oligarchy, "fascism", or "a dictatorship", amounted to much the same thing. If the "enemy" succeeded in dislodging the socialists from office before their mission had been completed, he declared on 23 July, they would seek "the conquest of power" by one of two routes. Either they would take the parliamentary one – having won a general election, they would rule alone and progress towards socialism within the framework of the Constitution, crushing the inevitably violent reaction of the forces of capitalism along the way – or else take the "revolutionary" one. The latter option, which would be adopted "against our will", would be undertaken only if the socialists considered themselves to have been removed from power unjustly or if the government sought to implant "a dictatorship or fascism". Given Largo Caballero's sensitivity to rank-and-file sentiment, this stance can be viewed as a response to the mounting radicalization of socialist workers throughout 1933. Largo Caballero himself now began to be acclaimed by left-wingers as "the Spanish Lenin", a comparison that did little justice to the Russian revolutionary's intellectual and organizational capabilities but which reflected the growing alienation of the socialists. Despite everything, the socialist minister still believed that the democratic framework established under the Republic represented the best way forward. However, the warning to the republicans was clear; if the socialists were "thrown out of the Constitution" for being "workers, for being socialists, for being a party of class", then they would have to seek power "by other means". Consequently the Azaña administration may have been undermined during the summer of 1933 by the Radical–Socialist dissidents, but Largo Caballero and his supporters threatened to take events much further. The stance of the socialist leader restricted the Prime Minister's room for manoeuvre, while sharpening the already considerable tensions within the ruling majority.[60]

By the end of August, the republican–socialist government had virtually run into the sand. Its key project, the Lease bill, had so far made pitiful
progress. This was due partly to the unyielding opposition of the
Agrarians. "The tenacious obstruction," as Gil Robles later boasted, "not
only impeded the passing of many laws, but also wore down the left-wing
governments extraordinarily." However, the Azaña administration's
shortcomings were also a result of the ineptitude and divisions of the
ruling majority. The minister concerned, Marcelino Domingo, remained
as inhibited and inactive as ever, while the parliamentary commission also
acted as a brake – "more than all the opposition forces together",
according to the Prime Minister – through a combination of the obstinacy
of its President, the dissident Radical–Socialist Ramón Feced, and the
pedantry of the socialist Lucio Martínez Gil. Furthermore, the government deputies were wilting amidst the stifling summer heat. During the
month of August, rarely a hundred were to be found at any one time in
the parliamentary chamber.[61]

On 25 August the Prime Minister himself reminded the left republican
and socialist deputies in the Cortes that the government's continuity
depended on them. Yet on the last day of the month there were only 14
Radical–Socialists, 82 Socialists, and less than half the premier's own
party present. The ruling coalition, in fact, was in a precarious state. Many
Galician deputies were up in arms at the proposed commercial treaty with
Uruguay as this would favour the wine and olive oil industries of the centre
and south of Spain at the expense of the cattle-breeders in the north.
Simultaneously, the Catalans were outraged over the latest valuation of
the powers to be transferred from Madrid to Catalonia. To make matters
worse, the Radical–Socialist dissidents returned to the fray. On 9 August
the National Executive Committee not only declared the agreements taken
by the parliamentary party on 2 and 3 August to be null and void but also
called for a Special Congress. These decisions, however, were contested
by the parliamentary party. As a result, a prolonged process of consultation with the regional bodies was initiated. The future of the PRRS, and
of its support for the republican–socialist administration, was clearly in
the balance. As if that was not enough, the socialists' own fidelity to the
government was weakening as a result of the growing clamour against
them. Besieged from without by the Radicals, the right, the CNT, and the
patronal, and undermined from within by the Radical–Socialists, the
ORGA, and Catalans, the Azaña administration found itself on the defensive. Having completed the bulk of its programme, the government's
continuity was now in jeopardy. A constructive solution to the crisis
would have been to negotiate the exit of the socialists from power so that
an all-republican administration could be formed. On the one hand, the
socialists would have been placed outside the government, but not necessarily outside the ruling majority – this would depend on the deal struck

with the republicans. On the other hand, a strictly republican government would have had the undoubted advantage of attracting the moderate, hitherto disenchanted, middle classes, thereby providing the regime with a greater measure of stability. The Prime Minister himself was well aware of the possibility that the Radicals, if perpetually spurned by the left republicans, might turn to the right in the search for allies. However, blinded by his own ambitions and goals, he did little to prevent it. Nor did the Radical *jefe*, absent for most of the summer from Madrid, do much to further the establishment of an all-republican administration. When criticized by Joaquín Pérez Madrigal, a Radical–Socialist dissident, for his passivity in relation to developments within the PRRS, Lerroux replied "my task is to wait. I am sure that my hour will arrive". The Radical leader's strategy could scarcely have been less apposite. The deep-seated lack of trust and understanding that characterized relations between the Radicals and the left republicans demanded a pro-active willingness to work towards an agreement rather than a re-active waiting game.[62]

The government's slump during the summer did not augur well for the elections, on 3 September, to the Court of Constitutional Guarantees, when fifteen of its twenty-five members were to be chosen by the *ayuntamientos*. To avoid the contest being turned into a plebiscite on the ruling alliance, the Cabinet adopted a strictly neutral attitude, but this was to no avail as the opposition, including the Radicals, seized on the election as a referendum on the Azaña administration. Worse still, the government's hands-off approach exacerbated the divisions within the republican–socialist majority. In many provinces, the ruling parties, despite the setback of the municipal elections five months earlier, failed to unite. The resulting fragmentation of the governing coalition was an unmistakable sign that it was breaking up. For the most part, the Radicals, as in the April elections, either stood alone or joined forces with conservative republicans. Like the right, the Radical Party viewed the poll as an opportunity to deliver yet another blow to an administration that was under siege.[63]

The Radical-based coalition, by winning 32 per cent of the vote, almost matched the right-wing one at 32.6 per cent, but the republican–socialist alliance, despite its lack of unison, won a greater proportion at 35.4 per cent. However, the distribution of members favoured the right, which won six of the fifteen, while the republican–socialist coalition secured five and the Radical one four.[64] The outcome was similar to that in the April municipal elections, but on this occasion the Prime Minister could not dismiss it as the product of "rotten boroughs". The ruling coalition had been roundly defeated. The principal claim of the Radicals' opposition since early 1932 – that the country was divorced from the Cortes – was, for the first time, probably true. For the Radical Party, moreover, the elections were a triumph. It achieved the highest total for any republican party: 14,495 votes, as opposed to only half that sum – 7,611 votes – for the PSOE, while Acción Republicana obtained 5,477 and the strife-torn PRRS a mere 2,750.[65] Overall, the Radical Party had captured just under 30 per cent of the entire vote. However, as in the April elections, the party's success – in Andalusia, Aragon, the Canary Islands and Valencia – was limited largely to traditional areas of strength rather than embracing new ones. The psephological physiognomy of the September results indicates that there were many parts of the country from which the Radicals and conservative republicans were unable to dislodge the right. *El Progreso* was quick to point out that "when – unfortunately – the right itself achieves a triumph over the government, everything that is said and done to justify the failure is puerile, arbitrary and illogical". For the Radical press, the party had arrested the advance of the regime's "manifest enemies", who, far from accepting it, "prepare themselves to fight it by all the means at their disposal". Had it not been for the Radical Party, the Court of Constitutional Guarantees would have been transformed, *El Progreso* concluded resoundingly, into "a rightist redoubt against the Constitution and the Republic". In short, the Radicals' role in averting a right-wing backlash made the formation of an all-republican government more urgent than ever. There was, in fact, much to be said for the Radical argument. Whereas the republican–socialist coalition of June 1931 would have won the September vote with ease, its divisions made the regime's supporters vulnerable to the right. Moreover, the September vote strengthened the impression gained in April that the Radicals might well hold the balance of power between left and right in the next general election. If they failed to reach an understanding with the left republicans, the Radical Party could well turn to the right in the search for allies that, unlike the conservative republicans, could provide them with a ruling majority. The Azaña administration had to take note. The premier himself was well aware of the danger of allowing the Radicals to slip from the left republicans' orbit. The solution was not necessarily the establishment of a strictly republican government as this would have been staunchly opposed by the socialists, but at the very least the strengthening of the ties between the republicans was absolutely essential.[66]

The September election had left the government, Azaña admitted to the President, "worn out, undone, crushed". Nevertheless, on 6 September the Prime Minister defended the continuity of the government before the Cortes, attributing the defeat to "the disorganization of the republican electorate". By contrast, the Radical leader insisted that if the ruling coalition carried on "it will lose the municipal elections, the general election and the Republic". The already brittle relations within the Cabinet gave way to mutual recrimination. Indeed, Largo Caballero told the Cabinet that the republican–socialist alliance was, in effect, over. If that was the case, the Prime Minister replied, he was not prepared to oversee "a disaster" in the partial elections in October and in the municipal elections a month later. Before the matter could be resolved, the President, citing the government's electoral defeat as the motive, withdrew his confidence from the Cabinet on 7 September.[67]

VII

The Quest for the Centre
The Radical Party in power,
September 1933 to April 1934

The President called on the Radical leader on 8 September 1933 to form a government with the Constituent Cortes which would re-establish the "fraternal understanding between all the republican groups". Lerroux, in accepting the request, placed himself in an extremely awkward position. He would have to seek the collaboration of his erstwhile opponents not only in order to create a government, but also to rule over a parliament which, as he had repeatedly pointed out, "is hostile to me", and for whose dissolution he had been calling since late 1931. Having secured the collaboration of Acción Republicana, on the understanding that the new administration would continue the work of the Constituent Cortes, but not that of PRRS, he set about, much in the style of the *ancien régime*, to create a Cabinet of notables, approaching public luminaries such as Felipe Sánchez Román, José Ortega y Gasset, and Salvador de Madariaga, as well as a number of left republicans on a purely individual basis. It was difficult to see how such a coalition could win over parliament, unless of course Lerroux was already looking forward to its dissolution. Acción Republicana, realizing that the Radical leader had dispensed with the parties, now withdrew its support. Brought to order by the President, Lerroux again invited the left republican parties to form a government. Reassured by the Radical *jefe*'s change in tack and wary of the danger of dissolution if a government was not forthcoming, the left republicans entered the Cabinet. On 12 September, a Radical-dominated administration, comprising seven Radicals, five left republicans, and one independent, was finalized. After nearly fifty years in the service of the republican cause, Lerroux had, at last, reached the top of the "greasy pole".[1]

On 2 October, the Prime Minister presented his Cabinet to the Cortes. He then proceeded to criticize the Azaña administrations' record, to reiterate that parliament was divorced from public opinion, and to conclude that he could not govern with the current chamber. He was requesting the backing of a body which he at once rejected. "He has come to the Cortes to say from the government," Azaña replied, "the same as he said in opposition." His position, as Martínez Barrio notes, was "evidently false". In effect, Lerroux, as indicated too by the very perfunctoriness of the programme which he outlined, was soliciting a vote of confidence from a Cortes which he intended to dissolve. The Republic, Azaña warned, should not revert to "the customs of the monarchy, in which the decree of dissolution was used as the triumphal instrument of a party". As a result, the left republicans and socialists did not vote for the government. The administration was over before it had begun. Lerroux promptly slid back down the "greasy pole" far faster than he had crawled up it.[2]

President Alcalá-Zamora, however, did not grant the decree of dissolution to the Radical leader. Nor did he fall back on the left republicans. Instead, determined still to create a centrist administration under his control, he busily set about trying to create a Cabinet of notables himself, calling on a succession of eminent public figures, but, as could have been foreseen, the opposition of the left doomed the President's initiative from the start.[3] Lerroux, who had already drawn up his list of ministers, expected, at last, to be granted the decree of dissolution.[4] Alcalá-Zamora, he believed, had in any case made the tacit offer of the decree should the Radical leader's government not obtain a parliamentary majority.[5] The President, however, had other plans. He did indeed turn to the Radical Party to assemble a government, but not to Lerroux. Rather, he asked the party's deputy leader, Martínez Barrio. The President, according to Martínez Barrio, was unable to call on Lerroux again as he had lost a vote of confidence. This, indeed, was the interpretation of the Constitution that predominated amongst the Cortes' legal experts, but Alcalá-Zamora himself, like the Radical chief, flatly rejected such a view.[6]

The truth is that Alcalá-Zamora did not want to give Lerroux the satisfaction of organizing the elections.[7] He also sought someone accommodating enough, especially after the trying experience of the independently-minded Azaña, to allow him a greater say in Cabinet affairs. Martínez Barrio, whom he had got to know during his contacts with the Radical opposition, was his man. Underlying this choice was the desire of the President to further his own political agenda: whereas the Radical leader was a conservative republican rival, Martínez Barrio might be converted into an ally, perhaps even allowing him to divide and rule the Radical Party. Clearly Alcalá-Zamora was not resigned, as Lerroux comments, to "the discreet abstention and neutrality that corresponded to the head of a republican parliamentary state as guarantees of his impartiality", though the original problem lay in the Constitution's failure to limit or specify the functions of the president sufficiently.[8] No wonder that César Jalón, a crony of the *jefe* and future Radical minister, refers to Alcalá-Zamora in his memoirs as "Alfonso XIV" and "A cheap imitation of Don Alfonso".[9] Yet, there was also a sound political reason for choosing Martínez Barrio rather than Lerroux; following the Radical leader's violent parliamentary confrontation with the left republicans and socialists on 2 and 3 October, his deputy would be much more likely to form a broadly-based government.

Lerroux was livid. In *La pequeña historia* he gives full vent to his spleen, denouncing the "ignoble conspiracy" of "the young lion", Indalecio Prieto, "the serpent", Manuel Azaña, and, last but certainly not least, "the monkey", Alcalá-Zamora. He claims that "never had anything similar been seen, a more cynical disloyalty, a more shameless betrayal". The conspiracy had been designed to "break me" by ritual slaughter on the parliamentary altar before appointing as premier a man "without name, without history and without worldy qualities". His bitterness towards the President is understandable insofar as the latter's original intention, according to Martínez Barrio, was to exhaust the Radical leader's credibility as Prime Minister before giving the decree of dissolution to someone else. Lerroux's rancour towards Martínez Barrio, however, is totally unjustified. Indeed, this begs the question as to why the Radical leader allowed his deputy to accept the President's offer in the first place. He claims that the decision was taken "without consulting me", but it is unthinkable that Martínez Barrio would endeavour, let alone be able, to undertake such an enterprise without the express approval of his *jefe*.[10] In fact, the Radical boss not only gave his consent – Jalón recalls him exclaiming that "giving power to Martínez Barrio is for me as if I had passed it on to my son Aurelio" – but he also went to extreme lengths to facilitate the formation of a government. Most strikingly, he agreed to the Radical–Socialists' condition, following a dramatic late-night visit from Martínez Barrio in the company of Azaña and Domingo, that an approach be made to the socialists, having previously vetoed their collaboration. Probably, Lerroux calculated that by rejecting the Radical–Socialists' request he might prejudice the Radicals' chances of overseeing the election altogether. Immediately after, Martínez Barrio scurried back to the Cortes in order to put the offer to the PSOE. By this stage, the socialist deputies' polemical reading of article 75 of the Constitution, according to which no minister of a government that had lost a vote of confidence could preside over its successor, had been reversed. At a meeting between the three former socialist ministers with Azaña, Domingo, and Besteiro, a formula was then found to justify the socialists' change in tack: the parties that had voted against the Lerroux government would all back a proposition stating that the vote of censure had been directed against the Prime Minister, but not Martínez Barrio. Consequently the way was clear for the resurrection of the republican–socialist alliance of 1931. Straight after, the socialist Executive Committee voted in favour of collaboration, if only "with a view to electoral supervision". At the subsequent reunion held between the socialist ex-ministers, Azaña, Besteiro, and Martínez Barrio, Indalecio Prieto set about drawing up the public statement which would explain the socialists' *volte-face*, but eventually declared himself unable to find the right wording. Despite the fact that a formula had already been agreed upon and that immediately afterwards Prieto composed a lengthy note elucidating the PSOE's final position with, in Vidarte's words, "brilliance and ease", the socialists had stumbled at the very last hurdle.[11] The socialists, "already embarked on the rhetoric of revolution", as Santos Juliá observes, had effectively declined Martínez Barrio's offer.[12] An historic opportunity had been missed. As Julián Besteiro noted at the time, "the Republic has lost out". The upshot was that the Martínez Barrio administration, being made up of three Radicals, three Radical–Socialists, two members of the erstwhile Agrupación al Servicio de la República, and a member each from Acción Republicana, the Izquierda Radical–Socialista, the Progressive Party, and the Esquerra, was a veritable mosaic of republican parties.[13]

A government headed by the Radicals would, therefore, organize the general election, even if Lerroux was not its leader. Though the practice of blatantly rigged elections may have belonged to the Restoration, the central government still wielded formidable electoral influence. An insight into the realities of republican politics is provided by the confidential report submitted to the Radical *jefe* by General Gonzalo Queipo de Llano, organizer of the party's campaign in Salamanca. Having admitted that the Radical Party was of "scarce importance" in the province, the General none the less stressed that "if the governor is changed" the party would be able to take on the Agrarians and even to sideline the socialists.[14] In other words, a suitably partisan civil governor could still make or break a party. Nationally speaking, the Radical National Council was convinced that the party would reap "a splendid victory". The fact that the Minister of the Interior, Rico Avello, was not a Radical but a member of the now-defunct Agrupación al Servicio de la Republica, did not dent the Radicals' confidence. At a lunch held at Lerroux's San Rafael estate on 15 October 1933, Martínez Barrio himself predicted that the party would fulfil its own expectations. "We will win", he affirmed.[15] This, however, did not mean that the Radicals would secure an outright majority – the party fielded around 221 candidates for the 470 seats, though this was nearly double the number in 1931 – but that they would become the leading parliamentary force.[16] Publicly, the Radical premier also forecast that the party would become the single largest entity in the next legislature, thereby allowing it to form a government with a "strong parliamentary majority". The unaligned Minister of the Interior conceded too that the Radical Party would win "many more seats" than in 1931. Martínez Barrio, Lerroux disclosed to party members, "is collaborating with me". "We will make the elections", he confidently forecast, "we will win them". As an "eminent Radical personality" assured *El Sol*, the party aimed to net around 170 seats, including twenty or so independents who would join once the Cortes met, while the right, the second largest force, would obtain between 70 and 80 deputies.[17] The optimism of the Radicals was based on much more than the government's potential electoral machinations. Above all, the Radicals aimed to reap the reward of their two-year opposition campaign to the Azaña administration which, as the electoral successes of 1933 had already demonstrated, had found a powerful echo amongst Spanish public opinion.

The overarching theme of the Radical electoral campaign was that the party offered a haven of centrist tranquillity far from the madding crowds of left and right. "Either them – Hatred – or us – Peace", as *Renovación* declared.[18] The Radicals explicitly rejected the extremist language, "the voice of war", deployed on both the left and the right.[19] The Radicals would usher in peace, as opposed to perturbation. "Spain needs a centre government", Guerra del Río averred in Albacete on 23 October. Or, as Lerroux put it a week later in Valencia, "I am the centre solution of Spanish politics". "Liberal democracy is us", the Radical programme insisted. A centre force, the party inevitably looked both ways, as summed up in its slogan of "Republic, order, liberty, social justice, amnesty".[20]

Elaborating upon the party programme by drawing on the Radicals' propaganda is unrewarding as the speeches and manifestos are invariably long on demagogic promises and short on detailed proposals. The Radical Party's inter-classist appeal was crystallized in the calls for harmony between the workers and *patronal* ("our principal mission", Lerroux declared in Madrid), for the regime to be made truly "national", for the workers to be raised up to the level of the "powerful classes and attain human solidarity", for, in sum, "a Republic for all Spaniards".[21] This stress on accommodating distinct and often conflicting interests contained an essentially centrist promise that eschewed the extremes of left and right. Beyond this catch-all, populist discourse a distinctly conservative agenda can be discerned. The "re-establishment" of law and order and of the need to "lend prestige to authority" were uppermost in the Radical campaign. So, too, was the need to meet the protests of the *patronal* by raising the economy from its "prostration" on terms that accommodated the workers' demands only insofar as they did not, the Radical leader specified in Murcia, "go against" the economy – a formula that suggested that industrial relations policy would be drawn up largely on the *patronal*'s terms.[22] Another objective was listed simply in the party programme as an "amnesty". It was understood that this would benefit above all the insurgents of 10 August 1932. However, moderates such as Martínez Barrio and Guerra del Río avoided the issue altogether, while the *jefe* made only an oblique reference to it in his final speech.

Yet the Radicals were far from denying the reforms of the first biennium. As the party leader stressed in Caceres on 26 October, the Radicals
proposed to modify that legislation from the first biennium characterized
by its "sectarian spirit". However, this would not, as he spelt out, amount
to a *tabula rasa* of the reforms, many of which the Radicals had voted for.
The educational reforms, for example, were criticized by Lerroux on the
grounds that the timetable for the substitution of church schools by yet-
to-be built state ones was unrealistic – a fact of which the authors of the
Law on Congregations were well aware. Following Azaña's attempt to
"destroy" the army, he announced the Radicals' intention to undertake
its "reorganization", but without proferring any details. Far from overturning the Agrarian Reform Law, the Radicals aimed to create many
more property owners. In fact, this represented, Guerra del Río underlined in Cordoba on 28 October, "the supreme ideal of the Radical Party"
as it would erect "an invincible bulwark that will defend the Republic at
all costs". The creation of "the greatest number possible" of small property owners, the Radical *jefe* explained in mid-campaign to the French
publication *L'Intransigent*, would require further measures. While invariably stressing that change should be undertaken "by steps not leaps", he
specified that for it to be "efficient" a Lease Law would be required – a
potentially much more radical measure than the Agrarian Law of
September 1932. He also spoke of reforming the economic and social
laws, but only singled out one, the Law on Municipal Boundaries, which
was widely unpopular outside socialist circles and had already been modified by an all-republican government. The quintessentially centrist
aspirations of the Radicals were underlined by Lerroux's speech in
Valencia on 30 October. On the one hand, he trusted that a major republican force would emerge to the right of the party. On the other hand, he
hoped that the left republicans would form a single entity, providing a
buffer between the Radicals and the organized working class. Naturally,
this would leave the Radical Party in the centre of the political spectrum
– as arbiter between left and right.[23]

The principal target of the Radicals' criticism was their former allies in
the provisional government, especially the socialists. Portrayed as
sectarian and classist, they were denounced by Guerra del Río in Albacete
as "a positive danger" which had caused the country to suffer a "devia-
tion". *Renovación* railed against them for causing plummetting
productivity and soaring unemployment, as well as for "the only motors
of the socialist march on the state"; namely, "jobs-for-the boys and the
inside deal". Lerroux, in Valencia, put it more bluntly: "Spain," he
declared, "does not agree with the socialist conscience." In reality, the
party was striving to take advantage of the middle-class backlash against
the socialists, blamed in large measure for the mounting social agitation
and the decline in the economy, that the Radicals themselves had done so

much to foment. What Martínez Barrio termed the "reconquest" and Lerroux the "reconstitution" of the new regime was required so that it was transformed, in Guerra del Río's words, into "the Republic of the republicans". Nevertheless, the left republicans were heavily rebuked, too. Martínez Barrio lambasted them in Cordoba on 10 November for regarding themselves as "the personification of the regime" and of "the *Patria*". Moreover, the *jefe* made it clear that an all-republican electoral alliance had failed to emerge as a result of the "trap" set by the left republicans in order to bring down his Cabinet. Relations with the left republicans, in short, had reached their nadir.[24]

By contrast, the right received a much more benevolent treatment. Admittedly, Guerra del Río warned against the dangers of a regime "of sacred water and the scapular", while the Radical leader condemned "reactionism". Yet Lerroux in particular went out of his way to welcome the concourse of the right, though specifying that he would only share power with those "within the republican orbit". The Radicals, motivated in part by the fact that they shared certain concerns in common with the right such as the defence of law and order, but also by the breakdown in relations with the left republicans, were extremely sensitive to the electoral resurgence of non-republican conservatism. The party's thinking had been spelt out by a leading, if anonymous, Radical in an interview published in *El Sol* on 18 October. On the assumption that the party would emerge as the largest parliamentary entity, the non-republican right as the second, and that the socialists and left republicans would win far fewer seats than before, the Radicals calculated that, together with the *Mauristas* and the right, they would command about 300 seats. In other words, the Radicals already foresaw the necessity of some sort of parliamentary understanding with the right. In his address to the party's Madrid candidates on 8 November, Lerroux was even more explicit. He estimated that the Radicals would be unable to form a majority with the support of the conservative republicans alone and that the party would have to choose between left and right. Given that an alliance with the socialists was out of the question and that the left republicans would "scarcely" be represented, he indicated that the Radicals were most likely to join forces with the right. This required a declaration of republicanism by the latter, something which he did not regard as "difficult". As he declared in Barcelona on 15 November, the Radicals would not be "against this right-wing orientation". On the contrary, they would endeavour to "channel it, attempt to attract it" on the grounds that "within the Republic all men can be accommodated". Having leaned to the left in 1931, the Radical Party was now preparing, due to the change in the political landscape, to lean the other way. In effect, the party aimed to take advantage of its centrist position to convert itself into the arbiter of Spanish politics.[25]

For the Radicals, the right was at once a potential partner and an electoral rival, as both were competing largely for the middle-class vote. This represented a redoubtable challenge for the party. Whereas in mid-1931 the right, to the advantage of the Radicals, had been demoralized and disorganized, by the end of 1933 it had been reborn and reunited. Indeed, the right-wing coalition, the broadest on offer, was to unleash by far the most sophisticated and well-resourced campaign. In Oviedo, to take an example, the republicans were astounded at "the magnificent" organization of its propaganda effort, which included glossy posters and plane drops. In Madrid alone, the right spent more than one million pesetas, far more than either the left or centre could possibly muster. For Spain as a whole, the CEDA printed 10 million leaflets and 200,000 colour posters, as well as deploying radio adverts, mobile film units, and littering the land with leaflets from the air.[26]

To an extent the Radicals and the right were appealing to different constituencies: the Radicals to the secular, moderate middle classes, the right to the rural and urban Catholic ones. However, Lerroux was acutely aware that, as he underlined in Valencia, the republican parties still had to consolidate the support of "this invasion of elements that have come from all parts", who may be wavering between the republicans and the right. Further, the Radicals had to embrace the women's suffrage. This had transformed the electoral landscape as the number of voters more than doubled to 13.187 million. In the provinces there were 4 per cent more women than men, while in the provincial capitals the ratio stood at 112:100, this climbing to 119:100 in the case of Madrid. Both the socialists and the right had voted in favour of the female suffrage in the conviction that it would favour their own interests. By contrast, the Radicals, given the pervasive presence of Catholic culture amongst middle-class women, were terrified at the prospect. The women's vote, Herminio Fernández de la Poza, Radical deputy for Leon, exclaimed in a report to Lerroux, "is the most important thing of all". "In Spain," he claimed, "90 per cent or more of women are Catholic and 60 or 70 per cent is monarchist." Moreover, the right was better organized amongst women than any other political force. In Fernández de la Poza's own, admittedly conservative, constituency not only were the men outnumbered by 117,000 to 110,000, but the Agrarian Party had a "very big" women's network, with a group "in nearly all the *pueblos*". The female vote in Leon, he predicted, would go "wholesale to the right" and the right would reap a "great triumph". The women's suffrage, the deputy concluded, "frightens me". Much the same could be said for the party as a whole. To counteract the appeal of the right the Radicals vigorously defended a regime of law and order, attempted to mollify Catholic opinion over the anticlerical reforms, and constantly stressed that, in Lerroux's words, "in the Republic there is room for all citizens, there is room in the Republic for all Spaniards". The Radical *jefe*, in his closing speech in

Madrid, explicitly courted monarchist sympathizers by insisting that the king had gone for good and by pleading with them to accept that the popular sovereignity of the Republic was "the only element of guarantee for the interests that they represent". In this regard, the campaign was given a major boost by the incorporation into the party of the former monarchist minister Santiago Alba, an informal ally of the Radicals since the outset of the Republic. Like Lerroux, Alba, as he explained in a public letter, sought to integrate those that aimed to work in "peace" into the new regime by means of "economic and agrarian reconstruction". His adhesion epitomized the Radicals' aim of consolidating the Republic by widening its base.[27]

The 1933 Electoral Law placed a premium on the formation of the broadest possible electoral alliances. In the first round, at least one candidate had to obtain a minimum 40 per cent of the vote; if not, a second ballot was held in which only those that had won 8 per cent or more of the vote in the previous round were eligible. The new system placed an even greater emphasis than the old on the creation of coalitions. Ideologically, the most natural allies for the Radical Party were the conservative republican parties, but, as the earlier elections in 1933 had demonstrated, they were allies of limited clout. A much more serious proposition was the left republican parties. However, they remained hopeful that an alliance with the socialists would be struck, but this proved vain as the PSOE, despite having voted for the Electoral Law and despite the blandishments of their former governmental partners, refused to reach a nationwide agreement.[28] The Socialist Party did leave the way open for local-level alliances, but the deterioration in grassroots' relations between the socialists and left republicans resulted in the establishment of few coalitions.[29] One exception was Bilbao, where Indalecio Prieto, the champion of socialist-republican collaboration within the PSOE, offered a place on the ticket to Azaña. Still the republicans, despite the co-operative spirit that reigned within the government, were reluctant to ally. While Lerroux himself seems to have done little, if anything, to re-establish relations in the wake of the Cortes clash of 2–3 October, Martínez Barrio claims to have sounded out, on his own initiative, both the PSOE and left republicans,[30] but the patent lack of interest, both on the left and within the Radical Party, thwarted the endeavour. Acción Republicana, at its congress in mid October, empowered its local organizations to ally with any republican force that it saw fit, but Azaña, despite his acute awareness of the disaster that awaited the republicans if they did not join forces, appears to done have nothing to secure a national-level pact with the Radicals.[31] The result was that the left/republican–Radical government did not generate its electoral equivalent. The Martínez Barrio administration, in consequence, was reduced to the role of a mere polling committee bereft of any political significance. For the left republicans, the failure of an all-republican alliance to emerge was an egregious error. Lacking an electoral arrangement with either the socialists or the Radicals, the left republicans made themselves vulnerable to a serious electoral reverse, while allowing the Radicals to shift ever further to the right. This was a short-sighted and sectarian decision, a continuation of the politics of exclusion practised by the left republicans in relation to the Radicals, that did little to consolidate the regime. By contrast, a broad middle-class alliance of the left republicans and Radicals, backed by the government, would have been a leading electoral contender. Nor had the Radicals done enough to establish an electoral understanding with their former allies. As a result, the Radical Party failed to reach a national-level pact with any other party. By contrast, the non-republican right, a major rival for the middle-class vote, had drawn up an electoral committee that ranged from the accidentalist CEDA to the Alfonsists, Agrarians, and even the Carlists.

In many provinces, the selection of Radical candidates brought to the surface virulent tensions within the party, especially between new and old republicans. A candidate for Orense, Justo Villanueva Goméz, was denounced to the national leader by a local activist on the grounds that he was a former follower of the monarchist ministers Bugallal, De la Cierva, Calvo Sotelo and Alba. "This austere republican", he continued sarcastically, had lost his life-long position as a state lawyer "for embezzling . . . a certain quantity". Another Orense contender, Antonio Casar Echevarrieta, one of the local leaders of the dictatorship, was allegedly kicked out of the army for corruption.[32] There were protests, too, at the grassroots recruits. "One now bumps into many people who call themselves republicans," wrote an activist from Albacete, "but they are not: they have affiliated to the parties of our regime in order to realize their vanities and their ambitions, but nothing more."[33] Hostility to the non-republican right was evident in numerous sections of the party. Eloy Soriano Díaz, writer and party supporter, warned Lerroux that in Badajoz many of the Radicals "of the 14th of April" had not only collaborated with the dictatorship but were currently associated with the CEDA, the Jesuits, and other religious groups. The right, which was campaigning against "all that the republican form of government signifies", was consequently backed by those who, "in an arriviste fashion", had infiltrated the party. The traditional Radicals, he stressed, were "horrified" as "we should not play the game, not even indirectly, of the reactionary forces".[34] Local leader Manuel Martínez complained that the Albacete party had not followed the national leadership's instructions of "alliances with purely republican parties, but nothing with socialists or monarchists, disguised or otherwise" as a result of an envisaged arrangement with the Agrarians, who, he contended, aimed, "at the appropriate moment, to destroy" the republicans. The crux was whether the Radicals should "reconquer" the Republic or allow "those that on the first occasion will assassinate us?".

The party's current strategy, he judged, was a "big mistake".[35] However, there were many parts of the country where the Radical Party, even if it allied with the left and centre republican parties, could aspire to no more than the minority placings. Leon province provides a clear-cut example. Local deputy Herminio Fernández de la Poza explained to the *jefe* that the bulk of the male electorate comprised small landowners who believed that "their properties and their produce" were best defended by the Agrarian Party, while the overwhelming majority of the female electorate, in his estimate, would also vote for the right. Only if the Radicals joined forces with the Agrarians would they obtain seven seats; otherwise, the Radical Party, in harness with the PRRS and the remnants of the Al Servicio de la República group, could set their sights no higher than the three minority places. In many constituencies, such decisions made the difference between contesting the majority seats or scrapping for the minority placings.[36]

The cornerstone of the Radical Party's electoral alliances was the centrist republican conservative parties. Of the thirty three constituencies where the Radicals allied with another party, over two-thirds, or 24, involved centre ones. Four were with left republican parties alone and five solely with right-wing ones. The coalitions with the centre and left republican forces were often forged in the face of strong socialist or right-wing opposition. Those made with the right invariably represented, as in the case of the southern provinces of Badajoz, Caceres, Granada and Jaen, an effort to overturn formidable socialist candidatures. In somewhat under half, or twenty-four, of the fifty-eight main constituencies the Radical Party stood alone.[37] Approximately one half of these, including Castellon, Huesca, Seville, Valencia and Zaragoza, was a demonstration of the Radicals' strength, but the other half, including Barcelona, Lerida, Gerona, Palencia, and Vizcaya, reflected their weakness. The vicissitudes of the Radical ticket in Barcelona provided a desultory comment on the party's decline there. At first, the party tried to ally with the left-wing Esquerra, but was rejected; next, it was rumoured that the Radicals would not run at all but back the right-wing Lliga; finally, Lerroux tried to foist his own list on the Barcelona organization, only to provoke a protracted polemic that would not be resolved until shortly before polling day, while in the other Catalan constituencies the Radicals failed to produce a complete list. Nationally speaking, the shortcomings to the party's growth over the previous two-and-a-half years was evident: in up to a half of the constituencies, the party was weakly represented.[38]

The Radicals, despite the circumscribed scope of their alliances, emerged after the first round as the republican frontrunner with seventy-nine deputies. By contrast, the left republicans had been decimated, obtaining a mere five deputies, while the PSOE did not make forty. The only party to surpass the Radical total was the CEDA: Acción Popular, the coalition's centrepiece, had won sixty-seven seats alone.[39] Forces further to the right had won considerably less: the monarchist Renovación Española twelve and the Carlists just two. The triumph of the non-republican right prompted the Minister of Communications, Emilio Palomo, to attempt to bring together the Radical Party, Acción Republicana, and the PSOE in a coalition in "defence of the Republic" for the second round. Initial soundings, he claimed, had met with the approval not only of Azaña but also that of Lerroux, who had allegedly declared his willingness to make "all kinds of personal sacrifices" in order to establish the alliance. The Prime Minister, who revealed that in his home constituency of Seville the Radicals would unite with Acción Republicana and the socialists in the next round, claimed that the Radical leader had greeted the idea of resurrecting the republican–socialist coalition with "great satisfaction". The premier was "frankly optimistic" that such a deal would be struck. Within twenty four hours, however, all hope of reviving the 1931 republican–socialist coalition had been dashed. The socialists, unenthusiastic from the outset, issued a statement on 22 November in which they lambasted the Radicals and in particular Lerroux for allying with the non-republican right. The Radical *jefe*, meanwhile, withdrew his support for Palomo's proposal. Politically, he considered an alliance with the socialists at this late stage to be untenable. Strategically, he realized that the Radicals would have to depend on the right, not the left republicans, for a majority in the next parliament. He did not want, therefore, to prejudice that collaboration by competing against the right in the second round.[40] Moreover, both the Radicals and the accidentalists had been struck by the fact that the centre–right coalitions of the first round had successfully overturned socialist majorities in the south – the PSOE plummeted from thirty-eight seats to just eleven in Badajoz, Caceres, Granada and Jaen – while separate lists for the Radical Party and CEDA in Huelva and Madrid had allowed the socialists to triumph. Gil Robles was particularly impressed by the "extremely grave error" of separate candidatures for the centre and right in the capital as together they had won more votes than the left.[41] The CEDA leader had no doubts as to the importance of a "circumstantial alliance" with the centre, maintaining that unless a centre–right deal was struck the socialists could gain 50 extra deputies, thereby evening out the forces in parliament. The Radical Party and CEDA were consequently brought together not only out of mutual self-interest but also out of a common hostility to the socialists. The Radical leader, on the day that he rejected the Palomo initiative, 21 November, entered into negotiations with Cándido Casanueva of the CEDA. He later declared that the party was prepared to ally with those "within the scope of republican legality" – he no longer, as in the address of 8 November to the Madrid candidates, demanded that they make an explicit declaration of their republicanism

– which, as further contacts with Casanueva made clear, meant the non-republican right. Lerroux's word, moreover, was final. All the provincial organizations' electoral deals would have to be approved by the Executive Committee, "represented", he clarified, "in this case by me". In reality, the Radical leader had taken a brutally pragmatic, though scarcely improvised, decision.[42]

The second-round pact between the Radical Party and the CEDA affected nearly half the fifteen constituencies concerned. By contrast, in the first round, the two parties had joined forces in only one in nine of the electoral districts. The Radicals' refusal to share a ticket with the monarchists led the CEDA to expel them from the alliance in Alicante and Granada. Elsewhere, however, the Radicals effectively traded off with the monarchists: in Ceuta and Melilla the Radicals were given a free hand in exchange for withdrawing from the two Madrid constituencies, where the monarchists formed part of the right-wing candidature. Of the remaining constituencies, the Radical Party was too weak in four of them to justify a joint list.[43] The lurch of the party to the right was vividly illustrated in the pages of *Renovación*. Before the first round, the conservative forces were excoriated for having "degraded the magistrature, dishonoured the army, plundered the public finances, lost the colonies, auctioned the bureaucracy, made money out of vice, promoted illiteracy". It was, the paper concluded, "absolutely useless . . . to enter into dialogue with these people".[44] After the Radical leader had indeed talked "with these people", *Renovación* quickly drew a distinction between the non-republican right and "the dead voice of the monarchist past" while equating "fascism" with the socialists.[45] Yet there was still serious resistance in the provinces to an electoral arrangement with the right. From Malaga, Pedro Gómez Chaix, the veteran Radical leader and biographer of Lerroux's early political mentor, Manuel Ruiz Zorrilla, protested vehemently that such an understanding would not only be "very difficult" but that the Radical rank-and-file would refuse to vote for it in both the province and capital. On the day of the election, the alliance having gone ahead, the local party officials withdrew in disgust from the polling stations. In Murcia, too, there was considerable opposition to collaboration with the right, while in Madrid a thwarted attempt was made to hold a special congress that would clarify the party's position. The dissenters, however, were unable to prevail over the national leadership.[46]

The second round was an emphatic triumph for the centre–right coalition. The rerun elections brought the Radicals another twenty-five seats, giving them a final tally of 104. The CEDA, with a total of 117, was the only party to outstrip the Radicals. As a whole, the centre parties had achieved a modest rise, up from 152 seats to 177, while the non-republican right had soared from a mere 41 deputies two years earlier to 201 in 1933. The left, accordingly, had plunged from a majority of 247 in 1931 to under a hundred, the PSOE winning 58 deputies, Acción Republicana five, and the PRRS a mere two.[47]

Immediately after the first round, the left, faced by the prospect of a resounding defeat, cried foul. The socialists, beneficiaries of official protection in 1931, were quick to denounce the abuses of civil governors, the Civil Guard, and of their political opponents. *El Socialista* affirmed that in Badajoz, for example, the intimidation of working-class voters involved everything from the buying of votes to the threat of machine guns. Similarly, in the Cortes, José Prat, socialist deputy for Albacete, decried the excesses of the Radicals in Seville.[48] Such claims of fraud underscored the series of frantic appeals to the President and the Prime Minister to overturn the result. While Juan Botella Asensi, the Minister of Justice, abandoned the Cabinet after losing his seat and urged the President to annul the election by decree, Gordón Ordás, the Minister of Industry, pleaded with him to dissolve the Cortes.[49] On 4 December, following the second round, Manuel Azaña pressed the Prime Minister to suspend the Cortes, constitute a government of all the republican forces, and hold the election anew. The premier, however, counteracted that "to know how to lose was our immediate obligation". The next day Azaña, Casares Quiroga, and Marcelino Domingo sent a letter to the President and Prime Minister alike which called for the establishment of a republican government which would be able to assure public opinion that "the course of the Republic is not going to deviate dangerously". Meanwhile, Juan Negrín, on behalf of the socialist parliamentary group, incited Alcalá-Zamora to form another republican government, pass a new electoral law, and thereby ensure the left's victory in a rerun poll. Largo Caballero wanted parliament to be dissolved. The President, struck above all by the socialists' "mad desire to regain power", viewed the efforts by the left to reverse the electoral outcome as nothing less than attempted *"coups d'état"*. Having suffered a terrible defeat, the left republicans and socialists were attempting to return to power by anti-democratic means – exactly the kind of behind-the-scenes manoeuvrings which Azaña, for one, had deplored in the Radicals during the first biennium.[50]

Undoubtedly serious fraud did take place, such as in the Galician provinces of Orense and Pontevedra, as well as in Badajoz, Granada, and Valencia in the south. One of the worst areas was Valencia where a ferocious struggle erupted between the PURA and the DRV which involved not just the breaking of ballot boxes, but also the use of bombs and bullets, resulting in the deaths of at least three DRV officials.[51] By the standards of the Republic, however, the general election of 1933 was probably the fairest of all. Certainly the Prime Minister and the Minister of the Interior appear to have been less interventionist than their peers in 1931 and 1936. Indeed, both the Interior Minister and his under-secretary lost their seats. Equally, the Radical–Socialists forfeited fifty three of their fifty-eight deputies – including three of their four ministers. The Prime Minister himself would have been bereft but for a friend who gave his seat up.[52]

The fundamental reasons for the defeat of the left do not lie in the abuses of the electoral system. Most importantly, there had been a definite shift of the electorate to the right. The conservative forces, discredited and in disarray in 1931, had since reorganized themselves, mobilizing the Catholic vote above all. Moreover, their resurgence had been greatly favoured by the transformation of the electorate with the introduction of the women's vote. Rosa María Capel, in her study of the female suffrage under the Republic, concludes that women, of whom only "a minority" backed the left, "collaborated in the electoral victory of the right".[53] Second, the republican–socialist alliance had disintegrated. The socialists, despite having voted for the Electoral Law of 1933, which heavily favoured broad coalitions, and despite the entreaties of their former left–republican allies, committed the monumental mistake of fighting the election alone, thereby prejudicing not only themselves but the republicans, too. Yet not even the republicans were able to reach an agreement. Whether anarcho–syndicalist abstention contributed to the left's electoral disaster has been hotly debated. Macarro Vera affirms categorically that "the importance attributed to the abstention of the CNT is a myth", yet fails to explain in his study of Seville why abstention was highest in 1933.[54] In Zaragoza, another anarcho–syndicalist stronghold, participation in both 1931 and 1936 was over 70 per cent, but in 1933 sank to 55.12 per cent. The most notable case of abstention was Cadiz, where only 37.3 per cent of the electorate voted. This is inexplicable without reference to the widespread support there for the CNT and the backlash against the Republic over the tragedy of Casas Viejas, a local *pueblo*.[55] Nationwide, Irwin has calculated that anarcho–syndicalist abstention accounted for 545,000 votes, or 6.02 per cent of the total vote, a significant slice of the electorate. According to these figures, the CNT's stance may have deprived the republicans, both of the left and the centre, of around 75 deputies.[56] Of those CNT affiliates that did vote, there is evidence that some may have backed the Radical Party. Certainly the Radicals' campaign was suffused by populist-permeated appeals to the working class, this being directed not just at the party's own minority working class base but also at the anarcho–syndicalists. The Radical Party thereby drew on its remaining links with the CNT as well as on their shared enmity towards the socialists. In Zaragoza, the *Cenetistas* were exhorted by the Radicals not to favour the "cave-dwellers" by abstaining and to punish the socialists for the "crimes of Arnedo, the Park of María Luisa and Casas Viejas".[57] Both the Radical minister Rafael Guerra del Río and the deputy for Malaga, Pedro Armasa, later claimed that the party had benefited from CNT collaboration. Further, at a meeting between the Radical Party and the CNT's regional committee for Barcelona, the latter offered its electoral participation in exchange for "compensation", to which the Radicals were disposed as long as there were no "acts beyond the law".[58] In conclusion, and on the basis of the available statistics, the left, even if united, would not have won the 1933 poll.[59]

Of all the parties, the Radical Party made the most efficacious use of its resources, doing better than any other force in terms of the number of votes cast for each deputy: while the PSOE had to secure 10,000 votes for each seat, the left republicans 8,000, and the right 6,000, the Radical Party had to garner a mere 4,000. Its success was still heavily concentrated in the party's traditional bulwarks; namely, the Canary Islands, Galicia, Aragon, Seville, and Valencia. Altogether, these five areas accounted for 47 deputies, or 45 per cent of the parliamentary party. By contrast, there was a vast area in the north where it was scarcely represented: between the regions of Asturias, the Basque country, Leon, and New Castile, the party cornered a mere brace of seats. As in 1931, it did extremely badly in Catalonia, securing just a single deputy. Altogether, the party was without representation in over a third, or 24, of the constituencies. On the other hand, the party enjoyed a substantial improvement in the south, soaring from 25 seats in Andalusia and Extremadura two years earlier to 45: that is to say, from 27 per cent of the Radical deputies to over 43 per cent. It is noteworthy that many of these gains had been made in first-round arrangements with the right. These include Granada and Jaen in Andalusia, where the party won an extra eight seats, and Badajoz and Caceres in Extremadura, where the Radicals rose from two to ten. Important advances were also made in harness with the right in the second round.[60] In comparison with 1931, the Radicals had clearly extended their electoral base into the countryside, shifting the party to the right. The impact of the alliance with the right had, together with the party's growth over the previous two years as well as its many local schisms, enormously altered the make-up of the parliamentary group. Over 60 per cent of the Radical deputies were new to the republican Cortes. "Many of them were unknown to me, new recruits attracted by the magnet of power", observes Martínez Barrio.[61] In overall terms, the party had risen by ten seats, a frankly disappointing return on two years of opposition. Had it not been for the fact that the Radicals had the best ratio of votes to seats, the result would have been noticeably worse; fifty two seats, if the left republicans' ratio is applied, or sixty nine, if that of the right is taken. Essentially, the mobilization of the right had, along with the weakness of the party's first-round alliances, gravely undermined the Radicals. Indeed, judging by Irwin's calculations, both the Radicals and the left republicans – who, despite having secured so few deputies, had still won over one million votes in comparison with 800,000 for the Radicals – many well have fared better had the all-republican administration of Martínez Barrio been matched by an equivalent electoral pact. The republicans, in short, had paid a heavy price for their disunity. Otherwise, they could have shifted the balance of the Cortes decisively towards the centre.

Neither the relative fairness of the election nor the upstanding example set by Martínez Barrio as premier was of any comfort for the Radical leader. On the contrary, he was, to judge by *La pequeña historia*, mortified by the outcome. He considered it "catastrophic" and a thorough indictment of Martínez Barrio's failure to complete the "special and principal mission" for which he had been entrusted: that of securing the largest parliamentary group. In his memoirs, the *jefe* assails the "two invalids" held responsible – Martínez Barrio, "a local councillor converted into the head of government" and a "wretch", and Rico Avello – for the disaster. Unlike Martínez Barrio, Lerroux would not have not been obsessed by displaying his "clean hands", but would have set about the business of manufacturing a victory. Statesmen, he later claimed, should not "sacrifice the state and the nation to scruples". The key to the entire situation, he concludes, was the decree of dissolution. This, due to the President's "envy and hostility", had been given to the Radical deputy leader, not to the *jefe*. Had it been otherwise, "national politics would have prospered". In reality, the Radical leader's own role in the election, as his correspondence with local leaders and civil governors makes clear, was far from negligible, but there is little doubt that he would have done considerably more as premier than Martínez Barrio to influence the result. As it happened, "the government had come out of it defeated". For Lerroux, this was the root of all his subsequent problems as it condemned him to live "at the mercy of others"; that is to say, the right.[62]

Following the election, the Radical chief was invited by the President to form a "purely republican" government which embraced those parties which had made explicit their "adhesion to the regime".[63] Clearly Alcalá-Zamora felt that the CEDA, despite having the biggest parliamentary group, was not yet close enough to the regime to assume such an undertaking.[64] Gil Robles himself had advised Alcalá-Zamora on 16 December 1933 that a centre government under Lerroux should be constituted.[65] The President's instructions notwithstanding, the Cabinet included the Agrarian José María Cid Ruiz-Zorrilla, a personal friend of Alcalá-Zamora and descendant of the republican leader Manuel Ruiz Zorrilla – but a monarchist, none the less. Martínez Barrio immediately objected to the appointment, going so far as to request his own omission from the government. Only by threatening not to assemble an administration at all did the Radical *jefe* persuade him to take part.[66] The collusion was an early indication of their differing views of the party's relationship with the non-republican right. This latent tension would be further exacerbated by the Radical leader's decision to extend the Cabinet's support beyond the parties that made it up. The eight Radicals, one Agrarian, one Liberal Democrat, one Progressive, and two independents that comprised the government commanded only one-third of the Cortes' votes. Lerroux, in order to secure a majority, proposed to seek that of the accidentalist CEDA. Such a strategy, he firmly believed, would consolidate the regime by incorporating the non-republican, as opposed to monarchist, right.[67] This momentous decision had not been taken on the spur of the moment. In his address of 8 November to the Madrid candidates, Lerroux had anticipated that neither the left nor the conservative republicans would win enough seats in order to form a majority together with the Radicals. As a result, he had forecast, the party would probably have to reach an agreement with the right. There was an important personal dimension to this strategy. Lerroux had expected, but failed, to achieve power in 1931, and then again in 1932. Having finally obtained it in September 1933 he had, in his view, been betrayed by the left republicans. This enmity, together with the left's much-reduced parliamentary presence, the strong showing of the right, and his own advanced years, was, for the Radical *jefe*, an opportunity not to be foregone.

The offer of an informal parliamentary alliance by the Radical Prime Minister was readily taken up by the CEDA leader. All too aware that the CEDA held less than a quarter of the deputies and that the non-republican right did not muster enough votes to command a majority, Gil Robles had further calculated that if he refused to buttress the Radical-led adminis-tration the latter would be obliged to join forces with the left and thereby prepare "the revolution from above". Even before the second round, he had declared his willingness to support a centre government from the outside. However, in exchange for the CEDA's support, as Gil Robles made plain to the premier before the Cabinet was presented to the Cortes, the government would have to fulfil the right's "minimum demands". These included an amnesty, the revision of the religious and labour legis-lation, as well as a drastic overhaul of the agrarian reform that would eliminate its "nationalizing" aspect.[68]

The Prime Minister, in presenting his Cabinet to the Cortes on 19 December, duly committed the government to undertaking the revision of the first biennium's legislation, which, he declared, had been character-ized by "party passion or an excessive spirit of class". An amnesty for the insurgents of 10 August 1932 would also be passed. The overriding objec-tive of the Radical-led administration, and the chief justification for the alliance with the right, was to "nationalize the Republic, to consolidate the Republic, to reconcile, within the law of the Republic, all Spaniards", so that "the *Patria* and the Republic" would be one. "An interior satis-faction" would thereby be restored not only to the army but also to the church as solutions were sought to those problems which had agitated "the spiritual peace of the country". The government would also respond to the needs of the *patronal* by enforcing law and order and by reducing public spending.[69] The speech mostly reflected, especially in its emphasis on nationalizing the Republic within a framework of law and order, the moderate vision which the Radical Party had espoused since the outset of the regime. At the same time, the programme signalled a slight shift to the right for the Radicals, not least in the stress placed on the revision of the reforms of 1931–3. Such compromises, however, were inevitable for a centre party in search of a parliamentary majority. Had the Radicals been dependent on the left republicans, they would just as easily have leaned the other way. Plainly, the Radicals promised a revisionist, but not a reactionary, administration. Indeed, the extent to which the legislation of the first biennium should be revised would become the key issue at dispute between the Radicals and their allies. This perennial tension would be shaped by the profound ideological differences between the two partners. Whereas the CEDA, intimately aligned with the Catholic Church, aspired to a confessional state, the Radical Party, which harboured numerous Masons, aimed at a secular one.[70] Consequently they held not only differing views of the church but of education, too. Economically, the Radicals, widely supported by industry and commerce, were more inclined to a *laissez faire* approach, while the *Cedistas*, drawing largely on the agrarian economy, were more protectionist. On the other hand, the Radicals were much more inclined to social welfare spending than the Catholic right. Crystallizing their distinct visions of state and society was the fact that the Radicals, in contrast to the accidentalists, had voted for the Constitution of 1931. As Gil Robles later wrote of the Radical leader, "an abyss separated me from his ideology".[71]

Underlying the deal struck between the Radicals and the right over a minimal programme of government lurked the CEDA's strategy-for-power. The accidentalists, Gil Robles explained, would achieve power by exhausting all other possibilities; in other words, they would first collaborate with the Radical Party from without the Cabinet, then from within, and, finally, take it over. "All ideals are realized by stages", he proclaimed. In other words, the rise of the right was predicated upon the fall of the Radicals. Moreover, the strategy was underpinned by the latent threat of violence should the CEDA be foiled in its designs. The accidentalist leader, in an interview with *Renovación*, declared that if his party was not allowed to govern at the appropriate moment "we shall seek other solutions" while explaining "to the people that the path of democracy serves no use whatsoever". Consequently the symbiotic relationship between the Radical Party and the CEDA, though consistent with Lerroux's conviction that the Republic had to be consolidated through the incorporation of the non-republican right, was a marriage of convenience between two parties that were at once allies and adversaries. The parliamentary majority, as the Radical César Jalón later noted, "was not bound together by a creed, not even by a common political thought, but by a fortuitous strategy". Naturally, this mix of ideological and strategic differences was a recipe for instability and conflict rather than the "peace" that the Radicals aspired to.[72]

Lerroux was none the less confident that the authoritarian ambitions harboured by the CEDA, which obviously represented an implicit threat to the democratic principles that were consubstantial with the Republic, would be disarmed through collaboration. A policy of "understanding, accommodation and confidence" would, he believed, integrate the right into the regime. His mission, indeed, was to achieve the "greatest number possible of adherences". This reconciliatory spirit was embodied in the appointment of Santiago Alba, the erstwhile monarchist minister who had recently joined the party, as speaker of the Cortes. This policy of accommodation gained an early success when the reconstructed Agrarian Party, which had won thirty-six seats in the general election, declared its formal adherence to the Republic on 21 January 1934. Though this prompted the departure of five deputies, including the former monarchist Prime Minister the Conde de Romanones, the influential landowner from Palencia Abilio Calderón, and General Fanjul, the bulk of the party, many of whom were former followers of Santiago Alba, including Cid, remained.[73]

The most immediate challenge faced by the government was the CNT's third, and greatest, uprising under the Republic. The anarcho–syndicalist movement, mightily disillusioned by two years of parliamentary democracy, had greeted the general election not only with a vigorous campaign in favour of abstention but also with the commitment, under the slogan of "In opposition to the urns, the social revolution", to launch an insurrectionary movement should the right triumph. On 8 December, the day the Cortes opened, the CNT revolt was unleashed. It was centred above all in Aragon[74] but also extended to localities in Andalusia, Catalonia, Extremadura, Leon, Logroño, the Levante (where many *pueblos* were organized along libertarian lines), while there were also strikes in Andalusia, Asturias, Castille, and Galicia. Despite being the most thoroughly prepared of the movement's risings under the Republic, it proved no match for the army and Civil Guard. There were numerous sanguinary clashes. In Villanueva de la Serena (Badajoz) twenty militants under the command of Sergeant Pío Sopena took over an army recruiting centre. They held out until the building was crushed by artillery. Seven people were killed. The insurgents also derailed a number of trains, most notably the Barcelona–Seville express at a cost of thirteen lives. In all, 89 people, comprising eleven Civil Guards, three Assault Guards, and seventy-five civilians, died in what Murray Bookchin has described as "the most destructive exercise in futility ever undertaken by the CNT and the FAI". Anarcho–syndicalist centres were closed the length and breadth of the land while thousands of activists were imprisoned. Not only did the rising exhaust the movement's already depleted ranks, but it also demonstrated the bankruptcy of the FAI's "revolutionary gymnastics". It was no coin-cidence that, over the next two-and-a-half years, the CNT would undertake no large-scale insurrectionary actions.[75]

Just as the revolutionary spirit of the CNT was waning, that of the socialist movement was in the ascendant. Socialist disillusionment with the Republic had begun in 1933 as a reaction to the shortcomings of reform, to the impact of the depression, but above all at the prospect of losing power as the republican–socialist coalition crumbled.[76] The possi-bility of embracing "revolution" should the socialists be ejected from the government had been raised by Largo Caballero at the Socialist Youth's summer school in August 1933. Following the collapse of the Azaña administration a month later, the PSOE Executive Committee had, on the 11th of that month, formally broken with the republicans for having formed a government – the first Lerroux administration – without them.[77] "For the socialists", observes Santos Juliá, "it was enough for them to feel excluded, expelled from the responsibility of governing in order to announce their new political intentions: this change, still incipient, is incomprehensible if one does not take into account that they all regarded the Republic as their own creature and they all believed that they had the right, above and beyond the elections and the popular vote, to govern it". After the first round of the general election, the socialists broke with the Republic, too. At a joint meeting of the PSOE and UGT Executive Committees on 25 November 1933 it was decided that if the "reactionary elements" won power the socialists would "rise up vigorously".[78] The decision to revolt at the coming to power, or "provocation", of the right was ratified the following day by the PSOE National Committee. At heart, this was a defensive strategy designed to keep the non-republican right out of power. Yet it was rejected in no uncertain terms by the left republicans. Azaña, as he told Fernando de los Ríos on 2 January 1934, did not believe that the Radical government, however reprehensible, justified an insur-rectionary response. In any case, the idea that a socialist-style uprising, comprising a general strike together with the support of sympathetic mili-tary elements, could triumph was "chimerical" given the strength of the state security forces and the fact that only one-fifth of the country was socialist.[79] Not only was such a rebellion doomed to failure, but it would also put both the Republic and Spain "on the brink of ruin". Even in the unlikely event that the rising succeeded, no republicans would support it. Meanwhile, the socialist moderates would be displaced by extremists, thereby causing a "terrible reaction". Nor did Azaña accept Largo Caballero's contention that he was merely acting, as was his duty, on the desires of the rank and file; on the contrary, the "duty" of the leaders was to guide and, if necessary, modify such sentiments. In short, the repub-lican leader not only rejected the insurrectionary option but was also convinced that it would be utterly counterproductive. The socialists paid their erstwhile ally no heed. Largo Caballero later dismissed, in a speech, those that permitted themselves to "give advice" in relation to matters that did not concern them. On 13 January, a ten-point revolutionary programme was drawn up by the PSOE Executive which included nation-alization of the land and the dissolution of the religious orders, the army, and the Civil Guard. Two weeks later, the supporters of Julián Besteiro, who were opposed to an uprising, were replaced on the UGT Executive by those of Largo Caballero, the chief advocate of "revolution". Largo Caballero himself took up the post of general secretary. He now headed both the party and the trade unions. In February, the *Caballeristas* also seized command of the largest union in the UGT, the FNTT. Control of the crucial Madrid party followed. Still in February, a revolutionary liaison committee was set up under the party leader. Ultimately, the social-ists believed that the insurrection would never take place; in other words, it was a threat that, by thwarting the entry of the CEDA into the govern-ment, they hoped never to fulfil. However, it was a high-risk strategy that not only depended on the collaboration of the President – Largo Caballero could not be sure that Alcalá-Zamora would continually resist the CEDA's demands to join the Cabinet – but also played into the hands of the right by leaving the timing of the rising to it.[80]

Central to the socialists' rejection of the Republic and of the republi-cans was the conviction that the Radical Party was a "reactionary" force that would dismantle the reformist achievements of the first biennium. Certainly the Radicals were revisionists, but they were not reactionaries. On the contrary, they intended to steer a centrist course that struck some sort of a balance between the conflicting social and political forces. This was illustrated by the Radical approach to the *patronal*. The electoral victory of the centre–right had been heralded by the employers' associa-tions as the long-awaited opportunity to satisfy their grievances; namely, to establish "law and order" and to modify, if not overturn, the socialist-inspired labour legislation. *Labor*, for example, denounced the Constituent Cortes for having "sown hatred and vengeance with the poli-tics of class". The *patronal* rejected not just the socialists – "the anti-republic" – but also the left republicans. Sánchez Castillo, director of the National Association of Contractors of Public Works and a Radical–Socialist, censured his own party for having displaced the indus-trial and commercial sectors from its heart as a result of its "socialist orientation". "What did they do?", he asked rhetorically, "for the benefit of the small employer, of the small industrialist, of the modest farmer, of the small capitalist and, in general, for all the productive and mercantile classes of the country, which in April 1931 gave their votes to the repub-licans?" The employers, echoing the Radicals, called for "a Republic for all Spaniards", which meant, as *Labor* explained, that "one can be repub-lican" and still "be against the ill-fated politics embodied in the dissolved

Cortes". Thus the *patronal* expected, Sánchez Castillo observed, "real rectifications" that demonstrated that within the republican parties "there is room for all social and economic aspirations".[81]

The Radicals promptly addressed the principal complaint of the *patronal*: the mixed juries. On 11 January the government changed the procedure by which the presidents of the juries, who held the casting vote, were chosen. During the first biennium, the system had been heavily attacked by the employers as the Ministry of Labour, headed by Largo Caballero, had nominated the presidents, thereby often ensuring a built-in majority for the workers. The Radicals, too, had found fault with the juries for being politically biased. It was now specified that the president could not be a member of a trade union or an employers' association, but should belong either to the legal profession or the civil service. In addition, they had to be chosen at random and not hand-picked. Given the generally conservative outlook of the legal profession, this modification in the mixed juries probably shifted the balance of power towards the employers. However, the Radicals' partial reform was not so much a frontal assault on the juries as a genuine attempt to make them more independent. That the decree did not meet the expectations of the *patronal* was shown by the inquiry conducted into the juries by the Minister of Labour in early 1934. While both the CNT, opposed to the juries on principle, and the UGT, innately hostile to the Radicals, would not take part in the inquiry, the employers, disgruntled at having to state their views once again, urged the government to make the juries purely conciliatory, as opposed to arbitral, bodies (unless both parts submitted themselves voluntarily), as well as to withdraw their powers of inspection. That done, the Lerroux administration failed to act on the *patronal*'s recommendations. Neither did a bill appear before parliament. Nor were any further decrees forthcoming. On the contrary, the mixed juries, despite having been roundly condemned by the employers' associations, continued to function as arbitration committees.[82]

The impatience of the *patronal* became greater still as a result of the government's handling of a major construction strike in Madrid. This pitted the CNT, which had initiated the stoppage in September 1933, and the UGT against the formidable Federación Patronal Madrileña. The strikers' chief goal was to secure the 44-hour week as a means of combatting ever-rising unemployment. Disillusioned by the "passivity of the government", the *patronal* had reached a provisional agreement with the unions in November 1933. However, the dispute flared up again, developing into a general strike, as a result of continuing dismissals. Eventually, on 17 February, José Estadella, the Minister of Labour, decreed the implementation of the 44-hour week. The Federación was stunned. It considered the measure not only illegal but a humiliating defeat. Eight days later, the Madrid *patronal* held a massive meeting of all the employers, ranging from the construction bosses to café owners and those in clothing, that had been affected by a spate of recent strikes. The assembled employers held the "professionals of politics" responsible for their woes, seizing on José Estadella in particular for heading "a sectarian ministry at the service of a class" – in this case the working class, not the middle class. Once more, they demanded the overhauling of the labour legislation, the overturning of the strike law, and, finally, "a profound reform of the Ministry of Labour, promoter of the present social state of the country on account of being where the socialist virus nests". The alienation of the *patronal* was further manifested in the birth of the Bloque Patronal, a "united front" of the Madrid employers which would form the basis of a nationwide organization. Brought together by a shared sense of crisis as a result of the economic depression and the strikes, the members of the Bloque soon fell out over the organization's strategy and goals. Nor was it representative, being limited to commerce, hostelries, and the construction trade. In other words, the Bloque was at once a demonstration of the *patronal*'s unity and divisiveness. "Neither in the economic nor the social sphere", noted Sánchez Castillo, "do the *patronos* think the same".[83]

A measure of confidence was restored in the *patronal* as a result of the government's response to the "ABC" strike of March 1934. Originally sparked by the hiring of non-union labour at *ABC*, the monarchist daily, the action subsequently blew up into a general walkout of the print workers. While the Minister of the Interior, Salazar Alonso, regarded it as "a revolutionary tactic", union propaganda viewed the conflict as "the decisive battle against reaction and fascism". The deployment of black-legs together with the authorities' backing settled the confrontation in favour of the newspaper owners.[84] When, however, the Madrid construction dispute was reignited by the refusal of management to abide by the 44-hour week, even the right-wing Salazar Alonso was obliged in March to imprison recalcitrant employers.[85] That same month, a strike wave was unleashed in the capital which ranged from the cafés to the clothing and wood industries. Worse still, there was a stoppage in the metallurgical industry in defence of, amongst other things, the 44-hour week. The Federación Madrileña expressed its disgust by proposing to name José Estadella as "citizen of honour" in his capacity as "the minister of the 44 hours". Clearly the Radicals' industrial policy was still in the making, but it was evident that they were not prepared simply to do the *patronal*'s biding, even though the latter formed the cornerstone of their social base. On the contrary, the Radical Party appeared to be seeking a middle way that would build a consensus between the *patronal* and the workers. Yet the Radicals' centrist approach had already lost them the trust of the Madrid employers. The Radical government, in short, had declared "war on the *patronal* class".[86]

In the countryside, the Radicals undertook a less equitable approach. Many landowners had interpreted the electoral result as a personal defeat for the workers which justified the overthrow, or at least eschewal, of the reforms of 1931–3. A number of measures from the first biennium were soon revised or repealed. First, the mixed juries, as outlined above, were modified in January 1934. Second, the law of *términos municipales* was heavily altered once the Radicals came to power. Under Lerroux's fleeting administration of 12 September to 3 October 1933, the property owners in twelve southern provinces were permitted to hire labour from anywhere within, though not from outside, each individual province. The move elicited a widespread outcry. The Prime Minister received numerous letters from workers pleading with him to reconsider the measure. A UGT branch in the province of Logroño, for example, claimed that the proposed revision would "increase the employers' *caciquismo*, facilitating the persecution and denial of work of which we, the workers, are victims, and contributing as well to the destruction of the new regime".[87] Yet the Minister of Labour, Ricardo Samper, declared the intention of the Radicals to repeal the measure because, by increasing unemployment and inhibiting productivity, it had benefited neither the labourers nor the landowners.[88] In fact, many workers, especially those in the CNT or not in a union at all, had opposed the measure as favouring the socialists. Malefakis describes it as "universally unpopular" outside socialist ranks.[89] Accordingly, a bill to overturn the law completely was presented to parliament in January 1934. Lastly, the Radicals revoked the *turno rigoroso* arrangements from the previous year. This limited legislative revisionism was surpassed by the government's "reaction-by-omission" whereby the authorities turned a blind eye to violations of the existing laws. As a result, socialist activists were discriminated against, wages dropped, and the legislation was not applied as before.[90] In this way, the Radical Party appeased their accidentalist ally by allowing the socio-economic forces of the right, as well as those landowners that now militated within Radical ranks, to regain some of the power so far lost under the Republic. In January 1934, the socialist deputy and president of the FNTT, Lucio Martínez Gil, pleaded with the government to fulfil the regulations and to prevent the persecution of workers for refusing to join "the entities that the *patronos* are creating". Still, the clock had not been set back to monarchist times. Wages fell to around the level of 1932, unemployment did not soar, and, in institutional terms, the socialists continued to defend their interests through the mixed juries, the town and village councils, and, as a last resort, through the deployment of the strike.[91] Moreover, conditions appear to have varied a good deal from one province to another. The new contract for the province of Seville, for example, paid even more than that of 1933, while the use of machinery during the harvest was restricted. Salaries in Cordoba province were higher, too, than during the previous year. By contrast, conditions appear to have deteriorated notably in provinces such as Granada and Jaen. In February 1934, socialist leader Indalecio Prieto denounced before the Cortes the situation in Jaen, where, he claimed, the labour legislation was being widely abused, the Civil Guard intimidated the workers, and where, since the general election, over 400 workers had been imprisoned. That same month, a Radical minister admitted that "in many *pueblos* they presently live in a full-blown dictatorship of the old *caciques*".[92]

Revisionism of the first biennium's reforms was none the less regarded by the Radical Party not only as consistent with its centrist appeal but also as a necessary price to pay for the support of the non-republican right. The backing of the CEDA and its allies gave the Radicals direct and unprecedented access to the public spoils system. Largely as a result of the *cal, yeso y cemento* scandal of 1910, the links with Juan March, and the fact that the party was later engulfed by a major scandal, the Radical Party has long been regarded, in Stanley Payne's apposite phrase, as the "pork-barrel" party of Spanish politics *par excellence*.[93] This view, however, must be qualified somewhat. First, the Radicals have been reviled for their clientelism, or what *El Socialista* denounced as their "nepotism".[94] There is no doubt that a great many party members were appointed in a partisan fashion to positions in the gift of the authorities. "They all want jobs, they all ask for posts", exclaimed the Galician leader Gerardo Abad Conde in a letter to Lerroux which, as if to make his point, contained a list of requests for positions in areas as far flung as Galicia, Madrid, and Valencia. What counted was not so much the suitability of the candidates for the job as their fidelity. For example, a veteran Radical, who had been tried five times under the monarchy for his activities in defence of the republican cause, requested the post of chief tax inspector in Vizcaya in April 1934 on the grounds that no one could "supersede me in terms of political merit".[95] The Radical leader himself, much like a dynastic politician, spent a considerable part of each day receiving numerous people with requests of both a party and personal nature. In a typical example, an activist wrote to the *jefe* to explain that he had been unable to see him as a result of "the innumerable people who ask to see you daily".[96] Joaquín Chapaprieta, who became Prime Minister in 1935, was astonished at the length and detail of the letters that Lerroux regularly addressed to him on behalf of other people.[97] Shortly after the Radical leader came to power in December 1933, he was visited by a commission to press the claims of party members in relation to the appointments made to leading public posts. That month, the Ministry of Education named numerous Radicals as chief inspectors and head teachers. Similarly, eight Radicals were appointed to the Lozoya canal project. In July 1934, the workers' representatives on the board of the Monte de Piedad, a savings bank, were allegedly replaced by a brother of Dámaso Veléz (the political secretary of Lerroux), an intimate friend of Santiago Alba (the Radical President of the Cortes), a brother of Sánchez Fuster (Lerroux's personal secretary), and a friend of Aurelio Lerroux (the adopted son of the Radical leader).[98] The opposition press accused the Radicals of acting in the same fashion in relation to the mixed juries, hospitals, and many other positions in the gift of the state. Even the apparently austere Martínez Barrio, who has strenuously denied embracing such practices, was not immune. According to Alcalá-Zamora, he secured a position on the Council of State for the colleague that gave up his parliamentary seat for the then Prime Minister in the 1933 general election.[99]

Such examples were pounced upon by El Socialista as proof of "Radical voracity". On 24 February it published an article headlined "The Activity of the Radical Committees" in which it alleged that these were "today masters of the state" as a result of their "business" with the Radical parliamentary group and the ministers. The stance of the socialist daily was pure humbug. Both the left republicans and socialists took massive advantage of their rise to power to place their own card-carrying members in an enormous variety of public positions. Evidence of this is provided by the huge piles of "recomendaciones" (letters of recommendation) addressed to politicians in the Civil War Archive. These range from Radicals such as Lerroux, Martínez Barrio, and César Oarrichena to other republicans such as Alvaro de Albornoz, Marcelino Domingo, and Pita Romero. The President, who himself regularly petitioned ministers on behalf of his own clientele, records that the competition for public positions within the Radical–Socialist parliamentary party led to "real and frequent brawls". If the Radical leader's "recommendations" managed to install a niece in the Geography Institute, another in the Bank of Spain, and his nephew in the civil service, there is no doubt that the left republicans and socialists also indulged in exactly the same sort of "euphoria", as El Socialista dubbed it.[100] Indeed, in 1933, the Federal deputy, Joaquín del Moral, published a book appropriately entitled Oligarquía y enchufismo ("Oligarchy and Favouritism"). Del Moral, who had been under-secretary in the Ministry of the Economy, reveals the aggregate income of the deputies of each party, embracing not just their remunerations as parliamentarians – which stood at 1,000 pesetas a month – but for all the public positions which they exercised. Thus the Radical–Socialist deputies received on average of 5,063 pesetas a month, the socialists 6,421, while those of Acción Republicana over 10,000. By contrast, the Radicals, then out of office, earned a mere 1,389 pesetas a month from their public service.[101] Also provided is a detailed breakdown of the posts held by a number of deputies. One of the most notorious cases was that of the socialist Manuel Cordero, who, as well as being a deputy, also found time to be a town councillor for Madrid, a regional deputy, a board member of the state petroleum company, CAMPSA, the President of the

Commission of Responsibilities, and the head of four different mixed juries; in all, he managed to juggle no less than fourteen jobs. In reality, the socialists had become accustomed to the perks of the state sector under the Dictatorship of Primo de Rivera. By collaborating with the military regime, they had benefited above all from the creation of the *comités paritarios*, which were replaced in 1931 by the *jurados mixtos*. While Largo Caballero was at the Ministry of Labour, UGT members were invariably favoured over non-socialist ones for public works contracts. Complaints against the socialists for monopolizing employment on these contracts continued into the second biennium. The socialists were sometimes prepared to use violence to protect their privileges. For example, the Radical Party branch in Cañete la Real (Malaga), where the PSOE controlled both the local council and court, claimed that the socialists, who had cornered a public works contract, coerced Radical workers not only by attacking their centre, but also by firing shots at them and "even setting fire to the farm that they were working".[102] Such sectarian practices contradicted the socialists' much-vaunted claim to represent the "working class" as they constantly deployed the resources of the state to further the interests of the PSOE and UGT at the expense of other working-class organizations. All in all, the corporatist labour policy pursued by Largo Caballero in the 1920s and '30s can be seen as an institutionalized form of clientage. Moreover, as the example of Manuel Cordero shows, the socialists had greatly extended their networks under the new regime. Not surprisingly, the prospect of being excluded from the public spoils system was an additional motive for the radicalization of the socialists in 1933. In conclusion, the socialist as well as the republican parties, like the monarchist ones before them, were characterized by extensive clientelist practices. For many individuals, indeed, such considerations overrode those of ideology or political affiliation.[103]

One of the principal sources of state patronage was local government. The Radicals, from the moment they achieved power, exhibited an intense interest in wresting control of both local and provincial authorities from their opponents. As the civil governor for Caceres wrote to the Prime Minister days after he had presented his government to the Cortes, "I dismissed the town council legally and completely. I will now see if I can do the same with the (provincial) Junta". Similarly, *El Socialista* reported that in Santafé in Granada province the socialist town council had been forcibly replaced by the Civil Guard with Radicals who were former monarchists. This, the socialist organ claimed, was "an example of what is happening throughout Spain".[104] There is no denying that the Radical deputies, as shown by the agitated meeting of the parliamentary party on 27 December 1933, constantly pressed ministers to extend the party's dominion over local government. Not only was this perceived as strengthening the party's presence in the provinces but it was also regarded as yet another means of providing employment for Radical affiliates. Martínez Barrio, as Minister of the Interior in early 1934, was frequently criticized by fellow deputies at the meetings of the parliamentary group for his "passive resistence" in not dismissing more opposition *ayuntamientos*. This practice further exacerbated tensions with the CEDA, though not because it was considered unprincipled. On the contrary, Gil Robles complained to the Prime Minister on numerous occasions that his party had not received its share of the steering committees that were being created. For example, he protested to the premier in a letter in January 1934 that in various provincies the participation of the right on the committees was "derisory" or ignored altogether, leaving his ally "spurned, with a minimal representation, which could appear as alms".[105] This sectarian policy, however, was far from exclusive to the Radicals. It should be remembered that Miguel Maura, Minister of the Interior from April to October 1931, had overthrown thousands of rural councils by dubious means in order to "republicanize" the countryside. Another 316 town and village councils, at a rate of roughly fourteen a month, were dismissed by his replacement, Casares Quiroga, over the following two years. The initial scale of Radical dismissals, in comparison with Casares Quiroga, was slightly less: Rico Avello overturned 40 in three months, whilst Martínez Barrio replaced only six in another three.[106] The toppling of *ayuntamientos* aside, local Radicals, like the left republicans and socialists before them, were ever eager to obtain material benefits for their home town or *pueblo* in order to strengthen both their clientage networks and their popularity. To take an example, in March 1934 the Radicals of Sama de Langreo in Asturias requested "some local improvement" from Lerroux so that they would be regarded as "beneficial mediators" and win "many supporters". Similarly, the civil governor for Cadiz wrote to the *jefe* in February 1934 that the Radicals would be unable to maintain their support in the locality of Castellar de la Frontera "unless material advantages were obtained for this *pueblo*".[107] In this way, the party replicated the role of the *cacique* as intermediary agent between Madrid and the provinces.

There was one area, however, where the Radicals stood apart from their erstwhile left republican and socialist colleagues: the exploitation of the public sector for their own business or pecuniary ends. In the first decade of the century, the Lerrouxists, lacking the resources of the monarchist parties, had taken advantage of the public purse to finance their party. During the following decade, politics merged into business as the party became a means for personal enrichment. The *cal, yeso y cemento* scandal of 1910 in particular was to seal the Radicals' reputation for graft. Both before and during the Republic, the socialists and left republicans – eager to distance themselves ethically from the allegedly "corrupt" monarchy – regarded this as a reason for distancing themselves from the

Radical Party, too. Yet while the Radicals were in government in 1931 not a single case emerged of the party's malfeasance. By contrast, once the party came to power in 1933, numerous allegations were made by the opposition press, especially *El Socialista*, in relation to the Radicals' alleged venal practices. For example, the socialist organ contended on a number of occasions in 1934 that Radical politicians had received bribes. The most detailed instance concerned the appointment of the secretary to the Court of Constitutional Guarantees. According to *El Socialista*, three Radical deputies – Fernando Rey Mora, Basilio Alvarez, and Emiliano Iglesias – had each been paid 30,000 pesetas by a Señor Serrano in order to secure the post for his son. Although the charge was vehemently denied, the paper reproduced a letter supposedly written by the father in which he stated that the Radical deputies "are the ones that arrange everything". The Radicals were also accused of peculation. The Radical mayor of Huelva, for example, was accused in a newspaper report of June 1934 of having embezzled the town hall's funds. At the national level, the personal secretary of Basilio Alvarez was put on trial for having purloined 15,000 pesetas worth of taxpayers' money. In the summer of 1934 *El Socialista* conjectured that the PURA deputy Pascual Martínez Sala, a former agent of Juan March, was involved in smuggling operations, the paper adding for good measure that he was also the economic protector of Sigfrido Blasco Ibáñez.[108] Greater speculation surrounded the Radicals' supposed abuse of public contracts. The most widely publicized case of 1934 was the "rice and maize" affair, according to which a number of Radicals received illegal commissions for the exportation of rice and the importation of maize. Funds were supposedly syphoned off during the rebuilding of the port of Melilla, too. State protection for the private business affairs of Radical Party members was also denounced by the opposition press. "Distribución Orphea Film", a company presided over by the Radical leader himself, was on the point of collapse by March 1934, but it was then bailed out by the Ministry of Industry.[109] Another Lerrouxist enterprise to benefit from state backing was "Autoestaciones", a bus company whose well-being was based on a substantial public contract. Similarly, the "Trasátlantica" company, which was run on Lerroux's behalf by his right-hand man in Catalonia, Juan Pich y Pon, whose own financial involvement in the company apparently amounted to no less than 300 million pesetas, received public subsidies. None of these company cases, in themselves, is evidence of wrongdoing. The same cannot be said for the dispute between the wine trade and the sugar industry over the profitable CAMPSA oil contract. Apparently, wine was a far better additive for the oil than sugar, but the government decided in favour of the latter. It was surmised that the reason for this unexpected resolution was that the Minister of the Economy, Manuel Marraco, was a leading shareholder in the largest of the sugar companies, "La Azucarea Aragonesa", and that his son was the company manager.[110] Finally, *El Socialista* claimed that casinos, banned under the Dictatorship, were tacitly permitted under the Radicals. In January 1934, a casino, the daily averred, opened in Ciudad Real, though this was swiftly closed down. It was later said that several more were allowed to operate in Madrid throughout the summer of 1934. One reporter even provided an eye-witness account of a casino in the Plaza de Santa Ana – a popular square right in the heart of Madrid, a short walk from the Cortes. One such locale was unveiled in the elegant Basque resort of San Sebastian in September 1934, but was shut down within a matter of hours on the orders of the Radical Minister of the Interior, Salazar Alonso. *El Socialista* speculated that the casino had been permitted to open in the first place on account of the intervention of "a nephew or son who acts as frontman for his father or uncle" – an unmistakable reference to Lerroux's adopted son, Aurelio. Further conjecture was thwarted by the decision of the public prosecutor to seize any edition of the socialist organ that dealt with the matter.[111]

These claims of Radical corruption have to be treated with a certain scepticism given that they were made by a hostile source, *El Socialista*, which was eager to discredit the Radicals in order to further its own political agenda. For example, the paper had to retract the accusations made against the PURA deputy Martínez Sala. Though such claims knowingly exploited the Radicals' venal reputation, and though there is insufficient evidence for each case to be properly evaluated, they probably contain an important element of truth. Lerroux later admitted in exile that, amongst those that surrounded him, there were "many parvenus who went into politics in order to make money". The scale of the Radicals' graft, while accepting that such practices are notoriously difficult to detect and demonstrate, should not be unduly exaggerated. The reason for this was given by the Radical leader's right-hand man, Emiliano Iglesias, in a private exchange during the summer of 1934 with the monarchist politician Pedro Sainz Rodríguez. Iglesias did not deny that there was some basis to the party's reputation, but claimed that it was "very difficult to do business in the present circumstances". He, for example, had been on the verge of investing between two and three million pesetas – a considerable amount of money – in the importation of eggs from Turkey, but the number of people who had got wind of the operation, including the editor of the daily *La Libertad* and a number of deputies, and who demanded a cut in exchange for their silence, had made it unprofitable. The downcast Radical concluded that the vigilance of the press together with the scrutiny of parliament "and all the individuals who find out about everything" meant that "there is no way of doing anything".[112] Moreover, the pork-barrel approach to politics did not characterize all the party; in reality, it typified the Barcelona party, the PURA, and the Radical leader's inner circle, above all. Nor should the differences between the

Radicals and their former government partners be blown up out of proportion insofar as they all strayed into areas of questionable, but not illicit, activity. For example, the adjudication of a public contract to a company in which a Radical politician had an interest may have been unethical, but it was not strictly illegal. Allowing a socialist deputy to hold up to fourteen public positions was also unethical, but neither was it illegal. The dividing line between the Radicals and their former allies was sometimes thin indeed.

The venality of the Radicals underlined their essentially pragmatic approach to the exercise of power. The party possessed no major reformist ambitions, not even, in true populist style, a clearly defined programme. Instead, the Radical agenda consisted of shifting the Republic towards the centre ground by opening up the channels of influence to the middle classes and by revising, but not rejecting, the reforms of 1931-3. The rationale of this strategy is that both the party and the regime would be consolidated by the integration into the Republic of the heterogeneous middle classes. Consequently the Radicals viewed their rule as a period of stabilization as the regime's base was broadened and a more consensual politics emerged. The pragmatism of the Radicals was no doubt enhanced by the performance of its ageing leader, Alejandro Lerroux, who is invariably portrayed as lacking drive and determination as premier. According to Alcalá-Zamora, he never understood "the most fundamental aspects of the position" while exhibiting a "total and constant inhibition". In the Cortes, the oft-absent Prime Minister was distinguished, Gil Robles recalls, by his "tiredness" and "indifference" as well as failing to "set any sort of course for the legislative tasks". As a result, parliament "scarcely functioned" during this period.[113] The Radical ministers were not much of an improvement. Often lethargic and ineffectual, the President describes them as "deplorable administrators". In particular, he dismisses Lerroux's second government as "a bad administration". Meanwhile, the parliamentary group attempted to improve on its ill-disciplined performance of the first biennium, but to little avail. On 3 January 1934, only two weeks after the Radical *jefe* had assumed office and on the day of a major Cortes debate, the party's deputies were urged by the leadership to ensure their regular attendance in the chamber. That very afternoon, however, a meeting with the Prime Minister had to be cancelled because too few deputies appeared. By all accounts, the Radicals' lack of discipline was to be a permanent feature of their rule.[114]

From the very outset, the Radicals' manifest moderation and ideological differences with the CEDA created tensions within the alliance. On 4 January, in an incident provoked by the anti-Catalanist remarks of the proto-fascist Dr Albiñana, the Radicals leapt to the defence of the Republic – the Minister of the Economy leading the "*Vivas!*" from the front bench – in contrast to the CEDA. By the end of the month's first week, the government's partners, according to the CEDA leader, were already exhibiting "a growing impatience". The right was especially anxious over the amnesty, but the Prime Minister informed Gil Robles that there was resistance to it from within the party. The CEDA *caudillo*, constantly harassed himself by the monarchists, lobbied the Cabinet on virtually a daily basis. On 24 January, the CEDA sided with the Radicals in opposing a monarchist bill, but exploited the incident in order to apply even greater pressure. This was complemented by *El Debate*'s unflagging criticism of the ministers' alleged lack of energy and efficiency. It seized on the Minister of the Economy in particular for his "tropical indolence", warning that if a coherent economic policy was not presented forthwith "it will be disastrous for the country and for the government". On 5 February, Gil Robles gave a threatening speech in Seville. He boasted that with 117 deputies "the responsibility of provoking catastrophes and over-throwing governments each week is greatly felt", before issuing a sharp warning: either the government undertook a "total rectification" of its trajectory or else the right would "perhaps" be obliged to take over soon.[115]

Clearly the Radical Prime Minister was dragging his heels over the demands of the CEDA. Quite simply, the Radical Party had little to gain from being pulled to the right. This would weaken the party's centrist appeal and correspondingly strengthen that of its allies. Ground would be given on a particular issue or policy only insofar as it was necessary to maintain the parliamentary majority. Consequently the Radical Party and the CEDA were condemned to a constant tug-of-war as their differing agendas pulled them this way and that. Even so, the Radical deputy leader, Martínez Barrio, harboured profound misgivings about the alliance. He had first protested at sharing the Cabinet with the Agrarian José María Cid as his party had yet to declare itself republican (it did so a month later). He had then clashed with Lerroux over the formation of a parliamentary majority in collaboration with the right.[116] Hereon, the tension between the Radical left and the CEDA was unremitting, as demonstrated by the confrontation of 4 January. At a banquet on 12 January the Radical *jefe* tried to placate the doubters by assuring them that the arrangement with the accidentalists would not undermine the regime. On the contrary, he claimed, the incorporation of the right into the Republic would be the Radical Party's "greatest and supreme service". Moreover, the party would not endanger the Republic through its collaboration with the CEDA and its allies under any circumstances: "death rather than surrender to reaction", he cried stirringly. Martínez Barrio was not convinced. He replied by denouncing the "catastrophic solutions" of those that aimed to "overthrow the government" – a reference to the left as well as to the right – and by insisting that under the present legislature the party should "be its own succesor". Ten days later, Martínez Barrio

Alejandro Lerroux as a radical newspaper editor in 1897.

Multitudinous picnics, like this one on the Coll mountain near Barcelona in 1903, were one more means of populist mobilization. Standing to Lerroux's right is his alter ego, Emiliano Iglesias.

Lerroux addressing a Barcelona crowd in support of those imprisoned following the "Tragic Week" of July 1909. Those at the table include Pablo Iglesias, the socialist leader, and Benito Pérez Galdós, the renowned writer and republican.

The Radical leader delivering a speech in the Madrid bullring during the tumultuous events of 1917.

Members of the provisional government on 14 April 1931, the day the Second Republic was proclaimed. From the left, Manuel Azaña, Alvaro de Albornoz, Niceto Alcalá-Zamora, Miguel Maura, Francisco Largo Caballero, Fernando de los Ríos, and, finally, Alejandro Lerroux.

A full house in Madrid for Lerroux's speech of 21 February 1932.

The Radical leader's first Cabinet following the 1933 general election files out of the Royal Palace.

Radical deputy Basilio Alvarez, seen here in April 1933, was conspicuous not only as a cleric within an historically anticlerical party but also for his flamboyant oratory.

The tension shows at the critical meeting of 18 May 1934 between the Radical leadership and the dissidents headed by Diego Martínez Barrio. To the far left is Rafael Guerra del Río and to the far right Antonio Lara. Martínez Barrio is seated second from the right. Standing to Lerroux's left is Rafael Salazar Alonso.

The Huelva Radical Youth group proudly exhibits a portrait of the party''s founder-figure and leader.

The Palencia Radical Party. In the background, to the left, is a portrait of Lerroux, and, to the right, the regime's muse, "La república española".

Radicals from the *pueblo* of Real de la Jara in Seville province.

elaborated upon his position in a speech in Madrid, rejecting both the pact with the non-republican right as well as the possibility that the latter might govern under the present legislature. Instead, he advocated a middle way between left and right through the union of the republicans. On 4 February he delivered an even more damning appraisal of the alliance in *ABC*'s Sunday magazine, *Blanco y Negro*. Decribing the political situation as "imprecise and confused", he called for the left's revolutionary threats to be dealt with not by "the repressive mode", but by means of political dialogue. Further, he insisted that the CEDA should not be permitted to make demands on the government until the non-republican right had declared itself republican. This was a warning shot across Lerroux's bow.[117]

The conflict mounted as, three days later, Martínez Barrio clashed head on with Gil Robles in the Cortes. The CEDA *jefe*, having announced that the Radical deputy leader's comments to *Blanco y Negro* had created a "political problem", stated bluntly that if the right encountered "obstacles . . . along the path of legality" it would turn to violence. This threat gave even greater moral authority to Martínez Barrio's call for the government to be "master of all its movements". The Prime Minister endeavoured to accommodate both sides by reiterating that he aimed to "extend the base of the Republic" while governing "in a republican manner"; that is to say, he would collaborate with the right as long as the regime was not threatened.[118] The key point at dispute between the two Radical leaders was the refusal of the non-republican right to declare its adherence to the Republic. Whereas Martínez Barrio, scarred by years of conflict with the monarchists in Seville, regarded this as a question of principle, Lerroux, who had long ago reached a modus vivendi with the monarchy, trusted in the quotidian realities of political give-and-take in order to reach a satisfactory arrangement with the accidentalists. For Martínez Barrio, recognition of the regime was the minimal price of collaboration, while for his pragmatic *jefe* this was preferable, but not essential. The Prime Minister reiterated to the press in February that cooperation with the CEDA had been thrust upon him as a consequence of the general election. "It's not my fault", he lamented. On the other hand, he defended the coalition as a means of nationalizing the regime and thereby contributing towards its consolidation; "I am a national man", he averred.[119] The obvious danger of the alliance was that it might represent the thin edge of the wedge as more and more ground was ceded to the right without any identifiable limit being set. The Radical leader's constantly shifting definition of what "in a republican manner" meant was indicative of the dilemma. By contrast, the deputy leader's clear cut stance not only provided the regime with a greater measure of security but would also allow the Radical Party to re-establish its links with the left republicans rather than mortgage its future to the non-republican right.

The outspoken remarks of Martínez Barrio to *Blanco y Negro* were shrilly censured by *El Debate* as "a ministerial 'sabotage'". Worse still, Gil Robles began to refer dismissively to the coalition with the Radicals as "the experiment" and to bully the government with undisguised contempt. On 19 February, in a speech in Pamplona, he issued what was virtually an ultimatum. "Señor Lerroux", he declared, "the experiment is being exhausted": either the government rectified its course or "we will have to withdraw our support from the government". A week later in Salamanca, he pilloried the Cabinet for its "total sterility" while reiterating that the situation was "unsustainable". On 23 February a CEDA statement criticized the Lerrouxist administration for having "abandoned one problem after another, plunging Spanish political life into an extremely dangerous decline from which it is urgent to emerge at all costs". *El Debate* echoed these complaints by describing the executive as "inert, while the problems become graver" and by rejecting the Radical dissidents for opposing "the only policies possible". The CEDA barrage eventually succeeded in dividing the Radical Party against itself. Martínez Barrio and other critics of the right, including the Minister of the Economy, Antonio Lara, found themselves increasingly isolated at the meetings of the Radical parliamentary group in February. Having resisted the pressure of his allies for weeks, the Prime Minister finally made the necessary sacrifice: at the beginning of March, he let the two fractious ministers go.[120]

Typically, President Alcalá-Zamora seized on the reshuffle to settle one of his many personal scores. The Minister of Education, Pareja Yébenes, who had had the temerity to name an "enemy" of the President as rector of the University of Seville, was replaced by Salvador de Madariaga, the international diplomat and academic who was not a member of the Radical Party but whose services its leader had previously sought in September 1933 in order to add some intellectual ballast to his administration. On that occasion, Madariaga had made his Cabinet entry dependent on the establishment of good relations with the socialists and the promise not to pass an amnesty for the insurgents of 10 August 1932, but now, with neither condition met, he joined Lerroux's third administration all the same. Antonio Lara gave way to the dour Aragonese businessman with close links to the *patronal*, the veteran Lerrouxist Manuel Marraco. Finally, Martínez Barrio was replaced by the thrusting lawyer from Madrid, Rafael Salazar Alonso, aged only 38, who had converted himself into a personal favourite of the Radical leader through his unswerving loyalty and energy. Described by fellow minister Guerra del Río as "a terrible man", Salazar Alonso was a hardline replacement for the liberal Martínez Barrio. A Manichean view of politics, according to which a struggle had been unleashed between "the revolution" and "the state", placed him firmly on the side of the "friends of order". His evident sympathy for the right was soon made manifest by the decision to super-vise personally the security arrangements for the celebrated Easter procession in Seville.[121]

The March Cabinet marked a shift to the right. Both Salazar Alonso and Marraco were considerably more conservative than the two dissident ministers. However, the government crisis' most extraordinary feature is that, after only two months in power, the Radical leader was prepared to eject from the Cabinet not only his deputy leader but also the Minister of the Economy at the bidding of the CEDA. The overweening manner in which Gil Robles had engineered the previous Cabinet's downfall made the CEDA already appear as the dominant and bullying partner. Nevertheless, the Prime Minister welcomed the new administration on the grounds that "my greatest task" was the incorporation into the regime of "the forces that were not in it". From this perspective, the reshuffle symbolized "a further step in the consolidation of the Republic". Shortly after, at his birthday banquet, Lerroux added that the party had conceded "nothing of its programme", while reiterating that the Cabinet's renewal gave "stability to the Republic".[122] In effect, the Radical leader had sacri-ficed the internal unity of his own party to the maintenance of relations with the right. The change in government was none the less an ominous development in both practical and psychological terms as the Prime Minister had failed to exploit fully the symbiotic nature of the relation-ship with the right. He was unable either to place the alliance on a more equitable footing, or, more importantly, to offer the regime sufficient guarantees against the CEDA's authoritarian ambitions. In sum, the centrist promise of the Radical Party was in danger of being undermined by the lack of a centrist strategy.

Soon the unrelenting pressure of the right yielded results in both the policy-making and legislative arenas. For the right it was essential that the anticlerical reforms of the first biennium should be revised or overthrown. Already, the Radicals had turned a blind eye to the Law of Congregations by allowing religious schools to continue to function. In January 1934, the government also initiated negotiations with the Vatican with a view to drawing up a new Concordat. Moreover, following the Cabinet reshuffle in March, the Cortes began to discuss the partial restoration of the *haberes del clero* whereby the state would provide for the salaries of small-town priests over the age of 40 at two-thirds the 1931 rate. This was scarcely an extreme move as the first Azaña administration would have passed a similar measure in late 1931 but for the intemperate inter-vention of Alcalá-Zamora.[123] Still, the left attacked the proposal as a further concession to Catholic opinion. Numerous Radical deputies also resisted the use of the "guillotine" in order to hasten the bill's progress. In spite of this, it was passed into law on 4 April by the government parties in alliance with the right. That same month, the Cortes undertook discussion of a far-reaching measure: an amnesty that would embrace those involved in the attempted *coup d'état* of 10 August 1932, most notably General Sanjurjo. This was not simply a compromise incurred as a result of the alliance with the right, but was also an unacknowledged debt acquired with the insurgents by the Radical leader himself. During the debate over the bill, a confrontation between the socialist spokesmen Indalecio Prieto and the Liberal-Democratic Minister of Justice, Ramón Alvarez Valdés, who had refused to defend the rising of December 1930 against the monarchy, together with the subsequent public outcry, resulted, on 13 April, in yet another minister abandoning the government. The Minister of Education, Salvador de Madariaga, temporarily assumed the Justice portfolio as well. The government clashed repeatedly with the right, which endeavoured to broaden the scope of the amnesty, and the socialists, who opposed it altogether. The final measure, passed by the Cortes on 20 April, covered not only the rebels of August 1932 and collaborators of the Dictatorship but also the anarcho–syndicalist insurgents of December 1933.[124]

The President, however, refused to sign the bill. He objected that it undermined the Republic by setting its enemies at liberty. In any case, he had informed the first Cabinet formed after the general election that he would not accept an amnesty for the *Sanjurjada* rebels. At the time, Lerroux had readily acceded, only to go back on his word later. The President, stung by the premier's duplicity, tried to have the bill returned to the Cortes for reconsideration, but, according to article 84 of the Constitution, he required the backing of at least one minister. Having subjected the Cabinet to one of his infamous outpourings of rhetorical eloquence, the President discovered, to his amazement, that not a single minister, not even his friend and personal appointee Cirilo del Río – "Not even you, Cirilo?" – was prepared to second his initiative. Thwarted, Alcalá-Zamora, in an unconstitutional fit of pique, attached a 34-page note to the bill outlining his personal objections. The pervading sense of crisis during the April showdown was reflected in the attempt on the life of Salazar Alonso and the widespread rumour that the President was to be kidnapped by Assault Guards under the orders of the Minister of the Interior and Gil Robles.[125]

The CEDA thereupon proposed that the ruling majority pass a vote of confidence in the Prime Minister, which, in the circumstances, would amount to a vote of censure against the President. The same stance was defended to deafening applause by Salazar Alonso before the Radical parliamentary party, though Martínez Barrio, who reminded it of the understanding originally reached between the President and the Cabinet, dissented. The goal of the CEDA was to force Alcalá-Zamora's resignation and replace him, most likely, with Lerroux. However, the wily Radical leader refused to cooperate, realizing that such a move would undermine his party while easing the path to power of its thrusting ally. In fact, the CEDA strategem, designed to remove the Radical *jefe* from parliamentary politics, was a rerun of the socialist ploy to elect him as president in 1931. Following the dispute over the Amnesty bill, the Radical Prime Minister offered his resignation to the President as a matter of protocol but, to his surprise, Alcalá-Zamora accepted. Even more surprisingly, the President then invited the Minister of Labour, Ricardo Samper, to form a new administration. This was humiliating for the *jefe*. The bald, bespectacled Samper, who was a lawyer and prominent figure in the Valencia-based PURA, was not, despite his ministerial status, a leading figure within the Radical Party. Few would have predicted such a choice. Lerroux's inner circle urged him not to allow Samper to take up the invitation, but the Radical leader assented, the only condition being that Salazar Alonso, now on bad terms with Alcalá-Zamora for having criticized him over the amnesty, should remain in the Cabinet. The defence later given by the *jefe* of his failure to dispute the President's choice – that he did it for the sake of the country and so as not to embarrass the President by forcing him to return to Lerroux as premier – is unconvincing. Once again, as in September 1933, he lacked the stomach to confront President Alcalá-Zamora, even though he was in a stronger position than before. As a result, the relatively unknown Ricardo Samper formed the third Radical-led administration in four months.[126]

The April crisis marked a watershed in the relationship between the President and the ruling majority. The unnecessary and unjustifiable reshuffle had been a product of his excessive interventionism. In fact, it was the second time that he had removed the Radical leader, whom he clearly regarded as a rival, in an arbitrary fashion. Having largely lost the support of the left and already won the hostility of the right, he was in danger of forfeiting the backing of the centre, too. His growing isolation further destabilized a regime that required exactly the opposite. Furthermore, Alcalá-Zamora, by not allowing the parliamentary system to function properly, was accentuating the inbuilt fragility of the governing coalition. As a result, the Radicals had staggered from one Cabinet crisis to another in the space of just two months. Nor was the presidentially-ordained Samper administration likely to improve matters. On the contrary, the President, by appointing a secondary figure from within the Radical Party, aimed to enhance his ability to interfere in the affairs of government. This proclivity to divide and rule had already been made evident during the first biennium, but the relative cohesion of the republican–socialist coalition, as demonstrated in the crisis of June 1933, had limited the damage. Under the ordinary Cortes, however, the President had greater scope for such ploys as the ruling majority was more fragmented. Even before Lerroux formed the first post-electoral administration, Alcalá-Zamora had suggested to Gil Robles that the CEDA should be split in two. By converting Ricardo Samper into Prime Minister, the President had created an inherently weak administration. Samper, not being party leader, lacked authority from the outset, while it was natural that the Radical Party would want its *jefe* to return as Prime Minister before long, not least to upset Alcalá-Zamora's plans. Moreover, the April crisis had highlighted another destabilizing development: the Radical leader's debt to the insurgents of 1932 as a result of his willingness to consider the insurrectionary option as a route to power.[127]

VIII

The Price of Pragmatism
The schism of May 1934

The successful, if turbulent, passage of the Amnesty bill was to be a turning point for the Radical dissidents led by the party's deputy leader, Diego Martínez Barrio. Their differences with the *jefe* had first been made manifest in December 1933 when Martínez Barrio had handed the premiership over to him. At the time, Martínez Barrio had called for a Radical-based government formed in alliance with parties that were "unequivocally" republican. He believed that the republicans and, to a lesser extent, the socialists, still represented the only viable foundation for the consolidation of the Republic. "I am convinced", he declared, that the republicans and socialists would have to reunite "in defence of the postulates and dictates of democracy". Clearly Martínez Barrio was extremely wary of the right. By contrast, Lerroux, in aspiring to a centrist government that would be extended "as far as possible", made no mention of the republican parties. He was implicitly prepared to rely on the support of the non-republican right in order to form a parliamentary majority.[1] It did not take long before the divergent visions of the two Radical leaders brought them into conflict. Martínez Barrio initially opposed the appointment of the Agrarian José María Cid Ruiz-Zorrilla as Minister of Communications on the grounds that he was not a republican. The Radical deputy leader was also dismayed that Santiago Alba, the former monarchist who had just joined the Radical Party and who was regarded by him as a "venal" politician, was made speaker of the Cortes. Indeed, Martínez Barrio asked Lerroux to be left out of the Cabinet so that he would be better placed to maintain ties with the left republicans, but the Radical leader would have none of it, even threatening not to head a government at all if his deputy did not fall in.[2] Martínez Barrio thereupon tried to convince him that the Radicals had no option but to establish a minority administration that pursued its "own policies" as the party's prospective right-wing allies had not yet declared their allegiance to the Republic. By compromising with non-republican forces, he argued, Lerroux would ultimately be serving the interests of the right at the expense not just of the Radicals but of the Republic itself. The Radical premier, however, was unmoved. Collaboration, he insisted, would effectively incorporate the right into the new regime, thereby extending the Republic's base and providing it with greater stability.[3] As a result, Martínez Barrio resolved to "rectify" the government's course by acting "in defence of the regime". In fact, on 22 December 1933, shortly after the Prime Minister had presented the government's programme to the Cortes, Martínez Barrio held a meeting with Lerroux in which, according to Renovación, he urged "a change in the Radical trajectory towards the republican left". From this time on, the rumours of a rift within the party were to fly thick and fast. The denials were to be just as insistent. Renovación eventually exploded that, "for once and for all", neither Martínez Barrio nor any other Radical deputy was in fundamental disagreement with the jefe. Such denials, however, were to be contradicted by the mounting symptoms of conflict within the party's ranks. Policy differences were immediately evident. The dissidents criticized the hard line on law and order, the politically-motivated replacement of local councils, the reversing of the anticlerical legislation, and the turning of a blind eye to violations of the labour legislation in the countryside. Economics minister Antonio Lara, an ally of Martínez Barrio, denounced the "spirit of revenge" of many landowners in the wake of the general election as "dangerous". The only means of avoiding, or at least of delaying, "the social revolution", he believed, was to defend "the just rights" of the working class. Martínez Barrio himself was disturbed above all by the envisaged amnesty for the insurgents of 10 August 1932. Early in January 1934, he confronted the Prime Minister in Cabinet over the bill. He argued, according to El Socialista, that the time was not ripe for such an initiative and that, if taken, the government should be extremely cautious about who was included. On this occasion, the Cabinet majority backed Martínez Barrio – Lerroux, Cid Ruiz-Zorrilla and Alvarez Valdés voted against him – but this was merely to prove a temporary reprieve.[4]

Resistance from within the party to the direction taken by the government soon gained momentum. On 8 January 1934, the PURA deputy Julio Just, who, like Martínez Barrio, contended that the republicans should seek to unite rather than divide their forces, had already reached the conclusion that the dissidents would be "obliged to abandon the discipline" of the Radical Party. The misgivings of the Radical liberals were given greater voice at a banquet held to honour Lerroux on 12 January 1934. In his speech, Martínez Barrio contended that the left republicans' electoral calamity had converted the Radicals into "the only possible solution in Spain". Within the current Cortes, therefore, "there is no solution beyond the Radical Party" as there did not exist any "replacements". As long as this parliament lasted, he reiterated, the Radical Party had to be "its own succesor". The non-republican right, in other words, was effectively barred from governing as it was not republican. Likewise, Martínez Barrio rejected the "catastrophic solutions" of both left and right as they would only result in "civil war". Nine days later, in a speech in Madrid, he further criticized the government for "pacting all its steps" instead of relying on its "own inspiration", affirming that it was better to adopt "a firm position, and be defeated, rather than be directed or humiliated". "No one", he insisted, "will govern by means of us". The climax to Martínez Barrio's public dissent as a minister was his outspoken declarations to *Blanco y Negro* on 4 February 1934. On the one hand, he rebuked the left for its "narrow and sectarian criteria". On the other, he upbraided the right for striving to demonstrate that the government "lives because they allow it to". Only if the CEDA declared its allegiance to the Republic could it enter the Cabinet, though Martínez Barrio himself would refuse to serve in such an administration as he did not believe it "convenient" for the country. He concluded that the current political situation was "lamentable" and "sterile" and that the sole solution was for the government "to react".[5] This prompted yet another meeting with the Radical leader, who was also confronted by Antonio Lara and the veteran leftwinger Guerra del Río. While Lerroux played down the brewing conflict with an ingenuous "Crisis? What crisis?", Martínez Barrio insisted that the government had to define "its attitude clearly". No doubt his unyielding attitude contributed towards a more open exchange of views within the party as a whole. Pérez Madrigal, for example, publicly defended the arrangement with the right on the pragmatic grounds that it had facilitated the Radical Party's seizure of power. The ongoing debate acquired parliamentary status with the clash of 7 February between the CEDA *caudillo* and Martínez Barrio, who maintained that the electoral alliance with the right did not make their governmental collaboration inevitable and that the Radicals should not rule at the behest of "other ideas".[6]

The dispute within the Radical Party was played out during the second half of February 1934 largely within the confines of the parliamentary group. The party, as one deputy put it at the meeting of 16 February, was divided into two by differences of "doctrine and the approach of the government". Lerroux tried to reconcile them at the meeting of the 20th by contending that the government was neither of the left nor of the right but of a "national character". He assured the malcontents that the electoral devastation of the left republicans had forced him to reach an understanding with the non-republican right and that his own politics remained unchanged. He promised them, furthermore, that no party, unless it was "truly" republican, would enter the Cabinet. The following day, Martínez Barrio was assailed by several deputies for having overseen an electoral campaign that was "frankly anti-rightist" as well as for not having dismissed more socialist *ayuntamientos* as Minister of the Interior. Indeed, Martínez Barrio did not share the eagerness of many Radicals to overthrow public bodies in the hands of opponents. As Minister of the Interior, he had refused, despite the concerted pressure of his fellow deputies, to sack provincial and local authorities on spurious grounds. On the contrary, he had insisted that each case of alleged corruption or mismanagement should be judged strictly on its merits. His performance as minister, as he wrote in a letter in February 1934, may have left "unsatisfied" those that believed that a change of government permitted "all kinds of outrages", but he was determined not to become "its vehicle". Within the parliamentary group, Lerroux sought to win the disaffected over by affirming that the right would not betray the Republic, "of that I am sure". Should they do so, he would not hesitate to use the "greatest violence". The government, he insisted, still embodied the aspirations of 14 April 1931. Such rhetorical reassurances, however, did little to alter the reality of the alliance with the non-republican right.[7]

Martínez Barrio's objections to the Radical-led government were not purely ideological in nature. He was strongly influenced, too, by the venal practices of one of Lerroux's closest associates. Since November 1931, when Emiliano Iglesias had been declared morally incompatible with the Cortes, Martínez Barrio had felt a "moral repugnance" for the corrupt cabal centred on the Radical leader's lieutenant. This embraced, he was convinced, not just Iglesias' Galician cronies but also the PURA, along with isolated individuals such as Manuel Marraco and those deputies, such as Tomás Peire, that formed part of Juan March's web within the Radical Party. Indeed, the "common denominator" of the entire group, he claimed, was March. Despite the attempt of "'Marchism'" to undermine him and despite a private resolution, made in the summer of 1933, to abandon the party "the day" that Iglesias returned (which, in the election of 1933, he had), Martínez Barrio was held back by two considerations: his personal consideration for Lerroux and the fact that the Radical Party remained a "useful instrument" for the regime.[8]

The burgeoning strife within the Radical Party was pounced upon by Gil Robles in his major public speeches of 19 and 26 February, when he threatened to bring the government down should it not purge itself of the CEDA's critics. The accidentalists' pressure soon paid off. On 27 February, Radical sympathizers of the right issued a manifesto in which they called for the uncompromising defence of law and order, the reestablishment of the death penalty, negotiations with the Vatican, and for the revision of the Constitution. Most pointedly, they demanded the departure from the Cabinet of "any" minister who did not agree with these proposals. At the parliamentary group's meeting later that day neither the rightists nor the rebels would give ground. The CEDA assault together with the opposition to Martínez Barrio and his followers from within the Radical Party combined to make the position of the nonconformist ministers untenable. At the beginning of March, Martínez Barrio and Lara resigned from the Cabinet.[9]

Opposition to the alliance with the right was not circumscribed to the parliamentary group alone. The Radical civil governor for Huelva, for example, resigned in March 1934 on the grounds that "I cannot live from the alms of an Inquisitorial clown such as Gil Robles". He was convinced that the Radicals had become the "keeper of an order which only benefits our adversaries". Many other activists felt exactly the same.[10] One member attacked Lerroux in a letter for his "thousand defections and cowardly acts", for being a "prisoner of the right", and for having handed the regime over to "the clerics". If this had been done in war, he concluded dramatically, "they would shoot you in the back, traitor". Considerable grassroots support for the stance of the dissident deputies can be found in many parts of the country, including Andalusia, the Canary Islands, and Galicia. Further, the national-level dissidence encouraged, and drew on, that of a number of provincial parties which shared much in common with Martínez Barrio's stance but whose protest, strongly shaped by local considerations, was to adopt a different trajectory. The party in the Levante provides the most outstanding illustration. In Alicante, the Radicals had effectively been split over the question as to whether they should collaborate with the right as early as January 1934 following the election of Rafael Blasco as President of the Provincial Junta. Blasco, as head of the dissidents, struggled to win over the Alicante rank and file in the face of the concerted opposition of the loyalists, led by deputy César Oarrichena. At the congress of 1 April, the Alicante city organization was dissolved and Oarrichena expelled from the party. While the dissidents had the backing of 85 branches, the loyalists had that of the civil governor, Adolfo Chacón de la Mata. In May, Blasco denounced to Martínez Barrio "the right-wing labour initiated by the civil governor and inspired by Oarrichena". "With the Radicals", he concluded despondently, "I cannot be left-wing because they are not. Nor do the leaders let me guide the party to the left. I believe, therefore, that there is no solution but to abandon politics".[11] While the majority of the Alicante city members joined Martínez Barrio, the rest of the local party continued to fight for control of the provincial organization. Another fierce struggle ensued in the neighbouring province of Valencia. Many *Blasquistas* were outraged by the Radical government's religious reforms and the proposed amnesty. PURA deputy Vicente Marcos Miranda abandoned the Radical Party in February 1934, in anticipation, as he wrote to Martínez Barrio, that "new events, which are destined to occur, will lead me elsewhere". In reality, his resignation was designed to bring matters within the PURA to a head at the meeting of the Federal Council on 17 February. This, however, proved inconclusive. None the less, 70 per cent of the Valencia city branches called on the PURA to withdraw from the Radical Party. Battle recom-

menced at the meeting of the city congress on 8 April. Once again, Marco
Miranda urged the *Blasquistas'* withdrawal from the Radical Party, while
Ricardo Samper defended the status quo. Eager to avoid a split, the pro-
Lerrouxists managed to postpone a decision until the provincial congress
took place on 28 May.[12]

The determination of Martínez Barrio to forge a republican alternative
to the Radical Party–CEDA axis was underlined by the series of meetings
which he held in March, following his resignation as minister, with the
conservative republicans Felipe Sánchez Román and Felix Gordón Ordás,
both of whom were linked to Miguel Maura. Documents from Martínez
Barrio's Archive reveal that the three men discussed a common
programme with a view to future collective action. Gordón Ordás, in a
letter of 17 March, congratulated the Radical politician for the document
which he had drafted, and, ten days later, Sánchez Román reminded
Martínez Barrio of the imperative need to maintain "our conversations"
and to develop "the content of your aforementioned notes".[13] These meetings were none the less regarded by the Radical deputy leader as
complementary to his struggle within the party rather than as a sign that
he had effectively broken with it. Thus in a letter of 19 March he pleaded
with a disgruntled activist not to abandon the party on the grounds that
"acts of dissidence generally begin badly and end up even worse". On the
contrary, Martínez Barrio urged him to help save "an organization that
is indispensable for Spain and for the Republic". In the meantime, Lerroux
made little apparent effort to resolve the brewing confrontation. With his
blessing, Martínez Barrio spent much of March and April outside Madrid,
staying at a friend's house in Huelva as well as visiting Seville and the
Spanish territories in north Africa.[14] As a result, the Radical *jefe* scarcely
saw his deputy, while making no reference to the conflict in public and
discouraging the parliamentary group from debating the issue. One of his
lieutenants explained to the press that Martínez Barrio had to appreciate
that the government's policies were determined by "the force of circumstance" and that they were not in any way "anti-republican". There was,
accordingly, no possibility of "profound divergences".[15] Evidently, the
Prime Minister believed that there was nothing left to discuss. Probably,
he calculated that, as a last resort, his legendary powers of persuasion and
his personal sway over Martínez Barrio would win the latter over.
Certainly Martínez Barrio felt torn between an "undiminished affection
for Lerroux" and the "pressure of the republicans and patriots".[16]

Martínez Barrio's public silence was broken by a speech in Seville on
1 April, followed by another in Ayamonte (near Huelva) on 9 April. He
lambasted the governing bloc for its policies, its patronage activities, but
above all for its dependence on the CEDA. Though collaboration with the
right was denounced as the most immediate danger to the Republic,
Martínez Barrio also made clear his opposition to the "spectre of a

socialist dictatorship". Only if the republicans united, he reiterated, could the twin threats of left and right be averted. The time had come for the republicans to forge "our own policies, with their own characteristics and profile, so that we are not the pupils of anyone". It was not too late for the Radical Party to change course. "I will sacrifice everything," he concluded emotionally, "rather than produce disunion amongst the republicans, and in particular – why not say it – amongst the republicans who, like me, live within the discipline of the Radical Party."[17] This was at once a plea and a warning. Lerrouxist loyalists responded to Martínez Barrio's hard-hitting declarations in an ambivalent fashion. "Neither dissidence nor rebellion", proclaimed *Renovación* in an attempt to down-play the issue. In a similar vein, several Radical ministers welcomed the speeches for having healed, rather than deepened, the party's wounds, while a number of deputies chose to dwell on Martínez Barrio's loyalty. Others, however, published a pamphlet that sought to refute the deputy leader's claims by insisting not only that the Lerroux-led administration reflected the will of the electorate but also that it had consolidated the Republic by extending its base. There was, they concluded, no alternative to the trajectory undertaken "for the supreme good of Spain, for the pres-tige of the Republic, and out of devotion to the ideals of democracy". By contrast, the dissidents viewed the speeches as signalling "the reconquest" of the party's programme. There were even those, such as Luis Fábregas, a deputy for Orense, who criticized Martínez Barrio for his "excessive subordination of a sentimental type" towards Lerroux.[18]

A striking characteristic of the growing dissidence was the lack of debate within the party. Both the Executive Committee and the parlia-mentary group were effectively muzzled. Thus an attempt to raise the issue at a meeting of the latter on April 18 was smartly quashed by Lerroux's henchman Juan José Rocha, who declared that it should be left for a better moment in "the complete confidence that this will not create any sort of conflict for the Radical Party". The poor attendance at the meetings reflected a fundamental lack of democratic accountability and participa-tion within the party. In April, for instance, the average attendance stood at under half, even during the government crisis.[19] Nor did the Radical press act as a forum for debate. *Renovación*, far from acting as an arena for discussion, endeavoured to unite the party by constantly attacking a common foe, the Socialist Party, and by dwelling in incongruously reli-gious tones on the virtues of the "apostle and prop of the Republic" and "the Christ of our time" – Alejandro Lerroux. In the same vein, the issues raised by the April Cabinet crisis were reduced to one of personal loyalty, for "Alejandro Lerroux is the Spanish Republic". In sum, the Radical lead-ership, and in particular the *jefe*, was not prepared for the party to resolve its differences by democratic means.[20]

Events, moreover, appeared to be moving against the dissents. On 4

April the ruling majority voted into law the bill on Assets of the Clergy. This partial rectification of the anticlerical legislation was naturally regarded by the dissidents, especially as many of them were Masons, as a devastating blow. The mounting crisis within the Radical Party was brought to a head later in the month by the showdown over the Amnesty bill. On 27 April, at a meeting of the parliamentary group, Martínez Barrio reminded his colleagues of the unwritten agreement between President Alcalá-Zamora and Lerroux's second Cabinet never to concede an amnesty for the August 1932 insurgents. Salazar Alonso called for the overthrow of the President, while Pérez Madrigal attacked the deputy leader for fomenting the Radicals' disunity. Worse still, the bulk of the deputies flatly rejected the arguments of Martínez Barrio.[21] The next day, the Amnesty bill having been signed by the President, the Samper administration was formed. Martínez Barrio's despair is reflected in a letter he wrote at the time to a friend. He lamented that "the match is about to be decided and I have lost. Within the Radical Party there remains little or nothing for me to do. The Radical Party, its leadership jubilant and joyful, is going to get married with Gil Robles and that which his party represents; me no". As he later wrote, "it was then that I said to myself that my permanence in the Radical Party had become impossible".[22]

Still, the Radical deputy leader had not yet given up all hope. On 13 May he wrote to a dissident that "the discrepancies" still depended on a "final decision" in the near future.[23] However, despite a gathering in Lerroux's house, a celebrated lunch at the "Fuente de la Reina" restaurant, and a National Committee meeting on 16 May, the two sides were unable to bridge their differences. These were succintly put by Martínez Barrio: "I believe that the right is trying to introduce itself into the regime in order to gain power and organize a *coup d'état* when it judges the moment appropriate. Don Alejandro says that these elements are republicans and that his duty is to attract them to the regime." Or, as the Radical leader declared, "everyone is now at liberty to establish their position".[24] Indeed, the dissidents, as they explained in a manifesto published on 19 May, had deserted the party because it had strayed from "the old Radical ideology" and, in the process, failed to maintain the "necessary, cordial, unbreakable solidarity" with the republican parties. Martínez Barrio was even more explicit in a speech of 17 June 1934. He insisted that Lerroux had abandoned the Radicals' centrist politics for that of a "sectarian" right which rejected the regime's "liberal and democratic postulates". As a result, the fundamental division within the Republic was not that between left and right but between "the defenders of the regime and its enemies".[25]

Numerous underlying reasons have been adduced for the schism in the Radical Party. There is no doubt that Martínez Barrio in particular was distanced morally from the party by the way in which certain Radicals exercised power; that is to say, by their venality and the demands of their clientage networks. He did little, on the other hand, to criticize or combat such practices before the Radicals came to power, though as Prime Minister and as Minister of the Interior he does appear to have stood up to the party on this issue. Yet this was a contributory, not a sufficient, cause of his dissidence. Nor was the scheming of President Alcalá-Zamora, eager to divide and rule the Radical Party and thereby enhance his own sway over the governing majority, more than a secondary stimulus.[26] Most attention has been focused on the Masonic connection as the hidden cause of the split. Many contemporaries and subsequent commentators have speculated that Martínez Barrio, Grand Master of the Gran Oriente Español at the time of the Radical Party's break up, acted at the behest of the Masonic lodges. Such suspicions predate the schism itself. In Seville, on 1 April, Martínez Barrio denied publicly that he was at the "dictate of a hidden power". At the final meeting between the dissidents and the loyalists on 16 May, Martínez Barrio was asked directly if he was following Masonic instructions, to which he retorted elliptically that his stance was due to an "imperative of conscience". For El Debate, there could be no doubt. "Beyond the party, the affection for Lerroux, and Spain's convenience," it pronounced, "lay the hidden order, the secret call, the imperious sign made from the shadows."[27] Lerroux, himself a lodge member, also attributed the party's division to the machinations of the Masons, but the argument of La pequeña historia is largely deductive and insubstantial. However, Alcalá-Zamora, no friend of the Radical leader, and Juan-Simeón Vidarte, a socialist deputy and Mason, defend this interpretation, too. Further credence is lent to this hypothesis by the fact that in 1930s Spain the Masonic movement was a decidedly liberal and anticlerical organization whose parliamentary members were almost exclusively republicans or socialists.[28]

Certainly Martínez Barrio, originally elected as Grand Master in 1931 before being reelected in June 1933, was severely criticized within the lodges as a result of his stewardship of the 1933 general election. Juan-Simeón Vidarte, for example, dubbed him the "great organizer of defeats". Worse still, the Radicals then entered into an informal alliance with the Masons' arch enemy, the Catholic right, or, as the "Vicus" lodge put it, "the foreign policy of Rome". The Masons were afraid that they might meet the same fate as their persecuted colleagues in Nazi Germany and Austria. The change of climate within the Gran Oriente Español was signalled by the adoption of a new disciplinary measure in January 1934 which stated that any lodge member implicated in "a strategy of approximation with reactionary forces" could be expelled. Directed at the Radicals, this obviously placed those that were Masons, especially leading figures such as Martínez Barrio and Antonio Tuñón de Lara, the Deputy Grand Master, in an extremely delicate position. A potent mix of outrage,

dread, and the desire to bring the Cortes to a prompt end produced a ferocious backlash within the Masonic movement against the Radicals, and
in particular the Grand Master. In February 1934, for example, the Grand
Regional Lodge of Morocco, headed by the Radical–Socialist Cristóbal de
Lora, approved a motion stating not only that the government could not
be described as "republican" but also that the Grand Master should leave
it with a view to forcing a political crisis that would result in the dissolution of the Cortes. It was no coincidence that this replicated the response
of the left in the immediate aftermath of the general election. Nevertheless,
Martínez Barrio's Cabinet exit in early 1934 cannot be put down to the
Masons. "Nothing allows one to suppose," Gómez Molleda observes,
"that the decision was due to the desires expressed by the lodges." In fact,
the resignation had been due above all to the cumulative pressure of the
CEDA together with the collusion of the Prime Minister, who, on this
occasion, was willing to let Martínez Barrio go.[29]

Yet there can be little doubt that Martínez Barrio's Masonic obligations made his situation within the Radical Party increasingly untenable.
As Grand Master, he had been distinguished by calls for harmony between
the republicans and by the defence of the Masons' liberal and democratic
ideals above and beyond their individual party affiliations.[30] As a politician, he had also defended the paramountcy of the ties between the
republicans while criticizing collaboration with the non-republican
CEDA. Naturally, the Radicals' rejection of the left republicans for the
alliance with the Catholic right placed him in a terrible dilemma, which
could only become more acute with time. The Radical leader, he even
suspected, aimed to poison his relations with the left. As he divulged later
to Azaña, "Lerroux wanted to dishonour me. Yes, yes; he wanted to
compromise me with some dishonourable political operation . . . That's
why I left". He was further undermined as Grand Master by the socialists' decision to register their disgust at the Radicals, "our worst enemies",
by resolving that those involved in the preparation of the revolutionary
movement could no longer remain in the lodges.[31] Consequently, the
longer the Radicals collaborated with the right, the less viable the position of the Grand Master was likely to become. Throughout these months
the Permanant Commission of the Council was inundated by a flood of
complaints at "the political performance of certain brothers of ours who
are . . . in open dispute with fundamental postulates of our ideology". The
widespread opposition to the Radicals was to culminate in Martínez
Barrio's resignation as Grand Master at the Grand National Congress on
26 May 1934, a mere ten days after the Radical split.[32]

To what extent Martínez Barrio's separation from the Radical Party
was due to the influence of the Masons is extremely difficult to say, especially given his own evasive testimony. Undoubtedly his liberal
convictions were powerfully shaped by the struggle with the right in

Seville, for whom Martínez Barrio was the *bestia negra*. Yet his Masonic militancy lent an institutional dimension to his ideological dissension. In effect, the lodges, by sharpening the dilemma, accelerated the process of divorce from the Radical Party. For the sheer brevity with which Martínez Barrio manifested his misgivings – a few weeks after the Radicals assumed power – and then disengaged himself from the party was out of character with his cautious and conciliatory temperament. In all probability, the Masonic connection played a notable role in catalyzing the rebellion of Martínez Barrio.[33]

The influence of the Masons may have accentuated the disintegration of the Radical Party but it cannot be regarded as a sufficient cause of the split. Of the 19 deputies who left the party, twelve were Masons, along with one of the two socialist deputies that joined them.[34] However, the majority of Masons within the parliamentary party, including the left-winger Guerra del Río and the veteran Eloy de Vaquero, together with many other leading figures such as Gerardo Abad Conde and Pedro Armasa, did not abandon the party. Most strikingly of all, Antonio Tuñón de Lara, Martínez Barrio's deputy as Grand Master who was "totally trusted by him", failed to join the rebels. Similar divisions can be found at the local level, too. In Alicante, for example, the leaders on both sides of the split, along with the loyalist civil governor, were all Masons. The sway of the lodges therefore varied a great deal according to the individual (as Martínez Barrio recognized in his speech of acceptance as Grand Master in June 1933). In all likelihood, the movement exerted a greater influence on the more progressive Masons if only because it magnified the contradiction between their liberal convictions and the alliance with the Catholic right. Still, for those politicians affiliated to the lodges, such as Carlos Esplá, Felipe Sánchez Román, Fernando de los Ríos, Juan-Simeón Vidarte, and Fernando Valera, their Masonic ideals were generally subordinate, if complementary, to their politics. In short, they gained power through the parties, not the lodges. When the socialists made membership of the Masons incompatible with that of the PSOE, none of those affected forfeited the latter. As he explained to the Grand Congress upon his resignation, Martínez Barrio himself had been so preoccupied with his political affairs that he had simply not had "the energy and time necessary" for his Masonic duties.[35]

As a result of the May split, seventeen deputies, including five from Seville, three from Galicia, three from Tenerife, and two from Valencia, in addition to the National Secretary and former deputy, Manuel Torres Campañá, abandoned the Radical Party. To these must be added Vicente Marco Miranda and Julio Just, who had left the party three months earlier. The Radical Party had thereby lost just under a fifth of its parliamentary group. Furthermore, numerous leading lights in the Spanish Confederation of Radical and Republican Youth, including its president, as well as a founder-member of the Radical Party, who wrote to Lerroux to express his disgust at "the handing over of the Republic to its enemies", resigned. However, not all of the Radical deputies that had sympathized with, or been one of, the detractors had left the party. These included José María Alvarez Mendizábal and the ex-deputy Pedro Gómez Chaix, whom Martínez Barrio had exhorted in a letter not to become a "prisoner" by remaining at Lerroux's side. Numerous civil governors also stepped down, either because they were appointees of Martínez Barrio, as in the examples of Almeria and Palencia, or else for ideological reasons, as in the cases of Alicante, Cadiz, Ciudad Real, Seville, Tenerife and the Ceuta delegate. Another high-level recruit for the dissenters was the mayor of Madrid and former Acción Republicana deputy, Pedro Rico.[36]

The dissidents formed the Radical–Democratic Party under the leadership of Martínez Barrio. They were joined by a brace of socialist deputies and one from Miguel Maura's Conservative Republican Party. In purely parliamentary terms, the new force was, with twenty-two deputies, the largest opposition republican force.[37] It marked another stage in the reorganization of the republicans in the wake of the 1933 general election. Only a month and a half earlier, Izquerida Republicana, which represented a fusion of Acción Republicana, the Independent Radical–Socialist Party, and the Galician Republican Party, but did not include the Radical–Socialist Party under Gordón Ordás, had been established under the leadership of Manuel Azaña.[38] Two months after the Radical Party split, Julio Just, Vicente Marco Miranda and Faustino Valentín, along with the former deputy Héctor Altabás, formed Esquerra Valenciana.[39] For his part, Martínez Barrio aimed to bring all the progressive republican forces together under one roof. A step towards this goal was taken in September 1934, when the Radical–Democrats merged with Gordón Ordás' Radical–Socialists to create Unión Republicana.[40]

Gauging the impact of the schism in the provinces is more difficult given the unrepresentative nature of the material in the party archive (there is scarcely a word in favour of the dissidents) and the fact that local studies pay little attention to the matter. Splits are recorded for Alicante, Almeria, Avila, Cadiz, the Canary Islands, Catalonia, Cordoba, Huelva, Madrid, Malaga, Mallorca, Melilla, Salamanca, Santander, Seville, Valencia, Valladolid and Zamora, but their precise extent is often unclear.[41] Even the relatively well-documented Valencia case lacks precision. Although the breakaway group lead by Just, Marco Miranda and Valentín received a good deal of publicity, there are no reliable details. While Marco Miranda refers to a "considerable mass" following him, Gerardo Carreres, the new National Secretary, claimed that the PURA split had not been of "great importance".[42] Certainly it cannot be assumed that the fissures at the national level corresponded with those at the provincial level. In Lugo and Orense, for instance, the majority of the rank and file went over to the rebels, but only one of eight deputies.[43] An indication of the schism's spread is provided by the fact that sixteen Provincial Committees had been established by the Radical–Democratic Party before the end of May. Publicly, the Radical leadership insisted that the split amounted to no more than a handful of individuals. Privately, Carreres complained to Lerroux of "the great deal of work" that the breach had caused. For a start, the bulk of the Galician party appears to have jettisoned the party: overwhelmingly so in the case of La Coruña and Lugo and to a lesser extent in Orense, though in Pontevedra the grassroots remained loyal. In Seville and Santa Cruz de Tenerife the great majority of branches turned their backs on the Radical Party.[44] Majority backing in the cities of Malaga and Alicante was also found. From Almeria, Antonio Tuñón de Lara lamented to Lerroux later in the summer that the local party's lack of unity was so chronic that "I'm beginning to feel defeated in this tyrannical struggle against everyone". In Cadiz, two-fifths of the city councillors left the party along with half those in Jerez as well as the civil governor. The damage to the party was sufficient to force the election of a new Provincial Committee in May.[45] By contrast, some provinces were affected little, if at all. In Leon, according to the party secretary there, not one of the province's 80 committees joined the rebel ranks, while in Huelva only one local branch joined the dissidents.[46] A precise picture of the split's magnitude cannot, on the basis of the available material, be given, but, four months later, the PRD had already managed to establish 557 local branches. A year on, Unión Republicana – the product of the merger of the PRD with the PRRS – claimed to have around 200,000 affiliates, which was more than Acción Republicana in its heyday, but less than the PRRS at its alleged peak. Attracting the bulk of the grassroots in some areas and an indeterminate number in others, it would appear that around one-sixth of the Radical Party had been lost to the dissidents.[47]

The May 1934 schism reduced the Radicals to 85 parliamentary deputies – fewer than in 1931. Especially coming so soon after its rise to power, the nationwide rupture was a devastating blow to the party's morale and prestige. The split not only shifted the party *to* the right, but also made it more dependent *on* the right. On the other hand, the party's internal and ideological unity was enhanced. Yet the loss of the dissidents further eroded the Radicals' credibility with the left and made a future *rapprochement* with the opposition republicans even less likely. That said, by abandoning the party, Martínez Barrio and his followers made the Radicals more vulnerable than ever to the exigencies of the right. In purely pragmatic terms, the schismatics would have done more for the republican cause by remaining within the Radical Party.[48]

As a result of the split, the Radical Party was forced to undertake, in the words of the National Secretary, "with all urgency . . . the reorganization of the party throughout Spain". In the event, the leadership would take advantage of the schism to tackle the state of neglect into which much of the party had already fallen. In Avila, for example, it was "totally abandoned", in Huesca it had collapsed into an "anarchic state", while in Mallorca it proved incapable of a "useful and efficient labour". Progress, however, was sluggish, as shown by the unusually critical comments of the National Committee in June. Two months later, the National Secretary was still complaining at his never-ending workload and at the inertia of certain provincial bodies. In Seville, for instance, where swift action was required in order to offset the advances of the rebels, it was not until August, following a period of "disorientation", that the first branches of the restructured party were set up. That same month, a deputy informed the Radical leader that the Lugo and La Coruña parties were losing "the little that remains". Consequently, the party reacted to the schism in organizational terms in a tardy and uneven manner.[49]

In terms of morale, the Radicals sought to reunite through the traditional resort to the Lerrouxist personality cult. Indeed, the schism vividly illustrates the central role played in the life of the party by its charismatic chief. *Renovación* estimated prior to the split that 45 of the party's deputies were "Lerrouxists" above and beyond their status as "Radicals". In its immediate aftermath, the parliamentary group organized a banquet for the *jefe* "in adherence to his person". In the same vein, a "national homage", which would climax with a mass rally in Madrid, was projected as an act of "unbreakable adherence" to Lerroux "in this hour of unjustified desertions and of inexplicable ingratitude". In the meantime, the Radical leader was fêted by ministers and deputies alike at the Círculo de Bellas Artes and at Baños de Montemayor.[50] The grassroots' response, as illustrated by the letters sent to Lerroux, was also overwhelmingly personalistic in nature. Few of those that wrote to their leader attempted to explain the dissidents' action, though some attributed it to the influence of the Masons and others to Martínez Barrio's "disproportionate ambition". Rarely is the *jefe* himself held responsible in any way. While some expressed their approval for his "policy of attraction, of understanding, of proximity" and for his "policy of regeneration", most are concerned only to reaffirm their personal devotion. Lauded by many as "the indisputable *JEFE*" and the "ONLY *Jefe*", there were even those that suggested that the party should be renamed the "Lerrouxist Party" because "the Radical Party is Lerroux, it is you, only you". As one activist put it, "one cannot be Radical, without being Lerrouxist beforehand". The same fervour characterized the response of many that had been, or were, Radical deputies. "My Lerrouxism is superior," wrote Fernández de la Poza, "to all party discipline."[51] For most Radicals, therefore, the dispute within the party was a question of personalism rather than policy. The dissidents, a life-long party member explained to Martínez Barrio, may have won the political argument, but "one is obliged to die Lerrouxist". As another exclaimed, "only with Lerroux and for Lerroux alone will we struggle until the final moment". The Radical leader, as Martínez Barrio himself admitted, had become "something so consubstantial with the Radical Party that without him it would not exist".[52] Not surprisingly, the Radical media, too, viewed the schism in largely personalistic terms. For *Renovación*, the dissidents' desertion of the party was above all else a personal affront to the *jefe*. Characteristically, the paper claimed that Lerroux, described as the "axis and nerve and brain and heart" of the party and as "the most outstanding and serene figure" of Spanish republicanism, was still capable of forgiving "the moral decrepitude" of those that were "envious and cruel". The fortunes of the Radical Party, as the May 1934 split had vividly demonstrated, were indissolubly linked to the vision and guidance of one man. The resulting dilemma was inadvertantly put in the letter of one loyalist. "Personalism is the evil that afflicts the parties", he averred. "My ideal is pure Lerrouxism".[53]

IX

Trapped between Left and Right
The Samper administration of May to October 1934

Ricardo Samper made it plain from the outset of the administration formed by him in the wake of the April 1934 Amnesty crisis that he did not intend to act as a puppet of either the Radical leader or the CEDA *caudillo*. Like Lerroux, Samper believed that the Radical Party should strive to incorporate the non-republican right into the Republic. He called on the opposition to accept that only by means of "a politics of moderation" could the right be accommodated and "cooperation between the political forces" be established. Unlike Lerroux, Samper, whose own politics were shaped by the struggle in Valencia between the PURA and the CEDA-affiliated DRV, appealed for constraint on the part of the Radicals' allies: "the forces of the right should take note of the dangers for all and especially for them that would result from a tendency to abuse their power and if they tried to denaturalize the genuinely republican direction that suits Spain". Moreover, he claimed that, even if the CEDA joined the Cabinet, a majority government could not be formed as other right-wing forces were unacceptable to the Radical Party. In any case, governmental collaboration with the CEDA could not be "more than a circumstantial union". The premier, strongly encouraged by the President, was determined to steer a more independent course than his predecessor and thereby integrate the right into the regime on more equitable terms. As Lerroux later lamented, Samper did not continue "the policy initiated by me in order to attract and incorporate into the new regime" the right. "I am moderate and I am concerned with a sense of balance", as the Prime Minister declared on the presentation of his Cabinet to the Cortes on 2 May 1934. It was cruelly ironic that the Radical Party should have split shortly after Samper assumed the premiership as this deprived him of valuable support. He himself was none the less proof that, despite the schism, there still remained those in the party that were extremely wary of its coalition partners. However, the Prime Minister's room for manoeuvre was limited: he not only had to contend with the non-republican right, upon whom his administration depended for its parliamentary survival, but also a sizable, pro-rightist sector within the Radical Party. The Cabinet itself was divided between sceptics of the right, such as Guerra del Río, and its sympathizers, spearheaded by the strident Salazar Alonso.[1]

Initially, the Samper administration was well received by the right. The new premier's greater drive and energy compared to Lerroux together with his keen interest in economic affairs, as reflected in the creation of the National Economic Council and the evident concern to draw up the budget as soon as possible, impressed the CEDA. The speech given by the Prime Minister in Valencia on 22 May elicited the approving remark from *El Debate* that "it is not frequent that our men of government pay attention to the study of economic questions". The Radicals' allies were also mollified, two days later, by the modification of the *términos municipales* law. A further cause for celebration was the first fruits of the April amnesty, as the extreme right-wing leader José Calvo Sotelo returned from exile in May and lands were returned to the nobility.[2]

Yet conservative opinion was soon disconcerted by the Samper administration. While the rise to power of the Radicals had restored considerable confidence in the economy, as reflected in rising investment and productivity from the beginning of 1934, they had still to meet the *patronal*'s demands for the overhaul of the socialist-inspired labour legislation. Gravely disappointed by the timid reform of the mixed juries in January 1934 and by the resolution of the Madrid construction workers' strike two months later, the employers' associations had reason to expect a more sympathetic hearing from Samper. In Valencia, he had acted as their lawyer as well as heading the Ateneo Mercantil. Nationally, he was a founder member of the Confederación de Entidades Económicas Libres y Círculos Mercantiles de España. Earlier in the year the *patronal* had reiterated, in an inquiry mounted by the Ministry of Labour, that the juries should be used purely for arbitration purposes, that they should not have the power of inspection, and that their involvement in the drawing up of contracts should be strictly limited. To the *patronal*'s exasperation, the Minister of Labour, José Estadella, proceeded to shelve the findings. A further blow was the outcome of the long-standing metallurgical strike in June, whereby the unions, with the explicit backing of the Minister, secured the 44-hour week. In September, this was extended by Estadella to 1 December 1934. Such "injustice" led the metallurgical companies to protest anew at the "impossibility of the *patronal* of bearing the new burden", profits having plunged since 1930.[3]

The Radicals' industrial relations policy was clearly still in the making. On the one hand, they had settled conflicts in favour of the workers, as shown by the construction and metallurgical disputes. On the other hand, as in the *ABC* stoppage in Madrid and the general strike in Valencia, they had come down decidedly on the side of the *patronal*. They further benefited the employers by reducing the number of work inspections from an average of 33,468 in 1932/3 to 21,135 in 1934.[4] Yet the disenchantment of the *patronal* was patent from the outset of 1934, as later manifested by the foundation of the Bloque Patronal in May.[5] Moreover, during the spring and summer of 1934 the employers were to be constantly up in arms at the attempts of the government to solve the unemployment crisis by increasing the financial burden on them, and by, in their view, extending, rather than reducing, the power of the mixed juries. The *patronal* was aggrieved, in short, at its unexpected "lack of political protection".[6] Indeed, the Radical approach signalled the "collapse of the representation of its class interests".[7] Yet the small and middling business community constituted the cornerstone of the party's social base. The Radicals had lost the support of the *patronal* through a combination of their inter-classist vision, according to which a balance should be struck between the claims of the employers and those of the workers, and the lack of a well-developed industrial relations policy. The centrist administrations' relatively even-handed approach, which satisfied neither the *patronal* nor the unions, meant that the Radicals fell, in effect, between two stools.

If anything, relations between the Radicals and the *patronal* deteriorated even further as a result of the endeavours of the Lerroux and Samper administrations to assuage the rising unemployment. Despite the fact that the economy had begun to pick up in 1934, the number of those without work continued to climb. According to official figures, over 700,000 workers, or 18% of the active working population, were unemployed in May 1934. This estimate was based on the returns from the trade unions, but not all workers were affiliated to a union, while the CNT generally refused to cooperate. "We do not have the means to compile statistics in Spain", the socialist Julián Besteiro pointed out in the Cortes. The real level of unemployment was probably double the official figure – at around 1.4 million. Strikes in favour of a reduced working week, as in the Madrid construction industry, had aimed to create more jobs, but greater state intervention was obviously required. In January 1934, Lerroux, then Prime Minister, had announced a four-year plan of public works, targetted above all at the construction of public buildings, with a total outlay of 1000 million pesetas. This would be financed by an extraordinary budget. Over the following weeks, projects designed to aid other sectors of the economy, such as the railways and shipbuilding, were put forward. It was also envisaged that other industries, such as the electrical and aeronautical ones, would be embraced by further plans. A mini-Cabinet, presided over by the Prime Minister himself, was set up in order to oversee these myriad schemes. This wide-ranging programme of state intervention was partly stimulated by a number of purely circumstantial developments: a greater awareness, and acceptance, by early 1934 of the benefits of deficit-spending, the reduction in the deficit inherited from the Dictatorship, and the continuing growth in unemployment. In seeking to improve relations between workers and management, the initiative also reflected the centrist dimension to Radical politics. Indeed, the party had been unique in calling since 1932 for the creation of an extraordinary budget in order to combat the recession. The Radicals' plan was kick-started, to the general delight of the business community, by a lowering of the interest rate.[8]

The Radical strategy to combat the recession was far more enterprising in scale and scope than anything attempted during the first biennium. The budget for Lerroux's initial project, for example, was much greater than that for the relatively ambitious plan of August 1931. Spending on construction alone would offset "in good part" the depression in Spain. While certain business sectors, such as the Federación de Industrias Nacionales, warmly welcomed the government's scheme, many others did not. Influential publications such as *Economía Española* and *El Trabajo Nacional* rejected it (though without offering an alternative), largely on the grounds that an "organic plan" had not been drawn up and that a deficit budget would cause "the ruin of the country". In a letter of 27 March 1934 to the Prime Minister, Unión Económica lambasted the proposals on much the same grounds. Such criticism, together with the passive resistance of the right, the general climate of political instability, and, it has to be said, a lack of will on behalf of the Radicals, resulted in a greatly diluted bill being presented to the Cortes on 30 June. The latest scheme was, the Minister of Labour admitted, "extremely modest". The bulk of the bill, passed by the Cortes on 7 July, was given over to the creation of a National Junta of Unemployment to oversee the fight against unemployment. In August, the Junta recommended that 24 million pesetas should be spent on public works, of which 1.3 million would be dedicated to the construction of public buildings – a mere 0.13 per cent of the budget outlined by the premier back in January. The law of 7 July had also urged the government to present a bill that included an insurance scheme and other measures designed to alleviate the plight of the unemployed but the obstruction of the CEDA along with the tumultuous events of the summer sidelined the proposition. On the other hand, a credit of 9.6 million pesetas that was exempt from parliamentary scrutiny was granted to the coal industry in August, while expenditure on main and secondary roads was higher than in 1931 and 1933, if slightly lower than in 1932. Yet there could no escaping the fact that the July law was but a shadow of the Radicals' original blueprint. Daniel Riu, director general at the Ministry of Labour and principal architect of the plan presented in January, criticized it as "completely inefficient". Needless to say, this fell far short of a genuine anticyclical boost. At least the Radicals had made an attempt to offset the escalating unemployment, but they had been stymied by the opposition of the *patronal* and the lack of support from left and right alike.[9]

The Radicals' labour policy in the cities contrasted markedly with that in the countryside. The enforcement of legislation in the rural areas was inherently more difficult than in the urban ones as a result of the limitations of the weakly-resourced Spanish state and the corresponding strength of local élites along with the lack of a tradition of trade-union bargaining. Relations between the left republicans and socialists had deteriorated greatly at the grassroots level in 1933 precisely because the agrarian and labour legislation had not been upheld. Since the Radicals had assumed power, there had been an unbroken stream of complaints at violations of these laws in the rural arena. In truth, the workers, now bereft of party protection at the national level and alarmed at the rise of the right, were much more inclined to protest at the shortcomings of the Radical administrations than those of the republican–socialist ones. The defensiveness of the labourers was accentuated by the ever-rising unemployment – an increase of 50 per cent in the rural economy over the last two years – and by the weakening of the unions.[10] Above all, the landowners had embraced the success of the right in the 1933 general election as *their* triumph over the workers. The property owners' ensuing offensive against the labourers was facilitated by the Radical authorities' tendency to turn a blind eye. In effect, the Radical Party implicitly recognized that rural Spain was the domain of the right. The upshot was a decline in labour conditions. In February 1934 the FNTT, the landless labourers' UGT-affiliate, had warned the government that if the regulations were not fulfilled, the *turno rigoroso* not implemented, and the use of machinery not restricted by harvest time, the union would go on strike that summer. It was plain that the legislation was being widely abused in many areas. In the province of Toledo, the socialist deputy Blázquez claimed in the Cortes, the new contracts had still not been drawn up, the mixed juries were scarcely operating, and many workers had not even been paid for the previous harvest. Those that had found work in Talavera de la Reina were being paid a miserly three pesetas a day. Moreover, many of the province's workers were forced to join Acción Popular. On 12 May the FNTT National Committee produced a ten-point list which not only included demands in relation to the harvest but also others concerning the enforcement of the Agrarian Reform Law. Rejection of the programme would, the union warned, result in a national strike in early June.[11]

The Samper administration, faced by the prospect of a nationwide stoppage at harvest time, made a genuine effort to resolve the FNTT's grievances. Both the Minister of Agriculture and the Minister of Labour, along with the Prime Minister, tried to avert the strike by enforcing the extant legislation. On 24 May, the field inspectors were instructed to ensure that labourers were hired fairly. Contracts which were, in Edward

Malefakis' words, "favourable to the workers" were to be drawn up by the *jurados mixtos*. These also set minimum wages at the same level as those for 1931–3. On 2 June, the government reinforced the regulations that made landowners contract workers through the employment offices. Further, the field inspectors were told to place extra workers with employers wherever unemployment was high. These reconciliatory advances were partly offset by the hostile actions of the Minister of the Interior, Salazar Alonso, who prohibited FNTT meetings and arrested union leaders while denouncing the workers' mobilization, in inflammatory tones, as a "frankly revolutionary movement". Finally, in the last week of May, he decreed the harvest a "national service" and the stoppage, therefore, illegal.[12]

Certainly the FNTT's approach to the strike was complicated by its ambivalent rhetoric, which, like that of the socialist movement as a whole, swung between reformist moderation and revolutionary messianism. Upon election in February 1934, the FNTT's pro-Largo Caballero leadership had proclaimed, "We declare ourselves for the Revolution!" Moreover, for many rural workers, the promise of reform had given way by mid-1934 to the belief that the only means of obtaining meaningful change was by revolution. Consequently there was a widespread belief that a stoppage in the countryside would trigger a nationwide walkout, thereby ushering in the social revolution. The landless labourers, as the socialist deputy Juan-Simeón Vidarte noted mournfully, "in their desperation took its realization for granted". As 5 June loomed, the government, which had accepted all the union's principal demands, seemed to be on the verge of a settlement. However, the FNTT, loathe to give in to a figure as reviled as Salazar Alonso, to relinquish the recently formed alliance with the Andalusian CNT, and anxious, in Vidarte's words, to demonstrate its "enormous force" and achieve a "triumph", suddenly produced a new list of exigencies on 3 June. These, which included the unprecedented demand that harvest conditions, including wages, should pertain to the whole year, were predictably rejected by the Cabinet. Only the day before the Minister of Agriculture had been optimistic that an agreement would be reached. What had begun as a dispute over working conditions had become a showdown between the socialists and the Radical-run state.[13]

The FNTT strike, the greatest in Spanish agrarian history, was unleashed on 5 June. Altogether, stoppages were proclaimed in more than 1,500 municipalities, but tools were actually downed in only 435 of them. Union support was undermined by the disorientation within its ranks at the shifts in policy and by the fact that the government's reconciliatory initiatives had won over many moderates. In any case, the protest was doomed from the outset by the absence of a simultaneous action by the urban unions and the national CNT. The isolation of the FNTT ensured its defeat. The Minister of the Interior's vigorous preventive measures – during the course of the conflict thirteen workers died, though mostly through confrontations between unionists and blacklegs – also played their part. Expectations of revolution were totally unrealistic given the lack of alliances and the lack of preparation for an armed struggle (highlighting the contradiction between reformism and revolution within the socialist strategy). The strike was, as Vidarte laments, "a senseless movement which we could not halt". By 20 June, the strikers had succumbed.[14]

Up to 7,000 labourers were imprisoned, many of whom were allegedly starved and tortured. Some were made to walk up to 100 kilometres from one jail to another. All of them, however, were released within a month. Meanwhile, the collection of strike funds was impeded and the entry of Portuguese blacklegs facilitated.[15] The parliamentary immunity of four socialist deputies was also infringed by an unrepentant Salazar Alonso (for whom they had committed "a crime against the state"), thereby causing a terrible rumpus in the Cortes. The fact that the level of conflict had not been greater was due to the moderation not only of the socialists but also of certain ministers. The Prime Minister, for example, refused to let Salazar Alonso declare a state of war in the province of Jaen, despite his protestations that the stoppage there was characterized by "great violence". Following the strike, the zealous Minister of the Interior, eager to take political advantage of events, dismantled much of the socialist network in the south. The FNTT in particular did not recover until 1936. As a result, the landowners had largely re-established their pre-1931 socio-economic hegemony while the balance of local power had shifted towards the centre–right as numerous left-wing town councils were overthrown. The socialist movement, bereft not only of its strongest union but also of its infrastructure in its main area of support, had been dealt a shattering blow, especially as regards its preparations for a "revolutionary" uprising should the CEDA enter the government. The stoppage had clearly been a dreadful blunder. Nor, however, was the crushing of the FNTT a victory for the Samper administration. Conciliation, as embodied in the endeavours of the Ministers of Agriculture and Labour, had given way to the repressive methods of the Minister of the Interior. In effect, the hawks had triumphed at the expense of the doves. The strike, by radicalizing the political climate, had undermined the centrist cause of the Prime Minister while enhancing that of the Radical right-wingers and their allies. *Renovación*, for example, assailed the socialist action as a "vile procedure" designed to spread "ruin and hunger", while the FNTT's defeat by Salazar Alonso, who was "consubstantial" with the party, was hailed as the victory of "youth, of the qualities of a ruler". In short, the stoppage had strengthened the Radical hardliners and the right alike while making the realization of the Prime Minister's centrist aspirations more difficult than ever.[16]

Of immediate benefit for the Radical Party was the Ministry of the Interior's overturning of numerous socialist town councils in the wake of the stoppage in favour of largely Radical-run interim administrations, thereby enhancing the party's presence in the provinces. Deputy Ruiz del Toro claimed in parliament that nearly all the councils in Murcia had been replaced under the direction of Salazar Alonso, who, he believed, aspired to the status of *"l'enfant terrible* of the Republic". *El Socialista* expostulated that Salazar Alonso's "dictatorial whim" had left scarcely a socialist, left–republican, or even Conservative Republican Party *ayuntamiento* standing. By the end of June, for example, the paper claimed that not a single socialist-dominated council in the province of Alicante remained.[17] The 30–odd cases highlighted by the socialist organ must be set against a nationwide total of nearly 10,000 local councils. Salazar Alonso, according to the figures issued by his own Ministry in mid-August, had so far dismissed 249 councils, as opposed to Martínez Barrio's six, Rico Avello's 40, Miguel Maura's 88, and Casares Quiroga's 316. None the less, Quiroga's rate of disqualification, at 14 a month, was far lower than Salazar Alonso's, at nearly 50. However, in *Bajo el signo de la revolución*, Salazar Alonso, who was restrained from further substitutions by both the Prime Minister and the President, laments that "I am not concerned at . . . the *ayuntamientos* which I dismissed, but at those which I did not dismiss". However, the blatantly partisan nature of the policy, denounced in the Cortes, undermined the Radicals' much-vaunted commitment to the legal order. Presumably as a result, *Renovación*, always eager to trumpet Radical advances, eschewed the subject altogether.[18]

No sooner was the FNTT strike over than the Samper administration's conciliatory will was again put to the test. On 12 April the President of the Generalidad, Luis Companys, had promulgated the Law on Contracts of Cultivation passed by the Catalan parliament. This empowered the *rabassaires*, renters and sharecroppers who were mostly concentrated in the wine-growing sector and who formed a key electoral constituency of the ruling Esquerra party in Catalonia, to buy land which they had worked for fifteen years in addition to providing them with a greater degree of tenant security. The Catalan right, with the backing of the CEDA and its allies, sprang to the defence of the landowners. It lobbied the government to ascertain whether the Generalidad, in accordance with the Constitution and the Statute of Autonomy, could indeed legislate on agrarian affairs. The question of conflicting powers between Madrid and Barcelona was, from the outset, a political football. Back in 1932, the contending parties had adopted diametrically opposed positions: the Esquerra had maintained that the Cortes would have to draw up the relevant law, while the right-wing Lliga had argued that this was the province of the Catalan parliament. On 4 May, the newly-installed Samper government, confronted by the intrinsically complex judicial question of competing legislative powers and under pressure from the right, duly passed the matter on to the Court of Constitutional Guarantees. On 8 June, the Court, by a close-run decision of thirteen votes to ten, upheld the contention of the right that the Law of Cultivation was both unconstitutional and in violation of the Autonomy Statute.[19]

A prompt attempt to defuse the confrontation was undertaken by the President. Before the verdict of 8 June was delivered, he met Amadeu Hurtado, the widely respected Catalan lawyer who had defended the Generalidad before the Court. Alcalá-Zamora, an expert in administrative law, suggested that, if the Law of Cultivation was declared unconstitutional, the Catalan parliament should pass another, slightly different, one. The Prime Minister, Hurtado established, was of the same opinion. In this way, the government, eager to avoid further conflict, would have a motive – the political cost to be derived from continuing with the legal challenge – not to declare the law unconstitutional. Hurtado passed this suggestion on in person to Companys. Rather than regard the advice as constructive, he replied belligerently that "the dignity" of the Catalan parliament would not consent to a comma of the original law being altered, even if it could be considered unconstitutional in some respects. He added that he would defend the measure no matter what the consequences. On 12 June, the Catalan parliament debated the decision of the Court of Constitutional Guarantees. Outside, Companys addressed an expectant crowd in such a way, an eye-witness recalls, as to "inflame and instigate intransigent positions and, in the end, open revolt". Inside, the Catalan President referred to the recent declarations of the Prime Minister, who had reiterated that, if certain changes were made to the Law of Cultivation, a solution to the conflict could be found. Either the Law was constitutional, or it was not, riposted Companys. For good measure, he denounced "the offensive against our liberties" and the "monarchist" powers that had taken control of the state. Patriotism, he concluded, would not allow for compromises, even though the situation might reach "a state of force". The parliament duly passed a law which was identical to the previous one.[20]

Samper was flabbergasted. The Esquerra had reacted to the first important dispute over the Statute in a volatile and unyielding fashion. Indeed, the Generalidad, rather than exploiting the premier's known sympathy for its position, provided the government with even less room for manoeuvre, thereby playing into the hands of the right. Worse still, the clash between the Generalidad and the central authorities was, for left and right alike, a highly emotive issue. Traditionally, much of the progressive opposition, especially the socialists, had shown little sympathy for the cause of Catalan autonomy. However, the strength of the republican movement in Catalonia had led the Revolutionary Committee to recognize the Catalans' right at San Sebastian in August 1930. This was embodied first in the 1931 Constitution and then, the following year, in a Statute of Autonomy. As a consequence, the routing of the left republicans and socialists in the 1933 general election bestowed on the Generalidad – retained by the Esquerra in the January 1934 provincial elections despite having won fewer seats than the Lliga in the national poll two months earlier – a potent symbolism. Indeed, the left elevated the Generalidad into the last bastion of republican resistance to the unholy alliance of the centre–right. In June, Azaña defended the Catalan government as "the last republican power that still stands in Spain". The cause of the Generalidad was therefore converted by the left, wounded by the crushing of the FNTT strike that month, into its own. At stake was not just the autonomous rights of the Catalans but a particular vision of the Republic. Accordingly, the government's attempt to resolve the dispute through the Court of Constitutional Guarantees was interpreted by socialists and left republicans alike as yet another demonstration of the Radicals' subordination to the right and of their assault on "the entire work of the Constituent (Cortes)". For the right, the matter was no less significant. Together with its innate hostility to Catalan claims as subversive of the Spanish nation-state was the added grievance of the challenge to the hegemony of the landowners over renters and sharecroppers. Those who backed the Generalidad were viewed by the right not only as defying the popular will, as manifested in the 1933 election, but also, and more importantly, the authority of the state.[21]

The Radical Party, as in the case of the Autonomy Statute, was strongly divided over the issue. The party's spokesman on Catalan affairs, Juan Palau, fulminated against the Generalidad's "anti-constitutional and anti-statutory and, in addition, anti-republican" stance. For Palau, the crisis was nothing more than a "conspiracy" of the left.[22] Yet there was also considerable support within the party for the Catalans' rights of autonomy. Foremost amongst them were the PURA deputies, who included, of course, the Prime Minister. In addition, three Radicals on the Court of Constitutional Guarantees had voted in favour of the Generalidad.[23] Finally, there was within the government itself a strong current of opinion in favour of a conciliatory approach. The Prime Minister, along with Rafael Guerra del Río, Vicente Iranzo, and Filiberto Villalobos, sought a settlement that was acceptable to both sides, while others, including the Progressive Cirilo del Río and, inevitably, Rafael Salazar Alonso, opposed them. The reaction of the Generalidad on 12 June to the decision of the Court, along with the withdrawal of the Esquerra and PNV deputies from the Cortes, had obviously reduced the government's room for manoeuvre. Still, Samper continued to pursue a consensual solution. Indeed, the Prime Minister, following the Esquerra's abandonment of the Cortes, made it plain in parliament not only that he agreed with the Law of Cultivation, but also that he did not seek a conflict with Catalonia. On the contrary, he called on the Esquerra, whose absence from the chamber he lamented, to collaborate in the search for a "prudent solution that avoids friction" by means of a "spirit of mutual understanding". For both left and right, the Catalan contention was too charged an issue, and the political stakes too high, for it to be susceptible to a mere question of goodwill. Socialist spokesman Indalecio Prieto accused the Prime Minister of being befuddled and bewildered. Similarly, Gil Robles ridicules the premier in *No fue posible la paz* for allowing his "weak temperament" to confuse "judicial solutions" with "surrender". In short, the Prime Minister was caught between the hostility of the left and that of the right. The CEDA leader pressed Lerroux, who was taking the waters at Baños de Montemayor, to return posthaste to Madrid as "Samper is not succeeding". Despite the opposition of the CEDA, Samper held a parliamentary debate on the issue on 25 June. On the one hand, he reassured the government's allies that it would uphold the sentence passed by the Court of Constitutional Guarantees. On the other hand, he spoke of a negotiated solution. In effect, the Prime Minister was endeavouring to appease the right while reaching a settlement with the Generalidad. Shortly afterwards, on 30 June, Gil Robles addressed a long and detailed letter to Samper in which he pleaded with him to "impose respect for the law and protect the prestige of the state". To that end, the CEDA leader exhorted him to seek a vote of confidence that would allow the government to suspend the Cortes while it sought a solution. This, indeed, is exactly what Samper did. On 4 July, the government secured the necessary vote amidst tumultuous scenes as CEDA and socialist deputies not only traded punches but even brandished pistols, including the socialist spokesman, Indalecio Prieto.[24]

The vote of 4 July suited the premier's ambivalent strategy admirably for it permitted him to satisfy the right while striking a deal with the Catalans. In fact, secret discussions with the Generalidad had already begun. Though the regional government continued to make defiant gestures, such as passing the regulations for the enactment of the Law of Cultivation on 10 July, it was clearly willing to reach a compromise. On 14 July, it declared that it would draw up "rules" which would permit it to "regulate" the Law of Cultivation and "allow" its application in accordance with the Constitution. In the meantime, the government demonstrated its good faith by continuing to transfer powers to Catalonia, such as those concerning taxation on 12 July. Both Samper and Companys sought, Salazar Alonso recalls, a "friendly solution". The Prime Minister himself was closely involved in the negotiations, as was Hurtado, while the President played an active role, too. However, the talks did not produce the swift and binding settlement demanded by the CEDA. The accidentalists' mounting disillusionment, as reflected in the pages of *El Debate*, gave way first to anger and then to outright outrage. By contrast, the government continued to exude optimism. Guerra del Río, following a visit to Catalonia in early August, praised the "good disposition" of Companys. Several other ministers assured public opinion that a deal was at hand, while reproaching the right for failing to keep faith with them. The Naval Minister Juan José Rocha claimed that the feud was simply a matter of "cordiality" and that the Prime Minister's gradualist approach was the only one possible. None the less, the Catalan question took an enormous toll on the Cabinet during the summer of 1934, absorbing vast amounts of its time and energy while detracting from other tasks. Indeed, the dispute, by trapping the government between left and right, greatly impeded the development of its centrist agenda. Yet the Radical premier emphatically demonstrated that a centre administration could work alongside the left. Even Salazar Alonso admits that both Samper and Companys, despite considerable pressure from their respective camps, kept to a "path of equanimity and serenity". On the other hand, the search for a centre–left solution made a showdown with the right inevitable.[25]

Just as the Prime Minister was in the throes of the Catalan dispute, another regional conflict, this time in the Basque country, blew up. On coming to power in December 1933, the Radicals had initially gained the parliamentary support of the leading Basque nationalist party, the PNV, by promising, in accord with the Constitution, to pass an autonomy statute for the region. For the Radicals, however, this was not an urgent matter as the twelve PNV deputies were not indispensable to the government's survival. This, together with the filibustering of the right, kept delaying the bill. In contrast to the first biennium, when a left-wing government had collaborated with the like-minded Esquerra in order to deliver the Catalan Statute, the PNV found that, despite its Catholic and deeply conservative outlook, it lacked support amongst the national right-wing parties. For example, in the dispute in February 1934 over whether or not Alava should be included in the proposed Statute, the Radicals sided with the Basques, Catalans, and socialists in opposition to the CEDA and its allies. For the Catholic right, obsessed by the unity of the Spanish state, Basque rights of autonomy, like those of the Catalans, smacked of separatism. "Our enemies today," as the PNV deputy Manuel Irujo commented, "are the forces of the right." Once the Catalan dispute erupted in April 1934, the PNV became more wary than ever of the ruling majority's intentions. As a result, once the Esquerra retired from the Cortes on 12 June, the Basque nationalists joined them.[26]

The PNV's act of solidarity swiftly translated into a defence of the Basques' own interests as a result of the fiscal proposals of the Minister of the Economy, Manuel Marraco. He had first tried to collect new taxes approved in 1933 without reaching a prior agreement with the Basques. Then, on the prodding of the right, he decided to alter the tax on wine. This would effectively slash the income of the local authorities in Vizcaya and Guipuzcoa by about a half. Such a move, as the provincial steering committees for the Basque provinces pointed out on the very same day that the PNV withdrew from the Cortes, would undermine the *conciertos económicos*, the most important of the Basques' remaining historic rights. The issue highlighted the fissures within the Radical Party over the autonomy question. For example, the Basque steering committees, which had criticized the minister's fiscal plans, were all dominated by the Radicals. Within the Cabinet itself, two hardline centralists, Marraco and Salazar Alonso, were outnumbered by those, including the Prime Minister, in favour of a more flexible approach.[27]

On 3 July, the Cabinet, following the lobbying of Samper, Lerroux, and Marraco by Juan Gallano, Radical President of the Vizcaya *Diputación* (provincial government), agreed to reappraise the impact of the wine Statute on the Basque country. "It is not a question of annuling the current *concierto económico*. Nor are the taxes on the wines going to be reduced", declared a recalcitrant Marraco. The government also promised to present a bill, in accordance with article 10 of the Constitution, that would facil- itate the holding of provincial elections in the Basque country for the first time since 1922. This was because the *ayuntamientos* rejected the *Diputaciones* as legitimate representatives as these had been nominated by the government (resulting in a patent over-representation of the Radicals). The town councils, at a meeting in Bilbao on 5 July, reacted by nominating a provisional committee "for the defence of the *concierto económico*", which, on 29 July, called for the holding of elections on 12 August in order to choose a definitive committee. Such a decision was entirely legal as it concerned an administrative, as opposed to political, issue. None the less, the Radical civil governor for Vizcaya, the volatile Angel Velarde, banned the elections. He was seconded by his superior and ally, Salazar Alonso, for whom this was yet another affront to the authority of the state.[28]

The heavy-handed approach of Velarde together with the government's misunderstanding of the elections – it believed that they were regular elec- tions and not that for a committee – complicated the situation enormously by converting it into a question of competing powers. Thus *Renovación* rejected the Basque claims outright in an editorial of 8 August as the mani- festation of an "agitating nationalism", while dismissing the actions of the PNV, which displayed "the fascist spirit of the Esquerra", as a ploy to "discredit, derail the Republic". Like the Minister of the Interior, the Radical organ concluded that the entire matter was simply a question of authority. *El Debate*, already disillusioned by the Samper administration's perceived back-pedalling over the Catalan conflict, also demanded firm action in the face of such "coercions of the state". The government's room for manoeuvre had been greatly reduced by the unneccesary confronta- tion over the 12 August elections. Once again, as in the Catalan dispute, the Prime Minister, as Juan Pablo Fusi writes, "saw himself trapped between the hostility of the left and the pressure of the right". None the less, Samper, as in the case if the Generalidad, persisted in seeking a negotiated solution. The Cabinet, in a statement published on 8 August, declared the elections "absolutely illegal" but added that, in the first session of parliament, a bill would be presented so that the provincial elections could be held. Over the next two days the Prime Minister assured the Basques that the government did not want to restrict the application of the *concierto* "in the slightest", that there existed "the desire to reach an agreement" over the new taxation arrangements, and that the town councils could name their commissions in ordinary sessions. He also stressed his willingness to "listen to as many commissions as present themselves in order to express their complaints and aspirations by legal means". He was even prepared to resign over the issue. When he asked Salazar Alonso to moderate Velarde's comments on the PNV, the minister reacted by offering his resignation. Samper responded by threatening to do the same. Only the intervention of the Radical leader overcame this clash between, in Salazar Alonso's words, his own "firmness" and the Prime Minister's "conciliatory formulas". The government's accommodating approach none the less failed to dissuade the Basques from attempting to hold the elections.[29]

The crux of the problem is that the conflict had become much more than one between the PNV and the government. Leadership of the *ayuntamientos'* protest was in the hands of the left, in particular those of the *Azañista* mayor for San Sebastian, Fernando Sasiaín, and the republican–socialist town council of Bilbao, initially headed by the socialist Fermín Zarza. From the left's point of view, at dispute was not just the autonomous rights of the Basques but its very conception of the Republic. And just as the left had made the Generalidad's cause its own, so it was determined to do the same with the Basque issue – despite the fact that it had hitherto regarded the Basque nationalists as little more than clerical reactionaries. As a result, the left embraced the Basque cause, out of a mixture of principle and opportunism, as one more means, within an ever-widening opposition front, of attacking the Radical administration. While the authorities claimed that the 12 August elections had been prevented in 74 of Vizcaya's 115 town councils, in 43 of Guipuzcoa's 87, and in the Alavese capital, Vitoria, the Basques insisted that in the first two provinces polling had taken place in the great majority of local councils. For the Samper government, this was an illegal act rooted in the oppositional strategy of the left. For the Basques, in the words of PNV leader José Antonio Aguirre, Madrid had undertaken "an attack" on the pact between the Basque country and the Spanish state.[30]

In reality, the PNV, though it had seconded the *ayuntamientos'* protest, was keen neither to collaborate with the left nor to flirt with illegality.

Indeed, José Horn, head of the PNV's parliamentary group, had sought a formula prior to the elections whereby the Prime Minister might accept them. Similarly, following the elections, Aguirre met Samper in an effort to find a solution. The PNV leader put forward a proposal whereby the provincial steering committees would resign and new ones would be chosen by the town councils, while the premier still dwelt on the government's "high-minded and understanding spirit". Aguirre stressed that they were endeavouring to reach an agreement "with understanding and tolerance". Both men, in other words, sought a solution. Before this could be realized, an assembly was held on 2 September in the Guipuzcoan *pueblo* of Zumarraga which brought together PNV and Catalan deputies as well as members of the recently-elected commissions, while the socialist Indalecio Prieto acted as moderator. Symbolically, the gathering represented the union of the Basque nationalists, the Esquerra, and the national left against the Radical–right governing coalition. Yet the meeting failed to meet expectations as no concrete agreement emerged. Of greater political resonance was the attempted disruption of a PNV homage to the Catalan deputies in Guernica, the home of Basque nationalism, by the police on the orders of Velarde. This prompted the collective resignation of *ayuntamientos* throughout Vizcaya and Guipuzcoa. Shocked at the turn which events were taking, the PNV now drew back from the conflict. Despite the fact that during the month of September town councils were being replaced by steering committees, that hundreds of local councillors were being put on trial, and that mass resignations by local functionaries were being enacted, the PNV refused to join the left in taking the struggle on. Indeed, Aguirre, wary of being implicated in the socialists' revolutionary preparations, announced that his party would return to the Cortes once it reopened on 1 October, while expressing the view that the Autonomy Statute could still – in spite of everything – be achieved under the centre–right. The PNV would later vote in favour of the next Cabinet, formed in early October. However, the hardline approach of Salazar Alonso and Velarde, buttressed by the CEDA and its allies, had effectively sabotaged the efforts of Samper in favour of a reconciliatory outcome.[31]

The essential moderation that had characterized the Prime Minister's dealings with the socialist–republican opposition was complemented by a similar approach to the legislative achievements of the first biennium. There was, in fact, a strong element of continuity. Agrarian policy provides a paramount example. The zeal of many *Cedistas* and Agrarians, together with the monarchists, to demolish the rural reforms of 1931–3, was offset by the determination of the Radicals and other moderates, notably the Progressive Minister of Agriculture, Cirilo del Río, to alter, rather than annihilate, the extant legislation. The very heterogeneity of the ruling coalition, as Edward Malefakis points out, "prevented a wholesale repudiation of the Azaña heritage". To this must be added the capacity of the left, whose presence in the current parliament was much greater than the right's had been in the previous one, to defend its own interests, whether in committee, in the Cortes, or on the executive council of the IRA, the body responsible for applying the Agrarian Reform Law. Thus the attempt by the right in February 1934 to expel the *yunteros* given access to land by the civil governor of Extremadura was thwarted by the Radicals and the left. Likewise, in June 1934 a number of *Cedistas* tried to exploit the climate of confrontation created by the FNTT stoppage to axe the funds of the IRA, but once again the Radicals joined forces with the socialists and opposition republicans to foil the strategem. The only measure of 1931–3 that was rejected outright was the generally discredited *términos municipales* law. Admittedly, Del Río restructered the IRA, but this was largely in accordance with a blueprint drawn up by the Radical–Socialist Marcelino Domingo. Furthermore, neither the IRA's budget was cut, nor was any of the confiscated land handed back to the old owners. Most importantly of all, the pace of expropriation under the Radicals was far superior to that under the Azaña administration. Whereas an average of 275 peasants were settled per month on 24,203 hectares between September 1932 and December 1933, the first nine months of 1934 saw 81,558 hectares distributed amongst an average of 700 peasants per month – more than double the rate under the left. In truth, this was entirely in accord with the promises made by the Radicals during the election campaign. That said, they did little to fulfil their propaganda pledges of further reform. Lacking both the will and the programme for substantial change but in any case shackled by the right, the Radicals had none the less defended the legacy of the left.[32]

Another crucial area where the Samper administration endeavoured to continue the work of the Cortes, despite the fetter of the right, was education. The republican goal of wresting education from the control of the Catholic Church through the creation of a secular state system had lain at the heart of the modernizing reforms of the first biennium. Equally, the Catholics were determined, following the 1933 election, to overthrow or at least drastically modify the laicizing legislation. Gil Robles, upon the presentation of the Radicals' post-electoral administration, had called for "a rectification of . . . all that refers to education, which is for us a vital question in relation to which we cannot give any ground at all". The Minister of Education, Dr Filiberto Villalobos, a long-standing republican and reformist who was a member of the Liberal Democratic Party, found himself, therefore, in an extremely difficult position. On the one hand, he aimed to fulfil the legislation of the first biennium. "I will do whatever is necessary", he declared before the Cortes, "to fulfil strictly the Constitution and the Law of Congregations". On the other hand, he was confronted by the zealous opposition of the right. A vivid illustration was provided by the declaration of CEDA leader Cándido Casanueva before an assembly of the Women's Association of Civic Education that "you have the unavoidable obligation to pour a drop of hatred every day into the hearts of your children against the Law of Congregations and their authors".[33]

The key issue at dispute was the replacement of church schools by state ones. According to the Law of Congregations, this had to be carried out by 31 December 1933 for the primary schools and by 1 October 1934 for the rest of the educational system. In practice, the lack of time, money, and buildings, along with the resistance of conservative town and village councils, had made these targets unrealistic from the outset. Needless to say, applying this legislation was made even more problematic for the Radical-led administrations of 1934 as a result of their parliamentary dependence on the right. Most immediately, the government could not pass the educational budget, to be scrutinized by the Cortes in June, without the consent of its allies. Villalobos decided to tackle the dilemma by offering a credible state alternative to the church-run system rather than by shutting down the religious schools; that is to say, through competition rather than closure. Such an approach allowed him to strengthen the state system without incurring the outright opposition of the right. This was a truly centrist compromise insofar as it aimed to satisfy both left and right. It had the added virtue of being faithful to the Radicals' electoral promises. As it happened, the inherent difficulties of replacing the church schools would later be recognized by the Popular Front government of 1936. The substitution of religious schools, the Minister of Education would admit, had to advance "with prudence and discretion" and the state "should respect and even protect private education". In the meantime, Villalobos' strategy allowed him, following the Cortes debate of 26–28 June 1934, to secure the budget.[34]

Despite the constraints of the alliance with the right and a patent lack of continuity – there were three different ministers of education in four months – the Radical governments of 1934, due overwhelmingly to the efforts of Villalobos under the Samper administration, considerably extended the state system set in motion during the first biennium. Not only did the number of teachers rise from 46,260 in 1933 to 50,260 in 1934 but Villalobos, unlike the left, raised their minimum salary – earned by more than half of the nation's teachers – from 3,000 to 4,000 pesetas. The number of primary school pupils increased from just under 2.4 million in 1933 to a shade over 2.5 million a year later, while that of secondary school students climbed by 13,991 to nearly 64,000. Admittedly, the construction of primary schools had dwindled during the first four months of 1934, but under the Samper administration this picked up again: between the end of April and that of August, 16 million of the 25 million-peseta budget was dedicated to the building of elementary schools. Meanwhile, the number of inspectors increased from 322 to 377, thereby improving the ratio between them and the teachers. Overall, the Radical-led governments of 1934 spent a higher proportion of the national budget on education – 7.08 per cent – than the left-wing administrations of 1931–3.[35]

Not only did Villalobos build on the statist foundations laid during the first biennium but he was also prepared to defy the right through further secular reforms. Three decrees in July and August, executed while parliament was suspended, completely reorganized the secondary school *bachillerato*, largely in accordance with schemes outlined, but only partially realized, under the Azaña administration. A measure of his daring was the fact that the new *bachillerato*, as Rodríguez de las Heras observes, "culminates the influence in official educational circles of the Institución Libre de Enseñanza", the influential body which had promoted secular education in Spain since 1876. The right was furious. *El Debate* lambasted the edicts not only for excluding the teaching of religion and treating private education "disdainfully", but also for breaching the deal struck with the ruling majority over the June budget whereby the new plans for the secondary system would be presented to parliament in October. The CEDA organ put this down to "a new tactic of the defeated forces of the biennium, who continue being masters of the Ministry of Education". A sustained campaign of Catholic protest was launched against the Minister, now viewed as a dangerous liberal. The Federación de Amigos de la Enseñanza (Federation of the Friends of Education, the FAE), created under the auspices of *El Debate*, criticized Villalobos for not having suppressed coeducation in the secondary system, for leaving the National Council of Culture, an advisory body, in the hands of "socialists and people who are enemies of the church", and for tolerating "Communist and socialist propaganda in the schools". The Minister, it concluded, "does not respond, not in the least, to the national conscience, nor to the patriotic sense". Once again, the centrist policy of the Samper administration had incurred the ire of its allies.[36]

Less enterprising was the Radicals' approach to the armed forces. Diego Hidalgo, appointed as Minister of War in January 1934, was principally motivated by a desire to return "peace and tranquillity" to the army following the sweeping series of measures enacted by Manuel Azaña. This was entirely in accordance with the spirit of the Radicals' goal of ruling "for all Spaniards". Hidalgo did little to alter the reforms of the first biennium. Nor did he undertake any major structural changes of his own. On the contrary, he limited himself largely to generating support for the Radicals by undoing many of the promotions frozen by Azaña and by improving the situation of non-commissioned officers and sergeants. Although this has been dismissed as "party politics", it at least had the virtue of enhancing support for the regime. Much the opposite has been said of Hidalgo's key appointments. Yet he did not promote avowed monarchists. Rather, he tended to favour republican figures not closely associated with Azaña, such as General López Ochoa, a well-known Mason, or those regarded essentially as apolitical "professionals", a category which embraced, for example, General Batet, and, arguably, the young General Franco, promoted to Major General in March 1934. As a result, the Radical minister's appointments, "timid, like his performance as a whole", as Cardona notes, was not so much anti-republican as anti-Azaña. Hidalgo further boosted support within the army by bringing the state arms industry more under the military's control and, to the inordinate delight of Lerroux, a convinced, if frustrated, imperialist, by overseeing the reoccupation of the tiny enclave of Ifni in southern Morocco. In the meantime, the minister resisted right-wing calls for the re-establishment of the Courts of Honour. It is well established that Azaña's unpopularity with the armed forces lay not so much in his reforms as in his politics and condescending, sometimes openly hostile, attitude. The more urbane and conservative Diego Hidalgo probably inspired greater confidence amongst the military. Moreover, his reforms may have been limited and lacking in vision, but they were not reactionary. Indeed, the Radicals' military policy, like that in other areas, was distinguished by its moderation and the attempt to strike some sort of centrist balance.[37]

It should also be stressed that the Radicals were not devoid of their own reformist initiatives. In fact, the party's most original legislative project was exactly the kind of social measure which might have been undertaken by the left. In 1931, the Radical Party, in common with Acción Republicana, had committed itself to the creation of a Ministry of Health but, once in power, the Radicals, like Acción Republicana before them, had aborted the proposal, principally for financial reasons. In March 1934 they did at least move the health service from the Ministry of the Interior to the more appropriate one of Labour. Moreover, the Radicals did not abandon the health system, by now in a catastrophic state – there having been no wide-ranging public health law since 1857 – altogether. On the contrary, a bill was presented in June that was designed, first, to coordinate the health services more effectively. It was imperative, as the former Radical deputy González y Fernández de la Bandera observed in parliament, that the system's "real anarchy" should come to an end. Overlapping services at the national, provincial, and local levels had resulted in an expenditure that was "infinitely superior to that which should be realized and on the other hand the practical results are completely nil". The second goal was to tackle the appalling, and notorious, plight of the rural doctors. Funded by the local councils, their salaries were negligible and invariably in arrears. Many had not been paid for over five or six years; nationally, they were owed over 50 million pesetas.[38]

The bill for the Coordination of the Health Services was eventually voted into law on 20 June. Fault was found with it on the grounds that the restructuring was inadequately conceived. One deputy went so far as to assert that "this law is completely impractical. It will be the constant target of debate and lawsuits and misunderstandings between the representatives of the state and the provincial and municipal corporations". Furthermore, the scheme's financial provisions still left the local councils to bear the brunt of the doctors' pay. In Aragon, for example, the councils responded by holding a meeting of protest on 24 June. The Radicals had nevertheless made a start in relation to one of the most neglected areas of state welfare. Public health, the Minister of Labour pointed out, had at last become an "essential function of the state".[39] The Radicals had also acted to the benefit of one of the many professional groups that supported it. *La Voz Médica*, the journal of the rural doctors, reacted with undisguised glee, while doctors applauded the law as "our economic salvation . . . it will release us from misery and slavery" and acclaimed the Radical leader as "the defender of justice and of the humble". More generally, the party was congratulated for being "the first and only one that has focused on modern health with a clear and effective vision, advocating a health policy of which we are in such need".[40]

In overall terms, the Radicals' revision of the legislation of 1931–3 was – despite the unyielding harassment of the right – comparatively moderate in nature. In some areas, such as religion, this involved concessions, often of a limited nature, to the Catholic right, but in general terms the Radicals upheld, and sometimes advanced, the gains of the first biennium. They even undertook reformist initiatives of their own. The constant battles between the Radicals and their allies over policy making and over the handling of the regional and labour disputes also highlighted the extent to which the Radical Party did not share the counterreformist goals of the non-republican right. Clearly the diverse forces that made up the ruling majority lacked a common agenda and programme. Their uneasy, and often uncertain, relationship had inevitably ushered in a period of political instability.

By mid August, the Samper administration was struggling to keep its conciliatory aspirations alive amidst an increasingly radicalized political climate. The FNTT strike, the regional conflicts, and the extensive labour agitation meant that the government now faced an opposition front that ranged from the Basque nationalists and the *patronal* to the socialist trade unions, the left republicans, the anarcho–syndicalist movement, and the Socialist Party. The tension was further heightened by the resurgence of the extreme right in the shape of the proto-fascist Bloque Nacional under the leadership of the belligerent José Calvo Sotelo, who had returned from exile in May as a beneficiary of the April amnesty, and José Antonio Primo de Rivera's Falange, converted into the shock troops of the monarchists following the latter's secret deal with the Italian dictator Benito Mussolini in March 1934. Street violence was also fomented by the revolutionary stance of the Socialist Youth (Juventud Socialista), together with its resolute determination to avoid being crushed like its counterparts in Germany, Austria, and Italy. The first fascist youngster was killed in November 1933 and by the summer of 1934 another seven had fallen. Falangist death squads, aptly dubbed the "Falange of Blood", accounted on 10 June 1934 for Juanita Rico, who was given a mass funeral as the "the first victim of fascism". The ultimate goal of the Falangists was, as the discovery of a huge cache of arms and explosives in July underscored, to provoke the intervention of the army by creating an atmosphere of fear and disorder. The anxiety of the opposition republicans was manifested by the meetings that took place between Manuel Azaña, Miguel Maura, Felipe Sánchez Román and Diego Martínez Barrio during the summer of 1934. This led to a visit by the Radical–Democratic leader to the President on 7 July in which he beseeched Alcalá-Zamora to facilitate the formation of an alternative government as a prelude to a general election and, hopefully, the reversal of the 1933 result. In the same spirit, Azaña met the socialist leaders a week later in an attempt to resurrect the republican–socialist alliance, but, like Martínez Barrio, his endeavour came to no avail, as Largo Caballero firmly rejected his advance.[41]

Of most immediate concern for the Prime Minister was the fact that the support of the CEDA, always precarious, was fast beginning to ebb. On 14 August, Gil Robles, fresh from his honeymoon, met two CEDA vicepresidents, Lucia and Aizpún, to discuss the political situation. Much in the style of a teacher reprimanding a wayward pupil, he severely criticized the government's handling of the Basque and Catalan conflicts as well as its record on public order, though exempting the CEDA's faithful ally, Salazar Alonso, from any blame. If, he let it be known, the Cabinet continued in the same vein the CEDA would withdraw its support once the Cortes reopened on 1 October. Nor did the Radical leader offer much succour. In interviews with *El Debate* and *Renovación* he characterized the CEDA's stance as "completely correct". On 21 August, the CEDA *caudillo* informed the premier that he considered the administration's performance, in the words of *El Debate*, "totally mistaken". The rapidly dwindling credibility of the Samper administration within the ruling majority was indicated by the constant to-ings and fro-ings of Radical ministers between Madrid and Lerroux's San Rafael estate, by the frequent consultations between prominent Radicals and the CEDA *jefe*, and, finally, by the fact that the comments of Salazar Alonso, who was scuttling constantly backwards and forwards between the two leaders as a go-between, were of more interest to the press than those of the Prime Minister. Though Samper felt like the "good Christian" who contemplates "without fear the hour of his death", he was still determined to defend his administration's record before the Cortes.[42]

During the first half of September the enveloping sense of crisis was accentuated by a number of high-profile protest meetings, a swarm of strikes, and a series of dramatic arms finds. On 8 September, a rally of the agrarian associations was organized in Madrid by the Catalan landowners' body, the Instituto Agrícola Catalán de San Isidro, recently coopted by the CEDA. A joint stoppage by the Communists, CNT, and socialists, which included a shoot-out with the security forces that left a number of workers dead, tried – in vain – to halt the event. The objective of the meeting, which was addressed by Gil Robles and Martínez de Velasco as well as by Calvo Sotelo and the monarchist Antonio Goicoechea, was to pressure the government over the Catalan dispute. The following day, the CEDA's youth organization, the JAP, held a quasi-fascist rally at Covadonga in Asturias. As the site from which the reconquest of Spain from the Arabs was launched, Covadonga symbolized the CEDA's militant Catholicism and its Spanish nationalist ideals. Opponents would also readily interpret the choice of location as a metaphor for the CEDA's ambition to "reconquer" Spain from the Republic. The UGT and CNT attempted to thwart the meeting, this time through derailments, the blowing up of bridges, and even the use of firearms, but still it went ahead. The CEDA orators confidently predicted that the party would soon be in power, from where it would crush the regional nationalist movements. By now, Gil Robles, acclaimed by the serried ranks of the JAP as "¡jefe! ¡jefe! ¡jefe!", had reached the conclusion that it was better to face the revolution "from above before the adversary finds himself better prepared".[43]

On 14 September the Socialist Youth held their own rally in Madrid as the climax to a campaign in protest at a decree of the Minister of the Interior prohibiting those under sixteen from joining political organizations, a measure that, Salazar Alonso admits in *Bajo el signo de la revolución*, was designed to circumscribe the left.[44] The meeting, attended by 80,000 people, was notable as the first one organized in conjunction with the Communist Party, thereby fuelling rumours of a forthcoming working-class revolution. Indeed, earlier in the month, the authorities had uncovered a number of socialist arms caches. In particular, the security forces had intercepted a ship, the *Turquesa*, off the north coast of Spain on 11 September as it was delivering arms to the Asturian workers. This enterprise involved a number of socialist deputies, most notably the former minister Indalecio Prieto, who narrowly escaped arrest at the point of delivery. An exultant Minister of the Interior admitted that he might have been considered "mad or a fantasist" for his "arbitraries or caprices", but the finds were – at last – evidence that there did indeed exist an "extensive revolutionary plan of attack against the state". For *Renovación*, were it not for Salazar Alonso – "a real man" – Spain would be "on the edge of the abyss". A wave of strikes in September further exaccerbated the climate of confrontation. Furthermore, the government and the opposition clashed over the transfer of the remains of Galán and García Hernández, the military martyrs of the Jaca rising of December 1930 against the monarchy, to a central location in the capital. Salazar Alonso also persuaded his Cabinet colleagues on 14 September, the day of the Socialist Youth rally, to suspend all political meetings from the following day onward as a security measure.[45]

By this point, a beleaguered Prime Minister was struggling to contain a wide-ranging opposition front, while contending with the disagreements of hardline Cabinet colleagues, the waxing impatience of Lerroux to return to power, and the increasingly vociferous criticism of the CEDA. In fact, the question at stake within the Radical Party was not if, but when, Samper would resign. While the premier still aimed to defend his record before the Cortes, a growing number of Radicals urged the formation of a new government before parliament reconvened. However, the Cabinet itself was sharply divided over the issue: Samper, backed by Guerra, Iranzo, and Villalobos, was confronted by Salazar Alonso, while Diego Hidalgo and Rocha preferred to leave the decision to Lerroux. At the Cabinet meeting of 11 September, the Minister of the Interior explained that he – like Gil Robles – wanted to bring the socialist "revolution" forward by having the CEDA enter the government before parliament met. He even contemplated declaring a state of war to provoke the socialists because "it was the government's opportunity . . . to finish with evil".[46] Earlier in the month, exasperated by what he regarded as the premier's dilatory and faint-hearted approach to the Basque problem (an assault, in the minister's view, on "the motherland herself"), he had attempted to bring the government down by resigning. He wanted Lerroux to return as Prime Minister because, as he explained to Gil Robles, "they did not let him act". The resignation, however, was overriden by the Radical *jefe* as premature. Yet he also wanted a reshuffle before the Cortes assembled, but, at a Cabinet meeting on the 13th, the President made it plain that if a "third party" – that is to say, Lerroux or Gil Robles – prompted the government's fall before parliament met, he would exclude him from the premiership.[47] On 13 September, as a result, the Radical parliamentary group, on Lerroux's cue, gave the government a vote of confidence to deal with the situation as it saw fit and then report to parliament. Samper, after all, would be able to defend his record before the Cortes. It was none the less symbolic of his administration's isolation that its fall had been averted through the intervention of the President, not that of the CEDA or of the Prime Minister's own party. The Radical vote of 13 September, as *El Debate* pointed out, was not a mandate "to govern" but to choose the "moment to resign".[48]

Four days later, however, Gil Robles told the President that, in contrast to the Radical Party, the CEDA wanted a reshuffle before parliament reopened. This was backed up by the official withdrawal of the CEDA's support from the government on the 26th. Furthermore, the accidentalists seized upon their divergences with Samper to announce their intention of fulfiling the second stage of their strategy-for-power; namely, by entering the Cabinet. On 28 and 29 September the Radical deputies met to consider their stance in relation to the forthcoming crisis. In *No fue posible la paz*, Gil Robles claims that the Radical Party not only reaffirmed its acceptance of the CEDA's collaboration "by unanimity" but also embraced Salazar Alonso's position that the *Cedistas* should be incorporated into the next Cabinet.[49] In reality, there was substantial opposition to the CEDA's ministerial debut. Earlier in the month, Guerra del Río, the Minister of Public Works, had maintained in a speech that the Radical Party should be the dominant ruling party because it was the only major republican force left in the Cortes. What is more, he opposed the formation of a more conservative administration. "Not one more step to the right", he had cried defiantly. He therefore exhorted the Radical Party to exploit the mutually dependent nature of the relationship with the CEDA: "our votes are needed and we will not give them to any government that goes any further to the right than the present one".[50] At the meetings of the parliamentary group on 28th and 29th, the CEDA's right to form part of a government was questioned on the grounds that it had not voted for the Constitution of 1931. "The Grand Old Man", as Lerroux was known amongst the party faithful, retorted that whether or not the CEDA had declared itself republican or backed the Constitution was irrelevant. "They are republicans," he confusing, "if they support republican governments."[51] Somewhat confusingly, the Radical statement on 29th declared the party to be compatible with all those "that have explicitly accepted republican legality". The Radical *jefe*, while accepting the *Cedistas*' claim to a stake in power, admitted at the meeting that same day that "it would be preferable . . . that the CEDA did not form part of the government". Altogether, many shared Eloy Vaquero's position on the CEDA: "without it, better. If not, with it". Lerroux was given a vote of confidence to resolve the reshuffle in accordance with this stance. Unlike a minority within the parliamentary party, the "Grand Old Man" defended the right of the accidentalists to join the Cabinet, but, in common with the majority, he was determined to put this off as long as possible. He would, in consequence, endeavour to persuade the *Cedistas* not to enter the government "so that they do not exhaust themselves to the same extent as us in the exercise of power". Naturally, he was alarmed at the prospect of sharing power with his avaricious ally as this would undermine the appeal of the Radical Party by dragging the government to the right. Executive collaboration with the CEDA would also hamper the pursuit of "politics as business" as well as access to the public spoils system. Greater than the Radical leader's fear of the *Cedistas*' Cabinet participation, however, was that of the Cortes' dissolution. The end of the legislature, he had declared before the party on the 29th, would be a matter of "gravity . . . for the country, for the Republic and for us". This anxiety, however, was unfounded. President Alcalá-Zamora would almost certainly avoid dismissing parliament for a second time within a year, especially as the Constitution permitted him just two opportunities. The daring which had distinguished the Radical leader in his political youth had, in old age, almost completely deserted him.[52]

Why, ultimately, was the most historic of the republican parties prepared to let the CEDA, which had not only refused to declare itself republican but also harboured authoritarian ambitions incompatible with the Republic's democratic ideals, into the government? This question was especially poignant as the socialist movement promised to unleash a revolution should the right enter the Cabinet. Such a prospect would destabilize the Republic, if not threaten its existence. There are many reasons for the Radicals' acceptance, however unwilling, of the *Cedistas* as ministerial partners. The marked change in the Radical Party's parliamentary make up as a result of the 1933 election, along with the dissident exodus in May 1934, had, by shifting the party to the right, made it more sympathetic to the CEDA. Also, certain leading veterans, most notably Rafael Salazar Alonso and Emiliano Iglesias, had, whether out of opportunism or genuine political conviction, become fervent advocates of the right.[53] The path towards their collaboration was eased by the fact that both parties were eager to replace the Samper administration and both were perturbed by the regionalists' claims and the burgeoning threat of the left. The most important reason was the inescapable reality of the Radicals' parliamentary dependence on the accidentalists. Without the CEDA, the Radicals could not continue in office, and they dreaded the prospect of a general election. In this sense, the Radicals had reached a point of no return.

On 1 October, Samper was at last able to defend the actions of his administration before the Cortes. His principal argument was that the settlement of the Catalan dispute was at hand, the regional parliament having passed, on 26 September, the regulations for the application of the Law of Cultivation in accordance with the Constitution and the Autonomy Statute. This solution was rejected by the CEDA leader as nothing less than surrender. Gil Robles, having viciously dismissed the Prime Minister's efforts on the grounds that "not in the form, not in the substance, not in the content, nor in the procedure have you been accompanied by luck", announced the withdrawal of his party's backing and called for a government that reflected the parliamentary majority. Bereft of support, the government resigned.[54]

To a greater extent than Lerroux, Ricardo Samper had attempted to steer a middle way between the exigencies of the Catholic right and the opposition of the left. His administration had failed to sustain its momentum in part because of the executive and legislative shortcomings that still characterized the Radical Party. The government's bills, for example, continued to be criticized by its allies for their tardiness, for often lacking an adequate explanatory preamble and sufficient administrative guidelines, and for, in many cases, lacking cogency. Some of the most important measures, such the reform of the state bureaucracy and the budget, were savaged for their incoherence and inattention to detail. Nor did the Radical parliamentary party provide the government with much relief. Radical deputy Mariano Arrazola rebuked his own colleagues in the Cortes for their lax attendance. During the previous day's session, he noted, only half-a-dozen Radicals had been spotted in the chamber. "This cannot continue", he exclaimed: "I accept that the CEDA and the Agrarians are right in saying that they are the ones that prop the government up".[55] The Radicals' manifest lack of interest in the proceedings of parliament obviously did little for the Samper administration, while permitting the more disciplined CEDA a greater say in affairs. Nor did the administration of May to October 1934, despite its fundamental moderation, find much succour on the left. The Esquerra, its oppositional statements notwithstanding, eventually came round to collaborating with Samper, but the Basque left absolutely refused to do so while the national republican parties offered only sporadic backing. Moreover, the socialists viewed the government from the outset with extreme hostility, regarding the Radical Party as the stooge of the right. In this spirit, the UGT manifesto of 1 August denounced the Samper administration as "a regime of white terror", while El Socialista judged that Spaniards lived "in a full-blown dictatorial regime".[56] Yet the Radical Party was unable to realize its centrist aspirations above all as a result of the opposition of the Catholic right, without whom it could not survive in office. Though the accidentalists' strategy made the government's fall a death foretold, the conciliatory approach of the Prime Minister in particular brought the political crisis forward. To this must be added the lack of support for Samper from within the Radical Party itself. Menaced from within by Salazar Alonso throughout its period in office, the Samper administration also failed to muster sufficient support from the Lerroux-led parliamentary group in September.

Consultations over the new government took place within an atmosphere of extreme political tension. The high anxiety of the left was reflected in the fact that the ordinarily equitable Martínez Barrio warned the President on 27 September that General Franco planned to kidnap him while Salazar Alonso was preparing a coup d'état.[57] At the founding congress of Unión Republicana (the merger of the Radical–Democratic Party and the PRRS) on 30 September, Martínez Barrio also called on the President not to heed "those who, believing themselves victors, announce the imminent destruction of the Republic".[58] Both the left republicans and the socialists urged him to dissolve the Cortes and to hold a general election.[59] For the left, the CEDA was a Trojan horse which threatened to demolish the Republic from within. The socialists had made it plain that, should the CEDA join the Cabinet, they would declare a "revolution" that would aim to topple not just the government but the "bourgeois Republic" itself, El Socialista speaking of the need to "possess" and "supersede" the regime by means of a "war against those that have caused the ruin of Spain". "Next month", warned the socialist organ, "could be our October".[60] The underlying rationale of this strategy was that the President, confronted by such a catastrophic prospect, would refuse to allow the accidentalists into the Cabinet.[61] This was an extremely risky assumption which, if proved wrong, effectively left the timing of the socialist uprising in the hands of the right – a blunder of which the CEDA was all too aware.[62]

For his part, the President realized full well that the socialists looked to him as a bulwark against the perceived fascist threat of the CEDA. While he had his own doubts as regards the CEDA's democratic convictions, he also opposed its elevation to the executive on the more prosaic grounds that this would strengthen the governing bloc and thereby reduce his own room for manoeuvre. Offsetting these objections was the President's determination, which he shared with the CEDA, to reform the Constitution (as detailed in his unequivocally entitled book Los defectos de la Constitución de 1931). Such an opportunity, given that the CEDA was the largest parliamentary minority, might not present itself in the next legislature. Besides, the left did not offer him any alternative. In any case, he was loathe to call on the left republicans, especially Azaña, for personal reasons. In sum, Alcalá-Zamora's attitude towards the non-republican right was not totally hostile, but ambiguous.[63]

In the event, the President did try to avert the accidentalists' entry into the government. On 2 October, he told Gil Robles that, in his opinion, the Samper administration should remain in office and, even more importantly, that the CEDA should forego power under the current parliament. By means of compensation, he insinuated that he would permit Gil Robles to become the dominant figure of the following parliament, but this carrot-and-stick approach made no impact on the CEDA leader. Foiled, the President tried to limit the Cedistas to a single ministry but Gil Robles, anxious, in his words, to "boost the governmental performance, which the congenital weakness of the Radical group made ever more necessary", insisted, at his meeting with Lerroux the next day, on three Cabinet seats. The Radical leader apparently acceded "easily". Unwilling to exhaust his last chance of dissolving the Cortes and lacking any other option, Alcalá-Zamora, too, gave way. Invited to form the next government, the Radical jefe endeavoured to limit the CEDA's ambitions. He cavilled at the accidentalists taking over the Ministry of Agriculture as they might adopt "a simple, regressive criteria" as well as objecting to the appointment of José Oriol Anguera de Sojo since the Catalans viewed the former civil governor of Barcelona as hostile to their interests.[64] The implacable Gil Robles, however, refused to give way. All three CEDA ministers – Manuel Giménez Fernández at Agriculture, José Oriol Anguera de Sojo at Labour, and Rafael Aizpún at Justice – were regarded as moderates, but, from the point of view of the left, they occupied key positions in the struggle against the organized working class. The fact that the Cabinet majority still lay with the Radical Party and that Salazar Alonso had been removed as a result of Alcalá-Zamora's "maniacal hostility" was of little comfort.[65]

The new Cabinet was announced on 4 October. Shocked at the inclusion of the CEDA and fearing the reaction of the socialists, Martínez Barrio visited the President two days later to plead with him to hand power over to the left for the sake of the regime. But Alcalá-Zamora was unmoved.[66] That same day, the socialists declared their "revolution". For the Socialist Youth, this may have been equated with a Bolshevik-style seizure of power and the overthrow of the "bourgeois" state, but for the mainstream socialists, including UGT leader Largo Caballero, this amounted to the declaration of a general strike together with the uprising of sympathetic military elements.[67] The socialists' ill-conceived *pronunciamiento* model was again, as in 1917 and 1930, found wanting. Neither the strike nor the armed assaults, invariably little more than skirmishes, posed a threat to the state. The single, spectacular, exception was a full-blown insurrection in Asturias.[68] The Asturian socialists, together with the local CNT, not only stormed Oviedo, the capital, but also forcibly occupied much of the region. They thereupon declared the establishment of "libertarian communism", which included the abolition of money, the collectivization of the mines and factories, and the redistribution of the land. The Cabinet, as astonished by the scale of the revolt as the socialist leadership, fell back on the army.[69] The Minister of War sent General López Ochoa to crush the rebellion,[70] his first choice of General Franco having been rejected by the Cabinet.[71] However, Franco was appointed as "advisor" by Diego Hidalgo and installed in an office next to him. In reality, Franco, rather than López Ochoa or the Azaña-appointed Chief of the General Staff, General Masquelet, oversaw the military operations.[72] In effect, Franco converted himself into the Chief of Staff and even, it has been argued, as de facto Minister.[73] The workers, taking advantage of the region's rugged, mountainous terrain and the miners' know-how with dynamite, put up a fierce struggle, but after two weeks they admitted defeat. A second, but logistically unrelated, insurrection erupted in Catalonia. Under considerable popular pressure, the Generalidad had half-heartedly declared a Catalan state within "the Spanish Federal Republic" on the evening of 6 October. The local garrison under General

Batet took control of the Generalidad and, in a matter of hours, had overcome the main body of resistance.[74]

The uprisings of October 1934 were at once a demonstration of the unity and division of the opposition to the centre–right ruling majority. United by a shared antagonism to the Radical–CEDA axis, the socialists, left republicans, and Catalan nationalists were none the less divided by the lack of a common strategy or vision. The socialists had striven to keep the "revolution" to themselves, spurning the advances of both the left republicans and Catalan nationalists, and drawing on the Alianza Obrera (Workers' Alliance), to the dismay of other working-class forces such as the BOC and CNT, only insofar as it served their interests. The socialist rebellion was further undermined by the immobilization of the UGT's most powerful union, the FNTT, as a result of the summer strike, as well as by the failure – with the exception of Asturias – to enlist the CNT. The Catalan revolt, too, was severely handicapped by the absence of the anarcho–syndicalists. The general strike and Asturian insurrection confirmed that, for the socialists, parliamentary democracy, as embodied in the Republic, was not an end in itself but a tool for the achievement of meaningful reform. Once the regime no longer served their interests, the socialists were prepared to break with it. Yet their strategy amounted to a horrendous error of judgement. Not only did they achieve none of their aims, but they also played directly into the hands of the right. Accordingly, they had gravely undermined the Republic at no benefit either to themselves or their former allies, the republicans. For the centrist aspirations of the Radical Party, the uprising, by polarizing the political climate to an unprecedented extent, was a devastating blow. Up to then, the Radicals, dependent on the parliamentary support of the CEDA, had inevitably made concessions to the right, but they had also protected or even advanced many of the reforms of 1931–3 in their defence of a centrist politics. The October events signalled a crushing loss of legitimacy for the Radicals and a corresponding gain in authority for the right. Indeed, October 1934 was to mark a watershed in the relations between the Radical Party and its right-wing allies.

X

Allies and Adversaries
The Centre–Right government of October 1934 to April 1935

The uprisings of October 1934 were a monumental blow for the centrist aspirations of the Radical Party. On the one hand, the right, the real victor of the October events, was in the ascendant. Its burgeoning strength was enhanced by the ongoing repression and by a corresponding shift in power away from the civilian authorities towards the military ones. On the other hand, the left, having suffered a shattering setback, had been politically marginalized. The socialist movement had been suppressed, the Esquerra leadership was behind bars, and the national left–republican parties had broken with the institutions of the regime. The political climate, therefore, had been radicalized to an unprecedented degree. The Radicals' all-embracing vision of "a Republic for all Spaniards" had been seriously discredited and with it their goal of "centring" the regime through the creation of a broad-based consensus.

The entry of the CEDA into the Cabinet was, nevertheless, defended by Radicals of all shades as a step in the consolidation of the regime. The veteran Radical Eloy Vaquero, now Minister of the Interior, lauded Gil Robles as an indisputable republican whose "political strength derives from the purest democracy". The right, far from compromising the Radical Party's principles by joining the government, had, Joaquín Pérez Madrigal claimed, sought to consolidate "a revolutionary labour", which was inseparable from "the democratic ideal" of the Radical Party. Indeed, the Republic, in the words of the liberal Minister of Labour, José Estadella, had shifted "further towards real democracy".[1] By contrast, the Radicals were sharply divided over the course to be undertaken by the new government. Some wanted the left to be crushed altogether. In a speech before the Unión Mercantil the Radical deputy Enrique Izquierdo Jiménez, having thundered that "revolutionary Marxism" and "international masonry . . . have left the *Patria* in shreds", clamoured for the anarchist, socialist and communist movements to be banned from public life. Others assailed the left republicans. Pérez Madrigal, on his return from Asturias in October 1934, rashly declared that "my first conclusion is that Azaña has a grave responsibility in what has occurred". Still others were quick to discredit the Catalan Statute. Juan Palau deplored it in a speech in Barcelona as a threat to the unity of Spain and Catalonia, while Emiliano Iglesias asserted that the Statute, which, in his opinion, had been anti-constitutional from the start, had failed "tragically and absurdly". The time had come, he concluded, for the rulers, "as men and as Spaniards", to ensure that the Statute would prevail neither "as self deter-mination, nor as a concession". Some Radicals were even prepared, in the rarified political atmosphere, to jettison the party's ideological founda-tions. Minister Eloy Vaquero wrote in the pages of *Renovación* that the liberal and democratic tenets of the nineteenth century – the cornerstone of the Radical Party's political philosophy – were "bankrupt". He believed that, in common with the authoritarian right, the situation "demands a strong state in all its aspects".[2] The most vehement critic of the left was Salazar Alonso. The October events, according to his Manichean outlook, represented a confrontation between "two bands: one, those that defend the state, and the other, those that attack the state". The governing bloc's overriding priorities, he insisted, were to confront the continuing threat of "the revolution" and to defend "the national ideal", not forgetting the "historic destinies of our motherland".[3] Such sentiments brought him closer to the CEDA than ever. In a similar vein, *Renovación* castigated the left republicans for permitting Marxism and separatism to "denaturalize, adulterate and corrupt the liberal and democratic Republic". Naturally, the socialists were viewed with greater hostility than ever. The state-employed teachers of Asturias were vilified in an editorial article of 10 November 1934 for contributing to the uprising by allegedly indoctri-nating their pupils to chant "long live Lenin", to recite the International, to raise clenched fists, and even to insult "the *Patria*". The children of Asturias, in short, had been brainwashed into "a blind instrument designed for destruction and devastation". As a consequence, the Radical organ proposed that the teaching profession should be purged, the socialist unions banned, new legislation introduced, and the Marxist indoctrinator replaced by "the dignified *maestro*, responsible, priest of an inextinguishable learning". In addition, *Renovación* backed the reform of the Constitution, welcomed the socialists' and left republicans' absence from parliament, and called for an "iron surgeon" to "root out from the school the malignant tumour of destructive Marxism".[4]

Yet there was also a redoubtable section of the Radical Party that was plainly horrified at the turn of events. Many Radicals promptly recognized that reconciliation, not revenge, was required if the political climate was not to be further polarized. Once the Cortes reopened on 5 November, Ricardo Samper, now Minister of Foreign Affairs, pleaded with his fellow deputies to proceed as if the left-wing opposition was still present. Another minister, Rafael Guerra del Río, not only called for the complete rein-statement of the PSOE, but also insisted that the workers' demands should be met not by repression, but reform. As an immediate palliative he urged the provision of employment, "whatever it costs". In the same spirit, there were those Radicals who called for the modification, as opposed to the effective abolition, of the Catalan Statute. Such Radicals perceived that the socialists and left republicans had to be reincorporated into the polit-ical mainstream as a counterweight to the right in order to bolster the party's centrist cause. "Now we need the left", as Guerra del Río remon-strated. There were even those, such as Basilio Alvarez, who advocated the dissolution of the alliance with the right. Further, *Renovación*, despite its belligerent stance towards the left, was still extremely wary of the right.[5] In an editorial of 22 November 1934, the party daily urged the Radicals to provide for the small property owners and peasants and "not a few workers", otherwise they would swell the ranks of "fascism". The regime's consolidation, it contended, required the Radical Party to call on the workers and peasants so that they would not join the forces of "reac-tion". In sum, the party had to "renew itself" in the face of "great social and political convulsions".[6] Lerroux himself adopted an ambiguous line that was designed to placate simultaneously the party faithful and their coalition partners. On the one hand, in a speech in Seville on 17 December, he defended the Catalan Statute, downplayed the repression, and portrayed the Radical Party as a reconciliatory mediator between left and right. On the other hand, he reassured the CEDA not only by welcoming its rise to power as the decisive stage in the consolidation of the Republic, but also by affirming his willingness to collaborate with the right, if, and when, it formed a Cabinet.[7]

The key issue for the ruling majority was the nature and extent of the repression. The first death sentences, handed down by the military courts in the midst of the Asturian rebellion, concerned Major Enrique Pérez Farrás and two captains by the names of Escofet and Ricart, all of whom had been involved in the Barcelona uprising. The Cabinet, to the acclaim of the right, voted in favour of the executions on 17 October. The President responded by summoning the ministers to a special meeting at the palace the following day. He urged them to reconsider their decision by arguing that it would be counterproductive to create martyrs "for the enemy" as well as by drawing attention to the fact that they had pardoned the insurgents of 10 August 1932. The Cabinet, however, was unmoved. Alcalá-Zamora thereupon invoked article 102 of the Constitution, according to which the President could commute sentences relating to "crimes of extreme gravity" following a favourable report from the Supreme Court. The Constitution specified that for the Court to review a sentence the "proposal" of the government was required; in practice, this meant that the President had to secure the support of at least one minister.

Yet not a single Cabinet member, not even Martínez de Velasco or Pita Romero, Alcalá-Zamora's eyes and ears in the government, would back him. Undaunted, the President decided to keep the Cabinet in the palace until a satisfactory decision had been reached. "The entrapment was complete", as the Minister of Communications, César Jalón, recalls. In the end, the government, despite the opposition of the three CEDA ministers, voted in favour of a report from the Supreme Court. At a further Cabinet meeting on 31 October, the President wore the ministers down through sheer persistence. Even though the report of the Supreme Court had not been favourable, the Prime Minister signed the commutation.[8]

Lerroux later regretted his action. "Neither my will nor my heart," he wrote in *La pequeña historia*, "put anything into that act of clemency."[9] Similarly, Jalón criticizes the Radical leader in his *Memorias* for being "inconceivably weak".[10] Certainly the Prime Minister's climbdown had not been in keeping with the "law and order" stance associated with conservative republicanism and which had its origins in the disorder of the First Republic and the example of the French Prime Minister Louis Thiers, who had crushed the Paris Commune in 1871. Indeed, Melquiades Alvarez had urged the premier on the day the Cortes reopened, 5 November, to save "the Republic, the institutions . . . and law and order" by treating the left-wing opposition in the manner of Thiers.[11] The remorse of the Radical leader was perhaps due to the fact that, as he was writing while the Civil War still raged, he wanted to ingratiate himself with the Nationalists, themselves little given to acts of clemency. He justifies the pardon in *La pequeña historia* on the grounds that he did not want to appear less merciful than the President.[12] In all likelihood, he realized that a hardline repression would undermine the Radicals' centrist appeal while enhancing that of the right as well as that of a victimized left. By contrast, a softly-softly approach would foster a political climate more in accord with the aspirations of the Radical Party. Nevertheless, the Radicals' refusal to undertake a more severe approach strengthened the right in its belief that republican democracy was inherently weak and unreliable, especially when faced by a revolutionary threat from the left. For the left, the repression was confirmation that the Radical Party was little more than a stooge of the anti-republican right. The Radical Party was more isolated than ever. Not surprisingly, the repression was to be the fundamental point of political reference until the general election of February 1936. More immediately, it was to be the focal point of the struggle within the ruling majority between the Radicals and the CEDA for the next six months.

Such was the CEDA's disgust at the commutation of Pérez Farrás' sentence that Gil Robles made it known to sympathetic generals that he would not oppose a "solution by force" in order to restore "the legality violated by the president". The CEDA, as Cándido Casanueva, one of those involved, later disclosed, was willing to "follow the path that the army itself indicated"; that is to say, to second a *coup d'état*. However, Generals Fanjul and Goded, having sounded out like-minded colleagues, told the CEDA to accept the Pérez Farrás pardon and remain in the government because the army could not guarantee that "power would not fall into the hands of the left, which in a few days would destroy us". Thus the coup attempt was simply abandoned out of pragmatism; namely, the fear that the left, having alarmed the military through the strength of its resistance in Asturias, would overwhelm the armed forces altogether.[13]

Sharp on the heels of the Cabinet dispute over the Pérez Farrás case followed a costly clash between the Radicals and the right in the Cortes. This began with an assault by the extreme right, including an excoriating indictment by the Bloque Nacional leader José Calvo Sotelo, on the former Prime Minister Ricardo Samper and the Minister of War Diego Hidalgo for having allegedly failed to prepare the state sufficiently for the uprisings of October 1934. Both ministers vigorously contested the charges, but the CEDA, far from defending their allies, assumed the leading role in the campaign against the two ministers, climaxing with Gil Robles's call on 15 November for the government to ditch them.[14] Though the Prime Minister tried to resist their removal, especially that of Diego Hidalgo, "such a friend of mine", the withdrawal of the CEDA's support proved decisive.[15] While Lerroux fulfilled a life-long ambition by taking over the Ministry of War, his faithful if undistinguished companion Juan José Rocha, then Minister of the Navy, lived up to his nickname of "Miss Ministry" by taking on the Ministry of Foreign Affairs as well.[16] As a result, only a month into his third administration, Lerroux had abandoned two Radical ministers at the behest of his principal ally. The success of this opportunistic attack was an ominous sign of the shift in power that had taken place between the allies since the October events. Diego Hidalgo was so aggrieved by his dismissal that he published a book – bluntly titled *Why was I thrown out of the Ministry of War?* – as a rejoinder to his right-wing critics. Like Diego Hidalgo, Samper attributed his expulsion from the government to "a shady political manoeuvre" of the right. Unlike Diego Hidalgo, he pleaded with his *jefe* to rally the left republicans in defence of the regime.[17]

A month later, the CEDA set upon yet another minister. This time the target was Filiberto Villalobos, the Minister of Education who had so outraged Catholic opinion with his liberal edicts during the summer. In November, *El Debate* had heavily criticized him on the grounds that a "Marxist and revolutionary policy" still dominated the Ministry of Education and that the nefarious influence of socialist and left republican teachers had done even more harm to "the *Patria*" than the October insurrections.[18] On 21 December, CEDA deputy Jesús Pabón attacked the educational reforms for their dangerous secular proclivities. The hitherto conciliatory Villalobos responded emphatically that "they want to boycott the ministers who defend the Republic loyally".[19] The CEDA *caudillo* reacted by provoking the downfall of the minister. "It was the second partial crisis", Gil Robles claims in his memoirs, "that I felt obliged to provoke since the majority government was formed".[20] In reality, the CEDA, having toppled its third minister in as many months, was steadily eroding the foundations of the Radical administration in order to facilitate its own rise to power. Despite the ongoing battle with the Radicals over the repression, the CEDA strategy was making promising progress. On the first anniversary of the 1933 general election, *El Debate* published a major appraisal of the alliance with the Radical Party. While the first stage of the CEDA's plan had been satisfactorily completed, the second – support of the Radicals from within the Cabinet – was "in full and joyful execution". Moreover, the third stage – "to substitute Lerroux", as the accidentalist organ candidly put it – had been accepted as inevitable by the Radical leader himself. Clearly collaboration with the Radicals was little more than an ends to a means, a circumstantial necessity. The efficacy of the CEDA approach, the Catholic daily continued, was demonstrated by the expulsion of Martínez Barrio and his followers from the Radical Party, by the downfall of the Samper administration, and by the dismissal of those ministers that had since incurred the CEDA's wrath. Given that the right's lack of a parliamentary majority had made it impossible "to progress with greater rapidity", the strategy, *El Debate* concluded exultantly, had been "an enormous success". Such self-congratulation highlighted the fact that the ruling coalition's instability had been engineered in large part by the CEDA, thereby undermining the credibility of a regime which had yet to be consolidated.[21]

On 28 November the government, following a report by a Cabinet committee, presented a bill to the Cortes recommending that the Catalan Statute should be suspended for no longer than three months after full constitutional guarantees had been restored throughout the country. In the meantime, a governor general, who would assume the functions of the Generalidad and have the power to appoint the regional government, would rule Catalonia. The degree of autonomy to be permitted until full rights had been restored would be determined by another committee. In parliament, the monarchists proposed the complete overthrow of the Statute – a blatantly anti-constitutional move – while the Lliga, together with Martínez Barrio's Unión Republicana and a Radical minority, called for its immediate re-establishment. The monarchist initiative, with the backing of a number of CEDA deputies and the Falange, failed to muster sufficient support. The CEDA leadership advanced more surreptitiously as it was aware that, if a conflict with the President was provoked, neither the Radical Party nor the Lliga would take the accidentalists' side. Indeed, on 11 December the Prime Minister defied the CEDA by asserting that the

Radical-dominated Cabinet rather than the Cortes should determine the length of the transitory regimen. As a result, the CEDA reached a compromise, "painfully elaborated" recalls Gil Robles, with the Radicals. According to the law passed on 14 December, the Statute was suspended indefinitely until the government, in agreement with parliament, took the decision to reactivate it. Despite this deal, the administrative powers hitherto transferred to Catalonia were to be reclaimed by the state, while the Law of Cultivation Contracts was annulled, thereby prompting the eviction of numerous *rabassaires*. In effect, the entire region was being punished for the Esquerra's rebellion, a procedure that was almost certainly unconstitutional.[22] Meanwhile, the President of the Generalidad, Luis Companys, and his collaborators were sentenced on 6 June 1935 to thirty years in prison for "military rebellion".[23] Appointed as governor general was a wily veteran of the monarchist Liberal Party, Manuel Portela Valladares, who had served a similar function under the *ancien régime* as provincial governor of Barcelona. All in all, the Radicals had not exactly treated Catalonia with benevolence, but at least they had limited the worst excesses of the right.

By comparison with Catalonia, the repression in Asturias was much fiercer. Many people were detained for up to two months, "savagely mistreated", and then released without charge. Several insurgents died as a result of their ill-treatment, while at least one committed suicide. Even those investigating such incidents were at risk. A journalist known by the pseudonym of "Luis de Sirval", who had exposed the atrocities of Yagüe's troops, was arrested under false pretences and then shot by a member of the Foreign Legion. Neither the commission of investigation sent to Asturias nor the government itself ever discussed the death of the journalist, even though it was passionately debated in the Press Association – the President and Secretary of which were none other than Alejandro Lerroux and César Jalón.[24] Nor did the Cabinet discuss what Jalón himself describes in no uncertain terms as "our Casas Viejas". This took place when General López Ochoa had a number of insurgents shot for failing to give up their arms as well as for the assassination of a Civil Guard captain. The reality of the repression in Asturias, despite the limitations on reporting, eventually became known, in part as a result of the findings of a commission of left–republican and socialist deputies. The resulting outcry led to the transfer of Major Lisardo Doval, the most notorious torturer, in early December 1934, though even then the abuse of prisoners did not cease altogether.[25]

By radicalizing further the political climate, the repression in Asturias was profoundly counterproductive for the Radicals' centrist cause. There are a number of reasons for this apparently contradictory approach. The stronger backlash in Asturias was to be expected insofar as the uprising there was far more violent and prolonged than that in Catalonia or elsewhere. The greater involvement of the army inevitably made the repression more brutal, especially as this included the Army of Africa, battle-hardened by the colonial war in Morocco. The tendency to regard Asturias as an army affair was accentuated by the fact that, unlike Catalonia, it did not possess any special powers, such as those of autonomy, which would have made it a focus of political debate. The lack of civilian control was further exacerbated by the difficulty of communication with this remote, mountainous region. Oviedo, the Asturian capital, was over 400 kilometres from Madrid. Still, the excesses of the army and Civil Guard reflected on the government. The Minister of Communications, César Jalón, was astonished that the Cabinet could function "in such total ignorance of the facts", such as the massacre at Sama de Langreo. Underlying this hands-off attitude lay the manifest respect of conservative republicans such as Lerroux, impressed by the example of French republicans like Clemenceau, for the hard-line tactics of the army in times of social upheaval. Possibly, the Radical leader was also influenced by the fact that the Asturian revolt, in contrast to that in Catalonia, was spearheaded by the Radicals' arch-enemies, the socialists. None the less, the Radicals realized, too late, that they had made a grave mistake. The decision of the Cabinet to transfer Doval was taken, Jalón relates, "without discussion" as the public outcry over the suppression of the insurrection had left the ministers "inwardly crushed". In fact, the repression of the Asturian rising was to haunt the Radicals for the rest of their days in power. "Asturias! Always Asturias!", exclaims Jalón in his memoirs. "The nightmare of the revolution and nightmare of Spain," he cries, "was to be the ghost that followed us until overthrowing us." Even so, the Radicals, initially prodded by an obstinate but clear-sighted Alcalá-Zamora, were too lenient for their allies.[26]

Undoubtedly the repression of the October 1934 uprisings was arbitrary and excessive. The mass detentions and torture in Asturias, the widespread replacement of local authorities, the closure of numerous socialist and anarcho–syndicalist centres, the arrest of workers unrelated to the insurrections, the suspension of the Catalan Statute, and the protracted period of censorship were all highly questionable, if not illegal, measures. One of the most glaring individual injustices was the arrest and imprisonment of former Prime Minister Manuel Azaña. Having gone to Barcelona for the funeral of Jaime Carner, Minister of the Economy from 1931 to 1933, he was seized for his alleged involvement in the Catalan insurrection. The Prime Minister, who had earlier sent a telegram to the authorities in Barcelona asserting that the erstwhile premier was involved in subversive activities,[27] boasted to the press that "very extensive documentation" had been found on the left–republican leader that confirmed the existence of "an important . . . enterprise".[28] In reality, Azaña was not merely uninvolved in the Catalan rising but he had attempted to prevent it. Apparently, Lerroux was well aware of this fact, but acted otherwise.[29] While he awaited justice, Azaña suffered the indignity of being incarcerated on a ship in Barcelona harbour. It is difficult to see how such a flagrant act of injustice could be anything other than counterproductive for the Radicals. Alcalá-Zamora, no friend of Azaña, tried to persuade the Radical Prime Minister against his vendetta, but Lerroux – who claimed to have let the socialist leader Indalecio Prieto escape to France – was too consumed by "hatred" to heed the President's advice.[30]

There was at least one respect in which the October risings were to prove of enormous benefit to the Radical Party – the toppling of local authorities allegedly involved in the October events to the advantage of the Radicals and their allies. The special powers governing Catalonia enabled the Radicals to reassert their hegemony in Barcelona and to break new ground by becoming the leading force in the Catalan provinces. The party's aim, according to its regional chief and now mayor of Barcelona, Juan Pich y Pon, was "a grand labour of reconstruction". Part and parcel of the new regime was a massive exploitation of the public spoils system, causing opponents to dub Pich y Pon as the "dictator of the Town Hall". The Radicals' use and abuse of local Catalan government was denounced in the Cortes by the Lliga as "monstrous". The Lliga leader, Francisco Cambó, whose own party had lost out in the post-October upheaval, claimed that "I have never belonged to a chamber that was so insensitive as the present chamber to the damage caused to the public interest".[31] In national terms, over 2,000 socialist and left republican *ayuntamientos* – 20 per cent of the total – were replaced with centre–right steering committees. One-eighth of all mayors were also dislodged.[32] The Radicals thereby made huge gains at the local level. In Badajoz, for example, the party eventually controlled 161 of the province's 163 local councils. Not one left–republican or socialist authority was left standing in Alicante. Former Radical Alvaro Pascual Leone accused the Lerroux administration in parliament of continuing the partisan policy initiated by Salazar Alonso, while the monarchist Honorario Maura upbraided the government for its "arbitraries" in relation to the town and village councils. Both article nine of the Constitution and the Municipal Law of 1877 were invoked by the opposition, but to no effect. Control of the *ayuntamientos* was crucial to the Radicals' power in the provinces and in particular their clientage networks. It was a policy that responded, as Martínez Barrio observed, to "necessities, conveniences and exigencies".[33]

The advance of the Radicals in the provinces should not disguise the fact that in many areas of government their centrist aspirations were being steadily undermined. Of critical importance in this respect was the drastic decline in labour relations. Employers, both in the cities and the countryside, went on the offensive after October 1934 in an effort to overturn the gains made by the workers over the previous three-and-a-half years. The mixed juries ceased functioning, contracts from the first biennium were not recognized, and many thousands of workers were indiscriminately "selected" – that is to say, dismissed – for their trade union militancy or for having participated in the October events. The condition of the land-less labourers, already badly hit by the defeat of the FNTT strike in June, deteriorated swiftly as salaries plunged and unemployment soared. *El Debate* itself reported that in Badajoz the labour regulations were being thoroughly abused, that droves of Portuguese workers had been drafted in to gather the harvest at starvation-level wages, and that the Spanish workers had no option but to accept the landowners' terms. During the cereal harvest, the day labourers' legally-entitled pay in Badajoz stood at 9.75 pesetas per day, but in reality they were being paid between 3 and 4.50 pesetas.[34] A devastating indictment of the situation in Badajoz was penned by José Carlos de Luna, the civil governor, for Manuel Giménez Fernández. "In synthesis, the situation is this", he wrote, "absolute peace, hunger, humility on the part of the poor and arrogance, wretchedness and incomprension on the part of the majority of the rich". He concluded despairingly that "the obstinacy and the egoism of these ferocious landowners" was "a suicidal approach that will ruin everything that has been achieved". The Catholic unions, which believed that their hour had finally come, were to be rapidly disillusioned. The workers' organization of the *Cedistas*, Acción Obrerista, stressed at its national congress in March 1935 that the working class was "sick of verbiage" and beseeched the CEDA to "put into practice the postulates of the social Catholic doctrine" that it defended. Equally, the Gremio de Campesinos del Sindicato, despite its avowedly anti-Marxist lineage, soon began to complain bitterly at the exploitative practices of the landowners.[35]

The politics of persecution also distinguished the reaction of the *patronal*. The rejection of the mixed juries and of outstanding contracts together with the victimization of union activists sent wages tumbling while pushing unemployment ever upwards. As a result, the watershed in industrial relations lay not in December 1933, when the Radicals came to power, but in October 1934. By ignoring the widespread violations of the labour legislation and by modifying the latter to the advantage of the employers, the government aided and abetted the dramatic deterioration in working conditions within the urban and rural economies alike. No doubt this shift to the right was facilitated by the fact that the Ministry of Labour was no longer in the hands of the Radical Party, but that of the CEDA. The new minister, José Oriol y Anguera de Sojo, provisionally suspended the mixed juries as well as refused to intervene, in contrast to his predecessors, in industrial conflicts, while the 48-hour week promptly returned to the construction and metallurgical industries. Further, in early November, the government passed the "abusive strike" decree which restricted all stoppages to strictly labour, as opposed to political, matters.

The most damaging proposal of all was Anguera de Sojo's bill of January 1935, designed to replace Largo Caballero's Law of Professional Associations, which, according to Mercedes Cabrera, would have condemned to "illegality the workers' parties and unions". The decided intervention of the Radicals, however, ensured that the CEDA's authoritarian initiative was thwarted.[36]

The pursuit of revenge by the employers in the wake of the October 1934 insurrections naturally caused unemployment to rise even further. *Renovación*, in an editorial entitled "Misery, misery and misery", denounced the plague of child beggers which had descended on Madrid as well as the extensive poverty in Andalusia where people, in their desperation, robbed olives from the large estates and where infants were to be found working from "sunrise to sunset" for a mere fourteen reales a day. The only youngsters found to be laughing in the *pueblos* of the south were "the offspring of the rich". The Radical organ criticized the authorities for being too remote "in terms of distance and memory". But it was not just the south. The civil governor for Madrid province estimated at the beginning of 1935 that as many as three-quarters of the workers and peasants were unemployed. Some sectors in Orense, such as construction, had 90 per cent of the workforce laid off. *Renovación* urged the government to tackle the "misery" with "all our passion and all our compassion".[37] Radicals and *Cedistas* alike professed extreme concern at the situation. For Lerroux, it was "an enormous preoccupation", while for *El Debate* "this plague of the unemployed" had to be eliminated for the sake of "Spanish proletarian children". Yet no attempt was made to match or resurrect the Radical proposals of 1934: the ascendancy of the right put paid to such thoughts. In February 1935 a bill that was designed to spend up to 250,000 pesetas on individual public works projects was passed. Given the scale of the problem, this was a drop in the ocean. The next month, the CEDA deputy Dimas de Madariaga exhorted the front bench to form a special commission in order to tackle the problem. The Minister of Labour assured his colleague that the level of unemployment was lower than the official statistics indicated – it was, in fact, much higher – and that the Cortes should await forthcoming proposals. Madariaga retorted that immediate action, not words, was required because "the people are asking us for bread". Similarly, the Radical Basilio Alvarez criticized the government's approach for being outdated and for "the slow workings of the bureaucracy". The patent shortcomings of the measures undertaken were reflected in the constant stream of delegations from the provinces pleading with the central authorities to alleviate the plight of the unemployed.[38]

The divergences within the ruling majority over the work crisis were symptomatic of a broader lack of agreement on a common agenda. This was vividly illustrated by the failure to reach a consensus over economic policy and in particular over the next budget. In December 1934, the Cabinet, having been unable to elaborate a shared formula, had to extend the budget that was already in force for the next three months. Reflecting, but also compounding, these differences within the coalition was the avoidance of parliament by the Radical ministers. The Prime Minister was frequently criticized. "He never comes", exclaimed one deputy. "Why is Señor Lerroux not on the front bench?", asked another, "so that Spain sinks?" Ministers were also censured for not addressing the questions put to them in person. It was once remarked that the absence of the Minister of the Economy was hardly surprising given that he had been seen drinking for the previous one and a half hours. Lliga leader Francisco Cambó commented that "we are witnessing in Spain a period of weakness in the public authorities perhaps like no other which we have lived through". Or, as another deputy put it, "we are not doing a thing here".[39]

Accentuating the lack of policy direction was the perennial interventionism of the President. A typical example was the clash over the attempt by the CEDA Minister of Justice, Rafael Aizpún, to reform the Supreme Court. The right, which regarded the Court as containing too many left-wing and presidential appointees, aimed to modify its composition by specifying that its members could not belong to a party or any association of a political character. Alcalá-Zamora's opposition to the resulting bill, which was read before the Cortes in December 1934, was such that he threatened to veto it altogether. In the end, his decided hostility, together with the change in government later in the year, left the Court untouched. An aggrieved Gil Robles concluded that the President was "one of the gravest problems to peace in Spain".[40] Indeed, Alcalá-Zamora was still bent on sharpening the divisions within the ruling majority by engineering a split within the CEDA. The President, having failed to convince Gil Robles in 1933 of the necessity of breaking up his party, set to work on the CEDA Minister of Agriculture, Manuel Giménez Fernández, but he, too, refused to succumb to Alcalá-Zamora's wiles.[41]

Symptomatic of the heightened rivalry within the ruling majority was the *Cedistas'* public scrutiny of the Radicals' hegemony of the state spoils system. So far, a tacit agreement had existed whereby the Radicals had gained privileged access to the public administration in exchange for pursuing the minimal policy demands of their right-wing backers. This unspoken arrangement was challenged by an *El Debate* editorial of 8 November which questioned "the use, for life, of the national representation and the drawn-out occupancy of public positions" – an unmistakable reference to the Radicals. In particular, it insisted that the appointment of a civil governor – nearly all of whom were in the hands of the Radical Party – should not be regarded as "a prize for the services lent to a party and even less the payment of a debt of friendship". This thinly-veiled attack on its ally reflected the CEDA's new-found muscle following the events of October 1934 as well as its impatience for more power. Its thirst for a greater share of national and local government was hardly surprising. According to the Radical minister César Jalón, the CEDA did not control one civil governorship or one mayorship "of medium-sized importance".[42]

In December the CEDA leader met Lerroux to manifest his unease at the progress of the government. *El Debate* kept up the pressure by berating it for its "mode, rhythm, fortitude and efficiency" and by insinuating that this was due to its absorption in the spoils system. Lerroux shrugged off the reproaches of his ally by reiterating that the accidentalists' incorporation into the Cabinet meant that "we have taken the firmest step towards democracy". He pointed to the acrimonious disputes between the CEDA and the monarchists as proof that the former was on the side of the Republic. Nevertheless, on 30 December the CEDA leader set out his demands in a letter to the Prime Minister. These included stronger repressive measures against the left, an increase in the CEDA's Cabinet presence, and the control of a number of civil governors. Moreover, he requested that General Franco be appointed Chief of the General Staff, and that Major Doval, the chief torturer in Asturias, be made head of the Civil Guard. If these demands were not met, the CEDA would abandon the government.[43] Further meetings took place the following month in which Gil Robles raised the question of constitutional reform, urged Lerroux to accelerate his legislative labours as well as to grant the CEDA more ministers. The Prime Minister made reassuring noises in relation to the first two matters, but was much more reticent about the third. As he explained in a meeting with high-ranking Radical officials, he would do everything possible to dissuade the CEDA *caudillo* from altering the status quo. If that failed, "we will try to pull one over them".[44]

In fact, Lerroux tried to limit the CEDA's advance by appointing just one more CEDA minister. However, at a meeting of the coalition leaders on 16 January, Martínez de Velasco, quite possibly under the influence of his friend the President, insisted on another seat for the Agrarians – otherwise they would leave the government. Yet the Prime Minister was loathe to accommodate the Agrarians as this would place the Radicals in a minority. Gil Robles, rather than aggravate the situation, left Lerroux to resolve the matter as he saw fit. On 21 January, the premier simply kept Rocha at Foreign Affairs and replaced him at the Naval department with yet another Radical, the Galician Gerardo Abad Conde. In effect, he had taken advantage of the divisions within the right to boost the Radicals' presence. The "absurd" outcome astonished Gil Robles. Having been wrong-footed, the CEDA leader was more determined than ever to force a major change in the government.[45]

Despite the favourable nature of the Cabinet reshuffle, the Radicals were to find themselves increasingly besieged as the year wore on. First, the party's centrist appeal of "a Republic for all Spaniards" continued to be compromised by the fallout from the repression. On 28 December 1934 Azaña was released from his confinement on the "Alcalá Galiano" in Barcelona harbour, despite the efforts of Lerroux to retain him there, on the order of the Supreme Court. This did little to enhance the government's standing. On the contrary, it appeared as if Azaña was being persecuted by his former allies. As Jalón recollects, the Cabinet, upon hearing the news, "passed over the matter as quickly as possible". Despite this humilliation, in March 1935 the Cortes scrutinized Azaña's role in the illegal supply of arms to the Portuguese revolutionaries. The Prime Minister, having failed to ensnare the left–republican leader over the October 1934 risings, instructed his deputies to back an accusatory proposition of the CEDA. He cynically defended this move not as an act "of hostility" but as an opportunity for Azaña to defend himself – though adding that he, Lerroux, thought that the former Prime Minister was "responsible". However, the parliamentary commission that was set up to examine the charges was slow to report as a result of the delays occasioned by its Radical members, who were less than eager to convict the erstwhile premier. Indeed, the vote on the commission's final recommendation, which took place on 20 July 1935, failed to achieve the required majority due to the abstention of the Radicals. For Gil Robles, this was yet another example of the Radicals' "policy of appeasement of the revolutionary elements". In the end, the political sensibilities of the party had triumphed over the personal ones of its leader.[46]

However, from the beginning of 1935 the repression in Asturias – "Asturias, Always Asturias!", Jalón bemoans – returned to haunt the Radical Party. A petition in January 1935 signed by 564 prisoners from the jail in Oviedo drew attention to the continuing torture. A public letter sponsored by intellectual luminaries such as Miguel de Unamuno and Ramón Valle Inclán added to the outcry. Moreover, the protest over the human rights abuses had by now acquired an international dimension. A member of the British delegation that visited Asturias, Leah Manning, published a book, *What I Saw in Spain*, which contained a damning account of the "pacification", including over 50 pages of detailed appendixes,[47] while a leading French socialist had a highly-publicized meeting with the Prime Minister in February 1935 to denounce the security forces' excesses. Scarcely surprisingly, the Cabinet was aware that, Jalón writes, "we enjoyed a very bad world press".[48] An account sent to the Prime Minister of the coverage in Argentina related that the repression in Asturias had received "immense diffusion". Spain, it was widely believed, had returned to "the worst times of Fernando VII".[49] Although all the death sentences bar two – a sergeant by the name of Diego Vázquez, who had joined the insurgents in Asturias, and a worker, "El Pichilato", accused of taking advantage of the upheaval to murder seven women, were executed in February 1935 – had been commutted, the continuing repression of the left was proving profoundly counterproductive.[50] Not only were the Radicals undermining their own appeal while enhancing that of the right, but they were also fostering a new spirit of unity amongst the opposition. Republicans and socialists alike were brought together by the common experience of repression. Indeed, the President had warned the government "uselessly" against this very danger.[51] As Martínez Barrio relates, the persecution of Azaña was the catalyst for the coming together of Izquierda Republicana, the National Republican Party, and Unión Republicana in March 1935, which, in turn, gave rise to a joint statement on 12 April 1935. At the same time, socialist leader Indalecio Prieto had initiated contacts with the republicans with a view to resurrecting the republican–socialist alliance.[52] Yet the Prime Minister continued to defend the arrangement with the right ardently. In a speech in Alicante he acclaimed it as the salvation of "Spain, the Republic and Liberty". Still, there was also an awareness within the Radical ranks that a certain distance had to be kept from the right if the party was not to dig its own grave. *Renovación*, in keeping with the leadership, maintained that the Radical Party had "republicanized" its allies and that Lerroux, accordingly, was "the saviour of the Republic", but it also manifested its wariness by publishing articles that criticized "the reactionary pressure" of the CEDA while reviling *El Debate* as "the Jesuit serpent". In fact, the Radical organ was highly critical of both left and right for converting October 1934 into the quintessential point of political reference: "the civil war attracts them, it captivates them, it obsesses them equally", it observed. The apparent polarization of Spanish politics could only be offset, *Renovación* concluded, by ensuring that "the Centre Party, which is the Radical one" headed the government.[53]

There could be little doubt that the centrist appeal of the Radicals was being undermined by the "reactionary pressure" of the CEDA. This was demonstrated to devastating effect by the fate of the reforms put forward by the Minister of Agriculture, Manuel Giménez Fernández. This square-set, moustached law professor from Seville stood out within the CEDA for his liberal views and in particular for his republicanism. His proposals, far from aiming to demolish the reforms of the first biennium, revealed a moderately reformist bent. On 20 December 1934, he extended the occupation of previously untilled land by the 25,000 *yunteros*, or ploughmen, of previously untilled land in Extremadura. Although a decree in January 1935 prohibited forcible expropriations, the settlement target of the minister, at 10,000 families per annum, was exactly the same as Azaña's for 1933. Moreover, while Giménez Fernández remained in the ministry, this target was met. The third, and most important, measure was designed to improve the prospects of the *arrendatarios*, or tenant farmers. Giménez

Fernández himself was a stout defender of the small farmer, as opposed to the big landowners, whom he dubbed the *"conservaduros"* – a play on *conservador* (conservative) and *duro* (hardliner) – and whom he criticized for "regarding the law merely as the best means of preserving their privileges and their wealth". According to the bill, discussion of which began on 5 December 1934, tenant farmers would be entitled to purchase the land which they rented after twelve years. The price would be determined by agreement with the owner or else by means of independent arbitration. Those that did not buy up the land would be granted six-year leases, have their rents fixed by independent courts, and suffer eviction only as a result of the non-payment of rent. These scarcely revolutionary proposals, which elaborated upon a scheme first drawn up by Cirilo del Río, provoked a bitter and protracted parliamentary debate. The wrath of the extreme right, for whom the minister was nothing less than a "disguised Marxist", was to be expected, but the bill's discussion also brought the latent divisions within the CEDA to the surface. Initially, the party backed Giménez Fernández, but this eventually gave way to outright hostility.[54] Members of his own party branded him a "white Bolshevik" for daring to challenge the paramountcy of the big landowners. Opposition from within the CEDA and in particular the Seville party, where he was dubbed "Lenin" by the Farmers' Circle, led him in January 1935 to tender his resignation to Gil Robles.[55] Although the CEDA *caudillo* refused to let Giménez Fernández stand down, he failed, despite his own "social Catholic" nostrums, to stand up to what he himself described in a letter as the "great hostility" within the party to the minister's projects. On the contrary, he increasingly criticized the combative Giménez Fernández for the ardour with which he defended his initiatives.[56] During the course of February and March 1935, the bill's most progressive features were stripped away one by one. The DRV deputies, often portrayed, like Giménez Fernández, as Christian Democrats, contemplated the besieged minister with an "almost total silence".[57] The measure which was finally approved on 15 March provided the tenant farmers with four-year leases, but deprived them of the right of purchase, while establishing total liberty in relation to the fixing of rents. The Law, as Jacques Maurice observes, "re-established the all-embracing power of the landowners by overturning all the previous legislation – even that of Primo de Rivera – on subleasing, collective tenancies, evictions, and the revision of rents". Giménez Fernández's original blueprint had been virtually obliterated.[58] The Radicals, having stressed that they did not agree with the bill, none the less voted for it as a result of the "regime of permanent transactions" that characterized the ruling coalition: that is to say, to placate the majority of the CEDA and Agrarian deputies. In an effort to save face, the Radical leader promised to pass a law rectifying the current one at an unspecified point in the future.[59]

The Radical-led government was to be further weakened by a propaganda offensive of the CEDA in February and March of 1935. Doubts were raised by the accidentalists as to the Radicals' fitness for power by drawing attention to their clientelistic practices. This was highlighted by Gil Robles in a speech in Granada in which he asserted that "this policy of pleasing unspeakable interests above and below . . . does not bother us", while taking care to distance his own party from such activities. "We are not," he insisted, "a party born of the official favour." He even claimed that the *Cedistas* had not featured more prominently in the Cabinet hitherto because, in implicit contrast to the Radical Party, they did not require sinecures and other public posts. As usual, *El Debate* was more explicit, rebuking the Radicals for subordinating the well-being of the nation to its own partisan interests.[60] A curious feature of the CEDA's extra-parliamentary campaign was that it played down the party's authoritarian leanings. Indeed, its organizing principle was the Confederación's commitment to "social justice". "It is not the party of one class," Gil Robles declared, "but it seeks the harmony of all within a politics of social justice." Private property, for example, should fulfil "its social function". The CEDA leader also revealed an unexpected sympathy for the causes of the October insurrections. Neither the use of force nor the rigid application of the law, he averred – in stark contrast to the bellicose declarations of the previous months – was sufficient to eradicate the wellsprings of the uprisings. On the contrary, "we have to take on board", he effused, "the spirit, the desire of justice and charity that beats in the heart of these revolutionary movements". "Or justice inspired in Christ," he concluded, "or revolution inspired by injustice." This uncharacteristic outburst of compassion was perhaps intended to divert the attention of the CEDA's own tenant supporters from the party's opposition to Giménez Fernández's Lease bill as well as to accentuate the divisions and disorientation within the Radical Party and possibly even to counter the resurgence of the left. It may also have been designed – with one eye on the next Cabinet reshuffle – to allay the President's fears in relation to the CEDA's authoritarian ambitions.[61]

By this stage, the Radical Party and the CEDA had become locked in a bitter battle in the provinces. The Radicals were struggling to defend their control of local government against the encroachments of their allies. The Toledo Radicals were aggrieved at the extent to which they were being "sacrificed" to elements from the "most extreme reactionism". The Radical mayor, for example, had lost the vice-presidency of the mixed juries to the right, while the Radical members of the Provincial Junta for Charity had all been dislodged.[62] In March the Jaen Provincial Committee complained to the national headquarters at its "surrenders and sacrifices" for the sake of the right. In many *pueblos*, including Alcaudete, Baeza, Chiclana de Segura, Santo Tomé, Pontones, Ubeda, and Vilches, the

Radicals, having reached an agreement with the right, had failed to secure their share of councillors on the steering committees. The Radicals were also forfeiting influential public positions such as the Provincial Delegate of Labour and the presidency of the mixed juries for Ubeda. In the same vein, local *Cedistas*, who were "robustly" protected, boasted that the Radicals would obtain nothing from the CEDA ministers.[63] In Salamanca, the division of power within the new Diputación (provincial government) led a local leader to complain to Lerroux that the Radicals "were going to be in a position of inferiority" as opposed to that of "preponderance" to which they believed themselves entitled.[64] Not only were the Radicals fighting to maintain their hegemony of local government but also their own social base. On the island of Mallorca, for instance, the Radicals faced a concerted campaign by the right to win over their supporters, but found themselves severely handicapped by a lack of organization, dismal propaganda, and a generalized inertia. The Mallorca party was lambasted by *Renovación* for having become entrapped in a "paralysis" of its own making. The fact that the right, together with its greater organizational and propagandistic resources, had gained the political initiative as a result of the October 1934 risings made it difficult for the Radicals to eschew ever greater internal conflicts. In January, the Junta of the Madrid party was overthrown. By April, the conflicts within the Basque Radical Party had became so overwhelming that Lerroux, having dismissed the Vizcaya organization two months earlier, dissolved the entire party in order to rebuild it from scratch.[65]

By the spring of 1935, the Radicals had been put on the defensive by the counterproductive consequences of the repression and by the increasingly overt struggle with the CEDA at the national and provincial levels alike. "So much discussion, so much energy and so much time lost!", exclaimed the CEDA organ.[66] None the less, the CEDA *caudillo* remained confident that his strategy was advancing smoothly. "Two years ago, in whose hands was Spain? Today, into whose hands it is falling?", he asked rhetorically at a rally. The CEDA would conquer the government once it was obvious that no other force could "carry out the programme that Spain needs". Moreover, he predicted that "we are nearer power than many believe", while warning both the Radicals and the President that if the *Cedistas* were not given power, "we will go to the people". In other words, the CEDA would not be intimidated by the prospect of a dissolution of the Cortes.[67]

This precarious balance did not last long. In March, twenty death sentences were handed down by the military courts. These included two prominent socialists from the Asturian rising, Teodomiro Menéndez and, more importantly, Rafael González Peña, the trade unionist and national deputy who had been the rising's leading figure. The right naturally demanded that the government approve the sentences, but the socialists, left republicans, the President, and many Radicals were in favour of clemency. The CEDA leader warned the Prime Minister on several occasions that a pardon in this instance would provoke the break-up of the ruling majority. On 29 March, the premier, determined not to give the President "the initiative" in relation to the question of "compassion", recommended to the Cabinet that clemency be shown. All seven Radical ministers, in stark contrast to the Pérez Farrás case, voted in favour of commutation "without reserve", unlike the *Cedistas*, the Agrarian and the Liberal Democrat. Yet Lerroux refused to reconsider the matter. On 3 April, the three CEDA ministers walked out of the Cabinet. Another reshuffle loomed.[68]

Underlying the uncompromising clash over the death sentences lurked a struggle over the drive and direction of the Radical-led administration. *El Debate* lamented its "slowness in the task of liquidating the revolution" and its lethargy in "reconstructing the state". The Radicals' pragmatic approach clearly fell far short of the CEDA's authoritarian agenda. The CEDA organ also subjected the Radicals' alleged venality to further censure in an effort to discredit them. "The lack of activity in the government," according to *El Debate*, "does not have any other origin . . . than the legacy consented to by a number of old-fashioned politicians of traditional modes of thinking." As if that were not explicit enough, the CEDA mouthpiece referred baldly to the "the advantages of power" enjoyed by the Radical Party, such as "lucrative posts" and "influential positions of power", and concluded damningly that it had failed to "liberate itself from the prison of its history". Having extended its hold over local and provincial government to unprecedented levels in the aftermath of the October risings, the Radical Party was also under considerable pressure from the CEDA to redistribute that power more equitably. Naturally, the Radicals realized that if the *Cedistas* tightened their grip on the Cabinet, they would be in an even stronger position to enhance their presence in the provinces. "There was a struggle of aspirations", the former Radical Antonio Lara observed, the CEDA aiming to extend "the ambit" of its "participation and its predominance". The clash over the González Peña case was merely a stand-off in the battle for the control of the government.[69]

On being consulted by the President over the new government, the CEDA *caudillo* demanded five Cabinet seats, including the Ministry of War. Not wanting a further shift to the right, Alcalá-Zamora called on Lerroux to assemble a Cabinet of reconciliation that extended as far as the left. For a majority administration to be formed, the Radical leader still required the accidentalists' support, but Gil Robles categorically refused to collaborate with any of the republican parties that had underwritten the public statement of 6 October 1934 in protest at the CEDA's entry into the government. The President, too, failed to persuade the

CEDA leader to take part. Alcalá-Zamora thereupon entrusted Martínez de Velasco to establish a government of "republican conciliation", but Gil Robles still refused to share power with the 6 October signatories. Consequently Martínez de Velasco secured the backing of Lerroux, Cambó, and Melquiades Alvarez before returning to the CEDA *jefe*. Under the influence of Alcalá-Zamora, for whom Gil Robles was a "dangerous reactionary", Martínez de Velasco insisted that the Agrarians should have four seats, including the premiership and the Ministry of War. This was interpreted by the CEDA leader as a veto on his party's claims. He refused to cooperate.[70]

Still the President would not give in to the CEDA. He found a willing ally in the Radical leader. They cobbled together a Cabinet of presidential "recommendations" and Lerrouxist loyalists, and, in accordance with the Constitution, closed the Cortes for a month. Probably to appease the President but also perhaps to apply pressure to the right, the Prime Minister drafted in General Masquelet, Azaña's Chief of Staff, as Minister of War and the head of the IRA, Juan José Benayas, as Minister of Agriculture. Lerroux, who "loved arrangements designed to win time", probably hoped, like Alcalá-Zamora, that the CEDA would modify its demands at the prospect of a dissolution upon the Cortes' resumption in May. By exploiting the symbiotic nature of their relationship with the accidentalists, the Radicals were attempting to call the CEDA's bluff. In any case, the Radical *jefe* did not expect the government to last long. In trying to persuade the young economic expert Alfredo Zabala to become Minister of the Economy, he wittily explained that he was not offering to make him a minister "but something even better – an ex-minister" – an illusion to the ministerial pension. Unaccountable to parliament, but welcomed by the left, the so-called "government of experts" illustrated the essential moderation of the Radicals once they were beyond the reactionary orbit of the CEDA. First, the regime of martial law was brought to an end on 9 April. Second, the Generalidad was re-established with all its autonomous powers intact except for public order. The regional government, the new President of which was Juan Pich y Pon, was to be run by the Radicals in collaboration with the Lliga.[71]

The CEDA retaliated by launching a massive campaign of protest. A telegram was dispatched to all sections of the party instructing them to prepare for the probable dissolution of the Cortes. Over 8,500 telegrams of support were received in a single day by the national leadership. The vast majority of CEDA officials in the provinces resigned en masse. Meanwhile, the JAP published a manifesto demanding "All power for the *jefe*!" and held a quasi-fascist rally in Madrid on 23 April which highlighted the CEDA youth's "new spirit of politics". The pressure was kept up throughout April by meetings the length and breadth of the land, with 197 held on the last day of the month. It appeared that the Radical bluff had been called. "Señor Gil Robles", a former Radical noted, "had pronounced sentence of death on the government".[72]

It did not take long for Lerroux to realize that the CEDA was prepared to face a dissolution. By contrast, the Radical Party was not. Confronted by a hostile left and an aggrieved right, the Radicals would be in an extremely vulnerable position, not least because the political climate remained strongly polarized. To avoid a dissolution, the party had to cut a deal with the CEDA. The Radicals' opening gambit was for Santiago Alba to explore the possibility of the CEDA backing the government from the outside. Gil Robles rejected the proposal out of hand. A week later, on 12 April, the Prime Minister, whose anxiety at a dissolution was heightened by the fact that the left was beginning to stir itself – that very day, Azaña, Martínez Barrio, and Sánchez Román issued a manifesto – exchanged views with the CEDA *caudillo* regarding the reconstruction of the old alliance. Eight days on, Lerroux tried to persuade Gil Robles that the government should seek the support of parliament, but he rebuffed the Radical leader once more. Further meetings followed in which the Prime Minister continued to defend a "certain predominance" of the Radicals in the Cabinet. By 27 April, the four majority leaders had still not decided whether or not the administration should be presented to parliament. Yet two days later, the Prime Minister, obsessed by the possibility of a dissolution, indicated his willingness not only to accept a reshuffle before the Cortes met but also a Cabinet that reflected the parties' parliamentary strength: which, of course, would give the CEDA more seats than the Radical Party. On the other hand, he insisted that the CEDA could occupy neither the War nor Naval ministries. All in all, the tug-of-war over the April administration had merely demonstrated that, if a majority government was to be formed, there was no alternative to the Radical–CEDA axis.[73]

The Cabinet resigned on 3 May. To general surprise, if not alarm, Gil Robles now expressed an interest in becoming Prime Minister himself. However, he was not only aware of the opposition of the President, who had cited the CEDA leader's excessive youth as an obstacle as well as the hostility of "the good republicans" and who had attempted to appease Gil Robles by indicating that he would be "the man of the next parliament", but he also realized that the Radicals would take less than kindly to the leapfrogging of Lerroux. As a result, and so as not to provoke a dissolution in the hands of the left, the CEDA *caudillo* backed down. The Cabinet received the news "like balm". Asked to form the next government, the Radical leader did not heed the call from erstwhile premier Ricardo Samper, who urged the formation of an administration "of republican reconciliation that supersedes the antagonisms between right and left". Instead, he approached the CEDA, attempting to parry Gil Robles's demand for five ministries by pressing for parity at four each, but the implacable accidentalist leader refused. The CEDA eventually accepted five ministries, while the Radicals were down to only three of the thirteen. The Agrarians, with nearly sixty deputies less, had two ministries. Lerroux's fifth administration, announced on 6 May, was the seventh to be headed by a Radical in only twenty months.[74]

The new administration marked the eclipse of the Radical Party. In all the Cabinets formed since 12 September 1933, the Radicals had commanded an absolute majority, but they were now reduced to less than a quarter of the ministries. Even worse, they had been dislodged from heavyweight departments such as Economy and War for the peripheral ones of Public Works and the Navy. Both numerically and qualitatively, the 6 May government signalled a major shift to the right. Most ominously, Manuel Giménez Fernández had been replaced by the Agrarian Nicasio Velayos, a wealthy landowner from Valladolid who belonged to the crustacean right. Gil Robles, who had already demonstrated his readiness to collaborate with military insurgents, secured the Ministry of War. The centre–right axis of the last seven months had, therefore, given way to a right–centre, if not reactionary, one.

The drawn-out crisis of March to May 1935 marked the high point of the Radicals' rearguard action in the wake of the October 1934 risings to stem the advance of the right. In trying to shore up the centre ground, the Radicals had become embroiled in a struggle with the right that was centred above all on the repression and the counter-reform. Underlying this lay a confrontation over the distribution of power both in the provinces and at the national level. Due to the incessant pressure of the CEDA in particular and lacking the presence of the left as a counterweight, the Radical Party gave ground in the partial reshuffle of November 1934, in that of a month later, and in the full-blown crisis of April to May 1935. Although Lerroux's administration of October 1934 to March 1935 had been the longest-lasting of those formed since the general election of 1933, it been characterized by its chronic instability. Moreover, the government's record was largely a negative one: the excessive repression of the left, the dismantling of the reforms of 1931 to 1933, and the onslaught on the workers. The verdict of one of the ministers concerned was uncompromising: "Zero in economics. Zero in administration. Zero in social policy". Finally, the incorporation of the CEDA into the Cabinet had, despite the sanguine forecast of the Radical leader, ushered in a period of lesser, rather than greater, stability.[75]

The Radicals were caught in a terrible dilemma. On the one hand, the heavy-handed response to the uprisings had burnt the party's bridges with the socialists and left republicans. On the other hand, the Radical Party could not govern with the CEDA, but nor could it govern without it. In reality, the Radicals were doomed to deal with the right, which was at once its ally and its antagonist. The outcome to the April stand-off merely deepened the political crisis. The CEDA, the first two stages of its strategy completed, was on the verge of securing the third, and final, one. "In the long run – and right now it does not seem so long – victory is certain", *El Debate* enthused. For the left, the May government heralded, in the words of the Communist deputy Bolívar, "the arrival of fascism". The left republican Ramos Acosta, in Manichean terms that have characterized the left's view of the Radical Party then and since, denounced the Radicals for having unleashed a "systematically destructive labour" of the reforms of the Constituent Cortes in order to resurrect "the legislation of the monarchy", leaving Spaniards "already divided in two perfectly separated groups" and the left with no option but to form "an anti-fascist front".[76]

In fact, there was widespread consternation within the Radical Party itself at the new government. Particularly outraged was the PURA. "A disastrous solution", exclaimed *El Pueblo*, "the impression throughout Spain is one of extreme distress". The reaction of the PURA was strongly shaped by the challenge to its position in Valencia of the local CEDA-affiliate, the DRV. The catalyst was the appointment of Luis Lucia, the DRV leader, as Minister of Communications. Sigfrido Blasco Ibáñez, the PURA *jefe*, limited himself to stating that there would be "repercussions". More explicit was *El Pueblo*. "It is the augury of a second blow in favour of a clerical dictatorship", it warned. The shift of power towards the CEDA, the PURA organ concluded, revealed that "it is not our Republic".[77] Such was the agitation within the party that, as Ricardo Samper's diary reveals, the *Blasquistas* were "inclined to separate" from the Radical Party.[78] Tempestuous meetings of the parliamentary party followed, but without a solution being found. Yet the opposition within the Radical ranks was not confined to the *Blasquistas* alone: a quarter of the deputies abstained in the vote of confidence on the new administration. A third of these were *Blasquistas*. However, the Radical leader overcame the PURA dissidence at a meeting of the parliamentary group on 11 May. Exactly how Lerroux did this is not known, but he may have promised them further public positions.[79] In any case, the PURA, having wrecked its relations with the left by taking undue advantage of the post-October repression, had few other options.[80] Other sections of the party had reached much the same conclusion. In Vigo, Emiliano Iglesias called upon the classes of conservatism to unite in the face of the ever-present danger of the left. The swing to the right under the new government was soon apparent in a number of localities. In Seville, for example, the Radical majority on the town council was promptly overturned by the CEDA.[81] The implications for the Radical Party's power in the provinces, for its clientage networks, and for its future electoral standing were ominous indeed.

XI

Compromise and Confrontation
Resisting the Right, May to October 1935

Despite the setback of the May administration, the Radicals continued to defend the alliance with the right with conviction. In a speech in Cordoba on 25 May the Radical *jefe* justified the recent Cabinet reshuffle as yet another step in the consolidation of the Republic as a truly representative regime. His undiminished determination to integrate the non-republican right into the Republic was exemplified by his claim that the day would come when "my friends had converted themselves into my enemies and these into my friends". In his view, the Radical Party, by aspiring to bring together all Spaniards within a "national" framework, served an essentially moderate and reconciliatory role. "With my policy of appeasement," he insisted, "I have achieved for the Republic the spirit of tranquillity." His rhetoric, however, clashed jarringly with the reality of the abuse of workers' rights, the press censorship, the overthrowing of socialist and left republican town councils, the states of alarm, and the persecution of political opponents such as Azaña. Furthermore, Lerroux's vision of a harmonious alliance with the right was belied by the recent, drawn-out Cabinet crisis and by the ongoing struggle within the alliance in parliament and the provinces alike. The legitimacy of the Radical strategy was also brought into question by the fact that the party was now speaking from a position of patent weakness. The Radicals, though they continued to resist the exigencies of the right, were clearly in retreat. Symptomatic of the consequent unease within the party was its tendency to focus on a common external enemy – in this case, the left – as a means of fostering unity, rather than to tackle questions of policy and principle, often a source of division. In addressing the Madrid Radical Circle on 15 May, Antonio Marsá, editor of the *Libro de Oro*, dwelt on the past – describing the first biennium as a period of "horrors that threatened civil war and the ruin of Spain" – rather than confronting the present.[1]

Ideologically and strategically on the defensive, the Radicals were more dependent than ever on their capacity to meet the demands of their clientelist networks. Under the Republic, politicians were still judged to a great

extent by their ability to extract material concessions from the authorities, above all from those located in Madrid and from the civil governors,
and in particular to generate employment for their supporters by securing
state sector jobs as well as public works contracts. The *pueblos* of
Logroño, for example, were characterized by a local Radical as being "of
no political depth and of an egoism so refined that one has to do for them
everything that they ask". The advance of the CEDA and Agrarians at the
national level, and their corresponding demand for a greater share of local
and provincial government, constituted a direct threat to the Radical
Party's control of public patronage. The loss of the Radicals' Cabinet
majority in May 1935 made them more sensitive than ever to the ambitions of their allies. At stake was not just the Radicals' patronage
possibilities but their very position in the provinces. This defensiveness
was enhanced by the fact that they were still struggling in many areas to
consolidate the power acquired as a result of the overturning of opposition *ayuntamientos* in the wake of the October 1934 risings. As a result,
a bitter struggle unfolded in the provinces during the summer of 1935
between the Radical Party and its coalition partners. In the province of
Avila, for instance, the right, especially the *Cedistas*, vied fiercely with the
Radicals for supremacy. The civil governor explained in correspondence
to Lerroux that the Radical Party, "which did not exist here", had been
built up through his exertions from a mere 20 branches to over 200 (with
more than 23,000 affiliates), by enticing "small landowners, tenant
farmers, shopkeepers, and industrialists" away from the right. Such
support, he stressed, depended to a great extent on the Radicals retaining
power in the province, yet this "great preponderance" was imperilled by
the propaganda offensive of their allies during the summer of 1935
together with the resurgence of the republican opposition. In June the
governor pleaded with the Radical leader to make an appearance in the
province so that the party could repulse the "tenacious pressure" of the
right. "All protection is little", he concluded alarmingly.[2]

As the Avila example indicates, a crucial role was often played in the
battle for a province by the civil governor. Their far-reaching powers, a
function of the Spanish state's Napoleonic-inspired centralism, could
make or break a party, especially one, such as the Radical Party in Avila,
that enjoyed little local tradition. A sympathetic civil governor, the Soria
Radical Party wrote to Lerroux, was the "only means of being able to
organize a strong party": otherwise, "no one pays us any attention". Any
attempt by the right to replace a Radical governor with one of its own was
vigorously resisted, above all in those provinces where the Radical Party
had yet to consolidate its support. A prime illustration is provided by the
province of Logroño. Prior to October 1934, the party had been weakly
implanted there, but the installation of a Radical governor had facilitated
its "upward growth", even though 70 per cent of the town and village

councils were controlled by the CEDA and the Radicals had to contend with the *"Supercacique"*, a local accidentalist deputy. Hardly surprisingly, the prospect of a CEDA governor was regarded by the Radicals as nothing less than "catastrophic". In the same vein, the Leon party disclosed to the national leader that it had made "notorious progress" under the auspices of the current civil governor, but if he was replaced "it will go into decline".[3] Similarly, the governor for Almeria, E. Peyró, warned Lerroux that if he lost his job, the local Radical Party, locked in dispute with the CEDA, would face the "dismantling and possible disappearance of the Radical positions". "I want to avoid," he underlined, "the overthrow of the positions conquered by the Radical Party." Equally, the Orense party stressed that if the governorship fell into the hands of another force the effect would be "deplorable". "The doors," it exclaimed, would be "hermetically sealed against all hope." On the other hand, the *Cedistas*, bereft of civil governors themselves, were naturally aggrieved at the extremely partisan use to which the Radicals put them. "In many provinces," Gil Robles later complained, "our members were unashamedly persecuted by the civil governors at the service of the Radical Party." At dispute were not just the governorships and the steering committees, but all those public positions in the gift of the authorities. To take a typical example, an employee of the Provincial Labour Office in Huesca urged the Prime Minister not to substitute certain representatives and inspectors on 1 June 1935 with members of the CEDA. To be replaced by "antagonists", he claimed, would produce "disastrous results", as the CEDA cooperated with the Radicals "exclusively for their own political ends".[4]

Inevitably, political and personal tensions within the local Radical organizations were sharpened by the ideological and institutional gains of the right. The confrontation within the Palencia party during the first half of 1935 between the provincial committee and that in the capital, described by the latter as "more personal than political", brought the party there to the verge of rupture. Earlier in the year, the Radical leader was bluntly informed by Perfecto Díaz, a deputy from the first biennium, that the Toledo party "is sinking". Provincial entities were also being torn apart by blatant errors of the party's own making. The Gerona party in Catalonia, for instance, was up in arms during the summer of 1935 at the attempt of the regional boss, Juan Pich y Pon, to bring it more firmly under his sway by designating one of his own men as its president. Not only were the local members outraged at "the absorption by Barcelona" but, to make matters worse, the new president allegedly placed his personal ambitions above those of the party. He failed, despite promises to the contrary, to have its debt paid off, while exploiting his position to become the Provincial Labour Delegate. The upshot was that this "impudent upstart" and "undesirable", who had occasioned numerous resignations, had "greatly" set back the Gerona party's revival. Pich y Pon was soon made to pay a price of sorts for his self-serving favouritism. Having made a multitude of inappropriate appointments first as mayor of Barcelona and then, since April 1934, as governor general of Catalonia, both the efficacy and the policy-making capacity of the respective authorities had been severely compromised. Such was his failure to take charge of the situation in Barcelona once the CNT reemerged during the early summer that two ministers, including an exasperated Gil Robles, had to be dispatched to Barcelona in June in order to reestablish order.[5]

The escalating conflict between the Radical Party and the CEDA in the provinces placed their collaboration in both the Cortes and the Cabinet in jeopardy. Something had to be done. At the end of June Gil Robles returned to Salamanca, his home town and constituency, to attend a Civil Guard ceremony. The local Acción Popular party took advantage of their *jefe*'s visit to organize a banquet in his honour. Neither event called for the presence of the Prime Minister but Lerroux, along with another Radical minister, Manuel Marraco, attended both. This outward display of unity has subsequently been referred to as the "Pact of Salamanca", though in fact there was no signed accord or explicit agreement. However, the mere presence of the Prime Minister at a banquet for the CEDA leader on his home territory was an unequivocal reaffirmation of the ruling alliance. "A decisive step", Lerroux declared at the time, "in the consolidation of the Republic". Or, as he later recalled, "it was necessary to present ourselves as united before public opinion". In part, the show of support by the two leaders was to offset the resurgence of the republican opposition as Azaña, Martínez Barrio, and Sánchez Román addressed a series of high-profile mass meetings in May and June. Above all, the Salamanca acts were designed to counteract the conflict between the CEDA and the Radical Party in the provinces. For Lerroux, their governmental cooperation had to be extended "throughout the whole country". Thus the "Pact" was a signal to the party that collaboration with the CEDA had to be maintained at all costs, while Gil Robles, José Antonio Primo de Rivera noted, "puts up with the Radicals as undesirable, but for the moment indispensable, partners". At once allies and antagonists, the two parties were brought together by their mutual dependence. The "Spirit of Salamanca" was subsequently embodied in a highly personal, if not personalistic, decision taken by Lerroux in relation to the parliamentary group. He informed it that, though amendments could be presented to bills and discrepancies with its allies be aired, it was forbidden to vote against the government.[6] This extraordinary measure underscored the extent to which support for the right had waned amongst the Radical ranks. Indicative of the growing disillusionment was the resignation of Clara Campoamor, the Radicals' only female deputy, from the party in February 1935. She accused her leader of betraying everything that the party stood for by placing it at the behest of the right – as witnessed at first hand in her capacity as Director General of Charity at the CEDA-run Ministry of Labour. The importance of the *jefe*'s directive to the deputies was illustrated by the reaction of the accidentalists to the parliamentary vote of 28 June, when the Radical Party played a crucial role in obtaining a quorum for the government. "There does not exist," effused *El Debate*, "a shadow of a doubt, and the task undertaken will neither fail nor be truncated." In the same spirit, Lerroux reaffirmed the alliance with the CEDA in a speech on 5 July in Pontevedra.[7] This highlighted a crucial distinction between the Radical leader and the CEDA chief: whereas Gil Robles had frequently attacked, and not infrequently ridiculed, the Radicals, both in parliament and outside, Lerroux, for all his differences with the CEDA, had remained outwardly loyal. Though the refusal of the Prime Minister to combat the CEDA publicly was to be a notable constraint on the Radicals' antagonism towards their coalition partner, this did not mean that other sections of the party did not clash openly, and repeatedly, with the right in 1935.

The credibility of the Radical Party, having staked its reputation on the promise of social peace and political stability within the framework of "a Republic for all Spaniards", was further undermined in 1935 by the deterioration in the conditions of employment as landowners and *patronal* alike sought to turn the clock back to the days of the monarchy. The offensive of the landowners against the day-labourers and leaseholders was to reach unprecedented levels, especially in the centre and the south. The labour legislation was extensively abused, wages plummeted, and known left-wingers were often discriminated against at the time of hiring. In the case of Andalusia, which accounted for nearly a third of national unemployment at the end of 1934, the situation was exacerbated during the summer of 1935 by a severe drought. Trade union and other left-wing activists were physically intimidated, some even being killed, and they were subjected to house searches. The property owners' backlash was, as even the Francoist historian Ricardo de la Cierva admits, "genuinely ferocious".[8] With the rural unions underground, numerous socialist and opposition republican *ayuntamientos* overthrown, censorship still in force, and the PSOE deputies largely absent from the Cortes, the workers' means of fighting back were strictly limited. Their struggle was made even more painstaking by a further change in the labour legislation. In July the composition of the mixed juries, few of which were functioning, were modified in favour of the Catholic unions. On the other hand, the juries' essential functions, to the dismay of the employers, were not altered. Symptomatic of the mass suffering were the swarms of people reduced to begging and the heightened security surrounding the southern estates so that the needy could not gather firewood and olives. In Extremadura, the hungry took to stealing the acorns fed to the pigs – only to be shot at by the Civil Guard. One of the most revealing commentaries upon the state of the south in 1935 is provided by the correspondence between Carlos de Luna, the civil governor for Badajoz, and Diego Hidalgo, the former minister and Radical deputy for the province. According to what the governor described as "the egoism" of the landowners and what Hidalgo termed the "psychology . . . of our rich Extremadurans" the situation had already declined greatly by the beginning of 1935. Appeals by De Luna to the landowners' comprehension and "a little material sacrifice" met with their utter inflexibility. As far as the well-to-do were concerned, the law was simply an instrument by which "to defend their wretchedness and their prerogatives". By the end of 1935, De Luna was still pleading in vain with the government for the legal means by which to oblige "the rich to fulfil their duties as citizens, imposing by force the most elemental of all: that of charity and love for their fellow man".[9] The failure of the Lerroux administration to heed such exhortations from within its own ranks was a manifestation of the extent to which the new Cabinet was identified with the interests of the big landowners. The latter, as one CEDA activist wrote to Giménez Fernández, "would give anything for their money. They would sell Christ again for thirty pieces, or perhaps for less". The CEDA leader himself would later admit that the rebirth of the left was due in great measure to the "egoism and indescribable conduct of the social classes" of the right.[10] Like the landowners, the *patronal*, despite entreaties from the government, widely abused the labour laws. Left-wing activists were discriminated against and contracts ignored as wages fell, hours lengthened, and unemployment continued to climb. The erosion in working conditions was not as excessive as in the rural economy, but it was extreme none the less.

The forces of the right, now that they dominated the Cabinet, were determined to translate their ministerial hegemony into legislative terms. Their zeal to dismantle the reforms of the first biennium was underscored by the new administration's frenzied parliamentary schedule: the majority of laws passed between 1 October 1934 and 26 July 1935 were executed during the first three months of the May government. Such haste was reflected in the badly drafted legislation and the flouting of parliamentary procedure. In the Cortes, former Radical González y Fernández de la Bandera upbraided the ruling coalition for constantly presenting legislation that was characterized by its "defects", "vices", and the "lack of study, as well as the lack of consideration for the parliamentary parties".[11] The ascendancy of the right found its most emphatic expression in the Agrarian Reform bill presented in July. This proposed not only that the price of compensation for expropriated land should be fixed at the market level, thereby virtually sabotaging the process of indemnification, but also that the budget of the IRA should be slashed. Falange leader José Antonio Primo de Rivera was not too far off the mark when he claimed that the agency would require another 160 years to carry out its task. Finally, by ditching the inventory of properties vulnerable to expropriation, the Minister of Agriculture, Nicasio Velayos, effectively exempted eight-tenths of the land from reform. "This governmental bill," observed Claudio de Albornoz, the moderate Izquierda Republicana spokesman, "simply signifies the annulment of the agrarian reform." To the opposition of the left republicans was added that of two former ministers of agriculture, Cirilo del Río and Manuel Giménez Fernández, as well as that of the Radicals – in short, moderates who were prepared to amend the Azaña law but not to emasculate it. The government largely defused the moderate opposition – which, in collaboration with the left republicans, would have been capable of holding the bill up until the summer recess – by making a number of concessions. Moreover, once the left republicans abandoned the Cortes in protest at the measure, the Radicals' resistance soon crumbled. Whereas the 1932 Law had been hammered out over the course of five gruelling months, that of 1935 swept through the Cortes in a mere five days. Nevertheless, the Radicals had managed to insert a far-reaching clause into Velayos' otherwise reactionary Law. The state, according to the draft sponsored by José María Alvarez Mendizábal, could expropriate any type of land for reasons of "social utility". Under the right this naturally lacked all meaning, but under the left, as the Popular Front government of 1936 would subsequently demonstrate, this Radical-inspired measure would have revolutionary repercussions.[12]

By contrast, the Radicals did little to challenge the CEDA's shake up of the armed forces. Unlike the Radicals, Gil Robles, the incoming minister, made no attempt to strike a balance between right-wingers and liberals as regards the key appointments. On the contrary, the monarchist Fanjul was made under-secretary, Goded was converted into Commander-in-Chief, and Franco, following his direction of the Asturian repression, was nominated Chief of Staff. Known republicans were sistematically sidelined. Alcalá-Zamora, but not Lerroux, repeatedly clashed with Gil Robles over the promotion of "open adversaries or very weak adherents of the regime". Also undertaken was a major rearmament programme as well as manoeuvres in preparation for an internal rebellion. In essence, the reforms were designed to ensure the political objectives of the right by equipping the army for the suppression of domestic opposition and by making a coup redundant or, if required, a straightforward matter. Undoubtedly, the changes wrought by the CEDA minister greatly facilitated the military rebellion of July 1936. Yet Radical resistance to these changes was limited. This was partly because the Radicals, being ultimately responsible for the repression in the wake of the 1934 risings, were themselves implicated in the shift of power from the civilian to the military authorities. In any case, the post-October climate made it difficult for the Radicals to dispute measures ostensibly designed to improve internal security and which, moreover, had been drawn up by the leader of their principal ally. It has to be said that Gil Robles did not raise the stakes by mounting a wholesale assault on the reforms of the first biennium. Despite the flurry of decrees that tumbled forth from the Ministry of War during the summer of 1935, the CEDA *jefe* did little to modify Azaña's achievement. Finally, the Prime Minister himself appears not to have questioned Gil Robles's plans. Indeed, Lerroux's sympathy for the insurrectionary option, together with his collaboration with the CEDA, suggest that he would not necessarily have objected to the surreptitious preparations for a rightist *coup d'état*.[13]

The Radicals' indifference to the military reforms should not obscure the fact that they clashed with the CEDA over a whole series of leading issues. A prominent bone of contention was unemployment. According to the authorities, this stood at 732,000 in April 1935. The Minister of Labour variously claimed that these statistics were false, that no true figures existed, or that unemployment had actually fallen by about 200,000 since the right had come to power. The official estimate, in fact, was based on the returns of only 70 per cent of the *ayuntamientos*, Madrid not being included. Further, as the Radical Rafael Guerra del Río, the former Minister of Public Works, pointed out in parliament, "a great workers' organization, the CNT", had not collaborated in the compilation of the data. The true level of unemployment was, probably, around one and a half million. Certainly there was no lack of ostensible concern from within the ruling majority for those without work. For *El Debate*, this was a matter of the utmost urgency; for Gil Robles it was his "greatest concern", and for the government this should be tackled "to the extent that is necessary".[14] The bill presented to parliament on 15 May belied such rhetoric. Overall, it was proposed to spend 200 million pesetas on the unemployed, of which 65 million would be disbursed in 1935. The rest would be deployed in 1936, by the end of which, the minister estimated, the "work crisis" would have "disappeared" – that is to say, been reduced to a "normal" level. The bulk of the budget, 108 million pesetas, was to be given over to subsidies for construction projects carried out by public and private entities alike. Only 20 million pesetas, as opposed to the 1000 million envisaged by the Radicals in January 1934, was to be invested in the construction of public buildings. The bill was immediately attacked by the Radical Basilio Alvarez on the grounds that "on account of the meanness, the limitedness, the reduced level, it's almost ridiculous". He calculated that the budget for 1935 would either provide for a total of 36,000 workers until the end of the year (at a rate of 5 pesetas a day), or else sustain all the unemployed for a period of one solitary week. The situation was made even more serious, he added, as the money sent back to Spain by emigrants to Latin America – an important source of income for many families before the world recession – had largely dried up. Alvarez's home region of Galicia had, he reckoned, lost 300 million pesetas as a result. An equally damning criticism of the bill was made by Guerra del Río. While 65 million was to be spent on those without work in 1935, he observed, "50 or 60 million are to be saved on public works in the Ministry of Public Works". "This," he concluded, "appears a mockery." He protested that, like the Constituent Cortes, "we are going to sacrifice our unchanging programme to balancing the budget at all costs".[15] In fact, the project was designed not so much to alleviate the plight of the unemployed as to stimulate the depressed construction industry.[16] Shackled by Lerroux's injunction not to vote against the government, the Radicals, despite the fact that, as the party spokesman admitted, their "observations" and "suggestions . . . appear to be in contradiction", backed the bill. However, a group of Radicals tried to tack on to it an article which would have added thousands of millions to the budget. This brought the Minister of the Economy, who confronted Guerra del Río angrily in parliament, to the point of resignation, but Lerroux, as Prime Minister, backed him against the Radical manoeuvre. As a result, the right-wing dominated government did little to alleviate the hardship of the unemployed.[17]

The government's tepid response to the mounting work crisis reflected the shift in economic priorities under the right away from the creation of employment towards the balancing of the budget and the defence of the agrarian oligarchy's interests. This was crystallized in the strenuous, if not always successful, efforts of the Minister of Agriculture – Gil Robles believed that he was simply not up to the job – to regulate the wheat market during the summer of 1935.[18] The quest for a balanced budget had culminated with the appointment of the "technocrat" and former monarchist Joaquín Chapaprieta as Minister of the Economy in the May government. He aimed to lower public expenditure, and, in the process, wipe out the deficit, by cutting costs as well as by eliminating fiscal fraud and corruption, but without raising taxes.[19] By means of the Law of Restrictions, approved by parliament on 26 July, Chapaprieta made a substantial saving by trimming the number of ministries from thirteen to nine, a measure to be applied two months later. Not that the minister proposed to slash all areas of government spending. Illustrative of the priorities under the right was the fact that the budget proposals for the second half of 1935 foresaw a reduction in education and for the anti-reformist Ministry of Agriculture, while expenditure on the armed forces and the Ministry of the Interior was projected to rise by over 74 and 77 million pesetas respectively for the year. The budgetary commitment to the security forces was powerfully complemented by the May government's legislative agenda: while 27 of the new laws concerned the armed forces, only four dealt with public works and just one with education. There could be little doubt that, given the widespread suffering engendered by the work crisis, the biggest cutbacks in state spending had been carried out at the least appropriate time.[20]

Support for Chapaprieta's plans to reduce the number of ministries was to be found in the Prime Minister, but the Radical ministers were clearly unhappy at the measures. The Minister of Public Works, for example, collided with Chapaprieta over the number of public service posts to be made available in the future.[21] The Minister of the Economy's overall reform package, as embodied in the 1936 budget and the 26 bills complementary to it, strongly divided the Radical Party. Indeed, the parliamentary debates during the summer of 1935 over Chapaprieta's cost-cutting crusade provide a vivid illustration of one of the most salient contradictions within the Radical Party: whereas the *laissez faire* business sector generally welcomed a slim-line state, those employed by, or in some way dependent on, the public sector were adamantly opposed. In fact, the bulk of Radical politicians, themselves public employees, were opposed to sweeping economies. The Radicals, Gil Robles observes, "clung to the public positions as if they were their only means of salvation". This was partly because many Radicals were mortified at the prospect of their clientelist networks being drastically curtailed by the streamlining of the public sector. An example is provided by the Lozoya Canal project near Madrid. It had been hoped, an advisory group informed Lerroux in June 1935, to deploy a hundred Radical workers on the venture but so far only three had been taken up. As a result, the workers began to question the promises made by the Radicals. While affirming that the party was not "an Employment Agency", the group stressed that "this policy" was like "sowing" and that it "always gives good results". Not only would this enhance the party's support but also improve its "bad" economic situation by permitting working-class members to pay their dues. This, it was pointed out, was clearly not possible when the workers had not got enough to feed their own families. An additional reason for the Radical opposition to the cutbacks was that the party's attachment to certain public-sector policies remained strong. The *jefe* himself had consistently defended the expansion of the state educational system since the advent of the Republic. In the same vein, the Radicals' prize legislative achievement, the Law for the Coordination of the Health Services, represented the only attempt so far under the regime to tackle the grievous shortcomings of the public health system. In fact, the Law was meant to have been implemented at the beginning of 1935, but, in December 1934, in the midst of the repression, it had been suspended for four months. However, in May 1935, the Radical deputy Antonio Tuñón de Lara demanded a new public health law that would rectify "our chaotic health organization" as well as the creation of a Ministry of Health. In Caceres province, for example, the *Diputación* was said to owe more than 600,000 pesetas to the suppliers and other bodies. In Plasencia hospital, one deputy claimed, the bedding was changed only once a month, the sheets were used to make shirts, and the patients sometimes had to sleep on hay mattresses full of "bedbugs and other plagues".[22] The Radical campaign at least elicited the promise from the government, to the undisguised delight of the rural doctors, to reactivate the Health Services Law in July. As one doctor wrote to Lerroux, this was a "great favour and justice" that would "liberate us from the clutches of the *caciques*". Given the commitment of many Radicals to the public health sector it is not entirely surprising to discover that the budgetary proposals of Chapaprieta, for whom the Radicals felt "the liveliest annoyance", made extremely painful progress. Not one of the 26 bills that were complementary to the budget had, by the end of the summer, been passed.[23]

Other right-wing legislative proposals, too, met with the determined opposition of the Radicals. An outstanding example was the press bill. Originally, this had been drawn up in the shadow of the October risings by the Radical Minister of the Interior Eloy Vaquero, but, once the May government had been formed, the CEDA leader made the project his own. The redrafted bill, however, was heavily attacked by the Radicals. On 16 May, José López Varela criticized it on the grounds that it would cause "an enormous damage". Even more outspokenly, Basilio Alvarez rejected the project for its "constant admonitions, innumerable precepts *a priori*, fines, suspensions, special courts, prisons and all the terrible *atrezzo* of a draconian monstrosity". It was, he concluded, "reactionary . . . a repressive arm against the press". The Radical protests, together with the obstruction of the left, eventually forced discussion of the bill to be abandoned altogether.[24]

Nor could the Radicals and their allies see eye to eye over the central issue of electoral reform. In January 1935 the Cabinet had approved a CEDA-backed scheme in favour of proportional representation. The author of the bill, Giménez Fernández, believed that this would free Spaniards from a majority system that forced them to choose between a false set of opposites: "revolution and counter-revolution, Republic and Monarchy, socialism and Catholicism". A setup that avoided the pendular swings of the prevailing one would appear, on the surface, to have been enormously attractive to a centrist force such as the Radicals. Indeed, in 1921 the party had, in opposition to the *cacique*-controlled system of the monarchy, presented a bill in favour of proportional representation. Now, however, the party, spearheaded by the Galicians under Emiliano Iglesias, backed the majority option. Understandable as this was insofar as Galician politics was still largely in hock to the gerrymandering practices of the Restoration, the rest of the party probably followed suit as a result of its success under the prevailing format in the 1931 and 1933 elections. Santiago Alba justified the Radical stance on the grounds that Spanish society was too immature for a system of proportional representation and that this would only create further instability for the regime. Once the parliamentary commission began its deliberations in February, the opposition of the Radicals and Agrarians to the CEDA initiative soon became apparent. In March, the leaders of the governing coalition tried, but failed, to negotiate a compromise. They hoped, instead, that the Cortes would come up with one. Following the formation of the May government, the ruling coalition, Gil Robles relates, "could not reach a single agreement, not even inside the commission". A special commission attached to the Prime Minister's office was created in June, but the recalcitrance of the Radicals was reflected in the belief of the commission's President, the Radical Pedro Armasa, that "we would be digging our own grave" by passing a proportional representation law. On 6 July, a deal was reached between the four majority leaders, only to be promptly undermined by further disagreements. Under the Chapaprieta government, formed in September, little further progress was made. By now, there were more proposals than parties. The Radicals, as disclosed by the discussion on 1 October within the parliamentary group, remained firmly in favour not just of the majority system but of smaller constituencies – something which, it was thought, would favour traditional, *cacique*-style methods. On 16 November the majority bosses strove again, in vain, to hammer out an agreement. While the CEDA and Lliga continued to favour proportional representation, the Radicals, Agrarians, and Liberal–Democrats were staunchly opposed. Yet another meeting in late November failed to break the deadlock. The Radicals, despite the perennial danger that the centre parties might be squeezed by broader coalitions of the left or right, took the short-term view that, having done well out of the system so far, they should stick with it.[25]

More seriously still, the Radicals obstructed the CEDA's cherished project of reforming the Constitution. On 5 July, Prime Minister Lerroux presented a CEDA-backed bill to the Cortes, discussed in Cabinet the previous month, which called for the reform of forty articles, including those concerning religion, education, the family, property, autonomy, and the monocameral parliamentary system. Many Radicals were horrified by such a far-reaching revision of the founding charter. Yet the greater the *Cedistas*' ambitions in relation to the Constitution the less likely it was that the ruling majority would ever be able to agree on its overhaul. Further complications arose as a result of the President's growing conviction that the CEDA – which, in reality, wanted to complete a series of other reforms before tackling the regime's charter as alteration of the latter would automatically result in a parliamentary dissolution – was not committed to changing the Constitution after all. An exasperated Alcalá-Zamora claimed that in 35 years as a lawyer he had never had to deal with "incidents, replacements, nullities and delay-making exceptions comparable to those in that political dispute". Once the Cortes reconvened in

October, the bill became buried in the parliamentary commission headed by Samper. By this stage, the Radicals had reached the same conclusion as the President; namely, that the current initiative should be restricted to article 125 alone, which dealt merely with the *way* in which the Constitution had to be reformed.[26]

These strategic and doctrinal divergences within the ruling majority reflected the lack of a common agenda. The CEDA *caudillo* records that the Radicals' collaboration during this period was "not at all enthusiastic" and that their support in parliament was "practically nil". Time and time again the stresses and strains between the Radicals and the *Cedistas* brought the alliance to the brink of "rupture". Only Gil Robles's energetic crisis-management and the authority of Lerroux within the Radical Party held the coalition together.[27] Yet at precisely the moment when the ruling majority was becoming increasingly divided, the opposition was becoming ever more united. These variegated forces, which included conservative, moderate, and left-wing republicans and which was joined by the liberal wing of the Socialist Party under Indalecio Prieto, were brought together above all by their shared experience of the repression. In May and June the leading signatories to the April "Manifesto", Manuel Azaña, Diego Martínez Barrio, and Felipe Sánchez Román, had launched a nationwide campaign to "recover" the Republic. Undoubtedly the Radicals, in spite of resisting the more extreme demands of the right, had greatly undermined their own cause by not halting the atrocities in Asturias earlier and by taking opportunistic advantage of the clampdown to replace hostile *ayuntamientos* with Radical-dominated steering committees. Moreover, many restrictions remained. Martial law had been brought to an end in most of Spain, but the states of alarm or prevention persisted in sixteen provinces. The constant extension of the states was brought into question by former Radicals, who, given the absence of the socialists from the Cortes and the sparse presence of the left republicans, often constituted, ironically, the opposition. On 6 June, for example, Alvaro Pascual Leone attacked the government for the continuing suspension of constitutional guarantees in numerous parts of the country. There was, he insisted, no justification for the measure. Another extension in July prompted him to inquire why the authorities persisted with the suspensions if, as they constantly asserted, order had been re-established. This, he concluded, had nothing to do with the threat of disorder and everything to do with an attempt to "kidnap liberty and pursue politics for the benefit of the governing parties". In Catalonia, he claimed, few workers' centres had been reopened by the end of May, even though the Minister of the Interior had undertaken to open those not implicated in the October rising and to review the situation of the rest. Minister Portela Valladares retorted that the first republican branches had in fact been permitted to renew their activities, but that the workers' centres were being treated with greater caution as they were inclined, he commented revealingly, to "what is called the social struggle, which generally degenerates into a fight against crime". Although the restrictions on the workers' movements were more severe than on the republicans, the scale of the curbs should not be exaggerated. Lerroux, for example, turned down an invitation to speak in Avila during the summer on the grounds that as long as public meetings were suspended "it doesn't seem to me right", as he wrote to the civil governor, "that the governmental parties should have a monopoly".[28] The ongoing constraints were also designed to appease the ruling majority's own supporters, preoccupied with the maintenance of "law and order", while guaranteeing a peaceful transition to normal political life. Nevertheless, there can be little doubt that the restrictions were enforced for too long, thereby diminishing the Radical Party's centrist appeal while playing into the hands of the right and opposition alike. In this regard, the Radicals sacrificed short-term gain for a serious loss of credibility in the medium term.

For the Radicals, the rejuvenation of the left-wing opposition was at once a bane and a blessing: it presented yet another political challenger, while providing a much-needed counterweight to the right. Much the same could be said of the Radicals' own coalition partners: the CEDA and others were indispensable allies, but they were power-hungry rivals, too. The CEDA strategy, as El Pueblo succinctly put it, was: "First part: support Lerroux (already done). Second part: collaborate with Lerroux (there now). Third part: replace him (next stop)". In May and June a swarm of public meetings were held by the accidentalists partly to counteract the reemergence of the left but also to prepare the ground for their next major target of reform: the Constitution. Having once voted on the bill on Restrictions, the agrarian reform, a raft of army bills, and having modified the mixed juries, the CEDA, as El Debate spelt out in an editorial on 3 July, would then aim to overhaul the regime's founding charter once the summer recess was over. This determination to recast the Constitution in accordance with the CEDA's authoritarian philosophy was backed up by the threat of violence should it not get its way. At the Confederación's fascist-style rally at Medina del Campo, its caudillo defended the party's collaboration with the Radicals as "the guarantee of victory" while asking rhetorically, "What need do I have of the army in order to triumph?". In other words, the CEDA's adherence to the Republic's democratic nostrums was merely a strategic option – Gil Robles referred to it as the "legalist tactic" – not a matter of principle or conviction. Alcalá-Zamora, despite his own deeply conservative outlook, was aghast at the backing of the CEDA leader for the party's "fascists", who aimed at "the total and totalitarian upheaval" of the Constitution.[29]

The revival of the left in addition to the ascendancy of the right further exacerbated the disorientation and divisions within the Radical provincial organizations. The most troubling case for the national leadership was that of its principal electoral bastion, the PURA. Although the breakaway of the PURA from the Radical Party in May had been averted, the discontent within the party remained manifest. Partly to appease the dissenters within the PURA, but also to offset the impact of the speeches given in Valencia by Azaña (in May) and Gil Robles (in June) the Radical leader, too, spoke there, on 9 July. His Valencia speech constituted an impassioned defence of the Radical Party's centrist politics. From the very outset of the Republic, the Radicals had realized that the regime had to be, in Lerroux's words, "of order, of cordiality, of accommodation, of social coexistence, or it could not last". Only by converting the regime into a truly "national" one would the republicans "make good use of democracy" by avoiding "passions exalted" by those "who want to do everything, as if by providential labour, in an instant". For the sake of the Republic, the Radicals had therefore sacrificed themselves by compromising first with the left, and then with the right. Collaboration with the latter, the Radical leader claimed, had been made inevitable by the outcome of the 1933 general election. To have dissolved the Cortes and held another election, as the left demanded, would have been a "stupidity" that would have resulted in "civil war". In any case, the Republic would not be "definitively" consolidated until the right had been integrated into it. By means of the alliance with the Radical Party, the forces of the right had evolved into republicans. "As gentlemen and men of honour," Lerroux insisted, "they cannot be traitors to their pledge nor to the Republic and they are identified with the Republic for good." What is more, the Radical Party had achieved this conversion without violating a single one of its republican principles. On the contrary, it had refused to build the regime "on abdications or by backing down". Now that the Radical mission was "on the point of completion" the right was fully entitled to govern alone. In the meantime, the Radical *jefe* exhorted the *Blasquistas* to join "the immense *falange* that tomorrow has to oppose any retreat and which has to be a stimulant and spur so that the parties of the right become conservatives of the Republic". A second challenge, however, awaited the Radical Party that required "as much tact, as much abnegation, as much spirit of sacrifice, as the first"; namely, "to reestablish the peace between all the republicans". Despite holding the left responsible for leaving "law and order destroyed, authority discredited, the economy in ruins", Lerroux appreciated that the Republic needed the left as much as the right. The opposition republicans had to return to "the path of reason", reorganize their parties, and reintegrate themselves into the political life of the regime. To that end the Radicals were prepared to offer their "loyal, generous and disinterested" collaboration, going so far as to cooperate in the construction of a "truly left-wing party". The Republic would thereby possess, to the right, "this *falange* that might govern tomorrow", and, to the left, "these foundations of republican tradition that also constitute an instrument of government". The Radicals, having finally consolidated the regime through "indispensable compromises", would thereupon recover their liberty of action.[30]

Certainly there was a good deal to be said for the Radicals' pragmatic approach to the right during their first year in government. By making the CEDA and its allies give ground on a whole range of issues, the Radicals were forcibly educating the forces of the right in the art of democratic compromise. However, the insurrections of October 1934 had swung the balance of power within the ruling majority heavily against the Radicals, dramatically reducing their leverage over the right. The task was made more difficult still by the excesses of the repression, for which they were ultimately responsible, but also the right for its revengeful and recidivist stance. Alcalá-Zamora judged that the right had simply taken advantage of the post-October 1934 climate "to persecute enemies, accentuate their conservatism and maintain themselves in power".[31] Indeed, there was little reason to believe that the *Cedistas* in particular, the majority of whom remained bent on transforming the Republic into a corporatist, Catholic state, had become republicans at all. Further, the Radicals' prospects of reforging relations with the opposition republicans, for whom the Radical Party had acted not as a brake on the right but as the stepping stone for "fascism", were exceedingly dim. Such hopes were scarcely improved by Lerroux's comparison in Valencia between, on the one hand, a loyal and accommodating right and, on the other hand, a sectarian and intransigent left. Despite the blatant shortcomings of the right's "republicanization", the Radical leader remained confident that a republican left and right would emerge, thereby leaving the Radicals, untrammelled by the exigencies of their allies, to pursue their own agenda.

The question of the party's future was again addressed by the Radical *jefe* at a lavish banquet held for over 1,500 people at Baños de Montemayor on 25 August. As in Valencia, he enjoined the opposition republicans, through their unification, to forge an instrument of government, and the *Cedistas*, through their collaboration with the Radical Party, to become "the great conservative party of the Republic". Once this "objective" had been achieved, he disclosed, "it is possible that in a short while I will say to you goodbye". A fortnight later, at the homage organized in Barcelona – "The Day of Lerroux", the party dubbed it – he referred once more to the fact that he would "have to retire" at an unspecified time in the future, though he added that this would not signal the end of the Radical Party.[32]

Such intimations of political mortality by the Radical leader can have done little to assuage the party's strife in the provinces. The Galician Radical Party, by all accounts, was in a lamentable state. The La Coruña party, Lerroux was briefed in July, "is very deficient, lacks order, organization and is greatly abandoned". Little had changed four months later when he was informed of the party's "disorganization" and of the fact that in the *pueblos* "we don't hear anything but laments and complaints".³³ In Santiago, where the Radicals had been at loggerheads for a considerable period, the party was, local members reported, "disorganized", the activity of the provincial committee "completely nil", and the municipal council characterized by its "disastrous performance". In reality, the Santiago Radical Party, the activist concluded, was "living off the favours of the right". In Orense, the party, according to the local executive committee, had been given over to "people who did not even find either shelter or protection in the old gangs of the monarchy". "This confusion," the committee bemoaned, "is the death of the party." In a similarly gloomy vein, the mayor of Pontevedra lamented that, as far as the *pueblo* was concerned, the party had achieved nothing.³⁴ The Aragonese party was also plunged in despair. In July, the former Radical deputy for Teruel José Borrajo wrote to Lerroux that the "trajectory" undertaken by the provincial party together with "the intrigue and unscrupulousness" that had taken hold of the organization had effectively sentenced it to "a rapid and inevitable death", leading him to abandon the Radicals. Equally, the Huesca party, where all 147 branches had been long neglected, was endangered, a local leader divulged to the Radical *jefe*, by "personal intrigues . . . lack of understanding, impatience and egoism". Meanwhile, a Zaragoza deputy, Dario Pérez, pressed the Radical leader in August to replace the civil governor by one "of aptitude and merits" so that the party could recover "a prosperity that it had and which, now, it lacks".³⁵ The following month the Madrid party was rocked by the resignation of the president and seven other members of the provincial junta as a result of a dispute over the reorganization of the Diputación's steering committee. The decision, dissidents explained to Lerroux, had been a direct result of the national leadership's "lack of consideration". That same month, the Radical mayor for Bilbao, along with two councillors, resigned, too.³⁶

Meanwhile, in Catalonia, the struggle for control of the Gerona organization between the Barcelona leadership and the local party continued unabated. Pedro Sastre Gener, a member of the National Council, denounced to the Radical *jefe* "the Barcelona absorption" which, "shamelessly" and "ignoring the most elemental democratic procedures", was destroying the Gerona party. "One day, not before long," he warned, "its men will have to confront Barcelona." A measure of the Radical Party's lack of consolidation was the fact that there were still internal disputes over the entry of former monarchists. Expulsion of the Radical mayor and president from the Medina del Campo party in Valladolid province led a group of local veterans to complain that they had been taken over by "old monarchist *caciques*". "Few of the old republican Radicals remain," they explained, "given that co-existence with these elements is impossible for us."[37]

In the south, the Radical Party was also afflicted by disputes and divisions. The Cadiz party, having failed to win a parliamentary seat in the 1933 election (it had cornered five in 1931), suffered numerous splits in 1934, but, following the October risings, the Radicals, with the partisan backing of the civil governor, Luis de Armiñán, again assumed a prominent role in the province as opposition *ayuntamientos* and other bodies were overthrown to the party's advantage. None the less, throughout 1935 the party was plagued by internal conflicts. The Sevillian party was striken by a multitude of defections, too. One of its most prestigious figures, Manuel de Terán, abandoned the party in June on the grounds that it had become "a pretence . . . without collective ends, amorphous". The Alicante party, having done reasonably well in both general elections, was also beset by splits and mass resignations throughout 1935.[38] An outstanding illustration of the unravelling of the Radical Party in 1935 is provided by the Badajoz organization. For most of the second biennium, the Radical Party controlled 157 of the province's 162 local councils. In 1935, however, the party was simply overwhelmed by events. As the Radical deputy Diego Hidalgo wrote to José Carlos de Luna, the civil governor, the provincial committee consisted of "old men" who were "hardly practical", while the Radical mayor of Badajoz was "old" and "somewhat slow". Numerous schisms took place as supporters flooded into the CEDA. "Rare is the *pueblo*," Luna noted in the summer of 1935, "in which the party finds itself united."[39]

The disunity and disorientation within the Radical ranks was in large measure due to the unremitting pressure of the *Cedistas* for ever greater power. The Radical deputy for the north African enclave of Ceuta, Tomás Peire, informed Lerroux in August of the CEDA's "attitude of open hostility towards our party" and of "the continuous attacks and malicious comments that . . . they direct incessantly at our people". If these did not cease, he warned, "the absolute rupture and separation between both parties in Ceuta will be unavoidable in the very near future". "This is one more symptom," he observed, "of the many that are appearing in other places." Indeed, Ramón Salgado denounced the CEDA before the parliamentary party for the "enormous preponderance" which it had acquired since the reshuffle in May 1935. "All the posts are for their members", he exclaimed. Any recommendation of the Radical Party, "because it's from the latter, is not heeded". While admitting that the CEDA had secured "many minor positions", the Radical leader defended the arrangement on the grounds that the accidentalists had not obtained a single civil governor.[40] This did not mean, however, that the governorships were not a constant source of dispute between the two parties. In August, for example, it was rumoured that the civil governor of Ciudad Real was about to be replaced. A mayor from the province promptly urged the Radical Prime Minister not to allow the governor to be removed on the grounds that he was "the man required" and that his influence, along with that of the local deputy Francisco Morayta, had ensured that 90 per cent of Ciudad Real's *pueblos* had Radical branches. Alarm also swept through the Almeria party as a result of the efforts there to replace the civil governor with a CEDA member. "The desire of all the Radicals", the governor himself wrote to Lerroux, is "to maintain the political hegemony" of the party and to avoid "the definitive defeat of Almerian republicanism, today flourishing and solid", while the president of the Radical provincial committee denounced "the deplorable game of intrigues and disloyalties" of the *Cedistas* in relation to the civil governorship. "All that is organized in our party", he insisted, "and, as a result, its future life, is endangered". The Radical president, for whom not a single *Cedista* in Almeria could be described as a republican, lambasted the party's allies as "our worst enemies".[41]

One of the greatest bones of contention between the Radicals and their "worst enemies" was that control of the civil governors had ensured the Radical Party's sway over many of the steering committees nominated in the wake of the October risings. In Andalusia, for example, ferocious disputes between the Radicals and *Cedistas* over the distribution of seats within the committees were a constant feature of the political landscape. In Seville, Radical leader Moreno Calvo, backed by the civil governor, Manuel Asensi, refused as a general principle to grant the CEDA more than 30 per cent of the seats. Naturally, this permitted the Radicals to swell their clientage base while undermining support for their increasingly frantic allies. In a report drawn up in November 1934 for the CEDA leadership, two Cadiz deputies protested that they were no longer able to "resist the pressure" of their rank and file, especially as the Radicals were "making fun of us, with the oldest and most discredited underhand methods of politics". Such was the tension between the two that the CEDA broke off all relations with the provincial Radical leader and the civil governor while demanding from Gil Robles "a share in *all* the nominations".[42]

The last thing that the strife-ridden Radical Party would have wanted at this stage was the dissolution of the Cortes. This was a lurking fear upon which the CEDA leader had repeatedly played. On 1 September, he declared before a JAP rally in Santiago de Compostela that he aspired to the "total revision" of the Constitution. If, he added menacingly, the Cortes did not accede, "they are a dead Cortes which must disappear" – a task which he, personally, would undertake by forcing their dissolution. The authoritarian tone of the meeting was heightened by Gil Robles's delirious dreams of empire. The CEDA *caudillo*, in a rhetoric that echoed that of Mussolini or Hitler, and against the background of the burgeoning

Italo-Abyssinian conflict, bragged of "the superiority of our religion, of the superiority of our language, of the superiority of our culture and of our spirit". Such sentiments scarcely entitled the CEDA to Lerroux's description of it as "the republican right". On the contrary, the style and content of the rally were outwardly fascistic. Equally, Gil Robles's bombastic threats against the Constitution, underpinned by the assertion that his party "controls parliament", hardly vouched for the party's democratic character.[43]

That the *Cedistas*, despite the jactitations of their *jefe*, were not masters of the situation was to be demonstrated by the Cabinet crisis of 20–25 September. Lerroux's fifth administration, in addition to the differences over constitutional reform, the electoral system, a new press law, the public works' budget, and the distribution of power and patronage in the provinces, had been divided, too, over Catalan autonomy. This ongoing tension culminated, on 19 September, in the resignation of the Agrarian Minister of the Navy, the fervent anti-Catalanist Antonio Royo Villanova over the transfer to the Catalan authorities of the control of the state highways. Partly out of solidarity, but also as a result of the rift with Gil Robles over wheat policy, fellow Agrarian Nicasio Velayos, the Agriculture Minister, stepped down as well. The Prime Minister, having lost the backing of the Agrarians, felt obliged to present his own resignation.[44] Inexplicably, the President, rather than ratify his confidence in Lerroux, turned to Santiago Alba, the speaker of the Cortes, thus making him the third Radical politician other than the party leader to be invited to form a government. Having constituted a Cabinet on the evening of the 23rd, Alba, following a consultation "with the pillow", desisted, much to the chagrin of his *jefe*, on the morning of the 24th, largely because neither Melquiades Alvarez nor Martínez de Velasco would provide him with the ministers he solicited. The next prime ministerial candidate was the President's long-time friend and political ally, Martínez de Velasco, but, lacking ambition, he proved unwilling to assemble an administration. Alcalá-Zamora then called on Joaquín Chapaprieta, the erstwhile Minister of the Economy, to undertake the task. Chapaprieta, who headed a small group of republican independents in the Cortes, baulked at the offer on the grounds that he could not count on the majority parties. As Prime Minister, he would find himself in the unusual position of being, he observed drily, "completely alone".[45] Undeterred, the President indicated that he would bring the Cortes to an end if the parties did not cooperate. Begrudgingly, Lerroux and Gil Robles, both of whom feared a dissolution under Alcalá-Zamora's favourite, Manuel Portela, acceded. Obviously aware that he could not rule without the adherence of those forces that had made up the previous administration, Chapaprieta was especially concerned to appease the Radicals, for whom the removal of their *jefe* from the premiership was a grave and unexpected blow. Having obtained

Lerroux's approval, Chapaprieta duly approached Santiago Alba for the high-profile post of Minister of the Interior but he, embittered by the lack of assistance for his own Cabinet initiative, bluntly turned him down. The Prime Minister-to-be therefore considered Joaquín de Pablo-Blanco, who, though he had renounced his seat following the May reshuffle, was still a member of the Radical Party. This choice was endorsed, if unenthusiastically, by the Radical leader as De Pablo-Blanco was a *persona grata* of the President – indeed, Alcalá-Zamora had originally recommended him to Chapaprieta. As a means of compensation, the "indispensable" Rocha was appointed Minister of Education. To Chapaprieta's dismay, the Radical chief himself now withdrew from the Cabinet. Having originally refused to join, and then been persuaded otherwise by Gil Robles, Lerroux had since come under considerable pressure from the parliamentary group not to collaborate with Chapaprieta at all, or at the very least not to become a minister. He had subsequently lapsed into a "great depression". Such symptoms of incipient Radical resistance, together with the unwelcome appointment of De Pablo-Blanco, made it more imperative than ever for Chapaprieta to include the Radical leader. Only by threatening not to form an administration at all was Chapaprieta able to persuade him to participate. Still, Chapaprieta's doubts in relation to the Radicals led him to buttress the government by incorporating a minister from the Lliga. The Cabinet, in accordance with Chapaprieta's own administrative reforms, possessed nine as opposed to thirteen ministries, of whom three were for the Radicals, three for the CEDA, and one each for the Agrarians and Lliga, while Chapaprieta retained the Ministry of the Economy in order to oversee his prized economic projects. The *Cedistas*, partly to avoid a dissolution but also to accommodate the Radicals, had accepted a slight reduction in their ministerial presence, but at least Portela, Alcalá-Zamora's key ally, whose inclusion had been vigorously opposed by Lerroux and Gil Robles, had been dropped.[46]

The new Prime Minister, who was distinguished by his small stature and outsized head, was intimately identified, both personally and ideologically, with the right. From the outset he was noticeably dependent on Gil Robles, whom he would met on virtually a daily basis as well as briefing him before Cabinet meetings, to the extent that the CEDA leader knew "all my thoughts and there's no need to say my plans and projects". Similarly, the premier's relationship with Martínez de Velasco was of an "absolute understanding". By contrast, Chapaprieta had little time for the Radicals. Not only had he crossed swords with them in his home province of Alicante, but he also claims to have harboured grave ethical doubts about them. In fact, he had rebuffed the blandishments of Lerroux to enter the Radical Party on several occasions since the advent of the Republic. The upshot of the reshuffle, therefore, was that the right still retained a firm grip on the Cabinet.[47]

On the surface, the Cabinet reshuffle appeared to be yet another demonstration of the President's Machiavellian prowess. After all, Alcalá-Zamora, in appointing a premier that owed his position to the President rather than to parliament, had increased his leverage over the government. There was, however, an additional motive. On asking Chapaprieta to form the administration, Alcalá-Zamora divulged that Lerroux could not continue as premier on account of the corruption of his "relatives and friends". He did not proffer any details, nor did Chapaprieta, despite the enormity of this decision and his own alleged reluctance to become premier, probe any further.[48] By contrast, the Radical leader was all too aware of what the President was referring to. Not long after the "Day of Lerroux", possibly 16 September,[49] the President had confronted him over a dossier, dated 5 September, which had been dispatched from Holland by a certain Daniel Strauss.[50] Together with Joaquín Gasa, the owner of the Olympia Theatre in Barcelona, Strauss had promoted the heavyweight boxing match the year before between the Spaniard Paulino Uzcudun and the German Max Schmeling. According to the 26-page account sent to the President, in May 1934 Gasa had introduced Strauss to the Radical boss in Catalonia, Juan Pich y Pon, who in turn had presented him, in Madrid, to Aurelio Lerroux, the adopted son of the Radical leader. There, Strauss had proceeded to give a demonstration in the exclusive Hotel Ritz – where he was staying – of a game, the "Straperlo" (a neologism forged from the names of the two inventors, Strauss and Perla). Looking much like a roulette wheel, the "Straperlo" none the less differed insofar as it did not depend on chance; on the contrary, the number on which the spinning ball eventually rested could be calculated. The inventors claimed that, despite appearances, the game was profitable because in the hubbub of a crowded casino hall people made hasty estimates which often proved erroneous. Strauss asserts that the dry-run at the Ritz was witnessed not only by Pich y Pon and Aurelio Lerroux but also by Miguel Galante, the former soldier at the Radical leader's estate on the night of the "Sanjurjada" who was a crony of Aurelio, as well as Gasa, and Uzcudun. Aurelio Lerroux himself proposed to obtain the necessary licence from the authorities – a far from straightforward matter as gaming had been banned prior to the Primo de Rivera Dictatorship – by exploiting his contacts within the party, starting with his father and Salazar Alonso, the Minister of the Interior. Pich y Pon undertook to pay 100,000 pesetas to Salazar Alonso and 50,000 to his under-secretary, Eduardo Benzo, in order to secure their cooperation, while Galante would persuade José Valdivia, a close personal friend, who, as Director General of Security, would be responsible for the technical and legal reports that were essential for the game's authorization, by slipping him 50,000 pesetas. Galante himself would receive another 50,000. A contract establishing a company to exploit the "Straperlo" in Spain was subsequently drawn up in June 1934 between Strauss, Pich y Pon, Gasa, and Uzcudun. At the Radical *jefe*'s San Rafael estate, Strauss adds, it was agreed that Alejandro Lerroux would receive 25 per cent of the profits and Pich 10 per cent, while Aurelio Lerroux, Galante, and the journalist Santiago Vinardell, another crony of Aurelio, would obtain 5 per cent each. Strauss then gave a further demonstration to Salazar Alonso and Benzo at the Ministry of the Interior. In the meantime, Sigfrido Blasco Ibáñez, the PURA leader, spoke to the Prime Minister, fellow *Blasquista* Ricardo Samper, who promised his collaboration in exchange for 400,000 pesetas. On 25 August 1934, Strauss, on the suggestion of Aurelio Lerroux, bought Salazar Alonso a gold watch just like the one he had already purchased for Alejandro Lerroux. That same day, Salazar Alonso, having received both the watch and the Prime Minister's consent, signed the authorization.

On 12 September 1934, the "Straperlo" was finally unveiled at the San Sebastian Casino, Strauss having spent "a fortune" refurbishing it. Three hours later, a pistol-brandishing policeman charged into the crowded Casino in order to bring the game to a halt. It later emerged that this had been done on the orders of the civil governor, Emeterio Muga, himself acting on a telephone call from the Minister of the Interior, Salazar Alonso. Strauss alleges that he was told by an associate of Aurelio Lerroux that Salazar Alonso would not have prohibited the game had he been paid "a healthy sum". Following the fiasco at the Basque resort, Strauss relates that Aurelio assured him that his father would authorize the game as soon as he returned to power. Once Lerroux had regained the premiership in early October, his son informed Strauss that his father had instructed both Vaquero, the new Minister of the Interior, and Benzo, to grant the authorization. Another contract was thereby drawn up between Strauss, Gasa, Uzcudun, and Aurelio Lerroux (though the latter's name does not appear on the document). Already, arrangements were under way for the game to be introduced on the island of Mallorca with the connivance of the civil governor. The collusion of Diego Hidalgo, the Minister of War, and of General Franco, military governor of Baleares, was also secured. The collaboration of the military authorities was fully assured once Lerroux added the War portfolio to the premiership. The "Straperlo", following another costly outlay by Strauss, opened in mid October at the Hotel Formentor but, eight days later, the operation was again aborted on the orders of the Ministry of the Interior. It was later established that Vaquero had acted on the protest of the CEDA leader, who had been tipped off by a local deputy. Although 3,000 people had passed through the casino, Strauss insists that he had run up an "immense deficit". Altogether, Strauss claims that the débâcle of the "Straperlo" in Spain had cost him eight months' work, two major contracts in Brussels, and "much more" than half a million pesetas. Had he met all the Radicals' demands for bribes, he insists, he would have forfeited at least two million pesetas. "In other words," he laments, "it's a real catastrophe." Nor had he heard anything since from either Aurelio Lerroux, the chief fixer, or Eduardo Benzo, the under-secretary at the Interior Ministry. In the meantime, he was seeking compensation and expenses from Alejandro Lerroux of 425,000 pesetas. That is to say, two premiers, three ministers, a brace of junior ministers and the head of state security had allegedly been bribed, and two casinos completely refurbished, for around half a million pesetas. Enclosed in Strauss's dossier were the 1934 contracts, receipts for the gold watches, as well as a number of letters, press clippings, and photos.

Far from denying Strauss's charges to Alcalá-Zamora, Lerroux retorted that it was not his role to defend those implicated and that, in any case, it would be difficult to prove any direct contact between himself and Strauss.[51] He added that similar accusations could be levelled at Indalecio Prieto, the socialist leader.[52] Two days later, the President broached the subject again. On this occasion, the premier revealed that he had been sent the dossier early in the year, probably in January,[53] and that he had endeavoured to strike a deal with Strauss's Paris-based lawyer, Henri Torres, but had failed. Lerroux concluded by dismissing the affair, to Alcalá-Zamora's consternation, with contempt.[54] The President replied that "these things worry me a great deal", and that he was concerned that the matter might be raised in parliament. The Radical *jefe*'s reaction, Alcalá-Zamora would later claim, had made a Cabinet reshuffle "inevitable". For his part, the Prime Minister suspected a "manoeuvre" of the President, noting that he "was in a hurry".[55]

Once the Cabinet fell in September, the Radical *jefe* realized that the President, having avoided asking him to head up another government and in view of the deleterious state of their relationship, might well use Strauss's accusation against the Radical Party. Before a new administration emerged, Lerroux disclosed the matter to the party's ministers and former ministers. Fears that the issue might develop into a scandal were fuelled by speculation in the opposition press that the real reason for the change in government was not the dispute over Catalan Autonomy but "a shady affair". Additional precautionary measures were taken by the Radical leader at a meeting of the parliamentary group on 26 September when it was agreed not only that the party should be reorganized but also that a national congress should be celebrated as soon as possible (Radical congresses, it would seem, were held not in keeping with the party's regulations but at the leader's behest). On 1 October, Prime Minister Chapaprieta, in his account before the Cortes of the recent reshuffle, did not mention the Strauss affair. Yet the whiff of scandal was already in the air. Basilio Alvarez inquired "if Don Alejandro did not commit a political offence, why was he demoted in the hierarchy? And if he committed an offence, why does he continue with a portfolio?". At the meeting of the parliamentary group held to decide whether or not it should vote for the government, there were calls to withdraw from the ruling coalition along with outspoken criticism of the CEDA. But the *jefe*, having praised the "absolute loyalty" of his principal ally, quelled the rebellion by indicating that the party should back the Chapaprieta administration.[56]

Only now, during the first days of October, did the President disclose the details of the Strauss dossier to the Prime Minister. Chapaprieta was horrified. Had he known of the affair beforehand, he would not have formed a government, and, if he had, Lerroux would not have been included in it. The Prime Minister noted that Strauss's letter was not only written in native Spanish but also that it revealed an intimate knowledge of domestic politics. There was no doubt in his mind that "rancorous political motives" lay behind the letter and that it was deliberately designed to create a "huge scandal". Alcalá-Zamora, having avoided informing Chapaprieta before precisely in order to get him to head a government, now asked the premier how he should proceed. The Prime Minister replied that the appropriate legal channel for a redress was the courts, not the presidency, that the motive for the action was clearly polit-ical, not legal, and that Strauss, a figure unknown in Spain and an adventurer, was not to be trusted. He recommended that the case be shelved, to which the President agreed "without reserve". Alcalá-Zamora, having successfully dislodged Lerroux from the premiership – as he had done in April 1934 and tried, but failed, to do with Azaña in June 1933 – was apparently content to take the issue no further. The Radicals, it seemed, had been saved from a potential scandal.[57]

Everything was to change as a result of a homage held for the Radical leader on 9 October. Organized by his party, the event, which took the form of a banquet at the Hotel Ritz, embraced the entire Cabinet as well as numerous deputies. As a show of support for the erstwhile premier the homage embodied an implicit criticism, if not rebuke, of the President. Both Chapaprieta and Gil Robles opposed the accolade as an unnecessary provocation to the extraordinarily suspectible Alcalá-Zamora, but an aggrieved Lerroux would not hear of cancelling it. The Cabinet therefore attended the celebration so as not to damage the ruling coalition. At the banquet, Gil Robles proclaimed supportively that "it's easy to fall into errors and weaknesses" but that these could be forgiven when, like Lerroux, "one has loved a great deal". He then embraced the Radical leader effusively. The Radical *jefe*, in toasting the President – and in stark contrast to the glowing eulogy dedicated to him in Valencia three months earlier – drew a none-too-subtle distinction between the person and the position. Alcalá-Zamora, as Chapaprieta dreaded, was mortified.[58] At the Cabinet meeting the following day the President set upon the Prime Minister, Lerroux recalls, "like a wolf on a lamb"; he "confronted" Gil Robles, and, finally, he attacked the Radical leader in the "most passionate" way.[59] Much more damagingly, Alcalá-Zamora informed

Chapaprieta that, having reflected further on the Strauss case, he had decided to pass it on to the Cabinet. Once again, the Prime Minister urged Alcalá-Zamora to ignore the matter, but to no avail. At a meeting on 12 October between Chapaprieta, Gil Robles, Martínez de Velasco, and Alcalá-Zamora, the latter, despite the pleadings of the Prime Minister and CEDA leader to return, shelve, or destroy the Strauss dossier, was, if anything, even more adamant about handing it over to the government.[60] All of which suggests that Lerroux's banquet barb was a terrible blunder. Alcalá-Zamora's request to see Giménez Fernández in relation to an "extremely important and urgent" matter on the day of the banquet, and then to reveal the existence of the complaint, would appear to confirm the impression that, having exploited the incriminating documentation to remove Lerroux from the premiership, it was only now that he was prepared to act further on the case.[61]

The implications of the President's change of tack were digested at the meeting of the three majority leaders with Alcalá-Zamora on the 12th. They concluded that Lerroux and Rocha would have to leave the Cabinet, that this would force the Lerrouxist loyalists into opposition, but that the bulk of the Radical Party would still support the government, thereby guaranteeing its survival. Privately, and more realistically, the Prime Minister speculated that the Radicals would make it impossible for him to complete his economic reform programme. On 18 October the Cabinet agreed, unanimously, to send the Strauss file on to the prosecutor's office at the Supreme Court. However, the President, nervous that the issue might be raised in the Cortes and, in common with Chapaprieta and Gil Robles, that Azaña, in his major speech at Comillas two days later, would expose the Strauss imbroglio, urged the government to act. Later that same day, the Cabinet issued a low-key statement, declaring that it had received "a complaint" against "certain persons" as a result of "supposed irregularities", and that this had been passed on to the prosecutor.[62] The impact, as Lerroux foresaw, was "enormous". The story had broken. As a result, Azaña made no more than a slight allusion to it in his speech. Worse, indeed, was to come.[63]

Two days after the Comillas speech, on 22 October, the Cortes debated Strauss's claims.[64] Lerroux implicated Azaña by quoting from a letter of 30 June 1935 from Strauss to Luis de Guzmán, a trusted collaborator and friend of the Izquierda Republicana leader, in which he declared that the matter was of "paramount importance. Above all for Azaña". In reply, the Radical leader disclosed, Guzmán affirmed that it was indeed of great "political" interest, but his colleagues reserved the right to use the information when they saw fit. Nevertheless, Lerroux, who later admitted that "in two hours I lived a hundred years", did not press his case. In particular, he failed to replicate the wealth of detail concerning the opposition's involvement which he had presented that very morning to the Cabinet.[65]

Instead, having denounced the whole affair as a "great intrigue", he made it clear that the "conjectures" of "blackmailers" and "intriguers" were not worthy of a reply. He took no further part in the proceedings. Nor did any other Radical unmask the alleged conspiracy. On the contrary, the Radical deputies undertook a damage limitation exercise by pleading that any misdemeanours, which they were "the first ones interested" in clarifying, should be restricted to the individuals concerned and not affect the entire party.[66] Both the extreme right and the left, eager to undermine the governing bloc by discrediting the Radicals, pressed for a parliamentary commission, to which the Prime Minister agreed straightaway. Meanwhile, the CEDA hurriedly distanced itself from the Radicals, claiming that it was interested only in the truth.[67]

The very next day, 23 October, the commission set to work. It was discovered that Strauss was a "skilful conman" who had fled Mexico eight years earlier following the exposure of "various dirty business deals", including the alleged robbery of a diamond worth $3000.[68] The "Straperlo", it also transpired, had already been successfully exploited by Strauss at three Dutch resorts in the summer of 1933. Both Emeterio Muga, the civil governor for Guipuzcoa, and Rafael Picavea, a local deputy, clarified that repeated efforts to reintroduce gambling into San Sebastian, a potentially lucrative source of income for the Basque resort, had been foiled. Picavea swore that Strauss had told him that he had obtained the licence because of his "friends" and "influence". Documents in the power of the commission disclosed, too, that the Minister of the Interior, Salazar Alonso, had authorized the "Straperlo" on 25 August 1934 on the grounds that, as an internal judicial report of 13 June 1934 concluded, it was not one of "luck, betting, nor chance" and, therefore, did not violate the extant legislation. Salazar Alonso now admitted that it "could be" that he had given his conformity, but stressed that he had not intended the "Straperlo" to be deployed as a "betting game". At the commission's disposal was a handwritten note of the Minister, dated 3 September, which overturned the decision of 25 August as well as instructing the civil governors to ban the game. This order, however, was not to be implemented, according to the note scrawled on it by the Director General of Security, José Valdivia, until 15 September – that is to say, three days after the game had been unveiled in San Sebastian. Salazar Alonso's order of 3 September, in consequence, appeared to be a retrospective act. The "Straperlo", Muga revealed, had been approved for use in the San Sebastian Casino after he had consulted Eduardo Benzo, the Ministry's under-secretary, who, none the less, denied this. More perplexing still, the Ministry of the Interior, in response to the commission's probings, stated that there was no record of an application from Strauss. Salazar Alonso's authorization, in sum, would seem to have been fraudulent. As far as the Straperlo's eight-day run in Palma de Mallorca was concerned, a CEDA deputy, Luis Zaforteza, claimed that despite the eye-catching adverts in the local press, including the offer of free transportation to the Hotel Formentor from all over the island, the civil governor had done nothing to halt it. However, the Minister of the Interior, Eloy Vaquero, had stopped the "Straperlo" as soon as it had been brought to his attention by the CEDA leader, Gil Robles.[69]

The verdict of the commission, following an all-night sitting, was delivered at 7 a.m. on 26 October. It confirmed the existence of acts not in accord with the "austerity and ethics" expected of those in public office. The CEDA criteria that responsibility should be limited to the accused, as opposed to their party, was adopted by the commission, but a Radical motion that no one should be declared guilty until proven otherwise did not prosper. The government promptly dismissed all those under suspicion from their public positions. On 28 October parliament debated the commission's findings. In his defence, the Radical leader again assumed a self-righteous posture. Whatever the Cortes and the courts decided, he asserted, the Radical Party would take the measures necessary to satisy "its conscience". Once more, he failed to reveal the nature and extent of the left-wing plot against the Radical Party. In effect, he threw himself on the mercy of the ruling majority by defending it as the "only possible instrument". Yet the martyr's role adopted by Lerroux was unlikely, in the circumstances, to find much favour with the house. Nor was the performance of Salazar Alonso, who continued to maintain that he did not sign the original authorization, any better. Blasco Ibáñez's intervention was more feeble still. The CEDA, determined above all to demonstrate their "unimpeachable conduct", offered the Radicals little succour. The Cortes condemned Blasco Ibáñez by 190 votes to 70. Salazar Alonso was more fortunate. Although lacking the unanimous backing of the Radicals, he was zealously defended by the CEDA and extreme right, including both José Calvo Sotelo and José Antonio Primo de Rivera. At least this was one issue on which all the forces of the right could agree. The former minister was thereby saved by a mere three votes – 140 to 137. The remaining Radicals lost the verdict by 166 votes to 14, the party having abandoned the chamber.[70]

The next day Lerroux and Rocha, whose brother was tangentially involved in the affair, resigned from the Cabinet.[71] The President again turned to Chapaprieta to constitute a new government. The subsequent consultations exposed the disorientation within the Radical camp. Santiago Alba informed the premier that Lerroux had made him the party's plenipotenciary for the reshuffle, but Chapaprieta, on establishing contact with the Radical *jefe*, discovered that this was not the case. Further, Alba, in defiance of the Prime Minister's instructions, failed to inform his leader of the three Radicals to be appointed to the Cabinet. By the time Lerroux found out, the Cabinet list had already been drawn up.

A disgusted parliamentary group approved two of the ministers – those of the state lawyer Luis Bardají to the Ministry of Education and of the engineer Juan Usabiaga to Agriculture, Industry and Commerce – but dissented from that of De Pablo-Blanco, partly because it was felt that he should have resigned in solidarity with his Radical colleagues and partly because he was seen as an agent of Alcalá-Zamora. From the outset, therefore, Chapaprieta's second administration lacked the full support of the Radicals.[72]

Judicial investigation of the Straperlo affair, initiated on 6 November 1935 by the special magistrate, Ildefonso Bellón, shows that there can be little doubt as to the cupidity of the Radical leader's coterie. Two groups were essentially involved: a section of the Barcelona old guard, headed by the inevitable Juan Pich y Pon, and "the Aurelio Clan". This motley crew, otherwise known as "the Customs Post" (as it controlled access to the Radical leader), included Miguel Galante, José Valdivia, Santiago Vinardell, and Sigfrido Blasco Ibáñez.[73] What united these two gangs was, of course, the Godfather-like figure of Alejandro Lerroux. "All in the family", as Strauss put it.[74] Others had also colluded in the scam, most notably Rafael Salazar Alonso. According to the evidence amassed by the magistrate, Salazar Alonso signed the authorization of 25 August 1934, despite his later claim that this had been forged. Moreover, he himself pointed out under interrogation by Bellón that the handwritten note of 3 September had in fact been drawn up on the 13th – that is to say, once the public outcry over the game's introduction in San Sebastian had prompted him to ban it. In other words, Salazar Alonso acted *after*, not before, the event.[75] In this regard, the Straperlo affair was a perfect illustration of Emiliano Iglesias' observation that the vigilance of the press and parliament meant that "there's no way to do anything". Furthermore, having denied before the commission that he did not know who was behind the "Straperlo", Salazar Alonso admitted that he had spoken to Aurelio Lerroux of the device on at least one occasion. At best, the former minister was covering up for the Radical leader, to whom he was fiercely loyal, at worst he was a willing collaborator in the entire enterprise.[76] Nor can there be any doubt that Lerroux was – at the very least – abreast of developments. That such a racket, involving, amongst others, Pich y Pon, Blasco Ibáñez, Salazar Alonso, and, above all, his own son, was not known to the Radical leader is extremely difficult to credit. In all likelihood, the *jefe* was not only well aware of what was afoot, but also expected his cut.

Invariably characterized as a "Jewish Dutch adventurer" by Spanish contemporaries and many historians since, Daniel Strauss was, in fact, neither Dutch, nor, so he claimed in a public letter of 4 January 1936, a Jew.[77] In any case, as Lerroux, to his credit, pointed out in parliament, "it's the same to me whether he's a Jew or a Christian".[78] Strauss, who was in his mid forties, was in reality of German origin and had been nationalized as a Mexican.[79] On the other hand, he was certainly an "adventurer". Having fled Mexico under a cloud, he had then become embroiled in further illicit dealings in Denmark. These culminated in the "Monte Carlo" affair of November 1931 in Flensburg, which resulted in two trials, both of which he lost. As a result, he switched his operations to Holland and from there branched out into Spain.[80] The Straperlo, in short, was merely the latest in a series of scandals for the wheeler-dealing Strauss.

Undoubtedly the Straperlo case was not an isolated instance of venality for the Radical Party, either. Both Alcalá-Zamora and Chapaprieta were first-hand witnesses to the Radical leader's money-making machinations. For example, the President was scandalized to discover in 1935 that Lerroux, as Prime Minister, intended to benefit personally from a national subscription set up in the wake of the October 1934 risings. The wily Lerroux assured Alcalá-Zamora that he would only accept those donations from Radical supporters, while the rest of the money would be used for "a particular purpose". What this was, however, the President never found out. In fact, half a million pesetas from the subscription ended up in the Radical *jefe*'s own "particular" pocket. Two other schemes, one of which would have brought admininistrative services and public works under the personal direction of the Prime Minister's office and another which involved arms sales, were nipped in the bud by the President, according to his own account. In a similar vein, Chapaprieta found, on becoming premier, that his predecessor had not accounted for all the money withdrawn from the so-called "reserve funds". Nor did he adequately justify the expenditure of nearly a million pesetas from a second fund. On the contrary, only days before leaving office, he had paid out 90,000 pesetas to Miguel Galante, the sidekick of Aurelio, and to members of his office. Such doings were perhaps not so much illegal as irregular. A more blatant example of Lerrouxist venality concerned the state tobacco company, the Compañía Arrendataria de Tabacos. Each year this purchased a quantity of Cuban tobacco by auction. It so happened that the Radical leader's secretary, Antonio Sánchez Fuster, was the agent for a Cuban company that aspired to the Spanish government contract. Sánchez Fuster, having gained access to the Prime Minister with the aid of a lengthy letter from his *jefe*, divulged that the company's real representative was none other than Lerroux himself. To twist the Prime Minister's arm even further, Sánchez Fuster added that the contract was of vital importance to his employer as he was on the verge of bankruptcy. Gil Robles, too, was well aware of the Radicals' improprieties. He, for instance, joined the Cabinet of May 1935 having vetoed the participation of Rafael Guerra del Río as a result of the alleged aberrations regarding a railway contract. Radical sources, if anything, tend to confirm this picture.

Emiliano Iglesias complained to the monarchist politician Pedro Sainz Rodríguez in 1934 that it was extremely difficult "to do business in the present circumstances". Once in exile, the Radical leader confessed not only that the party had attracted numerous arrivistes, but also that such individuals had characterized his inner circle. He explained, by way of example, that if he ordered twelve shirts, only four would find their way to his wardrobe as the other eight would be pilfered along the way by his intimates! The Radical Party, Martínez Barrio affirms, was set apart from the other republican parties by a "moral climate" which he vividly described as a "bad smelling and abject plague".[81]

In *La pequeña historia* Lerroux counters that there were innumerable cases of corruption, involving everything from the supply of oil from Russia, the arms trade, the construction of barracks, agricultural produce such as rice and oranges, the colonies, the customs posts, to greyhound racing and wheat imports, to which the President had turned a blind eye. In particular, he points the finger at Indalecio Prieto. Accusations levelled at the socialist leader in 1932 that he had favoured his business ally, Horacio Echevarrieta, in relation to a government contract were, it is true, never investigated as a result of the Azaña administration's refusal. Moreover, Alcalá-Zamora was aware that the socialists had illegally procurred 25,000 pesetas towards the purchase of a printing press for *El Socialista*. He suspected, too, that wrongdoings had been committed during the first biennium at the Ministry of Agriculture.[82] The available, if scant, evidence – this being a subject that has scarcely been scrutinized – indicates that the Radicals differed from the other republican parties if not in kind, then at least by degree. Public funds were originally plundered by Lerroux during the 1900s in order to finance his party (a thoroughly modern initiative, it has to be said). For some Radicals, however, politics became a source of personal enrichment – the business of politics as business, to rephrase Calvin Coolidge. The Barcelona Radicals in particular never purged themselves of the party's venal origins. For the likes of Juan Pich y Pon, the republican motto of "liberty, equality, fraternity" was interpreted, as César Jalón puts it, "in the sense of making themselves free, equal and brothers of Morgan or Rockefeller".[83] In this respect, the Radical Party possibly had more in common with the dynastic parties than the republican ones, though more research is required before any firm conclusions can be reached.

Yet how extensive was the corruption within the Radical Party? To start with, this embraced both the Barcelona and Valencia parties. Indeed, the PURA was rocked in the summer of 1935 by a scandal concerning a contract for the construction of primary schools. Like the Straperlo scam, this never prospered due its exposure by the press. Both the Barcelona Radicals and the *Blasquistas* were linked to the Mallorcan magnate Juan March, as were, according to Martínez Barrio, a number of leading individuals within the party such as Manuel Marraco and Tomás Peire. None the less, the extent of the party's graft should not be exaggerated. The CEDA leader judges that this affected a "sector" within the Radical Party, while Chapaprieta limits it to Lerroux's "intimates" and "relatives". Martínez Barrio, who had good reason to magnify the scale of the party's malpractices as this was a major motive for his dissidence, reckons that "not even a major part of the leaders" was implicated. Similarly, Alcalá-Zamora, no friend of the Radicals, asserts that "the great majority, if not almost the totality" were clean.[84] It should be stressed that Emiliano Iglesias' transgressions in relation to the Commission of Responsibilities in 1931 were originally denounced by a fellow Radical from Catalonia. Equally, the PURA leader Ricardo Samper was untouched by the Strauss affair, despite being Prime Minister at the time. In any case, the Straperlo racket, which was scuppered before it could flourish, amounted in the end to no more than a bunch of bribes. Not without reason, the special investigating magistrate for the Strauss case, Ildefonso Bellón, concluded that, in comparison with the Stavisky affair in France of 1934, it was "small change".[85] Of this there can be little doubt. Stavisky had been murdered in January 1934 in order to cover up the fact that the forged bonds which he had been floating on the Paris stock exchange had benefited leading Radical politicians. This sparked right-wing demonstrations which prompted the fall of Chautemps' government. Further protests followed on 6 February as a result of the decision of the incoming premier, Daladier, to sack the conservative Prefect of the Paris Police. At the demonstration, over a dozen people were killed and more than two hundred were wounded, causing Daladier's fall the next day. The tragedy, which stimulated fears on the left that the right would attempt an insurrectionary takeover, triggered the process which culminated in the formation of the "Popular Front". The question to be asked, therefore, is why the relatively insignificant Strauss case had such far-reaching consequences, above all for the Radical Party.[86]

The transformation of this modest episode into a scandal of national proportions is inseparable from the manner in which it was exposed. First, the left-wing opposition played a fundamental role in the unfolding of the drama. The conspiracy, the Radical leader later claimed, was hatched at a meeting between Strauss, Indalecio Prieto, Azaña, De Guzmán, and a friend of Alcalá-Zamora at the Brussels Exhibition. This is lent a certain credibility by the President's admission that a friend of his saw Prieto in September.[87] What is more, during the summer of 1935 Azaña travelled to France, Belgium and Holland. Chronology, however, is not on Lerroux's side. Azaña left Madrid around 10 September – in other words, once the claim had been sent. On the other hand, he did hold "mysterious meetings" during his month-long trip, according to the Prime Minister's sources, as well as establishing contact with Strauss or a representative of his. In any case, Azaña's aide-de-camp, De Guzmán, had already been in touch with Strauss by correspondence. It is also known that the republican leader met the exiled Prieto during the second half of September. Spanish diplomatic staff established that the socialist leader, who was based in Belgium, had been in contact with Strauss, or his collaborators, during the summer of 1935.[88] In all likelihood, the exiled socialist had urged Strauss to send his documentation directly to the President. It also appears that Prieto had composed the claim – right down to the idiosyncratic grammatical errors.[89] That the document does not mention the early efforts to promote the Straperlo via the Esquerra, while constantly stretching the evidence in order to implicate the Radical leader, heightens this impression. In fact, both the President and Prime Minister believed that Prieto was the key figure behind the operation. This made it a politically-motivated matter from the outset. The fact that Strauss' Parisian lawyer, Henri Torres, was a left-wing parliamentary deputy who was well connected to the Spanish left, having acted for the Esquerra leader Francesc Macià as well as having raised money for the Asturian workers following the October 1934 insurrection, was probably not unrelated.[90] The left, therefore, played a central part in the scandal not only by bringing it directly to the attention of the President but also by choosing the timing of its exposure. Ironically, this was just the kind of behind-the-scenes intrigue that Azaña, in his diary, repeatedly laments in relation to the Radicals. Nor did this prevent the left from occupying the moral high-ground throughout the Straperlo debate. For the forces of the left, this was a "purely monarchist-style scandal" that demonstrated that they, and not the Radicals, were the only genuine republicans.[91]

The ploy of the left would not have borne fruit but for the connivance of Alcalá-Zamora. The President, as Chapaprieta quite rightly points out, was not a "letterbox" for compensation claims. Ordinarily, such a letter would have been returned to the sender with a recommendation that the claim should be pursued via the courts. Strauss, paradoxically, offered Alcalá-Zamora this option in his missive. The President, however, chose another route. Having first used Strauss's accusations to dislodge Lerroux from the premiership, he then, despite Chapaprieta's protestations, insisted on presenting them to the Cabinet. He later pressed the Prime Minister to act without delay before the matter was raised in parliament. From the point of view of the Radicals, the President elected, Lerroux notes, the "worst procedure".[92] In other words, the President played a key role in bringing the Strauss affair out into the public domain. This course of action was taken by Alcalá-Zamora in the knowledge that Prieto was intimately involved and that Strauss was a crook who was effectively blackmailing the former Prime Minister.[93] In fact, the Strauss accusation was grist to the President's mill. He had regularly tried to gain the complicity of other politicans by referring to the Radicals' "carefree politics" in an effort to debilitate the ruling majority and in particular the Radical Party. Likewise, the President had several stabs at splitting the CEDA.[94]

The success of "Operation Straperlo" was not due to the collusion of the President with the left alone. The doubts and divisions within the governing bloc were essential to the scandal's far-reaching outcome. The Prime Minister, for one, was an inadvertent collaborator of Alcalá-Zamora. Certainly Chapaprieta was not, despite Pérez Madrigal's claims in the Cortes, a puppet of the President. That said, Chapaprieta not only lacked a parliamentary base of his own, but was also a technical expert who was overwhelmingly focused on his economic programme while being unsure of his administration's overall direction. There can be little doubt that he was strongly influenced by the scheming President. At the meeting of 12 October, for instance, he met with Gil Robles and Martínez de Velasco to discuss their response to Strauss' complaint in the company of Alcalá-Zamora – the architect of the government's dilemma![95] Originally, Chapaprieta had argued that the Strauss file should be presented to the courts. Once it had been received by the Cabinet, however, he recommended that it be passed to the prosecutor, that a statement be issued, and that, most importantly of all, the matter should be deposited with parliament, where he immediately accepted the setting up of a commission of investigation. Finally, he permitted the Cortes to act both as judge and jury – a clear violation of the separation of powers.[96] As Salazar Alonso pointed out in parliament, the accused had been suspended from their public positions for an indeterminate period as a result of the evidence presented by one person, the far-from-disinterested Daniel Strauss. As a result, the republican Cortes had proceeded much like the monarchist courts of honour overthrown by the Constitution.[97] Moreover, the commission acted with extraordinary celerity. A total of ten witnesses, including two Civil Guards who had been on duty at the Ministry of the Interior in the summer of 1934, appeared before it, yet these did not include five of the eight men under suspicion – Aurelio Lerroux, Pich y Pon, José Valdivia, Santiago Vinardell, and Miguel Galante. The Prime Minister, who was palpably overwhelmed by events, acted largely in accordance with Alcalá-Zamora's desires, even though he was aware that the case was motivated by "rancorous political motives" and that it was designed to create a "huge scandal". In effect, Chapaprieta, despite his determination not to become a "plaything" of those who "hide themselves behind the adventurer", did just that.[98]

The path taken by the Prime Minister was not shaped solely by the President. Throughout the crisis, the inhibited Chapaprieta was heavily dependent on the domineering leader of the CEDA. Whenever, for example, the Prime Minister had to impart bad tidings to Lerroux, he would invariably be accompanied by Gil Robles.[99] The CEDA *caudillo* was eager to send the case to the prosecutor, to publish the statement, and to go to parliament. While Chapaprieta eschewed providing details of the case to the Cortes on 22 October, Gil Robles disclosed that it referred to events in the summer of 1934. Also, he refused, despite the entreaties of both right and left, to express his support for the accused. Likewise, the CEDA was determined to clear the matter up as rapidly as possible. Thus *El Debate* was the first newspaper to publish Strauss's claim, in a special edition on the 26th. This was partly to defend the CEDA's own reputation, but mainly to advance its cause at the expense of the Radicals. At a meeting of the CEDA Council on 16 October, two days before the government's statement was issued, it was agreed to "give account as soon as possible" of the affair, but to save the Radical Party from an "unjust condemnation" and to make Lerroux appear as "weak with his friends"; that is to say, to enervate, but not eliminate, the Radical Party. This was the strategy pursued by the CEDA throughout the scandal. Thus CEDA minister Luis Lucia threatened to resign before the debate on the commission's findings had even taken place unless Aurelio Lerroux and Miguel Galante, both state representatives responsible to Lucia's ministry, be dismissed. It is inconceivable that this move was undertaken without Gil Robles's assent. The CEDA *caudillo*, as Chapaprieta observes, was "second to no one in calling for the most energetic sanctions". Within the commission, the accidentalists pressed for responsibilities to be individualized so that only a partial crisis – the resignation of Lerroux and Rocha – would be provoked. This would strengthen the *Cedistas*' grip on the Cabinet while weakenening that of the Radicals, but without incapacitating them as allies. Indeed, what is striking about the stance of the ruling alliance during the unfolding of the affair is its manifest lack of solidarity. During the crucial days of 14 to 18 October the majority leaders not only failed to hammer out a damage-limitation strategy with Lerroux, but they were not even in touch with him. Nor did they then seek a common way out by, for example, outfacing the President, turning to the courts, or even blocking an inquiry as the Azaña administration had done in 1932. It is significant, too, that none of the parties defended the Radicals in parliament with any conviction. Altogether, the crisis reveals much about the inherent fragility of the ruling majority – a fact which the President was quick to exploit.[100]

It has to be said that the Radicals' predicament was made considerably worse by their own disastrous response to the scandal. Between mid September, when Lerroux learnt that the President had received Strauss's dossier, and mid October, when the Cabinet statement was made public, the Radicals failed to elaborate an effective strategy. In particular, their ministers did not challenge any of the steps taken by the Cabinet, such as the passing of the case on to the prosecutor, the holding of a Cortes debate only three days after the statement had been issued, the immediate establishment of a parliamentary commission, the dismissal of those implicated from their public positions, and the resolution that the ruling majority should have a free vote. The Radical approach was justified by its *jefe* on the grounds that he was afraid of being accused of a cover up. This reflects partly on the precarious state of the governing coalition but also on the defeatist spirit that pervaded the Radical Party and in particular its leader. On 23 September, Jalón found him "sad and aged", his hands trembling, and on 18 October crying. To the passivity of the Radicals in Cabinet must be added their lamentable performance in the Cortes. Just when a rousing *tour de force* was most needed from Lerroux, his nerve gave way completely. Yet the overriding reason for the discrediting of the Radicals was a left-wing manoeuvre that had prospered as a result of the President's complicity and a patent lack of support from their allies.[101]

The Strauss scandal, José Antonio Primo de Rivera concluded damningly, amounted to the "disqualification" of a party that should "disappear from public life". By removing the Radicals, the extreme right aimed to destroy the parliamentary majority, thereby causing the CEDA to abandon its legalistic tactic for the violent one of the "catastrophists". If the far right believed that the scandal confirmed the moral bankruptcy of the Republic, the left was convinced that the affair's exposure demonstrated the regime's moral superiority. At least both the left and the right agreed on one thing – that the only solution to the crisis was a general election.[102]

XII

The Fall from Power
The unravelling of the Radicals, November 1935 to July 1936

The Straperlo scandal's impact on the Radical Party was immediate. Meetings were cancelled, local branches dissolved, and desertions legion from this point on. In particular, the fall from grace of Juan Pich y Pon had a shattering effect on the Catalan party, built up on the ruins of the Esquerra's insurrectionary folly of October 1934, including the resignation of "Amichatis", the editor of *Renovación*. Temporarily recovering his nerve, Lerroux announced at a gathering of the parliamentary group on 6 November that a plan had been drawn up for the party's overhaul, that a commission would be named to study it, and that a national congress would be held soon. Optimistically, the Radical *jefe* heralded "a new era of fecund life". On the 13th, having presented the deputies with the blueprint for the relaunch, he observed that there existed a "high-mindedness and unity of purpose that had not existed in previous meetings, when passion had predominated over reason". Out of adversity was born a renewed spirit of party unity, or so it seemed. The initial recommendations of the commission, spearheaded by Santiago Alba, included the dissolution of the Catalan and Madrid parties and the setting up of reorganizing committees for those provinces that required them. By the end of November, however, the commission had already come under fire for its lackadaisical progress. Alba's shortcomings were compounded by Lerroux's deleterious influence. Not only did he swing disconcertingly between hope and immobilizing despair, but he was still in two minds as to whether to cede control of the party to Alba.[1]

The Radicals may have been down, but they were not out. After all, they still had three ministers, they continued to form a substantial part of the ruling majority, and, in Chapaprieta's words, they represented "an absolutely necessary centrist force". On the other hand, the radicalization of the political climate over the Straperlo affair had further undermined the Radical Party's centrism. Moreover, the patent differences over the handling of the scandal had severely strained relations within the governing bloc. As underlined by Pérez Madrigal's vitriolic parliamentary speech on 30 October, the day the new Cabinet was presented to the Cortes, the Radicals were aggrieved with Alcalá-Zamora, with Gil Robles, who was regarded as a traitor, and with Chapaprieta, who was viewed as a mere puppet of the President. Radical spokesman Ricardo Samper, having feebly de-authorized Pérez Madrigal, declared that the party would vote for the government with "great reserve, going against its thinking", while making its future support conditional on the administration's progress. In fact, most Radicals abstained on the vote. The hostility of the Radicals towards the premier and President, together with their grave reservations towards the CEDA, had left the ruling alliance in a fragile state. The resolution of these conflicts was made more problematic still by the Radical Party's own internal confrontations. Throughout November there were bitter disagreements within the parliamentary group over the path to be taken. On 21 November, to give a leading example, a vociferous debate erupted over whether or not the Radicals should back the Chapaprieta Cabinet. Only Lerroux's personal intervention ensured that the party would continue to vote for the government. In the same vein, the reorganizing committee had to plea with the deputies not to comment on their "supposed" divergences to the press.[2]

In reality, the Radicals' short-term recovery was focused not so much on their reorganization as a plot to bring the government down. The opening salvo had been fired by Pérez Madrigal's speech of 30 October in which he had made a vehement attack on the Prime Minister for his alleged favouritism and for benefiting certain business interests, to which he was linked, through his economic reforms. In particular, Pérez Madrigal claimed that Chapaprieta had knowingly failed to act on abuses brought to his attention at CAMPSA, the state petroleum company, as a result of a professional conflict. It transpired, however, that CAMPSA's state representative – a Señor Niembro – was a Radical, and that he had leaked a report, not yet seen by the premier, to Lerroux. This had duly been passed on to Pérez Madrigal, the Radical leader's front man. On 12 November Pérez Madrigal returned to the fray, but the Prime Minister exposed the Radicals' CAMPSA connection while threatening to resign should they continue to scheme against him.[3] The backfiring of Pérez Madrigal's bombshell gave way to a concerted campaign of Radical obstruction to Chapaprieta's economic reform programme, whether in Cabinet, committee, or the Cortes. There was, Radical minister De Pablo-Blanco told the Prime Minister bluntly, little prospect that the Radicals would support his legislation. Meanwhile, Santiago Alba, who, as speaker of the Cortes, had already aided and abetted Pérez Madrigal's assaults on the premier, stirred up unfavourable press coverage against Chapaprieta.[4] The Prime Minister also found himself under siege from the CEDA. In both committee and the Cortes, the *Cedistas* combatted his proposals with a view to replacing him as Prime Minister with Gil Robles. An increasingly exasperated Chapaprieta denounced the "obstacles, quarrels, passions" that strew his path in a speech in Zaragoza on 17 November.[5] Now that the accidentalists were unquestionably in the ascendant, relations between the CEDA and the Radical Party waned fast. On 21 November Gil Robles approached Lerroux over the "problem" of the civil governors, hitherto monopolized by the Radicals, only for the republican leader to respond defensively "he who rules, rules . . . ". That same day, in a speech in Madrid, Guerra del Río assailed his allies for their part in the Straperlo affair. More pertinently, he rejected the approach of the governing bloc, a "betrayal of our true ideal", on the grounds that the Republic "is no longer ours". Not surprisingly, Gil Robles was convinced that the Radicals' "hostility" for the Prime Minister along with their "feeble" support for the ruling majority could jeopardize its survival altogether. The centre–right alliance, as Guerra del Río put it, "was coming apart at the seams".[6]

In the provinces, too, the Radical Party's progress was beset with difficulties. The party's relaunch had encountered considerable resistance, leading in some instances to damaging splits. A breakaway in the Lerida party was headed by former minister and Radical veteran José Estadella. The chief of the Lugo party, Manuel Becerra, defected to Martínez Barrio's Unión Republicana, while other Radicals from the province joined Izquierda Republicana. Meanwhile, the party was being bled by a stream of defections. The Youth organization, which adopted a raft of uncompromisingly left-wing resolutions at its Congress on 1 December, appeared to have completely escaped the control of the national leadership. What the party required above all in order to heal its wounds was time – but time was not on its side.[7]

Just at the moment when the Prime Minister had been brought to the verge of resignation as a result of the lack of support from within the ruling majority, another scandal linked to the Radicals broke. This concerned a company, "Africa Occidental", which had obtained a public contract to provide a maritime connection for Spain's African colonies of Guinea and Fernando Poo. In September 1929 the contract had been cancelled by royal decree on the grounds of non-fulfilment. The owner, a Catalan by the name of Antonio Tayá, had appealed to the Supreme Court for compensation, and won. As the Court had not fixed a sum, the Directorate of Colonies proposed, in June 1931, that 524,000 pesetas be paid out. Alcalá-Zamora, then Prime Minister, had questioned the payment and sent the case on to the Council of State for further scrutiny. Eventually, Tayá returned to the Supreme Court, which, on 22 April 1935, found in his favour once more. Again, the court failed to set the amount of compensation. Civil servants calculated that this stood at three million pesetas, but, like Alcalá-Zamora before, they recommended that the Council of

State review the case. The Council concluded that compensation could be paid not for the service, as this had not been provided, but for the damages suffered as a result of the contract's cancellation, and that this should be done by means of an extraordinary credit approved by parliament.[8] On 9 July 1935, the matter reached the Cabinet, which had to establish the quantity, and means, of payment. The Prime Minister, Lerroux, backed the solution put forward by his under-secretary, the ex-*Albista* Guillermo Moreno Calvo, who, unlike the Council, believed that the pay out did not require the blessing of the Cortes. None the less, a mini-Cabinet of Chapaprieta, Gil Robles, and Royo Villanova was set up to reassess the case. Two days later, Royo Villanova, the only minister who had had time to review it, told Lerroux at the end of a Cabinet meeting that he had found no irregularities and that he seconded the under-secretary's proposal. The Prime Minister thereupon stipulated that Tayá should be paid by drawing on the so-called "colonial treasure" fund, but the civil servant entrusted with this task, Antonio Nombela, the Inspector General of the Colonies, refused to do so on the grounds that this represented a misuse of the money. Moreover, the following day, Nombela was to be found denouncing the envisaged payment in the corridors of the Cortes. His protestations came to the attention of Gil Robles, who, having hurriedly reviewed the case file, now realized that the payment would have amounted to an "enormous irregularity". At the Cabinet meeting of 16 July, he argued that the whole affair be reexamined, to which the government gave its unanimous approval. The matter appeared to rest there. The following day, however, Nombela and the Secretary General for the Colonies, José Antonio de Castro, were sacked. The dismissals did not go unnoticed. In the Cortes, on 26 July, the independent deputy Dionisio Cano López found serious fault with Moreno Calvo while implicating the Prime Minister as an accesory to the facts. Worse still, the former Radical premier Ricardo Samper also sprang to Nombela's defence, implicitly criticizing his own leader for "assaulting" the colonial fund. Once Chapaprieta became Prime Minister, Nombela took his grievance to him in person. The former Inspector General demanded that, as in the Strauss case, a parliamentary commission of inquiry should be established. The premier, unhappy at the way the Straperlo scandal had been handled, decided otherwise, for a number of reasons: proceedings had already been initiated, the Cabinet should not forfeit its executive powers, nor should it be seen to take sides, and, finally, he did not want the ruling bloc to be undermined any further. In the meantime, Nombela directed his complaint to the speaker of the Cortes, Santiago Alba. Later that day, 28 November, the Cabinet, under Gil Robles's influence and despite the Prime Minister's objections, decided that the case should be passed on to parliament. The "Tayá affair", as it became known, was debated the very next day. On the initiative of the Radicals, in an effort to clear their name, another commission was created, which, as in the Straperlo example, completed its task in a matter of days. This found Moreno Calvo, but not Lerroux, guilty of misconduct. The commission's findings were debated during the all-night session of 7 to 8th December. Again, the extreme right implored the *Cedistas* to abandon the Radicals for its anti-republican crusade. The accidentalists resisted its blandishments, but they did little to defend their republican allies. At dawn on the 8th, the Cortes condemned Moreno Calvo by 160 votes to 40, while a monarchist motion in favour of "a severe moral and political condemnation" for the Radical *jefe*, designed to discredit his party completely, was rejected by 119 votes to 60. Neither Nombela nor De Castro, by a count of 110 to 40, were to be reinstated. Barely a month after the Straperlo débâcle, the Radical Party had been rocked to its foundations by yet another corruption scandal.[9]

In assessing the Tayá affair there can be little doubt that Moreno Calvo, with the connivance of Lerroux, had attempted to make an illegal payment. In all probability, the Radical premier was trying to bend, rather than break, the rules. For example, he could have acted on Moreno Calvo's advice and then provided an account of his actions to the Cabinet. Instead, he chose to pass the case on to a mini-Cabinet. Similarly, when Gil Robles, following Nombela's visit to the Cortes, asked the Prime Minister if he could review the Tayá file, Lerroux not only acceded without demur but also pressed the CEDA leader to study it with care. Nor did the premier protest at Gil Robles's change of mind. In fact, the Prime Minister was fully aware, as he told the Cabinet, that the Tayá case was, potentially, a "prickly" affair. He was, therefore, eager, at the very least, to be seen to be doing the right thing. Still, Lerroux, steered by Moreno Calvo, had knowingly made an illicit payment. To this end, they had not only applied undue pressure on the Council of State, but also tried to avoid parliamentary scrutiny. This amounted to a more serious case of corruption than the Strauss racket insofar as it involved the misuse of public funds at the very highest level.[10]

The Tayá affair, like the Straperlo one, was initiated by an aggrieved party: in this instance, the defenestrated civil servants. The metamorphosis of these sackings into a nationwide scandal was, as in the Straperlo scandal, attributable to the machinations of the Radicals' political antagonists. Once again, the President had a leading role in the drama. Not only were the Tayá case and the "colonial treasure" fund well known to him (he had ring-fenced the fund from misuse by decree in 1931), but also a key ally of Nombela, the deputy Fernández Castillejo (who had presented Nombela personally to the Prime Minister), was a close friend of his. Alcalá-Zamora was also kept abreast of developments by the President of the Council of State – none other than Ricardo Samper. Whether Nombela actually met the President, as Pérez Madrigal asserted in the Cortes, is irrelevant insofar as he had a go-between. In all likelihood, Alcalá-

Zamora, who had discussed the Tayá payment with Lerroux on several occasions, encouraged or even instructed Nombela to seek redress in the Cortes. This was, legally speaking, highly irregular, especially as proceedings had been begun, but politically it made devastating sense. The President, in avid pursuit of his own agenda, was determined to break the Radicals through a second scandal.[11]

Once the affair broke, the Radicals were poorly served, yet again, by their allies. Convinced that the matter was designed to discredit them too – Nombela having alleged that Gil Robles had initially turned a blind eye to the corruption – the *Cedistas* distanced themselves post haste from the Radicals. An overriding objective of the *Cedistas* during the unfolding crisis was to establish their own probity, while disabling the Radical Party – that is to say, to further their own ambitions at the expense of the Radicals. It was, accordingly, Gil Robles who urged the Cabinet to pass the case on to the Cortes. Once in parliament, it was also he who insisted that, despite the Radical leader's absence, the issue had to be decided "as soon as possible, whatever". As in the Strauss debate, the CEDA *caudillo* called for the verdicts to be limited to the individuals concerned, a strategy designed to debunk the Radicals as a governmental force while retaining their support for the ruling majority. Consequently the *Cedistas* did not heed the siren calls of the extreme right to forego the Radical Party altogether. On the contrary, they aimed to seize the premiership by presenting themselves as the only viable political option left. Nor were the Radicals helped by the fact that their defence was even more wretched than in the Straperlo affair. First, they failed to defuse the affair back in July. Cano López had been prepared to limit his intervention of the 26th to a question should the Prime Minister indicate that the two civil servants would be reincorporated. Instead, Lerroux deliberately absented himself from the chamber, provoking Cano López to speak out, thereby leading to a full-blown debate. Second, the Radicals failed to exploit the chinks in their enemies' armour. Nombela had been outraged not only by the Tayá payment but also by the appointment of the brother of Rafael Sánchez Guerra, the secretary to the President, as an engineer in Guinea at a rate of 2,500 pesetas a day, or a minimum of 50,000 pesetas a month – at a time when the salary of a deputy stood at 12,000 per annum. The Radicals, Moreno Calvo's speech on 29 November aside, did not pursue this matter. Thus the commission did not consider the engineer's appointment. Nor, astonishingly, did the Radicals question the inclusion of no less than Fernández Castillejo, Nombela's ally, in the commission. Lastly, the Radical performance during the final debate was abject. At supper time Lerroux departed the chamber, saying as he went that "I will consult with my plate". In fact, as he confided to Melquiades Alvarez, "tonight I will not return". The Radical leader, though aware that his contribution "could be decisive", recalls that pleas for his return merely "irritated me".

At 12.30, two Radical deputies hurried to his house, only to be told that he had gone to bed. At 3 am the Radical deputies were informed that the *jefe*, who was "indifferent to whatever might come out of the debate", would definitely not reappear. The abandonment of the Radical Party's founder and father-figure was symbolic of the party's surrender. For Lerroux, still reeling from the Straperlo scandal, the Tayá affair was the last straw. The dauntless demagogue of old had given up without a fight.[12]

For the Radical Party, the Tayá affair was the *coup de grâce* – or that, at least, is what both left and right hoped. The left anticipated that the elimination of the Radicals would bring the ruling bloc tumbling down, thereby paving the way for new elections and the return to power of the left republican–socialist axis. The extreme right, too, calculated that the Radicals' removal would cause the governing alliance to implode. As a result, the CEDA would at last be obliged to join the "catastrophist" counter-revolution; that is to say, to reject its legalist tactic altogether in favour of a military solution. By contrast, the CEDA regarded the stigmatization of the Radicals as the climax of its strategy-for-power since this would allow the accidentalists finally to seize control of the government. The Prime Minister alone was interested in keeping the Radicals afloat, but he did not command the parliamentary base necessary to make a difference. Whether for the sake of the regime, the ruling majority, or for the honour of Spanish politics, all the major parties had a vested interest in the sinking of the Radical Party.[13]

The Tayá affair, on top of the Straperlo scandal, represented a veritable "double whammy" for the Radicals. Their vulnerability to such revelations was due in large measure to their own manifest shortcomings, including the failure to consolidate the party in the provinces and the leadership's poor crisis-management once the stories broke. To this must be added the fact that the Radical Party had been on the defensive since October 1934. But the Radicals were also undermined by their allies and by the head of state. The President had played a crucial role in fomenting both affairs with a view to disqualifying the Radical Party, or at least Lerroux, from office. The Prime Minister, for his part, never struck an apposite balance. He was too obliging towards Alcalá-Zamora in relation to the first scandal, but too passive in relation to the second. What really wrecked the Radical Party's chances of political survival was the lack of solidarity of its parliamentary allies. The Radicals were exposed above all as a result of their abandonment by the CEDA and the other parties of the ruling bloc. The shattering impact of the scandals also revealed the relative fragility of the republican regime. An illustrative comparison is furnished by the Stavisky Affair which had engulfed the Radical Party's namesake in France the year before. Of far greater proportions than the Straperlo and Tayá cases put together, the Stavisky scandal did not destroy the *Parti Radical*. On the contrary, the greater consolidation of both the party and the Third Republic ensured that the storm was weathered at relatively little cost.[14]

The day following the vote on the Tayá affair, 9 December, Chapaprieta resigned. He had reluctantly concluded that the resistance from within the governmental bloc to his reforms, the eruption of yet another scandal, and the speculation concerning further Radical corruption cases, made it pointless for him to carry on.[15] The formation of a new majority administration did not pose an insurmountable problem. Santiago Alba and Gil Robles had already reached an agreement of mutual support should one of them be appointed Prime Minister. However, the President turned to Martínez de Velasco to cobble together a Cabinet. He failed to win sufficient backing, above all from the CEDA.[16] The elimination of the Agrarians and the discredit into which the Radicals had fallen convinced the hubristic Gil Robles that his hour had finally come: "it only remained to hand over power to the CEDA", he later wrote. Yet the President informed the CEDA leader that he was inclined instead to a dissolution. Gil Robles was livid. He riposted threateningly that the sabotage of the CEDA's strategy-for-power would condemn the right to "violent solutions" and that whether the left or right triumphed in the next election "there was no alternative, unfortunately, to civil war".[17] The prophesy of the CEDA *caudillo* was fulfilled almost straight away. Following the President's rebuffal, Gil Robles's very own under-secretary, the monarchist General Fanjul, invited the Minister to back a *coup d'état* – to safeguard, naturally, "the spirit of the Constitution". Not for the first time, the CEDA leader expressed his willingness to pursue his political ends by violent means. However, Fanjul was stopped in his tracks by the Chief of the General Staff, the circumspect General Franco, who realized that the army still lacked the unity necessary for such a venture.[18]

The President had aimed to keep the Cortes going until the reform of the Constitution, his key policy objective, had been initiated so that the Cortes, in accordance with article 125 of the founding charter, could be brought to a close automatically. This would avoid the unwelcome prospect of impeachment for having dissolved the Cortes twice. Such a scenario, however, had become increasingly untenable under the Chapaprieta administration due to the diminishing support within the ruling majority.[19] Alcalá-Zamora himself had made the task more difficult still by prejudicing the Radicals. The alternative was to grant power to the CEDA, but, through a mixture of despair at its quasi-fascist proclivities and his dislike at having the Cabinet dominated by a single party – especially one that disagreed with him over the reform of the Constitution – he desisted.[20] Neither Miguel Maura nor Chapaprieta, to whom the President now turned, were able to muster a government that could oversee the dissolution of parliament. During the lengthy consultations, Gil Robles made it known that the CEDA and Radical Party were working in unison with a view to ensuring that he became Prime Minister. In reality, there was little cooperation between them. While Lerroux adopted a low profile, Alba, the Radical negotiator, was on bad terms with the CEDA as a result of Gil Robles's behind-the-scenes manouevres against him. What united the two parties, however, was a common hostility to a presidential solution. They assumed that, as in the crisis of April–May 1935, Alcalá-Zamora could be brought to his knees.[21]

The President, having failed to forge a centre–right Cabinet, opted instead for a purely centrist administration. His ultimate goal was to create a substantial body of moderate opinion in the next Cortes that would avoid the extremes of left and right by holding the balance of power. This, he reasoned, would "centre the Republic". The origins of the strategy were to be found in the refusal of Alcalá-Zamora, despite being head of state, to give up on his own party ambitions. His divide-and-rule approach to the ruling coalitions was partly designed to accentuate his leverage over them, but perhaps also reflected the fact that the President was thinking ahead to his return to party politics. More immediately, only by moulding a new force under his own tutelage would he be able to secure an administration that was both pliant and durable – something which, so far, had eluded him. These yearnings had been knowingly nurtured by Manuel Portela, a colleague of Alcalá-Zamora in the Liberal Party for around thirty years, while serving as Minister of the Interior in Lerroux's last Cabinet. The desired party, Portela insisted, could be manufactured through a combination of electoral know-how and official influence – much like the dynastic parties of the Restoration system.[22]

To draw up the envisaged centre government, Alcalá-Zamora first implored Joaquín Chapaprieta, but he turned the President down on the grounds that to divide the right and centre would merely facilitate the victory of the left. Nor could the loquacious Alcalá-Zamora persuade Manuel Giménez Fernández, ever wary of causing a schism within the CEDA, to undertake the task.[23] This was, it seemed, a "Third Way" with few future prospects. Finally, the President turned, successfully, to Portela himself. The new Prime Minister made a concerted effort to entice the Radicals into the Cabinet, ministries being offered to Diego Hidalgo, Pareja Yébenes, and Bardají, but the Radical Party, like the CEDA, rejected Portela's overtures. However, he managed to convince two Radicals, Manuel Becerra and De Pablo-Blanco, to enter the government on a personal basis and Alvarez Mendizábal to become Cabinet secretary – a further symptom of the party's disintegration. They were all immediately disowned by Lerroux.[24] The Portela administration, announced on 14 December, was made up of two dissident Radicals, the Agrarian leader, a Lliga member, a Liberal–Democrat, a Progressive, and a number of independents amongst whom was Chapaprieta. The backbone of the ruling majority since December 1933, the Radical–CEDA axis, had finally given way.

The challenge of the forthcoming general election was confronted by the Radical leadership at a meeting of the National Council on 21 December. The disorientation within the Radical ranks was exacerbated by the somewhat desperate decision to upgrade the gathering into a National Congress on the 22nd – technically, the party's first under the Republic. The climate of crisis was further heightened by Lerroux's declaration that should the party choose a new leader "some day" he would back Santiago Alba. Such remarks were extraordinarily inapposite. What the party required in the circumstances was leadership, not its questioning. On the other hand, the Radical *jefe* affirmed unwaveringly that the party would "continue in a centrist position, even in the electoral contest".[25] Yet this would make it the prime target for the electoral machinations of Portela, who had confidently predicted that the government-created Centre Democratic Party would amass 150 seats.[26] The Radicals would be even more vulnerable to Portela's predations if they were unable to realize their aim of joining the main right-wing coalition. However, Chapaprieta still hoped to bring the centre and right together in a broad alliance that would compete effectively with the left. Indeed, he not only won over Martínez de Velasco, Cambó, and De Pablo-Blanco to the idea, but also Gil Robles, and even Portela. The initiative was stymied by the President, who remained determined that a purely centrist force under his sway would be the arbiter of the next parliament.[27] The upshot was that the ministers in favour of a centre–right electoral arrangement were replaced on 30 December 1935 by personal appointees of Alcalá-Zamora and Portela. Ominously, the presidential prerogative had clearly overridden that of parliament. Of the dissident Radicals, Manuel Becerra was retained but De Pablo-Blanco, who had backed Chapaprieta, was replaced at Agriculture by Alvarez Mendizábal. Meanwhile, the Radical Party itself continued to crumble. Former premier Ricardo Samper resigned from the party in December, while Juan Pich y Pon, one of Lerroux's key henchmen since his beginnings in Barcelona, abandoned politics altogether. A glimpse of the disarray at the grassroots level is provided by a letter of 30 December 1935 to the Radical leader from the ex-civil governor Vázquez Limón, who related that demoralization amongst the rank and file was so great that many activists had fled to other parties.[28]

"Without a programme, without organization, and without masses", the tall, stooping figure of Portela with his shock of white hair – making him look much like a Grand Wizard – set about conjuring up a centre force through an electoral sleight of hand. Construction of the requisite electoral machinery had already got under way through the replacement of civil governors and steering committees, the appointment of loyalists to leading public positions, and the legally dubious toppling of hostile *ayuntamientos* and mayors. His original plan was to dissolve the Cortes well into February 1936 and to hold the general election towards the end

of April. Time, however, was against him, especially as the Republic's electoral system was not as easily rigged as that of the Restoration. To
facilitate matters the Cortes were suspended for a month on 2 January.
That same day, the monarchists and CEDA, with the backing of Maura
and some left-wing deputies, called for a meeting of the Permanent
Deputation, parliament's standing body, with a view to pursuing a charge
of "criminal liability" against the government for closing the Cortes. The
Radicals' response reflected their turmoil. Lerroux, in an interview with
Gil Robles on 3 January, forfeited all responsibility by saying that the
party would back whatever posture Alba adopted. However, the three
Radical members of the Deputation, which included the left-wingers
Guerra del Río and Blasco Ibáñez, were unlikely to follow suit. Guerra del
Río and Cantos, the other Radical member of the Deputation, had already
refused to back what they regarded as a monarchist manoeuvre. For his
part, Alba aimed, according to Portela, to use the Permanent Deputation
to recall parliament and impose his own government, or even to overthrow Alcalá-Zamora, thereby converting himself, as President of the
Cortes, into President of State. Such plans, if true, were thwarted by the
sudden dissolution of parliament on the morning of 7 January just before
the Permanent Deputation met. Two days later, Portela claims, Alba
endeavoured to recall the deputies and convert the Cortes into a convention as a further challenge to the President and premier. This manoeuvre,
too, was apparently foiled by the Prime Minister's swift intervention. The
prospect of further scheming by Alba made Portela give up on the idea of
delaying the election in order to give himself more time. As a result, the
Republic's third general election was scheduled for 16 February 1936.[29]

Given the recent scandals, the strife-ridden relaunch, and the floun-
dering leadership of Lerroux, the general election of February 1936 could
scarcely have come at a worse time for the Radicals. The loss of national
and provincial power by the party to its arch-rival, Portela, was obviously
a shattering setback, especially for a force that had become so dependent
on official favour for its support. The exigencies of the electoral system
made it imperative that the Radical Party attach itself to one of the two
main coalitions. Otherwise, like the left republicans and the socialists in
1933, the Radicals would be at a grievous disadvantage. The disparate
forces of the left, their marked ideological and strategic differences
notwithstanding, patched together the "Popular Front", while the parties
of the right, who could not even agree on a common programme, managed
to assemble the "Anti-revolutionary Coalition", or "National Bloc". An
alliance of the Radicals with the Popular Front was unthinkable. The
Radicals were reviled by the left as its persecutors in the wake of the
October 1934 uprisings – the leitmotiv of the electoral campaign – and
for acting as a bridge to power for the reactionary right in exchange for
access to the public spoils system. Politically, ideologically, and even

morally, the left felt utterly alienated from the Radical Party. For the right, the breakdown in relations at the national level following the Tayá scandal, the widespread conflict with the Radicals in the provinces, and the general discredit into which the party had fallen made it an unappealing ally. The Radical Executive Committee, following a meeting on 13 January 1936, left each provincial organization free to strike its own electoral deal while indicating that they should join forces wherever possible with the CEDA. The Radical leadership even suggested that it was prepared, in an unprecedented move that reflected its isolation, to reach an understanding with monarchists. Negotiations were held on 19 and 20 January with José María Cid, Miguel Maura, and José María Gil Robles, but – the extremely hard bargain driven by the accidentalist leader aside – few provincial CEDA organizations were inclined to a pact with the Radical Party. The fact that the Radicals were represented by Alba, and not Lerroux, scarcely improved matters. Alba, a convert to the party who lacked authority within it as well as the necessary base, failed to provide the leadership required.[30]

The obstacles faced by the Radicals in order to form part of the "Anti-revolutionary Coalition" are illustrated by the travails of the Alicante party. Already weakened by the defection of local leader Ruiz Pérez-Aguilas to Chapaprieta and by that of Cámara Cendoya to Portela, the Radicals found the *Cedistas*, in negotiating the creation of a centre–right alliance, to be "very intransigent", deputy César Oarrichena reported to Madrid. The Radicals believed that they could still muster 45,000 votes in the province, thereby justifying three places on the ticket, but the CEDA offered them just one. "This is not fair", Oarrichena protested. The Radicals' hand was further weakened by the incorporation of Cámara Cendoya onto the slate. That the monarchists and *Portelistas* should each have a candidate when "they don't have votes in this province . . . is inadmissible", wailed the Radical deputy to Santiago Alba. Worse was to come as the CEDA eventually reached an agreement with Portela that excluded the Radical Party altogether.[31] The Radicals' frail bargaining position was similarly exposed in their traditional stronghold of Zaragoza. There, the right would not even consider the former Radical minister Manuel Marraco, despite his eminently conservative credentials and prominent profile within the *patronal*, as a candidate. Next, the Radical Party endeavoured to team up with the centre–right coalition of the Agrarians, Conservative Republicans, and Progressives, but this initiative failed, too. Despite the opposition of the national leadership, the party finally tried to pact with Portela, but this also came to nothing. As in Alicante, the Radicals were forced to present an unaligned ticket. In Zaragoza province, the party hitched up its one candidate with a Portela appointee. In the neighbouring province of Huesca, another former bulwark, the party was rebuffed by both the republicans and the right.[32] The Radical Party, in consequence, put forward a solitary, unattached candidate. One of two provinces where the Radicals managed to get three candidates on a right-wing list was Badajoz. In the 1933 election, the Radical Party had won six seats there, as well as dominating the province throughout the second biennium. Nevertheless, the CEDA was far from eager to incorporate the Radical Party into the Coalition. Local deputy Diego Hidalgo was appalled by the negotiating stance of the CEDA *caudillo*, Gil Robles. "He was not a statesman, nor a diplomat, nor a politician, nor a man of government," Hidalgo observed scathingly, "but simply one more agitator, full of pride, empty of experience, politics, and knowledge, vain, haughty, conceited." "It pained me," he concluded, his own deeply conservative convictions notwithstanding, "that half of Spain might depend on the will of this man who did not have any of the qualities required to occupy in politics the role which destiny had assigned him." As the Alicante case demonstrated, a further hazard for the Radicals was the fact that the Prime Minister saw them as direct rivals to his own creation, the Centre Democratic Party. The government, Vázquez Limón warned Lerroux, was determined to "resort to all means in order to break our organization". One of Portela's subterfuges was to accentuate the divisions in the party by co-opting Radicals in exchange for official favours and influence. In Alicante, Almeria, Cuenca, La Coruña, Lugo, Orense, Pontevedra, and Valencia, Radicals were indeed induced to sign on for the Centre Democratic Party or another centre party. Altogether, 21 former Radicals stood as candidates. In the end, the Radicals, too, allied with Portela, who, lacking the time and resources to conjure up his grand electoral illusion, was disposed to ally not only with the centre and right, but also the left. The Radicals' electoral prospects were debilitated still further by the party's own rifts and ructions. In January, the Lugo section, which had returned four deputies in 1933, declared itself an independent republican entity under Manuel Becerra. In Murcia, local leader José Cardona, having being de-authorized by Lerroux, abandoned the party to calamitous effect. Of the party's 42 branches – one for each locality in the province – 41 joined Cardona's Independent Republican Party. Not surprisingly, the CEDA chose to ally not with the Radical Party, "for having extinguished itself", but Cardona. Murcia, too, had elected four Radicals in 1933. An even greater blow for the Radical Party was the estrangement of the PURA, electorally its strongest regional entity. The *Blasquistas*, having been repulsed by the Popular Front, formed a provincial alliance with the *Portelistas*.[33]

Nationwide, the Radical Party, disgraced and in disarray, was largely shunned by the other parties. The statistics speak for themselves. The Radical Party, in competing for 473 parliamentary seats, presented 78 candidates, in comparison with over 200 in 1933. Surprisingly, this was more than Martínez Barrio's Unión Republicana, at 52, and not too far short of Izquierda Republicana's 104. The distribution of Radical candidates, however, was horribly skewed. Only three coalition tickets – Badajoz, Madrid, and Pontevedra – contained more than one Radical. In all, twenty-three managed to squeeze onto the lists of the Anti-revolutionary Coalition, but few were highly placed. Overall, 70 per cent of the Radical candidates found themselves outside the two main alliances. As a result, the Radicals stood alone in 25 constituencies, while in another seventeen they did not run at all. Lerroux himself was considered too much of a liability by the Madrid party to be included on its slate. He took refuge in the Catalan Front of Order in Barcelona, as well as in Castellon, where he stood on an unaligned Radical ticket.[34]

The Radical Party's electoral campaign was extremely limited in scope. It was further marred by conflicting ideological stances. Some candidates reverted to the party's left-wing origins, while others delivered an unabashed defence of the right. Pérez Madrigal, for example, called for a "Spanish front" in defence of "patriotism". "Lerroux to save the Republic," he boomed, "and Gil Robles to save Spain." Alienated from the left and beholden to the right, the Radical leader upheld the party's alliance with the accidentalists – there was no "other remedy" – while denouncing the Popular Front for being "against the Republic". That aside, the Radical leader was strikingly moderate. He rejected reform of the Constitution (in contrast to when he was in power), called for the Catalan Statute to be respected, and emphatically rejected all coercive solutions – "no violence". Populist pleas for "a perfect society", for "the privileged class" to manifest "a little more charity and greater generosity", and for "harmony" between the capitalists and the workers were still to the forefront. In effect, Lerroux continued to defend "the central zone". Yet this was the low-key campaign of a discredited party. The Radical *jefe* – who was subjected to constant heckling over the Straperlo scandal – did not give a single meeting in Madrid, yet he failed to fill an indoor venue in nearby Segovia.[35]

The Radicals won a mere eight seats, of which six were returned in alliance with the right.[36] Lerroux was not one of the eight. Only Guerra del Río in Las Palmas and Villanueva in Orense were elected independently. The Radical total, following review, was shorn to five. Guerra del Río then joined the mixed parliamentary group. As a result, the party had been reduced to four deputies – ninety-nine less than in the last Cortes.[37] Nationally, the Popular Front triumphed narrowly over the Anti-revolutionary Coalition. In reality, given the inbuilt pendular effect of the system, the electorate had shifted from the centre–right to the centre–left. Indeed, the vote for the purely centrist parties seems not to have fallen greatly – from 22.3 per cent in 1933 to 21 per cent in 1936 – but it was badly damaged by the shortcomings of their alliances. However, the Radical Party's disaster was due simply to its drastic loss of support. It polled just 0.9 per cent of the votes cast, or less than 100,000 votes – roughly a tenth of those attracted in 1933.[38]

During the fractious spring and summer of 1936 the Radicals were little more than onlookers. The Popular Front collapsed soon after the election as the republicans occupied the government while the socialists and Communists went into opposition. The government and even the political parties were to be eclipsed by the trade unions as worker mobilization ensured that power passed from the state into the streets. Meanwhile, the non-republican right ditched the *Cedistas'* "legalistic tactic" for the "cata-strophic" solution, long advocated by the extremists, of a military uprising. Some Radicals feared for their future under the Popular Front. In the most extreme case, Angel Velarde, the hard-line governor of Asturias in October 1934, fled the country while being pursued by the police. His mentor, Salazar Alonso, who disclosed to Lerroux that "I'm going through very serious difficulties", considered starting afresh in a new country, but he was later made a director of the national daily *Informaciones*.[39] By contrast, the PURA came out in support of the Popular Front, Blasco Ibáñez welcoming it for having "removed the reac-tionary threat". Others, while not backing the Popular Front, were severely critical of the right, if only in private. Diego Hidalgo, who had fought the election in harness with the right, affirmed in a letter that the *Cedistas* "are not attached to either the Republic or democracy". He went on to blame the "negative and ill-fated politics" of the administrations of the second biennium for having "turned all the social classes against one another, disgusted the poor and the rich, the military and the civilians, those above and those below". On the other hand, Lerroux wrote confi-dentially that the situation was "very grave and very delicate", and that "we are enduring, more or less disguised, a dictatorship". Despite the party's links with the right and the fear of reprisals from the left, the Radicals did not embrace the "catastrophists". On the contrary, in early April the National Executive Committee, with a view to the municipal elections, announced that its compromises were over "with everyone". During the presidential election a month later, the party refused to back any one person so as not to exacerbate "the difficulties against which the Republic is struggling" while stressing that the candidates should be "defi-nitely and unmistakenly republican". In private, the Radical leader called for moderation in the face of the increasingly extreme political climate: "Nothing to do with fascism, nothing to do with falangism; salvation lies in the law and liberty." Whether the regime leant "more to the left or more to the right", the overriding goal remained "the survival of the Republic". The party should, therefore, seek "an understanding with liberal elements of all types" in the conviction that the answer to the Republic's turmoil lay in "liberal democracy".[40]

Not that the Radicals were any longer in much of a position to advance

such a solution. Once the attempted *coup d'état* of 17/18 July 1936 gave
way to civil war, violence polarized the populace as a "confused, many-
sided game" became transformed into a "bipolar one" as people were
"forced to choose sides", though of course many were given no option as
soon as their locality fell under the sway of one side or the other.[41] Scarcely
surprisingly, Lerroux's contacts with the insurrectionary right, already
evident in 1932, ensured that he received warning of the rising. He abandoned San Rafael on the evening of the 17th, the day before the mainland
revolt.[42] Other Radicals were not so fortunate. Salazar Alonso was seized
in Madrid, summarily tried, and shot. César Jalón, on holiday in the
Basque country, was imprisoned by loyalists, but lived to tell the tale.[43]
Diego Hidalgo, in Valencia for the wedding of Ricardo Samper's
daughter, went into hiding and eventually escaped, albeit 13 kilos lighter,
to France, from where he put himself at the service of the "great crusade"
under the "Head of State" – that is to say, the rebel leader, Franco – in
order to defeat the "Government of Terror".[44] Emiliano Iglesias and Juan
Pich y Pon found sanctuary abroad, too. All the eminent soldiers linked
to the Radicals joined the insurgency. Indeed, General Sanjurjo was its
figurehead, though he soon perished in a plane crash. Despite being a
Mason, General Miguel Cabanellas, elected as a Radical deputy in 1933,
helped secure Zaragoza for the Nationalists. The manic General Queipo
de Llano, active in the Radicals' 1933 electoral campaign, was critical in
securing Seville for the rebels before implementing a brutal repression
throughout Andalusia. He also played a notable, if eccentric, role in
Nationalist propaganda through his infamous radio broadcasts.[45] Yet
many of those that were Radicals at the outset of the Republic remained
faithful to it during the fratricidal conflict. Most prominent was Martínez
Barrio, who made a fated attempt as Prime Minister to win over the insurgents at the outset of the uprising. He was speaker of the Cortes during
the conflagration and, once in exile, was President of the Republic until
his death in France in 1962.[46] The vast majority of those that deserted the
party alongside Martínez Barrio in 1934 fought on the side of the
Republic, together with others that had remained loyal to Lerroux. Basilio
Alvarez, for example, toured the Caribbean and Latin America in support
of the Republic,[47] while Guerra del Río aided the republican war effort as
a deputy in the Cortes. By contrast, the Radical leader put himself at the
disposal of the "patriotic crusade" to save Spain, as he wrote to Franco,
from "anarchy and barbarism". Indeed, *La pequeña historia*, written in
1936–7 and in which Lerroux paid tribute to the "genius of Mussolini and
to the courageous labour of Hitler", was in many ways an apologia for
the Nationalist cause.[48]

Most Radicals, loathed more by the left than the right as a result of the
governments of 1933–5 – a period dubbed by the left as "The Black
Biennium" – probably followed the example of their leader insofar as they

were able. Yet the ambivalence inherent in the Radicals' centrism made them suspect, if not contemptible, for left and right alike. For example, the former Radical mayor of Avila supplied the Nationalist troops with boots but, unlike the majority of the town's Catholic businessmen, he did not receive payment for his services. Numerous pro-Nationalist Radicals, following the cessation of hostilites in April 1939, found their passage homeward effectively blocked as their Masonic ties were under investigation.[49] A notable example was Eloy Vaquero, the autodidact who learnt to read in the fields of Andalusia and who, as an exile, became Professor of Spanish Literature at Columbia University in New York. Lerroux warned Vaquero that, if he entered Spain, he would "fear for your life or at least for your tranquillity and security".[50] The Radical *jefe* himself, despite having congratulated the military dictator at the war's end on "the reconquest of Spain", was himself unable to go back to the *Patria*. Exiled in Estoril, near Lisbon, accompanied at different periods by Gil Robles and Juan March (who provided financial support), he languished while the Francoist regime weighed up both his political and Masonic past.[51] The Special Court for the Repression of Masonery and of Communism established that Lerroux had entered the lodges in 1886, that he was still paying his dues in 1932, and that he was affiliated to the La Unión Lodge in Madrid as late as January 1934. Worse still, there was no record of the Radical leader having left the movement nor had he presented a retraction in the meantime. Accordingly, he was sentenced on 1 December 1945 to two years and a day in jail. However, the Court recommended that the sentence be commuted as a result of the accused's "service in the cause of order and of the unity of the *Patria*" as well as a consequence of his "political rectification".[52] Not being absolved until June of the following year, Lerroux thereupon declared his intention to head for Spain "soon".[53] Yet he did not reach home until 1947, now 83 years old. He moved into a house in Madrid made available by another right-wing patron, the former Liberal Prime Minister the Conde de Romanones, but was dismayed to find that he lived "like a prisoner" with two policemen following him "day and night". Not even a journey to Seville was permitted.[54] He died on 27 June 1949. According to regime publications, the former anticlerical firebrand had passed away "in the bosom of the Catholic religion". He was even acclaimed within Spain as a "great Spaniard" for his "defence of the national cause". By contrast, the exiled republican publication, *Política*, greeted his demise as "a death without respect". He marked, it sentenced, "the highest point of Spanish dishonour". Controversy and polemic dogged Alejandro Lerroux, like his party, to the grave.[55]

Conclusions

There can be little doubt that the Black Legend which haunts the Radical Party has obscured its real significance during the Second Republic of 1931 to 1936. That the overwhelmingly negative image of the Radical Party as opportunistic, otiose, and sleaze-ridden must be qualified cannot be disputed. That the Radicals, as the leading republican entity in the governments of 1931, the main opposition party from 1932 to 1933, and as the axis of the administrations of 1933-5, played a crucial role in the history of the regime can no longer be denied either. This greatly modifies the view of the Republic as a regime rent asunder by rival ideologies of left and right. On the contrary, the centre of the political spectrum, which drew on civil servants, doctors, lawyers, teachers, landowners, and workers, but also the shopkeepers and small-scale industrialists who constituted the cornerstone of the urban economy, amounted to a formidable body of opinion. Of all the middling parties, such as the Derecha Liberal Republicana, the Liberal–Democratic Party, and the Lliga, the Radical Party was by far the largest. As a centrist force, the Radicals, whether they shifted to the left, as in 1931-3, or to the right, as in 1933-5, invariably endeavoured to extenuate the more extreme positions of their allies. Cynosure of the centre, the Radical Party played a crucial part in the unfolding of the drama of the Second Republic.

The moderating influence of the Radical Party was evident from the regime's outset. To a greater extent than the left republicans and socialists, the Radicals emphasized consolidation rather than change as the key to the Republic. This can be put down to the ideology of conservative republicanism, itself strongly shaped by the turmoil of the First Republic of 1873-4, by the touchstone paradigm of the French Third Republic, and by its mostly middle-class social base. However, the Radical stance also responded to a series of inescapable realities. First, the support for the republican cause of 1930-1 had to be converted from its anti-monarchist sentiment into a pro-republican one if the new regime was to be stabilized. Second, in many rural provinces, such as Albacete, Cuenca, Guadalajara, Leon, Palencia, Toledo, and Zamora, the republicans' presence in April 1931 was negligible. The paramount challenge confronting the republicans, therefore, was to transform the qualified allegiance of the cities and the limited allegiance of the countryside into a solid body of support for the Republic. Only in this way would the new regime rest upon firm foundations. Moreover, it was imperative that this should be done before the right, demoralized and disorganized in 1931, drew upon its vast institutional and financial resources in order to create a mass movement that could threaten the Republic. However, once the Radical Party set about broadening the base of the regime by incorporating landowners, including former monarchists, into its ranks, the socialists in particular denounced it not only as opportunistic but also as "right-wing" and "reactionary". This was wide of the mark. The Radicals' burgeoning conservatism, more sociological than ideological, cannot be equated with the politics of non-republican forces such as the Agrarians or the accidentalists, let alone the monarchists or extreme right. Besides, the left–republican parties, too, had grown considerably in the rural areas – yet they escaped the condemnation of the socialists. In fact, the expansion of the republicans amongst the landowning and shareholding sectors paralleled that of the UGT amongst the day labourers. The essential point is that it was to the regime's advantage that the rural middle classes entered a party that was *of* the regime rather than one that was *against* it. This fulfilled an integrative function that was fundamental to the Republic's consolidation. The May 1931 municipal elections were designed precisely in order to foment this process. Sidelining conservatives, the "neutral classes", and the undecided would only swell unnecessarily the ranks of the non-, if not anti-, republican right. In other words, the Radicals defended a strategy of assimilation that would underpin, not undermine, the regime.

For the forces of the left, change came before consolidation since reform was regarded as inseparable from the Republic itself. Indeed, the sectarian slant to certain reforms meant that the regime's support was knowingly diminished. Most notably, the alienation of the CNT was indissolubly linked to the socialist-inspired labour legislation. Whether or not the anarcho–syndicalists could have reached a modus vivendi with the Republic is highly debatable. That said, the panoply of statist projects designed to boost the UGT's interests at the expense of the CNT, together with the repression of the anarcho–syndicalist movement and the manifest uninterest of the republican authorities in negotiating with it, played directly into the hands of the FAI and other radicals at the expense of the syndicalist moderates. The ramifications of the CNT's rift, consummated in early 1932, should not be underestimated. In the 1933 general election, the anarcho–syndicalists, rather than vote for the left, abstained. More importantly, the revolutionary strikes and insurrections promoted by them greatly radicalized the political climate. Not only did this distance middle- and upper-class opinion from the regime, but it also accentuated the socialists' lurch to the left in 1933. The regime, in short, paid a heavy price for the alienation of the CNT.

In reality, the reforms of 1931–3 were not so much intended to construct a consensual framework for the regime as to give substance to the secular and modernizing ideals of the republicans and socialists. Yet the very nature and breadth of the agenda for change, embracing agrarian, anticlerical, educational, labour and military reforms, as well as regional autonomy, was bound to create a fallout. This was especially true given that the Republic was born in the midst of the Great Depression, that it inherited the biggest deficit in Spanish history, that the resources of its state were risible, and that its rulers were shackled by the orthodoxies of their economic outlook. There can be little doubt that the republicans took on too much with too few means and, as the Radicals pointed out, with too little support. The labour legislation, to take an obvious example, not only aggravated the CNT but also the *patronal*, which, unlike many landowning associations, was willing to work within the regime. Similarly, the sundry anticlerical laws ruptured the republican–socialist government in 1931, lost the regime much goodwill amongst moderate Catholic opinion, and presented the non-republican right with the ideal banner by which to rally its dejected troops. Politically ill-conceived, the religious reforms were profoundly counterproductive for the consolidation of the Republic.

For the Radicals, change and consolidation had to go hand in hand. Certainly their approach to reform was not "right-wing" or "reactionary". They participated with élan in the spirit of renewal that characterized the governments of 1931, while their own reformist proposals embraced education, health, religion, and public works. The Radical Party, being less doctrinaire than its left republican and socialist allies, also demonstrated that it was willing to accommodate them by shifting to the left. This went unnoticed. On the contrary, the party's greater moderation was taken as proof by the left that, in the absence of the right, it *was* the right. This distorted view was lent still greater force by the left's assumption that the regime had soon been consolidated. In 1932, Indalecio Prieto was already asserting that "the Republic as regards its form is indestructible", a belief that pervaded much of the left.[1] Such self-confidence blinded the left to the very real danger of the right's resurgence, a misjudgement that culminated in the socialists' decision to go it alone in the 1933 election in the conviction that they could win an outright majority. The implicit association of the Radicals with the right also proved an obstacle to the improvement of relations between the republicans. The reconciliation of the republicans was of especial importance for the stability of the regime once the left republican–socialist alliance collapsed on the eve of the 1933 general election. Although Azaña was well aware of the folly of the left republicans contesting the election on their own, he did little to foster an all-republican candidature. As a result, the left nudged the Radical Party to the right by marginalizing it within the republican camp through a combination of ideological prejudice, personal disdain, and strategic shortsightedness. In this way, the doubts and fears of the left in relation to the Radical Party became a self-fulfilling prophesy. The long-term stability of the regime was effectively sacrificed to short-term sectarian advantage. It can be argued that the creation of a broader consensus in favour of the Republic, much as the Radicals advocated, would have provided a greater guarantee for both the regime and its reforms.

Central to the division within the republican camp was the debate over the socialists' role within the regime. From the Radical point of view, the socialists, having secured their goal of the labour reforms, would best be deployed in the opposition as a vigilant reserve. In the meantime, a strictly republican government would restore the confidence of the middle classes, especially the business and financial sectors, and thereby provide the Republic with a greater measure of stability. Naturally, an all-republican administration would also benefit the Radicals by enhancing their presence in comparison with the republican–socialist governments of 1931. By contrast, the left republicans defended the PSOE's continuity in power not only because it was more in tune with their own reformist agenda but, more importantly, because the collaboration of the socialist movement was viewed as essential to the creation of a genuinely popular, and progressive, regime. More pragmatically, they estimated that while the socialists were in power the UGT could be kept under control, but once the socialists were out of power their unions would make life for the republicans impossible. Finally, both Acción Republicana and the Radical–Socialist Party had their own reasons for retaining the socialists in government: the left republicans' pivotal position between the Radical Party and the PSOE bestowed on them a prominence they would not otherwise have possessed.

In reality, both the socialist working class and the moderate middle classes were crucial to the future welfare and stability of the regime. A much greater effort to construct a framework for the accommodation of their interests should have been made. The Radicals' departure from the government in December 1931 narrowed the social base of the ruling majority to the socialist working class and the progressive, largely urban, middle classes. Ranged against the Azaña administration were not just the anarcho–syndicalists, the Communists, and Catholic opinion, but also the bulk of the liberal middle classes. Whether, as a result, the government ever had sufficient support to realize its far-ranging programme of reform in an extremely adverse economic climate is highly questionable.

On leaving the government in December 1931, the Radicals' overriding objective was to drive a wedge between the left republicans and the socialists by capitalizing on the anti-socialist backlash amongst the middle classes. This, in theory, would force the formation of a Radical-led all-republican administration. By focusing on the socialists as the source of economic ruin and political disruption, however, the Radicals implicitly censured the left republicans. Besides, the Radicals' growing stress on the divorce between the Cortes and the country made criticism of the left republicans ever more explicit. The ulterior motive of the Radical campaign – to mobilize conservative opinion – disenchanted the left republicans still further. Thus the closer the Radicals came to outright opposition, the greater the unity of the republican–socialist ruling majority became. By looking at once to the right and the left, in an effort to attract conservative opinion while appealing to the left republicans, the Radical Party fell between two stools. In reality, the courting of Acción Republicana and the Radical–Socialist Party required a greater identification with their reformist aims. Yet the Radicals' statesman-like stance in 1931 gave way to impatient and irresponsible posturings that climaxed with the *jefe*'s threat of a *coup d'état* in his Zaragoza speech of 10 July 1932. Nor can Lerroux's maladroit involvement in the failed uprising be attributed to a fixation with nineteenth-century praetorian politics. On the contrary, the conspiracy revealed the Radical leader's suspectibility to the sirens of the right, the insurgency having been directed by reactionary generals hostile to the regime. This egregious error blighted Lerroux's democratic credentials as well as shedding light on his personal motivation for collaborating with the non-republican right in 1933–5. To be sure, the insurrectionary option was far from exclusive to the Radical Party – all political options under the Republic embraced it – but it did little for the party's reputation or the regime's stability.[2]

The anti-government campaign of 1932 at least had the virtue, from the Radical point of view, of greatly boosting the party's support. There was, however, a grave shortcoming to its vertiginous growth. Indiscriminate recruitment and the hasty promotion of newcomers provoked innumerable feuds and fissures within the Radical ranks. It could be argued that this was a necessary price to pay for the party's expansion, and that, at the end of the day, it had more to gain than lose by such an approach. By comparison, Acción Republicana incorporated new recruits at the provincial and national levels alike on a more controlled and equitable basis. The same stewardship and clarity of purpose was often absent in the Radical Party, yet this was especially important given its social and ideological heterogeneity. The Radicals tended to sacrifice their own consolidated expansion to the mobilizing impulse of their populist, anti-socialist rhetoric. Yet the corrosive conflict between new and old members, which was never satisfactorily resolved, blurred the party's appeal and later undermined it while in power as well as affecting its judgement in relation to the right.

The repentant effort of the Radicals to reforge their links with the left republicans in the wake of the *Sanjurjada* of August 1932 through a concerted campaign of appeasement reached its apogee at the Congress of October 1932. This, the only one held by the Radicals during the Republic, highlighted the abyss between the party's democratic rhetoric and its oligarchic reality, as demonstrated by the weakness of its institutional structures and the personalistic, if not authoritarian, power of its leader. In terms of the Radicals' political strategy, the fatal flaw of the Congress lay in its timing. It could scarcely have been less apposite. With the party in disgrace, the right disarmed, and the ruling majority rejuvenated, a euphoric republican left had no need, at this juncture, of the Radicals.

The impatience of the Radicals for power was betrayed by the renewal of their opposition shortly after the Congress. That they should have taken advantage of the calamity of Casas Viejas in January 1933 to revive their flagging fortunes was not surprising, but their campaign was overlong, uncoordinated, and, ultimately, badly executed. It smacked, moreover, of opportunism. None the less, its apparent benefits were indisputable: in the April municipal elections the Radicals, despite their own alarmist forebodings, did surprisingly well, and again in the elections to the Court of Constitutional Guarantees in September. Nevertheless, a *rapprochement* with the left republicans was highly problematic as long as the Radicals kept up their destabilizing opposition. Yet once this ceased in June 1933, the onus for reconciliation lay on the left republicans. Despite the fact that the Azaña administration faced a wide-ranging opposition front, that the economy had sunk to a new nadir, that the socialists' waxing disenchantment presaged the establishment of a strictly republican government, and that, in any case, the ruling majority had achieved the bulk of its aims, the left republicans were unable to orchestrate a proper response. The Radicals insisted that an all-republican government would not only consolidate the regime's support amongst the increasingly disillusioned middle classes, but also would offset the rise of the right, thereby bringing stability to an increasingly fraught and fragmented regime. However, the government, determined to complete its programme and loathe to reward the opposition of the Radicals, stumbled on, despite its own divisions. Had the left republicans taken advantage of the Radicals' pragmatic willingness to compromise, a deal would almost certainly have been struck.

The failure of the republicans to settle their differences during the summer of 1933, and, later, during the crisis of September to October, was a turning point for the Republic. The rupture persisted under the all-republican administration of Martínez Barrio despite the determination of the socialists to go it alone in the general election and despite the ominous revival of the right. The resulting electoral isolation of the left republicans and the Radicals' partial alliance with the non-republican right marked a parting of the ways. The hung parliament that emerged as a result of the 1933 election led the Radicals to form a parliamentary majority with the right, thereby altering the course of the regime. Republican disunity, in other words, had had far-reaching consequences. Yet the republicans' divergences, which were more strategic and personal than ideological or sociological, had been far from insurmountable.

The rule of the Radical Party from 1933 to 1935 has commonly been portrayed as one of subordination to the reactionary diktat of the Catholic right. From this perspective, the Radicals amounted to little more than a stepping stone for "fascism". In reality, the role and coherence of the right has been unduly magnified, while that of the Radical Party – as mere cyphers of the counter-revolution – has been reduced to scant, if scathing, attention. Revealingly, many books still refer to the second biennium as "the right in power".[3] Yet this is a grave misrepresentation. From December 1933 to December 1935 Spain was governed by a coalition of centre and right-wing parties. As late as April 1935, moreover, the Cabinet was dominated by the Radical Party – not the right. The Radical–CEDA alliance in particular was always a marriage of convenience between two starkly contrasting forces which, despite both being rooted mainly in the middle classes, were separated by ideology, by culture, and by tradition. Needless to say, the Radicals were determined not to accommodate the right too readily as this would only undermine their own centrist appeal. At heart, the Radicals and *Cedistas* not only harboured two distinct visions of state and society, but they were also bereft of a common programme or strategy. Had they converged on a "counter-revolutionary" agenda – as the left often claimed was the case – they would have demolished the achievements of the Constituent Cortes before too long. In truth, the ruling majority was characterized by profound incompatabilities and perennial tensions. Thus the first four months of centre–right collaboration produced no less than three governments.

The very fact that the Radicals had reached a parliamentary understanding with the non-republican right was considered by socialists and left republicans alike as a betrayal of the republican cause. However, this was consistent with the Radicals' call before and after April 1931 for "a Republic for all Spaniards"; that is to say, with its conviction that consolidation of the regime required the integration not only of those forces that were clearly sympathetic to it but also of those that were undecided, unconvinced, or even hostile. Given the lacunae in republican support in 1931 and the challenge posed to the regime's consolidation by the Catholic right, there was much to be said for the Radical strategy.

Up to October 1934, the Radicals, in keeping with their declared aspirations, did not unleash an all-out assault on the reformist achievements of the first biennium. On the contrary, they sought to pilot a middle course that signified the preservation or modification, but not the emasculation, of the laws of 1931–3. There was a great deal of continuity, most evident in relation to agrarian reform, education, and industrial relations policy. In addition, the Radicals undertook an important reformist initiative of their own, the overhaul of the public health system. Other proposals, such as the unemployment package of January 1934, did not prosper due to a lack of support from right and left alike. The fact is that the number of laws dismantled by the Radical administrations up to October 1934 were few and far between. It was a "current cliché", as Prime Minister Samper observed in the Cortes on 12 June 1934, that numerous labour laws, amongst others, had been overthrown. "What series of social laws has the present parliament abolished?", he asked, "one can be cited: the law of *términos municipales*".[4] Yet this law, as Samper pointed out, was universally unpopular outside socialist circles. Of the new measures executed by the centre–right majority, the much-criticized passing of the *haberes del clero* had not only been on the verge of being approved by the Azaña administration in late 1931 but also was of limited importance. Not even the most retrogressive law of this period, the amnesty of April 1934, can be seen as an out-and-out concession to the right. Included in the Radical Party electoral programme, the amnesty was a Machiavellian debt incurred by Lerroux with the insurgents of August 1932. Right-wing pressure was probably decisive only insofar as the law's timing was concerned. Altogether, none of the legislative changes carried out by the Radicals during their first nine months in office were at variance with their electoral campaign. Nor, with the obvious exception of the amnesty, can any of them be described as overtly right-wing or "reactionary". In legislative terms, the Radicals had not only mapped out a centrist path but had done so despite the unremitting pressure of the right and the opposition of the left.

The greatest reverses suffered by the reforms of 1931–3 related to their lack of enforcement by the Radical administrations, the most serious violations concerning the labour laws in the countryside. The turning of a blind eye by the authorities to these abuses was undoubtedly a concession to the right. The application of the labour laws was none the less inherently problematic as a result of the entrenched nature of local elites and the lack of resources of the Spanish state – as the socialists, to their dismay, had discovered while in power. Moreover, the decline in working conditions was neither wholesale nor always acute. In fact, the Radicals did not mark a total break with the first biennium – they simply made an existing problem worse. Nor were the omissions in the rural areas characteristic of the Radical governments' overall approach to labour relations. On the contrary, the Radicals' adherence to the extant legislation lost them the support of the *patronal*, a grievous blow as the shop-keepers and industrialists formed the central plank of the party's social base. This can be criticized as a counterproductive, if not naïve, policy as it damaged the Radicals' standing with their own supporters, won little favour with the left, and debilitated the party in the face of the right. The failure of the Radicals to replace Catholic schools with public ones has also been seized upon as a glaring example of "reaction by omission". However, the manifold hazards of substitution were recognized from the outset by the left-wing authors of the original legislation, as they would be later by the Popular Front government of 1936. Besides, the Radical leader had warned of the difficulties during the 1933 electoral campaign. In any case, the Radicals, despite the harassment of the right, oversaw a rise not only in the number of schools, but also in those of teachers, pupils, and inspectors, as well as a 33 per cent increase in the salary of the majority of teachers. Indeed, the Radical administrations of 1934 and 1935 actually spent a greater proportion of the national budget on education than any of the leftist governments of 1931–3.

The Samper administration of April to October 1934 was even more determined than its Radical predecessors to follow a course that was independent of the right. The government's largely conciliatory approach to the FNTT strike, to the Basque and Catalan disputes, and its defence and even advancement of the reforms of the first biennium in areas such as education, health, and land redistribution made the pressure of the right greater than ever. Nevertheless, the government found little solace on the left. Outraged by the amnesty, legitimized by the Martínez Barrio schism, and convinced that the Samper administration was a craven caretaker Cabinet, the left republicans and above all the socialists were invariably hostile. Indeed, they took opportunistic advantage of the regional rifts in particular to attack the Radical-led administration. None the less, as the parliamentary vote on the *yunteros* in February 1934 and that on the IRA four months later demonstrated, the Radicals could defy the right with the backing of the left. Ultimately caught between left and right, the government was undermined, too, by the conflicting currents within the Radical Party. Yet by refusing to act as the mere executor of the CEDA's will and by highlighting the lack of a common agenda for the ruling majority, the Samper administration considerably accentuated the tensions within the centre–right alliance. But as long as the left remained within the institutions of the Republic, the Radical Party was able to maintain a certain balance of power with the right.

What wrecked the equilibrium between the Radicals and the right was the risings of October 1934. Both the socialists and the Catalans, trapped by their own rhetoric, embraced the insurrectionary option once the CEDA entered the government. The left has subsequently justified the rebellions as a courageous if doomed attempt to arrest the rise of the

authoritarian right. Yet the uprisings highlighted the limits to the socialists' democratic credentials. Nor, in purely pragmatic terms, was this the
way to halt the advance of the accidentalists. On the contrary, the events
of October 1934 devastated the left, gave the right an enormous fillip, and
greatly damaged the centre by radicalizing the political climate to an
unprecedented extent. "October 1934", therefore, marked a watershed
for the Radical–CEDA axis by shifting the balance of power heavily
towards the right. From this point on, the Radicals had to fight a rearguard action that revolved around two principal questions: the scale of
the repression and the scope of the counter-revolution. A bitter battle
ensued between the two allies at the national level and, even more explo-
sively, at the provincial level as the Radicals struggled to defend the centre
ground against the encroachments of the right.

  Despite the Radicals' insistence that collaboration with the right would
further the consolidation of the Republic, the irony of the CEDA's incorporation into the government was that it brought the ruling majority less,
not more, stability. Not only was the CEDA determined to press home its
advantage, but the more power it acquired the more reactionary it became.
For their part, the Radicals did themselves no favours through their
contradictory approach to the repression. Although resisting the more
extreme demands of the right, they pursued a personal vendetta against
Azaña while shackling the opposition press, parties, and unions for an
unjustifiable period. They also radicalized the political climate by permitting the labour laws to be wantonly abused. However, little legislation
from the first biennium was actually abolished. On the contrary, the
CEDA Minister of Agriculture, Manuel Giménez Fernández, put forward
reforms of his own rather than axing those of 1931–3. Though his efforts
were dashed by the CEDA majority, they highlighted the contradictions
and lack of clarity within the right's own ranks. Moreover, the Radicals
refused to act as mere flunkeys of their authoritarian allies. Indeed, the
party managed to protect its hegemonic position within the government
until the lengthy stand-off of March to April 1935. Once the right had
finally secured control of the Cabinet, it achieved one major legislative
coup by overturning the Agrarian Reform Law in July 1935. Still, there
was a whole raft of reactionary measures in relation to which the forces
of the right made little or no headway due to the resistance of the Radicals.
These included issues of outstanding importance such as the control of the
press, the overhaul of the electoral system, and, above all, the redrafting
of the Constitution. Over other matters, such as education and public
works, the Radicals acted as a brake on the reactionary designs of their
coalition partners. Consequently the progress of the ruling alliance during
the summer of 1935 was halting, uneven, and, from the point of view of
the right, profoundly unsatisfactory. Despite these partial successes, the
Radicals' future was far from bright. They had burnt their bridges with

the left, only to become ensnared in a conflictive and ultimately self-destructive relationship with the right. Ideologically besieged, alarmed by the resurgence of left and right alike, and lacking leadership, the party began to crumble during the summer of 1935, most visibly in the provinces. The defeatist speeches of the Radical leader in the late summer were at once a symptom and a cause of the party's decline.

That the Radicals should have been expelled from power by a brace of corruption scandals may, historically speaking, have come as no surprise. In reality, neither the Straperlo nor the Tayá affair, while exposing the cupidity of Lerroux and his coterie, was of major proportions. However, the opposition was able to exploit the scandals to great effect through the collusion of Alcalá-Zamora – whose excessive interventionism was to be an indelible feature of his sectarian and destabilizing performance as President – and the lack of solidarity of the right. In fact, the affairs laid bare not just the fragility of the ruling majority but also that of the political system as a whole. The scandals provide, too, a spectral snapshot of the Radicals at the close of 1935: disorientated, incoherent, and resigned to their fate. Their fall from grace and their heavily discredited centrist appeal gave them little chance in the February 1936 general election. During the spring and summer, they were reduced to the role of mere spectators as the irresolute premiership of Santiago Casares Quiroga allowed the attempted *coup d'état* of 18 July 1936 to explode into a nationwide conflagration.

The contribution of the Radical Party to the Second Republic was, it has to be said, exceedingly mixed. More clearly than their left republican and socialist allies, the Radicals appreciated the necessity of stabilizing the regime by extending and consolidating its base and by pursuing reform in accordance with its burgeoning support. Such an approach, given the adverse circumstances into which the Republic was born, the restricted resources of the Spanish state, and the lack of support for the regime, may ultimately have represented a greater safeguard for reform as well as eschewing the radicalization that eventually made some sort of national conflict inevitable. The Radicals' pragmatic defence of a broadly-based regime was an undeniably constructive proposal that went unheeded by a doctrinaire left that overestimated its own strength while underestimating that of its own, and the regime's, enemies.

The essential moderation of the Radicals and their willingness to compromise were put to the final test in their alliance with the non-republican right. On the one hand, the nature of the deal struck by the party with the right did not provide the Republic with a sufficient guarantee. The CEDA did not hide its disdain for democracy, the sheer instrumentality of its "legalist tactic", or of its correspondingly authoritarian ambitions. In exchange for their collaboration, the Radicals should have demanded a commitment to the regime's democratic founding principles.

This would have proven truly integrative by reassuring the left, silencing the party's own critics, and, above all, by providing the regime with a greater measure of security. Instead, the Radicals, bereft of a clear strategy and debilitated by their own divisions over the right, stumbled along without ever knowing quite where to draw the line. The chief culprit, for a party blighted by its overwhelming identification with the *jefe*, was Lerroux, who was too inclined to muddle along on a day-to-day basis rather than address the wider needs of the regime. The fact that he was prepared to sacrifice the left wing of the party to the alliance in May 1934 was damning evidence of his excessively accommodating approach. Altogether, the Radical strategy for the incorporation of the non-republican right into the Republic lacked the appropriate vision and safeguards. The ultimate failure of the party's integrationist scheme was that it patently failed to make the CEDA more democratic. The Radicals were found wanting not only in relation to the CEDA but also as regards the left republicans. Stabilization of the Republic, given that the regime was divided not into two irreconcilable camps but fragmented into myriad parties and interest groups, placed a premium on the skilful balancing and brokering of divergent forces.[5] Yet the Radicals' opposition of 1932–3 was often dogmatic. In particular, their dealings with the left republicans, especially during the pivotal period of the spring and summer of 1933, were not nearly deft enough. Finally, the Radicals' contribution to the consolidation of the Republic was also undermined by their own contradictions (in part a product of the party's heterogenous social and ideological make-up), by their patent lack of talent, and by the flagging leadership of the *jefe*. All in all, the Radical Party played a salient role in the collective failure of the republicans to consolidate democracy in Spain.

On the other hand, there is no question that on a purely quotidian level the Radicals constantly frustrated the ambitions of the right, whether by dragging their heels or by outright opposition. Up to October 1934, this approach, with the notable exception of the decline in rural labour conditions, was strikingly successful, not least because it drew on the counterweight of the left. Even after the left-wing risings of October 1934 had substantially unsettled the centre–right balance, the Radicals persisted in resisting the advance of the Catholic right on numerous fronts. The Radicals remained largely true to their centrist instinct and demonstrated in the process that the right could be made to compromise – even if that process was not taken far enough. While the failure of the Radicals to consolidate the regime was due in part to their inability to articulate a convincing vision of national regeneration, their mainly re-active, as opposed to pro-active, record was to a great extent a function of the fact that they were a minority administration caught between the imperatives of the right and the exigencies of the left. As a result, the Radicals' room for manoeuvre was limited by the conflicts created by one side or the other. Undermined from without and from within, the Radical Party was essentially a flawed force whose contribution to the Republic was, inevitably, ambiguous. The persecution of the Radicals by both the left and right during the conflict of 1936 to 1939 was to be an apposite, if tragic, metaphor of their quest to "centre" the Republic.

Notes

Prologue

1 The only overall study of the republican movement is Nigel Townson, editor, *El republicanismo en España (1830–1977)* (Madrid, 1994). The book coordinated by José A. Piqueras and Manuel Chust, *Republicanos y repúblicas en España* (Madrid, 1996), is, despite the title, almost entirely taken up with the nineteenth century.

2 On the struggle for the political and intellectual legacy of Azaña see, for example, Carlos Seco Serrano, "El mito azañista", in *El País*, 21 April 1997.

3 See Eduardo Espín, *Azaña en el poder: el partido de Acción Republicana* (Madrid, 1980) and Juan Avilés Farré, *La izquierda burguesa en la II República* (Madrid, 1985).

4 On the Catalans, see M. Baras i Gómez, *Acció Catalana (1922–1936)* (Barcelona, 1984); Joan B. Culla i Clarà, *El catalanisme d'esquerra: del Grup de l'Opinió al Partit Nacionalista Republicà d'Esquerra (1928–1936)* (Barcelona, 1977); M.D. Ivern i Salvà, *Esquerra Republicana de Catalunya (1931–1936)* (Monserrat, 1988); Josep M. Poblet, *Historia de l'Esquerra Republicana de Catalunya* (Barcelona, 1976); and Enric Ucelay da Cal, *La Catalunya populista: imatge, cultura i política en l'etapa republicana (1931–1939)* (Barcelona, 1982). On the Basques see, for example, José Luis de la Granja, *Nacionalismo y II República en el País Vasco: estatutos de autonomía, partidos y elecciones. Historia de Acción Nacionalista Vasca: 1930–1936* (Madrid, 1986).

5 José Alvarez Junco, *El Emperador del Paralelo: Lerroux y la demagogia populista* (Madrid, 1990) and Joaquín Romero Maura, *"La rosa de fuego": el obrerismo barcelonés de 1899 a 1909* (Madrid, 1982).

6 Alvarez Junco, in *El Emperador*, p. 431, dismisses the last forty years of the Radical leader's career as a "mere epilogue to his phase as a popular agitator in Barcelona. From the Tragic Week onwards, Lerroux lost all originality, all creative impulse".

7 Octavio Ruiz Manjón, *El Partido Republican Radical (1908–1936)* (Madrid, 1976). Joan B. Culla i Clarà's *El republicanisme lerrouxista a Catalunya (1901–1923)* (Barcelona, 1986), is an outstanding local study of the Radical Party up to the Republic.

8 Manuel Azaña, *Diarios, 1932–1933: "Los cuadernos robados"* (Barcelona, 1997).

I From Revolution to Reform

1 For the electoral campaign of 1901, Joaquín Romero Maura, *"La rosa de fuego"*, pp. 115–25 and Alberto and Arturo García Carraffa, *Españoles*

Ilustres: Lerroux (Madrid, 1918), pp. 146–9.

For the reaction of the Catalan industrial and financial elite against the Restoration, see Angel Smith, "Anarchism, Socialism and Catalan Labour 1897–1914", unpublished Ph.D. thesis, University of London, 1990, pp. 192–4. For the impact of the "Disaster" of 1898 on Spanish society and politics, see Sebastian Balfour, *The End of the Spanish Empire 1898–1923* (Oxford, 1997).

2   For Lerroux's early life and career, see José Alvarez Junco, *El Emperador*, pp. 25–176; Culla, *El republicanisme lerrouxista*, pp. 13–22; and Alejandro Lerroux's own *Mis memorias* (Madrid, 1963), passim.

3   For the state of Catalan republicanism in the 1890s, see Santiago Albertí, *El republicanisme català i la Restauració monàrquica (1875–1923)* (Barcelona, 1972), pp. 80–111; Culla, *El republicanisme lerrouxista*, pp. 23–34; Angel Duarte, *El Republicanisme català a la fi del segle XIX* (Barcelona, 1987), passim; Rosa Ana Gutiérrez Lloret, *Republicanismo en Alicante durante la Restauración (1875–1895)* (Alicante, 1990), pp. 273–82; Romero Maura, *"La rosa de fuego"*, pp. 162–82.

4   Enrique Montero Hernández, "The Forging of the Spanish Second Republic: New Liberalism, the Republican movement and the Quest for Modernization (1868–1931)", unpublished Ph.D. thesis, University of London, 1989, pp. 105–12; Romero Maura, *"La rosa de fuego"*, pp. 345–53.

It has been amply demonstrated by José Alvarez Junco that Lerroux drew on government slush funds and that, in addition, virtually all the republican parties – as well as others – adopted this practice. See Alvarez Junco, *El Emperador*, pp. 61–3, 216–17, and 336.

Lerroux tried to export the Barcelona model to other regions via, for example, the Municipal Assembly of February 1906 in Zaragoza, but to no avail.

5   "Populism" is an elusive, protean concept which has been used to describe many political forms, ranging from the agrarian protests of the late nineteenth century in the USA to the Russian narod-nichestvo movement and the state ideologies of twentieth century Latin America. There has been much debate as to whether "populism" is an ideology, a movement, or whether it exists at all. See José Alvarez Junco and Ricardo González Leandri, editors, *El populismo en España y América Latina* (Madrid, 1994); Margaret Cannon, *Populism* (London, 1981); G. Ionescu and E. Gellner, editors, *Populism* (London, 1960); Ramiro Reig, "Populismes", *Debats*, number 12, June 1985, and his book *Blasquistas y clericales* (Valencia, 1986), pp. 12–20; as well as Sagrario Torres Ballesteros, "El populismo. Un concepto escurridizo", in José Alvarez Junco, coordinator, *Populismo, caudillaje y discurso demagógico* (Madrid, 1987), pp. 159–80.

6   Lerroux took advantage of the fact that Catalanism was largely a conservative concern in the late nineteenth century to combat the Lliga Regionalista and attract working-class support. See Duarte, *El Republicanisme*, pp. 145–8; Culla, *El republicanisme lerrouxista*, Chapters, 1, 2, and 3. For the innovative aspects of Lerroux's appeal, see Alvarez Junco, *El Emperador*, pp. 226–65 and Angel Smith, "Anarchism, Socialism", pp. 215–18.

The ambiguity of Lerroux's revolutionary rhetoric can be seen in his response to the 1902 general strike, as Alvarez Junco, *El Emperador*, pp. 272–3, and Culla, *El republicanisme lerrouxista*, pp. 53–7, highlight.

7   Antonio Marsá Bragado and Bernando Izcaray Calzada, coordinators, *Libro de Oro del Partido Republicano Radical 1864–1934* (Madrid, 1935), pp.

27–42; Montero, "The Forging", pp. 100–1. The manifesto of the Federación Revolucionaria is in the *Libro de Oro*, pp. 26–7.

8 Montero, "The Forging", pp. 103–5; Alvarez Junco, *El Emperador*, pp. 315–32; Balfour, *The End of the Spanish Empire*, pp. 176–83.

9 Culla, *El republicanisme lerrouxista*, pp. 221–3, 246–50, 255–6, 307–10, 314, and 332; Joan Culla i Clarà, "Lerrouxismo y nacionalismo catalán, 1901–1923: elementos para una interpretación", in Manuel Tuñón de Lara et al., *España 1898–1936: Estructuras y cambio* (Madrid, 1984), pp. 425–32. For the foundation of the party in Santander, see the *Libro de Oro*, pp. 45–52.

10 Culla, *El republicanisme lerrouxista*, pp. 224, 245–6; Alvarez Junco, *El Emperador*, pp. 419–21. For the law degree, and the previous attempt to obain one in Granada, see Lerroux, *Mis memorias*, pp. 606–9 and Culla, *El republicanisme lerrouxista*, p. 342.

11 Joan Connelly Ullman, *La Semana Trágica: estudio sobre las causas socioeconómicas del anticlericalismo en España (1898–1912)* (Barcelona, 1972), pp. 343–505; Romero Maura, *"La rosa de fuego"*, pp. 501–42; Balfour, *The End of the Spanish Empire*, p. 130; *Libro de Oro*, pp. 72–6. For Lerroux's non-revolutionary stance, see his speech in the Cortes in July 1910, cited by Ruiz Manjón, *El Partido Republicano Radical*, p. 90.

12 Montero, "The Forging", pp. 114–15 and 119–20; Culla, *El republicanisme lerrouxista*, pp. 231–2 and 246.

13 Antonio Robles Egea, "La Conjunción republicano-socialista", in *El socialismo en España: desde la fundación del PSOE hasta 1975*, edited by Santos Juliá in *Anales de Historia de la Fundación Pablo Iglesias* (Madrid, 1986), I, pp. 109–39. See also Antonio Robles Egea, "La Conjunción republicano-socialista", unpublished Ph.D. thesis, Complutense University of Madrid, 1987.

14 José Rodríguez de la Peña, *Los aventureros de la política: Alejandro Lerroux (Apuntes para la historia de un revolucionario)* (Madrid, 1915), pp. 103–6; Montero, "The Forging", pp. 121–3. A less publicized aspect of the scandal involved a water contract.

15 Culla, *El republicanisme lerrouxista*, pp. 235–42, 270 footnote 225; Alvarez Junco, *El Emperador*, pp. 421–2. Rodríguez de la Peña, in *Alejandro Lerroux*, pp. 118–19, estimates that Lerroux spent the healthy sum of 469,000 pesetas on *El Radical* between 1910 and 1913.

Juan Pich y Pon built up a vast array of business interests, ranging from electrical supply companies to property and newspapers. He became a millionaire in the process as well as the long-standing President of the Chamber of Urban Property. See Nicholas Rider, "Anarchism, Urbanization and Social Conflict in Barcelona, 1900–1932", unpublished Ph.D. thesis, University of London, 1987, pp. 99–100 and 176; Culla, *El republicanisme lerrouxista*, pp. 246 and 300.

16 Culla, *El republicanisme lerrouxista*, pp. 242–5, 250–1, 257–85, 306; Montero, "The Forging", pp. 133–6, 139–41; Albertí, *El republicanisme*, pp. 361–70.

The questioning is by Culla, *El republicanisme lerrouxista*, p. 270. The Radical Party had previously tried to ally with the UFNR in the provincial elections of March 1913, but had been rejected. In the 1914 general election, the republicans lost 57 per cent of their 1910 vote, plunging from seven to two deputies.

17 Lerroux, *Mis memorias*, p. 631; Montero, "The Forging", pp. 148–9; Rodríguez de la Peña, *Alejandro Lerroux*, pp. 136–41; Alvarez Junco, *El*

Emperador, pp. 424–5; Culla, *El republicanisme lerrouxista*, pp. 311–13. See also Lerroux's *La verdad a mi país: España y la guerra* (Madrid, 1915).

The wartime venture involving the mules foundered, according to the correspondence between Lerroux and Dato, as cited by Ruiz Manjón, *El Partido Republicano Radical*, p. 110 footnote 88. A notable exception to the Radicals' Francophile sympathies was Juan Pich y Pon, who had strong economic links with Germany: see Culla, *El republicanisme lerrouxista*, pp. 311–13.

18 Montero, "The Forging", pp. 146–56; Gerald H. Meaker, *The Revolutionary Left in Spain, 1914–1923* (Stanford, Calif., 1974), pp. 62–98; J. A. Lacomba, *La crisis española de 1917* (Madrid, 1970), passim; Balfour, *The End of the Spanish Empire*, pp. 213–20; Ruiz Manjón, *El Partido Republicano Radical*, p. 114; Culla, *El republicanisme lerrouxista*, pp. 315–19; Lerroux, *Al servicio de la República* (Madrid, 1930), pp. 114–16.

19 Ruiz Manjón, *El Partido Republicano Radical*, p. 118; García Carraffa, *Lerroux*, p. 195; Culla, *El republicanisme lerrouxista*, pp. 305 and 322; DSC, 2 June 1913. In the 1918 election the Radical Party was also isolated, forming part of a broader republican ticket in Barcelona alone.

20 Culla *El republicanisme lerrouxista*, pp. 352 and 383–6; Shlomo Ben-Ami, "The Origins of the Second Republic in Spain", Ph.D. thesis, University of Oxford, 1974, p. 51.

21 Culla, *El republicanisme lerrouxista*, pp. 337–41. In reality, the army and the empire were traditional articles of faith for Lerroux, but he gave them even greater prominence in order to foment support amongst conservative circles.

22 Culla, *El republicanisme lerrouxista*, pp. 253–5, 310–11, and 342.

In relation to Lerroux's 1914 election, César Jalón, a Radical minister under the Republic, informed Ruiz Manjón that this had been the king's wish (Ruiz Manjón, *El Partido Republicano Radical*, p. 106 footnote 81), but Culla finds no definitive proof (*El republicanisme lerrouxista*, pp. 284–5).

23 Montero, "The Forging", pp. 136–7; Lerroux, *Mis memorias*, pp. 605–6; Rider, "Social Conflict in Barcelona", pp. 94, 98–9, 105–10; Culla, *El republicanisme lerrouxista*, pp. 300–4, 307, 349–50, 354–5. Rider underlines that numerous Radical politicians had a personal financial stake in the World Fair.

24 Culla, *El republicanisme lerrouxista*, pp. 339 and 345; Montero, *El republicanisme lerrouxista*, p. 180; Lerroux, *Mis memorias*, pp. 490–2; César Jalón, *Memorias políticas: periodista, ministro, presidiario* (Madrid, 1973), p. 51 footnote 2; Alvarez Junco, *El Emperador*, p. 426.

25 Culla, *El republicanisme lerrouxista*, pp. 280–96, 328–30, 335–7, 351–2.

For the 1920 Congress, see the *Libro de Oro* pp. 105–19; Montero, "The Forging", pp. 180–2; Culla, *El republicanisme lerrouxista*, pp. 362–3; Ruiz Manjón, *El Partido Republicano Radical*, pp. 121–2 footnote 21.

26 Alvarez Junco, *El Emperador*, pp. 426–7; Montero, "The Forging", pp. 193–4; Ruiz Manjón, *El Partido Republicano Radical*, pp. 123–4.

27 Ben-Ami, "The Origins", p. 28; Santos Juliá, "De cómo Madrid se volvió republicano", in José Luis García Delgado, coordinator, *Los orígenes culturales de la II República* (Madrid, 1993), pp. 338–9 and 342; DSC, 2 June 1913.

28 Culla, *El republicanisme lerrouxista*, pp. 352–5 and 366–79; Montero, "The Forging", p. 195.

29 Lerroux, *Al servicio*, pp. 235–6 and 244–7; Vicente Marco Miranda, *Las conspiraciones contra la Dictadura: relato de un testigo* (Madrid, 1975), pp. 25–7; Culla, *El republicanisme lerrouxista*, p. 381; Montero, "The Forging", pp. 219–20.

30 Ben-Ami, "The Origins", p. 48; Ruiz Manjón, *El Partido Republicano Radical*, p. 126

. Under the Presidency of Juan Pich y Pon, the influential Chamber of Urban Property in Barcelona was not only one of the first corporate bodies to seek authoritarian solutions to the unrest of 1918–1921, but also proved an enthusiastic supporter of Primo de Rivera's Dictatorship of 1923–1930. Indeed, the Chamber's powers reached their apogee under the military regime. See Rider, "Social Conflict in Barcelona", pp. 171, 174–7, and 182.

31 Lerroux, *Al servicio*, pp. 245–7; Ben-Ami, "The Origins", p. 45; Angel Marsá and Eduardo Carballo, editors, *Alejandro Lerroux ante el momento actual* (Barcelona, 1930), passim; Lerroux, *Mis memorias*, p. 541.

32 Ben-Ami, "The Origins", pp. 55, 70, 72–4; *Libro de Oro*, pp. 160 and 171–5; Lerroux, *La pequeña historia* (Madrid, 1963), pp. 54–5; Montero, "The Forging", pp. 263–4. The manifesto for the Alianza Republicana is in the *Libro de Oro*, pp. 146–7, and an extract in Lerroux, *Al servicio*, pp. 322–4. Acción Republicana was, according to the founding manifesto drawn up by Manuel Azaña, "the embryo of a party".

33 Lerroux, *Al servicio*, p. 344; Montero, "The Forging", pp. 259–60. Alvaro de Albornoz was in the Radical Party 1909–1914, being elected a parliamentary deputy for Zaragoza in 1910.

34 Ben-Ami, "The Origins", pp. 52–3, 59–60, and 73–6; Montero, "The Forging", pp. 260–6 and 299–301.

35 Ben-Ami, "The Origins", pp. 50, 52, and 77; Ruiz Manjón, *El Partido Republicano Radical*, pp. 137, 143–6, and 158–9.

36 Ben-Ami, "The Origins", pp. 36–44, 57–8, and 87; Ruiz Manjón, *El Partido Republicano Radical*, pp. 153–4. Early in 1930 Lerroux still maintained that a constituent Cortes should decide the country's future. His change of heart was reflected in an article in *El Progreso* of 6 July 1930. See Ruiz Manjón, *El Partido Republicano Radical*, pp. 143–4, 146, and 156.

The formation of the DLR is covered in Niceto Alcalá-Zamora, *Memorias (Segundo texto de mis memorias)* (Barcelona, 1977), pp. 132, 134 and Miguel Maura, *Asi cayó Alfonso XIII*, 2nd edition (Barcelona, 1966), pp. 56–7.

37 Manuel Azaña, *Memorias políticas y de guerra*, 4 vols (Madrid, 1976), I, 1 September 1931 and II, 7 June 1932; Lerroux letter of 26 August 1930, later reproduced in *El Progreso*, 2 August 1931 and cited by Ruiz Manjón, *El Partido Republicano Radical*, p. 150; Maura, *Asi cayó*, pp. 71–2 and 87; Culla, *El republicanisme lerrouxista*, p. 327.

Miguel Maura admits that he was affected by Lerroux's campaign against his father, but claims that this did not influence his political judgement: see *Asi cayó*, p. 86.

38 Lerroux letter of 26 August 1930 in Ruiz Manjón, *El Partido Republicano Radical*, pp. 151–2; Maura *Asi cayó*, pp. 86 and 88; *Destino*, 9 July 1949, AMB, L16 C82; Indalecio Prieto, *Convulsiones en España*, II (Mexico, 1968), p. 323.

39 Maura, *Asi cayó*, pp. 84–5; Alcalá-Zamora, *Memorias*, p. 144. Azaña, too, strongly opposed Lerroux's appointment as Minister of the Interior. See Ramón Franco, *Decíamos ayer*, pp. 72–3, cited by Montero, "The Forging", p. 299.

40 Alcalá-Zamora, *Memorias*, p. 145; Francisco Largo Caballero, *Escritos de la República*, edited by Santos Juliá (Madrid, 1985), p. 12; Maura, *Asi cayó*, pp. 92–3; Ruiz Manjón, *El Partido Republicano Radical*, pp. 157–8; Lerroux, *La pequeña historia*, pp. 60–2 and 68; Lerroux, *Mis memorias*, pp. 546–8; Prieto, *Convulsiones en España*, II, pp. 323–5.

41 Ben-Ami, "The Origins", pp. 45–7 and 88; Marco Miranda, *Las conspiraciones*, p. 80.

For the republican conspiracies in general, see Marco Miranda, *Las conspiraciones*. The Alianza also explored contacts with José Sánchez Guerra and Santiago Alba: see Ruiz Manjón, *El Partido Republicano Radical*, pp. 133–5.

42 Culla, *El republicanisme lerrouxista*, p. 451; Marco Miranda, *Las conspiraciones*, pp. 47 and 116; Ruiz Manjón, *El Partido Republicano Radical*, p. 133; letter, AS, P-S Madrid, C39 L704, cited by Ruiz Manjón, *El Partido Republicano Radical*, p. 133 footnote 2; Ben-Ami, "The Origins", p. 47; Maura, *Así cayó*, p. 86.
The manifesto for the December 1930 uprising, drawn up by Lerroux, is in Ruiz Manjón, *El Partido Republicano Radical*, pp. 159–61.
The existence of Lerroux's alternative revolutionary committee, the "Junta Revolucionaria", is revealed in the manuscript of Antonio Bartolomé y Mas, AS, P-S Madrid, C721, which was kindly brought to my attention by Eduardo González Calleja.

43 Maura, *Así cayó*, pp. 100, 105, 107, and 109; Lerroux, *La pequeña historia*, pp. 78–81; Ben-Ami, "The Origins", pp. 102–3.

44 Maura, *Así cayó*, p. 84. Many Radicals, including Lerroux, regarded the municipal elections as a trap, but the party participated out of loyalty to the Republican–Socialist Alliance (Montero, "The Forging", p. 403).
"Nobody believed," Lerroux later wrote, "nor expected in Spain that the change of regime would come about as a result of elections, and much less of municipal elections." See *La pequeña historia*, p. 32.

2 "A Republic for all Spaniards"

1 For the Republic's reception in Madrid, see Josep Pla, *Madrid – El advenimiento de la República* (Madrid, 1986), pp. 13–33 and Santos Juliá, *Madrid, 1931–1934: de la fiesta popular a la lucha de clases* (Madrid, 1984), pp. 7–21. For examples of its reception outside Madrid, see Diego Caro Cancela, *La segunda república en Cádiz: elecciones y partidos políticos* (Cadiz, 1987), pp. 79–80, Luis Germán Zubero, *Aragón en la II república: estructura económica y comportamiento político* (Zaragoza, 1984), pp. 235–6; Neil MacMaster, *Spanish Fighters: An Oral History of Civil War and Exile* (London, 1990), p. 44; Vicente Ramos, *La Segunda República en la provincia de Alicante* (Alicante, 1983), I, p. 172.
For the Second Republic as a whole, see in particular Gerald Brenan, *The Spanish Labyrinth*, 2nd edition (Cambridge, 1950), Gabriel Jackson, *The Spanish Republic and the Civil War, 1931–1939* (Princeton, 1965), and Stanley Payne, *Spain's First Democracy: The Second Republic, 1931–1936* (Wisconsin, 1993). For a brief overview, see Nigel Townson, "The Second Republic, 1931–1936: Sectarianism, Schisms, and Strife", in José Alvarez Junco and Adrian Shubert, editors, *Spanish History since 1808* (London, 2000). For the first biennium alone, see Santos Juliá, "La experiencia del poder: la izquierda republicana, 1931–1933", in Townson, editor, *El republicanismo en España*, pp. 165–92.
Alfonso XIII, having neither abdicated nor renounced his rights, hoped that his exile would be brief. For the reaction of the landowners' associations, see Montero, "The Forging", pp. 365–70.
There was one section of the non-republican right which welcomed the Republic unreservedly – the Carlists. See Martin Blinkhorn, *Carlism and Crisis in Spain 1931–1939* (Cambridge, 1975), pp. 3 and 40.

2 Martin Blinkhorn, "Spain", in Stephen Slater and John Stevenson, editors, *The Working Class and Politics in Europe and America 1929–1945* (London,

1990), pp. 201–2; Juan Hernández Andreu, *España y la crisis de 1929* (Madrid, 1986), passim; Francisco Comin, "La economía española en el periodo de entreguerras (1919–1935)", in J. Nadal, A. Carreras, and C. Sudrià, editors, *La economía española en el siglo XX* (Barcelona, 1987).

3 Avilés, *La izquierda burguesa*, pp. 47–9, 54–8, and 337. For a local example, see that of Albacete, in Manuel Requena Gallego, *De la Dictadura a la II República: el comportamiento electoral en Castilla-La Mancha* (Cuenca, 1993), pp. 25–6 and 133–4.

4 For the socialists under the Republic, see the extensive writings of Santos Juliá, particularly *Los socialistas en la política española, 1879–1982* (Madrid, 1997), and Paul Preston, *The Coming of the Spanish Civil War: Reform, Reaction and Revolution in the Second Republic*, 1st edition (London, 1978). For the anarcho–syndicalists, see John Brademas, *Anarcosindicalismo y revolución en España, 1930–1937* (Barcelona, 1974), and Julián Casanova, *De la calle al frente: el anarcosindicalismo en España (1931–1939)* (Barcelona, 1997), and for the Communist Party, Rafael Cruz, *El Partido Comunista de España en la Segunda República* (Madrid, 1987).

  Outstanding local studies of the workers' movement include Juliá, *De la fiesta*, José Manuel Macarro Vera, *La utopía revolucionaria: Sevilla en la Segunda República* (Seville, 1985), and Pamela Radcliff, *From Mobilization to Civil War: The Politics of Polarization in the Spanish city of Gijón, 1900–1937* (Cambridge, 1996).

5 *El Sol*, 30 April 1931 and Eduardo Guzmán, *La Segunda República fue así* (Barcelona, 1977), pp. 53–63.

6 José Carlos Gibaja Velázquez, *Indalecio Prieto y el socialismo español* (Madrid, 1995), pp. 19–25; Juliá, *Los socialistas*, pp. 125–58.

7 In fact, the PRRS suffered a minor split in May 1931. See Avilés, *La izquierda burguesa*, pp. 71–3.

8 Edward E. Malefakis, *Agrarian Reform and Peasant Revolution in Spain* (New Haven, Conn., 1970), pp. 166–70; Juliá, *Los socialistas*, pp. 168–73; Santos Juliá, "Objectivos políticos de la legislación laboral", in José Luis García Delgado, coordinator, *La II república española: el primer bienio* (Madrid, 1987), pp. 27–47.

  The desperate plight of the lower classes in Andalusia is vividly related in the "Report on the social situation in Andalusia", which was submitted to the government at the beginning of June 1931. See the Archivo de Barcelona in the Ministerio de Asuntos Exteriores, RE. 131, carpeta 3.

9 Mercedes Cabrera, *La patronal ante la II República: organizaciones y estrategia (1931–1936)* (Madrid, 1983), pp. 202 and 212; Casanova, *De la calle*, pp. 13–39; Rider, "Social Conflict in Barcelona", pp. 546–803; Blinkhorn, "Spain", p. 205.

10 Mercedes Samaniego Boneu, *La política educativa de la segunda república* (Madrid, 1977), pp. 146–9. Reliable nationwide figures, as in many other areas of Spanish life in the early part of the twentieth century, are difficult to come by.

11 Samaniego Boneu, *La política educativa*, pp. 96–103.

12 Payne, *Spain's First Democracy*, pp. 90–3.

13 *El Sol*, 9 June 1931.

14 Francisco Quintana Navarro, *España en Europa, 1931–1936: del compromiso por la paz a la huida de la guerra* (Madrid, 1993), pp. 17–18 and 37; *El Sol*, 15, 17, 21, and 26 May 1931.

15 *El Sol*, 21 May and 2 June 1931; Salvador de Madariaga, *Españoles de mi tiempo* (Barcelona, 1974), p. 42. In *La pequeña historia*, p. 99, Lerroux

mistakenly claims that he gave no account to the Cabinet.

16   Joaquín Chapaprieta, *La paz fue posible: memorias de un político* (Barcelona, 1971), p. 246; Jalón, *Memorias*, p. 39. The *Paris-Soir* article is in *Renovación*, 21 November 1933.

17   MA Egido León, *La concepción de la política exterior española durante la 2ª República* (Madrid, 1987), pp. 64–82; Quintana Navarro, *España en Europa, 1931–1936*, pp. 39–43; Shlomo Ben-Ami, *The Origins of the Second Republic in Spain* (Oxford, 1978), pp. 264, 266, and 269; AS, P-S Madrid, C40 L716; *ABC*, 24 and 25 April 1931; *Solidaridad Obrera*, 16 April 1931; *El Liberal*, 21 and 26 April 1931; Alcalá-Zamora, *Memorias*, p. 171; *El Sol*, 26 April 1931.

      Given Lerroux's clientelist reputation, it is noteworthy that he was one of only two ministers to back Alcalá-Zamora's initiative to cut back ministerial staff (Alcalá-Zamora, *Memorias*, 171).

18   Maura, *Así cayó*, 270. He refers, with vicious irony, to Domingo's "delicious clientele".

19   *El Sol*, 22 April 1931; Quintana Navarro, *España en Europa, 1931–1936*, pp. 39–43; Francisco Quintana Navarro, "Salvador de Madariaga, Diplomático en Ginebra (1931–1936). La película de la política exterior de la II república", *Historia Contemporánea*, 15, 1996, pp. 110–11; M.A. Egido León, *La concepción de la política exterior*, pp. 64–82. On Salvador de Madariaga, see also *Salvador de Madariaga, 1886–1986. Libro homenaje en el centenario de su nacimiento* (La Coruña, 1987) and Paul Preston, "Salvador de Madariaga and the Quest for Liberty in Spain", Taylorian Special Lecture, University of London, 1986.

20   *El Sol*, 5 and 7 May 1931.

21   *El Sol*, 5 May 1931; Lerroux, *La pequeña historia*, p. 91; Quintana Navarro, *España en Europa, 1931–1936*, pp. 37–8.

22   Lerroux, *La pequeña historia*, pp. 91–2 and 99; Manuel Marraco to Lerroux, 21 April 1931, AS, P-S Madrid, C621 L9 exp. 1659; Juan Giró Prat to Lerroux, 23 April 1931, AS, P-S Madrid, C44 L755.

23   *El Sol*, 17 April, 7, 14, 15 May, 6 June, and 29 November 1931.

24   Alvarez Junco, *El Emperador*, pp. 217–18; Balfour, *The End of the Spanish Empire*, pp. 76, 141 and 171; *El Sol*, 21, 30 April and 13 May 1931.

      The continuity of Basilio Paraíso within the party was not just ideological but personal – his son, also named Basilio, was elected in June 1931 as a Radical deputy to the Cortes.

25   *El Sol* and *El Progreso*, 5 May 1931.

26   *El Sol*, 19, 26, 39 and 31 May 1931; *El Debate*, 30 May 1931.

27   *El Sol*, 28 April 1931.

28   The first-hand accounts from within the government – which do not coincide on many details – are Maura, *Así cayó*, pp. 240–64; Diego Martínez Barrio, *Memorias* (Barcelona, 1983), pp. 36–8; and Alcalá-Zamora, *Memorias*, pp. 185–7.

      The Monarchist Circle was allowed to open on the authorization of the Director General of Security, Carlos Blanco, a die-hard monarchist, who had been the personal choice of Alcalá-Zamora. The owner of the monarchist *ABC*, Juan Ignacio Luca de Tena, was apparently behind the Monarchist Circle in the first place. See Maura, *Así cayó*, pp. 241–2.

29   Maura, *Así cayó*, pp. 294–7; Martínez Barrio, *Memorias*, p. 42; and Alcalá-Zamora, *Memorias*, pp. 188 and 190.

      At least Maura and Alcalá-Zamora agreed that Segura was, in Maura's

NOTES TO PP. 35–8

368

words, "an irreconciliable enemy". See Maura, *Asi cayó*, p. 298 and Alcalá-Zamora, *Memorias*, p. 184. Some monarchists positively welcomed the church burnings as playing into their hands. See Pedro Carlos González Cuevas, *Acción Española: teología política y nacionalismo autoritario en España (1913–1936)* (Madrid, 1998), p. 132.

30 Maura, *Asi cayó*, pp. 244 and 263; *El Sol*, 12 May 1931; Martínez Barrio, *Memorias*, pp. 36–7. Lerroux asked Martínez Barrio's opinion at a time – once he was in the railway station, ready to depart – and in such a way as to indicate that his mind was already made up.

31 Maura, *Asi cayó*, p. 263. At the time, Lerroux limited himself to saying, before leaving Madrid, that calm would be restored soon, and, on passing through San Sebastian, that "order" was fundamental to the Republic's "consolidation" (*El Sol*, 12 May 1931). In *La pequeña historia*, he claims that he only learnt of the incendiarism in San Sebastian, which is quite possible, but the point is that the situation was fast deteriorating when he abandoned the capital. He also claims to have spoken out in relation to the burnings at the Madrid Casino, but this speech took place before the May events. See *La pequeña historia*, pp. 97 and 101–3.

32 *El Progreso*, 14 April 1931; Isidre Molas, *El sistema de partidos en Cataluña (1931–1936)* (Barcelona, 1974), pp. 55–6; Manuel Tuñón de Lara, *Luchas obreras y campesinas en la Andalucia del siglo XX: Jaén (1917–1920) Sevilla (1930–1932)* (Madrid, 1978), pp. 155–64; Alfonso Alfonso Bozzo, *Los partidos políticos y la autonomía en Galicia (1931–1936)* (Madrid, 1976), p. 369; Leandro Alvarez Rey, *La derecha en la II República: Sevilla, 1931–1936* (Seville, 1993), p. 65; L. Aguilo Lucia, *Las elecciones en Valencia durante la segunda República* (Valencia, 1974), pp. 46–9; Jesús Bueno, Concepción Gaudó, and Luis Germán, *Elecciones en Zaragoza-capital durante la II República* (Zaragoza, 1980), pp. 67–73; Germán Zubero, *Aragón*, p. 230; *Heraldo de Aragón*, 14 April 1931; Francisco Bermejo Martín, *La II República en Logroño: elecciones y contexto político* (Logroño, 1984), p. 114; Ruiz Manjón, *El Partido Republicano Radical*, pp. 172–3; and Nigel Townson, "Algunas consideraciones sobre el proyecto 'republicano' del Partido Radical", in José Luis García Delgado, coordinator, *La II República española: bienio rectificador y Frente Popular, 1934–1936* (Madrid, 1988), pp. 53–69.

33 Cabrera, *La patronal*, pp. 33–5 and 38–40. The lack of data from many federations – itself a symptom of fragmentation – means that the real number of members in the Confederación Patronal may have been much higher. Unfortunately, Cabrera's study does little to delineate the links between the political parties and the *patronal*.

34 Take, for example, the background of the President of the Unión Económica, Ramón Bergé y Salcedo, as detailed by Cabrera, *La patronal*, p. 56 footnote 44. See also Cabrera, *La patronal*, pp. 48–9 footnote 34.

35 Ramón Bergé y Salcedo was on the National Junta of Acción Nacional in late 1931. See Cabrera, *La patronal*, p. 56 footnote 44.

36 Miguel Angel Cabrera Acosta, *Las Elecciones a Cortes durante la II República en las Canarias Occidentales* (Santa Cruz de Tenerife, 1990), p. 20 and *La II República en las Canarias Occidentales* (Santa Cruz de Tenerife, 1991), pp. 140–1; Manuel Ramírez Jiménez, *Los grupos de presión en la segunda república española* (Madrid, 1969), pp. 56–7; Culla, *El republicanisme lerrouxista*, p. 305 footnote 197. For a reductionist view of the relations between the PURA and the patronal in Valencia, see Aurora Bosch et al.,

Estudios sobre la seguna república (Valencia, 1993), pp. 212–14.

37 Germán Zubero, *Aragón*, pp. 154–5; Alcalá-Zamora, *Memorias*, p. 145; Lerroux, *La pequeña historia*, p. 72; Indalecio Prieto, *Convulsiones en España*, I (Mexico, 1967), pp. 323–4. See also Castán Palomar, *Aragoneses contemporáneos* (Zaragoza, 1934), and the *Gran Enciclopedia Aragonesa*.
    Marraco had long campaigned for a more ambitious economic development of Aragon. See, for example, his report on "La Nacionalización de las Obras Públicas" at the first National Congress on Irrigation in 1913 and his *Pensamiento económico aragonés* (written in collaboration with A. Giménez Soler). Equally, he was involved in the Confederación Sindical Hidráulico del Ebro of 1926. Closely linked to Marraco's economic plans for Aragon was Manuel Lorenzo Pardo, the engineer who published various works on the development of the Ebro valley and who became a Radical deputy in 1933. He was subsequently appointed Director General of Hydraulic Works.

38 Rafael Valls, *La derecha regional valenciana (1930–1936)* (Valencia, 1992), pp. 117ss; Azaña, *Memorias*, I, 5 July 1931; Juliá, *Los socialistas*, pp. 173–4; Prieto, *Convulsiones en España*, I, p. 101.

39 Manuel Marraco to Lerroux 21 April 1931, AS, P-S Madrid, C621 L9 exp. 1659 and Juan Giró Prat to Lerroux, 23 April 1931, AS, P-S Madrid, C44 L755.

40 *El Liberal* 21 June 1931; Germán Zubero, *Aragón*, pp. 157–8, footnote 44; and Bormejo, *Logreño*, pp. 453–4. FNTT membership rose rocket-like from a mere 36,639 members in June 1930 to 392,953 two years later. See Malefakis, *Agrarian Reform*, p. 292 and Preston, *The Coming*, p. 78.

41 Requena Gallego, *De la Dictadura*, p. 133; Eloy Soriano Díaz to Lerroux, 28 September 1931, AS, P-S Madrid, C40 L716; León de las Casas to Lerroux, 18 April 1931, AS, P-S Madrid, C43.

42 Requena Gallego, *De la Dictadura*, pp. 120 and 137–8, 149; Manuel Requena Gallego, *Partidos, elecciones y élite política en la provincia de Albacete 1931–1933* (Albacete, 1991), pp. 96–7, 100, 111, and 127.

43 Graham Kelsey, "Anarchosyndicalism, libertarian communism and the state: The CNT in Zaragoza and Aragon, 1930–1937", Ph.D. thesis, University of Lancaster, 1984, p. 551; *Heraldo de Aragón*, 4 June 1931. A veteran republican from Huesca noted that "thanks to the support of Lerroux . . . *caciques* and clerical elements, cut off from public affairs by the rigorous attitude of the people on 12 April, have managed today to return". Cited by Kelsey, "Anarchosyndicalism", p. 49.

44 *ABC*, 20 June 1931; José Antonio Alarcón Caballero, *El movimiento obrero en Granada en la II República (1931–1936)* (Granada, 1990), p. 129; Mario López Martínez, *Orden público y luchas agrarias en Andalucia* (Cordoba, 1995), pp. 179–80; letter from Librilla (Murcia) to Lerroux, 10 June 1931, AS, P-S Madrid, C40 L716; Dámaso Vélez to Lerroux, 16 February 1936, AS, P-S Madrid, C46 L770; Alcalá-Zamora, *Memorias*, p. 174; Javier Tusell, Genoveva Quiepo de Llano, and Octavio Ruiz Manjón, *Las Constituyentes de 1931: unas elecciones de transición* (Madrid, 1982), p. 34; Alvarez Rey, *La derecha*, pp. 65 and 68.

45 *El Socialista*, 19 April, 6 and 17 May, and 21 June 1931; *Heraldo de Aragón*, 3 and 12 June 1931.

46 Requena Gallego, *De la Dictadura*, pp. 137 and 148.

47 Requena Gallego, *De la Dictadura*, pp. 134, 137, and 139; *El Liberal*, 19 and 28 May 1931; Ben-Ami, *Origins of the Second Republic*, p. 268. See also the general articles denouncing the practices of the *caciques* in *El Liberal*, 15 and

17 May 1931 and *El Socialista*, 19 April and 6 May 1931.

48 Cited by Requena Gallego, *De la Dictadura*, p. 134

49 *El Sol*, 28 April 1931; Radical Party of Sarinena to Lerroux, 21 April 1931, AS, P-S Madrid, C621 L9; Radical Party of Munera to Lerroux, AS, P-S Madrid, C45, cited by Requena Gallego, *De la Dictadura*, p. 135; Radical Party of Albatera to Lerroux, 18 May 1931, AS, P-S Madrid, C41 number 2 L734; José Gallarder to Lerroux, 29 May 1931, AS, P-S Madrid, C43.

50 A. Albert y Nieto to Lerroux, 20 June 1931 and 14 August 1931, AS, P-S Madrid, C41 number 2 L732; S. Quintas to Lerroux, 25 April and 1 May 1931, AS, P-S Madrid, C46 L771.

51 Radical Party of Valdepeñas to Lerroux, 22 July 1931, AS, P-S Madrid, C44; *El Liberal*, 13 June 1931; Manuel Burgos y Mazo to Lerroux, 30 June 1931, AS, P-S Madrid, C1161 L713; *El Progreso*, 21 May 1931; Bermejo, *Logroño*, pp. 453–4.
   The dissidents in Ciudad Real fared better in the general election than the official party, electing two deputies as compared to one for the Radicals.

52 A notable exception is Shlomo Ben-Ami, "The Origins" pp. 278–83 and 320.

53 Maura, *Asi cayó*, p. 309 and Requena Gallego, *De la Dictadura*, pp. 141–2.

54 Maura, *Asi cayó*, p. 314; Ben-Ami, "The Origins", p. 278; and Requena Gallego, *De la Dictadura*, p. 146. Ben-Ami claims that at least 882 were annulled, while Requena Gallego estimates, more accurately, that it was over 2,000. 52.3% of the municipalities in Albacete, 47.4% of those in Ciudad Real, and 49% of those in Toledo had rerun elections. See Requena Gallego, *De la Dictadura*, p. 146. In Cadiz 59.6% of the local councils held elections anew, in Granada 69.5%, and in Seville 71.3%. See Caro Cancela, *Cádiz*, p. 80; López Martínez, *Orden*, p. 223; and Alvarez Rey, *La derecha*, p. 55.

55 Requena Gallego, *De la Dictadura*, p. 146.

56 Maura, *Asi cayó*, pp. 309–10 and Requena Gallego, *De la Dictadura*, pp. 142–4.

57 *El Liberal*, 24 May and 14 June 1931; Juan-Simeón Vidarte, *Las Cortes Constituyentes de 1931–1933* (Barcelona, 1976), p. 46.

58 Requena Gallego, *De la Dictadura*, pp. 142, 147–8.

59 For Valencia, see Fernando Alós, *Reorganización, supremacía y crisis final del blasquismo (1929–1936)* (Valencia, 1992), p. 87 and for the province p. 88, while for La Mancha see Requena Gallego, *De la Dictadura*, p. 149. For the other examples, and many others besides, see *El Debate*, 30 and 31 May, 2 and 3 June 1931, as well as Ben-Ami, *Origins of the Second Republic*, pp. 313–14.

60 Requena Gallego, *De la Dictadura*, p. 154 and *El Debate*, 2 and 3 June 1931.

61 Alvarez Rey, *La derecha*, p. 55; Requena Gallego, *De la Dictadura*, p. 152; Caro Cancela, *Cádiz*, p. 83; López Martínez, *Orden*, pp. 223–7; and Vicent Franch i Ferrer, *El Blasquisme: Reorganització i conflictes polítics (1929–1936)* (Valencia, 1984), p. 259.
   53 of the Cadiz seats were unidentified. The PURA total includes, somewhat confusingly, 22 from the Radical Party. If one assumes that all the independents were monarchists, then the non-republican right and monarchists together mustered 11 per cent of the seats.

62 Requena Gallego, *De la Dictadura*, p. 151.

63 Republican resentment over the municipal elections resurfaced during the elections for the municipal judges on 7 June 1931. The Radicals from Argamasilla de Alba in Ciudad Real province complained that "monarchists of-the-12th-of-April and republicans-of-the-14th-at-night" had, in preparing

for the elections of the local judges, actively encouraged the intimidation of voters, whether by means of the municipal guards threatening people with "sables and revolver", landowners threatening sharecroppers with eviction, or the poor being threatened with the withdrawal of charitable support. "If this is the Republic, we were better off with the monarchy", the local Radicals concluded. See AS, P-S Madrid, C40 L758.

64   The following account of the Radical electoral campaign is based on *El Progreso*, 13, 16, 23, and 28 June 1931; *El Sol* 9, 23, 24, 27 and 28 June.

At the national level, the campaign can be readily equated with the utterances of Lerroux, given his overwhelmingly dominant role within the party. At the regional and provincial levels, the propaganda was obviously shaped by local circumstances.

Ruiz Manjón's analysis in *El Partido Republicano Radical*, pp. 186–90, is limited to just three speeches: the two given by Lerroux in Valencia and the one in Barcelona.

65   Lerroux declared during the campaign that religion was not "a tyranny but a solace".

66   Tusell at al., *Las Constituyentes de 1931*, pp. 43– 4 and 53; Germán Zubero, *Aragón*, pp. 238–44; Alós, *Blasquismo*, pp. 87–8.

67   *El Debate*, 18 June 1931; *El Liberal*, 23 June 1931; Alfonso Bozzo, *Galicia, 1931–1936*, pp. 76–87; Ruiz Manjón, *El Partido Republicano Radical*, p. 662. For *La Zarpa*, see Ruiz Manjón, *El Partido Republicano Radical*, p. 663.

68   Luis Quirós y Arias to Lerroux, 18 June 1931, AS, P-S Madrid, C46, L771; Radical Party of Valdepeñas to Lerroux, 22 July 1931, AS, P-S Madrid, C44; *El Debate*, 9 June 1931; *El Liberal*, 23 June 1931.

69   *El Debate*, 9, 14, 17, 18, 19, 23 and 24 June 1931; Bermejo, *Logroño*, pp. 453–4; *El Liberal*, 23 June 1931; Tusell at al., *Las Constituyentes de 1931*, pp. 41–5.

70   See the *El Sol* editorials of 12, 23, 24, and 27 June 1931.

71   For coverage of Lerroux's campaign by the right-wing press, see *ABC*, 18, 19, 20, 23, 26 June 1931; *El Debate*, 27 May, 10, 11, 12, 14, 23, 24, and 26 June 1931. By contrast with the treatment of Lerroux, Azaña was an "enemy of the conservative Republic", as was Alvaro de Albornoz. See *El Debate*, 10, 12, and 21 June 1931.

72   Ossorio, *Memorias*, pp. 167–8; Jackson, *The Spanish Republic*, pp. 54–5; *ABC*, 18 June 1931; *El Debate*, 6 and 26 June 1931.

Sectors of the right, the Carlists in particular, endeavoured to discredit Alcalá-Zamora and Miguel Maura by highlighting their allegedly Jewish origins. See Blinkhorn, *Carlism*, p. 179 and Vidarte, *Las Cortes*, p. 35.

73   Detailed results for the Radical Party in Ruiz Manjón, *El Partido Republicano Radical*, pp. 192–6. The party presented around 150 candidates, there being none in Baleares, Jaen, Salamanca and few in the Basque country, according to Tusell at al., *Las Constituyentes de 1931*, pp. 40 and 52–3.

74   Cabrera Acosta, *Las Canarias*, pp. 147 and 150 as well as *Las elecciones*, pp. 34–7 and 107–12; Ben-Ami, *Origins of the Second Republic*, p. 317; Ruiz Manjón, *El Partido Republicano Radical*, pp. 196–200; Alvarez Rey, *La derecha*, pp. 57–61 and 65; Germán Zubero, *Aragón*, pp. 245–51; Caro Cancela, *Cádiz*, pp. 108–20; Alós, *Blasquismo*, pp. 93–6.

75   Ruiz Manjón, *El Partido Republicano Radical*, p. 594; Avilés, *La izquierda burguesa*, pp. 343 and 345; Espín, *Azaña*, pp. 288–92.

Lawyers formed 43% of the Radical parliamentary party, 42% of the PRSS, and 25% of AR. 14% of the PRRS were journalists and writers, compared to 8% for AR and 5% for the Radical Party. 36% of the AR deputies were academics. Outside the parliamentary group, the proportion of industrialists and shopkeepers in the Radical Party rose to around a quarter.

76 *ABC*, 30 June 1931 and *El Sol*, 30 June 1931. See also *El Debate*, 30 June 1931 and the *El Liberal* editorial of 1 July 1931.

3 The Struggle with the Socialists

1 *El Sol*, 1, 2, 4, 28 and 29 July 1931; Azaña, *Memorias*, I, 7 July 1931. Prieto was also motivated by his personal hatred of Lerroux. See Alcalá-Zamora, *Memorias*, p. 170.

2 *El Sol*, 5 July 1931.

3 *El Progreso*, 3, 5, 25, 29, and 31 July 1931; *El Sol*, 28 and 29 July 1931; Azaña, *Memorias*, I, 7 July 1931.
   Lerroux reiterated his extreme reluctance to become prime minister in speeches in Soria and Madrid, while in Valladolid he went even further, claiming that he would not want to be prime minister even after the Constitution had been passed. See *El Sol*, 11, 25, and 26 August 1931.

4 *El Sol*, 28, 29 July, 2, 11 August, 20 October, 26 November 1931; Azaña, *Memorias*, I, 9 and 25 August 1931; *El Progreso*, 12 July 1931.

5 *El Sol*, 11 July 1931; *El Progreso*, 12 and 16 July 1931; Azaña, *Memorias*, I, 7, 8, 10, and 13 July 1931.

6 *El Sol*, 11 and 14 August 1931.

7 *El Progreso*, 25 and 26 August 1931.

8 The Regulations can be found in AS, P-S Madrid, C570 L769 and *El Progreso*, 8 and 24 September 1931.

9 Martínez Barrio, *Memorias*, p. 107; Ruiz Manjón, *El Partido Republicano Radical*, pp. 601–27, 629–38.

10 Azaña, *Memorias*, I, 9, 25 August, 1 and 8 September 1931.

11 Azaña, *Memorias*, I, 21 July, 4 August, and 1 September 1931.

12 Azaña, *Memorias*, I, 4 and 28 August, 9 September 1931.

13 *El Progreso*, 11, 13 September, and 8 October 1931; Azaña, *Memorias*, I, 4 August and 9 September 1931. Azaña's speech is in *Memorias*, I, pp. 241–59.

14 *El Sol*, 13 September 1931. José Giral of AR also declared his support for the continuation of the Constituent Cortes after the Constitution had been passed. See *El Sol*, 13 August 1931.

15 *El Sol*, 15 September 1931 and *El Progreso*, 10 October 1931.

16 Azaña, *Memorias*, I, 2 and 16 September 1931; DSCC, 16 September 1931; Martínez Barrio, *Memorias*, pp. 49–50; editorial of *El Progreso*, 18 September 1931; Avilés, *La izquierda burguesa*, p. 93.

17 DSCC, 25 September 1931; Espín, *Azaña*, pp. 205–6; Martínez Barrio, *Memorias*, pp. 50–64; Avilés, *La izquierda burguesa*, p. 95. Largo Caballero's amendment was passed by 132 votes to 118 but the socialist leader then reached an agreement with the Esquerra. Only six AR deputies voted against it.

18 DSCC, 1 and 6 October 1931; Azaña, *Memorias*, I, 1 October 1931; Espín, *Azaña*, pp. 217–18; Azaña, *Obras*, IV, p. 165. Six AR rebels gave victory to the socialists and Radical–Socialists in the property debate.

19 *El Progreso*, 26 September 1931; DSCC, 21 October and 4 November 1931; Azaña, *Memorias*, I, 16 September 1931. Similarly, in October Martínez Barrio had to deauthorize the account given to the press by Emiliano Iglesias of a meeting of the parliamentary group. See *El Sol*, 17 October 1931 and Azaña, *Memorias*, I, 18 October 1931.

20 Azaña, *Memorias*, I, 28 August and 9 October 1931; Martínez Barrio, *Memorias*, pp. 70 and 82; Alcalá-Zamora, *Memorias*, p. 175.

21 DSCC, 28 August 1931. See also Clara Campoamor's *El voto feminino y yo* (Madrid, 1936).

22 DSCC, 28 August 1931. Basilio Alvarez's speech is reproduced in *Dos años de agitación política*, edited by Marcos Valcárcel (La Coruña, 1991), pp. 163–79.

23 Martínez Barrio, *Memorias*, pp. 64, 77 and 84; Quintana Navarro, *España en Europa, 1931–1936*, pp. 31–7.

24 Martínez Barrio, *Memorias*, pp. 83–4.

25 DSCC, 10 October 1931; Santiago Varela, *Partidos y parlamento y la II República española* (Barcelona, 1978), pp. 221–2; *El Sol*, 7 and 20 October 1931.
   On the centrality of anticlericalism to republican culture, see José Alvarez Junco, *El Emperador*, pp. 397–414 and "Los intelectuales: anticlericalism y republicanismo" in José Luis García Delgado, coordinator, *Los orígenes culturales de la II República* (Madrid, 1993), pp. 101–26.

26 Martínez Barrio, *Memorias*, p. 71; *El Sol*, 7 and 14 October 1931; María Dolores Gómez Molleda, *La Masonería en la crisis española del siglo XX* (Madrid, 1986), appendix on "Diputados de las Cortes Constituyentes Pertenecientes a la Orden", p. 513.

27 DSCC, 9 October 1931; Espín, *Azaña*, pp. 175–6. Azaña's speech is in *Memorias*, I, pp. 343–54. His claim that Spain was no longer Catholic referred to its culture, and did not dispute the fact that there were still many millions of believers.

28 *El Sol*, 13 October 1931; Alcalá-Zamora, *Memorias*, pp. 183, 190–2; Varela, *Partidos*, p. 221–2, footnote 42; Martínez Barrio, *Memorias*, pp. 71–8; Arxiu Vidal i Barraquer, *Iglesia y Estado durante la Segunda República española*, I, pp. 88, 253–5, 374–83, 391 and 404, cited by Varela, *Partidos*, p. 224 footnote 77.
   In his Santander speech in October, Lerroux claimed quite mendaciously that he had not voted on article 26 because of a technical hitch. See *El Sol*, 20 October 1931.

29 DSCC, 13 October 1931.

30 Azaña, *Memorias*, I, 14 October 1931.

31 *El Progreso*, 26 September 1931; Azaña, *Memorias*, I, 28 August, 1, 8, 9 September, and 14 October 1931.

32 Azaña, *Memorias*, I, 1 September and 14 October 1931; Martínez Barrio, *Memorias*, p. 90.

33 *El Sol*, 20 and 24 October 1931; Azaña, *Memorias*, I, 29 October 1931.

34 Letter of 19 November to Lerroux, AS, P-S Madrid, C43 L743; Radical Party of Chimeneas (Granada) to Lerroux, 9 November 1931, AS, P-S Madrid, C44 L755; Radical Party of La Cumbre (Caceres) to Lerroux, 16 September 1931, AS, P-S Madrid, C40 L716.
   For further complaints from the provinces in relation to the socialists, see the letters to Lerroux of 29 July and 5 September 1931, AS, P-S Madrid, C41 number 2 L733, that of 9 November 1931, AS, P-S Madrid, C44 L755, and that of J. Aguilera of 11 November 1931, AS, P-S Madrid, C41 number 1 L724.

35 *El Debate*, 30 October 1931; *El Socialista*, 25 October 1931; Azaña, *Memorias*, I, 29 October 1931; *El Sol*, 3 November 1931.

36 Still, Luis García Lozano, the Radical deputy for Burgos, left the party as a result. See *El Sol*, 23 October 1931.

37 Azaña, *Memorias*, I, 23, 28, 29, 30, and 31 October 1931; *El Socialista*, 3 November 1931.

38 *El Sol*, 3 and 4 November 1931; Martínez Barrio, *Memorias*, p. 89; *El Debate*, 1 November 1931.

39 Carolyn Boyd, "Responsibilities and the Second Republic, 1931–1936" in Martin Blinkhorn, editor, *Spain in Conflict 1931–1939: Democracy and Its Enemies* (London, 1986), pp. 14–39. On the long and eventful life of Juan March, see Manuel D. Benavides, *El último pirata del Mediterráneo* (Mexico, 1976); Arturo Dixon, *Señor monopolio: la asombrosa vida de Juan March* (Barcelona, 1985); Ramón Garriga, *Juan March y su tiempo* (Barcelona, 1976); Alfonso Piñeiro, *Los March: el precio del honor* (Madrid, 1991).

40 Boyd, "'Responsibilities", in Blinkhorn, editor, *Spain in Conflict*, p. 29; Garriga, *Juan March*, pp. 298–308 and 311–13; Vidarte, *Las Cortes*, pp. 247–51; Dixon, *Señor monopolio*, pp. 105–9; Azaña, *Memorias*, I, 5, 6, and 13 November 1931. *El Sol* published a résumé of the secret session on 7 November 1931.

41 Maura, *Asi cayó*, p. 109; Lerroux, *La pequeña historia*, pp. 78–9; *El Sol*, 7 November 1931; Piñeiro, *Los March*, pp. 73–4; Garriga, *Juan March*, passim; Culla, *El republicanisme lerrouxista*, p. 305 footnote 197; Dixon, *Señor monopolio*, p. 93; Azaña, *Memorias*, I, 5 and 13 November 1931; *El Socialista*, 24 February 1934.

42 Piñeiro, *Los March*, pp. 118, 121, and 130. The payment of the *Casa del Pueblo* by Juan March, and the money owed to him by the socialists, is in *La Tierra*, 11, 13, and 14 June 1931; Piñeiro, *Los March*, pp. 117–19, 123; and Joan Oliver Araujo, *La II República en Baleares: elecciones y partidos políticos* (Palma de Mallorca, 1983), p. 44, footnote 29.

43 Piñeiro, *Los March*, pp. 120–5 and 129–34; Azaña, *Memorias*, II, 3 April 1932; Lerroux, *La pequeña historia*, pp. 63–5.

44 Boyd, "Responsibilities", in Blinkhorn, editor, *Spain in Conflict*, pp. 29–30; Azaña, *Memorias*, I, 23 July, 5 August, 31 October, 3, 13, and 19 November 1931 and *Memorias*, II, 19, 22 February, 3 and 8 April, 14 June 1932; Payne, *Spain's First Democracy*, pp. 69–70.

45 Azaña, *Memorias*, I, 13 November 1931; *El Sol*, 14 and 19 November 1931; *El Socialista*, 13 November 1931.

46 *El Sol*, 7 and 13 November 1931; Azaña, *Memorias*, I, 13 November 1931; Vidarte, *Las Cortes*, p. 251. One who acted for March but was not of Lerroux's coterie was Tomás Peire. See Piñeiro, *Los March*, p. 385 and Azaña, *Diarios*, 2 March 1933.

47 Azaña, *Memorias*, I, 13 November 1931. Not only did the Radicals accept the socialists' half-hearted apology but they also published – illegally – their conciliatory words.

48 *El Progreso*, 1, 3, and 6 November 1931; *El Socialista*, 1 November 1931; Martínez Barrio, *Memorias*, p. 58; Alcalá-Zamora, *Memorias*, p. 191; Azaña, *Memorias*, I, 3 October 1931. On Lerroux's lack of leadership, see also Martínez Barrio, *Memorias*, pp. 64, 77 and 84.

49 Quintana Navarro, *España en Europa, 1931–1936*, pp. 31–7, 50–3, and 59–62; De Madariaga, *Españoles*, pp. 43 and 45; Salvador de Madariaga, *Memorias (1921–1936)*, 2nd edition (Madrid, 1974), pp. 293–4; *El Sol*, 7 and 13 October 1931.

50 *El Sol*, 12 September and 20 October 1931; Cabrera, *La patronal*, pp. 212–13. See also the statement sent to the Cortes by numerous employers' associations in July and published in *El Sol*, 31 July 1931.

51 Azaña, *Memorias*, I, 18 October 1931; *El Progreso* 12 July 1931; *El Sol*, 14 August 1931.

52 Azaña, *Memorias*, I, 2 and 18 October, 4, 7, and 13 November, 7 December 1931; Lerroux, *La pequeña historia*, pp. 114–17; *El Sol*, 1 November 1931. Neither *La pequeña historia* nor Martínez Barrio's *Memorias* reveal any hankering on Lerroux's part to be president.

53 *El Progreso*, 6 November 1931; Martínez Barrio, *Memorias*, pp. 91–3; Azaña, *Memorias*, I, 1 and 2 December 1931. For the Radical Party's official stance, see the statements published in *El Sol*, 3 and 6 December 1931. Curiously, Azaña, despite his eagerness to marginalize Lerroux by electing him to the presidency, did not press his case in Cabinet.

54 Azaña himself was well aware of Alcalá-Zamora's shortcomings, observing in his diary that he was "extremely dangerous" as he would create a "conflict every day" and that, if he acted as President as he had done as Prime Minister, he would not last long. See Azaña, *Memorias*, I, 4, 13 November, 1 and 10 December 1931.

55 *El Sol*, 19 and 24 November 1931.

Martínez Barrio repeated this stance to journalists in the Cortes on 26 November 1931 and at the Provincial Congress of the Madrid Radical Party on 30 November 1931. See *El Sol*, 27 November and 1 December 1931. In response to a questionnaire of *El Heraldo*, the Radical parliamentary spokesman, Rafael Guerra del Río, called for the continuation of the republicans and socialists in office as long as the prime minister remained a republican: see *El Progreso*, 29 November 1931.

56 *El Sol*, 17, 24, 28 November, 6 and 9 December 1931; Azaña, *Memorias*, I, 21 November, 1 and 7 December 1931; *El Progreso*, 24 November and 8 December 1931; *El Liberal*, 2 December 1931. By 6 December, however, Azaña – judging by the conversation which he held with the socialist leader Fernando de los Ríos – had changed his mind (Azaña, *Memorias*, I, December 6 1931).

57 *El Liberal*, 28 November and 5 December 1931; *El Sol*, 15, 26 November, 3, 8, 10 December 1931.

58 See the *El Progreso* editorials of 27, 29, 30 October and 14, 24, and 26 December 1931.

59 Azaña, *Memorias*, I, 2 November 1931; *El Liberal*, 27 and 28 November 1931; *El Sol*, 27 November and 15 December 1931.

60 Azaña, *Memorias*, I, 1 December 1931; *El Liberal*, 2 and 9 December 1931; *El Sol*, 3 December 1931; *El Progreso*, 8 December 1931. See the *El Liberal* editorial of 4 December 1931 on the complementary laws as a continuing bone of contention.

61 Azaña, *Memorias*, I, 9 December 1931.

62 Azaña, *Memorias*, I, 12, 13, 14, and 15 December 1931; Lerroux, *La pequeña historia*, pp. 127–8; *El Sol*, 15 December 1931; and Azaña in DSCC, 17 December 1931.

63 *El Liberal* and *El Sol*, 15 December 1931.

64 *El Sol*, 16 December 1931 and *El Liberal*, 20 December 1931. See also the article by the Radical deputy Juan Calot in *El Progreso*, 16 December 1931.

65 Azaña, *Memorias*, I, 14 December 1931.

66 *El Sol*, 8 December 1931. The *Ahora* interview was reprinted in *El Progreso* on 17 November 1931.

4 In Search of a Strategy

1 *El Financiero*, 29 January 1932. *El Noticiero Universal* and *La Nación* are cited by *El Financiero* on 4 March 1932.
2 *El Liberal*, 5 January and 2 February 1932; *El Sol* 12 January 1932.
3 *El Socialista*, 15 January and 16 August 1932; V. Aranqüena to Lerroux, 7 January 1932, AS, P-S Madrid, C41 number 2 L732; Germán Zubero, *Aragón*, p. 158; *La Tierra*, 1 February 1932.
4 Caro Cancela, *Cádiz*, p. 137; Requena Gallego, *Albacete 1931–1933*, pp. 155–6; *La Tierra*, 17 February 1932. See also the *El Socialista* editorial on republicans and *caciquismo* of 17 January 1932.
5 *El Progreso*, 3 January 1932; Martínez Barrio, *Memorias*, p. 111; Alicante party to Lerroux, 9 March 1932, AS, P-S Madrid, C41 number 2 L733; Mariano García Andreu, *Alicante en las elecciones republicanas, 1931–1936* (Alicante, 1985), p. 53.
6 Requena Gallego, *Albacete 1931–1933*, p. 156; *El Socialista*, 5 June and 27 September 1932; and Isidro Mateo to Lerroux, 3 June 1932, AS, P-S Madrid, C11 L713.
7 *El Sol*, 28 February and 4 March 1932; Azaña, *Memorias*, II, 19 February 1932. Lerroux claims that all those present at the banquet supported the party. *El Sol* reports that they were all from the business world with the exception of the Barcelona old guard, while the *Libro de Oro* states that there were "many señoras", p. 218.
8 A. Rodríguez de la Borbolla to Lerroux, 29 August 1932, AS, P-S Madrid, C1720 L672; A. Montaner to Lerroux, 26 July 1932, AS, P-S Madrid, C1720 L672; Bermejo, *Logroño*, pp. 223–5; F. Zuazo to Lerroux, 24 August 1932, AS, P-S Madrid, C1720 L672; *El Liberal*, 28 September 1932.
9 Tusell et al., *Las Constituyentes de 1931*, pp. 183–4; *La Tierra*, 1 February 1932; Manuel Rivera to Lerroux, 22 April 1932, AS, P-S Madrid, C41 number 2 L734; L. Sellés to Lerroux, 29 June 1932, AS, P-S Madrid, C1720 L672; Salvador Martínez Moya to Lerroux, 6 July 1932, AS, P-S Madrid, C1720 L672.
   A Radical branch from Murcia told Lerroux that it would back Rivera but not agents "of Ciervism". It also criticized the national leadership for converting the problem into one "without remedy" (AS, P-S Madrid, C40 L741).
   For another internal struggle in the neighbouring province of Alicante, see García Andreu, *Alicante*, p. 54 and *El Socialista*, 14 May 1932.
10 Quintanar de la Orden Radical Party to Lerroux, AS, P-S Madrid, C46 L771; José María Azpíroz Pascual, *Poder político y conflictividad social en Huesca durante la II República* (Huesca, 1993), pp. 63–70 and 72–5; Requeno Gallego, *Albacete 1931–1933*, p. 156; *El Liberal*, 15 March 1932.
11 Martínez Barrio, *Memorias*, pp. 106–7. See also the *El Progreso* editorials for 14 and 25 February 1932.
12 *El Socialista*, 9 March 1932; *La Tierra*, 27 April 1932; the Cañete la Real (Malaga) Radical Party to Lerroux, 25 March 1932, AS, P-S Madrid, C4 L746; letter to Lerroux, AS, P-S Madrid, C17220 L672; Radical Party of Chauchina (Granada) to Lerroux, March 1932, AS, P-S Madrid, C43.
   I find it extremely difficult to reconcile this last document with the interpretation given to it by López Martínez, *Orden*, p. 180.
13 "Informe confidencial" dated 17 July 1932, AS, P-S Madrid, C1720 L672; Domingo Alonso Jimeno was one of four socialist deputies elected for Toledo, as shown by Tusell et al., *Las Constituyentes de 1931*, p. 192. In combatting

the socialists, the Radicals sometimes colluded with the CNT. See, for example, Caro Cancela, *Cádiz*, p. 149.

14 See the Radical statement in *El Sol*, 16 December 1931; Lerroux, *La pequeña historia*, pp. 128–9; *El Sol*, 11 February and 4 March 1932.

15 Casanova, *De la calle*, p. 43; Francisca Rosique Navarro, *La reforma agraria en Badajoz durante la II República* (Badajoz, 1988), p. 231, has astonishingly little to say about the incident. For a recent reappraisal, see Martin Baumeister, "Castilblanco or the Limits of Democracy – Rural Protest in Spain from the Restoration Monarchy to the Early Second Republic", *Contemporary European History*, 7, I, 1998, pp. 1–19.

16 Concepción Muñoz Tinoco, *Diego Hidalgo: un notario republicano* (Badajoz, 1986), pp. 48–57; Elsa López, José Alvarez Junco, Manuel Espadas Burgos, and Concepción Muñoz Tinoco, *Diego Hidalgo: memoria de un tiempo difícil* (Madrid, 1986), p. 130–2; DSCC, 5 January 1932.

The tension between the two parties was heightened by the dispute in November 1931 as to whether Margarita Nelken, one of the organizers of the strike, was entitled to enter the Cortes as a socialist deputy (she was not a Spanish national). See López et al., *Diego Hidalgo*, pp. 122–5.

Even Martínez Barrio, one of the Radical Party's most liberal figures, maintained over twenty years later that the blame for the incident lay with the Pacense socialist leaders for their "rancorous impulse" rather than with the Civil Guard. See Martínez Barrio, *Memorias*, pp. 102–3 and 112.

17 Casanova, *De la calle*, pp. 43–4 and Martínez Barrio, *Memorias*, p. 104. The account of the massacre is based on the investigation carried out by the civil governor of Vizcaya, the details of which are given by Casanova, *De la calle*, pp. 44–6. On 30 January 1934 a military court absolved the lieutenant who ordered the shooting. In contrast to the national party, local leader F. Alonso called for the satisfaction of all the workers' demands, a move that was apparently in keeping with the mood of the Arnedo Radical Party as a whole. See Bermejo, *Logroño*, p. 224.

18 Azaña, *Memorias*, II, 23 January 1932; Casanova, *De la calle*, pp. 102–6, and, for his general reflections, pp. 124–31; Avilés, *La izquierda burguesa*, p. 124; Payne, *Spain's First Democracy*, p. 77.

Casanova relates that one of the deportees died from illness, while the rest had all returned to Spain by September 1932. In parliament, the Prime Minister turned the issue into a vote of confidence, at which point numerous Radicals abandoned the chamber. As a result, the government won by 159 to 14 votes. See Azaña, *Memorias*, II, 12 February 1932 and Juliá, *Azaña*, p. 170.

There was greater support for the deportees at the local level of the Radical Party. For example, the Radical Youth of Madrid called on the government to amnesty them as a gesture of goodwill on the first anniversary of the Republic, as did the branch in the district of Carabanchel, while the Puente de Vallecas branch, also in Madrid, called for an amnesty for all political crimes, especially the deportees. See *El Liberal*, 30 March, 3 and 7 April 1932.

19 DSCC, 13–19 January 1932 and 23 February 1932.

20 Azaña, *Memorias*, II, 13 March 1932; Martínez Barrio, *Memorias*, pp. 107, 109, 112; *El Sol*, 28 February 1932.

21 Pedro Sainz Rodríguez, *Testimonio y recuerdos* (Barcelona, 1978), pp. 154–5; Lerroux, *La pequeña historia*, p. 130; Azaña, *Memorias*, II, 29 January 1932.

22 Martínez Barrio, *Memorias*, pp. 107 and 109; Azaña, *Memorias*, II, 29 January 1932; *El Sol*, 4 March 1932.

In the interview with *El Sol* of 11 February 1932, Lerroux revealed that the meeting had been switched from Barcelona to Madrid at the government's request because of the CNT deportations, and that he would speak instead on 21 February in the Madrid bullring.

23 *El Progreso*, 13 January, 4, 5, 6, 7, 18, and 21 February 1932. Much the same adulation was heaped on Lerroux two months later on the first anniversary of the Republic. See *El Progreso*, 14 April 1932.

24 *El Progreso*, 23 February 1932 and Martínez Barrio, *Memorias*, p. 109. The speech is in *El Progreso*, 23 February 1932.

25 In *La pequeña historia* Lerroux insists that his speech was "without an accent of opposition" (pp. 129–30).

26 Andrés de Blas Guerrero, "El Partido Radical en la política española de la Segunda República", *Revista de Estudios Políticas*, 31–2, 1983, rightly stresses the Radical mission of "centring" the Republic.

27 *El Liberal*, 23, 24, and 25 February 1932; *El Progreso*, 23 February 1932; *El Socialista*, 23 and 24 February 1932; *El Sol*, 23 February 1932; Azaña, *Memorias*, II, 22 February and 5 March 1932.

28 In his diary for 7 January 1932, Azaña states that he wanted the republican–socialist government to last as long as possible before giving way to an all-republican one headed by Lerroux. See Azaña, *Memorias*, II, 7 January 1932.

29 Martínez Barrio, *Memorias*, p. 109; *El Sol*, 4 March 1932; Emiliano Iglesias to Lerroux, 8 February 1932, AS, P-S Madrid, C846 L742, cited by Ruiz Manjón, *El Partido Republicano Radical*, p. 288.

30 *El Sol*, 24 and 28 February 1932; Azaña, *Memorias*, II, 24 February 1932.

31 Lerroux also criticized Azaña's labours as Minister of War on account of the lack of preparation of the army. Martínez Barrio, *Memorias*, p. 111, records Azaña's hurt.

32 Azaña, *Memorias*, II, 5 and 25 March 1932; Lerroux, *La pequeña historia*, p. 128.

33 *El Sol*, 28 February and 4 March 1932; Payne, *Spain's First Democracy*, pp. 74–9; Cabrera, *La patronal*, pp. 205–6.

34 *El Sol*, 4 and 5 March 1932; Azaña, *Memorias*, II, 5 and 13 March 1932; Payne, *Spain's First Democracy*, p. 78.
   The newspapers had been suspended in accordance with the harsh Law of Defence of the Republic. The parliamentary motion criticizing the move had been signed by Gil Robles, the leader of Acción Nacional, and Lerroux, in his capacity as President of the Press Association.

35 Azaña, *Memorias*, II, 13 and 17 March 1932; *El Debate*, 29 March 1932; Espín, *Azaña*, pp. 93–4; Avilés, *La izquierda burguesa*, pp. 134–5.

36 Avilés, *La izquierda burguesa*, p. 134; Espín, *Azaña*, p. 95; Gómez Molleda, *La Masonería*, pp. 429–50; *El Progreso*, 11 March 1932.

37 *El Sol*, 12 April 1932; *El Liberal*, 15 March 1932; *El Progreso*, 22 March 1932. For the Acción Popular campaign, see José María Gil Robles, *No fue posible la paz* (Barcelona, 1968), pp. 67–76 and Preston, *The Coming*, pp. 48–58.

38 *El Progreso*, 22 March 1932; *El Sol*, 28 February and 15 April 1932.

39 *El Sol*, 12 April 1932; Alvarez Rey, *La derecha*, pp. 67–8.

40 *El Progreso*, 14, 25 February, 5 and 19 April 1932. See also Lerroux's speech to the Radical Youth in *El Progreso*, 8 March 1932 and the editorial of the party organ on 27 May 1932. For the offensive in the provinces see, for example, Caro Cancela, *Cádiz*, p. 138 and Requena Gallego, *Albacete*

1931–1933, p. 157. For Lerroux's view of the socialists' sectarianism, see *La pequeña historia*, p. 131.

41 The Radical leader habitually avoided the issue of the party's proposals for reform by asserting that "I have nothing to add to my programme". See, for example, his speech in Barcelona and his declarations to the press there in *El Sol*, 28 February 1932. In the same vein, see the *El Progreso* editorials of 13 January, 4 and 6 February 1932.

42 *El Progreso*, 22 March 1932; *El Sol*, 15 April 1932; Azaña, *Memorias*, II, 14 April 1932. For the Radical campaign as a whole, see *El Progreso*, 8, 9, 19, and 22 March, 8, 12, and 16 April 1932.

43 Alvarez Rey, *La derecha*, pp. 65 and 67; AS, P-S Madrid, C1720 L672; Requena Gallego, *Albacete 1931–1933*, pp. 152–4. By mid 1932 the Huesca party had branches in 122 pueblos. See Azpíroz Pascual, *Huesca en la II República*, p. 60.

44 1932 is the only year under the Republic for which there are complete figures on the number of Radical branches. According to the limited information available, the average Radical branch under the Republic had 100 members. This would give the party a total membership in 1932 of nearly 400,000, which is probably too high a figure. By contrast, the PRRS had 67 members per branch in 1932 but claimed that there were in fact 231. The former figure, if applied to the Radical Party, would give it 255,002 affiliates in 1932, the latter the unrealistic aggregate of 875,513 members. See AS, P-S Madrid, C44 L751; Ruiz Manjón, *El Partido Republicano Radical*, pp. 608 and 611–12; Espín, *Azaña*, p. 93; and Avilés, *La izquierda burguesa*, p. 144.

45 Caro Cancela, *Cádiz*, pp. 137–42 and 165.

46 Antonio Montaner to Lerroux, 26 July 1932, AS, P-S Madrid, C1720 L672; Pedro Loperena to Lerroux, 4 July 1932, AS, P-S Madrid, C1720 L672; *El Progreso*, 27 and 29 July, 3, 12, 16, 21 and 23 August 1932.

47 *El Progreso*, 8 March, 4, 5, and 6 July 1932; Ruiz Manjón, *El Partido Republicano Radical*, pp. 329–30, 348–51, and 364–6.

48 López Martínez, *Orden*, pp. 176–82; Alarcón Caballero, *Granada*, pp. 128–9; the letters of Fernando Gómez de la Cruz to Lerroux, AS, P-S Madrid, C1720 L672.

Gómez de la Cruz claimed that Pareja Yébenes had tried to enter the Socialist Party following the Republic's proclamation. In November 1932, Rafael Salazar Alonso appears to have persuaded the warring factions to reunite. Lerroux's contact with Pareja Yébenes predates the Republic, as evident from his letter to him of 11 September 1930, AS, P-S Madrid, C39 L700, cited by Ruiz Manjón, *El Partido Republicano Radical*, p. 153, footnote 20.

49 Cabrera, *La patronal*, pp. 163, 183–6, and 198–202.

50 DSCC, 11 May and 6 July 1932; Varela, *Partidos*, pp. 245–6 and 274 footnote 65. Despite his party, Diego Hidalgo presented one of the most coherent alternatives to the bill.

Martínez Barrio strongly criticizes the Minister of Agriculture, Marcelino Domingo, and his under-secretary, Santiago Valiente, in his *Memorias*, pp. 115–16 and 120, while Alcalá-Zamora contends that under Azaña "each ministry was like a canton and each minister a soloist, for better or worse, without a ministerial orchestra". See Alcalá-Zamora, *Memorias*, p. 212.

51 Rafael Salazar Alonso, *Bajo el signo de la revolución* (Madrid, 1935), p. 270; DSCC, 20 May 1932; Varela, *Partidos*, p. 139; Espín, *Azaña*, pp. 209–10.

52 Varela, *Partidos*, pp. 137–9 and 152–5; Azaña, *Memorias*, II, 8 July 1932;

Ruiz Manjón, *El Partido Republicano Radical*, pp. 309–16.
53 Azaña, *Memorias*, II, 19 and 22 February, 3, 8, April, and 14 June 1932; DSCC, 14 June 1932; Piñeiro, *Los March*, pp. 140–3; Garriga, *Juan March*, pp. 316–30.
54 Azaña, *Memorias*, II, 7, 10, 17, and 24 June, 8 July 1932, Lerroux, *La pequeña historia*, p. 128.
55 *El Sol*, 28 June 1932; Azaña, *Memorias*, II, 6 July 1932.
   For an example of the pressure on the Radical Party to defend Juan March, see the letter of Natalio Rivas, the former monarchist minister, to Lerroux in which he called on the Radical leader to release the Mallorcan magnate from his "cruel and arbitrary" internment for the sake of the "good name of Spain". See AS, P-S Madrid, C1161 L713.
56 Azaña, *Memorias*, II, 7 June, 6, 7 July 1932; Martínez Barrio, *Memorias*, p. 129.
57 Gil Robles in DSCC, 14 June 1932; Azaña, *Memorias*, II, 8 July 1932. For the way in which Azaña's meteoric rise shaped his view of politics, see Azaña, *Memorias*, I, 28 August and 1 September 1931.
58 *El Sol*, 12 July 1932. Lerroux did criticize Azaña, though not by name, in relation to the Military Academy in Zaragoza.
59 *El Socialista*, 15 July 1932; *El Debate* editorial 16 July 1932; *El Sol*, 16 July 1932; Azaña, *Memorias*, II, 11, 12 and 15 July 1932. *El Progreso* responded on 20 July 1932 that the socialist manifesto was "unconstitutional, inopportune, aggressive, unjust and antipatriotic". See also *El Progreso*, 16 July 1932.
60 DSCC, 19 July 1932; Azaña, *Memorias*, II, 11 July 1932. The contradictions in Lerroux's stance were highlighted by *El Sol* in its front-page editorial of 15 July 1932.

5 Plotting for Power

1 The insurgents were especially concerned to prevent the passing of the Catalan Statute. See Sainz Rodríguez, *Testimonio*, p. 325.
   The rising was brought forward to 10 August 1932, at 48 hours notice, because it was feared that it would be uncovered. See Julio Gil Pecharromán, *Conservadores subversivos: la derecha autoritaria alfonsina (1913–1936)* (Madrid, 1994), p. 110.
2 Azaña, *Memorias*, II, 3, 9 May, 22 June, 5 July 1932; Azaña, *Diarios*, 8 and 9 August 1932; Martínez Barrio, *Memorias*, p. 139; Alcalá-Zamora diary for June to August 1932, cited by Martínez Barrio, *Memorias*, pp. 138–9 and 152.
3 Eduardo González Calleja, "La radicalización de la derecha durante la Segunda República (1931–1936): violencia política, paramilitarización y fascistización en la crisis española de los años treinta", Ph.D. thesis, Complutense University of Madrid, 1993, p. 432.
   The only insurgent success in Madrid was to secure control of the depot of the monarchist-dominated Cavalry Corps. Several died in the assault. See González Cuevas, *Acción Española*, p. 168.
4 Joaquín Arraras, *Historia de la Segunda República española*, 4 vols (Madrid, 1956–1968), I, p. 522; Juan Antonio Ansaldo, *¿Para qué? (De Alfonso XIII a Juan III)* (Buenos Aires, 1951), p. 40.
5 González Cuevas, *Acción Española*, p. 169 and Vidarte, *Las Cortes*, pp. 457–9.
6 For events in Seville, see the first-hand material supplied by Martínez Barrio, *Memorias*, pp. 142–3 and 145–6, as well as the detailed reconstruction in Alvarez Rey, *La derecha*, pp. 252–61 and 264. There is also an account by

Sanjurjo's aide, lieutenant colonel E. Esteban Infantes, *La sublevación del general Sanjurjo* (Madrid, 1933).

7 González Calleja, "La radicalización de la derecha", p. 429.

8 Manuel Burgos y Mazo, *¿De República a . . . ?* (Madrid, 1931), p. 208, cited by González Cuevas, *Acción Española*, p. 166.

For the former Constitutionalists, and in particular Burgos y Mazo, see Alvarez Rey, *La derecha*, pp. 244–52. Of Melquiades Alvarez's involvement there is no doubt, despite the disclaimers of Maximiano García Venero, *Melquiades Alvarez: historia de un liberal*, 2nd edition (Madrid, 1974), p. 452. In fact, Melquiades Alvarez, Santiago Alba, and Burgos y Mazo drew up a manifesto for Sanjurjo, but this was discarded in favour of one written by Juan Pujol, editor of *Informaciones*. See Arrarás, *Segunda República*, I, pp. 464–5.

9 On Sanjurjo, see the pen portrait by his close friend, the monarchist intellectual and future Nationalist minister, Pedro Sainz Rodríguez, *Tesimonio*, pp. 251–2.

10 For Sanjurjo's disquiet and the pressure from the right, see Azaña, *Memorias*, II, 8, 11, and 17 January, and 3 February 1932. The General had been approached by Gabriel Maura, monarchist brother of the Minister of the Interior, in relation to the organization of a coup as early as August 1931, but it took another seven months before he committed himself. See Gabriel Cardona, "La conspiración", *Historia 16*, VII, number 76, p. 46.

The intermediary was Pedro Rico, who became an AR deputy and mayor of Madrid under the Republic. See his account in AMB, L9 C39. He was also asked by Sanjurjo to see the Prime Minister, but whether he did or not is unclear.

Sanjurjo tried to enlist General Francisco Franco, the future dictator, but he, with typical guile, promised nothing while adding that "I shall see what I can do according to the circumstances", as related by an eyewitness, Pedro Sainz Rodríguez in *Testimonio*, pp. 325–6. Franco confirms that he refused to take part in Francisco Franco Salgado-Araujo, *Mis conversaciones privadas con Franco* (Barcelona, 1976), p. 499, but the reasons given are not as convincing as that which he gave in late July 1932 at a lunch at the house of the Marqués de la Vega de Anzo – namely, that the rebellion was likely to fail. See Gil Robles, *No fue posible*, p. 235. Sainz Rodríguez believed, as late as 1936, that Franco aspired to nothing more than the position of High Commissioner in Morocco, but the President, in his diary of 18 May 1932, noted that he was suspected of aspiring "to be the most dangerous *caudillo* of the monarchist reaction". Cited in Martínez Barrio, *Memorias*, p. 138.

11 Alvarez Rey, *La derecha*, p. 249; González Calleja, "La radicalización de la derecha", pp. 427–9; Ansaldo, *Para qué*, p. 32; Martínez Barrio, *Memorias*, p. 139.

The Italian Ambassador related that General Barrera spoke of a popular plebiscite to determine the regime that followed the establishment of a provisional dictatorship. See Ismael Saz Campos, *Mussolini contra la II República* (Valencia, 1986), p. 39.

12 Gil Pecharromán, *Conservadores*, p. 110.

Albiñana wrote a book about his confinement, *Confinado en las Hurdes* (Madrid, 1933).

13 González Cuevas, *Acción Española*, p. 167; Azaña, *Memorias*, II, 21, 25, 27, 28 June; Alcalá-Zamora diary entry for 27 June 1932, cited in Martínez Barrio, *Memorias*, p. 138.

14 *El Socialista*, 13 and 14 August 1932; Vidarte, *Las Cortes*, pp. 446, 448, and 459; Martínez Barrio, *Memorias*, pp. 144 and 148; DSCC, 10 and 11 August 1932.

15 Alvarez Junco, *El Emperador*, pp. 36–42; Joaquín Romero Maura, "Terrorism in Barcelona and its impact on Spanish politics 1904–1910", *Past & Present*, 41, 1968; Montero, "The Forging", pp. 219–20; García Carraffa, *Alejandro Lerroux*, pp. 20, 26–9, 49–53, 56, 66, 81–4, and 91.

16 AMB, L9 C39. See also Martínez Barrio to Rico, 27 June 1953 and Rico to Martínez Barrio, 15 July 1953, AMB, L9 C39. The first meeting between Lerroux and Sanjurjo was the only one attended by Rico in person.

General Franco was of the same opinion as Rico, having learnt from Natalio Rivas, Lerroux's intimate ally, that Sanjurjo had seen the Radical leader the day before the Republic's proclamation. See Franco Salgado-Araujo, *Conversaciones*, pp. 89 and 121.

17 Lerroux, *La pequeña historia*, pp. 80–1; Rico to Martínez Barrio, 15 July 1953, AMB, L9 C39, as well as the comments of Martínez Barrio on the draft; Tusell at al., *Las Constituyentes de 1931*, pp. 141–7, and 179; Ruiz Manjón, *El Partido Republicano Radical*, pp. 202–3.

18 Azaña, *Memorias*, I, 2 July, 7 August, and 16 November 1931. Interest in a coup was also shared by the socialist intellectuals Luis Araquistain and Juan Negrín, as related in Azaña, *Memorias*, I, 28 August 1931.

19 E. Ballester to Lerroux, 16 October 1931, AS, P-S Madrid, C43; General José Fernández de Villa-Abrille to M. González Jonte, 8 August 1933, AS, P-S Madrid, C30 L447.

20 Lerroux, *La pequeña historia*, pp. 131–3; Martínez Barrio, *Memorias*, pp. 105–6. Lerroux says that Ubaldo Azpiazu, not Maura, was present, which is perfectly possible, but Martínez Barrio's *Memorias* are generally much more reliable.

21 Lerroux, *La pequeña historia*, pp. 132–4.

22 Martínez Barrio, *Memorias*, pp. 105–6; Lerroux, *La pequeña historia*, pp. 131–3; Azaña, *Memorias*, I, 2 July 1931.

23 Azaña, *Memorias*, I, 2 July 1931. Franco confirms that Sanjurjo had an "intimate friendship with Lerroux" in Franco Salgado-Araujo, *Conversaciones*, p. 499.

24 Martínez Barrio, *Memorias*, p. 154; Lerroux, *La pequeña historia*, pp. 132–5; Avilés, *La izquierda burguesa*, p. 154.

25 Martínez Barrio, *Memorias*, pp. 131–4 and 137; Azaña, *Memorias*, II, 22 and 25 June 1932.

26 Martínez Barrio, *Memorias*, pp. 132–3.

27 Martínez Barrio, *Memorias*, pp. 141–3 and 155. The more discreet Lerroux did not give the impression to the deputies that visited San Rafael that he was in favour of the *coup d'état*. His account of why he left Madrid was given to *La Libertad*, cited by Martínez Barrio, *Memorias*, pp. 154–5.

28 *El Socialista*, 28, 30, 31 August and 2 September 1932; Bergamín to Lerroux, AS, P-S Madrid, C1720 L672; Azaña, *Memorias*, II, 11, July 1932; Azaña, *Diarios*, 29 August 1932.

29 *El Socialista*, 14, 15, and 17 October 1932; *El Progreso*, 15 and 16 October 1932; Azaña, *Memorias*, IV, pp. 520–1; Azaña, *Diarios*, 15 and 20 August 1932. Azaña asked himself if Lerroux was "a brute, a madman or a malevolent person: or the three things together".

30 Azaña, *Memorias*, I, 2 July 1931, II, 20 and 22 July 1932. On a purely official level, Azaña wrote to Lerroux after the attempted *coup* to thank him for "your solidarity and adherence and that of your party at this difficult time for the Republic, for the defence of which we must always be in agreement", AS, P-S Madrid, C1720 L672.

31 DSCC, 10 August 1932; Azaña, *Memorias*, IV, 7 November 1937; Azaña, *Memorias*, II, 20 and 22 July 1932, III, 1 March 1933; Alcalá-Zamora, *Memorias*, p. 517.

32 Cabanellas' proximity to the coup preparations is revealed in the Burgos y Mazo papers, cited by Alvarez Rey, *La derecha*, p. 251. Indeed, the Minister of the Interior was so unhappy at his performance during the *coup* that he wanted Cabanellas replaced, but there was insufficient evidence to justify such a move. See Azaña, *Diarios*, 12 August 1932.

33 Azaña, *Memorias*, II, 23 January, 22 February, and 2 April 1932.

34 Garriga, *Juan March*, p. 333. Neither Benavides, *El último pirata*, p. 297, nor Piñeiro, *Los March*, p. 143, have any evidence either.

35 González Calleja, "La radicalización de la derecha", p. 431; González Cuevas, *Acción Española*, p. 165. The March publication lost the word "Militar" from its title on 26 March 1932.

36 González Cuevas, *Acción Española*, p. 173 and Piñeiro, *Los March*, p. 391. Burgos y Mazo claims that March never produced the money which had been promised, but March is more likely to have backed the purely monarchist strand of the conspiracy. See the Burgos y Mazo papers, cited by Alvarez Rey, *La derecha*, p. 245. Tomás Peire became, according to Piñeiro, one of March's "key men" in the post-Civil War years.

37 Azaña, *Memorias*, II, 15 July 1932 and Azaña, *Diarios*, 2 March 1933.

38 Azaña, *Memorias*, II, 22 February 1932. Lerroux also provided succour for those who, if not necessarily involved, at least knew of the rising. Amongst them was the owner of the influential monarchist daily *ABC*, Juan Luca de Tena, who wrote to the Radical leader while in detention on 21 August 1932 to thank him for his "affectionate letter" while describing him as a man "of good faith", AS, P-S Madrid, C1720 L672.

39 Azaña, *Diarios*, 22 July, 15 and 29 August 1932; Martínez Barrio, *Memorias*, pp. 153–4; Alvarez Rey, *La derecha*, p. 252.

40 Martínez Barrio, *Memorias*, pp. 139–43 and 145.

41 Martínez Barrio, *Memorias*, p. 148; Alvarez Rey, *La derecha*, p. 258; Vidarte, *Las Cortes*, p. 450, 454, and 457.
    Ironically, the Radical mayor of Seville, José González y Fernández de la Bandera, wrote to Lerroux on 27 August 1932 to explain that he had acted as the Radical leader would have wanted, AS, P-S Madrid, C1720 L672. The mayor's defiance would not be forgotten. On 10 August 1936 – four years to the day after the "Sanjurjada" – he was shot following the outbreak of the Civil War on the orders of General Queipo de Llano. The fact that the General was himself a Radical crystallizes the contradictions that characterized the party.

42 Alvarez Rey, *La derecha*, pp. 258–9 and 278–80; A. Rodríguez de la Borbolla to Lerroux, 29 August 1932, AS, P-S Madrid, C1720 L672. *El Socialista* also affirmed on 13 August 1932 that Torres Caravaca, vice president of the Radical Circle of Seville, put himself at Sanjurjo's disposition.

43 José Bermúdez de Castro to Lerroux, 19 August 1932, AS, P-S Madrid, C1720 L672; General Eduardo Pardo to Lerroux, 18 August 1932, AS, P-S Madrid, C1720 L672.

44 González Calleja, "La radicalización de la derecha", p. 434 footnote 241; Paul Preston, *Franco: "Caudillo de España"* (Barcelona, 1994), pp. 228–9.

45 Gil-Yuste to Lerroux March 1933, AS, P-S Madrid, C30 L447.

46 José Fernández de Villa-Abrille to M. González Jonte, 8 August 1933, AS, P-S Madrid, C30 L447. Fernández de Villa-Abrille kept his promise. Once the

Civil War erupted, he was condemned to death by Franco, but not, in the end, executed. See Antonio Alonso Baño, editor, *Homenaje a Diego Martínez Barrio* (Paris, 1978), p. 114.

47   Alfonso Serna, *Un proceso histórico: del 10 de agosto a la sala sexta del supremo* (Madrid, 1933), pp. 32–5; González Calleja, "La radicalización de la derecha", pp. 170 and 433–4; Azaña, *Diarios*, 25 August 1932; González Cuevas, *Acción Española*, p. 172.

48   González Calleja, "La radicalización de la derecha", p. 435; Gil Pecharromán, *Conservadores*, p. 113. The handful in favour of accepting the republican regime were also defeated in favour of the accidentalist formula. See Gil Pecharromán, *Conservadores*, pp. 113–14.

49   González Cuevas, *Acción Española*, pp. 172–4.

50   José Luis Rodríguez Jiménez, *La extrema derecha española en el siglo XX* (Madrid, 1997), pp. 115–16. The king continued to play the accidentalist card, too. See González Calleja, "La radicalización de la derecha", pp. 436–7.

That few monarchists abandoned the Sevillian branch of Acción Popular after the October 1932 Congress is attributed by Alvarez Rey to the fact that the local leader, the Conde de Bustillo, was, in his own words, a "convinced anti-republican and anti-democrat". See the Archive of Giménez Fernández, cited by Alvarez Rey, *La derecha*, p. 275.

6 The Ambiguous Courtship

1   DSCC, 18 August 1932; *Heraldo de Madrid*, 18 August 1932, cited by Ruiz Manjón, *El Partido Republicano Radical*, p. 327; Manuel Marraco to Lerroux, AS, P-S Madrid, C1720 L672; *El Progreso*, 7 and 10 September 1932.

2   Martínez Barrio, *Memorias*, pp. 160–1; Avilés, *La izquierda burguesa*, pp. 158–9; Malefakis, *Agrarian Reform*, pp. 236–40.

3   Martínez Barrio, *Memorias*, pp. 158–60; Avilés, *La izquierda burguesa*, 161 and 163. The Santander speech is in Azaña, *Memorias*, IV, pp. 115–32. The speech had been approved beforehand by the Cabinet.

4   Ruiz Manjón, *El Partido Republicano Radical*, pp. 352–52; *El Progreso*, 4 March 1932; Martínez Barrio, *Memorias*, pp. 158–9.

5   This, and the account that follows of the Congress, is based on the extensive documentation in the party archive, AS, P-S Madrid, C1720 L672 and C570 L4749, as well as on the *Libro de Oro*, pp. 223–40.

6   AR, like the PRRS, had already held two national congresses by this stage. In addition, the PRRS had held two special ones.

7   Lerroux's opening address is in the *Libro de Oro*, pp. 226–32. His closing speech was also characterized by its reconciliatory nature. He emphasized that the Radicals had left the republican–socialist government in December 1931 "over nuances that had more to do with questions of procedure than doctrine". This speech, too, is in the *Libro de Oro*, pp. 226–32.

8   The programme drawn up by the Congress is in Martínez Barrio, *Memorias*, p. 161.

9   Avilés, *La izquierda burguesa*, pp. 162–3 and Espín, *Azaña*, p. 96. Azaña's Valladolid speech is in *El Sol*, 15 November 1931.

10   Preston, *The Coming*, pp. 74–6 and 78–81. For the Asturian mines, a major arena of conflict, see Adrian Shubert, "Revolution in self-defence: the radicalization of the Asturian coal miners, 1921–1934", *Social History*, VII, number 3, 1982.

11   Ruiz Manjón, *El Partido Republicano Radical*, pp. 346–7; Nigel Townson,

"The Socialist Disengagement from the Socialist-left-Republican Alliance in 1933", MA dissertation, University of London, 1983; Martínez Barrio, *Memorias*, pp. 160 and 162.

12 Azaña, *Diarios*, 16 December 1932 and 24 May 1933; DSCC, 16 December 1932; *El Progreso* editorial, 18 December 1932.

13 *El Progreso* editorials, 10, 20, 24 and 27 December 1932; article by Juan Palau in *El Progreso*, 25 December 1932; Azaña, *Diarios*, 14, 16, 24, 29 and 31 December 1932.

A sector within the Radical Party, including Martínez Barrio and Lara, had grave reservations over the renewal of the opposition, as Azaña notes in *Diarios*, 16 and 24 December 1932.

Azaña's own contemporary account seethes with contempt for the Radicals. He lambasts the "hatred" and "vulgarity" of Lerroux and the lack of "ideas and statesman-like ability" as well as reviling the Radicals' ally Santiago Alba as "an intriguer, badly intentioned and rancorous". See Azaña, *Diarios*, 24 and 29 December 1932.

14 Jerome Mintz, *The Anarchists of Casas Viejas* (Chicago, 1982), pp. 201–25 and 253–76. A more succinct version in Casanova, *De la calle*, pp. 108–13, with general considerations on pp. 126–7.

15 Azaña, *Diarios*, 1 February 1933; *El Progreso* editorials 12, 15 and 20 January 1933. The quotes from *El Imparcial* and *El Pueblo* are in *El Progreso* 26 January 1933. The Martínez Barrio speech is to be found in *El Progreso* 26 January 1933 and the Riera Vidal article is in *El Progreso*, 25 January 1933.

16 *El Progreso*, 4, 17, 25, 26, 27, 31 January, and 1 February 1933. The speech of 28 January 1933 by Basilio Alvarez is in *El Progreso*, 1 February 1933 and *Dos años*, pp. 120–9. See also the speech by Fernando Rey Mora in Palma de Condado (Huelva) in *El Progreso*, 11 January 1933 and the article by a Radical deputy in *El Progreso*, 21 January 1933.

17 *El Progreso*, 1, 2, and 3 February 1933.

18 DSCC, 1 February 1933; Azaña, *Diarios*, 5 February 1933; *El Debate*, 5 February 1933. The Lerroux speech is in DSCC, 3 February 1933 as well as in Antonio Marsá Bragado, *El republicanismo histórico* (Madrid, 1933), pp. 89–118. The central thrust of *El Progreso* hereon was that "for the life of the Republic, the government should resign" and give way to an all-republican administration. See the editorials of 7, 11, 22 February, 1, 11, 12 March 1933.

19 DSCC, 3 February 1933; Azaña, *Diarios*, 24 December 1932 and 15 February 1933; *El Sol*, 8 and 22 January 1933. The speech is in *El Debate* 16 February 1933.

20 Azaña, *Diarios*, 13, 21, 22, and 23 February 1933.

21 Azaña, *Diarios*, 18, 20, 23, 24, and 28 February 1933. On 28 February 1933 Gordón Ordás, Valera, and Feced resigned as director generals (Azaña, *Diarios*, 28 February 1933).

22 Azaña, *Diarios*, 1, 2, and 16 March 1933; DSCC, 2, 15, and 16 March 1933. According to Azaña, Guerra del Río wanted to publish the statement of the Assault Guards in *El Imparcial*, which was sympathetic to the Radical Party, but Lerroux overruled him. As a result, Guerra del Río, in a fit of pique, allegedly tore up the envelope that contained the statement, at which point Lerroux exclaimed that he did not want to talk any further in the Cortes about either the statement or Casas Viejas. If true, this obviously reflects the tensions within the Radical Party. See Azaña, *Diarios*, 1 March 1933.

23 Mintz, *Casas Viejas*, pp. 260–4; Gérald Brey and Jacques Maurice, *Historia y leyenda de Casas Viejas* (Bilbao, 1976), pp. 61–2.
    Captain Rojas was tried in May 1934 and condemned to 21 years in prison for the killings, but he was released following the military rising of July 1936. He won a new reputation for brutality in the repression of the republicans in Granada during the Civil War. See Casanova, *De la calle*, p. 114.

24 Martínez Barrio, *Memorias*, pp. 175–6; Azaña, *Diarios*, 14 and 16 April 1933.

25 *El Progreso*, 26, 27, 28 and 31 January, 14 February, and 5, 15, and 28 March 1933.

26 On the Madrid party, see Payne, *Spain's First Democracy*, p. 168.
    The most comprehensive study of the ideology and organization of the CEDA is José Ramón Montero, *La CEDA: el catolicismo social y político en la II República*, 2 vols (Madrid, 1977). Starkly contrasting views can be found in Paul Preston, *The Coming*, and Richard AH Robinson, *The Origins of Franco's Spain: The Right, the Republic and Revolution, 1931–1936* (Newton Abbot, 1970).

27 For "accidentalism" and the influence of the church on the CEDA, see Preston, *The Coming*, pp. 27–30; Paul Preston, "The "Moderate" Right and the Undermining of the Second Republic in Spain, 1931–1933", *European Studies Review*, III, 4, October 1973; Robinson, *The Origins of Franco's Spain*, pp. 113–17.

28 Gil Robles, *No fue posible*, p. 79 and Payne, *Spain's First Democracy*, p. 170.

29 *El Progreso*, 10 March and 7 April 1933. See also the editorial of 23 March 1933 on "La cruzada reaccionaria" ("The Reactionary Crusade").

30 Azaña, *Diarios*, 27 March 1933; *El Progreso*, 5 and 23 March 1933. The elections concerned 2,653, or 28.65%, of Spain's municipalities, and 19,068, or 23.5%, of the 81,099 councillors, yet involved only 12.98% of the electorate, according to the *Anuario Estadístico de España* of 1934, p. 650.

31 *El Progreso*, 4, 25, and 29 April 1933; *El Debate*, 25 and 26 April 1933. The results are based on 84% of the returns, as provided by the Ministry of the Interior and published in *El Sol* and *El Debate* on 25 April 1933. According to Montero, the CEDA won as many as 4,906 councillors (*La CEDA*, II, p. 284).

32 Avilés, *La izquierda burguesa*, p. 175; *El Debate*, 5 May 1933; Azaña, *Diarios*, 2 May 1933.

33 Azaña, *Diarios*, 5 and 9 February, 8, 11, 12, 17 May 1933.

34 Azaña, *Diarios*, 11, 25, 28 and 31 May 1933. Alcalá-Zamora wanted the Radicals to let three bills be passed before he would force a reshuffle, but Lerroux refused to compromise. See Martínez Barrio, *Memorias*, p. 178.

35 Azaña, *Diarios*, 18 and 25 May 1933; Martínez Barrio, *Memorias*, p. 176.

36 *El Debate*, 1, 3, and 4 June 1933; *El Socialista*, 22 May 1933; Blinkhorn, *Carlism*, pp. 99–100 and 103–4; Preston, *The Coming*, p. 83; and Azaña, *Memorias*, III, pp. 460–1 and 479–87.

37 Azaña, *Diarios*, 25 May 1933 and Avilés, *La izquierda burguesa*, pp. 181–3.
    Though a split within the PRRS was eschewed, the histrionic Joaquín Pérez Madrigal joined the Radical Party at the end of July 1933. The morbidly susceptible Alcalá-Zamora was devastated when the correspondent of *The Times* – a fervent Catholic – indirectly inquired the day before the President signed the bill on Congregations if he had gone to Mass. See Azaña, *Diarios*, 5 June 1933.

38 Jalón, *Memorias*, p. 66; Martínez Barrio, *Memorias*, p. 181; Santos Juliá,

Historia del socialismo español (Barcelona, 1989), pp. 75–7; Avilés, *La izquierda burguesa*, p. 184; Azaña, *Diarios*, 10 and 11 June 1933.

Marcelino Domingo, swayed by the socialist vote and the antagonism towards the Radicals within his own party, did not even establish contact with the Radical Party. See *El Debate*, 14 June 1933 and Martínez Barrio, *Memorias*, p. 182.

39 *El Debate*, 7, 9, and 11 June 1933; Espín, *Azaña*, pp. 113–15; Martínez Barrio, *Memorias*, p. 182.

As a result of the reshuffle, José Giral was replaced by Luis Companys of the Esquerra while Francisco Barnés of the PRRS joined as Minister of Education. The Federal leader José Franchy Rosa was made head of the newly-created Ministry of Industry and Commerce, and Agustín Viñuales of AR Minister of the Economy. As Alvaro de Albornoz left the government on 14 July 1933 to take up the Presidency of the Court of Constitutional Guarantees, Casares Quiroga, Minister of the Interior, provisionally took over the Ministry of Justice.

40 Azaña, *Diarios*, 11 and 12 June 1933; Martínez Barrio, *Memorias*, pp. 181–2; DSCC, 14 June 1933. Azaña's speech is also in his *Obras*, II, pp. 759–70. Martínez Barrio also gave an ample account to the press. See *El Debate*, 14 June 1933.

41 Azaña, *Obras*, IV, pp. 644–5; Azaña, *Diarios*, 15 June 1933.

The proposed Lease Law would limit rents, establish contracts of at least six years, and permit occupiers to purchase the land after twenty years. Unlike the Agrarian Reform Law, this would not require a vast budgetary and bureaucratic outlay. Moreover, it would strengthen republican support amongst the small and middling peasantry at the expense of the right.

42 Manuel Tuñón de Lara, VV.AA., *La crisis del Estado: Dictadura, República, Guerra (1923–1939)* (Barcelona, 1981), cited by Casanova, *De la calle*, p. 56.

43 Juliá, "La experiencia del poder: la izquierda republicana, 1931–1933", in Townson, editor, *El republicanismo en España*, pp. 184–6; Malefakis, *Agrarian Reform*, p. 329 footnote 50.

The strike figures, provided by the Ministry of Labour, are incomplete. In reality, the picture was even more conflictive. Research has shown, for example, that in the province of Cordoba there were 95 stoppages, whereas the Ministry accounts for only 54. See Santos Juliá, *Historia económica y social moderna y contemporánea de España* (Madrid, 1991), pp. 69–72. For the organization of the right amongst the working class, see Colin Winston, *Workers and the Right in Spain 1900–1936* (Princeton, New Jersey, 1985).

44 Casanova, *De la calle*, p. 59. A salient argument of Santos Juliá, in *Madrid, 1931–1934* and "Economic crisis, social conflict and the Popular Front: Madrid 1931–1936", in Preston, editor, *Revolution and War*, is that the CNT in Madrid grew at the expense of the UGT.

45 The standard work on the working-class movements in Seville is José Manuel Macarro Vera, *La utopía*, pp. 314ss. See also Cabrera, *La patronal*, pp. 209–11; Alvarez Rey, *La derecha*, pp. 324–30; and *El Debate*, 9 May 1933.

Both *El Debate* and Cabrera claim that as many as 3,000 entrepreneurs and shopkeepers journeyed to Madrid from Seville, but Alvarez Rey's estimate of 1,000, based on a more detailed account, appears more reliable.

46 Cabrera, *La patronal*, pp. 213–14.

47 Cabrera, *La patronal*, pp. 156–8.

48 Cabrera, *La patronal*, pp. 216–17.

49   Alvarez Rey, *La derecha*, pp. 171–6 and Cabrera, *La patronal*, pp. 167 and
     188–91. Martínez Barrio's address to the FEDA did not so much reflect the
     proximity of the Sevillian Radicals to the Federation, which was firmly
     aligned with the non-republican right, as their generalized sympathy for the
     patronal.

50   *El Debate*, 15 March 1933; Angel Luis López Villaverde, *Cuenca durante la
     II República* (Cuenca, 1997), p. 90; *El Progreso*, 14 and 18 March 1933;
     Libro de Oro, pp. 327–33.

51   Avilés, *La izquierda burguesa*, pp. 191–3; Diego Hidalgo to Rafael Salazar
     Alonso, 30 October 1931, ADH. Azaña's diary mentions neither the visit
     which he received from the FEDA in May 1933 nor that of the Unión
     Económica Congress delegation on 23 July 1933. By contrast, on 27 June
     1933, he refers to the visit of two commissions of strikers.

52   Avilés, *La izquierda burguesa*, pp. 191–3; *El Sol*, 11 July 1933; *El Progreso*,
     12 July 1933.

53   Jalón, *Memorias*, p. 65; Lerroux, *La pequeña historia*, p. 139; Martínez
     Barrio, *Memorias*, pp. 184 and 187–8.
     Relations between Alcalá-Zamora and Azaña were worse than ever after
     the reshuffle. No longer would the President receive the Prime Minister at
     home (Martínez Barrio, *Memorias*, p. 184). An *El Sol* editorial of 13 June
     1933, which was highly critical of the President, was, the hypersensitive
     Alcalá-Zamora mistakenly believed, penned by Azaña himself, thus making
     the situation worse still. See Alcalá-Zamora, *Memorias*, p. 242 and Azaña,
     Diarios, 15 June 1933.

54   *El Progreso*, 27, 28, 29, and 30 July 1933; Azaña, *Diarios*, 27 July 1933.
     The *El Progreso* editorial of 29 July 1933 was emphatically entitled "It is
     Impossible to Govern after Dying".

55   This brings into question Azaña's judgement in allowing Domingo to stay on
     as Minister of Agriculture following the June 1933 reshuffle. For the Prime
     Minister's searing criticism of Domingo, see Azaña, *Diarios*, 16 June, 6, 27,
     and 28 July, and 8 August 1933.

56   Azaña, *Diarios*, 27 and 28 July 1933.
     The labyrinthine saga of the struggle over the national dailies can be
     followed in Azaña, *Diarios*, 29 June, 6, 15 and 27 July 1933, and Avilés, *La
     izquierda burguesa*, p. 190. Juan March offered the press to the government
     if it set him free, but Azaña rejected the offer as the sort of *ancien régime*-
     style deal which he abhorred. See *Diarios*, 28 July 1933.

57   *El Sol*, 1 August 1933; Azaña, *Diarios*, 7 and 27 July, 1 to 8 August 1933;
     Martínez Barrio, *Memorias*, p. 188; *El Debate*, 25 July 1933.

58   Azaña, *Diarios*, 30 July 1933. Divergent accounts of the lack of agreement
     between Azaña and the Radicals in Azaña, *Diarios*, 1 to 8 August 1933 and
     Martínez Barrio, *Memorias*, pp. 188–9.

59   Preston, *The Coming*, pp. 78–82; José Manuel Macarro Vera, "Sindicalismo
     y política", in Santos Juliá, editor, *Ayer*, 20, 1995, p. 158; Juliá, "Objetivos
     políticos de la legislación laboral", in García Delgado, coordinator, *La II
     República española: el primer bienio*, p. 158. See also the excellent introduc-
     tory study by Santos Juliá to Largo Caballero's *Escritos de la República*,
     edited by Juliá, pp. XXIII–LII.

60   *El Socialista*, 31 January, 15 and 26 March 1933. See also Juliá in Largo
     Caballero's *Escritos*, edited by Juliá, pp. XLV–LV, as well as Juliá's article,
     "Los socialistas y el escenario de la futura revolución", in Germán Ojeda,
     editor, *Octubre 1934: cincuenta años para la reflexión* (Madrid, 1985). Also

see Macarro Vera's article "Sindicalismo y política" in Juliá, editor, *Ayer*, 20, 1995, pp. 141–71.

61 Gil Robles, *No fue posible*, p. 60; Malefakis, *Agrarian Reform*, pp. 270–3; Azaña, *Diarios*, 1 to 8 and 15 August 1933; Azaña, *Obras*, IV, p. 644.

62 DSCC, 25 August 1933; Avilés, *La izquierda burguesa*, pp. 189–90 and 195–6; *El Debate*, 21 July 1933; *El Progreso*, 21 July 1933.
    Despite his criticism, Pérez Madrigal joined the Radical Party the following day (*El Progreso*, 22 July 1933). An increasingly suspicious Azaña speculated that Lerroux was behind the "intrigues" of Feced, who was linked to Gordón Ordás and Sánchez Román. See Azaña, *Diarios*, 27 July 1933.

63 Azaña, *Obras*, IV, p. 645; *El Progreso* editorial, 2 September; Espín, *Azaña*, pp. 119–24; Avilés, *La izquierda burguesa*, p. 196.

64 *El Sol*, 5 September 1933. The CEDA secured three of the six right-wing members elected in September 1933.

65 This does not include the votes won by the Radical–PRRS alliance in Extremadura. If one divides these equally between the two parties, the Radical Party won nearly 16,000 nationwide, while the CEDA almost reached 14,000. See Montero, *CEDA*, II, pp. 287–8.

66 *El Progreso*, 5, 6, and 7 September 1933.

67 Alcalá-Zamora, *Memorias*, p. 243; DSCC, 6 September 1933; Azaña, *Obras*, IV, pp. 645–6. According to the President, Azaña agreed that a new government was necessary, but he later changed his mind and tried to continue in power. See Alcalá-Zamora, *Memorias*, pp. 243–4.

7 The Quest for the Centre

1 Azaña, *Obras*, II, pp. 850–1 and Lerroux, *La pequeña historia*, pp. 152–3.

2 See the debate in DSCC, 2 and 3 October 1933. The Azaña quotes can also be found in Azaña, *Obras*, II, pp. 855–6. See also Martínez Barrio, *Memorias*, pp. 191, 194–5, and 199.
    Azaña rightly criticizes the Prime Minister's delay in presenting the government, in Azaña, *Obras*, II, pp. 843–4. In *La pequeña historia*, p. 156, Lerroux admits that "the least agreeable hypothesis" was that of having to govern with the Constituent Cortes. In his *Memorias*, Alcalá-Zamora refers to the left republicans' lack of support for Lerroux as "committing suicide" and as "suicidal madness", pp. 244 and 246. In the same vein, Martínez Barrio, *Memorias*, p. 201.

3 The luminaries called upon to form a government – José Manuel Pedegral, Gregorio Marañón, Felipe Sánchez Román, and Adolfo González Posada – are listed in Alcalá-Zamora, *Memorias*, p. 246 and Martínez Barrio, *Memorias*, pp. 199–200.

4 Lerroux, *La pequeña historia*, p. 162 and Martínez Barrio, *Memorias*, p. 201.

5 Lerroux, *La pequeña historia*, pp. 153 and 205. The President made it clear that the Radical Party should try to govern with the Constituent Cortes: see Alcalá-Zamora, *Memorias*, p. 244 and Lerroux, *La pequeña historia*, pp. 152–3.

6 Vidarte, *Las Cortes*, p. 662 and Martínez Barrio, *Memorias*, pp. 200–1.

7 Lerroux, *La pequeña historia*, p. 168.

8 Lerroux, *La pequeña historia*, pp. 151 and 161–2 and Varela, *Partidos*, pp. 101–2.

9 Jalón also refers to Alcalá-Zamora as the "the pocket-sized Machiavelli" and "Boots" in Jalón, *Memorias*, pp. 76–7.

10 Lerroux, *La pequeña historia*, pp. 158–9, 162, 169, and 182, and Martínez

Barrio, *Memorias*, pp. 195 and 205.

11 Jalón, *Memorias*, p. 74; Vidarte, *Las Cortes*, pp. 661–2 and 667–72.

12 Juliá, *Azaña*, p. 294; Vidarte, *Las Cortes*, p. 672.

13 Martínez Barrio, *Memorias*, p. 203 and Azaña, *Obras*, IV, pp. 647–8. Martínez Barrio was left mumbling "it's not the same, it's not the same", as related in Vidarte, *Las Cortes*, p. 672. Martínez Barrio does not mention Prieto's last gasp effort, while Azaña offers a more detailed and convincing account. The Acción Republicana leader believed that the Martínez Barrio government should govern with the Cortes for a while so that relations between the republicans and the socialists could be improved – an eminently sensible plan – but Martínez Barrio was not prepared to challenge the President over the dissolution.

14 Letter to Lerroux of 11 October 1933, AS, P-S Madrid, C51 L798.

15 Jalón, *Memorias*, pp. 80–1 and Martínez Barrio, *Memorias*, p. 207.

16 *Renovación*, 2 November 1933 and Ruiz Manjón, *El Partido Republicano Radical*, pp. 394–5.

17 *El Sol*, 18 October 1933; Jalón, *Memorias*, p. 77; and Lerroux, *La pequeña historia*, pp. 177–81. Rico Avello was possibly appointed, as Lerroux implies in *La pequeña historia*, p. 174, due to the influence of Alcalá-Zamora, who wanted to limit the Radicals' control over the electoral machinery.

18 *Renovación*, 5 November 1933. The quote was used in reference to the social-ists but, given the overall context of *Renovación*'s coverage, it can be applied to the right, too.

19 The quote is from a Martínez Barrio speech in Seville and can be found in *El Sol*, 14 November 1933. The same theme arises in his speech in Segovia and in Lerroux's Madrid address. See *El Sol*, 17 and 19 November 1933.

20 *El Sol*, 24 and 31 October 1933. The Barcelona party's programme is in *Renovación*, 15 November 1933.

21 The quotes are from Lerroux's Madrid speech, in *El Sol*, 19 November 1933, and Martínez Barrio's in Alicante, in *El Sol*, 24 October 1933.

22 *Renovación*, 2 November 1933 and *El Sol*, 31 October and 7 November 1933.

23 *El Sol*, 27, 29, 31 October, 1, 11, 16, and 19 November 1933; *Renovación*, 2 November 1933.

24 *El Sol*, 24, 27, 29, 31 October, and 19 November 1933; *Renovación*, 31 October 1933. For criticism of the socialists by *Renovación*, see the editorials of 3, 5, and 7 November, and the article of 2 November 1933. In the edito-rial of 3 November 1933, the Radical organ claimed that the "tabu" of 1931 – the monarchy – had been replaced by that of socialism.

25 *Renovación*, 16 November 1933 and *El Sol*, 9 November 1933. See also the interview with Lerroux in *El Sol*, 18 October 1933.

26 *Renovación*, 3 and 12 November 1933; *El Debate*, 3 November 1933; Robinson, *The Origins of Franco's Spain*, pp. 143–4, 147, and 333; Preston, *The Coming*, pp. 47–9.

27 Fernández de la Poza to Lerroux, 13 October 1933, AS, P-S Madrid, C39 L704 and *El Debate*, 18 October 1933. There were 6.849 million women voters to 6.338 million male ones.

28 Azaña, *Obras*, IV, p. 649 and Juliá, *Azaña*, pp. 303–5.

29 A development charted in my MA dissertation, "The Socialist Dis-engagement".

30 Martínez Barrio, *Memorias*, p. 207. In *La pequeña historia*, pp. 158–9 and 162, Lerroux lambasts the left republicans for their lack of solidarity.

31 Juliá, *Azaña*, pp. 302–9. Espín, in *Azaña en el poder*, pp. 135–8, offers no evidence to suggest that Azaña made a serious effort to win the Radicals over.

32 Saturnino Pugá Núñez to Lerroux, 30 October 1933, AS, P-S Madrid, C46 L771.

33 Manuel Martínez to Lerroux, 24 October 1933, AS, P-S Madrid, C41 L724.

34 Letter to Lerroux, 10 September 1933, AS, P-S Madrid, C40 L716.

35 Manuel Martínez to Lerroux, 24 October 1933, AS, P-S Madrid, C41 L724.

36 Fernández de la Poza to Lerroux, 13 October 1933, AS, P-S Madrid, C39 L704.

37 Eight alliances were forged with the left republicans, while ten were formed with the right. Ceuta and Melilla, the north African territories, are not included amongst the main constituencies. See Ruiz Manjón, *El Partido Republicano Radical*, p. 392–3.

38 Ruiz Manjón, *El Partido Republicano Radical*, pp. 390–1.

39 Gil Robles, *No fue posible*, p. 102 footnote 13. Many of those denominated "Agrarians", who secured eighty seats in the first round, belonged in fact to the CEDA. Indeed, the Agrarian Party's final tally was only thirty six.

40 *El Sol*, 21 and 23 November 1933. Lerroux's declarations to *La Noche* were reproduced in *El Sol* on 22 November 1933. See also the article, "El momento político", in *El Sol* on 22 November 1933.

41 *El Debate*, 23, 29, and 30 November 1933. The first round alliance between the Radical Party and the CEDA yielded 27 seats in seven constituencies. By contrast, the alliance between the left republicans and the socialists in 18 constituencies produced only two deputies. See Andrew Durgan, "The 1933 Elections in Spain", unpublished MA dissertation, University of London, 1981, appendix C. The failure of the left to obtain 40 per cent of the vote in Madrid meant that the election there had to be rerun. See Gil Robles, *No fue posible*, pp. 97–9.

42 *El Sol*, 22, 23 November, and 2 December 1933; *Renovación*, 23 November 1933; Gil Robles, *No fue posible*, pp. 102–3. Lerroux may well have reached some sort of agreement with Casanueva over the Radical Party's future political collaboration with the CEDA as the two men remained in contact after 21 November 1933. See *El Sol*, 21, 23 November, and 3 December 1933. *El Socialista* claimed on 26 November 1933 that they hammered out a detailed programme, including a Concordat, an amnesty, the repeal of the labour laws and the Agrarian Reform Law, as well as the return of all land confiscated in relation to the "Sanjurjada", but this is not corroborated.

43 Ruiz Manjón, *El Partido Republicano Radical*, pp. 393–4 and 401; Robinson, *The Origins of Franco's Spain*, p. 335; *Renovación*, 1 December 1933. The Carlists were forced to withdraw in Alicante and Malaga, as related by Blinkhorn, *Carlism*, p. 124.

44 *Renovación*, 3, 7, 10, and 19 November 1933.

45 *Renovación*, 24, 25, 28, and 30 November 1933. On 21 and 22 November 1933 *Renovación* attacked Azaña.

46 AS, P-S Madrid, C44 L755; AS, P-S Madrid, C811 L744; *Renovación*, 25 November 1933.

47 The results are in Ruiz Manjón, *El Partido Republicano Radical*, pp. 402–8.

48 DSC, 14, 15, 22, 29 December 1933 and 4 and 9 January 1934. For Badajoz, see *El Socialista*, 10, 15, 16, 17, 21 and 22 November 1933, and for illegal pressures elsewhere see *El Socialista*, 10, 15, 16, 17, 21, 22, and 30 November 1933.

49 *Renovación*, 29 and 30 November 1933; *El Debate*, 1 December 1933; and Alcalá-Zamora, *Memorias*, pp. 259–60.

50 Martínez Barrio, *Memorias*, pp. 211–12; Alcalá-Zamora, *Memorias*, pp. 259–60; Juliá, *Azaña*, p. 311.

51 López Martínez, *Orden público*, pp. 319–29 and Stephen Lynam, "'Moderate' conservatism and the Second Republic: the case of Valencia", in Blinkhorn, editor, *Spain in Conflict*, pp. 144–5.

52 Avilés, *La izquierda burguesa*, pp. 218 and 223; Alcalá-Zamora, *Memorias*, p. 259; Jalón, *Memorias*, p. 85; Martínez Barrio, *Memorias*, pp. 206–7 and 210. Alcalá-Zamora believes that the elections of 1933 were cleaner than those of 1931 as a result of the way in which the civil governors operated. See Alcalá-Zamora, *Memorias*, p. 259. Even Gil Robles, in *No fue posible*, p. 99, grudgingly acknowledges that the government was "pretty impartial".

53 Rosa María Capel Martínez, *El sufragio feminino en la Segunda República española* (Madrid, 1992), p. 245.

54 Casanova, *De la calle*, p. 115; Macarro Vera, *La utopía*, pp. 366–7 and 455–6; José Manuel Macarro Vera, "Octubre: Un error de cálculo y perspectiva", in Ojeda, editor, *Octobre 1934*, p. 270. Macarro Vera states that abstention in Seville stood at 42% in 1931 and 44% in 1933, while falling to 31.8% in 1936.

55 Germán Zubero, *Aragón*, pp. 286–7; Caro Cancela, *Cádiz*, pp. 179–81 and 191–208.

56 Caro Cancela, *Cádiz*, pp. 179–81, 194, and 191–208; W.J. Irwin, *The 1933 Cortes Elections* (New York, 1991), pp. 270–1, cited by Payne, *Spain's First Democracy*, p. 423, footnote 36. The figure of 75 deputies is based on Irwin's calculation that 7,000 votes were required for each republican deputy. By contrast, Andrew Durgan estimates in "The 1933 Elections", p. 24, that anarcho–syndicalist abstention did not cost the left more than 40 seats. Casanova questions the usual stereotypes over CNT abstention but admits that further local studies are required before any definite conclusions can be reached (*De la calle*, pp. 80–3).

57 Casanova, *De la calle*, p. 117.

58 *El Socialista*, 16 January 1934; *El Socialista*, 21 January 1934, cited by Robinson, *The Origins of Franco's Spain*, p. 337 footnote 240; AS, P-S Madrid, C41 L724. There is no record of the next Barcelona meeting between the Radical Party and CNT, so the final outcome is not known.

59 Irwin, *The 1933 Cortes Elections*, p. 269, cited by Payne, *Spain's First Democracy*, p. 180. Despite the obvious shortcomings of such an exercise – it cannot, for example, take into account the impact of a united left-wing appeal – it is none the less indicative of the extent to which the left was super-seded by the centre–right. Indeed, Durgan calculates that if the left republicans and socialists had joined forces throughout Spain they would not have won more than 133 seats ("The 1933 Elections", p. 22).

60 Ruiz Manjón, *El Partido Republicano Radical*, pp. 403–4.

61 Martínez Barrio, *Memorias*, p. 220.

62 Lerroux, *La pequeña historia*, pp. 169, 174–6, 179, 181, 184, 188–91, and 205–6. Lerroux criticizes Rico Avello for lacking "political experience", for not feeling "the passion of politics", and for his "independence". Such is Lerroux's fury that he concludes that Alcalá-Zamora should either have asked Gil Robles to form a government or else, "to rectify the mistake that he had committed", have given the Radical leader the decree of dissolution for a new round of elections.

63 Gil Robles, *No fue posible*, pp. 108–9.

64 Alcalá-Zamora probably also resented Gil Robles for having "usurped" him

as the principal Catholic leader, as pointed out by Blinkhorn, *Carlism*, p. 125. The President was keen to get the parties of the non-republican right to declare their allegiance to the new regime. See Alcalá-Zamora, *Memorias*, pp. 258–9.

65 Gil Robles, *No fue posible*, p. 108 footnote 23. In justifying the alliance with the Radicals, Gil Robles relates that he wanted to avoid a dissolution at all costs by having a viable government formed as it would have been "madness" for the President to have given the decree of dissolution to the CEDA given that it had not declared its adherence to the regime and given that the alliance with the monarchists was "still fresh". In other words, he implicitly accepted Alcalá-Zamora's arguments in relation to the unsuitability of the CEDA exercising power at this stage. See Gil Robles, *No fue posible*, p. 106.

66 Lerroux, *La pequeña historia*, p. 195; Jalón, *Memorias*, p. 88; Martínez Barrio, *Memorias*, p. 213.

67 Lerroux, *La pequeña historia*, pp. 205–6. For a critical overview of the Radical Party during the second biennium, see Nigel Townson, "'Una República para todos los españoles': el Partido Radical en el poder, 1933–1935", in Townson, editor, *El republicanismo en España*, pp. 193–222.

68 Gil Robles, *No fue posible*, pp. 105–6 and 108–9; DSC, 19 and 20 December 1933; Martínez Barrio, *Memorias*, p. 214. See also Gil Robles's declarations to *El Debate*, of 30 December 1933 and the *El Debate* editorial of 17 December 1933.

69 DSC, 19 December 1933.

70 According to the appendix on p. 513 of Gómez Molleda's *La Masonería* on the "Diputados de las Cortes Constituyentes Pertenecientes a la Orden", 42 of the 94 Radical deputies in 1931, or just under half, were Masons. However, she provides no overall figures for 1933–1935, though by drawing on the appendix and the information on page 503 it is apparent that at least 27 of the 104 Radical deputies elected in the 1933 election were lodge members.

71 Gil Robles, *No fue posible*, p. 164.

72 *Renovación*, 2 January 1934 and Jalón, *Memorias*, p. 104. See also the prompt criticism of the Radical-led government in the *El Debate* editorial of 20 December 1933.

73 Lerroux, *La pequeña historia*, pp. 185 and 198 and Robinson, *The Origins of Franco's Spain*, pp. 154–5. Alcalá-Zamora, in his *Memorias*, pp. 258–9, claims the credit for the "conversion" of both the Agrarian Party and the PNV.

74 For the Aragon rising, see Kelsey, "Anarchism in Aragon during the Second Republic: the emergence of a mass movement", in Blinkhorn, editor, *Spain in Conflict*, pp. 70–1; Casanova, *De la calle*, pp. 118–21; Azpíroz, *Huesca*, pp. 162–9. For the rising in general, Guzmán, *La Segunda República*, pp. 234–45; Peirats, *Anarchists*, pp. 91–2; Gómez Casas, *Anarchist Organization*, pp. 146–7; and Bookchin, *The Spanish Anarchists*, pp. 256–7.

75 Casanova concludes that, following the rising's suppression, the CNT was "broken, dearticulated, without means of expression" (*De la calle*, p. 123). By contrast, Kelsey believes that for the Aragonese activists the rebellion was "a source of great moral strength, a feat of arms to which they could and did look back on with pride". See his article, "Anarchism in Aragon during the Second Republic: the emergence of a mass movement", in Blinkhorn, editor, *Spain in Conflict*, p. 71.

76 Macarro Vera in *La utopía*, pp. 345–52 and his article "Sindicalismo y política", in *Ayer*, 20, 1995, edited by Juliá, pp. 157–61.

77 Juliá, *Los socialistas*, p. 196. On 2 October 1933 Indalecio Prieto declared before parliament that the socialists' compromises with the left republicans were at an end. Rejection of the first Lerroux government, however, did not prevent the socialists from nearly entering the subsequent Martínez Barrio administration. For the socialists' disillusionment with the left republicans as a result of their continuing collaboration with the Radicals, see *El Socialista*, 20 October 1933 and *El Obrero de la Tierra*, 21 and 28 October 1933.

78 Juliá, *Historia del socialismo*, pp. 79 and 85–6; Juliá, *Los socialistas*, pp. 199–200; Juliá in the introductory study to Largo Caballero, *Escritos*, edited by Juliá, p. LIII; Indalecio Prieto in DSC, 19 December 1933.

79 Azaña, *Memorias*, IV, pp. 156–9. In fact, the socialists won 19.84 per cent of the vote in the 1933 general election. See Irwin, *The 1933 Cortes Elections*, p. 269, cited by Payne, *Spain's First Democracy*, p. 180.

80 Juliá, *Los socialistas*, pp. 202–3 and Preston, *The Coming*, pp. 104–6.

81 Cabrera, *La patronal*, pp. 258–9.

82 Cabrera, *La patronal*, pp. 219–20.

83 Cabrera, *La patronal*, pp. 229–35.

84 Jordi Palafox, *Atraso económico y democracia: la Segunda República y la economía española, 1892–1936* (Barcelona, 1991), p. 236 and Salazar Alonso, *Bajo el signo*, pp. 51–4 and 63–73.

85 Cabrera, *La patronal*, p. 235 and Salazar Alonso, *Bajo el signo*, pp. 50–1.

86 Cabrera, *La patronal*, pp. 235–7 and Juliá, *De la fiesta*, p. 394. The quote at the end is from Sánchez Castillo, cited by Cabrera, *La patronal*, p. 260. For a detailed account of the strikes and the growing separation between the *patronal* and the Radical Party in Madrid see Juliá, *De la fiesta*, chapters eight and nine.

87 The forty-four letters received by Lerroux concerning the *términos municipales* decree – which are from all over the country – are in the party archive. All but two are from October 1933. See AS, P-S Madrid, C1627 L789.

88 *El Progreso*, 19 and 23 September 1933.

89 Malefakis, *Agrarian Reform*, p. 328 and Macarro Vera, "Octubre: un error de cálculo y perspectiva", in Ojeda, editor, *Octubre 1934*, p. 273.

90 For examples of abuses, see *El Socialista*, 3 January, 6 and 7 February 1934. Further examples are given in DSC, 3, 9, and 17 January 1934 as well as 6 March 1934. See also Preston, *The Coming*, pp. 94 and 103 in addition to his article, "The agrarian war in the south", in Preston, editor, *Revolution and War*, p. 175.

91 DSC, 16 January 1934 and Malefakis, *Agrarian Reform*, pp. 328–9.

92 Macarro Vera, "Octubre: un error de cálculo y perspectiva", in Ojeda, editor, *Octubre 1934*, p. 272; López Martínez, *Orden público*, pp. 347–54; DSC, 7 February 1934; and *El Socialista*, 17 February 1934.

93 Payne, *Spain's First Democracy*, p. 383.

94 *El Socialista*, 24 February 1934.

95 Abad Conde's undated letter is in AS, P-S Madrid, C51 L798 and that of the Radical veteran in AS, P-S Madrid, C43 L745.

96 M. Soriano Sánchez to Lerroux, 9 January 1934, AS, P-S Madrid, C40 L716. See also the civil governor of Burgos to Lerroux, 12 November 1934, AS, P-S Madrid, C47 L776 and D. Milán Carrasco to Lerroux, 27 October 1934, AS, P-S Madrid, C45 L764.

97 Chapaprieta, *Fue posible*, p. 246.

98 *Renovación*, 12 January 1934; *El Socialista*, 19, 23 January, and 6 July 1934; Alcalá-Zamora, *Memorias*, p. 259. Judging by Alcalá-Zamora's shocked reaction to the appointments to the Monte de Piedad, this would seem to be true. Amongst Lerroux's original nominations, Alcalá-Zamora recalls, was an "habitual scrounger". See Alcalá-Zamora, *Memorias*, pp. 308 and 310.

99 *El Socialista*, 17 January, 18 April, 6 July, 29 August, 4 September, and 3 October 1934; Alcalá-Zamora, *Memorias*, p. 213.

100 *El Socialista*, 24 February and 25 August 1934; Alcalá-Zamora, *Memorias*, p. 213.

101 Joaquín del Moral, *Oligarquía y "enchufismo"* (Madrid, 1933), pp. 92–3 and 104–9. I have corrected Del Moral's averages for the earnings of the deputies as they are wrong according to his own data. An "enchufe" is an electric socket. Thus "enchufismo" is the process of "plugging in"; that is to say, the process whereby a job is obtained not through competition but through an inside contact or personal recommendation.

102 Letter to Lerroux, 11 January 1934, AS, P-S Madrid, C43 L746.

103 On the *jurados mixtos* and their forerunners, see Juliá, *Los socialistas*, pp. 126–44 and "Objetivos políticos de la legislación laboral", in García Delgado, coordinator, *La II República española: el primer bienio*, pp. 27–47.

104 AS, P-S Madrid, file unmarked; *El Socialista*, 7 January 1934.

105 AS, P-S Madrid, C1709 L696; Gil Robles to Lerroux, 9 January 1934, AS, P-S Madrid, C30 L447.

106 *El Debate*, 18 August 1934. Salazar Alonso gives slightly different figures in *Bajo el signo*, pp. 116 and 121–2.

107 Asturian Radicals to Lerroux, 23 March 1934, AS, P-S Madrid, C47 L776 and that of the civil governor, AS, P-S Madrid, C43 L747.

108 *El Socialista*, 5 and 28 June, 20 and 22 September 1934.

109 *El Socialista*, 13, 16, 23, 25, 27, 30 and 31 May, 8 June, and 1 July 1934.

110 *El Socialista*, 2 and 9 May, 30 June, 30 August, 1, 7, 16, 18, 19, and 21 September 1934.

111 *El Socialista*, 10 and 21 June, and 18 September 1934.

112 Alós, *Blasquismo*, pp. 202–3. In the same vein, Salazar Alonso asserts that the letter reproduced in relation to the Court of Constitutional Guarantees affair was "false" (*Bajo el signo*, p. 265). For Lerroux's and Iglesias' comments, see Sainz Rodríguez, *Testimonio*, p. 157. He does not give the year of the encounter with Iglesias, but it would appear to be 1934.

113 Alcalá-Zamora, *Memorias*, pp. 244 and 261; Gil Robles, *No fue posible*, pp. 165–166; and Pemán, who denounced "months of sterility", in DSC, 6 March 1934.

114 Alcalá-Zamora, *Memorias*, p. 264 and *Renovación*, 4 January 1934. See also the criticism of *El Debate*, 4, 11, 13 January, 1 and 11 February 1934.

115 Gil Robles, *No fue posible*, pp. 110–15 and *El Debate*, 1, 6, and 11 February 1934.

116 Martínez Barrio, *Memorias*, p. 216; Jalón, *Memorias*, p. 88; Lerroux, *La pequeña historia*, p. 195.

117 *Renovación*, 13 January 1934 and *El Debate*, 23 January 1934. The *Blanco y Negro* interview is in *El Debate*, 23 January 1934.

118 DSC, 7 February 1934.

119 *Renovación*, 6 and 17 February 1934.

120 *El Debate*, 7, 20, 22, 24, and 27 February 1934; Gil Robles, *No fue posible*, pp. 116 and 118.

121 Salazar Alonso, *Bajo el signo*, pp. 16, 41–5, and 77; Alcalá-Zamora,

Memorias, p. 268; Jalón, *Memorias*, pp. 104–6; and *Renovación*, 7 March 1934. See also *El Debate*'s account of the reshuffle on 1 March 1934 and Lerroux's comments on the negotiations in *Renovación*, 4 March 1934.
122 *Renovación*, 6 March 1934.
123 Martínez Barrio, *Memorias*, pp. 91–2.
124 Gil Robles, *No fue posible*, pp. 118–20. The Amnesty Law covered acts up to the third anniversary of the Republic on 14 April 1934.
125 Martínez Barrio, *Memorias*, p. 214; Lerroux, *La pequeña historia*, pp. 220–1; Salazar Alonso, *Bajo el signo*, pp. 88–90, 96–7, and 101–8.
126 Lerroux, *La pequeña historia*, pp. 225, 227–9; Martínez Barrio, *Memorias*, pp. 220–1; Gil Robles, *No fue posible*, pp. 121 and 122; Salazar Alonso, *Bajo el signo*, pp. 93–6 and 112.
127 Gil Robles, *No fue posible*, pp. 108–9.

8 The Price of Pragmatism

1 *El Debate*, 17 December 1933 and Martínez Barrio, *Memorias*, p. 223.
2 Martínez Barrio, *Memorias*, p. 213. Martínez Barrio's resentment towards Santiago Alba does not appear, as Lerroux admits, to have been rooted in a desire to be speaker of the Cortes himself. See *La pequeña historia*, p. 185.
3 Martínez Barrio, *Memorias*, pp. 216 and 223–5.
4 *El Socialista*, 4 January 1934; *Renovación*, 23, 24 and 28 December 1933. See also the declarations by Antonio Lara in the same vein in *Renovación*, 18 February 1934.
5 *Renovación*, 9, 13, 19, and 21 January 1934, as well as *El Debate*, 23 January 1934. The *Blanco y Negro* interview is in *El Debate*, 6 February 1934 and an extract is in Martínez Barrio, *Memorias*, p. 217.
6 DSC, 7 February 1934; *El Debate*, 6 February 1934; and *Renovación*, 6 and 7 February 1934.
7 AS, P-S Madrid, C1707 L696; the letter of 26 February 1934 from Martínez Barrio to Dámaso Vélez in Martínez Barrio, L11 C45; *Renovación*, 21 and 22 February 1934; and Joaquín Pérez Madrigal, *Memorias de un converso* (Madrid, 1943–52), V, p. 137.
8 Martínez Barrio, *Memorias*, p. 185.
9 *El Debate*, 28 February 1934; *El Pueblo*, 28 February, 1 March 1934; and Martínez Barrio, *Memorias*, p. 217.
10 E. Zufra to Lerroux, 1 June 1934, AS, P-S Madrid, C39 L700; E. Malboysson to Martínez Barrio, 7 March 1934, AMB, L7 C33; Martínez Barrio to J. Marcial Dorado, 9 April 1934 in AMB, L3 C10.
11 See the somewhat confusing account in María Herrero Fabregat, "La masonería y la escisión del Partido Radical en 1934", in José Antonio Ferrer Benimeli, coordinator, *Masonería, Revolución y Reacción*, I (Alicante, 1990), pp. 328–31. See also García Andreu, *Alicante*, p. 56, and the two conflicting circulars concerning the dissident assembly of 10 June 1934, AS, P-S Madrid, C43.
12 The letter of Marco Miranda to Martínez Barrio, 15 February 1934 in Martínez Barrio, L7 C33; *El Liberal* (Seville), *El Socialista* and *El Debate*, 10 April 1934; Alós, *Blasquismo*, pp. 198–199; and Franch, *El Blasquisme*, pp. 151–3.
13 See the letter of Gordón Ordás to Martínez Barrio of 17 March 1934 in AMB, L4 C21, and that of Sánchez Román of 27 March 1934 to Martínez Barrio in AMB, L10 C40. For the meetings, see also *El Liberal* (Sevilla), 10 and 27 March 1934 and *Renovación*, 10 March 1934.

14 *El Sol* 1 april 1934, cited by Herrero Fabregat, "La masonería y la escisión del Partido Radical en 1934", in Ferrer Benimeli, coordinator, *Masonería*, pp. 327–8; and Martínez Barrio, *Memorias*, p. 217.

15 *Renovación*, 11 March 1934.

16 Letter of Martínez Barrio to J. Marcial of 9 April 1934 in AMB, L3 C10. In his *Memorias*, Martínez Barrio still writes of Lerroux with affection, despite the total rupture in their relations following the schism.

17 *El Liberal* (Madrid), 3 April 1934 and *El Liberal* (Seville), 3 and 10 April 1934. The quotes are from the Ayamonte speech. There are also sections of Martínez Barrio's speeches in Martínez Barrio, *Memorias*, pp. 217–18. Before the Seville meeting, Martínez Barrio issued a defiant statement in which he exclaimed that "after this one can now say: those that want to follow me, follow me!". See *El Liberal* (Seville), 1 April 1934. He reaffirmed his position in an interview with *Luz* during the first week of April 1934. See *Renovación*, 6 April 1934.

18 *Renovación*, 3 and 6 April 1934; *El Debate*, 4 April 1934; and *El Liberal* (Seville), 3 and 4 April 1934.

19 The Radical parliamentary group scarcely met in the lead up to the schism, yet a flurry of meetings were held after the split in an effort to limit the damage. See AS, P-S Madrid, C1709 L696. A deputy revealed to the party press that the parliamentary group was not allowed to make declarations on the matter. See *Renovación*, 10 May 1934. Lerroux himself asserted that the National Council would not meet until the conflict had been resolved, but the gravity of the situation later made him relent. See *El Debate*, 11 and 17 May 1934. During the crisis-ridden month of April 1934 an average of 48 deputies attended the parliamentary group's meetings.

20 For the eulogies dedicated to the Radical leader, see *Renovación*, 8 March 1934, 17, 22, 27, 28, and 29 April 1934, 3 and 4 May 1934. A forty-page special edition of *Renovación* on 22 April 1934 to celebrate the anniversary of the Republic was mostly given over to Lerroux, too. Criticism of the socialists is continuous throughout this period. To a far lesser extent, individual republican leaders were subject to criticism (Maura, 27 March 1934 and 17 May 1934, Azaña, 4 and 7 April 1934), as well as Izquierda Republicana (12 April 1934), and the republicans in general (4 and 19 April 1934).

21 Martínez Barrio, *Memorias*, pp. 220–1; Actas, AS, P-S Madrid, P-S Madrid, C1709 L696, 27 April 1934; and *Renovación*, 28 April 1934.

22 *Renovación*, 13 May 1934 and Martínez Barrio, *Memorias*, p. 223. According to Martínez Barrio, the decision was finally prompted by the opening parliamentary debate of the Samper government. See Martínez Barrio, *Memorias*, p. 223.

23 AS, Sección Masonería, L594 exp.40, cited by Herrero Fabregat, "La masonería y la escisión", in Ferrer Benimeli, coordinator, *Masonería*, p. 331.

24 *El Debate*, 11 and 17 May 1934; *El Socialista*, 10 May 1934; *Renovación*, 12, 17 and 18 May 1934. Although it is recorded that Martínez Barrio and Lerroux previously lunched on 28 April, there is no account of the meeting. See *El Debate*, 29 April 1934.

25 *ABC*, 19 May 1934 and Martínez Barrio, *Memorias*, pp. 226–7.

26 Lerroux, *La pequeña historia*, pp. 226–8, 250, and 265; Jalón, *Memorias*, pp. 101–4.

27 Martínez Barrio, *Memorias*, p. 217 and *El Debate*, 17 May 1935.

28 Lerroux, *Mis memorias*, p. 517; Lerroux, *La pequeña historia*, pp. 247–50; Alcala-Zamora, *Memorias*, p. 201; Juan-Simeón Vidarte, *El bienio negro y*

la insurrección de Asturias (Barcelona, 1978), p. 144. In attributing the split of May 1934 to the Masons, Lerroux – who wrote *La pequeña historia* during the early part of the Civil War of 1936 to 1939 – was probably aiming to appease the Nationalists, too. *El Radical*, a weekly published in Zaragoza, supported the Masonic conspiracy theory in its edition of 22 October 1934 with an article entitled "Don Diego, el Triángulo y el Mandil". For the liberal political afiliation of the vast majority of Masons, see the appendix on "Diputados de las Cortes Constituyentes Pertenecientes a la Orden" in Gómez Molleda, *La Masonería*, p. 513.

29 Gómez Molleda, *La Masonería*, pp. 482, 496, and 498–502; and Vidarte, *El bienio*, p. 75.

30 Gómez Molleda, *La Masonería*, pp. 483, 487–8, and 510. An editorial of September 1933 in the *Boletín Oficial del Supremo Consejo del Grado 33*, which called for "fraternal affection" rather than "petty sectarianism" within the lodges, may, Gómez Molleda speculates, have been written by Martínez Barrio.

31 Gómez Molleda, *La Masonería*, p. 491; Vidarte, *El bienio*, pp. 141–2; Azaña, *Obras*, IV, p. 310.

32 Gómez Molleda, *La Masonería*, pp. 484, 488–501, and 507.

33 Alvarez Rey, *La derecha*, p. 64. In the Seville speech, Martínez Barrio declared that "I was never a sectarian" (*Memorias*, p. 217). It is unfortunate that Gómez Molleda's account does not really explore the extent to which the Masons shaped the Radical split, surely one of the movement's most crucial moments under the Republic. Indeed, her study, despite being titled one about Masonry "in the Spanish crisis of the XX century", stops short in 1934.

34 The socialists were Hermenegildo Casas and Adolfo Moreno Rodríguez. Of the civil governors, those that represented Almeria, Ciudad Real, Cadiz, Seville and Tenerife were Masons (Gómez Molleda, *La Masonería*, p. 503). Gómez Molleda claims on page 504 that "all" the dissident Radicals that were Masons were also veterans of the lodges, but this is not so: José González y Fernández de la Bandera, for example, joined as recently as 1932, according to Alvarez Rey, "La masonería en Sevilla. Entre el compromiso y la militancia política (1900–1936)", in Ferrer Benimeli, coordinator, *Masonería*, p. 252.

35 Herrero Fabregat, "La masonería y la escisión", in Ferrer Benimeli, coordinator, *Masonería*, p. 328 and Gómez Molleda, *La Masonería*, pp. 485 and 507–8. Unfortunately, Gómez Molleda does not give complete figures for the number of Masons in the Radical Party following the 1933 general election.

36 *Renovación*, 18 May 1934; *El Debate*, 19 May 1934; *El Liberal* (Seville), 20, 22, 23 and 26 May 1934; *El Socialista*, 19 May and 8 June 1934; Martínez Barrio to Pedro Gómez Chaix, June 1934 in AMB, L4 C18; Martínez Barrio, *Memorias*, p. 228.

It was just as well that Gómez Chaix did not defect as, according to a local activist, he had "much support" in the province. See M. Avilés to Lerroux, 31 May 1934, AS, P-S Madrid, C41 number 2, L733. Despite not joining Martínez Barrio, Alvarez Mendizábal was denounced to Lerroux by a local rival from his constituency of Cuenca as a "pintoresque traitor", in AS, P-S Madrid, C39 L700 (letter undated). A. Alfonso Bozzo, *Galicia 1931–36*, p. 94, claims that the majority of the civil governors in Galicia also resigned, which is quite possible.

37 The *Maurista* was Luis Recasens Sitches, as *El Debate*, 31 May 1935 reports. The Esquerra had 18 deputies, the Conservative Republicans, 17, Acción Republicana 5, and the Independent PRRS 4, though the pro-government

Lliga had 24. See Gil Pecharromán, *La Segunda República española (1931–1936)* (Madrid, 1995), p. 200.

38   Avilés, *La izquierda*, pp. 232–7 and Martínez Barrio, *Memorias*, pp. 227–8.

39   García Berlanger and Pascual Leone also left the PURA, but stayed in the Radical–Democratic Party. Julio Just later joined Izquierda Republicana, according to Franch, *El Blasquisme*, p. 158. The founding manifesto of Esquerra Valenciana is in Alfons Cucó Giner, *El valencisme polític: 1874–1936* (Valencia, 1971), pp. 438–40.

40   Martínez Barrio, *Memorias*, pp. 227–8.

41   See the mountainous correspondence concerning the split in AS, P-S Madrid, C40 L721, C1627 L783 and 789. For nationwide coverage of the split see also *El Liberal* (Seville), 20, 22, 23, 24, and 31 May 1934 and 7 June 1934.

42   The letter of Marco Miranda, dated 12 May 1934, is in AMB, L7 C33 and that of Carreres, dated 7 August 1934, in AS, P-S Madrid, C43 L744.

43   However, two other deputies, Becerra and Azpiazu, declared themselves as independents. See Bozzo, *Galicia (1931–1936)*, p. 94.

44   *El Debate*, 25 May 1934; Gerardo Carreres to Lerroux, 7 August 1934, AS, P-S Madrid, C43 L744; Alfonso Bozzo, *Galicia (1931–1936)*, pp. 93–4; *El Liberal* (Seville) and *El Socialista*, 29 May 1934. A mere 15 per cent of the local branches in Seville province remained loyal to Lerroux. See Alvarez Rey, *La derecha*, p. 403.

45   See the letter of the civil governor for Malaga to Lerroux of 9 August 1934, AS, P-S Madrid, C46 L769; García Andreu, *Alicante*, p. 56; Antonio Tuñón de Lara to Lerroux, 5 August 1934 to Lerroux, AS, P-S Madrid, C45 L760; Caro Cancela, *Cádiz*, p. 224.
      The dissidents in Malaga formed the Radical Autonomous Group, which included a deputy (Eduardo Frapollí), the city's mayor, and four councillors. Five councillors remained loyal to the Radical Party. See *El Socialista*, 16 May 1934.

46   For Leon, see the letter of Fernández de la Poza of 18 May 1934 to Lerroux in AS, P-S Madrid, C40 L721 and for Huelva the letter of Rey Mora to Lerroux of 21 August 1934 in AS, P-S Madrid, C47 L773. In Logroño the impact also appears to have been minimal, according to Bermejo, *Logroño*, p. 349. The same can be said of Granada, where the only figure of note to leave was the general secretary of the Provincial Committee. See José Antonio Alarcón Caballero, *El movimiento obrero en Granada en la II República (1931–1936)* (Granada, 1990), p. 133.

47   Avilés, *La izquierda burguesa*, pp. 246 and 338; Ruiz Manjón, *El Partido Republicano Radical*, pp. 434, 608, and 611–12. If one takes the available figures, as provided by Ruiz Manjón, each Radical branch had 100 members. This gives the PRD a total membership of 55,700 – it had, in fact, 50,191 registered members. The problem, as with all the parties, is that the level of affiliation was decidedly lower than the level of militancy.

48   For the rightward shift of the Sevillian party, see J. T. Vázquez de la Cruz to Lerroux, 25 August 1934, AS, P-S Madrid, C47 L778; A. González de Rojas to Lerroux, 11 July 1934, AS, P-S Madrid, C44 L758; the letter of the Algamitas branch to Lerroux of 3 July 1934, AS, P-S Madrid, C41 Number 2 L733; and Alvarez Rey, *La derecha*, pp. 404–6.

49   Civil governor of Avila to Sánchez Fuster, 26 June 1934, AS, P-S Madrid, C1627 L783; M. Binefar to Lerroux, 29 May 1934, AS, P-S Madrid, C40 L721 and T. Paule to Lerroux, 17 May 1934, AS, P-S Madrid, C40 L721; the Radical Party of Manacor to Lerroux, 26 June 1934, AS, P-S Madrid, C1627

L783; G. Carreres to Lerroux, 7 August 1934, AS, P-S Madrid, C43 L744; M. de Terán to Lerroux, 30 May 1934, AS, P-S Madrid, C43 L747; *El Liberal* (Seville), 9 June 1934; Villanueva to Lerroux of 13 August 1934, AS, P-S Madrid, C548 L780.

For a more optimistic view of the Seville party's situation, see J. Lasarte to Lerroux, 14 August 1934, AS, P-S Madrid, C45 L762 and Romualdo Yáñez Gómez to Lerroux, 15 July 1934, AS, P-S Madrid, C46 L770. For the reorganizational efforts, see the meetings of the parliamentary group of 30 May and 6 June 1934 in AS, P-S Madrid, C1709 L696 and *El Debate*, 30 May and 25 July 1934.

50 *Renovación*, 28 April 1934; *El Debate*, 24 May, 2, 19 June, and 6 July 1934; Juan Pich y Pon to César Oarrichena, 26 June 1934, AS, P-S Madrid, C522 L4777.

51 The great bulk of the letters to Lerroux are in AS, P-S Madrid, C40 L721 and C1627 L783 and L789. See the letter of Herminio Fernández de la Poza of 3 May 1934, AS, P-S Madrid, C44 L752. One admirer, Mariano Gómez, affirmed in a letter of 18 February 1934 that "one cannot be Radical without being *Lerrouxista*" (AS, P-S Madrid, C51 L800), while the Radical Youth group for Hostafranchs in Catalonia proposed to name its new monthly publication *El Lerrouxista*, according to a letter of 9 July 1934 to Lerroux, in AS, P-S Madrid, C51 L800.

52 AS, P-S Madrid, C1627 L783 and L789, and C40 L721; *Renovación*, 13 January 1934.

53 *Renovación*, 16, 18, and 19 May 1934; and AS, P-S Madrid, C40 L721.

9 Trapped between Left and Right

1 DSC, 2 May 1934; *Renovación*, 6 and 18 May 1934; and Lerroux, *La pequeña historia*, p. 256.

2 *El Debate*, 10, 23 and 25 May 1934.

3 *El Debate*, 15 April 1934; *El Socialista*, 12 August 1934; Bosch, *Estudios*, pp. 212–14; Cabrera, *La patronal*, pp. 219–21 and 238–9; Juliá, *De la fiesta*, p. 396; and Palafox, *Atraso económico*, pp. 231–5. Profits for seven of the leading metallurgical companies had fallen by 30 per cent. See Cabrera, *La patronal*, pp. 239–40.

4 See Karin Nowak, "De la Dictadura a la República: continuidad y cambio en el Ministerio de Trabajo (1920–1936)", p. 12, footnote 30. Paper given in the Fundación Ortega y Gasset on 9 December 1997.

5 The founding charter of the Bloque Patronal is in Cabrera, *La patronal*, p. 234.

6 Cabrera, *La patronal*, p. 238.

7 Juliá, *De la fiesta*, p. 405.

8 Juliá, *Historia económica*, pp. 49–50 and Palafox, *Atraso económico*, pp. 250–2. The quote is from DSC, 14 June 1934.

9 Palafox, *Atraso económico*, pp. 252–6 and 263–4. Of the 23.97 million pesetas that the National Junta recommended should be spent, one million was to be devoted to the construction of roads and six million to reforestation. See *El Debate*, 31 August 1934.

10 The UGT was losing members – from just over one million in June 1932, of which 393,953 belonged to the FNTT, to 640,691 at the beginning of 1934 – and was therefore less able to direct the protest of the workers via legal channels. See Malefakis, *Agrarian Reform*, p. 292.

11 The Toledo example is in DSC, 10 May 1934. Work contracts in Huelva were

also abused, as revealed in DSC, 11 May 1934. See also Malefakis, *Agrarian Reform*, p. 336; Manuel Tuñón de Lara, *La segunda república*, 2 vols (Madrid, 1976), II, p. 67.

12 Malefakis, *Agrarian Reform*, p. 337 and Salazar Alonso, *Bajo el signo*, pp. 146–55.

13 *Renovación*, 3 June 1934; Malefakis, *Agrarian Reform*, pp. 337–8; Vidarte, *El bienio*, pp. 151 and 155. In parliament, the socialist spokesman on agrarian affairs, José Prat, recognized the "consensual labour" of the Ministers of Agriculture and of Labour, but insisted that their efforts had been sabotaged by the "policy of repression" of Salazar Alonso. See DSC, 30 May 1934. In an interview with the author in 1991, Prat expressed the view that Zabalza's personal ambitions also played a role in the decision to go ahead with the strike.

14 Malefakis, *Agrarian Reform*, pp. 338–9 and Vidarte, *El bienio*, p. 155.

15 For the repression, see the debate in DSC, 14 June 1934; Tuñón de Lara, *La segunda*, II, pp. 69–70; and Vidarte, *El bienio*, pp. 152 and 160. Margarita Nelken, a socialist deputy for Badajoz, claimed in DSC, 7 June 1934 that the state of the jails was "anti-humane".

16 *Renovación*, 27 May and 24 June 1934; Malefakis, *Agrarian Reform*, p. 340; and Salazar Alonso, *Bajo el signo*, pp. 165–81. Salazar Alonso insists that the Civil Guard discovered caches of arms in the *pueblos*.

17 DSC, 6 June 1934; *El Socialista*, 26, 30 June, and 14 July 1934.

18 These figures, from *El Debate*, 18 August 1934, are not quite the same as those given in Salazar Alonso, *Bajo el signo*, pp. 116 and 121–2. More detailed local studies are likely to show that the level of dismissals was higher than the official figures show. In the province of Granada alone, 127 local councils were partially or completely replaced by steering committees between September 1933 and February 1936. See Alarcón, *Granada*, p. 132.

19 DSC, 12 June 1934; Alberto Balsells, *El problema agrari a Catalunya: la qüestió rabassaire (1890–1936)* (Barcelona, 1968), pp. 229–45; and N. Jones, "Regionalism and revolution in Catalonia", in Preston, editor, *Revolution and War*, pp. 103–4. For the details of the new law, see Enric Jardí, *Companys i el 6 d'octubre* (Barcelona, 1997), pp. 27–30.

20 Amadeu Hurtado i Miró, *Quaranta anys d'avocat: historia del meu temps* (Barcelona, 1967), pp. 276, 281–2, and 288; Jardí, *Companys*, pp. 35, 39–40 and 42; and N. Jones, "Regionalism and revolution", in Preston, editor, *Revolution and War*, p. 104. For an eye-witness account of Companys' extra-parliamentary harangue see Manuel Cruells, *El 6 d'octubre a Catalunya* (Barcelona, 1970), p. 115, cited by Jardí, *Companys*, p. 38.

21 DSC, 12 and 25 June 1934; *El Debate*, 13 and 23 June 1934; and *El Socialista*, 2 and 13 June 1934.

22 *El Debate*, 14 June and 7 August 1934; *Renovación*, 8 and 28 June 1934, as well as 5 September 1934.

23 The support of Basilio Alvarez for the Catalan law was scarcely surprising given that he had not only fought for the rights of Galician peasants for twenty five years, but also that he had defended those of the *rabassaires* prior to the Republic. Indeed, he was a friend of the Catalan President, Luis Companys. For his picturesque career as a cleric, journalist – he was editor of *El Debate* in 1911 – and political agitator see his books *Abriendo el surco: manual de lucha campesina* (Madrid, 1976) and *Desde mi campo: el libro del periodista* (Madrid, 1912), as well as J. A. Durán, *Agrarismo y mobilización campesina en el País Gallego, 1875–1912* (Madrid, 1977); J. A. Durán,

Historia de caciques, bandos e ideologías en la Galicia no urbana (Rianxo, 1910–1914) (Madrid, 1972); and Manuel Portela Valladares, *Memorias dentro del drama español* (Madrid, 1988), pp. 27, 28, and 34. The support for the Generalidad of Fernando Gasset, a former monarchist, and of Gerardo Abad Conde, a veteran Lerrouxist, was less expected.

24 DSC, 25 June, 4 July 1934; *Renovación*, 24 June 1934; and Gil Robles, *No fue posible*, pp. 124–5. The letters are in AS, P-S Madrid, C39 L700.

25 For the ministers' declarations, see *El Debate*, 20 July and 1 August 1934; *Renovación*, 22 and 24 July 1934, and 3 August 1934. The mounting exasperation of *El Debate* can be followed in the editorials of 15, 20, and 22 July 1934, along with those of 3, 10, and 17 August 1934. See also Alcalá-Zamora, *Memorias*, p. 279; Hurtado, *Quaranta anys*, pp. 293–4; Jardí, *Companys*, pp. 45–7; and Salazar Alonso, *Bajo el signo*, pp. 269 and 272–3.

26 José Luis de la Granja, *Nacionalismo y II República en el País Vasco* (Madrid, 1986), pp. 463 and 467–8.

27 *El Sol*, 13 June 1934, cited by Juan Pablo Fusi, *El problema vasco en la II República* (Madrid, 1979), p. 113 and De la Granja, *Nacionalismo*, p. 475. The following account draws extensively on the lucid analysis of Fusi in *El problema vasco*, pp. 112–22.

28 *El Sol*, 2 August 1934. In relation to the dispute over the representativeness of the *Diputaciones*, Samper recognized that the local councils were "morally right". See *El Debate*, 26 August 1934. For the affinity between Salazar Alonso and Angel Velarde, see Salazar Alonso, *Bajo el signo*, pp. 201 and 219, in addition to Velarde's letter of 2 August 1934 on pp. 195–9.

29 *El Debate*, 8, 9, 10, and 11 August 1934; *Renovación*, 8 August 1934; Fusi, *El problema vasco*, p. 116; and Salazar Alonso, *Bajo el signo*, pp. 201–3. See also the commentaries in *Renovación* of 12, 14 August and 4 September 1934.

30 The authorities' figures are from Fusi, *El problema vasco*, p. 118. Salazar Alonso maintains in *Bajo el signo*, p. 208, that only 28 local councils in Vizcaya attempted to hold an election. The Basques claimed that polling had taken place in 100 councils in Vizcaya, in 72 in Guipuzcoa, and in 10 in Alava. See De la Granja, *Nacionalismo*, pp. 478–9. The quote is from José Antonio Aguirre Lecube, *Entre la libertad y la revolución, 1930–1935: la verdad de un lustro en el País Vasco* (Bilbao, 1976), p. 462.

31 *El Debate*, 26 August 1934; Aguirre, *Entre la libertad*, pp. 479–80, 494–7, 529–33; De la Granja, *Nacionalismo*, pp. 482–3, 488; and Fusi, *El problema vasco*, pp. 118–20.

32 Malefakis, *Agrarian Reform*, pp. 344–6. The comparison of the rates of expropriation is not quite accurate in that the first set of figures includes the initial four months of Radical rule. Much of this, however, was taken up by the caretaker administration of Martínez Barrio.

33 DSCC, 19 December 1933 and DSC, 27 June 1934. The Casanueva quote is from Antonio Rodríguez de las Heras, *Filiberto Villalobos: su obra social y política (1900–1936)* (Salamanca, 1985), p. 193.

34 Rodríguez de las Heras, *Filiberto Villalobos*, p. 195. An initial concession was made to the right with the decree of 1 August 1934 by which coeducation in primary schools was overturned.

35 Rodríguez de las Heras, *Filiberto Villalobos*, pp. 196 and 213–14; Mariano Pérez Galán, *La enseñanza en la segunda república española* (Madrid, 1975), pp. 285, 289, and 294. In 1931 5.69 per cent of the budget was spent on education, in 1932 5.92 per cent, and in 1933 6.57 per cent. This was lower,

too, than in 1935, when spending on education stood at 6.60 per cent. See Pérez Galán, *La enseñanza*, p. 282.

36 *El Debate*, 8, 29, and 30 August 1934, in addition to 26 September 1934; Rodríguez de las Heras, *Filiberto Villalobos*, pp. 210–12. By contrast, *El Socialista* believed that Villalobos had continued the "reactionary line" of the government and that the Jesuits "have invaded the ministry" (9 August 1934). Simplistic accounts of the reforms, such as that by Manuel de Puelles Benítez, *Educación y ideología en la España contemporánea (1767–1975)* (Barcelona, 1980), persist in denominating this period as one of "counter-reform".

37 Gabriel Cardona, *El poder militar en la España contemporánea hasta la guerra civil* (Madrid, 1983), pp. 197–202 and Espadas Burgos in López et al., *Diego Hidalgo*, pp. 152–62. Hidalgo had been impressed by Franco during a tour of the military installations of the Baleares islands in June 1934, where Franco was Commander. See Espadas Burgos in Elsa López et al., *Diego Hidalgo*, pp. 169–71. For a more critical appraisal of Hidalgo's appointments, see Paul Preston, *Franco: A Biography* (London, 1993), pp. 95–6, while Alcalá-Zamora, in his *Memorias*, p. 296, faults Hidalgo's "excessive attention to the technical criteria". For Ifni, see Alcalá-Zamora, *Memorias*, pp. 269–70 and Lerroux, *La pequeña historia*, pp. 323–5.

38 See the parliamentary debate of 19 and 20 June 1934 in DSC. A decree of 25 December 1933, converted into law on 16 March 1934, renamed the Ministry of Labour as that of Labour, Social Security, and Health.

39 DSC, 19 and 20 June 1934. See also Estadella's article in *Renovación* of 26 August 1934. He was able to draw on his experience as director of health and charity in the Mancomunidad from 1921 to 1923. See Culla, *El republicanisme lerrouxista*, p. 350.

40 *La Voz Médica*, 6 July and 17 August 1934.

41 *El Debate*, 10 June 1934; Arrarás, *Historia de la segunda República*, II, pp. 408–9; Payne, *Spain's First Democracy*, pp. 199–200; and Tuñón de Lara, *La segunda*, II, p. 73. A plan to assassinate the socialist leader, Indalecio Prieto – who, curiously, was a friend of José Antonio Primo de Rivera – was averted at the last moment, while the left made an attempt on the life of the Falangist leader. The monarchists' deal with Mussolini is in John Coverdale, *Italian Intervention in the Spanish Civil War* (Princeton, 1975), pp. 50–4; Gil Pecharromán, *Conservadores*, pp. 265–6; and Saz, *Mussolini contra la II República*, pp. 66–82.

42 *El Debate*, 15, 17, 22, 23, and 28 August 1934; *Renovación*, 17 and 23 August 1934.

43 See the *El Debate* editorial "A government is required" of 11 September 1934 and the Cabinet statement on public disorder of 12 September 1934. See also Gil Robles, *No fue posible*, pp. 129, 131; Jardí, *Companys*, p. 47; and Payne, *Spain's First Democracy*, p. 210.

44 Salazar Alonso, *Bajo el signo*, pp. 228–9 and the decree on pp. 236–7. The meeting was authorized against his will. *Renovación* judged that the Socialist Youth was being exploited as "cannon fodder" (30 August 1934), while *El Debate* fulsomely welcomed Salazar Alonso's initiative – "one cannot ask for more" (26 August 1934).

45 *Renovación*, 12, 18 September 1934; Gil Robles, *No fue posible*, pp. 130–1; Salazar Alonso, *Bajo el signo*, pp. 183–94, 240–51, 266, and 292–3.

46 *El Debate*, 28, 30 August 1934, 7, 14 September 1934; *Renovación*, 13, 14 September 1934; Salazar Alonso, *Bajo el signo*, pp. 313–21.

47 Gil Robles, *No fue posible*, p. 128 and Salazar Alonso, *Bajo el signo*, pp. 321–2.

48   AS, P-S Madrid, C1709 L411; *El Debate*, 14 September 1934; *Renovación*, 14 September 1934; and Salazar Alonso, *Bajo el signo*, pp. 322–3.

49   *Renovación*, 28 September 1934 and Gil Robles, *No fue posible*, pp. 131–3.

50   *Renovación*, 4 September 1934.

51   For the minutes of the meetings of the parliamentary group, see AS, P-S Madrid, C1709 C411.

52   *Renovación*, 30 September 1934 and Jalón, *Memorias*, pp. 117 and 119.

53   Quite why Salazar Alonso, a moderate life-long republican, should shift so dramatically to the right has never been satisfactorily explained. Alcalá-Zamora believes that he was transformed after coming into contact with the Badajoz landowners during the electoral campaign of 1933. See Alcalá-Zamora, *Memorias*, p. 283.

54   DSC, 1 October 1934 and Gil Robles, *No fue posible*, p. 136.

55   *El Debate*, 3 and 19 July 1934. Arrazola is cited by *El Debate* on 31 May 1934.

56   *El Socialista*, 29 July and 1 August 1934.

57   Alcalá-Zamora, *Memorias*, p. 282.

58   Martínez Barrio, *Memorias*, pp. 249–50.

59   *El Socialista*, 2 to 4 October 1934; Avilés, *La izquierda burguesa*, pp. 248–9.

60   See the *El Socialista* editorials of 25, 27 and 30 September 1934.

61   Juliá, *Historia del socialismo*, p. 125.

62   In his diary for 22 September 1934 Alcalá-Zamora notes that Largo Caballero believed that "the duty of everyone is to gather around me for the defence of the Republic as the most efficient guarantee". Cited in Martínez Barrio, *Memorias*, p. 247.

63   Lerroux comments in *La pequeña historia*, p. 256, that "if he had little affection for the party, he had even less for its *jefe*". Martínez Barrio contends in his *Memorias*, pp. 251–2, that Alcalá-Zamora was moved by the religious question and by his hatred for the members of the Azaña administrations.

64   Gil Robles, *No fue posible*, p. 137 and Jalón, *Memorias*, p. 121. Ironically, Prime Minister Manuel Azaña and his Minister of the Interior, Santiago Casares Quiroga, had held Anguera de Sojo – who was made public prosecutor under Azaña – in high esteem during the first biennium. See Azaña, *Diarios,* 10 May 1933 and Jardí, *Companys*, p. 57.

65   Gil Robles, *No fue posible*, pp. 138–9. For Salazar Alonso, see Alcalá-Zamora, *Memorias*, pp. 282–3; Jalón, *Memorias*, p. 123; Lerroux, *La pequeña historia*, p. 261; and Salazar Alonso, *Bajo el signo*, pp. 326–7. Salazar Alonso reveals that Gil Robles tried to keep him in the Cabinet, which is hardly surprising. The PURA was naturally opposed to the appointment of Luis Lucia, leader of its local rival, the CEDA-affiliated DRV, especially as Samper's fall had been orchestrated by the CEDA. See Gil Robles, *No fue posible*, pp. 137–8.

66   Martínez Barrio, *Memorias*, pp. 286–7.

67   See Santos Juliá, "Los socialistas y el escenario de la futura revolución", in Ojeda, editor, *Octubre 1934*, pp. 103–30.

68   The standard work on the causes and events of the Asturian rising is Adrian Shubert, *The Road to Revolution in Spain: The Coal Miners of Asturias 1860–1934* (Urbana, Ill., and Chicago, 1987). See also his article, "The epic failure: the Asturian revolution of October 1934", in Preston, editor, *Revolution and War*, pp. 113–36 and in particular pp. 128–33 for the events of October 1934.

69   That the government was prepared for a rising in Asturias was shown by the military exercises held in neighbouring Leon in the last week of September

1934. See Espadas Burgos in Elsa López et al., *Diego Hidalgo*, pp. 166–7.
70 Espadas Burgos in Elsa López et al., *Diego Hidalgo*, p. 169, claims that this was the decision of Lerroux, but gives no source.
71 With the exception of the CEDA ministers, according to Cardona, *El poder militar*, p. 203, though no source is given. The CEDA had earlier pressed for Franco's nomination as head of the General Staff, the move having probably been foiled by President Alcalá-Zamora. See Gil Robles, *No fue posible*, p. 140.
72 For Franco's appointment as "advisor" see Espadas Burgos in Elsa López et al., *Diego Hidalgo*, pp. 171–2 and Diego Hidalgo, *¿Por qué fui lanzado del Ministerio de la Guerra? Diez meses de actuación ministerial* (Madrid, 1934), pp. 79–81. Franco took direct control of operations from 7 October. See Cardona, *El poder militar*, pp. 204–5.
73 Gil Robles, *No fue posible*, p. 140; Espadas Burgos in Elsa López et al., *Diego Hidalgo*, pp. 173–5 ; and Vidarte, *El bienio*, p. 290.
74 Jardí, *Companys*, pp. 59–94. A much briefer account in Jones, "Regionalism and revolution", in Preston, editor, *Revolution and War*, pp. 106–8.
  The memoirs of the monarchist intellectual Pedro Sainz Rodríguez indicate that, if the government had been overwhelmed by the October 1934 risings, Lerroux might have endorsed a *coup* attempt by non-republican elements in the army. See Sainz Rodríguez, *Testimonio*, p. 156.

10 Allies and Adversaries

1 *Renovación*, 8 November 1934, 5 December 1934, 18 January 1935 and 24 January 1935.
2 *El Debate*, 27 January 1935, *Renovación*, 23 October 1934, 22 November 1934, 16 January 1935, and 14 February 1935. See also the speech given by Emiliano Iglesias in Barcelona, *Renovación*, 27 November 1934.
3 See Salazar Alonso's declarations in *Renovación*, 2 and 5 November 1934 as well as his article in *Renovación*, 27 December 1934.
4 *Renovación*, 10, 15, 16, 20 November 1934, 19 December 1934, and 9 January 1935.
5 Samper's views are to be found in DSC, 5 November 1934, *Renovación*, 18 January 1935, and the interview, originally given to *Heraldo de Madrid*, in *Renovación*, 20 November 1934. The other declarations are in *Renovación*, 10, 24 October 1934 as well as 2 and 11 November 1934. Somewhat contradictorily, *Renovación* called on 10 October 1934 for "mercy" for those republicans – or "former brothers" – that had committed crimes.
6 *Renovación*, 22 November 1934.
7 *Renovación*, 19 December 1934. See Lerroux's speech in Huelva, too, in *Renovación*, 18 December 1934.
8 *Renovación*, 20, 24, 30 October, and 2 November 1934; Alcalá-Zamora, *Memorias*, pp. 292, 294; Gil Robles, *No fue posible*, pp.141–4; Jalón, *Memorias*, pp.143–8; and Lerroux, *La pequeña historia*, pp. 281–8. Alcalá-Zamora claims on page 294 of his *Memorias* that he was prepared to go as far as resigning. For the government's pressures in relation to the Supreme Court, see Azaña, *Memorias*, IV, p.521.
9 Lerroux, *La pequeña historia*, pp. 308–10.
10 Jalón, *Memorias*, p. 159.
11 DSC, 5 November 1934.
12 Lerroux, *La pequeña historia*, pp. 288 and 315–17.
13 Gil Robles, *No fue posible*, pp. 145–8.

14 DSC, 5 November 1934; Gil Robles, *No fue posible*, pp. 152–3.
15 Lerroux, *La pequeña historia*, pp. 294–5.
16 Jalón, *Memorias*, p. 167.
17 Samper's declarations are in *Renovación*, 20 November 1934, from an interview originally given to *Heraldo de Madrid*. See also Lerroux, *La pequeña historia*, pp. 294–5 and Jalón, *Memorias*, p. 182.
18 *El Debate*, 21 November 1934. See also the editorial of 8 November 1934 and the commentaries of 15, 18, and 28 November 1934, as well as that of 14 December 1934.
19 DSC, 21 December 1934. Also see *Renovación*, 28 December 1934.
20 Gil Robles, *No fue posible*, p. 157.
21 *El Debate*, 18 November 1934. See also the editorial of 18 December 1934 on the party's aims.
22 DSC, 6 and 11 December 1934 and Gil Robles, *No fue posible*, p. 153–5.
23 Jardí, *Companys*, pp. 116–25, for the trial and sentence.
24 Jalón, though aware that this was a "prickly and oft-raised subject" within the Association, never raised the subject in Cabinet. See Jalón, *Memorias*, p. 176. In a similar vein, Alcalá-Zamora, in his *Memorias*, p. 298, claims that Lerroux promised to expel the assassin of "Luis de Sirval" from the Legion, but never did.
25 Jalón, *Memorias*, pp. 177–8. See also Ojeda, editor, *Octubre 1934*, passim, and J. A. Sánchez y García Saúco, *La revolución de 1934 en Asturias* (Madrid, 1974), pp. 139–45.
26 Jalón, *Memorias*, pp. 175–8, 182 and 185–6.
27 Barcia in DSC, 22 October 1935. He saw the telegram during the trial of the Catalan government.
28 *ABC*, 11 October 1934, cited by Juliá in *Azaña* p. 366. Azaña himself was convinced that the Radicals were responsible for his arrest, as related by Juliá, *Azaña*, p. 371.
29 Lerroux knew that Azaña was not involved but acted otherwise. See *Mi rebelión en Barcelona*, cited by Martínez Barrio, *Memorias*, pp. 262–3.
30 According to the account of Alcalá-Zamora, *Memorias*, p. 299.
31 DSC, 6 and 15 February 1935. Alcalá-Zamora comments in his *Memorias*, pp. 298–9, that the Radicals converted their undeserved hegemony into "the dictatorship of a type of viceroy".
32 Salazar Alonso, *Bajo el signo*, pp. 116–29.
33 DSC, 1 and 6 February, 1 March, and 17 July 1935; Carlos de Luna to Lerroux, 2 March 1935 ADH.
34 *El Debate*, 15 May 1935.
35 Alvarez Rey, *La derecha*, pp. 418–20.
36 Cabrera, *La patronal*, p. 223.
37 DSC, 29 January 1935 and *Renovación*, 26 January 1935. In Madrid 37.4% of the workforce was unemployed, according to the information in DSC, 15 March 1935.
38 DSC, 29 January, 27 March 1935; *El Debate*, 18 and 23 December 1934.
39 DSC, 23 January, 15, 22 February, 1, 15, 22, and 26 March 1935.
40 Alcalá-Zamora, *Memorias*, p. 300; Gil Robles, *No fue posible*, pp. 210–11; and Jalón, *Memorias*, pp. 173–4.
41 Jalón, *Memorias*, pp. 206–7.
42 *El Debate*, 20 October, 8 November 1934; Jalón, *Memorias*, p. 190.
43 For differing versions of the CEDA *caudillo*'s demands, see Gil Robles, *No fue posible*, pp. 166–7 and Jalón, *Memorias*, p. 191.

44 Gil Robles, *No fue posible*, pp. 166–7 and Jalón, *Memorias*, p. 191. For the meetings between Lerroux and Gil Robles, see also *El Debate*, 12, 13, and 15 January 1935, and *Renovación*, 12 January 1935.

45 Lerroux in DSC, 23 January 1935 and Gil Robles, *No fue posible*, pp. 169–71.

46 DSC, 21 March 1935; Alcalá-Zamora, *Memorias*, p. 300; Gil Robles, *No fue posible*, p. 171; Jalón, *Memorias*, p. 188; and Payne, *Spain's First Democracy*, pp. 230–1. In *La pequeña historia*, pp. 274–6, Lerroux claims that he was convinced from the outset that Azaña was not involved in the Barcelona rising and that he made this clear in Cabinet. He also denies pressuring the Supreme Court. The name of the ship is given by Jalón, *Memorias*, p. 157.

47 Payne, *Spain's First Democracy*, p. 229. Leah Manning, *What I Saw in Spain* (London, 1935). The appendices, however, were penned by two Spanish socialists – the former minister Fernando de los Ríos and left-winger Julio Alvarez del Vayo – as well as the left-republican leader Felix Gordón Ordás.

48 Jalón, *Memorias*, pp. 183–4.

49 See the letter of 5 April 1935 in AS, P-S Madrid, C852 L749.

50 Jalón, *Memorias*, p. 180.

51 Alcalá-Zamora warned the government "uselessly" against this very danger. In Alcalá-Zamora, *Memorias*, p. 301.

52 In the Cortes Martínez Barrio condemned both the Esquerra and the socialists for the risings of October 1934. See DSC, 16 November 1934, as well as Martínez Barrio, *Memorias*, pp. 254–5, 267–8, and 272–4.

53 The Alicante meeting is in *El Debate*, 27 January 1935 and the articles are in *Renovación*, 4 January and 2 February 1935. See also the editorial in *Renovación*, 13 January 1935. The calls for moderation are to be found in *Renovación*, 9, 10, 11, 18, 21, and 31 October 1934, 3 and 4 November 1934, 18 and 21 December 1934, and, finally, 1 and 16 January 1935.

54 Gil Robles, *No fue posible*, pp. 175–6 and 179–81; Jalón, *Memorias*, pp. 170–1; and Varela, *Partidos*, pp. 250–2.

55 Alvarez Rey, *La derecha*, pp. 420 and 423–4, as well as Javier Tussell and José Calvo, *Giménez Fernández: precursor de la democracia española* (Seville, 1990), pp. 101–3.

56 The quote is from Alvarez Rey, *La derecha*, p. 423 and the growing discrepancies are in Gil Robles, *No fue posible*, pp. 103–6.

57 Valls, *La derecha regional*, pp. 190–4. Stephen Lynam, "'Moderate' conservatism", in Blinkhorn, editor, *Spain in Conflict*, p. 148, offers a different reading of Lucia's stance, arguing that he fought for the measure at a local, as opposed to national, level. It has been argued that the "Christian Democrats" were not prepared to push the issue of social reform for fear of splitting the CEDA. See Lynam, "'Moderate' conservatism", in Blinkhorn, editor, *Spain in Conflict*, p. 148, and Varela, *Partidos*, pp. 247 and 249.

58 Tusell and Calvo, *Giménez Fernández*, pp. 70–100; Malefakis, *Agrarian Reform*, pp. 343–55; and Jacques Maurice, *La reforma agraria en España en el siglo XX (1900–1936)* (Madrid, 1978), p. 56. Gil Robles, in *No fue posible*, p. 182, tried to play down the opposition to Gimenez Fernández's proposals within the CEDA by defining it as a "minority within the parliamentary group".

59 Guerra del Río in DSC, 14 March 1935 and Valls, *La derecha regional*, pp. 193–4.

60 *El Debate*, 5 February, 19 March, and 26 March 1935. See also the editorial comments of 24 and 27 March 1935.

61 *El Debate*, 26 February 1935, 10, 12, and 19 March 1935.

62 According to a letter of 21 March 1935 to Lerroux, AS, P-S Madrid, C621 L811.

63 Letter of 4 March 1935, AS, P-S Madrid, C621 L811.

64 Letter of Germán Díaz to Lerroux of 5 February 1935, AS, P-S Madrid, C43.

65 *El Debate*, 10 February 1935; *Renovación*, 25 November 1934 and 8 January 1935.

66 *El Debate*, 19 February 1935.

67 *El Debate*, 5 and 26 February 1935. In a speech in Zaragoza, in *El Debate*, 12 March 1935, Gil Robles repeated the warning in relation to the *pueblo*.

68 Gil Robles, *No fue posible*, pp. 213–14, 216–17; Jalón, *Memorias*, pp. 193, 195–6; and Lerroux, *La pequeña historia*, p. 318. Alcalá-Zamora recalls in his *Memorias*, p. 301, that Lerroux voted "without hesitation". González Peña was not detained until 3 December 1934 before being condemned to death by a military court on 15 February 1935.

69 DSC, 8 May 1935 and *El Debate*, 27 and 30 March 1935.

70 Gil Robles, *No fue posible*, pp. 217–20; Lerroux, *La pequeña historia*, pp. 331–2.

71 Jalón, *Memorias*, p. 202; Lerroux, *La pequeña historia*, p. 323; and Martínez Barrio, *Memorias*, p. 273. The interview of Alfredo Zabala took place with the author on 8 June 1991. Six of the ministers were not deputies.

72 The CEDA campaign is in *El Debate*, 9, 23, 24, 25, 28, and 30 April 1935 as well as Montero, *La CEDA*, II, p. 32. The JAP manifesto is in *El Debate*, 7 April 1935, the telegrams in *El Debate*, 6 April 1935, and the resignations in *El Debate*, 5 and 12 April 1935. The ex-Radical, Antonio Lara, is in DSC, 8 May 1935 and the Radical bluff, as manifested by Emiliano Iglesias, in *El Debate*, 5 April 1935.

73 For the meetings, see *El Debate*, 18, 21 and 30 April 1935, and for the declarations of the CEDA and Radical deputies see *El Debate*, 23 April 1935. Also see Alcalá-Zamora, *Memorias*, p. 304 and Gil Robles, *No fue posible*, pp. 223–9.

74 See the DSC debate on the crisis of 8 May 1935, *El Debate*, 30 April 1935, as well as Gil Robles, *No fue posible*, pp. 224–5 and Jalón, *Memorias*, p. 205. The Samper quote is from *El Debate*, 5 May 1935. According to Jalón, *Memorias*, pp. 210 and 212, Lerroux hoped that Manuel Portela and Joaquín Chapaprieta, both independents, would act as de facto Radicals, but this proved to be misplaced. For the role of the Sevillian landowning oligarchy in ejecting Giménez Fernández from the ministry, see Alvarez Rey, *La derecha*, pp. 420–4.

75 Jalón, *Memorias*, p. 189. He was referring specifically to the period from December 1934 to February 1935, but the comment can be readily applied to the administration as a whole.

76 DSC, 8 May 1935 and *El Debate*, 7 May 1935.

77 *El Pueblo*, 7 and 10 May 1935.

78 Martínez Barrio, *Memorias*, p. 285.

79 Franch, *El Blasquisme*, p. 174, though he provides no sources.

80 Neither Franch, *El Blasquisme*, pp. 172–4, nor Alós, *El blasquismo*, p. 220, shed much light on the PURA crisis.

81 *El Debate*, 16 April 1935 and Alvarez Rey, *La derecha*, pp. 411–12.

11 Compromise and Confrontation

1 *El Debate*, 16 and 26 May 1935.

2 L. Ruiz Mosso to Lerroux, 7 May 1935, AS, P-S Madrid, C44 L758; civil governor of Avila to Lerroux, 22 January 1935 and 15 June 1935, AS, P-S Madrid, C46 L769.

3 Soria Radical Party to Lerroux, 25 January 1935, AS C40 L716; L. Ruiz Mosso to Lerroux, 7 May 1935, AS, P-S Madrid, C44 L758; Leon Radical Party to Lerroux, 15 January 1935, AS, P-S Madrid, C45 L760.

4 E. Peyró to Lerroux, 16 February 1935, AS, P-S Madrid, M1058 L3290; Orense Radical Party to Lerroux, 20 May 1935, AS, P-S Madrid, C46 L768; Gil Robles, *No fue posible*, p. 164; M. Olivés to Lerroux, 29 May 1935, AS C46 L768.

5 Radical Party of Palencia (capital) to Carreres, 23 June 1935, AS, P-S Madrid, C621 L811; Perfecto Díaz to Lerroux, 28 February 1935, AS, P-S Madrid, C43 L748; P. Sastregener Mercador to Carreres, 10 June 1935, AS, P-S Madrid, C621 L811; Gil Robles, *No fue posible*, pp. 277–9.

6 Lerroux, *La pequeña historia*, p. 249; *El Debate*, 6 and 25 June 1935; José Antonio Primo de Rivera cited by Preston, *The Coming*, p. 163.

7 Campoamor in AS, P-S Madrid, C519 L4772, cited by Ruiz Manjón, *El Partido Republicano Radical*, p. 468; *El Debate*, 26 June 1935; *El Debate*, 6 July 1935, cited by Ruiz Manjón, *El Partido Republicano Radical*, p. 480.

8 Palafox, *Atraso económico*, p. 265; Preston, "The agrarian war in the south", in Preston, editor, *Revolution and War*, p. 176; De la Cierva cited by Payne, *Spain's First Democracy*, p. 237.

9 Cabrera, *La patronal*, pp. 224–6; Preston, "The agrarian war in the south", in Preston, editor, *Revolution and War*, p. 176; Carlos de Luna letters in ADH.

10 Alvarez Rey, *La derecha*, p. 418 and Gil Robles, *No fue posible*, p. 302.

11 Gil Robles, *No fue posible*, p. 279 and DSC, 29 June 1935. See also Albornoz's outburst in DSC, 25 July 1935.

12 DSC, 26 July 1935; Malefakis, *Agrarian Reform*, pp. 356–63; Payne, *Spain's First Democracy*, p. 237; Varela, *Partidos*, p. 254.

13 Alcalá-Zamora, *Memorias*, pp. 334–5; Gil Robles, *No fue posible*, pp. 232–64; Preston, *The Coming*, pp. 157–9.

14 DSC, 15, 21 May, and 11 June 1935; *El Debate*, 11 May and 7 July 1935; Gil Robles, *No fue posible*, p. 273.

15 DSC, 11, 13, and 26 June 1935.

16 As pointed out by Cabrera, *La patronal*, pp. 244–7.

17 DSC, 21 June 1935 and Chapaprieta, *Fue posible*, pp. 176–7. The government's scheme would appear to have been blighted by the usual shortcomings. Employment on the public works projects often depended on a worker's political affiliation. In Castellon, to take one example, many mayors would apparently employ only those that were in the Radical Party, or who had at least promised to vote for the Radicals in the next election. There were also, it was claimed, considerable bureaucratic delays. The workers on one road-building project in Caceres, for instance, were purportedly owed over 60,000 pesetas, having not been paid for over six months. See DSC, 23 and 28 May 1935.

18 Palafox, *Atraso económico*, pp. 240–8 and 257–8; Gil Robles, *No fue posible*, pp. 268–73.

19 See chapter 3 of Chapaprieta's *Fue posible* for a detailed account of his aims.

20 DSC, 14, 18, and 25 June 1935. For the budget as a whole, see DSC, 11, 12,

14, 18, 19, 21, and 25 June 1935. The increase in police and defence spending accounted for nearly a third of the rise since the 1933 budget. See Palafox, *Atraso económico*, pp. 267–8.

21 Gil Robles, *No fue posible*, pp. 281–2; Chapaprieta, *Fue posible*, pp. 177–8 and 182–3. The latter claims that Lerroux, too, opposed the economy measures once he lost the premiership in September 1935.

22 Gil Robles, *No fue posible*, p. 164; Grupo Profesional to Lerroux, 14 June 1935, AS, P-S Madrid, C51 L800; Antonio Tuñón de Lara in DSC, 23 May 1935; Fulgencio Díez Pastor in DSC, 20 June 1935.

23 T. Rubio to Lerroux, 15 June 1935, AS, P-S Madrid, C47 L773; Gil Robles, *No fue posible*, p. 290.

24 Gil Robles, *No fue posible*, pp. 266–7; DSC, 15 and 16 May 1935; T. Rubio to Lerroux, 15 June 1935, AS, P-S Madrid, C47 L773.

25 Tusell and Calvo, *Giménez Fernández*, pp. 137–8, 140, 142–4; Gil Robles, *No fue posible*, pp. 324–7; Chapaprieta, *Fue posible*, pp. 313–14; AS C1709 L696, including the meeting of the parliamentary group on 21 November 1935.

26 Chapaprieta, *Fue posible*, pp. 311–12; Alcalá-Zamora, *Memorias*, pp. 335–56.

27 See Gil Robles, *No fue posible*, p. 290 and, more generally, the epilogue to his *Discursos Parlamentarios* (Madrid, 1971), p. 675.

28 DSC, 31 May, 6 June, 4, 23, and 25 July 1935; Lerroux to the civil governor of Avila, 15 June 1935 AS, P-S Madrid, C46 L769.

29 *El Pueblo*, 7 May 1935; Preston, *The Coming*, pp. 161–3; *El Debate*, 2 and 3 July 1935; Alcalá-Zamora, *Memorias*, p. 336.

30 Alós, *Blasquismo*, p. 220. The speech can be found in Franch, *El Blasquisme*, pp. 285–99, *El Debate*, 9 July 1935, and *El Pueblo*, 9 July 1935. For Lerroux's subsequent defence of collaboration with the CEDA, see *La pequeña historia*, pp. 344–5.

31 Alcalá-Zamora, *Memorias*, p. 338.

32 *El Sol*, 27 August and 10 September 1935; *El Debate*, 27 August 1935.

33 See the letters of 21 July 1935 and 27 November 1935 in AS, P-S Madrid, C44 L750 and C621 L811 respectively.

34 Letter of 19 June 1935 to Lerroux, AS, P-S Madrid, C621 L811; Orense party to Lerroux, 20 May 1935, AS, P-S Madrid, C46 L768; mayor of Pontevedra to Lerroux, 16 October 1935, AS, P-S Madrid, C46 L768.

35 José Borrajo to Lerroux, 2 July 1935, AS, P-S Madrid, C1716 L699; Teodosio Auseré to Lerroux, 15 November 1935, AS, P-S Madrid, C621 L811; Dario Pérez to Lerroux, 16 August 1935, AS, P-S Madrid, C1716 L699. In a further letter of 27 November Auseré comments that the reorganization will be "very laborious". See AS, P-S Madrid, C621 L811.

36 See the minutes of the Madrid Junta of 18 September 1935, AS, P-S Madrid, C1716 L694. For Bilbao, see Pablo Barrera to Lerroux, 27 June 1935, AS, P-S Madrid, C43.

37 Pedro Sastre Gener to Lerroux AS, P-S Madrid, C621 L811; Medina del Campo group to Lerroux, 16 August 1935 AS, P-S Madrid, C1716 L699.

38 Caro Cancela, *Cádiz*, pp. 219, 225 and 227; Alvarez Rey, *La derecha*, pp. 427–8; García Andreu, *Alicante*, p. 56.

39 Carlos de Luna to Lerroux, 11 March, 14 May, 6 June, 25 October, 6 and 18 November 1935, ADH; *Semblanzas*, pp. 3 and 6, ADH; Diego Hidalgo to De Luna, 10, 25 May, 29 August, 3, 30 October, 20 November, and 13 December 1935, ADH. See also the letters to Hidalgo from the *pueblos* on the same subject, in ADH.

40 Tomás Peire to Lerroux, 22 August 1935 AS, P-S Madrid, C1716 L699. The meeting of the parliamentary group on 3 October 1935 is in AS, P-S Madrid, C1709 L696.

41 D. Cortés, mayor of Puertollano, to Lerroux, 9 August 1935, AS, P-S Madrid, C43 L747; the civil governor and Radical presidents of the local and provincial committees to Lerroux, both letters dated 25 August 1935, AS, P-S Madrid, C1716 L699.

42 Alvarez Rey, *La derecha*, pp. 407–9.

43 Gil Robles's speech is in *El Debate*, 3 September 1935. Alcalá-Zamora told Giménez Fernández that "this is fascism". See Tusell and Calvo, *Giménez Fernández*, p. 148. For Alcalá-Zamora's concern at Gil Robles's fascist proclivities, see also Alcalá-Zamora, *Memorias*, p. 336 and Tusell and Calvo, *Giménez Fernández*, pp. 151 and 155.

44 Lerroux, *La pequeña historia*, pp. 365–6; Gil Robles, *No fue posible*, pp. 286–8. Royo Villanova had tried to leave the government several weeks earlier over the same issue.

45 Gil Robles, *No fue posible*, pp. 288–90; Alcalá-Zamora, *Memorias*, pp. 340–1; Jalón, *Memorias*, p. 229; Chapaprieta, *Fue posible*, pp. 212–13.

46 Chapaprieta, *Fue posible*, pp. 213–17; Jalón, *Memorias*, pp. 210 and 225; Gil Robles, *No fue posible*, p. 291; Lerroux, *La pequeña historia*, pp. 367–8.

47 Chapaprieta, *Fue posible*, pp. 205 and 234–6.

48 Chapaprieta, *Fue posible*, pp. 207–8 and 212–15; Gil Robles, *No fue posible*, p. 288.

49 According to Gil Robles, *No fue posible*, p. 299.

50 The following account of the affair is based entirely on the 26-page version sent to the President by Daniel Strauss, which can be found in ATS, Legajo 6239.

51 Alcalá-Zamora, *Memorias*, pp. 312 and 530; Lerroux, *La pequeña historia*, p. 264. The President took the precaution of checking the story out with Juan Rocha and Ricardo Samper, both of whom confirmed it. Indeed, Rocha's brother, Julio, had been paid a consultancy fee in his capacity as a lawyer by Strauss (Alcalá-Zamora, *Memorias*, p. 312).

52 Tusell and Calvo, *Giménez Fernández*, p. 151. Lerroux may have said this at the second meeting.

53 Jalón, *Memorias*, p. 221 and Gil Robles, *No fue posible*, p. 300, recall April, while Alcalá-Zamora, and Chapaprieta, *Fue posible*, p. 265, place it in January. In fact, Strauss's account refers to 21 January 1935 as the date by which Lerroux should pay him. See ATS, Leg. 6239.

54 Alcalá-Zamora, *Memorias*, pp. 312 and 530; Tusell and Calvo, *Giménez Fernández*, p. 151; Chapaprieta, *Fue posible*, p. 254. Lerroux's less plausible version – that he told Strauss' representative to catch the first train back to Paris – is in *La pequeña historia*, pp. 339–40.

55 Gil Robles, *No fue posible*, p. 300; Lerroux, *La pequeña historia*, pp. 355, 359; Alcalá-Zamora, *Memorias*, pp. 340 and 530.

56 Jalón, *Memorias*, pp. 219 and 222; Ruiz Manjón, *El Partido Republicano Radical*, p. 493; DSC, 1 October 1935.

57 Chapaprieta, *Fue posible*, pp. 243 , 254–6, and 266. On being presented with Chapaprieta's final Cabinet list Alcalá-Zamora had in fact commented that it would have been best not to include Lerroux, but without explaining why. See Chapaprieta, *Fue posible*, p. 229.

58 Chapaprieta, *Fue posible*, 257–61; Gil Robles, *No fue posible*, p. 294; Lerroux, *La pequeña historia*, pp. 374–6.

59   Lerroux, *La pequeña historia*, pp. 376–7. This, at least, is Lerroux's recollection. Gil Robles takes a more sober view of Alcalá-Zamora's "allusions" to him and of the "insinuations" made in relation to Lerroux. See Gil Robles, *No fue posible*, p. 295.

60   Alcalá-Zamora, *Memorias*, pp. 312–13; Chapaprieta, *Fue posible*, pp. 261–3. Gil Robles claims in *No fue posible*, p.296, that he first learnt of Strauss' claim at this meeting, but this is highly unlikely. Giménez Fernández – who was informed by Alcalá-Zamora on the 9th – promptly reported all conversations with the President back to his leader. As a result, Gil Robles would have learnt of the claim on the 9th or, at the latest, on the 10th.

61   Chapaprieta, *Fue posible*, pp. 265–6 and 309; Tusell and Calvo, *Giménez Fernández*, p. 151. The fact that during the September 1935 reshuffle the President had nominated another Radical, Santiago Alba, as Prime Minister, and had accepted Lerroux as a minister in the Chapaprieta Cabinet, further indicates that his principal aim was to remove the Radical leader from the premiership.

62   Chapaprieta, *Fue posible*, pp. 263–4, 267–8, 276; Gil Robles, *No fue posible*, p. 302; Jalón, *Memorias*, pp. 226–7; Lerroux, *La pequeña historia*, pp. 382–3.

63   Jalón, *Memorias*, p. 227 and Juliá, *Azaña*, pp. 414–15. The Cabinet statement was drawn up by Gil Robles, who gives the full text in *No fue posible*, p. 302.

64   Conflicting accounts of how this came about in Lerroux, *La pequeña historia*, p. 382; Chapaprieta, *Fue posible*, p. 269; Gil Robles, *No fue posible*, pp. 304–5.

65   DSC, 22 October 1935; Lerroux, *La pequeña historia*, p. 384; Gil Robles, *No fue posible*, p. 304.

66   See, for example, Andrés Orozco in DSC, 22 October 1935.

67   Chapaprieta, *Fue posible*, p. 269; Gil Robles, *No fue posible*, 302 and 304–5; DSC, 22 October 1935.

68   According to the version of the Spanish Ambassador to Mexico.

69   ATS, dossiers 1 and 2, Leg. 6239. The documentation in the ATS demonstrates that in reality Valdivia sent out the telegrams banning the game on the night of 17 to 18 September 1935.

70   Gil Pechamorrán, *La Segunda República*, p. 245; Gil Robles, *No fue posible*, pp. 297–8 and 306–10; DSC, 28 October 1935; Salazar Alonso, *Bajo el signo*, pp. 306–8 and 311; Jalón, *Memorias*, p. 231.

71   Differing accounts of the resignations in Gil Robles, *No fue posible*, pp. 308 and 310; Chapaprieta, *Fue posible*, pp. 274–5; and Alcalá-Zamora, *Memorias*, p. 313.

72   Chapaprieta, *Fue posible*, pp. 275 and 277–80; Gil Robles, *No fue posible*, p. 310. Usabiaga was no longer a deputy by this stage.

73   Jalón, *Memorias*, pp. 223 and 232. Aurelio allegedly described Blasco Ibáñez to Strauss as his "best friend". See Strauss' account in ATS, Leg.6239.

74   Strauss to Justo Oyarzabal, 14 December 1935, ATS, Leg.6239.

75   Salazar Alonso claims that the authorization of 25 August 1934 was forged, and that on 3 September he personally drew up an order denying the licence. See Salazar Alonso, *Bajo el signo*, pp. 307–8 and 311; Gil Robles, *No fue posible*, pp. 297–8.

76   Sainz Rodríguez, *Testimonio*, p. 157. According to Jalón, Salazar Alonso, like other Radical ministers, did not want to incur the displeasure of Alejandro Lerroux by spurning the requests of his adopted son. See Jalón, *Memorias*, p. 229.

77 Strauss' letter was later published in *ABC*, *El Socialista*, and *La Vanguardia*. The original is in ATS, Leg.6239. Fernando Jiménez Sánchez, in a recent example, refers to Strauss as an "Jewish Dutch adventurer". See *Detrás del escándalo político: opinión pública, dinero y poder en la España del siglo XX* (Barcelona, 1995), p. 59.
78 DSC, 22 October 1935.
79 As shown, for example, by his application to the Directorate General of Security for a gaming licence. See ATS, Leg.6239.
80 *Politiken* (Denmark), 30 October 1935. A copy of the article is in ATS, Leg.6239.
81 Alcalá-Zamora, *Memorias*, pp. 310, 313, 526–7, and 529; Gil Robles, *No fue posible*, p. 163 footnote 7; Lerroux, *Memorias*, p. 638; Chapaprieta, *Fue posible*, pp. 246–8; Sainz Rodríguez, *Testimonio*, p. 157; Martínez Barrio, *Memorias*, p. 186.
82 Lerroux, *La pequeña historia*, p. 351; Tusell and Calvo, *Giménez Fernández*, p. 151; Gil Robles in DSC, 22 October 1935; Alcalá-Zamora, *Memorias*, pp. 306–7.
83 Jalón, *Memorias*, p. 219.
84 Valls, *La derecha regional*, pp. 217–20; Martínez Barrio, *Memorias*, pp. 184 and 186; Gil Robles, *No fue posible*, p. 163; Chapaprieta, *Fue posible*, p. 245; Alcalá-Zamora, *Memorias*, p. 308.
85 Gil Robles judged it as "petty theft". This, and Bellón's view, are in Gil Robles, *No fue posible*, p. 297.
86 J. P. T. Bury, 5th edition, *France 1814–1940* (London, 1985), pp. 267–8 and Maurice Larkin, *France since the Popular Front: Government and People 1936–1986* (Oxford, 1988), pp. 50–1.
87 Lerroux, *La pequeña historia*, pp. 349 and 378; Alcalá-Zamora, *Memorias*, p. 312.
88 Chapaprieta, *Fue posible*, pp. 267–8 and Juliá, *Azaña*, pp. 423–4.
89 As even Alcalá-Zamora agreed. See Alcalá-Zamora, *Memorias*, pp. 312 and 531; Jalón, *Memorias*, p. 222; Chapaprieta, *Fue posible*, p. 268.
90 Chapaprieta, *Fue posible*, p. 268; Gil Robles, *No fue posible*, p. 303; Alcalá-Zamora, *Memorias*, pp. 530–1.
91 Jiménez Sánchez, *Escándalo político*, pp. 70–1, which includes the citation from *Política*.
92 ATS, Leg.6239; Lerroux, *La pequeña historia*, pp. 358 and 382–3.
93 The head of the presidential press office, Emilio Herrero, was a journalist at Prieto's Bilbao newspaper, *El Liberal*. Lerroux, in *La pequeña historia*, stresses not only that Strauss had a criminal record but also that he had been expelled from several countries. He claims that Alcalá-Zamora knew of the affair as early as August 1935, which is far from improbable. See Jalón, *Memorias*, p. 222 and Lerroux, *La pequeña historia*, pp. 342–3, 357–8, and 378.
94 Gil Robles recalls that this was the President's favourite topic of conversation during the consultations which they held, Alcalá-Zamora aiming to discredit Lerroux, a "declared enemy". See Gil Robles, *No fue posible*, pp. 163 and 288. See also Tusell and Calvo, *Giménez Fernández*, p. 148. It is significant that Alcalá-Zamora devotes less than three pages of the main text of his memoirs to the whole affair as well as being evasive and terse about his own role.
95 Alcalá-Zamora, *Memorias*, pp. 312–13; Chapaprieta, *Fue posible*, pp. 262–4.
96 Salazar Alonso, *Bajo el signo*, p. 311. Gil Robles agrees in *No fue posible*,

pp. 305–306, with Cambó's judgement at the time that the commission was anticonstitutional, but defends the decision on the grounds of "political passion".

97 See Salazar Alonso, Diego Hidalgo, and Andrés Orozco in DSC, 28 October 1935.

98 Chapaprieta, *Fue posible*, pp. 266–7.

99 In the same vein, Chapaprieta, in drawing up his Cabinet, had considered giving Lerroux the Ministry of the Interior, but Gil Robles persuaded him to allocate to the Radical leader the Ministry of Foreign Affairs instead. Yet Chapaprieta did this without so much as consulting Lerroux himself and despite the fact that the Radical *jefe* had been mortally offended by having been designated the same ministry in the provisional government. See Gil Robles, *No fue posible*, p. 290.

100 Gil Robles, *No fue posible*, p. 304; Tusell and Calvo, *Giménez Fernández*, p. 152; Chapaprieta, *Fue posible*, pp. 269–71; Lerroux, *La pequeña historia*, p. 382. *El Debate* reprinted Strauss' claim for good measure on the 27th. See Jiménez Sánchez, *Escándalo Político*, p. 66. In the Cortes, Gil Robles had hinted that Lerroux and Rocha should resign. See DSC, 28 October 1935.

101 Chapaprieta, *Fue posible*, pp. 267–71; Lerroux, *La pequeña historia*, p. 383; Jalón, *Memorias*, pp. 220 and 227.

102 Jiménez Sánchez, *Escándalo político*, p. 75.

12 The Fall from Power

1 Ruiz Manjón, *El Partido Republicano Radical*, pp. 529, 532 and 534; AS, P-S Madrid, C1709 L699; Chapaprieta, *Fue posible*, p. 381.

2 Chapaprieta, *Fue posible*, pp. 280–1 and 308; DSC, 30 October 1935; AS, P-S Madrid, C1709 L699. Only twenty-five Radicals backed the government on the vote of confidence, according to *ABC*, 31 October 1935 (as cited by Jiménez Sánchez, *Escándalo político*, p. 75).

3 DSC, 30 October 1935 and Chapaprieta, *Fue posible*, pp. 283–91. Nearly thirty years later, Pérez Madrigal revealed that he had drawn on "copious documentation" supplied by none other than Juan March in order to press his case. See Chapaprieta, *Fue posible*, pp. 420–1. Ironically, Pérez Madrigal brought out a satirical weekly in the summer of 1935 entitled "Clean Hands". See *El Debate*, 28 August and 5 September 1935.

4 Chapaprieta, *Fue posible*, pp. 283, 287–8, 292, 298–9, and 303–4; Gil Robles, *No fue posible*, p. 344.

5 Gil Robles, *No fue posible*, pp. 343–4, 347–9, and 351; Chapaprieta, *Fue posible*, pp. 292–303. Gil Robles counters Chapaprieta's charge by claiming, unconvincingly, that the premier was the intransigent one. See Gil Robles, *No fue posible*, pp. 341–3.

6 Gil Robles, *No fue posible*, pp. 344 and 347; AS, P-S Madrid, C735.

7 Ruiz Manjón, *El Partido Republicano Radical*, p. 540.

8 Gil Robles, *No fue posible*, pp. 329–30; Martínez Barrio, *Memorias*, pp. 285–91, which cites the diary of Ricardo Samper.

9 Chapaprieta, *Fue posible*, pp. 249–52 and 305–6; Gil Robles, *No fue posible*, pp. 329–41; and Antonio Goicoechea in DSC, 7 December 1935.

10 Gil Robles, *No fue posible*, pp. 330 and 333–4.

11 Alcalá-Zamora, *Memorias*, pp. 310–11; Gil Robles, *No fue posible*, pp. 329 and 337; Chapaprieta, *Fue posible*, pp. 305–7; and Lerroux, *La pequeña historia*, pp. 386–7 and 401.

12 Gil Robles, *No fue posible*, pp. 352–4; DSC, 29 November and 7 December 1935; Lerroux, *La pequeña historia*, pp. 400–1.

13 Jiménez Sánchez, *Escándalo político*, p. 90.

14 Lerroux, *La pequeña historia*, p. 389. The Prime Minister's sympathy for Tayá's cause was further indicated by his willingness to discuss the Catalan businessman's grievances with him in person. See *La pequeña historia*, p. 389. The first scandal, the "Straperlo", lived on in the collective memory in Spain as a synonym for "the black market".

15 Chapaprieta, *Fue posible*, pp. 308–9. A different slant in Gil Robles, *No fue posible*, pp. 355–8.

16 Chapaprieta, *Fue posible*, pp. 304–5, 325–6, and 330–2. Gil Robles denies that he refused to cooperate in *No fue posible*, pp. 359–60.

17 Gil Robles, *No fue posible*, pp. 360, 362–364; Alcalá-Zamora, *Memorias*, pp. 341 and 343. Alcalá-Zamora informed Gil Robles before the reshuffle that he would not entrust a government either to him or to Santiago Alba, but the *Cedistas* and Radicals evidently believed that they could force his hand. See Chapaprieta, *Fue posible*, p. 327.

18 Gil Robles, *No fue posible*, pp. 365–6. The CEDA leader's implicit backing was underlined by the fact that he was later hurt by the suggestion amongst right-wing circles that he had rejected the *coup* attempt "over a legal nicety". See Gil Robles, *No fue posible*, p. 378.

19 For Alcalá-Zamora's aims see Chapaprieta, *Fue posible*, p. 324.

20 Alcalá-Zamora, *Memorias*, pp. 341 and 344; Chapaprieta, *Fue posible*, pp. 311–12.

21 Chapaprieta, *Fue posible*, pp. 330, 333–44; Gil Robles, *No fue posible*, pp. 156–8 and 369–70.

22 Chapaprieta, *Fue posible*, pp. 345–6. For Portela's view of a centrist force that could hold the balance of power, see Portela, *Memorias*, pp. 152–3 and 156–7.

23 Tusell and Calvo, *Giménez Fernández*, p. 158; Gil Robles, *No fue posible*, p. 371, footnote 28; Chapaprieta, *Fue posible*, pp. 345–7.

24 Gil Robles, *No fue posible*, pp. 373–4. *El Pueblo*, 15 December 1935, cited by Ruiz Manjón, *El Partido Republicano Radical*, p. 547.

25 AS, P-S Madrid, C1709 L699 and Ruiz Manjón, *El Partido Republicano Radical*, pp. 548–50. The congress held in October 1932 was a "special" one.

26 Chapaprieta, *Fue posible*, p. 350 and Gil Robles, *No fue posible*, p. 431.

27 Chapaprieta, *Fue posible*, pp. 356–72 and Gil Robles, *No fue posible*, pp. 392–6. Portela's brief account refers evasively to "petty internal struggles". See his *Memorias*, pp. 158–9. Alcalá-Zamora wanted to protect himself against a parliamentary backlash over the second dissolution and any other attacks on his performance as president.

28 Ruiz Manjón, *El Partido Republicano Radical*, p. 550; Pich y Pon to Lerroux, 4 January 1936, AS, P-S Madrid, C846 L742; and Vázquez Limón to Lerroux, 30 December 1935, AS, P-S Madrid, C46 L770. Becerra was moved to the Ministry of Labour, Justice, and Health.

29 Gil Robles, *No fue posible*, pp. 396–400, 431; Portela, *Memorias*, pp. 160–3 and 167.

30 Gil Robles, *No fue posible*, p. 427; *El Debate*, 9, 14, and 31 January 1936. However, dissident Radicals, such as Manuel Becerra in Lugo, and, in the rerun election of 3 May 1936, Alvarez Mendizábal in Cuenca, did form part of the Popular Front. See E. Andicoberry to Lerroux, 19 December 1935, AS, P-S Madrid, C1727 L672 and López Villaverde, *Cuenca*, pp. 265, 290, 302 and 306.

31 AS, P-S Madrid, C522 and C569 L4769. See also Alba's letter to Oarrichena, AS, P-S Madrid, C569 L4768.

32 Ruiz Manjón, *El Partido Republicano Radical*, pp. 564–6.
33 Diego Hidalgo to Carlos de Luna, 4 March 1936 in ADH; Concepción Muñoz Tinoco, "Diego Hidalgo, política regional y política liberal en un periodo de convulsión", Ph.D. thesis, Complutense University of Madrid, 1985, p. 209; Lerroux, *La pequeña historia*, p. 422; Vázquez Limón to Lerroux, AS, P-S Madrid, C46 L770; Ruiz Manjón, *El Partido Republicano Radical*, pp. 562, 557–8 and 566–9; AS, P-S Madrid, C46 L770.
34 Ruiz Manjón, *El Partido Republicano Radical*. pp. 566–70 and *El Sol*, 11 February 1936.
35 *El Sol*, 4, 11, and 12 February 1936; Gil Robles, *No fue posible*, p. 426.
36 Those elected on a right-wing ticket were Picón for Avila, Bardají for Badajoz, Pérez Madrigal for Ciudad Real, Rozas for Jaen, Sierra Rustarazo for Cuenca, and Alba for Zamora. The exceptions were Guerra del Río for Las Palmas and Villanueva for Orense. See Ruiz Manjón, *El Partido Republicano Radical*, p. 574.
37 Ruiz Manjón, *El Partido Republicano Radical*, p. 577. The election of Tomás Sierra Rustarazo for Cuenca was overturned. See López Villaverde, *Cuenca*, pp. 264 and 272. Lerroux, having not been elected in the first round, did not even bother standing in the second.
38 Morlino, *Della democrazia*, p. 191, cited by Gil Pechamorrán, *La Segunda República*, p. 251 footnote 4. 0.9 per cent of the votes cast gives the Radicals 89,000, or 11 per cent of the 800,000 won in 1933, but all voting figures are approximate. Ruiz Manjón, drawing on the cases of Alicante, Castellon, and Valencia, speculates that most Radical votes went to the Popular Front, but these areas, traditionally strong republican ones, were not representative of the many other areas where the Radicals had gained support under the Republic. See Ruiz Manjón, *El Partido Republicano Radical*, pp. 573 and 576.
39 Velarde to Lerroux, 12 March 1936, AS, P-S Madrid, C46 L770; Salazar Alonso to Lerroux, 28 March 1936, AS, P-S Madrid, C46 L770; Ruiz Manjón, *El Partido Republicano Radical*, p. 579.
40 Diego Hidalgo to Carlos de Luna, 4 March 1936 in ADH; Ruiz Manjón, *El Partido Republicano Radical*, p. 587. The announcement that the Radical Party's compromises were over "with everyone" is from Lerroux's circular of 28 March 1936, the criteria of which were adopted by the Executive Committee. See Ruiz Manjón, *El Partido Republicano Radical*, pp. 582–4.
41 The quotes are adapted from the general observations of Sidney Tarrow in *Power in movement: Social movements, collective action and politics* (Cambridge, 1994), p. 104.
42 Lerroux, *Mis memorias*, p. 638.
43 See Jalón's, *Memorias*, pp. 251–422 and Lerroux's letter of 15 June 1936 to Diego Hidalgo concerning Jalón's fate, ADH.
44 Diego Hidalgo to Franco, 10 May 1937. See Francisco Franco Salgado-Araujo, *Mi vida junto a Franco* (Barcelona, 1977), p. 373 and López et al., *Diego Hidalgo*, pp. 195–216.
45 Culla, *El republicanisme lerrouxista*, p. 459 and Ian Gibson, *Quiepo de Llano: Sevilla, verano de 1936* (Barcelona, 1986), passim. According to Martínez Barrio, the exiled Clara Campoamor, despite her progressive credentials, flirted – unsuccessfully – with the Franco regime. See Capel, *El sufragio feminino*, p. 155 and Martínez Barrio, *Memorias*, p. 84.
46 Alonso Baño, editor, *Homenaje a Diego Martínez Barrio*, pp. 67–112; Martínez Barrio, *Memorias*, pp. 359–67 for the premiership, while pp.

356–423 cover the Civil War as a whole and exile.

47 See Basilio Alvarez's *España en Crisol* (La Coruña, 1989), including the introduction by José Antonio Durán, pp. 9–24. The book was originally published in 1937.

48 Lerroux to Franco, 18 July 1937 in Franco Salgado-Araujo, *Conversaciones*, p. 211; Franco Salgado-Araujo, *Mi vida*, p. 373; Lerroux, *La pequeña historia*, p. 517.

49 I should like to thank Enrique Montero Hernández for relating to me the story of the Radical mayor for Avila as told to him by the mayor's wife. A leading motive for the Nationalists to amass the documentation that now makes up the Civil War Archive in Salamanca was to identify the Masons and bring them to "justice".

50 See the brief account of Vaquero's life by Juan Ortiz Villalba in the introduction to Eloy Vaquero, *Del Drama de Andalucia*, pp. 226–31.

51 Franco Salgado-Araujo, *Mi vida*, pp. 381–2; Piñeiro, *Los March*, pp. 215 and 217–18. See also Lerroux's letter of 25 February 1938 to Franco in Franco Salgado-Araujo, *Mi vida*, p. 375.

52 The sentence is in AS, Sección de la Masonería, L14A Exp.18.

53 *España Nueva* (Mexico D.F.), 15 June 1946, as brought to my notice by Matilde Eiroa.

54 Juan Ortiz Villalba in the introduction to Eloy Vaquero, *Del Drama de Andalucia*, p. 229; Alvarez Junco, *El Emperador*, p. 631.

55 *Enciclopedia Univeral Ilustrada Europeo Americana* (Espase-Calpe), suplemento anual 1949–1952, p. 300; Culla, *El republicanisme lerrouxista*, p. 460; *Política*, 16 July 1949, which was kindly brought to my attention by Matilde Eiroa.

Conclusions

1 Martínez Barrio, *Memorias*, p. 160.

2 See the critical assessment of Enric Ucelay Da-Cal, "Buscando el levantamiento plebiscitario: insurrecionalismo y elecciones", in Juliá, editor, *Ayer*, 20, 1995, pp. 49–80.

3 For a recent example, see George Esenwein and Adrian Shubert, *Spain at War: The Spanish Civil War in Context, 1931–1939* (London, 1985), p. *v*.

4 DSC, 12 June 1934.

5 For reflections on the non-inevitability of civil war see Santos Juliá, "España sin guerra civil. ¿Qué hubiera pasado sin la rebelión militar de julio de 1936?", in Niall Ferguson, editor, *Historia virtual. ¿Qué hubierra pasado si . . . ?* (Madrid, 1998), pp. 183–210 and Edward Malefakis, "Balance Final", in Edward Malefakis, editor, *La guerra de España (1936–1939)* (Madrid, 1996), pp. 637–64.

Bibliography

I PRIMARY SOURCES

Unpublished sources

Archivo de Barcelona (in the Archivo del Ministerio de Asuntos Exteriores), Madrid
Archivo Diego Hidalgo, Madrid.
Archivo Martínez Barrio (in the Archivo Histórico Nacional), Madrid
Archivo de Salamanca, Archivo Histórico Nacional, Sección Guerra Civil, Salamanca

Parliamentary debates

Diario de sesiones de las Cortes Constituyentes de la República española, comenzaron el 14 de julio de 1931 (DSCC), 25 vols.
Diario de las sesiones de Cortes, Congreso de los Diputados, comenzaron el 8 de diciembre de 1933 (DSC), 17 vols.

Interviewees

Eduardo de Guzmán, José Prat García, and Alfredo Zabalza

Newspapers and periodicals (completely or partially consulted: dailies unless otherwise specified)

ABC (Madrid), March 1931 to February 1936.
El Debate (Madrid), March 1931 to February 1936.
Heraldo de Aragón (Zaragoza), March to December 1931.
El Liberal (Madrid), March 1931 to February 1936.
El Liberal (Seville), December 1933 to July 1934.
El Obrero de la Tierra (Madrid), weekly, September 1932 to September 1933.
El Progreso (Barcelona), March 1931 to September 1933.
El Pueblo (Valencia), March 1931 to February 1936.
Renovación (Barcelona), November 1933 to February 1936.
El Socialista (Madrid), March 1931 to February 1936.
El Sol (Madrid), March 1931 to February 1936.
Solidaridad Obrera (Barcelona), April 1931 to August 1932.
La Tierra (Madrid), April 1931 to August 1932.

Party publications and congress reports

Marsá Bragado, Antonio and Izcaray Calzada, Bernardo, editors, *Libro de Oro del Partido Republicano Radical 1864–1934* (Madrid, 1935).

Partido Republicano Radical, *Actuación de la minoría parlamentaria* (Madrid, 1932).

Partido Republicano Radical, *Asamblea nacional extraordinaria, Octubre 1932* (Madrid, 1932).

Partido Republicano Radical, *Bases de organización provincial* (Alicante, 1933).

Writings and speeches by contemporaries

Aguirre Lecube, José Antonio, *Entre la libertad y la revolución, 1930–1935: la verdad de un lustro en el País Vasco* (Bilbao, 1976).

Alba, Victor, *La Alianza Obrera* (Gijon, 1977).

Albornoz, Alvaro de, *El partido republicano* (Madrid, 1918).

Alcalá-Zamora, Niceto, *Los defectos de la Constitución de 1931* (Madrid, 1936).

——, *Memorias (Segundo texto de mis memorias)* (Barcelona, 1977).

Alvarez, Basilio, *Abriendo el surco: manual de lucha campesina* (Madrid, 1976).

——, *Desde mi campo: el libro del periodista* (Madrid, 1912).

——, *Dos años de agitación política en el parlamento* (La Coruña, 1991).

Alvarez del Vayo, Julio, *Freedom's Battle* (London, 1940).

——, *The Last Optimist* (London, 1950).

Ansaldo, José Antonio, *¿Para qué? (De Alfonso XIII a Juan III)* (Buenos Aires, 1951).

Azaña, Manuel, *Diarios, 1931–1933:"Los cuadernos robados"* (Barcelona, 1997).

——, *Obras completas*, 4 vols (Mexico, 1966–8).

——, *Memorias políticas y de guerra*, 4 vols (Madrid, 1976).

Ayuntamiento de Alicante, *Memoria de la secretaria municipal: 16 abril de 1931–31 diciembre de 1932* (Alicante, 1933).

Barea, Arturo, *The Forging of a Rebel* (London, 1972).

Batalla, Eduardo, *Mis memorias y mi lucha* (Barcelona, 1936).

Belausteguigoitia, Ramón de, *Reparto de tierras y produccion nacional* (Madrid, 1932).

Berenguer, Dámaso, *De la Dictadura a la Republica* (Madrid, 1946).

Borkenau, Franz, *The Spanish Cockpit: An Eye-Witness Account of the Political and Social Conflicts of the Spanish Civil War* (Ann Arbor, 1963).

Bowers, Claude G., *My Mission to Spain* (London, 1954).

Buckley, Henry, *Life and Death of the Spanish Republic* (London, 1940).

Camba, Francisco, *Lerroux: el caballero de la libertad* (Madrid, 1935).

Cambó, Francisco, *Memorias* (Madrid, 1987)

Carrillo, Santiago, *Juez y parte: 15 retratos españoles* (Barcelona, 1996).

Chapaprieta Torregrosa, Joaquín, *La paz fue posible: memorias de un político* (Barcelona, 1971).

Coca, Gabriel Mario de, *Anti-Caballero: una crítica marxista de la bolchevización del Partido Socialista Obrero Español* (Madrid, 1936).

Conze, Edward, *Spain Today: Revolution and Counter-Revolution* (London, 1936).

Díaz del Moral, Juan, *Historia de las agitaciones campesinas andaluzas*, 3rd edition (Madrid, 1973).

Estadella, José and Arán Horts, J., *El fracaso de los jurados mixtos: hacia una profunda reforma de los organismos de política social* (Madrid, 1935).

Esteban Infantes, Emilio, *La sublevación del general Sanjurjo: relato de su ayudante* (Madrid, 1993).

Fagoaga, C. and Saavedra, P., *Clara Campoamor: la sufragista española* (Madrid, 1981).

Foss, William and Gerahty, Cecil, *The Spanish Arena* (London, 1938).

Franco Salgado-Araujo, Francisco, *Mis conversaciones privadas con Franco* (Barcelona, 1976).

Franco Salgado-Araujo, Francisco, *Mi vida junto a Franco* (Barcelona, 1977).

García Carraffa, Alberto and Arturo, *Españoles ilustres: Lerroux* (Madrid, 1918).

Gil Robles, José María, *Discursos parlamentarios* (Madrid, 1971).

——, *Marginalia política* (Barcelona, 1975)

——, *No fue posible la paz* (Barcelona, 1968).

González Lopez, Emilio, *Memorias de un diputado de las Cortes de la República (1931–1938)* (La Coruña, 1988).

Gordón Ordás, Felix, *Mi política en España*, 3 vols (Mexico, 1961–63).

——, *Mi política fuera de España*, 3 vols (Mexico, 1970).

Hidalgo, Diego, *¿Por qué fui lanzado del Ministerio de la Guerra? Diez meses de actuación ministerial* (Madrid, 1934).

——, *Un notario español en Rusia* (Madrid, 1985).

Hurtado i Miró, A., *Quaranta anys d'avocat: historia del meu temps* (Barcelona, 1967).

Jalón, César, *Memorias políticas: periodista, ministro, presidiario* (Madrid, 1973).

Largo Caballero, Francisco, *Discursos a los trabajadores* (Madrid, 1934).

——, *Escritos de la República*, edited by Santos Juliá Díaz, (Madrid, 1985).

——, *Mis recuerdos* (Mexico, 1953).

——, *Posibilismo socialista en la democracia* (Madrid, 1933).

Lerroux, Alejandro, *Al servicio de la República* (Madrid, 1930).

——, *La pequeña historia* (Madrid, 1963).

——, *La verdad a mi país: España y la guerra* (Madrid, 1915).

——, *Mis memorias* (Madrid, 1963).

Luca de Tena, Juan Ignacio, *Mis amigos muertos* (Barcelona, 1971).

Madariaga, Salvador de, *Españoles de mi tiempo* (Barcelona, 1974).

——, *Memorias (1921–1936)*, 2nd edition (Madrid, 1974).

——, *Spain: A Modern History* (London, 1961).

Manning, Leah, *What I Saw in Spain* (London, 1935).

Marco Miranda, Vicente, *Las conspiraciones contra la Dictadura: relato de un testigo* (Madrid, 1930).

Marsá, Angel and Carballo, Eduardo, *Alejandro Lerroux ante el momento actual* (Barcelona, 1930).

Marsá Bragado, Antonio, *El republicanismo histórico* (Madrid, 1933).

Martínez Barrio, Diego, *Orígenes del Frente Popular español* (Buenos Aires, 1943).

——, *Páginas para la historia del Frente Popular* (Madrid, 1937).

——, *Memorias* (Barcelona, 1983).

Maura, Miguel, *Asi cayó Alfonso XIII*, 2nd edition (Barcelona, 1966).

Maurín, Joaquín, *Hacia la segunda revolución: el fracaso de la República y la insurrección de octubre* (Barcelona, 1935).

——, *Los hombres de la Dictadura* (Madrid, 1930).

——, *La revolución española* (Madid, 1932).

Mola Vidal, Emilio, *Obras completas* (Valladolid, 1940).

Moral, Joaquín del, *Lo del "10 de agosto" y la justicia* (Madrid, 1933).

——, *Oligarquía y "enchufismo"* (Madrid, 1933).

Morón, Gabriel, *El Partido Socialista ante la realidad política española* (Madrid, 1929).

——, *La ruta del socialismo en España* (Madrid, 1932).

Nin, Andrés, *Los problemas de la revolución española* (Paris, 1971).

Ossorio y Gallardo, Antonio, *Mis memorias* (Buenos Aires, 1946).
Pabón Suárez, Jesús, *Cambó*, 3 vols (Barcelona, 1952–69).
Peiró, Joan, *Escrits 1917–1939* (Barcelona, 1975).
Pérez Madrigal, Joaquín, *España a dos voces: los infundios y la historia* (Madrid, 1961).
——, *Memorias de un converso*, 9 vols (Madrid, 1943–52).
Pi i Sunyer, Carles, *La República y la guerra: memorias de un político catalán* (Mexico, 1975).
Pla, Josep, *El advenimiento de la República* (Madrid, 1983).
——, *Historia de la segunda República española*, 4 vols (Barcelona, 1940–41).
Portela Valladares, Manuel, *Memorias: dentro del drama español* (Madrid, 1988).
Prat García, José, *Memorias* (Albacete, 1994).
Prieto, Indalecio, *Cartas a un escultor* (Buenos Aires, 1961).
——, *Convulsiones de España*, 3 vols (Mexico, 1967–9).
——, *Dentro y fuera del gobierno* (Madrid, 1935).
——, *Discursos fundamentales*, edited by Edward E. Malefakis (Madrid, 1975).
——, *Palabras al viento* (Mexico, 1969).
Ramos Oliveira, Antonio, *Politics, Economics and Men of Modern Spain* (London, 1946).
Rivas Cherif, Cipriano de, *Retrato de un desconocido: vida de Manuel Azaña*, 2nd edition (Barcelona, 1980).
Rodríguez de la Peña, José, *Los aventureros de la política: Alejandro Lerroux (Apuntes para la historia de un revolucionario)* (Madrid, 1915).
Rosal, Amaro del, *Historia de la UGT de España 1901–1939*, 2 vols (Barcelona, 1977).
Saborit, Andrés, *El pensamiento político de Julián Besteiro* (Madrid, 1974).
Sainz Rodríguez, Pedro, *Testimonios y recuerdos* (Barcelona, 1978).
Salazar Alonso, Rafael, *Bajo el signo de la revolución* (Madrid, 1935).
——, *La justicia bajo la dictadura* (Madrid, 1930).
——, *Tarea: cartas políticas* (Madrid, 1934).
Senra, A., *Del 10 de agosto a la Sala Sexta del Supremo* (Madrid, 1933).
Rosal, Amaro del, *1934: el movimiento revolucionario de octubre* (Madrid, 1983).
Rosal, Amaro del, *Historia de la UGT de España (1901–1939)* (Barcelona, 1977).
Ruiz-Castillo Basala, José, *Funcionario republicano de reforma agraria y otros testimonios* (Madrid, 1983).
Trotsky, Leon, *La révolution espagnole 1930–1940*, edited by Pierre Broué (Paris, 1975).
Vaquero, Eloy, *Del drama de Andalucía: recuerdos de luchas rurales y ciudadanas* (Cordoba, 1987).
Vidal i Barraguer, Arxiu, *Església i Estat durant la Segona República Espanyola 1931–1936*, edited by M. Batllori and V. M. Arbeloa, 4 vols in 8 parts (Montserrat, 1971–1991).
Vidarte, Juan-Simeón, *El bienio negro y la insurrección de Asturias* (Barcelona, 1978).
——, *Las Cortes Constituyentes de 1931–1933* (Barcelona, 1976).
——, *No queríamos al Rey: testimonio de un socialista español* (Barcelona, 1977).

2 SECONDARY SOURCES

Monographs and general works

Aguilo Lucia, Luis, *Las elecciones en Valencia durante la segunda República* (Valencia, 1974).

Alarcón Caballero, José Antonio, *El movimiento obrero en Granada en la II República (1931–1936)* (Granada, 1990).

Albertí, Santiago, *El republicanisme català i la Restauració monàrquica (1875–1923)* (Barcelona, 1972).

Alfonso Bozzo, Alfonso, *Los partidos políticos y la autonomía en Galicia, 1931–1936* (Madrid, 1976).

Alonso Baño, Antonio, editor, *Homenaje a Diego Martínez Barrio* (Paris, 1978).

Alós Ferrando, V. R., *Reorganización, supremacía y crisis final del blasquismo (1929–1936)* (Valencia, 1992).

Alpert, Michael, *La reforma militar de Azaña (1931–1933)* (Madrid, 1982).

Alted, Alicia, Egido, Angeles y and Mancebo, María Fernanda, editors, *Manuel Azaña: pensamiento y acción* (Madrid, 1996).

Alvarez Junco, José, *El Emperador del Paralelo: Lerroux y la demagogia populista* (Madrid, 1990).

——, coordinator, *Populismo, caudillaje y discurso demagógico* (Madrid, 1987).

Alvarez Rey, Leandro, *La derecha en la II República: Sevilla, 1931–1936* (Seville, 1993).

Andrés Gallego, José, *El socialismo durante la Dictadura 1923–1930* (Madrid, 1977).

Arcas Cubero, Fernando, *El republicanismo malagüeno durante la Restauración (1875–1923)* (Cordoba, 1985).

Ardid Lorés, Manuel, *Propiedad inmobiliaria y actuación municipal en la Zaragoza de la Segunda República* (Zaragoza, 1996).

Aróstegui, Julio, editor, *Violencia y política en España* (Madrid, 1994).

Arrarás, Joaquín, *Historia de la segunda República española*, 4 vols (Madrid, 1956–68).

Artola, Miguel, *Partidos y programas políticos, 1808–1936*, 2 vols (Madrid, 1974–75).

Ayala, José Antonio, *Murcia en la II República* (Murcia, 1984).

Azpíroz Pascual, José María, *Poder político y conflictividad social en Huesca durante la II República* (Huesca, 1993).

Balbé, Manuel, *Orden público y militarismo en la España constitucional (1812–1983)* (Madrid, 1983).

Balcells, Albert, *Cataluña contemporánea, II (1900–1939)* (Madrid, 1984).

——, *Crisis económica y agitación social en Cataluña (1930–1936)* (Barcelona, 1971).

——, Culla, Joan, and Mir, Conxita, *Les eleccions generals a Catalunya, 1900–1923* (Barcelona, 1982).

——, *El problema agrari a Catalunya: la qüestió rabassaire (1890–1936)* (Barcelona, 1968).

Balfour, Sebastian, *The End of the Spanish Empire, 1898–1923* (Oxford, 1997).

Bardonnet, Daniel, *L'Evolution de la structure du parti radical* (Paris, 1960).

Bécarud, J. and López Campillo, E., *Los intelectuales españoles durante la II República* (Madrid, 1978).

Bermejo Martín, Francisco, *La II República en Logroño: elecciones y contexto político* (Logroño, 1984).

Bécarud, Jean, *La Segunda República española* (Madrid, 1967).

Ben-Ami, Shlomo, "The Origins of the Second Republic in Spain", Ph.D. thesis, University of Oxford, 1974.
——, *The Origins of the Second Republic in Spain* (Oxford, 1978).
Benavides, Manuel D., *El último pirata del Mediterráneo* (Mexico, 1976).
Beramendi, J., and Maíz, R., editors, *Los nacionalismos en la España de la II República* (Madrid, 1991).
Bizcarrondo, Marta, *Leviatán y el socialismo de Luis Araquistain* (Glashutten im Taunus, 1974).
Bizcarrondo, Marta, editor, *Octubre del 34: reflexiones sobre una revolución* (Madrid, 1977).
Blas Guerrero, Andrés de, *El socialismo radical en la II República* (Madrid, 1978).
——, *Tradición republicana y nacionalismo español* (Madrid, 1991).
Blinkhorn, Martin, editor, *Spain in Conflict 1931–1939: Democracy and its Enemies* (London, 1986).
——, *Carlism and Crisis in Spain (1931–1939)* (Cambridge, 1975).
Bookchin, Murray, *The Spanish Anarchists: The Heroic Years 1868–1936* (Cambridge, 1977).
Borrás, José, *Políticas de los exiliados españoles, 1944–1950* (Paris, 1976).
Bosch, Aurora, Cervera, Ama Mª., Comes, Vicent, and Girona, Albert, *Estudios sobre la Segunda República* (Valencia, 1993).
Brademas, John, *Anarcosindicalismo y revolución en España 1930–1937* (Barcelona, 1974).
Braojos Garrido, A., Parias, M. C., and Alvarez Rey, L., *Historia de Sevilla: el siglo XX (1900–1950)* (Sevilla, 1990), 2 vols.
Brenan, Gerald, *Personal Record 1920–1972* (London, 1974).
——, *The Spanish Labyrinth*, 2nd edition (Cambridge, 1950).
Brey, Gérald, and Maurice, Jacques, *Historia y leyenda de Casas Viejas* (Bilbao, 1976).
Broué, Pierre, and Témime, Emile, *The Revolution and the Civil War in Spain* (London, 1972).
Bueno, Jesús, Gaudó, Concepción, and Germán, Luis G., *Elecciones en Zaragoza-capital durante la II República* (Zaragoza, 1980).
Cabanellas, Guillermo, *La guerra de los mil días: nacimiento, vida y muerte de la segunda República española*, 2 vols (Buenos Aires, 1973).
Cabeza Sánchez-Albornoz, Sonsoles, *Historia política de la Segunda República en el exilio* (Madrid, 1997).
Cabrera, Mercedes, *La patronal ante la II República: organizaciones y estrategia (1931–1936)* (Madrid, 1983).
Cabrera Acosta, Miguel Angel, *La II República en las Canarias Occidentales* (Santa Cruz de Tenerife, 1991)
——, *Las elecciones a Cortes durante la II República en las Canarias Occidentales* (Santa Cruz de Tenerife, 1990).
Calero, Antonio M., *Movimientos sociales en Andalucía 1820–1936* (Madrid, 1976).
Campoamor, Clara, *Mi pecado mortal: el voto femenino y yo* (Madrid, 1936).
Camps i Arboix, Joaquín de, *El Parlament de Catalunya (1932–1936)* (Barcelona, 1976).
Cannon, Margaret, *Populism* (London 1981).
Cárcel Ortí, V., *La persecución religiosa en España durante la Segunda República (1931–1939)* (Madrid, 1990)
Cardona, Gabriel, *El poder militar en la España contemporánea hasta la guerra civil* (Madrid, 1983).
Carmona, Miguel, *Trayectoria política de Alejandro Lerroux* (Madrid, 1934).

Caro Carcela, Diego, *La Segunda República en Cádiz: elecciones y partidos políticos* (Cadiz, 1987).

Carod Rovira, Josep Lluis, *Marcel.li Domingo, 1884–1939: de l'escola a la República* (Tarragona, 1989).

Carr, Raymond, editor, *The Republic and the Civil War in Spain* (London, 1971).

——, *Spain 1808–1975*, 2nd edition (Oxford, 1982).

——, *The Spanish Tragedy* (London, 1977).

Casanova, Julián, *De la calle al frente: el anarcosindicalismo en España (1931–1939)* (Barcelona, 1997).

Castillo, Juan José, *Propietarios muy pobres: sobre la subordinación política del pequeño campesino en España* (Madrid, 1979).

Cobo Romero, Francisco, *Labradores, campesinos y jornaleros: protesta social y diferenciación interna del campesinado jiennense en los orígenes de la guerra civil (1931–1936)* (Cordoba, 1992).

Collier, George A., *Socialists of rural Andalusia: Unacknowledged revolutionaries of the Second Republic* (Stanford, 1987).

Contreras, Manuel, *El PSOE en la II República: organización e ideología* (Madrid, 1981)

Crow, John A., *Spain, the Root and the Flower: A History of the Civilization of Spain and of the Spanish People* (New York, 1963).

Cruz, Rafael, *El Partido Comunista de España en la Segunda República* (Madrid, 1987).

Cuadrat, Xavier, *Socialismo y anarquismo en Cataluña (1899–1911): los orígenes de la CNT* (Madrid, 1976).

Cucó Giner, Alfons, *El valencianisme polític: 1874–1936* (Valencia, 1971).

Culla i Clara, Joan B., *El republicanisme lerrouxista a Catalunya (1901–1923)* (Barcelona, 1986).

Dixon, Arturo, *Señor monopolio: la asombrosa vida de Juan March* (Barcelona, 1985).

Duarte, Angel, *El Republicanisme català a la fi del segle XIX* (Vic, 1987).

Durán, José Antonio, *Agrarismo y movilización campesina en el País Gallego (1875–1912)* (Madrid, 1977).

——, *Entre la mano negra y el nacionalismo galleguista* (Madrid, 1981).

——, *Historia de caciques, bandos e ideologías en la Galicia no urbana (Rianxo, 1910–1914)* (Madrid, 1972).

Durgan, Andrew, "The Alianza Obrera", unpublished research work at the University of London.

——, "The Elections of 1933", unpublished MA dissertation, University of London, 1981.

Egido León, María Angeles, *La concepción de la política exterior durante la II República (1931–1936)* (Madrid, 1987).

Elorza, Antonio, *La utopía anarquista bajo la segunda República española* (Madrid, 1973).

Esenwein, George and Shubert, Adrian, *Spain at War: The Spanish Civil War in Context, 1931–1939* (New York, 1995).

Espín, Eduardo, *Azaña en el poder: el partido de Acción Republicana* (Madrid, 1980).

Esteban Barahonda, Luis Enrique, *El comportamiento electoral de la ciudad de Guadalajara durante la Segunda República* (Guadalajara, 1988).

Fernández Clemente, Eloy, *Aragón contemporáneo (1833–1936)* (Madrid, 1975).

Ferrer Benimeli, José Antonio, *Masonería española contemporánea*, 2 vols (Madrid, 1980).

——, coordinator, *Masonería, revolución y reacción* (Alicante, 1990).

Fontana, Josep, *Cambio económico y actitudes políticas en la España del siglo XIX* (Barcelona, 1973).

Forner Muñoz, Salvador, *Industrialización y movimiento obrero: Alicante 1923–1936* (Valencia, 1982).

Franch i Ferrer, Vicent, *El Blasquisme: Reorganització i conflictes polítics (1929–1936)* (Valencia, 1984).

Fraser, Ronald, *Blood of Spain* (London, 1979).

——, *In Hiding: The Life of Manuel Cortés* (London, 1972).

Fusi Aizpurua, Juan Pablo, *El problema vasco en la II República* (Madrid, 1979).

—— and Palafox, Jordi, *España: 1808–1996: el desafío de la modernidad* (Madrid, 1997).

——, *Política obrera en el País Vasco, 1880–1923* (Madrid, 1975).

García Andreu, Mariano, *Alicante en las elecciones republicanas 1931–1936* (Alicante, 1985).

García Delgado, José Luis, coordinator, *España, 1898–1936: estructuras y cambio* (Madrid, 1984).

——, editor, *España entre dos siglos (1875–1931)* (Madrid, 1991).

——, coordinator, *La crisis de la Restauración: España, entre la primera guerra mundial y la II República* (Madrid, 1986).

——, editor, *La cuestión agraria en la España contemporánea* (Madrid, 1976).

——, coordinator, *La España de la Restauración: política, economía, legislación y cultura* (Madrid, 1985).

——, coordinator, *La II República española: el primer bienio* (Madrid, 1987).

——, coordinator, *La II República española: bienio rectificador y Frente Popular, 1934–1936* (Madrid, 1988).

——, coordinator, *Los orígenes culturales de la II República* (Madrid, 1993).

García García, Cristobal, *Partidos y elecciones: 1933 en Huelva* (Huelva, 1996).

García Prous, Concha, *Relaciones Iglesia-Estado en la Segunda República Española* (Cordoba, 1996).

García Santos, Juan F., *Léxico y política de la segunda república* (Salamanca, 1980).

García Venero, Maximiano, *Melquiades Alvarez: historia de un liberal* (Madrid, 1974).

——, *Santiago Alba: monárquico de corazón* (Madrid, 1963).

Garrabau, R., Barciela, C., and Jiménez Blanco, F. I., editors, *Historia agraria de la España contemporánea*, III (Barcelona, 1986).

Garriga, Ramón, *Juan March y su tiempo* (Barcelona, 1976).

Germán Zubero, Luis, *Aragón en la II República: estructura económica y comportamiento político* (Zaragoza, 1984).

Gibaja Velázquez, José Carlos, *Indalecio Prieto y el socialismo español* (Madrid, 1995).

Gil Pecharromán, Julio, *Conservadores subversivos: la derecha autoritaria alfonsina (1913–1936)* (Madrid, 1994).

——, *La Segunda República española (1931–1936)* (Madrid, 1995).

Gillespie, Richard, *The Spanish Socialist Party* (Oxford, 1989).

Gómez Casas, Juan, *Anarchist organization: The history of the F.A.I.* (Montreal, 1986).

Gómez Herraez, José María, *Voces del campo y ecos en la prensa: problemas agrarios en Albacete durante la segunda República* (Albacete, 1988).

Gómez Molleda, María Dolores, *La Masonería en la crisis española del siglo XX* (Madrid, 1986).

Gómez Navarro, José Luis, *El régimen de Primo de Rivera* (Madrid, 1991).

González Calleja, Eduardo, "La radicalización de la derecha española durante la

Segunda República (1931–1936): violencia política, paramilitarización y fascistización en la crisis española de los años treinta", Ph.D. thesis, Complutense University of Madrid, 1993.

——, and Moreno Luzón, Javier, *Elecciones y parlamentarios: dos siglos de historia en Castilla-La Mancha* (Castille La Mancha, 1993).

González Cuevas, Pedro Carlos, *Acción Española: teología política y nacionalismo autoritario en España (1913–1936)* (Madrid, 1998).

González Sobaco, Antonio, *Los partidos políticos durante la Segunda República en Castellón* (Castellon, 1986).

Granja, José Luis de la, *Nacionalismo y II República en el País Vasco* (Madrid, 1986).

Guzmán, Eduardo de, *1930: historia política de un año decisivo* (Madrid, 1973).

——, *La Segunda República fue así* (Barcelona, 1977).

Gutiérrez Lloret, Rosa Ana, *Republicanismo en Alicante durante la Restauración*, (Alicante, 1990).

Heiberg, Marianne, *The making of the Basque nation* (Cambridge, 1989).

Hennessey, C. A. M., *Modern Spain* (London, 1965).

Hernández Andreu, Juan, *España y la crisis de 1929* (Madrid, 1986).

Herr, Richard, *The Eighteenth Century Revolution in Spain* (Princeton, 1958).

Heywood, Paul, *Marxism and the Failure of Organised Socialism in Spain 1879–1936* (Cambridge, 1990).

Ionescu, Ghita and Gellner, Ernest, editors, *Populism: Its meanings and National Characteristics* (London, 1969).

Jackson, Gabriel, *Costa, Azaña, el Frente Popular y otros ensayos* (Madrid, 1976).

——, *The Spanish Republic and the Civil War* (Princeton, 1965).

Jardí, Enric, *Companys i el 6 d'octubre* (Barcelona, 1997).

Jiménez Sánchez, Fernando, *Detrás del escándalo político: opinión pública, dinero y poder en la España del siglo XX* (Barcelona, 1995).

Juana, Jesús de, *La posición centrista durante la segunda República española* (Santiago de Compostela, 1988).

Judt, Anthony, *Socialism in Provence 1871–1914* (London, 1979).

Juliá Díaz, Santos, editor, *El socialismo en España: desde la fundación del PSOE hasta 1975*, vol 1 (Madrid, 1986).

——, coordinator, *El socialismo en las nacionalidades y regiones* (Madrid, 1988).

——, *Historia del socialismo español*, vol. 3 (Barcelona, 1989).

——, *Historia económica y social moderna y contemporánea de España*, II (Madrid, 1991).

——, *La izquierda del PSOE (1935–1936)* (Madrid, 1977).

——, *Madrid, 1931–1934: de la fiesta popular a la lucha de clases* (Madrid, 1984).

——, *Orígenes del Frente Popular en España (1934–1936)* (Madrid, 1979).

——, *Los socialistas en la política española 1879–1982* (Madrid, 1997).

Kelsey, Graham, "Anarchosyndicalism, libertarian communism and the state: The CNT in Zaragoza and Aragon 1930–1937", Ph.D. thesis, University of Lancaster, 1984.

Lacomba, Juan Antonio, *La crisis española de 1917* (Madrid, 1970).

Ladrón de Guevara, María Paz, *La esperanza republicana: reforma agraria y conflicto campesino en la provincia de Ciudad Real (1931–1939)* (Ciudad Real, 1993).

Lamela García, V. Luis, *Pepe Miñones: un crimen en la leyenda (1900–1936)* (La Coruña, 1991).

López, Elsa, Alvarez Junco, José, Espadas Burgos, Manuel, and Muñoz Tinoco, Concha, *Diego Hidalgo: memoria de un tiempo difícil* (Madrid, 1986)

López López, Alejandro, *El boicot de la derecha a las reformas de la Segunda República: la minoría agraria, el rechazo constitucional y la cuestión de la tierra* (Madrid, 1984).

López Martínez, Mario, *Orden público y luchas agrarias en Andalucía* (Cordoba, 1995).

López Villaverde, Angel Luis, *Cuenca durante la II República* (Cuenca, 1997).

Macarro Vera, José Manuel, *La utopía revolucionaria: Sevilla en la Segunda República* (Seville, 1985).

MacMaster, Neil, *Spanish Fighters: An Oral History of Civil War and Exile* (London, 1990).

Malefakis, Edward E., *Agrarian Reform and Peasant Revolution in Spain* (New Haven, Conn., 1970).

Marcos del Olmo, María Concepción, *Voluntad popular y urnas* (Valladolid, 1995).

Marichal, Juan, *La vocación de Manuel Azaña* (Madrid, 1972).

Martí Gilabert, Francisco, *Política religiosa de la Segunda República española* (Pamplona, 1998).

Martin, Benjamin, *The Agony of Modernization: Labor and Industrialization in Spain* (Ithaca, New York, 1990).

Martín Vasallo, José Ramón, *Las elecciones a Cortes en la ciudad de Salamanca 1931–1936: un estudio de sociología electoral* (Salamanca, 1982).

Martínez Cuadrado, Miguel, *Elecciones y partidos políticos de España (1868–1931)*, 2 vols (Madrid, 1969).

Maurice, Jacques, *El anarquismo andaluz: campesinos y sindicalistas 1868–1936* (Barcelona, 1990).

——, *La reforma agraria en España en el siglo XX (1900–1936)* (Madrid, 1975).

——, and Serrano, Carlos, *Joaquín Costa: crisis de la Restauración y populismo (1875–1911)* (Madrid, 1977).

——, Magnien, B., Bussy Genevois, D., editors, *Pueblo, movimiento obrero y cultura en la España contemporánea* (Saint Denis, 1990).

Mavrogordatos, George Th., *Stillborn Republic: Social Coalitions and Party Strategies in Greece, 1922–1936* (Los Angeles, 1983).

Meaker, Gerald H., *The Revolutionary Left in Spain 1914–1923* (Stanford, Calif., 1974).

Meer, Fernando de, *La Constitución de la II República: autonomías, propiedad, iglesia, enseñanza* (Pamplona, 1978).

——, *La cuestión religiosa en las Cortes Constituyentes de la II República española* (Pamplona, 1975).

Mintz, Jerome R., *The Anarchists of Casas Viejas* (Chicago, 1989).

Molas, Isidre, *Lliga Catalana* (Barcelona, 1972).

——, *El sistema de partidos en Cataluña (1931–1936)* (Barcelona, 1974).

Montero, José Ramón, *La CEDA: el catolicismo social y político en la II República*, 2 vols (Madrid, 1977).

Montero Hernández, Enrique, "The Forging of the Second Spanish Republic: New Liberalism, the Republican Movement and the Quest for Modernization (1868–1931)", unpublished Ph.D. thesis, University of London, 1989

Muñoz Tinoco, Concha, *Diego Hidalgo: un notario republicano* (Badajoz, 1986).

——, "Diego Hidalgo, política regional y política liberal en un periodo de convulsión", Ph.D. thesis, Complutense University of Madrid, 1991

Nadal, J., Carreras, A., and Sudrià, C., editors, *La economía española en el siglo XIX: una perspectiva histórica* (Barcelona, 1987).

Nuñez Florencio, Rafael, *El terrorismo anarquista 1888–1909* (Madrid, 1983).

Ojeda, Germán, editor, *Octubre 1934: cincuenta años para la reflexión* (Madrid, 1985).

Oliver Araujo, Joan, *La II República en Baleares: elecciones y partidos políticos* (Palma de Mallorca, 1983).

Orihuela, A., Suárez, M., Anaya, L.A., Alcaraz, J., and Millares, S., *De la República a la Guerra Civil en Las Palmas* (Las Palmas, 1992).

Otero Ochaíta, J., *Movilización e inmovilismo en La Mancha de Ciudad Real (1931–1936)* (Ciudad Real, 1993).

Pabón, Jesús, *Cambó*, 3 vols (Barcelona, 1952–69).

Palafox, Jordi, *Atraso económico y democracia: la Segunda República y la economía española, 1892–1936* (Barcelona, 1991).

Payne, Stanley G., *Politics and the Military in Modern Spain* (Stanford, Calif., 1967).

——, *Spain's First Democracy: The Second Republic, 1931–1936* (Wisconsin, 1993).

——, *The Spanish Revolution* (London, 1970).

Peirats, José, *Los anarquistas en la crisis política española* (Buenos Aires, 1964).

——, *La CNT en la revolución española*, 2nd edition, 3 vols (Paris, 1971).

Pérez Galán, Mariano, *La enseñanza en la Segunda República española* (Madrid, 1975).

Pérez Yruela, Manuel, *La conflictividad campesina en la provincia de Córdoba 1931–1936* (Madrid, 1979).

Piqueras, José Antonio and Chust, Manuel, editors, *Republicanos y repúblicas en España* (Madrid, 1996).

Poblet, Josep M., *Historia de l'Esquerra Republicana de Catalunya 1931–1936* (Barcelona, 1976).

Portillo, Eduardo M. del, *Los hombres que trajeron la república: Lerroux, el reportaje de una vida fecunda* (Madrid, 1931).

Pradas Martínez, Enrique, editor, *8 de diciembre de 1933: insurrección anarquista en La Rioja* (Logroño, 1983)

——, *La segunda República y La Rioja (1931–1936)* (Logroño, 1982).

Prados de la Escosura, Leandro, *De imperio a nación: crecimiento y atraso económico en España (1780–1930)* (Madrid, 1988).

Preston, Paul, *Franco: A Biography* (London, 1993).

——, *Las derechas españolas en el siglo XX: autoritarismo, fascismo, golpismo* (Madrid, 1986).

——, editor, *Leviatán: antología* (Madrid, 1976).

——, *The Coming of the Spanish Civil War: Reform, Reaction and Revolution in the Second Republic* (London, 1978).

——, *The Politics of Revenge: Fascism and the Military in 20th Century Spain* (London, 1990).

——, editor, *Revolution and War in Spain 1931–1939* (London, 1984).

Puelles Benítez, Manuel de, *Educación e ideología en la España contemporánea (1767–1975)* (Barcelona, 1980).

Quintana Navarro, F., *España en Europa, 1931–1936: del compromiso por la paz a la huida de la guerra* (Madrid, 1993).

Rama, Carlos M., *La crisis española del siglo XX* (Mexico City, 1960).

Ramírez Jiménez, Manuel, *Los grupos de presión en la segunda República española* (Madrid, 1969).

——, editor, *Estudios sobre la segunda República española* (Madrid, 1975).

Ramos, Vicente, *La segunda República en la provincia de Alicante* (Alicante, 1983).

Reig, Ramiro, *Blasquistas y clericales* (Valencia, 1986).

Requena Gallego, Manuel, *De la Dictadura a la II República: el comportamiento electoral en Castilla-La Mancha* (Cuenca, 1993).

——, *Partidos, elecciones y élite política en la provincia de Albacete 1931–1933* (Albacete, 1991).

Rider, Nicholas, "Anarchism, Urbanization and Social Conflict in Barcelona, 1900–1932", unpublished Ph.D. thesis, University of Lancaster, 1987

Robinson, Richard, A. H., *The Origins of Franco's Spain: The Right, The Republic and Revolution, 1931–1936* (Newton Abbot, 1970).

Robles Egea, Antonio, "La Conjunción Republicano-Socialista", unpublished Ph.D. thesis, Complutense University of Madrid, 1987

——, editor, *Política en penumbra: patronazgo y clientelismo políticos en la España contemporánea* (Madrid, 1996).

Rodríguez de las Heras, Antonio, *Filiberto Villalobos: su obra social y política, 1990–1936* (Salamanca, 1985).

Rodríguez Jiménez, José Luis, *La extrema derecha española en el siglo XX* (Madrid, 1997).

Romero Maura, Joaquín, *"La rosa de fuego": el obrerismo barcelonés de 1899 a 1909* (Madrid, 1982).

Rosique Navarro, Francisca, *La reforma agraria en Badajoz durante la II República* (Badajoz, 1988).

Rueda, Germán, editor, *Doce estudios de historiografía contemporánea* (Santander, 1991).

Ruiz, David, *El movimiento obrero en Asturias* (Oviedo, 1968).

——, *Insurrección defensiva y revolución obrera: el octubre español de 1934* (Barcelona, 1988).

Ruiz Manjón, Octavio, *El Partido Republicano Radical (1908–1936)* (Madrid, 1976).

Salter, Stephen and Stevenson, John, editors, *The Working Class and Politics in Europe and America 1929–1945* (London, 1990).

Samaniego Boneu, Mercedes, *La política educativa de la Segunda República durante el bienio azañista* (Madrid, 1977).

Sánchez-Albornoz, Nicolás, editor, *The Economic Modernization of Spain, 1830–1930* (New York, 1987).

Sánchez y García Saúco, Juan Antonio, *La revolución de 1934 en Asturias* (Madrid, 1974).

Sánchez Sánchez, José and Mateos Rodríguez, Miguel Angel, *Elecciones y partidos en Albacete durante la II República, 1931–1936* (Albacete, 1977).

Sancho Calatrava, José A., *Elecciones en la II República: Ciudad Real (1931–1936)* (Ciudad Real, 1988).

Saz Campos, Ismael, *Mussolini contra la II República* (Valencia, 1986).

Serrano, Carlos, *Le tour du peuple* (Madrid, 1987).

Serrano, Vicente-Alberto, and San Luciano, José María, editors, *Azaña* (Madrid, 1980).

Shubert, Adrian, *A Social History of Modern Spain* (Cambridge, 1990).

——, *Road to Revolution: The Coal Miners of Asturias 1860–1934* (Urbana, 1987).

Smith, Angel, "Anarchism, Socialism and Catalan Labour 1897–1914", unpublished Ph.D. thesis, University of London, 1990.

Solé-Tura, Jordi, *Catalanismo y revolución burguesa* (Madrid, 1974).

Suárez Cortina, Manuel, *El reformismo en España* (Madrid, 1986).

——, editor, *La Restauración entre el liberalismo y la democracia* (Madrid, 1997).

Tamames, Ramón, *La República, la era de Franco* (Madrid, 1973).

Thomas, Hugh, *The Spanish Civil War*, 2nd edition (Harmondsworth, 1965).
Townson, Nigel, editor, *El republicanismo en España (1830–1977)* (Madrid, 1994).
——, MA dissertation, "The Socialist Disengagement from the Socialist-left Repúblican Alliance in 1933", University of London, 1983.
Tuñón de Lara, Manuel, *El movimiento obrero en la historia de España* (Madrid, 1972).
——, *Estudios de historia contemporánea*, 3rd edition (Madrid, 1982).
—— et al., *Historiografía española contemporánea* (Madrid, 1980).
——, *La España del siglo XX*, 2nd edition (Paris, 1973).
——, *La Segunda República*, 2 vols (Madrid, 1976).
——, editor, *La II República: una esperanza frustrada* (Valencia, 1987).
——, *Luchas obreras y campesinas en la Andalucia del siglo XX: Jaén (1917–1920) Sevilla (1930–1932)* (Madrid, 1978).
——, *Sociedad, política y cultura en la España de los siglos XIX–XX* (Madrid, 1973).
——, *Tres claves de la Segunda República: la cuestión agraria, los aparatos del Estado, Frente Popular* (Madrid, 1985).
Tusell Gómez, Javier, *La crisis del caciquismo andaluz (1923–1931)* (Madrid, 1977).
——, Queipo de Llano, Genoveva, and Ruiz Manjón-Cabeza, Octavio, *Las Constituyentes de 1931: unas elecciones de transición* (Madrid, 1982).
——, *La segunda República en Madrid: elecciones y partidos políticos* (Madrid, 1970).
——, *Las elecciones del Frente Popular*, 2 vols (Madrid, 1971).
——, *Historia de la democracia cristiana en España*, 2 vols (Madrid, 1974).
——, *Sociología electoral de Madrid: 1930–1931* (Madrid, 1969).
—— and Calvo, José, *Giménez Fernández: precursor de la democracia española* (Sevilla, 1990).
——, Gil Pecharromán, J., and Montero, F., editors, *Estudios sobre la derecha española contemporánea* (Madrid, 1993).
Ullman, Joan Connelly, *La Semana Trágica: estudio sobre las causas socio-económicas del anticlericalismo en España (1898–1912)* (Barcelona, 1972).
Valle, José María del, *Las instituciones de la República española en el exilio* (Paris, 1976).
Valls, Rafael, *La Derecha Regional Valenciana (1930–1936)* (Valencia, 1992).
Varela, Santiago, *Partidos y parlamento en la II República española* (Barcelona, 1978).
Various authors, *El movimiento libertario español* (Paris, 1974).
Various authors, *Primeras jornadas: Niceto Alcalá-Zamora y su época* (Priego de Cordoba, 1995).
Vega, Eulalia, *Anarquistas y sindicalistas, 1931–1936* (Valencia, 1987).
Venturi, F., *Roots of Revolution* (London, 1960).
Villacorta Baños, Francisco, *Profesionales y burócratas: estado y poder corporativo en la España del siglo XX, 1890–1923* (Madrid, 1989).
Winston, Colin, *Workers and the Right in Spain, 1900–1936* (Princeton, 1985).

Articles and lectures

Abercrombie, Nicholas and Hill, Stephen, "Paternalism and Patronage", *The British Journal of Sociology*, December 1976.
Alvarez Junco, José, "Cultura popular y protesta política", in *Pueblo, movimiento*

obrero y cultura en la España contemporánea, edited by Jacques Maurice et al., (Paris, 1990).

——, "Maneras de hacer historia: los antecedentes de la Semana Trágica", *Zona Abierta*, no. 31, 1984.

——, "Racionalismo, romanticismo y moralismo en la cultura política republicana de comienzos de siglo", in *Clases populares, cultura, educación: siglos XIX y XX* (Madrid, 1988).

Blas Guerrero, Andrés de, "El Partido Radical en la política española de la Segunda República", *Revista de Estudios Políticas*, 31–32, 1983.

Blinkhorn, Martin, "Anglo-American historians and the Second Spanish Republic: the emergence of a new orthodoxy", *European Studies Review*, 1973.

——, "Ideology and Schism in Spanish Traditionalism, 1874–1931", *Iberian Studies*, I, 1972.

——, "Carlism and the Spanish Crisis of the 1930s", *Journal of Contemporary History*, VII, 3–4, 1972.

——, ""The Basque Ulster": Navarre and the Basque Autonomy Question under the Spanish Second Republic", *Historical Journal*, XVII, no. 3, September 1974.

Cabrera, Mercedes, "Organizaciones patronales y cuestión agraria en España (1931–1936)", in José Luis García Delgado, editor, *La cuestión agraria en la España contemporánea* (Madrid, 1976).

Cardona, G., Abella, R., and Mateo, E., "La Sanjurjada", *Historia 16*, no. 76, 1982.

Cucó Giner, Alfons, "Sobre el radicalismo valenciano", *Hispania*, XXIX, 1969.

Culla i Clarà, Joan, "Lerrouxismo y nacionalismo catalán, 1901–1923: elementos para una interpretación", in Manuel Tuñón de Lara et al., *España 1898–1936: estructuras y cambio* (Madrid, 1984).

Gilmore, David, "Patronage and Class Conflict in Southern Spain", *Man*, no. 12, 1977.

Harrison, Joseph, "The Regenerationist Movement in Spain and the Disaster of 1898", *European Studies Review*, vol. 9, no. 1, 1979

Herrero Fabregat, María, "La masonería y la escisión del Partido Radical en 1934", in José Antonio Ferrer Benimeli, editor, *Masonería, Revolución y Reacción*, I (Alicante, 1990).

Juliá Díaz, Santos, "Comunidad y ruptura en el socialismo español del siglo XX", *Leviatán*, II, no. 17, 1984

——, "Corporativistas obreros y reformadores políticos: crisis y escisión del PSOE en la II República", *Studia Historia*, vol. I, 4, 1983

——, "Largo Caballero y la lucha de tendencias en el socialismo español (1923–1936)", *Annali della Fondazione Giangiacomo Feltrinelli*, 1983–84.

——, "La experiencia del poder: la izquierda republicana, 1931–1933", in Nigel Townson, editor, *El republicanismo en España (1830–1977)* (Madrid, 1994).

——, "La vigencia de Prieto", *Leviatán*, II, no. 15, 1984

——, "Orígenes sociales de la democracia en España", *Ayer*, no. 15, 1994.

Kaufman, Robert R., "The Patron-Client Concept and Macro-Politics: Prospects and Problems", *Comparative Studies in History and Society*, no. 6, 1974.

Kelsey, Graham, "Anarchism in Aragon during the Second Republic: the emergence of a mass movement", in Martin Blinkhorn, editor, *Spain in Conflict 1931–1939: Democracy and Its Enemies* (London, 1986).

Littlewood, Paul, "Strings and Kingdoms: the activities of a political mediator in Southern Italy", *Archives europeanés de sociologie*, no. XV, 1974.

Lynam, Stephen, "'Moderate' conservatism and the Second Republic: the case of Valencia", in Martin Blinkhorn, editor, *Spain in Conflict 1931–1939:*

Democracy and Its Enemies (London, 1986).

Mouzelis, Nicos, "Class and Clientelistic Politics: The Case of Greece", *Sociological Review*, no. 26, 1978.

Nadal, Jordi, "Spain, 1830–1914", in Carlo M. Cipolla, editor, *The Reemergence of Industrial Society* (London, 1973).

Powell, John Duncan, "Peasant Society and Clientelist Politics", *The American Political Science Review*, vol. 64, 1970.

Preston, Paul, "Alfonsist Monarchism and the Coming of the Spanish Civil War", *Journal of Contemporary History*, VII, nos. 3–4, 1972.

——, "El accidentalismo de la CEDA: ¿aceptación o sabotage de la República?", *Cuadernos de Ruedo Ibérico* (Paris), nos. 41–42, 1973.

——, "The "Moderate" Right and the Undermining of the Second Spanish Republic, 1931–1933", *European Studies Review*, III, no. 4, 1973.

——, "Salvador de Madariaga and the Quest for Liberty in Spain", Taylorian Special Lecture, University of London, 1986.

——, "Spain's October Revolution and the Rightist Grasp for Power", *Journal of Contemporary History*, X, no. 4, 1975.

Quintana Navarro, Francisco, "Salvador de Madariaga, diplomático en Ginebra (1931–1936). La película de la política exterior de la II República", *Historia Contemporánea*, 15, 1996.

Reig, Ramiro, "Populismes", *Debats*, no. 12, 1985.

Requena Gallego, Manuel, "Cambios en el comportamiento político y en la élite parlamentaria durante la II República en Albacete", in Rafel Villena Espinosa, coordinator, *Ensayos humanísticos: homenaje al profesor Luis Lorente Toledo* (Castille La Mancha, 1997).

——, "El triunfo monárquico en las elecciones municipales de 1931 en Castilla La Mancha", *Hispania*, vol. LV/2, 190, 1995.

Robles Egea, Antonio, "La Conjunción republicano-socialista", in Santos Juliá, editor, *El socialismo en España: desde la fundación del PSOE hasta 1975* (Madrid, 1986).

Romero Maura, Joaquín, "Terrorism in Barcelona and its impact on Spanish politics, 1904–1909", *Past & Present*, 41, XII, 1968.

Ruiz Manjón-Cabeza, Octavio, "El Partido Republicano Radical de Madrid durante la segunda República española", *Revista de la Universidad de Madrid*, XXII, 87, 1973.

——, "El radicalismo alicantino en la II República", *Anales de la Universidad de Alicante*, nos. 3–4, 1984–85.

——, "La Dictadura de Primo de Rivera y la consolidación del sentimiento republicano en España: una interpretación del Partido Radical", *Revista de Historia Contemporánea*, no. 1, 1982.

——, "La evolución programática del Partido Republicano Radical", *La Revista de la Universidad Complutense*, 1980.

Shubert, Adrian, "Revolution in self-defence: the radicalization of the Asturian coal miners, 1921–1934", *Social History*, VII, no. 3, 1982.

Torres Ballesteros, Sagrario, "El populismo: un concepto escurridizo", in José Alvarez Junco, coordinator, *Populismo, caudillaje y discurso demagogico* (Madrid, 1987).

Townson, Nigel, "Algunas consideraciones sobre el proyecto 'republicano' del partido radical", in José Luis García Delgado, coordinator, *La II república española: el bienio rectificador y Frente Popular, 1934–1936* (Madrid, 1988).

——, "The Second Republic, 1931–1936: Sectarianism, Schisms, and Strife", in José Alvarez Junco and Adrian Shubert, *Spanish History since 1808* (London, 2000).

——, "Una República para todos los españoles": el Partido Radical en el poder, 1933–1935", in Nigel Townson, editor, *El republicanismo en España (1830–1977)* (Madrid, 1994).

Weingrod, Alex, "Patrons, Patronage, and Political Parties", *Comparative Studies in History and Society*, no. 10, 1968.

Index

___